THE BANAT OF TIMIȘOARA

Edited by

Victor NEUMANN

THE BANAT OF TIMIȘOARA

A European Melting Pot

SCALA

CONTENTS

FOREWORD

I CONFESS THAT I have been waiting for this book for a long time. The Banat, as a civilisational space, seduced me in my youth, with its culture fanning out across the *triplex confinium*. This triple border became very real for me from the tower of Cenad Cathedral as I looked down on the convergence of Romanian, Hungarian and Serbian lands. In this volume, my old friend Victor Neumann – whose much-read and oft-cited book *The Temptation of Homo Europaeus* emerged out of a doctoral thesis that I recall with a feeling of intellectual joy – has gathered together 15 authors from Timișoara, Caransebeș, Novi Sad and Vrsac, Szeged and Belgrade. Thus, it is a multicultural and multinational volume that succeeds in reviving, in fascinating detail and with an inevitably broad context, a European image from the eighteenth to the twentieth centuries, which is fundamental to the modernity of the continent.

Research into regional history is illustrated in this volume, from the so-called *Landesgeschichte* of 1800 onwards, reshaped during the 1980s into a complex search for 'sub-' and 'transnational regions', 'Euro-regions' and 'frontiers' that have become objects of study for geopoliticians and historians.[1] It describes a Banat where, living alongside Romanians, were the Venetian Gerardo de Sagredo's Balkan and Benedictine monks from the Morisena monastery, Slavic and Oriental traders, Hungarian magnates, Ottoman commanders and Austrian architects working on von Erlach's projects. This Banat territory was, at various times, a proto-Romanian 'dukedom', Angevin land, Ottoman pashalik, Habsburg province administered by the Hungarian Diet, and finally, divided between Romania, Hungary and yesterday's Yugoslavia. Today it is a place that remains, geographically and spiritually, a cultural bridge, a connecting space.

In fact, Banat unites the European South-East, to which it belongs, with *Mitteleuropa* as imagined by Friedrich Naumann 100 years ago, and with an East-Central Europe from which it takes mental nourishment. It is a world descended from the Austrian autocracy of Franz Kafka, Stefan Zweig, Max Brod, Robert Musil, Czeslaw Miłosz and Milan Kundera, belonging, in my opinion, to a creative and active periphery of the West, but according to Jenö Szücs, to a 'third Europe'.[2]

The range of subjects covered in this volume on the Banat is diverse and carefully considered: the Enlightenment from the time of Brukenthal and Teleki; the age of Maria Theresa and Joseph II in which imperial Viennese policy led to the century's vastest European migration, thus creating a specific rural habitat of Swabian, Italian, Spanish, Czech and Slovak colonists in the region; the Freemasonry that was concentrated in an area between the Mureș and Tisza rivers; the bourgeoisie from Prague, Bratislava and Zagreb, not to mention those from the Germanic countries; the Freemasonry that included Francesco Griselini, author of one of the best-known histories of the Banat; the Romanian and Serbian Orthodoxy that represented a very real shelter for Transylvanian co-religionists; the Judaism so open to the kind of multilingualism that creates an elevated culture; the diverse education and the very active mass-media, mostly present in the centres with a South Slavic population; the urbanism, as well as baroque military, civil and ecclesiastical art, illustrated by the monumental citadel of Arad – which, hard as it is to understand, we are ignoring today – and the Catholic cathedrals of Timișoara and Lenauheim, the Serbian church of Timișoara and the Romanian church of Lugoj, the numerous statues of St Nepomuk, the frescoes in Brâncovenesc style from Săraca monastery or the neo-Gothic and Secession buildings – all of them acknowledging a syncretic cultural climate hard to find in other parts of Europe.

I have predominantly referred to culture, but I do not overlook that the political civilisation of modern Banat is accurately analysed here, with interesting emphases upon the 'passivity of the Banat' during the memorandist age and the little-known 'Banatian republic' from 1918 to 1919, an analysis constantly shaped by the thinking of Vasile Maniu and Alexandru Mocsonyi, Vincențiu Babeș and Constantin Diaconovici-Loga, Vasile Goldiș and Eftimie Murgu, pillars of the conceptual and geographical, historical and anthropological construct that bears the name of the Banat.

We owe this volume to a number of scholars whom I respectfully salute. I have learnt a lot from what they have written.

Răzvan Theodorescu
Vice-President of the Romanian Academy of Sciences

PREFACE

THE BANAT OF TIMIȘOARA: A EUROPEAN MELTING POT aims to promote an innovative perspective on the historiography of the region, with emphasis on an area whose identity, both past and present, derives from its geographical position, from the multi- and intercultural nature of the area, and from its civilisational diversity. The book relies on extensive research in the archives and libraries of Romania, Serbia, Hungary, Austria and Germany.

This history of the Banat proposes a vision free of linguistic, religious, ethnic or national constraints. It presents the sociopolitical, religious and cultural life of the region, along with events, dates and relevant facts from the eighteenth, nineteenth and twentieth centuries. This book provides the explanations necessary for an understanding of the regional and local administrations, and for describing community identity and ideologies, personalities and representative institutions. It is the result of a collective effort, in which the dates and facts described emphasize the common denominator of the people and ethnic groups who populated the Banat. Often, its pages lead the reader to discovery of a world where conscience plays an essential part. The interpretations are interdisciplinary, history being understood not only as a sequence of events and facts, but also as a recollection and evaluation of religion and education, arts and architecture, media and intellectual-political ideas, all of which have left an indelible mark on the region.

Due to the nature of the documentary information, the comparative studies and personal reflections, the history presented here is mostly focused on the problems and challenges of the region. The reader who seeks to understand the ethno-linguistic and religious diversity of the various groups that populated the Banat through history will notice that this aspect has been partially highlighted, as we have focused on the experiments relating to the amalgamation of population within the region. There is less emphasis on any kind of cultural or community segregation as the region has always been defined as a civic and intercultural phenomenon.[1]

The main objective of the editor and his team was to describe the inhabitants of the Banat and their mentality. It is an almost utopian area – comparable to Alsace-Lorraine (according to the Serbian writer Miloš Crnjanski) – where the cornerstone is the cultural code, the result of multiple legacies. We have proposed not only a presentation of the history but also a unitary coverage of the past of a region which after the Paris Peace Treaty of 1918 was divided between Romania, Serbia and Hungary. For this, we have included some of the most compelling descriptions from the Romanian, Serbian and Hungarian archives. As a result, we have been able to present in an objective manner the roles of the House of Habsburg, the Austrian Empire and the Austro-Hungarian Monarchy in the organisation, management and socio-economic development of the region.

The Banat of Timișoara: A European Melting Pot is a comparative work which presents an in-depth look at one fragment of an imperial, multi- and intercultural world. Despite being varied in style and interpretation, the studies in the book enrich and summarize the research conducted up to now, presenting the first history of the region, a hundred years after its division. Without following the normal construction of a book and presenting dates and events in chronological order, the studies describe the region by taking into account the results of the first modernisation process and focus on its features by contextualising them.

In *The Banat of Timișoara: A European Melting Pot* both the editor and his team present the positive and negative aspects of modernisation and the relationship between old and new. Its several hundred pages reveal the centuries preceding intolerant ethnonationalism, world wars and discriminatory legislation. (Although the main focus of the historical discourse and historiography is not on theories of political identity or on the totalitarian regimes of the twentieth century, it does not ignore the almost entire disappearance of the German and Jewish communities from the Banat and Central/Eastern European regions.) Its chapters recall the local–universal relationship along with the civilisation context in which the Banat was able to facilitate the reunion between West and East. The book often draws attention to the multiple cultural codes of the region, which gave a unique identity to the area, within the overall framework of Central and South-Eastern Europe. The tragedies caused by the First World War and the division of the region put an end to the first stage of modernisation. The continuities and ruptures during the interwar period are highlighted in the book's final chapters. The perspective submitted in this book is innovatory and the result of well-documented and carefully-thought-out research. I believe that the Europe we know today – not merely the states which benefited from the division of the Banat – has much to learn from this page of history.

Victor Neumann
Timișoara, February–March 2018

PART I
(INTRODUCTION)

I

BETWEEN ORTHODOX BYZANTIUM AND CATHOLIC EUROPE

The Banat and Its Multiple-Coded Cultural Legacies

Victor Neumann

THE BANAT IS WHERE some of the most fruitful exchanges occurred between the Romanian and European traditions, between the Orthodox and Roman Catholic faiths, and between the languages of local and neighbouring cultures. Many citizens of the Banat are proud of the positive relationships between the Christians, Jews and Muslims of the population. It is the place where Byzantium and Central Europe clashed, giving birth to a unique and diverse geography that embraced the entire world, and which became the cradle of a fascinating history. From the social, economic and political point of view, the Banat was a territory of experiments, social and liberal initiatives, humanist aspirations and the desire for material welfare. At certain times, the place belonged to individuals and communities who refused to obey the authorities or totalitarian regimes. The Banat has its own peculiarities, and invoking its historical realities is essential to any future projects. Cultural perspectives aside, a community has a future only if it has a past to which it can relate.

The Banat takes much pride in its heritage. It is only natural to wonder if the once-prosperous region crossed by the rivers Timiș, Cerna, Semenic, Almăj, Mureș and Tisza can be restored to its former status. This depends very much on the inhabitants of today and tomorrow, their values and belief in reconstruction. Taking into account the existence of the Bega Canal and the possibility of harnessing it as a bridge to Europe's great river, we might even dare to call it a 'Danube Region'. In other words, admitting that the Banat has a rich history and therefore an inherited identity, we are entitled to see its future through its past. Moreover, acquiring Western civic principles must be managed through education at home, in school and in the domain of public opinion.

The establishment of a responsible and pragmatic middle class is essential – one that is attentive to itself and to the community. The formation of professional elites is equally important. In short, there is significant human potential both in Timișoara and across the Banat. Its development depends on the collective investment of public and private institutions through creative minds and prolific production. Encouraging the young and talented is crucial for enabling cutting-edge industries (computer science, automation, electronics and telecommunications) to access European funds and to develop businesses in agriculture, trade and services. For example, the Banat has exceptional soil for growing not only grains – wheat, corn and oats – but also industrial crops such as cotton, flax, hemp, hops, rapeseed and sugar beet. In previous centuries, the agriculture of this region was the inhabitants' chief concern, as it contributed to the food supply of Europe and generated a high standard of living for the local population. If this area of activity is revived, the Banat will be able to participate and compete in the European market.

There were both prosperous and dark times in the history of the Banat region. Like other rich areas of Europe or the world, it attracted talented people and communities gained recognition due to the inventive spirit of its inhabitants. During the nineteenth century, Timișoara had a pace of development and growth similar to other regions in the Austrian Empire. Between 1880 and 1914, the city underwent a remarkable economic expansion, becoming the most important industrial, commercial, banking and cultural centre in the entire region. It also became a city admired for its multi-- and intercultural cooperation; for the multilingualism and civicism of its citizens; for its musical, literary and artistic creations; and for many scientific and technical innovations.

The eighteenth century brought a series of advances in the region and its natural resources were rationally exploited for the first time. The Bega Canal was built, the first factories were opened and, in turn, manufacturing and trade flourished. This accelerated further in the first half of the nineteenth century after construction of the first railway network. The periods 1718–79, 1804–40, 1849–60 and 1880–1914 saw declarations of regional identity in all forms. In the Banat, pluralism rather than singularity was dominant; it was defined not as one ethnic entity but as a space of religious, linguistic and cultural interaction. The presence of several active communities contributed to a rapid intellectual emancipation which resulted in numerous technical and artistic experiments.

After the First World War, the Banat was partitioned between Romania, Serbia and Hungary. This was the first sign that the region would lose some of the administrative and economic advantages brought on by Vienna's mercantilist policies introduced in the eighteenth and nineteenth centuries. Even so, between 1918 and 1938, cities such as Reșița, Arad, Lugoj and Timișoara – which have become part of Romania, along with the largest area of the region – played a key role in the continuity of large and small industries, including trade, mining and vehicle construction. For example, industry in the Romanian part of the Banat exported to overseas markets not only textile products, footwear, leather goods and hats, but also chemicals, steel, laminates, engines and dynamo generators, tools and equipment for the petroleum industry, steam locomotives, railway rails and bridge components. Elsewhere, the region continued to be highly appreciated for the diversity and quality of its agricultural products.

The partition of the Banat in 1918 triggered a fracture in administrative, economic and sociocultural affairs, as the words 'national' and 'nationalistic' became more frequently used. Despite this, the idea of regional identity – particularly in the Romanian and Serbian areas – has survived. The Banat's urban culture, schools, arts and crafts, along with the behaviour of its inhabitants, have conferred prestige on the region. The features that set the historical Banat apart, and the imperial heritage of the eighteenth and nineteenth centuries, continued to be exploited during the interwar period. The region and its people were admired throughout Romania for their individuality and civic values, inspired by the Central/Western European model. The Banat, and especially Timișoara, gained respect for its people and the quality of its products.

During and after the Second World War, the region was subjected to discriminatory measures, first from the Nazis and then from Soviet totalitarian regimes. During the Fascist regime, racist laws included the confiscation of Jewish wealth and the establishment of concentration camps. These were followed by discriminatory measures of the Communist and National Communist powers, which resulted in the deportation of petit bourgeois families of Romanian, Serbian and German origin to the southern part of Romania. These measures led to the marginalisation and erasure of an important part of the economic features, civic spirit, and multi- and intercultural particularities of the Banat. Moreover, the region lost its once thriving appearance in part because of the emigration of large social segments that had contributed to the functioning of institutions and training of craftsmen and professionals. Between 1950 and 1989, the Banat experienced a significant decrease in the elites who had contributed to the preservation of numerous sociocultural peculiarities. This phenomenon has escalated since 1989 – this time without regime constraints – leaving behind a noticeable void.

Starting with the first period of modernisation and early political movements, the cities of the Banat have made serious efforts to unravel segregation policies based on ethnic, racial or religious criteria, working in favour of the middle class and intercultural citizenship. The parts of the Banat which were integrated into Romania and Serbia were neither anti-national nor nationalist. They continued to play the 'cosmopolitan card' long after the partition of the region, not sharing the radical political principles belonging to those in search of ethnic purity. Timișoara excelled due to the civic spirit of its inhabitants, knowing how to adapt and capitalise on the ideas of the European Enlightenment and Viennese Josephism (see my Chapter 4 in this volume).

In societies where national institutions have created an authoritarian or totalitarian culture, regional differences have been neglected and often forgotten. A society built on these principles views such differences as aggression, hence its reaction is to be defensive or to reject it. Ideas of uniqueness and specificity that abound in textbooks, media and literature were – and still are – creators of myths. Therefore, it will take time for today's Romanian citizenry to accept the naturalness of things, the existence and rights of diversity of any kind, until the day comes when the idea of 'one flag, one nation' represents in the mind of every individual just one fragment of identity among many others. The flag might belong to a club (Rotary, Lions), to a profession (computer scientists, chemists, physicists, historians, cooks, construction workers, architects), to a city or a region, to a national state or to a continent. However, the flag itself represents only one of several means of expressing cultural identity.

Regionalism must not replace nationalism. The comparison of an inhabitant from the Banat with one from the Old Kingdom of Romania should be made properly, by researching and assuming the historico-political realities and accepting the cultural codes formed over the course of hundreds of years. For example, when assessing Romania, it is easy to see that it is a state born after the dissolution of the Ottoman, Austro-Hungarian and Tsarist empires, thus having regions with inherited languages, cultures, habits and mental reflexes of various origins: Slavic and Russian, Turkish and Ottoman, Byzantine and Greek, Austrian and German, Hungarian, Slavic and Serbian. We are looking at the supreme example of a space where differences and similarities interact and are at home with each other: a true melting pot. Analysed from the angle of regional history, Romania represents the multicultural features of Europe quite well. We can say that it has several types of culture since the different communities use several languages and belong to various churches. Similarly, it has several regions whose features are the result of the policies and influences exerted by dominant cultures from earlier times, before the establishment of a single nation or nation state. As a consequence, Romanian citizens are also defined by their regional identity: as inhabitants of the Banat, Bukovina, Transylvania, Moldovia, Wallachia or Dobruja.

There was a time when the association of Timișoara with Vienna and of the Banat with Austria was possible, as they had similar cultures that accepted and cultivated each other. It is also true that Vienna had intelligence and creativity in terms of its administration: it was interested in discovering the people of the region and the characteristics that set them apart, and it was also preoccupied with the geography, history and cultural products of the Banat. Vienna knew how to exploit the region, while providing the possibility of emancipation from feudal servitude. Those appointed to describe the geography and history of the region were imperial officials, scientists and explorers with remarkable experience in mapping the world they had researched. The writings of J.J. Ehrler and Francesco Griselini in the eighteenth century are exemplary, leaving a remarkable body of work describing how the House of Habsburg integrated the region between the Danube, Tisza and Mureș rivers.

What is the future of the Banat seen from a historical perspective? 'Futures past' – a phrase formulated by the historian Reinhart Koselleck in the title of a famous book[1] – convinces me that the solutions of tomorrow are to be found in the ideals and values inherited from our predecessors and in the ability to adapt to the dynamics of contemporary life. Once administrative decentralisation becomes the new reality for the states of East-Central Europe and regional centres have the right to decide on finance, strategies and economic investments, on cultural and architectural heritage, and on key educational institutions, there will also be hope of a revival. This is also the case with the Banat since it belongs to Romania, Serbia and Hungary, but at the same time has a certain degree of independence. Overcoming intellectual, economic, financial and demographic crises, as well as crises of conscience, depends on the inhabitants who establish themselves in the region and steer themselves based on existing human potential and on old and new aspirations regarding European integration. Since Timișoara has been chosen as the 2021 European Capital of Culture, the entire Banat is likely to benefit. It will probably mean a chance to rebuild the region in the near future. Directly or indirectly, the scientific research found in this volume also meets these aspirations, and aims to reclaim aspects unknown or little known regarding the history of the region.

It is possible and also necessary to establish a history of the Banat from the perspective of the Romanians, Serbs, Hungarians, Austrian-Germans and Europeans at the same time. The history of the region must be of interest to many people. In the pages of this book they will find new information, enabling them to discover people, places and topics less known or unknown, to understand events and facts, to question and enquire about the relationship not only between past and present, but also between past and future. Several historians have addressed this scientific approach, as it is necessary in order not only to enrich the factual descriptions of events, but also to understand the evolution in time and space of a social and historical reality in which the particularities of the two regions that are often viewed in parallel, the Banat and Transylvania, will be distinguished.

There are several questions which deserve our attention:

(1) What was the relationship between the enlightened despotism of the Habsburgs and the ideals of the Enlightenment?

(2) What were the consequences of the industrial development coordinated by Maria Theresa and Joseph II for the inhabitants of

the Banat and Transylvania?

(3) Was the transfer of an Austrian cultural code possible, offering these inhabitants a direction towards European integration?

(4) In these circumstances, can we speak of one identity for the Banat and another for Transylvania, of different interests and policies practised by the same empire in each of these regions?

The Banat had been multicultural since the Middle Ages – in other words, since it had been part of the Kingdom of Hungary and the Ottoman Empire. It was a region populated by Orthodox communities speaking Romanian and Serbian-Slavonic languages, Turkish-speaking Muslims, Armenians, Sephardi Jews, and Gypsies. In addition, as a result of Ottoman rule between 1552 and 1716, the nobility of the Banat disappeared along with older administrative structures. Religious congregations also were not stable. The Ottomans had an important fortress in Timișoara, a defence system and an elite military, but not an administration preoccupied with the organisation and management of the region. As a result, when Timișoara became part of the House of Habsburg, the Banat was completely reorganised according to imperial interests without encountering any local opposition. Despite actions which were inimical to regionalisation, evidence of remarkable progress in technology, industry, agriculture, arts, music and literature has been preserved.

In the nineteenth and twentieth centuries, historians used to write books in accordance with the political ideologies of the time. Even when research into the primary sources was impressive, and the collections of documents or some descriptions were outstanding, historians had to follow the path imposed by the public administration and the dominant class. There are sufficient examples to prove the absence of a historiographical assessment of the Banat, free from the constraints mentioned earlier.

The Banat has preserved an independent character based on its own institutions and church hierarchies. Since it had a population practising many religions and speaking several languages, it cannot be identified with a single demographic situation or a single nation. The cohabitation of Catholic and Orthodox bishops was a historical and religious reality of the Banat, which distinguished it from other regions or areas of Central and East-Central Europe. The Orthodox archdiocese of Karlowitz/Sremski-Karlovci had a long and stable history, with a broad autonomy obtained as a result of agreements with the imperial administration of Vienna, and also with the diets of Pressburg (Pozsonyi/Bratislava) and Buda. All the information registered in the historiography of the Banat indicates a social and political physionomy which was multicultural and multi-confessional, intercultural and border-specific. Old administrative policies reveal that Timișoara did not deviate from the path imposed by Vienna for more than two hundred years, and that its status as a royal free city was special, its autonomy recognised by the central power.

When the counties were founded, Vienna was preoccupied not only with colonisation, but also with the population's standard of living. The unitary organisation of the Banat region, rather than its division, was the focus of attention. What the Imperial Chancellery envisaged was the development and balanced distribution of labour, along with the establishment of counties similar in geographical size and in status. Education was given special attention, mainly the foundation of schools. The primary objective was to introduce similar rules, to establish a common cultural code through the emancipation of different social classes living in the regions under Habsburg rule. The project covered two forms of education: one 'for the noblemen' and the other 'for the common people', both aimed at promoting respect for rules and work ethics by all citizens of the empire (see Chapters 5 and 6 by László Marjanucz in this volume).

Without these important fragments of Central European history, it would be difficult to understand either the evolution of the empire or status of a region such as the Banat with multiple linguistic and religious affiliations. It is a region that transformed an experiment into reality, in the sense of a mixed identity between the European Enlightenment and the first period of modernisation. From an administrative point of view, we can better understand that the Banat had several command centres. In the past, there was Vienna, Pressburg/Pozsonyi, Ofen/Buda and Karlowitz/Sremski-Karlovci. Today, there is Bucharest, Belgrade and Budapest and, depending on the historical period, these centres were and still are the main political, religious and cultural references for the inhabitants of the region. In the case of such research topics – regardless of the volume of documents, analyses and observations of facts – the researcher is always faced with the challenge and difficulty of interpretation. The linguistic and religious diversity of the community, along with the mercantilist approach of imperialism, ensured the Banat and Timișoara a place and an identity specific to Europe in the eighteenth century. Those who administered the aforementioned imperial conglomerate did so by accepting the multilingualism and multiple religious confessions, and by generating a set of rules characteristic to this region, many of which have been preserved – perhaps to a lesser extent – but are recognisable even in today's Banat.

Vienna's policies sought to develop the regions equally, promoting the strategies of absolute but enlightened monarchies that were characteristic of Europe in that period. Being an imperial possession (*Kronland*) without a governing diet or administrative institutions to mediate between the imperial administration and local inhabitants, the Banat had social and economic policies and its own demographic situation, which was different from those of Transylvania and Hungary. For example, a nobility or privileged class did not exist in the Banat as a result of the previous Ottoman rule (1552–1716).

Baroque art was promoted in the cities and towns within the Banat in the eighteenth century, thus playing a key role in the region's cultural identity. The Baroque style characteristic of the Banat was the result of the ideas of the Enlightenment, opposing medieval prejudices and suggesting instead the possibility for renewal in society, political thinking and economic development. This particular type of art represents the culture and manner of thinking specific to Central Europe.

The Banat's version of the Baroque represents a projection that shapes the geographical space in accordance with the mentalities of European society. Baroque art appeared in the Banat in the eighteenth century and synthetised the evolution of art in Central Europe, suggesting the existence of a local expression of Baroque. Evidence of this localised adaptation of the universal Baroque can be found in both Catholic and Orthodox churches of that era. Baroque art of the eighteenth century demanded changes and adaptations that can be seen in the well-known *sensus allegoricus* (allegorical sense), a visual image found in several creations in the region.

The purpose of the imperial authorities was the integration of the Banat into the dominant culture of Central Europe, which was why Vienna paid attention to the reconfiguration of the Oriental image of the region that was a legacy inherited from the Ottomans. As a consequence, interest in urban programmes appeared, and the art and architecture of the urban centres of the House of Habsburg served as models (see Chapter 9 by Mihaela Vlăsceanu in this volume). During the Habsburg period painting workshops combined Byzantine church art with the Baroque models of Central and Western Europe. The interactions mentioned earlier had shaped figures and clothing, landscapes, and depictions of traditional Orthodox iconography. During the Enlightenment period there was a perception of some elements of Western art, which explains the fact that the Orthodox Church in the Banat is the result of multiple interactions between Byzantium and Catholic Europe. This phenomenon is visible everywhere in territories situated between Central and South-Eastern Europe, or between East and West, which were influenced by both cultures and stages in the evolution of civilisation (see Chapter 10 by Adrian Negru in this volume).

Complementing the research dedicated to Baroque and church art is the research related to the evolution of architecture. In the Banat there are brilliant examples from the past, allowing a thorough understanding of the habitat and thus recovering a distinctive feature of the region's history. These studies reflect an interest in understanding the construction of houses, palaces, churches, streets and symbols. We must remember that urban architecture was (and still is) fundamental to modern culture, and this manifested itself fully in the Banat and demonstrates that in the eighteenth and nineteenth centuries architecture types represented the image of modern society, aspirations of the inhabitants and integration of the Banat into European civilisation. The regional architecture of the previous centuries was usually iconic, inspired by the art of the buildings of the Habsburg Empire and later of the cities in the Austro-Hungarian Empire. There are several steps that marked the evolution of architecture, the variety of styles and the transition from one style to another – for instance, the change from the impressive and provincial Baroque, present over a long period of time, to eclecticism. Through the art of their buildings, the two most important cities of the region – Timișoara and Arad – demonstrate a stylistic pluralism and unitary architecture similar to those of Central European cities (see Chapter 7 by Gabriel Szekely in this volume).

While the village Baroque style combined with eclectic influences perpetuated in rural areas, after 1900 the buildings in urban areas benefited from ideas of modern art, namely the desire to promote a 'national architecture'. The iconic, spontaneous architecture from the years of monarchy continued to exist, but was also slowly set aside during the interwar decades and the Second World War, as national art inspired by folklore started to replace it. The historians of architecture even spoke of 'a conflict between the Central European culture characterised by an iconic style and the national trends of the people from South-Eastern Europe' (see Chapter 9 by Mihaela Vlăsceanu in this volume). We believe, however, that this process was a slow one and that the many social classes which inhabited the region managed to generate a local identity and a common culture.

As far as the rural habitat is concerned, it is presented according to the traditions of the Banat and of the colonised populations, in connection with the demographic policies of the Habsburgs in the eighteenth and nineteenth centuries and in relation to their construction plans. The study contains a review of the social and cultural realities, along with a typology of rural settlements in the Banat. The different manners of organising the habitat are the result of the many layers of cultures and civilisations developed throughout history and from the multicultural reality that has characterised the region since the Middle Ages – that is, several centuries before the integration of the Banat into the Habsburg Empire and before the colonisation processes began. Along with the technical descriptions concerning the architecture of villages, the amalgamation of typologies became a habit of the region's inhabitants just as in the case of urban styles, during the period when they were trying to establish their own cultural code. In this case, as in others, the *longue durée* of history indicates that populations have tended towards a form of coexistence defined by 'complexity and variety'. According to Teodor Octavian Gheorghiu (see Chapter 8 in this volume), there were few cases where a single typology functioned, the majority being mixed, indicating how typology of social and intellectual life was structured in the region during the period of modernism.

The Banat school system, as part of the Austrian Empire, focused on the establishment and practice of Serbian-language schools, which changed their affiliation from the church schools that dominated from 1790–1810 to the secular schools that became important in the years 1810–48 (see Chapter 12 by Grozdanka Gojkov in this volume). The educational system in the Banat, in the case of the Serbian population, was a process encouraged first by the nobility, then by urban society and finally by representatives of the Orthodox Church. Urban intellectuals were not only present in the process but under the influence of imperial policy, and played a very important role in the development of the education system and its convergence with other cultures from the Banat. We must take into consideration that in the nineteenth century, the Serbs in the Banat paid great attention to the preparation of teachers and professors, those who have always been the milestone for any education system to function well. A special place was granted to this profession in the period of the nation's Romantic affirmation, and later when literacy and the education of inhabitants became important for the purpose of acquiring a general culture. For example, the School of Pedagogy of Sombor is symptomatic but not unique as the Serbian education centres of the empire multiplied in the decades before and after the Revolution of 1848. The Austrian administration and education system as well as the establishment of German-language schools in many places in the Banat stimulated the educational process. This explains why the Banat benefited earlier than neighbouring regions from schools of various levels; from an interest in education and culture, in emancipation and socio-economic modernisation; and from a political thought that was in line with European trends of the time.

The education system in the Austro-Hungarian Monarchy was researched using Hungarian documents and bibliographical information; its main references are the laws that led to the development of the education system in its eastern regions, especially the development plans for elementary and secondary schools established in the Banat during 1867–1914, as well as the curricula and statistics concerning teachers and students. In that period, the foundations of a modern education system were set up and the state and municipal school networks were created, all proving the existence of education in multiple languages – Hungarian, German, Serbian, Romanian – until towards the end of the nineteenth century. It was the period in which imperial policies became almost one with the national ideal, losing the neutral status they had previously held. In the new school networks founded in the Banat, part of the old symbiosis of multicultural reality had survived, but that did not mean authorities in Budapest at the time understood or truly practised the meanings of multicultural diversity.

Students chose secondary schools based on the professional or intellectual opportunities they provided and therefore frequently opted for an education in the Hungarian language, voluntarily renouncing their mother tongue as 'studies conducted in a language other than Hungarian would impact negatively on the future careers of the graduates . . . to speak Hungarian fluently was a mandatory condition for application to a university'. Discussing the weaknesses but also the positive aspects of the education system established by the government in Budapest, we can conclude that in the years 1867–1914 a rapid modernisation of the school network occurred; its purpose was to raise the level of education of the inhabitants in accordance with economic development and the need to professionalise most of the domains of activity. Concerning education in the Banat, 'with the exception of university studies, the education system was able to meet local needs, from the primary education of peasant children to the higher demands of intellectuals. From analyses of the curricula we can see that they were established so graduates could be prepared not only for their chosen profession, but also to meet the expectations of society at that time' (quotations from Chapter 16 by Áron Kovács in this volume).

If significant progress was registered in the case of professionalisation, the same cannot be said regarding multicultural education. The Hungarian education system in the years 1867–1914 did not take into account the fact that it addressed a variety of populations from the eastern part of the monarchy, not only Hungarian-speaking communities. It neglected or treated lightly the problems arising from multilingual social realities of the multicultural monarchy. József Eötvös, the most avant-garde Hungarian intellectual and politician of the time, pointed out the importance of nationalities within the empire and how they should be approached. Both he and his theory were ignored (see my Chapter 14 in this volume).

Newspapers and magazines in particular have played a major role in uniting local cultural values with European and universal ones. Borrowing the model of the German press, the numerous magazines from the Banat contain a true chronicle of the life of the local inhabitants. The many perspectives regarding ethnonational ideas, the revolutionary movement and the civil war that took place in the region between 1848 and 1849 were indicators of the different political, intellectual and military interests of people of Serbian, Hungarian and Romanian origins. The discourse on identity propagated social, linguistic and religious differences. The theme is fascinating not only from a historical point of view, but also because it represents a way of clarifying the so-called 'ethnicity', a source of political propaganda that led to cultural, regional, national and European divisions in the following decades. The emancipation of the Southern Slavs, the association between Serbs and Croats, and the cultural and political programmes known as the Illyrian movement all were described as the main issues of the decade preceding the Revolution of 1848 (see my Chapter 14 in this volume).

In each case, the main idea relied on a collective identity based on language, origins and historical criteria. Sometimes, the same idea was also related to social modernisation.

As far as the Banat is concerned, this study brings a series of documentary evidence, as well as useful explanations regarding the reorganisation of the region after the multiple conflicts generated in 1848. The region became reorganised within the empire, the Viennese authorities taking into account the demands expressed by the Serbian leaders at the Karlowitz Assembly in 1848. 'The Imperial Patent founding the Voivodeship of Serbia and the Banat of Temeswar' was officially published on 18 November 1849. The new state entity was separated from Hungary and reported directly to the Ministry of the Interior in Vienna. According to the Imperial Constitution of 4 March 1849, 'The Voivodeship of Serbia and the Banat of Temeswar will be ordained such that the Church and nationalities are guaranteed protection under the old privileges and imperial ordinances.' The territorial division was made into the following counties: Bodrog, Torontal, Timiș, Caraș, Ruma and Ilok from the Srem County. The prefectures, named Timișoara, Lugoj, Torontal, Sombor and Novi Sad, were subdivided into praetoriums and communes. At that moment the Banat returned to its eighteenth-century status as a region directly subordinate to Vienna, thus becoming independent from the Hungarian political authorities. Its new regional administration was established in Timișoara, and General Ferdinand Mayerhofer was appointed its governor while Field Marshal Lieutenant Johann Coronini was named head of the military. The multicultural nature of the population continued to be a distinctive feature of the region, including Romanians, Germans, Serbians, Hungarians, Croatians, Slovaks, Bulgarians and Jews. In the mid-nineteenth century, they all had similar ideals oriented towards their own social emancipation.

The imperial administration balanced between the former medieval cosmopolitan, multicultural, multilingual idea and the modern right to differ in terms of origin, language and religion. The Banat was also involved in this ideological dispute. However, both orientations generated discussions among intellectuals in the propaganda of politicians caught between the aspirations of their communities and those of the monarchy which provided them with a legal framework and means of expression. The pleas of some personalities were accompanied not only by the voices of supporters or by a strong echo in the media, but also by an excess of zeal that fed nationalism and extremism before the First World War. It was a context in which the Banat experienced similar ideological divisions. Activism and passivism reflect especially the involvement of regional politicians of the Romanian community, such as Andrei and Alexander Mocsonyi. These two draw our attention in the context of political life during the Austro-Hungarian Monarchy. The principles and political thinking proved their ability to conceptualise the phenomenon of

Romanian ethnoculturalism and ethnonationalism in the Banat, and also useful changes in regional administration.

The Jews were also part of an emancipation process. The ones from the Banat – like those from other regions of East-Central Europe – were involved in a long period of struggle to acquire citizen rights. We consider it useful to see why this group was treated differently in the context of the Austrian Empire and the Hungarian government of which, for a period of time, the Banat was also part. Jewish reform was strongly represented in the Banat by Aron Chorin (1766–1844), rabbi of Timișoara and Arad. It was no mistake that the intellectual circles of both Jews and non-Jews had been drawn to debate on the emancipation theme, with the Banat benefiting from this experiment entirely. In fact, as an emancipated community – a status acquired through the imperial law of 1868 – we can observe a different evolution of the Jewish community within the Romanian regions, as well as the difficulty of integrating it under the same constitutional framework as the United Principalities of Wallachia and Moldavia (see my Chapter 4 in this volume).

Indeed, the peace treaties decided to divide the Banat according to linguistic, geographical and strategic criteria. The old imperial status, with a unified administration and particular identity, was completely ignored. The principles formulated by Woodrow Wilson as well as the claims of the three new entities established – Romania, Serbia and Hungary – generated disputes that resulted in the partition of the Banat. The major changes occurred in the years of the First World War and those immediately following, resulting in military operations, ethnonationalist policies, diplomatic games, endless political negotiations and decisions of the major political powers at the Paris Peace Conference, which resulted in partitioning the Banat between Romania, Serbia and Hungary. Serbian historiography, and also that of Romania and Hungary, has debated the problem of the Banat only from a nationalist point of view for more than a century, which has not allowed a proper understanding of the region's history. Historians' efforts must be directed towards the recovery and 'shaping [of] a complete and plausible image of the region's past' (see final chapter in this volume written by Slobodan Bjelica). This will be possible only through mutual understanding of the contributions of the three historiographies, by multiplying the analytical studies, and by formulating hypotheses and interpretations free of the old and 'dusty' ideologies from previous centuries (see Chapters 18 and 19).

The Banat, as an image of multicultural and intercultural realities of the area, must be understood in relation to its geography and dependence on the relationships between cultures and civilisations. We point this out to show that the values of a region formed on the border of two former empires and three contemporary national states are an amalgam. To conclude, every regional history – as well as national ones – should contain facts and events shown from multiple perspectives. Surely, in this way, the images of past and present will overcome the prejudices born out of a fictional, cultural, linguistic or religious uniqueness.

PART II

2
TIMIŞOARA UNDER THE SIGN OF PRINCE EUGENE OF SAVOY

Victor Neumann

THIS CHAPTER FOCUSES ON Prince Eugene of Savoy's contribution to the conquest of the Banat and the citadel of Timişoara, his virtues not only as a military man but also as a thinker and enlightened reformer who played an influential role in the entire Habsburg Empire.[1] In addition to bibliographical research, meticulous documentation was conducted in Viennese libraries and museums, exploiting recent information, proposing analyses and interpretations on the history of art and architecture, the history of books and the history of a generation of intellectuals that opened the horizon of modern knowledge. The references are mostly from the eighteenth century, in which despotism – the Habsburg case being a well-known example – was coupled with the ideas of the Enlightenment. The cultural elements which contribute to a more complex understanding of Eugene of Savoy's personality and his relationship to the Danubian regions and to Timişoara also were researched. A number of palaces and libraries were studied, as well as collections of paintings, design pieces, sculptures and maps associated with him. All these sources allowed for a larger perspective, one in which the traits of Eugene of Savoy can be understood in the context of his own thoughts and the ideas distinctive to his time: the events, facts and personalities that facilitated the progress and transition from medieval to modern in eighteenth-century Eastern and Central Europe, establishing an administration and a cultural code which would transform Timişoara into a royal free city.

The history of Timişoara and the Banat has been described in chronicles and monographs, sometimes presented in elaborate studies and books.[2] Prince Eugene of Savoy's connection to Timişoara is rarely mentioned, though, more attention being given to the siege and conquest of the citadel. Among the aspects that have been ignored were the reconstruction of the citadel under Eugene's influence and that of Governor Claude Florimond de Mercy; the role of Vienna and the Viennese Baroque, from not only an artistic but also a political point of view; defining the city's cultural code; and the integration of the inhabitants into a European set of behavioural and civilisational values.[3] Starting from the earliest contributions,[4] our study will present an image of the East-Central European world of the eighteenth century, in which administration, urbanism, people's concerns and mentalities interact to emphasise Timișoara's transition to modernity and Europeanism. We will offer a series of hypotheses on the relationship between the outstanding military man, supporter of Enlightenment ideas, and the city situated on the banks of the Bega. This novel perspective is based on relevant bibliographical and documentary sources, aiming for an interpretative contribution, the result of which will be what Marc Bloch recommended, namely 'a continuous contact with men' and 'the vast experience of human diversities'[5] – in other words, revealing and understanding the past in a rational manner, according to cultural, economic and sociopolitical realities. In writing about Timișoara and Eugene of Savoy, I considered the circumstances in which he was formed and matured as a military man and politician of Enlightened Europe. Tangentially, I acknowledged his military feats described in chronicles or history books, though I paid more attention to his intellectual formation, the administrative reforms, and cultural products created by his initiative or under his coordination, which impacted the renewal of Timișoara and its transformation from a Turkish Oriental city into a town bearing the marks of the first European modernity. Having the allure of a great aristocrat among military men and that of an erudite among the creators of the Austrian Baroque, Prince Eugene of Savoy was and remained a symbol for the majority of people belonging to the House of Habsburg after the peace treaties of Karlowitz and Passarowitz.

TIMIȘOARA: A CITY BETWEEN WORLDS

Timișoara, one of the European cities of modern Romania, traces its beginnings to the thirteenth century. The city's history tells of different strata, cultural and civilisational, from medieval to modern. Situated at the border of the former Kingdom of Hungary and the Ottoman and Habsburg empires, at the boundary of three contemporary countries – Romania, Serbia and Hungary – inside a geographical area in which the three great monotheistic religions – Christianity, Islam and Judaism – met, and where different communities and linguistic cultures coexisted, Timișoara is a Central/South-Eastern European city unique for its multiculturalism and interculturalism, multilingualism, competition and innovative spirit. Throughout history, the Banat[6] has played an important role in the area of Central and South-East Europe, and Timișoara was its economic, political, administrative, military, industrial, cultural and commercial core. The Banat of Temeswar (Timișoara)[7] first became known to Europe by this name in the eighteenth century, following its integration into the Habsburg Empire and due to its discovery and portrayal by Enlightenment travellers and explorers.[8]

Starting in the Middle Ages, the citadel and later the city witnessed some major European events: wars against the Ottomans; the late Crusades; ascension of Hungary; fall of the Ottoman Empire; unprecedented expansion of the Habsburg Empire; disappearance of the Austro-Hungarian Monarchy; and genesis of the Romanian, Serbian and Hungarian nation states. In every century Timișoara was transformed, the role of the city highlighted by the written testimonies of political, military and cultural personalities. The different royal, imperial and national administrations succeeding each other over the course of seven and a half centuries created an urban identity particularised through different layers of culture and civilisation, namely by the multiple identities of its inhabitants. This began in the fourteenth century, when the kings of Hungary from the Anjou dynasty built a citadel in place of an ancient settlement. During Charles Robert's reign, the city developed a great deal, being 'populated and rich, able to offer a proper hosting to the royal family'.[9] Charles Robert had colonised families from different parts of Europe in the region, an experiment which would be resumed by the Habsburgs in the eighteenth century.

Between 1552 and 1716, Timișoara and its surrounding region were occupied by the Turks, the city playing an important role for the Ottoman Empire, both militarily and commercially. Mosques, houses, baths and bazaars were built in Timișoara, symbolising not only a religious culture but also one of dwellings and laissez-faire competition. The Turkish baths – one of which, perfectly preserved, was discovered in the city's centre during archaeological excavations between 2013 and 2015 – was a hygienic concept superior to the Scandinavian sauna, capable of rivalling the modern spa.[10] As for the bazaar, it encouraged transparent relations between buyer and seller, a place where accumulation of capital was already present in the sixteenth century. Just as we acknowledge the existence of multicultural and intercultural social environments occupied by the Ottomans, we have to observe the genesis of obvious signs of modernity. Francesco Griselini says – and many of his successors agree – that the Turks did not plan to modernise the Banat.[11] In the case of both Timișoara and some other regional cities like Lipova, Lugoj and Ineu, things turned out differently. It is true, though, that the Ottoman Empire declined in the second half of the seventeenth century, hence the shortcomings found there by the following conqueror, the Habsburgs.

The location and people of Timişoara appealed to the Ottomans because they were placed at the interface of East and West. Generally, Europe represented, in the eyes of the Turks, an exotic, popular and interesting space.[12] By understanding Timişoara, they found out more about European diplomatic culture, architecture and everyday life. The city of Buda had been in the hands of the Ottomans for almost 200 years, which facilitated their assimilation of European customs and cultures. Some historians state that, by means of direct contact with the cities of Central and East-Central Europe, the Ottomans borrowed some of their lifestyle. Recent archaeological discoveries carried out in 2013–15 in the central squares of Timişoara (Freedom, St George and Union) demonstrate the existence of small communities who bore Turkish Oriental and Baroque Occidental cultural values. The virtues of Baroque and mostly Rococo decor – visible in the architecture of Central European cities – reflect both secular aristocratic and popular Muslim aesthetics.[13] Johann Bernhard Fischer von Erlach, the renowned architect of the House of Habsburg, had influenced not only Central European but also South-Eastern European architecture. During the Austrian-Turkish War of 1683–1716, he inspired even the style of Constantinople's significant buildings, such as the Nurosmaniye mosque and the Ragib Pasha Library. Europe, too, benefited from the Turkish-Oriental influences. It was fashionable in eighteenth-century France, in the German states, in the Kingdom of Poland and in the central regions of the continent to take Turkish baths. The European nobility acquired the Turkish turban and Turkish cuisine.[14]

The hegemonies were always military and diplomatic – the Habsburg and Ottoman Empires making no exception – meaning that not everything happening in peoples can be explained by a dominant minority, political actors or the religion preached by clerics. The reality is more complex, which prompts us to think that economic, religious and cultural transformations are not limited to a certain period. Despite the administrative, economic and cultural Ottoman presence mentioned, during the seventeenth and most of the eighteenth century, people living in cities in Central/South-East Europe were sensitive to change coming from Vienna. Things often fall into place by themselves, a scenario in which ideas and patterns arise as a result of great intellectual movements and interactions.

Destroyed during the Austrian-Turkish battles, Timişoara was literally refounded during the military and civil governance exercised directly from Vienna between 1719 and 1779. Following the integration of Timişoara into the Habsburg Empire, a multilingual administration was created; important military constructions were built; different European-language communities were colonised; unprecedented economic development and social experiments were planned. This resulted not only in peculiarities but also giving Timişoara cultural and behavioural similarities with other European areas.

Timișoara entered the Western sphere of influence in 1719–79. As early as the nineteenth century, Romanian historians such as August Treboniu Laurian sensed that, as soon as they became possessions of the House of Habsburg, the city and the region entered a new order of things.[15] The Austrian administration would transform the city, also reforming the whole land. The Enlightenment ideal cultivated by the Habsburgs made possible not only the restoration of the old settlements in the Banat, but also the founding of new ones. Governor Claude Florimond de Mercy founded many villages and populated them with Germans, Italians and Spaniards. Under his administration, Sînpetru, Zădărlac, Beșenova Nouă, Peciul Nou, Deta, Kudrić, Pișchia, Guttenbrunn, Biserica Albă, Mercydorf, Aradul Nou and Giarmata were founded.[16] Mercy's intention in colonising the villages was to exploit the rich lands of the Timișoara plain by promoting new agricultural branches, by stimulating crafts and by practising active commerce with Europe. In order to achieve such projects, he 'calls experienced farmers and skillful artisans to the Banat, especially Italians, and provides them with generous support'.[17] Some of these projects would enhance local manufacturing and, later, the industrialisation of Timișoara.

The cohabitation of several religious and cultural-linguistic communities was a reality that generated mutually advantageous interhuman relationships and undogmatic perspectives.[18] We are talking about not only the policy of Vienna, but also the options and manifestations of people who wished to settle in Timișoara and the Banat. Also in this latter case, the emphasis falls rarely on segregation on communitarian criteria, but more on inter-confessional and intercultural relations. These were understood by less wealthy people, by those who had a job and wanted to secure their everyday life, by those who accepted competition as a fundamental principle of existence. From a social perspective, Timișoara and the Banat quickly adopted the cultural and civilisational meanings that charcterise the eighteenth century and express the desire for absolute good. Much of what happened in those years was linked to the projects formulated by Eugene of Savoy and put into practice by Claude Florimond de Mercy.[19] The role of the prince, a shining example of Western Enlightenment, and in particular of the Austrian *Auflklärung*, was fundamental to the genesis of the first administration of 'Banat Country'.[20]

EUGENE OF SAVOY: BETWEEN MILITARY DISCIPLINE AND HIGH CULTURE

The reconstruction of Timișoara and early modernisation of the city and the region can be better described and understood if we focus on Prince Eugene of Savoy's personality, drawing upon some biographical data and examples of his military genius and political acumen in the eighteenth century. Known by many names, François Eugene de Savoy, Eugenio di Savoya Carignano, Eugene von Savoy, the prince would prefer the trilingual signature Eugenio von Savoy, consonant with his family's multicultural and intercultural allegiance. He was born in Paris on 18 October 1663, the son of Maurice, prince of Savoy and count of Dreux. His mother, Olimpia Mancini, was the niece of Cardinal Mazarin. In 1683 Eugene decided to pursue a military career and asked King Louis XIV of France for command of a regiment. The king's refusal, on the pretext that his small stature was inappropriate for a military career, prompted the young prince to take his chances at other European courts. Shortly thereafter he went to Vienna, where his brother Louis Julius was serving as an officer in the imperial army.

After Eugene of Savoy had established himself as a great personality, Louis XIV radically changed his opinion, stating: 'The prince is an inimitable example for all the rulers and the statesmen. I cannot sufficiently respect his iron loyalty and devotion to his sovereign, the feeling of pure patriotism and the strong dedication to the fulfilment of his duties. Also, I cannot sufficiently deplore the loss France has suffered since his leaving.'[21] Truly, the prince had become loyal to the Austrian imperial house, which welcomed his service and offered him the opportunity to display his extraordinary military talent, unmatched generosity and raw courage.

Eugene of Savoy had family ties with the House of Habsburg. His grandfather, Thomas Francis, founder of the Savoy-Carignan branch of the House of Savoy, was the son of Catherine Michelle, daughter of King Philip II of Spain. Eugene distinguished himself in battle in 1683, the year when the Ottomans besieged Vienna. He asked Emperor Leopold I for the right to fight in the imperial army and, following the emperor's consent, he attended the great Habsburg battle against the Ottomans, led by the Duke of Lorraine and backed by John III Sobieski's Polish army. This was the background on which the prince's impressive career began.

Successively ranked major general (1685), lieutenant general (1687), cavalry general (1690) and field marshal (1693), Eugene of Savoy became the pre-eminent military leader in 1697 when the president of the Imperial War Council, Count Max Stahrenberg, assigned him the role of supreme commander of the imperial troops. He would become a military leader who reorganised the army with the help of radical reforms, and achieved great results. When Emperor Leopold I ordered him to stop Sultan Mustapha II's march to Transylvania, Eugene attacked the Ottoman army at Zenta, while the sultan was crossing the river Tisza. The battle took place on 11 September 1697,[22] and the Habsburg victory transformed Eugene of Savoy into a well-known figure who envisioned the potential unification of Europe under a single monarch – one of the first in the modern age to do so. He believed – like Napoleon and other adventurers from a time closer to ours – in continuous revolt against historical legacies and in a novel theory on morality and politics. In his utopian projects, he seemed to be inspired by the philosophers and writers of the Enlightenment.

Eugene was attributed the merits of rigorous coordinator, believer in soldierly discipline, an ideal of human honesty, i.e. free from any feelings of hatred, jealousy or malice.[23] Yet his military qualities defined him best. The exaggerations – and they are not few – have the tendency to mislead. What kind of warrior could be free of hatred? Could this be the naivety of historians, or a temptation to prolong the echo of legends? In 1716, at the height of his career, the prince was entrusted with the main role in the Austrian-Turkish War, whose goal was, among others, the conquest of Timișoara and the Banat and their integration into the Habsburg Empire. In addition to an outstanding military career, Eugene of Savoy's true greatness comes from his attachment to arts and science, architecture and philosophy. He cultivated relationships with the Enlightenment philosophers Montesquieu, Voltaire, Rousseau and Leibniz, buying some of their manuscripts and books.

The Belvedere palace in Vienna, a monument of Baroque architecture, is the result of one of the most important architectural projects of the era that the prince endorsed. His interest in art and philosophy resulted in the establishment of some great collections and reveals an education and exquisite taste acquired in one of the prestigious European noble houses of political power and great wealth. Eugene of Savoy represents a rare example in history when a military genius acquires a thorough interest in books, is in dialogue with famous writers and philosophers, and is engaged in promoting and supporting them. From this perspective also, he belongs to the elite of the Enlightenment. His personal library is a testimony to his interest in humanist culture, in flagship artistic, literary, philosophical and theological creations. With the help of a professional librarian he had hired, the prince selected and bought numerous rare books, founding the so-called Bibliotheca Eugeniana. In that period, 1723–26, the emperor had invested money in establishing and inaugurating one of the most beautiful libraries in the world, the Imperial Library of Vienna. It was built according to the plans of the architect Johann Bernhard Fischer von Erlach, and executed by Joseph Emmanuel Fischer von Erlach. Upon his death, Bibliotheca Eugeniana, whose stock numbers over 15,000 volumes, was bought (in the year 1738) by Emperor Charles VI. It was integrated into the Imperial Library, which numbers 200,000 volumes and has since represented the universally valued historical collection of the Austrian National Library (Österreichische National Bibliothek).[24]

Why do we mention this monumental library? Because its architecture and art represent the imperial Baroque, or the Central European Baroque, which has always been an inspiration for the Baroque of Timișoara and Banat; because it defines the heterogeneous preoccupations of an elite and the artistic style of a culture; because the interiors, balconies, doors, windows, furniture, frescoes of this monument were created especially for it; because it is a place where the attention is directed not only to the symbolistic or cult of the emperor, but mostly to meditation, to the dialogue between theological, science and philosophy initiates; because in the paintings and the books the prince and his congeners (noblemen, priests, servicemen, architects, geographers, civil servants) had been collecting, we identify the messages of the new Europe; because Eugene of Savoy's books are situated in one of the most generous of spaces in this true Bibliotheca Europea, specifically below the 30-metre-high arch adorned with Daniel Gran's frescoes. Lastly, the library represents a way of thinking, a manner of being consonant with the utopian projections of the eighteenth century. We are talking not only about the prince's intellectual contributions, but also about the reception and multiplication of the ideas of his time. We are talking about accepting a cultural and civilisational code that personalised Europe during the Enlightenment and that was spread in the new territories conquered by the Habsburg Empire. It is a similar process to that of the early nineteenth century, when, during the Napoleonic Wars, the organisational, juristic and economic reforms initiated in post-Revolutionary France were introduced in all regions subordinated to it.

In all that Eugene of Savoy accomplished during his life and also in his legacy there is a dramatic tension, a permanent battle with the contradictory aspects of the human being, a dispute between military discipline and the high culture proposed by the freedom of Baroque; an amalgam of material and spiritual life. He lived in an age of great European culture, characterised by a monumental festive pathos, excessive ornamentation, an elevated level of artistic craft;[25] one defined by reality and illusion, by search and transformation. During this historical moment, Timișoara was besieged, conquered and integrated into European values by the legendary Eugene of Savoy, the Habsburg emperors and their representatives. It was the beginning of a century in which the individualities discovered a deeper European East and South-East for the first time, redrawing the map of these spaces. In the same period, the first topographical map of Timișoara's Banat was being designed.

THE AUSTRIAN-TURKISH WARS: THE CONQUEST OF TIMIȘOARA

Although the city of Timișoara was conquered in war, many European historians believe that the year 1716 was one of the 'happy moments' in local history: it meant an annexation to Habsburg possessions, and a relocation of the city and region inside Christian Europe. On the one hand, these historians take into account the conqueror's perspective; on the other, the changes that took place after the Banat of Timișoara had entered the Viennese and European sphere of influence. But let us look at the facts: following the victory of Petrovaradin,[26] Eugene made the decision to conquer the city of Timișoara, prolonging his expedition. His march towards Timișoara started on 14 August 1716. His war council examined the city and assessed the difficulties the soldiers might encounter during a fight. Under Eugene's command, the imperial army conducted a lot of complicated manoeuvres. A testimony from that time reads:

> After he and the troops had camped for a few days on the shores of the Danube . . . Prince Eugene decided to make a move. Because the heat impeded the infantry from making very long marches every day, Eugene went ahead with his cavalry until the infantry arrived. Finally, on 25 August the prince, his dragoon regiment and the one led by the Prince of Württemberg arrived at the camp in front of Timișoara. The next day, the entire army joined them. As soon as they arrived, the troops spread out to their designated positions. To establish a communication between the different command points, they built bridges over swamps.[27]

Therefore, at the beginning of the eighteenth century the city was at an advantage due to its geographical setting. On the other hand, it was often threatened by 'contagious emissions risen from so many stinking and mouldy waters', 'by all kinds of epidemic fever [which] was only one of the smaller nuisances that had to be endured by the inhabitants of the Banat'.[28] The conquest of Timișoara entailed very good military management and knowledge of the city, of its castle, fortresses, water moats and defensive walls. Throughout time, Timișoara held an important and strategic position, something not overlooked by anybody. According to Johann Nepomuk Preyer, the city's strength lay not so much in its fortifications, but 'mostly in its natural setting in the swamps of Bega and Timiș rivers'.[29]

Many generals of the imperial army took part in the siege of Timișoara, some of whom were political personalities in eighteenth-century Central Europe: Count Claude Florimond de Mercy, the Count of Stahremberg, Prince Alexander von Württemberg, Count Franz Paul von Wallis, Count János Pálffy, Prince von Bevern, Portuguese Prince Emanuel, Prince Albert von Braunschweig.[30] All were attached to the imperial plans for conquest and followed Eugene of Savoy's orders. The Austrian–Turkish battle for Timișoara was one in which both parties took a great interest. Along with the hundreds of elite Janissaries who were camped inside the city, the Turks had gathered a large army to defend the castle against the Austrians. The whole Turkish army numbered many thousands of soldiers of Turkish and Tatar origin, representing 'the elite of the sultan's Janissary troops'.[31]

The battles started on 28 August 1716 and finished with the imperial victory on 12 October the same year. The first attack was upon the 'resort house' of the pasha, located in one of Timişoara's suburbs. Before abandoning it to the imperial forces, the Turks burned the house and the entire suburb.[32] The next day, 29 August, Eugene ordered an attack on a mosque near Palanca. Being defenceless, it was also quickly conquered.

When the real battle started, on 20 September 1716, Eugene rallied two battalions from the Virmont regiment, a battalion from Ottokar Stahremberg's regiment, three companies of grenadiers, the armour regiments of Stainville and Neipperg, Palffy's Hussars, and in the following days (23 and 24 September) Count Max Stahremberg's brigade, composed of 11 battalions and 24 cannons,[33] Alexander von Württemberg's troops of 3,000 grenadiers, supported by 30 battalions and 2,700 pontoniers.[34] In short, the most important Austrian troops were stationed in the area. Eugene of Savoy's plan aimed at coordinating the attack near the city gates, and for that he demanded digging of trenches, soldiers assuming attack positions, building redoubts for weapon deposits, building bridges over swamps, setting up cannon batteries, etc.[35]

> Prince Eugen, somehow informed about the Ottomans' intentions, arrived at dusk to Pálffy's position. He gave orders for Count Max Stahremberg's brigade to march . . . Half an hour later, the Turks attacked the positions with loud shouts, as was their custom. The imperial cavalry, placed along the fortification, resisted the first blow with extraordinary force, making the Turks withdraw. But that didn't discourage the Turks. They repeated the attack twice more, being dismissed each time . . . By the number of deaths on the battlefield, one can deduce that the Turks' losses were important.[36]

The battles of 25 September and 4, 6 and 12 October were the bloodiest. The army commanded by Eugene of Savoy showed a lot of bravery in confronting the impressive Ottoman force.

> The dreadful bombardment started on 11 October . . . The Turks' response was anaemic, their batteries already having been destroyed by the earlier shooting. On 12 October, the Turks managed to repair their batteries, and their cannons were firing frighteningly, accompanied by the very intense shooting of muskets, until dusk. The Austrians feared the conclusion of the whole action, no matter how vigilant Prince Eugene had been and no matter how good his decisions were. The soldiers kept up their courage, but the weather had changed, and the continuous rain was threatening to flood the trenches, forcing the besiegers to retreat. Prince Eugene was losing hope when, on 13 October, on the forty-eighth day of the siege, the white flag was raised on one of the city's ramparts. The Prince of Württemberg, who was standing guard, immediately notified Eugene, who was pleased that the Pasha was willing to send some of his officers to the imperial camp.[37]

Griselini states that an unusual mobilisation of officers and soldiers of the imperial army was needed in order to be victorious in the battle. The reason for this was the Muslims' skill in handling the sword and also their principle of not leaving any place where they had built a mosque.[38] After a forty-eight-day siege, the Turks capitulated. They lost 3,000 of the 18,000 men they had at the beginning of the siege, while Eugene of Savoy lost roughly 2,000.[39] The Turkish commander surrendered on 13 October, the day when the white flag was displayed on the bastion of the city.[40] Prince Eugene of Savoy entered the city five days later. 'To Eugene came Ahmed Aga, commander of the city, and Ali Effendi. He sent Count Wallis and Count Filippi to the city, to remain there until the capitulation would be regulated at Prince Eugene's command post.'[41]

In the following year, 1717, Eugene also conquered the city of Belgrade, and peace was established, registered by the Treaty of Passarowitz[42] in 1718, which stated the annexation of more regions from the north and south of the Danube to the House of Habsburg. The treaty confirmed occupation of the Banat and Oltenia, thus the Habsburgs reached the largest extension of their empire. The conditions of capitulation were instituted by representatives of the belligerent parties and provided that Turks might leave Timișoara with their families including children, their belongings and a thousand carts. Soldiers were given the right to leave with their weapons and flags, and were escorted to Belgrade. Along the road, they were joined by the garrisons and the Muslim inhabitants of other cities and villages from the Banat. The Turks were forced to leave hostages in Timișoara, along with their artillery, ammunitions and supplies, until the safe return of the escort. Protected by the Austrian authorities along the route from Timișoara to Belgrade, they benefited from low-priced supplies of food from the villagers. Good understanding between the parties governed the whole process of capitulation, thus the retreat went as planned.[43] Christians who had turned to Islam were not obstructed from leaving, except for those who had deserted during the siege. The Serbians, Armenians, Jews and other inhabitants that the Austrians had found inside the city were granted the right to stay or to leave Timișoara.

Speaking of a conditional surrender, the treaty also included the Ottoman's proposals. According to the evidence of Franz Paolo von Wallis – the first military commander of the city in the period immediately following its conquest by Eugene of Savoy[44] – the population of Timișoara numbered 466 Serbians, 35 Armenians and 144 Jews.[45] Inside the city, there lived an undefined number of Romanians, Greeks, Turks and Gypsies.[46] Some defended the city during the Austrian-Ottoman conflicts, and, according to those inscribed in the act of surrender, they were allowed to sell their goods if they decided to leave the city.

What did Eugene of Savoy and his armies find in Timișoara and its neighbourhoods? A city in urgent need of reconstruction, of administrative institutions, of Christian churches (Catholic and Orthodox),[47] houses and drinking water. In the surrounding area, they found great natural resources: fertile land, virgin forests, large pastures 'overgrown everywhere by groves and reeds', but which represented wealth. They realised the enormous agricultural potential of the region, and the way in which Timișoara could capitalise on it by processing, industrialising and selling its natural resources. They were forced to note that at the time there was no concern for productivity by local people. They found peasants practising a subsistence agriculture: 'the people were growing only what was necessary for their families', the sale of agricultural products being unfamiliar to them.[48] They saw that the science, techniques and crafts developed in Europe had not penetrated the city. Initially, in the eyes of the imperial forces, it seemed that the recovery of Timișoara and the Banat would take centuries. In reality, though, in less than six decades, under the reigns of Charles VI, Maria Theresa and Joseph II, the people and the land had changed, recording a similar progress to other European cities and regions of the time that had made the transition to modernity.[49]

Before leaving Timișoara and going to Vienna to inform and persuade Emperor Charles VI on the importance of the integration and governance of the Banat, Prince Eugene had entrusted the command of the city to Franz Paolo von Wallis and the command of the region to Count Claude Florimond de Mercy.[50] The Jesuits' courageous and efficient involvement in supporting the Austrian army during the siege of Timișoara elicited Eugene's admiration. Therefore, immediately following the establishment of the imperial administration, these missionaries were entrusted with the reorganisation and coordination of religious services. Lacking a diocesan seminary and a specialist clergy, the German-speaking Jesuits ruled the diocese of Timișoara. Bishops Ladislau Nadasdy (1711–29), Adalbert Freiherr von Falkenstein (1730–39), Nicolas Stanislawich (1739–50) and Franz Anton Engel von Wagrein (1750–77) followed.[51] As the Banat was subordinated to Vienna, Timișoara's Catholic Church operated based on an administration independent of Hungary. These confessional frictions were not unique; the Reformed Church and other Catholics had similar problems. They existed between noble families and the imperial houses, and between Hungary and Austria – and, from time to time, these disagreements also impacted the administration of the Banat of Timișoara.

As for the Orthodox Church, representing Byzantine Christianity, it accepted subordination to the administration of Vienna. Under the Habsburgs, it was a fundamental landmark of the spiritual lives of the old inhabitants of the city and of the majority who populated the region. During the entire eighteenth century, the metropolitan church of Karlowitz was a strong institution of Orthodoxy, acknowledged by Vienna and responsible for the Serbian and Romanian communities. Its role was equal to the Roman Catholic bishoprics, its presence being felt in the dynamics of social life, in cultural and educational reforms, in the foundation of educational institutions and in the emancipation of people. The double subordination of the Orthodox Church of the Banat of Timișoara to Vienna and to St Petersburg granted the population a special status. Thus, more types of reforms were born, as well as countless possibilities of redefining the identity of Timișoara and the Banat.[52]

Lastly, 'the cultural corridors' of the eighteenth century show how the city and the region were penetrated alternately by a diversity of cultural expressions, either Byzantine Orthodox or Central and West European Baroque. Enlightenment ideas penetrated not only the besieger, playing a role in their grasping of new ideas and in the great transition, but also the besieged.[53] Many of those who had populated the Turkish city chose to stay following the Habsburg conquest. Like the colonists, they would become co-participants in the reforms of Timișoara and the Banat. In other words, the process of modernisation started in 1716 was owed to the merit of Eugene of Savoy's Viennese projects, his followers, the Catholic Church, and also of the reforms accepted and promoted by the religious Orthodox authorities.

The city of Timișoara was destroyed during the Austro-Turkish battles, and the population grew dissatisfied with the economic and governmental conditions. The historians blamed the Turks for the inefficient governance of the city and region, for the depopulation and disappearance of many settlements, the economic underdevelopment, the countless swamps which extended over vast surfaces during the 164 years of Ottoman domination, offering a desolate view.[54] Not having an infrastructure comparable to other territories of the empire, the cities of the Banat needed partial or total reconstruction. This was a strong argument for Eugene to immediately propose the imperial rules of administration. He recommended that a military and a civil governor, directly subordinate to Vienna, should rule the region, with his residence in Timișoara. Military governance was most important, the only thing capable of overcoming local shortcomings, large and small.

Not by chance, among the priorities of the first government was the design and completion of the Bega Canal,[55] which would offer Timișoara and its contiguous area the possibility of industrial and commercial development. The first stage of the draining of the swamps and the sewage of River Bega was finalised in 1730, ensuring the supply of drinking water for the people of Timișoara and also the beginnings of river transportation for surplus goods produced in the Banat. The main contributor to the reconstruction of the city and of the future town was Count Claude Florimond de Mercy. Griselini wrote that 'he was endowed with all the right attributes to elaborate and accomplish the grand plan [of reconstructing the city]. In him, military virtues were interwoven with deep political knowledge, all completed by his own experience. In a word, Mercy was a great genius and a great friend of the people, who deserved to be in the service of the best monarchs.'[56]

Like Prince Eugene of Savoy, Claude Florimond de Mercy was born in France and joined the Austrian army as a volunteer. He fought in Vienna during the Ottoman siege, and later was named an officer of the imperial army. During the anti-Ottoman campaigns in Hungary, he became captain of cavalry, later reaching the rank of field marshal. He was prized by the people of the Banat of Timişoara and also by the Viennese court for his remarkable contribution to the military, administrative and economic fields. Mercy's first political-administrative activities took place under Eugene's direction. Among the most memorable was the preoccupation with assigning the cavalry and the artillery that would defend the Banat, especially in the Danube area, where the Ottoman border was located.[57] As governor (one of the most long-lasting – he would hold the position until 1734), Mercy takes credit for the reorganisation plan of Timişoara and the Banat, one that would prove unexpectedly fruitful.

The region was divided into twelve districts: Timişoara, Becicherecul Mare, Cenad or Sânnicolau, Ciacova, Lugoj, Vršac, Lipova, Făget, Caransebeş, Orşova or Mehadia, Panciova and Palanca Nouă. They were subordinated to the central command of the Banat. This was the framework in which the ideas of Governor Mercy were born. He summoned to Timişoara different craftsmen from Italian cities, silversmiths, tin makers, blacksmiths, shoemakers, tailors, hatters, drapers. He opened a paper mill, a wire-draw for iron wire, Dutch press workshops for squeezing oil; he founded a draper's factory, bought stoves for silk manufacturing, looms, etc.[58] Lastly, he invested interest and money in building houses, at the same time inviting citizens to build their own dwellings inside or outside the city. Simultaneously, he drew attention to the fertile plain around Timişoara,[59] to the extensive cultivation of wheat, corn and grape vine, their harvest contributing to the supply of the empire.

The same Claude Florimond de Mercy was also responsible for organising the first colonisations of the Banat with people from all over Europe, in 1717–24, 1724–27 and 1727–34.[60] This was a special programme designed by the House of Habsburg through which Catholic populations were transferred to the Banat. The principles of this programme were conceived and formulated in the Commission of Newly Acquired Territories, later Einrichtungswerk des Königreichs Ungarn (Facilities of the Hungarian Kingdom). Most colonists were Swabian, a German-language community.[61] Other communities of French-, Italian-, Spanish-, Czech-, Slovakian-, Hungarian- and Bulgarian-speakers joined. At that time, though, the main identitifying feature was religion rather than language, origins or history. Because the House of Habsburg was Roman Catholic, the main reason for accepting the colonists was their religion. Ensuring the existence of proper places of worship was one of the first measures taken by the imperial power. This was no easy task because the city had only mosques when it was conquered. These were transformed into Christian churches, 'the most spacious mosque becoming a Jesuit church, also serving the bishop of Cenad, Ladislau from Count Nádasdy's family'.[62] It was also used as an episcopal cathedral, where the bishop celebrated mass.[63] Francesco Griselini speaks of a second mosque which was conceded to monks of the Franciscan order who had come from Bosnia.

> It was placed close to the Arad gate, today [1780] named Prince Eugene's gate, because it was through here that the hero entered the conquered city. These monks were granted a piece of land in front of the Lugoj gate, inside the Palanca Mică, opening missions in Lugoj and Panciova, and sending their brothers in the order from the Bulgarian province of Caransebeș to run the mission.[64]

All this information proves the strength of the involvement of the Roman Catholic Church in Viennese politics, the administration and reorganisation of the city, and in the colonisation that occurred during the eighteenth century.

It goes without saying that the urbanism of Timișoara changes the view of local and regional history. By pursuing architecture and urbanism, the historian benefits from a better understanding of Timișoara's social and cultural set of values.[65] The city and the region experienced a large transformation in the decades in which the Banat was named a distinct region of the empire, a domain of the crown, having its own administration (*Landesadministration*) subordinate to Vienna. Remarkable progress was made in agriculture, industry and commerce. The Banat became one of the largest grain producers in the empire, while plans were made to reconstruct Timișoara. The city attracted engineers, designers, architects, military men, as well as several artisans from the neighbouring or further regions of the empire. All would contribute to the reconstruction of the city. For example, they built barracks, impressive for the time – the Transylvanian Barracks, 483 metres in length.[66] During the same decades in which the modernisation of Timișoara and the region began, the Bega sewerage was designed and built, which offered Timișoara and its contiguous area possibilities of industrial and commercial development. The reconstruction of the urban centre, with defending walls, straight streets and lots of squares[67] was planned according to Viennese ideas and Eugene's influence. Timișoara's architecture has features that cannot be compared to those of the neighbouring cities: Arad, Lugoj, Vrsac or Szeged. Those urban centres inherited medieval elements while Timișoara was not only demolished and reinvented, but designed and built under imperial norms and according to the requirements of the time, borrowing the Central European Baroque model.

Comparisons to the Viennese Baroque can be made within the limits of common sense and respect for the truth, or by taking into account the imperial projects that transformed Timişoara into a military city but also an administrative, socio-economic and political burgh similar to others in the Habsburg Empire. We have to see and understand that the projects aimed for total reconstruction and integration into Central European culture and civilisation, which in itself subordinated to the urban models of Western Europe. Also, we must understand that the geography of Timişoara remained the same, and that local values continued by reforming and sometimes accepting – but at other times refusing – imperial ideas.

The reconstruction plan of the *Innenstadt* (inner city) of Timişoara was adopted in 1725.[68] The fortifications were of the Vauban type, Timişoara being mostly known for its military barracks. Transport and communication between Timişoara's barracks were important for the reconstruction plans, not only for the defence of the city but also because they accommodated the military institutions which were protecting the south-eastern borders of the empire.[69]

The great innovation of the Baroque, in urban terms, was the *corso*, a space of meetings, walks and socialising, which personalised Austrian Baroque cities. It made possible the emancipation of people and the articulation of diverse social segments; it polished the collective mentality and oriented it to European behavioural culture. People benefited from the meetings facilitated by the Baroque *corso*, their minds became freer, better informed, and more receptive than of those living in closed cities. To Jews – the most oppressed population of medieval Europe, often living in ghettos – Timişoara offered the opportunity to live not only in suburbs, but even inside the city. In exchange for some taxes and a health certificate, Jewish craftsmen, merchants and tradesmen were granted the right to settle in the immediate vicinity of the *corso*. On one of the streets parallel to the Cathedral Square, where the dominant architecture was represented by the Catholic and Orthodox churches along with the governor's palace, the first synagogue for the believers of the Sephardic and Ashkenazi communities was erected.[70] It was an imperial favour granted thanks to Baron Diego d'Aguilar (Mozes Lopez Perera), the administrator and the general intendant of the Austrian tobacco monopoly, protector and Maecenas of the Sephardic Jews of Timişoara'.[71]

Vienna had their own engineers design other aspects of the city partially or totally, thus impeding the rebirth of medieval structures. Inside the city were already two squares, the Parade (today, Liberty) and Cathedral (today, Union) – one for the military parade, the second, where the Catholic and the Orthodox cathedrals and the governor's palace were placed. From an architectural point of view, Timişoara's important buildings in the eighteenth century were the Roman Catholic cathedral, the Orthodox episcopal cathedral and the governor's palace (the Baroque palace) in Union Square along with the city hall and the general's house in Liberty Square.

Let us remember that 'The Jesuit and Franciscan churches, which were placed there [Liberty Square], and also the Transylvania Barracks, represented important landmarks. Each of the three edifices had a Baroque decorated tower, rising above neighbouring buildings.'[72] The size and style of the houses and palaces, their aesthetics, suggest the importance Vienna gave to the new regional centre. More important, though, was the fact that the two churches in Cathedral (Union) Square, Catholic and Orthodox, faced each other, inviting a peaceful cohabitation between the two different denominations. One celebrated mass in Latin and German, the other in Slavonic Serbian. The mutual religious tolerance was a sign of fraternity, one that led to the multiplication of Enlightened ideas, to the birth of Timișoara's spirit. The transformations that happened then and later were based on the reciprocity of services and on closeness, communication and understanding between representatives of the two Churches. This understanding went beyond administration and politics. The Baroque had offered similar attitudes, a *concordia discordans* (a discordant harmony), one hard to imagine in other European regions.

Timișoara became a citadel, and later a royal free city, in accordance with the ideas of the governor appointed by Eugene and of the Enlightenment despots, and with the politics of Charles VI, Maria Theresa and Joseph II, but mostly in accordance with the aspirations of its inhabitants. Catholic and Orthodox, Christian and Judaic, eighteenth-century Timișoara bears the sigil of the geography in which nothing is defined by the singular or the specific. It is a city and a world living at intervals, bearing ambivalent cultural and behavioural values, Eastern and Western.

Not all things would be made according to the reconstruction plan, but, after six decades of Viennese patronage, the emancipation of Timișoara and the Banat from the old religious, cultural and political servitudes is clearly visible. The city and the region became known in Europe, the contributions of intellectuals from Eugene of Savoy's inner circle being noteworthy. For example, those of Claude Florimond de Mercy, who changed the face of Timișoara and the region; of Francesco Griselini and Johann Jakob Ehrler, who explored the region and compiled the first scientific works about it; of Mathäus Heimerl, who published the first local newspaper in 1771, *Temeswarer Nachrichten*;[73] of Ștefan Stratimirović, the Orthodox bishop of Karlowitz,[74] of Austrian-German-Russian orientation, who writes in an inimitable manner about Orthodox, Catholic and Protestant relations, about the intercultural phenomenon of the Banat of Timișoara. Equally important and under the same Eugenian-Josephinist influence are the historical and philological writings, two decades later, of Romanian intellectuals Nicolae Stoica of Hațeg, Paul Iorgovici, Constantin Diaconovici-Loga, and Nicolae Tincu-Velea.

CONCLUSIONS: FROM EUGENE OF SAVOY TO JOSEPH II

How can one explain Eugene of Savoy's success and the projects of his collaborators? What share did the Viennese imperial administration have in the reconstruction of Timişoara and in redefining its identity? How substantial was the role of the local administration in the process of individual and communitarian emancipation? Was it Enlightenment ideas that influenced the reform, modernisation and first European integration of certain Central/Eastern European regions? What was the role of the emperors?

Through wise military strategies, understanding the people and mobilising the armies under his command, Eugene had decisively contributed to the transformation of the Habsburg Empire into a great European power. From an Austrian and even a European perspective, he was perceived as a legend in his lifetime and in the period that followed. At the same time, he acted as a Maecenas, understanding, cultivating and collecting[75] Renaissance and post-Renaissance painting and sculpture, the core of his collection being Italian Baroque art. The diversity of eighteenth-century Baroque creations would put its unmistakable mark upon Vienna and the cities under its influence.

In all that Eugene did – in spite of being a foreigner adopted by Austria[76] – he encouraged the monarchy to adopt a new world view and start the transition towards modernity. His thoughts and actions were echoed not only in the minds of the emperors he served – Leopold I, Joseph I and Charles I – but also in those who followed them, Maria Theresa and Joseph II. As we have mentioned, the conquest of Timişoara was among Eugene of Savoy's most important plans. Apparently, the plans referred to new lands for the Habsburgs and to the strength of the emperor. As the monarchy had become among the most powerful forces in Europe during the eighteenth century, such conquests also can be regarded as an extension of European culture and civilisation. Let us not forget that, in addition to the exploitation of opportunities to benefit the conqueror and the various realignments according to that spirit, schools were founded and the values of Western humanist arts and culture spread. They would have great impact upon the society of the Banat of Timişoara. In other words, we should understand Timişoara not simply as a place where one military supremacy was replaced by another, but also as a city and region that benefited from the new 'cultural corridors' in adopting the messages of modernity.

Unlike other cities, Timişoara's residents did not oppose the urban plan designed by Vienna and implemented by the governors appointed there by the Habsburgs between 1719 and 1779. On the contrary, it was regarded as a chance for change, as an impulse for overcoming the backwardness of the region. The primary municipalities at the beginning of the eighteenth century were

Vienna and Prague, the first becoming a reference point for those who wanted to rebuild from scratch. That was also Timișoara's situation.

The continuity of Eugene of Savoy's reforming ideas, and the way in which they were put into practice, are masterfully illustrated by Joseph II's *Reveries*. This is what the future emperor wrote in 1765:

> I believe we must work to convert the provinces and make them see how useful the limited despotism, which I propose, would be to them. To this end I should make an agreement with the provinces, asking them [to yield to me] for ten years full power to do everything, without consulting them, for their own good . . . Many individuals will not be at all happy with it, but the main body of the nation should be preferred to this portion.[77]

This was a point of view contrary to that of the nobility, but it stimulated emancipation from the feudal servitude for the majority of social segments, thus hastening the formation of the middle class. The Romanians from Timișoara's Banat – like Serbians and Germans of modest means – were the most receptive to novel ideas. Josephinism prepared for great change by founding schools in many languages and for all denominations, by installing Romanian, German and Serbian border regiments, and by promoting some of the norms for a modern economy. There was no nobility in the region so people in Timișoara and the Banat adopted the ideas of Josephinism and European civism in a relatively short time.

During Joseph II's visits to the Banat and Transylvania in 1768, 1770 and 1773, the myth of the good emperor was outlined. Actually, it replicated the image of a personality for whom individual freedom and good of the people were important, as well as the statehood which would assure people's progress.[78] Inspired by Eugene of Savoy,[79] Joseph II would deepen Enlightenment reforms, synthetised in his *Reveries*. In the life of the Romanian and Serbian population, and in that of the German, Italian, Spanish, Hungarian, Slovak, Bulgarian colonists, we find the legacy of Eugene of Savoy and Claude Florimond de Mercy, but also the ideal of Joseph II.[80] If Eugene started the reconstruction of Timișoara, then Joseph II contributed to its integration in an Enlightened Europe.[81]

PART III

3

THE ENLIGHTENMENT AND THE POLICIES OF THE HABSBURG EMPIRE

Case Studies of Transylvania and the Banat[1]

Victor Neumann

THE CONCEPT OF 'ENLIGHTENMENT' relates to education, knowledge, progress, social emancipation, the liberation of man from the servitude of nature in order to reconcile nature with man's own actions. Just as legend was replaced by history, so the separation of philosophy from myth was essential, not only because philosophy promoted analysis and reasoning based on science but also because it contributed to the genesis of the cultural code of the modern world. Although many ideological and political developments separate us from the phenomenon of the Enlightenment (also known as the Age of Enlightenment), it must be analysed within its historical context, philosophical orientations and the principles of society which formulated or adopted it. The Enlightenment did not propose an overestimation of scientific and literary facts nor did it focus on the utilitarianism and consumerism of our contemporaries. It is an exaggeration to compare it with the totalitarian ideas of the twentieth century, as Max Horkheimer and Theodor W. Adorno have done, influenced by the tragedies of the Second World War. They believed that 'enlightenment throughout the liberalistic period has always symphatised with social coercion' and that 'enlightenment is totalitarian as only a system can be'. The falseness of their statements does not amount to what their Romantic enemies have always accused them of, that is, the analytical method of reducing everything to elements, the destructive reflection, but is supported by the fact that the nature of things is determined from the very beginning.[2]

Even when they set out to discuss the concept, Horkheimer and Adorno intentionally neglected the entire period, dwelling on shortcomings inherited from previous times or from those born during later periods. They believed that, with the help of mathematics, automation and organisation, the Enlightenment period sacrificed thinking, while it retaliated against the people who have forgotten it.[3] As far as the criticism developed during the Enlightenment is concerned, Horkheimer and Adorno criticise it harshly. They say that the instrument of the Enlightenment was an abstraction, a constraint of people, and that language was used as a calculation tool, etc. Even if critical thinking did develop during the Enlightenment, it did not become the most important factor of change or transition from medieval to modern, to new social and political reforms.

However, by studying the phenomenon of time, we may see that thinking, critical-rational, or speculative, was one of the major themes of the Enlightenment. Its interest consistently favoured autonomy and the renewal of thought, if focused on the benefits of detachment from any kind of domination, illustrating the importance of a tolerant spirit. The representatives of the republic of letters and Freemasons from bourgeois or aristocratic circles were attracted not only by social and political changes, but also by the elevation of the soul, by mystery, magic and the inaccessible. The famous work of Adorno and Horkheimer, philosophers of the Frankfurt School, did not focus enough on these matters, which, seen as aspirations of the Enlightenment, deepen and define more precisely the human being with his old and new cultural and religious beliefs, his new set of values that have redefined his cultural behaviour. Each historical period and each historical region has its own features, this being the reason for which evoking and understanding the temporal and spatial contexts are important.

Reinhart Koselleck, one of the most important interpreters of the Enlightenment, was tempted to extrapolate references regarding the German Principalities or France to the largest areas of Europe. Starting from historical and philosophical texts of the eighteenth century, he began to formulate ideas and assumptions about society, institutions and the political changes during the transition period from medieval to modern, by taking into consideration the religious communities, civic and intellectual associations, the manner of thinking elaborated by the elites, and the attitudes which stimulated the society in Central and Western Europe. Secondly, he agreed with Horkheimer and Adorno that the attention towards the faults of critics has altered the meaning of concepts such as revelation, religion, faith, church, authority, secularisation, as they were perceived by many scholars from the Enlightenment.

Koselleck widely debated the theory according to which man was subdued by the dominant power during the Enlightenment, but the power itself was free from any religious and moral constraints. He focused on the secularisation of morality as a premise, considering the great theme of the eighteenth century to be the decrease in religiosity. 'By neutralising consciousness through politics, the secularisation of morality was favored. The spread of ecclesiastical antinomies which were characteristic to the absolutist state made possible the gradual expansion of the idea of a world based on nature and reason.'[4]

If we agree that Europe of the eighteenth century can be analysed from the perspective of several constitutional bodies, of changes in society and the renewal of each religious community, we will see that the Enlightenment phenomenon can be approached from various angles. There are multiple meanings attributed to the Enlightenment concept, depending on the historical heritage and the stage of development of local or regional cultures. Even if scientific discoveries have multiplied and rationalist ideas have gained ground, even if history began to identify with the reflective concept, the imperial or royal state institutions in Europe in the eighteenth century were not alienated from religion or from the moral code promoted by the Church. The example of the Habsburg Empire shows that imperial institutions not only cooperated with the Church, but also relied on these relationships and even benefited from its cultural heritage when, after the wars with the Ottoman Empire, the Habsburg Empire extended its rule in Central and South-Eastern Europe. The settlements of the eighteenth century were made with a Catholic population whose integration was accomplished based on the religious and moral relationships which had developed between the Habsburg Empire and the Roman Catholic Church. This occurred in the eighteenth century, in the region located between the Mureș, Tisza and Danube rivers, known as the Banat. The Habsburgs established new churches in order to subordinate the newly conquered territories and populations according to their own interests. This was the case with the Greek Catholic Church, subordinated to the Vatican and based on common values, both Orthodox and Catholic. The phenomenon occurred in regions such as Transylvania, Ukraine and the Banat, the result of cooperation between Church and State. The Habsburgs also spread the ideas of the Enlightenment from top to bottom in order to be able to control its effects. The emperor had to take into account the rules imposed by churches, by natural law, and by traditional and legal conventions. The autonomy of the Lutheran and Calvinist communities would not have survived in the eighteenth century if the old legal rules of religious, social and institutional hierarchies, founded in preceding centuries, had not been respected. In other words, there are regions in Europe where the renewal promoted by Enlightenment ideas must be perceived as an amalgam of continuities and discontinuities in relation to the structures of medieval thinking, and not as simple discontinuities.

In a study dedicated to the history of the concept of Enlightenment and the meaning attributed to it by Koselleck, Hans Erich Bödeker considers that the absolutist state has been perceived by historians as being extremely problematic,[5] as the conceptualisation of Enlightenment requires an understanding based on political, social, cultural and civic realities. Or, as we know, every period of time – and also every region, community and state – has its own peculiarities. Sometimes, Koselleck would extrapolate from his own references and knowledge related to the German principalities, France, etc., to larger areas where things did not occur in the same manner. In the eighteenth century, where state measures are concerned, we may talk about the ambivalent character of the Enlightenment, about the preservation of tradition, but also about renewal through literacy, emancipation and reform, and less about the dialectics between morality and politics.

The problem of the institutions at that time was a complex one. Not all European regions had experienced separation from the premodern era, as Koselleck had estimated. Often, national reform occurred from within. We cannot say that throughout the old continent radical and revolutionary measures had been adopted; however, the desire to modernise was visible in many communities. The change could become reality only through the intervention of an organised power. As a result, the intelligentsia often cooperated with the structures of the absolutist state, hoping to implement reform programmes related to justice, economy and politics. On the other hand, the mercantilism of kings and emperors was profoundly influenced by the political ideas of the Enlightenment, ignoring therefore revolutionary movements which were seen as dangerous or counterproductive. Not only were the French despots of the eighteenth century favourably disposed towards Enlightenment ideas, so were those of Prussia and Austria. They all agreed with the reforms, opposing all revolutions which were in accordance with Enlightenment principles. The differences between the countries can be understood by reading the policies from Vienna and Frankfurt – policies which could not be compared with those established in Paris in 1789 or 1848, policies which did not revolutionise the two historical moments. Despite the differences between the intellectual ideas and meanings granted to the sociopolitical phenomena, innovative thinking appeared in every region of the old continent of Europe, facilitated by the 'cultural paths' left behind by the colonising empires, administrators, merchants, intellectuals or their subordinates, who had contributed to the dialogue between Western and Eastern Europe.[6] We must also mention that the characteristics of geography, history and the cultural behavioural code of the elites had to be reviewed in order to formulate new judgements.

The transition from medieval to modern – a period in which exploring the unknown, innovation, the mixture of revelation and reason, the aspirations defined by historians through the concept of the Enlightenment were predominant – can be seen from the point of view of the intelligentsia, the political regimes and the diversity of the social segments. It is known that the intellectual elites of the eighteenth century were associated with science, but they were also interested in religion and, most importantly, the renewals due to exploration and knowledge perspectives did not undermine the religious ideas and beliefs. Enlightenment claims were directed towards acquiring religious tolerance. According to Reinhart Koselleck, the Enlightenment sought to prevent institutionalised churches and sects already prepared to make abuse of their power. It was the era of universal religiosity that was confronting similar problems to the previous generation: the omnipotence of God, the immortality of the soul, justice and freedom of conscience. Koselleck questioned whether Enlightenment partisans were prepared to practise the tolerance claimed from the Church. Recognising that the concept contained ambiguous meanings, Koselleck insisted on the unsolved conflicts present from one historical period to another. A different approach during the Enlightenment did not change the contradictions between the Church's mission and the social order. Hence his observation according to which the social organisation conceived and promoted in the eighteenth century would have been incurred even by his contemporaries.[7]

THE AUSTRO-PRUSSIAN AUFKLÄRUNG AND ITS IMPACT ON CENTRAL EUROPEAN CULTURE

We believe that to take into consideration this manner of regarding the historical process would be an exaggeration and would suggest also a personal controversy, especially since, in terms of culture, ideology, social and administrative policies, things seem to have been different. Even where continuities are more visible than discontinuities, the linearity of historical times must be questioned in the same manner as we must analyse the cause and effect relationship from every angle. From the Enlightenment perspective, progress cannot be seen only from a critical point of view, nor can we assume that the eighteenth century saw a great rupture with the past all around the world. The intellectual creation which characterises the Enlightenment should be seen in relation to attitudes, to social structures which did not have access to elite culture, but which constituted the majority in the eighteenth century. The majority participated in various manners in the renewal of thought – a fact which was not emphasised during the intellectual concerns of the time nor in the exegeses resulting from these concerns.

Without underestimating the role of literary scholars, philosophers and thinkers in general who have promoted the need for change, it is equally important to focus on the problems related to state policies, on the relationship between intellectuals, religion, Church, individual and community. These must have been more significant than the degree of importance accorded them by Koselleck in his interpretation of the Enlightenment. The concept of the Enlightenment must be seen from the perspective of various geographical contexts, regions, social and cultural forms of existence, different encounters and convergences between people, ideas and beliefs; that is, by accepting all its ambivalent meanings. We shall invoke an example from the intellectual history related to Enlightenment thinking which raises the following questions: What was the religious dialogue between Christians and Jews in the eighteenth century? What are its consequences in terms of the Enlightenment? The answers are more complicated than initially appears.

We think that novelty must not exclude the limitation that exists in every reevaluation of the past and present. At least in the case of the German *Aufklärung* concept there is a theological origin. We have identified the first explanation of this ambivalent concept of noetics in the work of Moses Mendelssohn, *Bestimmung des Menschen* (*The Destiny of Mankind*). Mendelssohn is the *Aufklärer* that focused on the theological origin of the concept, referring to *Mishna*, the Jewish Treaty that has guided him towards understanding the phenomenology of impurity. Mendelssohn had been preoccupied with the initiation of intellectuals from Berlin, with the ideas of diversity and the sophistication of the current. Pleas for the rehabilitation of Spinoza had taken place and concern for the essential truth of a system of a pre-established harmony[8] had arisen. The circle of *Berlinische Monatschrift* along with the Jewish newspaper *Ha Meassef* had to prove that Judaism was compatible with the modern world, while its German emancipation would have been unimaginable without the contribution of Moses Mendelssohn. According to Dominique Bourel, one of the interpreters of his work, Mendelssohn was an exceptional person, 'a person doubly loyal' both to German culture and to the Jewish spiritual heritage, who understood and applied the principles of the Jewish *Haskalah*, identifying its compatibility with the Prussian *Auflklärung*.[9]

Mendelssohn, a leading representative of religious and philosophical thought of the eighteenth century, the 'founding father' of an impressive social segment of the German world of which aristocrats, bankers, industrialists, lawyers, officers, politicians, professors, theologians and a famous composer were a part, helped to clarify the meanings of the term 'Enlightenment' seen from the perspective of the *Auflklärung*. By comparing his thinking to that of his congeners, we discover the religious, cultural and moral implications and the importance of the relationship between Jews and Christians for the Enlightenment concept of the eighteenth century. Viewed in the context of the Prussian and European Enlightenment movement and the Jewish *Haskalah* movement, the contributions of Moses Mendelssohn facilitate the evaluation of the *Aufklärung*. These movements have opened the path for new explanations regarding the analysed current. He claims that his work must be seen in the context of the intellectual movement in his country, Prussia, not only in relation to Judaism. He invites us to compare the *Aufklärung* with the *Haskalah*, a movement similar to the Jewish *Auflkärung*, a manner to translate the concept *Auflkärung* and Enlightenment.[10] Mendelssohn was convinced that it was possible to reconcile faith and reason, which was also compatible with philosophy. He embraced the idea of universal human fraternity opposed to the physical and spiritual ghetto, to such an extent that he became the spokesman of the German and Jewish symbiosis which spread in the 1800s and after the end of the First World War.[11]

Why is it useful to include Moses Mendelssohn in this discussion? Firstly, due to the terminological accuracy and clarifications made in his text *Über Die Frage: Was heißt aufklären?*,[12] which analyses the verb, the action and the illumination. For the three key concepts, *Aufklärung*, *Bildung*, *Kultur*, Mendelssohn makes an in-depth analysis, claiming that they are relatively new to the German language and, therefore, that the middle-class man understands them only partially. '*Aufklärung* dates from the early eighteenth century, *Kultur* is a translation loan from Latin and *Bildung* is derived from the old verb *bilden* (to shape, to cultivate and to train).' Arguably, *Bildung* and *Kultur* express a certain German specificity, a semantic *Sonderweg* (exceptional). The meanings given by Mendelssohn to the three terms indicate 'changes in social life, the efforts of industry effects and the improvement of their social status'. In conclusion, the 'culture decomposes into civilisation and Enlightenment'. Man must become 'means and end to all aspirations towards which we should focus ourselves should we wish to not lose sight of what is important'. The Enlightenment is for civilisation what theory usually is to practice, knowledge for morality, critics for virtuosity. What is fundamental is that the Enlightenment is universal, since it focuses on the human being as he is, without conditions, while the man of the Enlightenment seen as citizen changes depending on various conditions and profession. Mendelssohn did not grant a special interest to educating humans, unlike Lessing. Mendelssohn advanced towards the conceptualisation of the changing phenomena, reason for which, a pressing matter such as cultural identity associated with political identity had been approached with a suppleness of unmistakable thinking.[13] Acceding to revelation, the concern for the immortality of one's soul, defending the uniqueness of Judaism and the criticism brought to atheism along with superstitions are all reflections which emerge from his great books: *Phädon oder über die Unsterblichkeit der Seele in drey Gesprechen*, *Morgenstunden oder Vorlesungen über das Daseyn Gottes*, *Jerusalem oder über Religisöse Macht und Judenthum*. Both philosophical and theological, they tend to explain some of the major disputes of the time. As for *Was heißt aufklären*, it is a special text with reference to the meaning attributed to the Enlightenment, and presents an alternative to that of Immanuel Kant in *Was ist Aufklärung?*. His originality lies in the fact that he sensed the possibility and necessity of cultural European amalgamation and of the racial genesis. The integration of his work into the analysis dedicated to the Enlightenment is required not only to define the concept, but especially to assess the intellectual capacity and predictability of the eighteenth century.[14]

ENLIGHTENED DESPOTISM: CASE STUDIES OF TRANSYLVANIA AND THE BANAT REGION

Transylvania and the Banat region must be presented in a European context and not as two distinct regions, just like any other historical areas. Therefore, it might be useful to ask the following questions: What does 'Enlightenment' under the domination of the House of Habsburg and the Austrian Empire mean? Are we able to equate the enlightened despotism of the Habsburgs with the ideals of progress of the Occidental Enlightenment? To which social segment did the mercantile spirit address in Transylvania? To whom was the Industrial and Commercial Development Programme, coordinated by the Imperial Chancellery during the reign of Maria Theresa and Joseph II, addressed and what was its impact on the life of the inhabitants of Transylvania and Banat? Could it all be traced back to the attempt of borrowing the Austrian cultural code manifested through the Roman Catholic Church, otherwise seen as the Europeanisation of the inhabitants from these regions – Europeanisation accomplished by appropriating books, sciences, trades and human rights? Can we talk about two separate identities in Transylvania and the Banat region in the context in which the inhabitants of both parts were asked to prove their loyalty to the same Austrian Empire? How much truth and how much mythology lies in the historical discourse focused on local, regional, ethnic and ethnonational identities?

Although there are well-documented studies, the historiography of Transylvania lacks records concerning the evolution of the mental, social and political life of the inhabitants. Secondly, at this point the interest in primary sources is irrelevant, together with the understanding of the relationship between the transmitter and the receiver which meant to reveal the dialogue between Eastern and Western Europe. Thirdly, the concepts, notions and meanings of these dialogues are not sufficiently known by the general public.[15] Finally, in the exegesis referring to the European regional histories, society and politics were often ignored because of time and space constraints; then, there is the matter of regions characterised by two or more cultures and civilisations or the originality and prospects of particular and universal, of asymmetrical relations between centre and edge, of aspirations related to identity, otherness, admitting or integration, all concepts and notions we must also take into account.

The Romanian historiography of the past decades had taken a direction towards the Transylvanian region of the eighteenth century, often defined as one in which the Enlightenment ideas manifested at their fullest. A particular concern was shaped around the Greek Catholic Church (the Church united with Rome), whose establishment coincides with Vienna's intention to assimilate the Transylvanian majority population of Orthodox faith with the cultural and religious values of Central Europe, namely those of the Roman Catholic religion.[16] Defining these changes, which took place in Transylvania, required an analysis taking into account the policies of their time, the confrontations between the Habsburg and the Ottoman Empires, the conflicts between the Christians and the Muslims, and the distinctions between the dogma of the Western (Catholic) Church and that of the Eastern (Orthodox) Church. The friction, which occurred at the border of the Habsburg and the Ottoman Empires, identifies the local and regional particularities as a place where several cultures and civilisations collided. The Enlightenment ideas perceived and practised in Transylvania and the Banat region in the eighteenth and nineteenth centuries should be seen as closely connected with the imperial message and, equally, that of the churches. Therefore, these ideas focus on the relationship between the religious and political hierarchies and their willingness to cooperate, depending on inclusion or exclusion of the majority sectors of the community and those of various religious affiliations and language, but also based on the perception of the other's culture, which highlights the differences.

From the eighteenth century, the Roman Catholic Church in Transylvania and Banat was considered the state religion.[17] It sought to impose its own representatives at the top of the hierarchy of Transylvania, creating animosity among the elites and locals for whom the confessional representation was essential during the former independent principality. Immediately after the inclusion of Transylvania and the Banat regions within the Empire, controversies appeared with regard to religious affiliation or denominational identities. Throughout history, we can see that these denominational identities particularised the inhabitants of the region by conferring on them an identity. This explains the attention paid to the reorganisation of the Roman Catholic Episcopacy of Transylvania and of the Roman Catholic Episcopacy of Cenad/Timișoara (from the Banat region), a topic which would become of paramount interest at several periods: (1) in Transylvania during the reign of Emperor Leopold I; (2) during the anti-Habsburg uprising led by Francis Rákóczi II; (3) the appointment of the governor of the region.[18] In the Banat region, the situation was different, as the local and regional institutions had been completely rebuilt and directly subordinated to Vienna after the defeat and withdrawal of the Ottomans from the region. The disputes among the Calvinist Reformed Catholics, the Evangelical Lutherans, and the Unitarians were specific to Transylvania and they indicated the struggle for political power and not the focus on the exclusion of religious diversity. This highlights the cultural identities from Transylvania in the premodern era, cultures that have survived during the Empire rule, despite the transfer from the Calvinist Protestants to the Roman Catholics. The new orientation was supposed to be an imperial one whereas Catholics had to play the role of mediators. Even when referring to the aspirations of the House of Habsburg, to speak about an Austrian influence is still an overstatement. For that period of time, the intention mostly likely was to join the cultural and civic value code of Central Europe. This process was conducted slowly throughout the entire eighteenth century. Due to the development and stability of the new administration, new economic, social and political reforms were possible.

Latin was the official language of both the Catholic Church and the Imperial Chancellery. Promoting the German language among the Empire's regions occurred in the second half of the eighteenth century, in order to facilitate communication with the populations of the Empire, not for the benefit of any national idea. The ethnonationalism concept did not refer to the idea of a single nation defined in the modern era, implying the existence of the state. This concept appeared in Transylvania and the Banat regions once the romantic literary and historical writings were adapted to the local context. The ethnonationalism concept benefited from knowledge brought by the Enlightenment, but it opposed the aspirations expressed by its representatives. The Enlightened absolutism of the eighteenth century – to which the Habsburgs aspired – was concerned with organising individuals, groups and activities, while also taking into account religious and social criteria. The historian D. Prodan observed that the elements on which the Empire was built were dynasty, administration and army. However, he is not right to consider that these elements, along with the dominance of the Catholic religion, should have been encouraged in order to substitute for the absence of national unity.

With regards to the genesis and role of the Greek Catholic Church – we are referring to the largest linguistic community from Transylvania, the Romanian one – therefore, the Habsburg policies were meant to take over the old confessional groups. Under no circumstances were linguistic, historical and ethnographic segregations encouraged. With few exceptions, the governors of Transylvania in the eighteenth century were Catholic.[19] The same can be said about the ones from the Banat. Positions in the regional administration were not awarded based on memberships to the Hungarian, German, Romanian or Serbian communities. Confessional identity was highlighted in the eighteenth century and bore other meanings to the ones imagined by Herder, Fichte or Hegel, such as the nation of citizens or the ethnic-linguistic nation, through the concept *Volk*. Therefore, it is desirable to evaluate the intellectual aspirations which produce social and political changes, admitting that the Enlightenment ideas in Transylvania and the Banat regions were accompanied by strong Romantic influences. The latter generated a set of unusual references by the amalgamation of the Enlightenment and Romantic ideas, unimaginable in the Western European cultures, as both movements spread contradictory messages. The presence of this amalgam in Eastern and Central Europe was due to the rapid spreading of the German culture in the last decades of the eighteenth century and the reception through it, of an identitary thinking that triggered the underlining of linguistic differences.

As far as Enlightened absolutism was concerned, it facilitated the access to books, scholars and artists. Vienna had implemented several reforms in accordance with Enlightenment ideology and in this sense, the contributions of its two great chancellors, Friedrich Wilhelm von Haugwitz and Wenzel Anton von Kaunitz, must be acknowledged. The universalisation of modern philosophical concepts was visible throughout the empire, without interrupting the local peculiarities. In Transylvania, along with the nobility, school and culture have made possible the formation and affirmation of the elites.[20] Such intellectuals were familiar with the new scientific and ideological orientations of German, but also of French, origin, some of them being preoccupied by culture, which had proved valuable in order for them to occupy public positions, or to be involved in the publishing of articles, books and documents. Interestingly, the first segment with such preoccupations was that of the nobility, who read, wrote and collected books and paintings, avoiding the imperial censorship that did not allow Western influences, especially those with reference to the French Revolution. Samuel von Brukenthal, Ignác Batthyány and Samuel Teleki were outstanding figures from the nobility and clerical environments, and also of the intellectual and political life of Transylvania. They were drawn not by the new meaning given to the concept of nation after 1789, nor by the Napoleon epopee, but by the means designed to increase the progress spread by Enlightenment ideas. Their ideal was an Occidental *homo novus*, accomplished through a reform which would not affect the political system. In their view, these transformations were possible only from top to bottom, through Enlightened absolutism.[21] Transylvania would express its own idea of modernisation, the transition towards it being driven by the aspirations of the elites, and not by the townspeople who were working towards a civil society. The social discontinuities within the region were obvious, preventing the formation of an authentic bourgeoisie until the second half of the nineteenth century.

The example of Baron von Brukenthal is more than representative. Surrounded by specialists, he created a meritorious spiritual effervescence in Sibiu, which was highly appreciated by his congeners, Chancellor Teleki from Targu Mures and the clergy, nobility and intellectuals of Transylvania. Under his protection, a historiographical movement was developed, sustained by the works of Johann Filtsch, Daniel Filtsch, Johann Michael von Soterius Sachsenheim, Georg Hirling and Michael Conrad von Heydendorff, all concerned with the multiple identities and cultures of the region. The renowned historian József Benkö thanked him for facilitating the research conducted during that period.[22] The considerable number of works in his collection indicate Brukenthal's interest in history.[23] Along with the collection of books on theology, which continued to be one of reference, among Brukenthal's other volumes in Sibiu were books on geometry, geology, medicine, geography, astronomy, microtechnology and optics. This was possible due the abolition of Jesuit censorship and state policy regarding the secularisation of life established by Joseph II. Brukenthal's thinking was similar to the ideas promoted by the Austrian Enlightenment absolutism, but only to a certain extent.

The atmosphere under the patronage of Brukenthal must not be mistaken for the state of mind of the Transylvanian Saxon community, Fundus Regius. The Enlightenment ideas embraced by the baron were not always understood by the local feudal society. Only a small circle of people had benefited from Brukenthal's private collections. The Occidental travellers who saw these collections in the nineteenth century were very impressed not only by the sophistication promoted within the intellectual environment in Sibiu, but also by the European clothing adopted by the masters of the 'House', as represented in the paintings of the baron and his wife by the Viennese artist Martin von Meytens.[24] However, the masses did not understand or actively participate and therefore, did not take part in the European cultural endeavour proposed by Brukenthal. Even the musical and literary soirées had been rejected by the local bourgeoisie, 'Only those collections with a clear orientation towards Transylvanian Saxon tradition with focus on researching the past, had an extraordinary significance in the cultural life of Brukenthal's contemporary city: Sibiu.'[25] Another century would pass before the philosophy of Brukenthal and his work would be entirely understood.

As will be seen in the following chapters of this book, the series of transformations that the Banat region has undergone were influenced by a multitude of factors. Among them, we must mention the lack of a nobility, which not only facilitated the formation of the bourgeoisie, but also stimulated intellectual competition, technical and scientific discoveries, industrial initiatives and cultural experiments. Local populations along with those colonised by the Habsburgs were going to build – in a shorter period of time by comparison with Transylvania – an acceptable standard of living from a social and economic point of view, and a society interested in the reconciliation of cultural-linguistic and religious differences. Intellectuals – teachers, professors, priests, philologists, historians, actors – who were the pioneers of emancipation, entirely understood this ongoing phenomenon. They advocated for a unique experiment at the 'gates' of the Central European Empire – one that would succeed, despite some attempts to propagate community segregation.

THE ENLIGHTENMENT AND ROMANTIC AMALGAM

The problems of the Romanian community from both Transylvania and the Banat regions in the eighteenth century were related to religion and the social status of its members. It was the Empire's intention to constantly supervise the assimilation of the Orthodox population, especially where it had fragile institutions. This phenomenon should be seen not only as the expansion of Catholicism, but also as a means of integrating the majority of Orthodox people into the socio-economic policies and cultural norms of the Empire. However, the majority of Orthodox worshippers from Transylvania accepted the papacy by accepting the new religious institution of the Greek Catholic Church. As already mentioned, the House of Habsburg considered Greek Catholicism as a bridge towards the European values, and also as a counterweight to the old and powerful religious institutions in the region: Lutheranism, Calvinism and Unitarianism. The policies of Vienna in the eighteenth century were meant not only to consolidate power in the newly integrated territories acquired after the wars with the Ottoman Empire, but also to keep the peace between the inhabitants of the areas of various religions and languages. The well-organised communities based on the rules respected by parishioners, admitted guiding cultural institutions, even if they were not subordinate to the Roman Catholic Church. An example in this regard is the Serbian Slavonic Church whose Metropolis of Karlowitz was recognised as representing Orthodox Christianity in the Empire. This became an institution of reference with highly appreciated figures – Orthodox Hierarchs Stefan Stratimirovici and Moise Putnik among them – a symbol representing the inhabitants and the principles of peaceful coexistence in a multi-confessional and multilingual region: the Banat region. Although the Christian institutions manifested hostility towards Judaism, that religion was still tolerated at the time. The Sephardic and Ashkenazi Jewish rituals are attested in the eighteenth century in Alba-Iulia, during the time when Transylvania functioned as a principality, but also in the following century, when Transylvania was under the Habsburgs.[26] In the Banat region, Timișoara accepted both rituals and preserved them for a long period of time. Despite centralism and the spread of Catholicism in the eighteenth century, the Habsburg Empire took into account the multi-confessional aspects of its regions, and Transylvania and the Banat regions were no exception from this political thinking.[27]

The claims made on the behalf of the Romanian-speaking population in the mid-eighteenth century by the Greek Catholic Bishop of Blaj, Inochentie Micu-Klein, prepared the genesis of an intellectual regional movement in the late eighteenth century which gained notoriety in the following centuries: the Transylvanian School. It was formed by a group of intellectuals with similar preoccupations for theology, literature, history, politics, attending

Catholic and Protestant colleges in Latin, German and Hungarian from Transylvania and other regions of Central and Western Europe. Gheorghe Sincai, Ion Budai-Deleanu, Petru Maior, Samuil Micu, Ignatius Darabant and Ioan Piuariu Molnar are the most representative names of the Transylvanian School, intellectuals who worked to bring together the Enlightenment and Romanticism movements, as in these regions they intertwined. The Greek Catholic Church created the framework for the political discourse and, according to it, a hierarchy of Romanian-speaking population was shaped. The intellectuals came from the gentry, teachers, soldiers, priests and officials. Their relations with the peasantry were sketchy in terms of ideological messages and therefore their role in social benefits of this segment was minor as well.[28] The Transylvanian peasants, regardless of their language – Romanian, German or Hungarian – remained ignorant. In consequence, a question remains: for whom was the Transylvanian School intended?

The revolt of Horea was not motivated by national problems or ethnic nationalism. As for the political document called *Supplex Libellus Valachorum* (1791), its content does not highlight a dialogue between the peasants and elite nor does it show that the peasantry has legitimised the petitioners to speak on its behalf.

D. Prodan associated the idea of the social contract, of aspirations to equality and freedom expressed by Rousseau and Voltaire with the Transylvanian political thinking of the elite, although real similarities between Eastern and Western Europe were relatively few at the time. Instead, differences may be identified in the historical, demographic, sociocultural, administrative and political peculiarities. Despite their merits in highlighting the social shortcomings, the Romanian intellectuals from Transylvania in the years 1780–1800 seemed to have been the emissaries of their own claims. The intellectuals were very careful not to destroy the relationships between the existing social structures, nor to diminish the power of the nobility or that of Vienna, as happened in France. So the movement was not entirely guided by Enlightenment ideas, but nor was it as revolutionary as the French ideology in 1789. The concern of the Romanian intellectuals was not to distance themselves too much from state law, from the political identity that was conferred on them by the Empire. This perspective was formulated based on a fragment from *Supplex*: 'Of course . . . the intention of supplicants [the group that formulated the intellectual claims] was not to obtain for the plebs more than they rightfully deserve.'[29] Did this group of people see themselves as part of the nobility, different from the 'plebs', but representing their interests, even if they had not been appointed to carry out such a task? It was a fact that literacy was much delayed among the mass, and therefore the concept of citizenship was still new, as compared with that of the populations in Western Europe, even compared to the surrounding areas: Bukovina and the

Banat regions. Hence, there is a preoccupation for community citizenship, commencing from top to bottom.

In general, the claims formulated in the *Supplex* contain arguments on cultural-linguistic matters, as fragments of history were presented depending on the political interest of the moment. These arguments did not capture the attention of the imperial administration, which was eager to preserve the balance between the Estates of Transylvania and resist segregation based on language, culture, history and origins. However, the requests containing Enlightenment ideas with a universal character were accepted. The revolutionary ideas, namely those based on linguistic identity or ethnonationalism, were contrary not only to the regulations of the House of Habsburg, but also to the Enlightenment movement. From the reports submitted to Emperor Joseph the Second, we find that his administration was preoccupied with the following: the foundation of schools, regulating taxes and their use, the functioning of postal services, health control, nobility paying their debts, the law and justice system to be enforced regardless of social class, settling the conflicts between communities and Guberniu (Government), solving the Orthodox community disputes and litigations with the Catholic and Protestant confessions, revising constructions.[30] They indicate the reforms specific to the Enlightened absolutism from top to bottom, because they were possible only through the intervention of the central government.

The works of the Romanian, Transylvanian Saxons and Hungarian intellectuals from Transylvania promote the Romantic ethnonationalist ideology, one that would spread very quickly. The political ideology in question was present in many regions of Eastern and Central Europe. Patriotism and organicism were in accord to each other. Therefore, the themes of identity contained in the Transylvanian *Supplex* of 1791 should be discussed in relation to the Romantic and nationalist ideas, and not only in relation to the Enlightenment movement. The meaning imprinted on identity through the theory of differentialism was not a simple game of erudition or aesthetics, but the construction of an ideology inspired by the Romantic mystique, which would be reflected in political thinking of the following periods.[31]

The Habsburgs did not prevent communities from defining themselves based on wealth and religion, the nobility and the clergy giving them various names. With the spread of Herder's texts and ideas, regional languages and different ethnographic expressions were discovered. Underlining the differences between communities despite their similarities and convergences was due to intellectual activism. The relations with German schools, with the sociopolitical environments from the northern Protestant principalities, and with German writers and scientists all played an important role in shaping the ideological thinking of the elites in both Transylvania and the Banat regions. The German language, and not French, was essential in this process of identity assertion. Community feelings and instincts were encouraged. Herder's interpretations met the ideas and expectations mentioned above. His influence was exerted through the spread of some of his works, through translations and due to the press and his discourses focused on the idea according to which people have the right to develop their own culture, their own 'specificity' based on the peculiarities of language or dialect, but especially based on a common origin, history, folklore and cohabitation in the same territory. The new regional elites discovered and spread the notion of a cultural ethnonationalism, each superior to that of the neighbouring community, identifying it with the idea of nation. As a consequence, ideological and political conflicts appeared which compromised the peaceful cohabitation of several groups in the same space. The same happened especially in Transylvania, in the first half of the nineteenth century, when competition and antagonisms among the Romanian, Hungarian and Transylvanian Saxons became more and more visible.

Underlining the differences depending on languages, customs, folklore and history ignored the words inherited from other languages; the quasi-identical habitat between the populations in the region was forgotten; common regional history and culture was neglected; in many cases, religion made room for ethnonationalist ideology and national state policy. The differences highlighted the discrepancies, causing the isolation of Eastern Europe from Western Europe as the concept of nation was contrary to that of citizenship, and therefore contrary to a democratic nation. The alternative to the new identity and political thinking in the nineteenth century was the cosmopolitan tolerant thinking of the Habsburgs, which promoted a culture based on Enlightenment ideas, in which local and universal characteristics intertwined.

4

JOSEPHISM AND JOSEPHINISM[1]

Modernising Reforms[2]

Victor Neumann

THE BANAT HAD BEEN A MULTICULTURAL REGION long before the Habsburgs integrated it within their administrative system in 1718. It was a region where the Christian Orthodox population, speaking Romanian and Slavic-Serbian languages, was dominant, and coexisted with Turkish Muslims, Romanian and Serbian Orthodox Christians, Armenians, Sephardi Jews speaking Ladino (Spanish) and Gypsies. At the beginning of the eighteenth century, the region had neither nobility rule nor solid administrative structures. In these respects it was similar to Transylvania, which was an autonomous principality in the late sixteenth and seventeenth centuries. The nobility of the Banat had disappeared because of Ottoman domination, the lands of the region becoming the property of the sultan. The religious congregations did not have continuity, while the local administrations were only represented in the south of the region (the Banat of Lugoj and Caransebeș), which for short periods were included within the Principality of Transylvania. The Ottomans had an important citadel in Timișoara, a system of defence and a military elite, but no administration concerned with regional organisation and management. When Timișoara became part of the Habsburg Empire, it was therefore possible for the Banat to be completely reorganised according to imperial requirements and with no opposition from the local population.

JOSEPHISM AND JOSEPHINISM IN THE BANAT: THE GENESIS OF MODERN SOCIETY IN TIMIŞOARA

One of Joseph II's secret documents – the *Reveries* written in 1765 – played an essential role in the reformation of the Habsburg Empire. The *Reveries* indicates the beginning of the ideology known as 'Josephism', manifested during Joseph II's reign and continuing until 1849. Simultaneously, the genesis and evolution of Freemasonry occurred in Timişoara, the Banat and Transylvania took place, among many other changes. As for the *Reveries*, one paragraph of this document reveals the Habsburg policy and firm stance on reform:

> I do not believe it is very beneficial that there should be little kings and great subjects who live at their ease, not caring what becomes of the state. I believe it to be fundamental that every man, as a subject, owes to the state, which maintains him, protects him and secures his rights, such services as the state, whose spokesman is the sovereign, considers him capable of – and not what suits his convenience or pleasures. I believe it to be fundamental that, in order to direct the great machine, a single head, even though mediocre, is worth more than ten able men who have to agree among themselves in all simple operations . . . I believe we must work to convert the provinces and make them see how useful the limited despotism, which I propose, would be to them. To this end I should make an agreement with the provinces, asking them [to yield to me] for ten years full power to do everything, without consulting them, for their own good . . . Many individuals will not be at all happy with it, but the main body of the nation should be preferred to this portion.[3]

In order to convince the regions within the empire to accept such a policy, Joseph intended to gather together all the social, religious and cultural groups around the kingdom. The administration played a very important role through its own civil and military institutions, as did the support of the Roman Catholic and Orthodox churches. Given this context, the emperor could turn his attention to Freemasonry, whose reforming purpose was beneficial to the state. The nobility's mindset was rather hostile and it had to be quickly overcome by an original method of conceptualising modernity. Masonic lodges developed in the big cities of Central Europe, quietly encouraged by the imperial power. At Timişoara, the founding of the Three White Lilies lodge is proof of such a coming together of the civic, reformist, cosmopolitan structure with both the reforms of Josephism and the wider European Enlightenment movement.

Who were the members of the Three White Lilies lodge? What were their professions and to which institutions did they belong? What is the relationship between this lodge and the administrative, political and economic structure of the time? One contemporary document mentions that between 1776 and

1783 the lodge included Freemasons from a variety of professions: medicine, pharmacy, surgery, administration, military, engineering, accounting, archives, finance, entrepreneurship, typography, judiciary and commerce.[4] Often, the profession was mentioned alongside the institution from which the Freemason came, indicating an association with, or even a direct involvement in, the local or central Viennese administrative institution: the secretary general and the chief prosecutor of Timiș County; the chief bank commissioner; the chief revenue officer of Cenad County; the imperial commissioner for alimentation; the imperial commissioner of grain reserves from Ciacova, among several others.[5]

Alongside real names, mostly of German but also of Slavic, French, Italian and Hungarian origin, there is a list of aliases of the lodge's members, such as Horatio, Scipio, Livius, Plutarch, Socrates, Plato, Seneca, Democritus, Cicero, Spinoza and Diderot. It is notable that the Freemasons were rarely members of the nobility, but represented a bourgeoisie transferred to Timișoara during the eighteenth century from Vienna, Prague, Brno, Bratislava, Buda, Cracow, Zagreb and Szeged. Secondly, Timișoara hosted a strong military garrison, the citadel being designed between 1718 and 1752 and reconstructed between 1754 and 1779, hence the significant representation of military men and topographers in the Three White Lilies lodge. Moreover, Vienna had conferred on the new regional administrative region (*Landesadministration*) responsibility for the restoration and enlargement of the citadel, for erecting churches, for founding commercial companies, printing houses and schools. Shortly after its liberation from Ottoman domination, Timișoara experienced a series of radical changes, as a result of being included in the imperial fortification system. Alongside the project and the building of the Bega Canal, manufacturing and industry flourished.

Of great significance was the formation of border regiments in the Banat, which played an important part in the relationship with Vienna. For example, the Romanian regiment of Caransebeș contributed to the improvement of the imperial defence system, and also to the first emancipation, modernisation and European inclusion of the Romanian communities of the Banat. The same phenomenon occurred with regard to regiments of Swabian and Serbian soldiers. All these transformations required military men, officials, cartographers, doctors, priests and professors – all of whom formed associative and liberal groups. The Three White Lilies lodge operated with the consent of the emperor and the role of the Freemasons was directly connected to his mercantile policies. The data shows that the lodge facilitated the relationship with Vienna, contributing to the penetration of Joseph's reforms, the changing of mentalities, and the diffusion of the imperial baroque style in Timișoara and the Banat. The appreciable rise in the number of Freemasons within the Three White Lilies lodge was due to the initiatives of members belonging to the topographic body of the imperial army who were transferred to Timişoara with the purpose of mapping the Banat region.

FRANCESCO GRISELINI AND IGNAZ VON BORN: THE WRITING OF THE FIRST HISTORY OF THE BANAT OF TIMIŞOARA

At the same time as Freemasonry appeared for the first time in Timişoara, the Venetian historian Francesco Griselini was making a long and fruitful journey to the Banat (1774–77), followed by the drafting of a history of the region. The title of this book, according to the original Italian manuscript, was *Lettere odeporiche di Francesco Griselini, ove i suoi viaggi, e le di lui osservazioni spettanti all'Istoria naturale, ai costumi di vari popoli, e sopra più altri interessanti oggetti si descrivono* (*Travelling Journal of Francesco Griselini: Observations upon the Natural History, Customs of Different Communities and Description of Other Interesting Objects*).[6] The book was included in the historiographical circle thanks to its German translation by the mineralogist Ignaz von Born,[7] entitled *Versuch einer politischen und natürlichen Geschichte des Temesvarer Banats im Briefen an Standespersonen und Gelehrten.*[8] Many years before he finished his monograph, Griselini had told Born about the details of his journey and his intention to publish his research,[9] and the two had agreed upon the translation of the work. In a footnote in the German edition, the author mentioned that it 'was made under the supervision of the Wise Gentleman and Cavalier, Councillor Ignaz von Born'. The Romanian editions reproduced the German version either fragmentarily or in its entirety, publishing it under the title, *An Essay on the Political and Natural History of the Banat of Timişoara.*[10]

The intellectuals Francesco Griselini and Ignaz von Born came from Venice and Vienna, respectively. They were celebrities at the time, their studies and writings being acknowledged by eighteenth-century European academies and societies of savants. They were interested in the message of fraternity and, as Freemasons, had the opportunity to meet in one of the Viennese lodges, the True Concord. In everyday life, they were preoccupied by the knowledge and integration of the European set of values of the newly conquered Habsburg regions. Their letters show us their aspirations, their scientific cooperation, the results of their work, and their desire to harmonise local and universal features.

Two decades before he started to write the first history of the Banat, Francesco Griselini revealed his sympathy with the ideals of Freemasonry, defending them in the comedy *I liberi muratori* (1754). Often compared to Carlo Goldoni's *Le donne curiose* (1753), the comedy displays an understanding of the origin, activities and benefits of the Masonic lodges, whose presence is recorded in almost all the important cities of the Italian peninsula during the eighteenth century.[11] Despite the fact that the two popes who led the Catholic Church in the mid-eighteenth century – Clement XII (1730–40) and Benedict XIV (1740–58) – opposed fraternal societies, regarding them as alien to the Vatican and its dogma, and condemning them in papal bulls (for example, *In eminenti*, 1738), Masonic lodges were tolerated and even openly accepted by Italian urban society.

According to Francesco Griselini, the secrecy of association was entirely inoffensive, more amusing than dangerous. For this reason, he supported Freemasonry without hesitation. This theme was often discussed with his friend, the celebrated dramatist Goldoni. Both researched the meanings of the messages and hierarchies, metamorphosing them in plays.[12] At one point in *I liberi muratori*, Griselini depicts the initiation ceremony of Freemasonry, emphasising its signs and gestures, the hierarchy of the lodge in which the main role is held by the venerable master and the officers, and the mysterious ambience within it. He was familiar with the norms of the Masonic lodge, the vows and the principles that animate the fraternity: compliance with rituals; acknowledgement of brothers by their signs and gestures; payment of a membership fee; existence of a code of conduct for relations inside and outside the lodge; the reason behind the absence of women in the lodge. He built the play around the ceremony of initiation. An illustration included at the back of the published play depicts the two candidates, Dorante and Sganarello, blindfolded with swords directed at their chests. On the title page, Francesco Griselini claims his own affiliation to Freemasonry.[13]

This closeness to the fraternal movement meant cultivating the idea of total freedom, understood apart from professional, family or religious constraints, but with a profound sense of citizenship. Here its partial identification with Enlightenment ideas – particularly with those that laid the basis for reform and modernisation – is significant.[14] I believe that Griselini's orientation towards Freemasonry was relevant when he explored the Banat of Timișoara. Relations with Vienna, the journey to the eastern regions of the Empire, the letter exchange with contemporary scholars and Griselini's friendship with Ignaz von Born prove that Masonic ideas contributed to the multiplication of scientific information in the eighteenth century, at the same time playing the role of a catalyst in the scientific and cultural life of the time. It is worth remembering that the meetings between the Enlightened explorer and the imperial representatives were intermediated by the renowned True Concord lodge from Vienna, one of whose members was Born.[15]

Griselini's *Lettere odeporiche* was produced on the orders of the House of Habsburg (he was sent to the Banat on an official mission), but it was also written under the impulse of Freemasonry.[16] Considering the period in which it was drafted, the book provides an excellent and detailed presentation of the region's geography, history, economy and population. It is important for Italian and Romanian culture, and for Austrian and Central European intellectualism and politics, because it depicted for the first time the civil, antique, medieval and modern condition of the region, presenting its monuments and artworks; discussing the emergence of industry in the Banat, and the character of its population; and showing the level of ignorance or knowledge of the people in trade or agriculture.[17] The book will remain forever among the main bibliographical references to the Banat, highlighting its geographic peculiarities and areas of potential development. Griselini's approach is interdisciplinary and encyclopedic – typical of the eighteenth century – its value deriving mostly from the novelty and reliability of information.[18] It should be noted that, after spending some years in the Banat (1774–77), the Venetian author left a very well-documented legacy, promoting the book among Western academics in Milan, Florence, Venice, Vienna, Sweden, France and Germany. We can observe this in the names of the scholars and academies mentioned in every chapter of the book. The chapters are written in epistolary style, with insertions of discoveries pertaining to different scientific fields.

We should mention that, in the second half of the eighteenth century, regions such as Dalmatia, Croatia, Transylvania and the Banat were unknown to Europeans. From his book, it appears that Griselini was a supporter of imperialism, Venice and its cultural and economic interests not having been prejudiced by its experience of Habsburg domination. Griselini's activity in one of the Venetian lodges facilitated his interaction with intellectuals, writers, historians, naturalists, doctors and journalists. Some of them collaborated on the *Giornale d'Italia*, a publication edited by Griselini between 1765 and 1776, which achieved a certain notoriety by publishing information about exploration and scientific discoveries.

The chronicles and letters concerning the Banat, the knowledge gathered about the Central and East European regions, the discoveries made while travelling down the River Danube highlighted the origins of the Romanian population and its relation to Western Roman civilisation. The author compared and exemplified the closeness between the Romanian and Italian languages. In the end, his contribution does not come down simply to a bridge between different places of the old continent, but also to the assertion of a historiography of the Banat, one which has inspired many later historians and ethnographers, concerned about the region's multicultural and intercultural realities.

It is interesting that the Italian edition comprises five more chapters than the German version, offering new data regarding the history, demographic movement, religions, mentalities, geography, ethnography and the general aspect of the region. The foreword of the Italian edition is written in such a way that the reader 'can formulate his idea relating to the region's physical geography, but also to the succession of events'.[19] The intention is to facilitate access to facts and events that had occurred in Timișoara and the Banat in the eighteenth century, some of which were directly known to the author.[20] It proves, by irrefutable examples, the proximity between the Western Latin world and the East-Central European one, between the languages and cultures of Romania and Italy.[21] Griselini was interested in sending a clear message about the little or barely known regions of Europe. Timișoara and the Banat have thus become important landmarks from not only the imperial but also the European perspective, the richness and diversity of linguistic and religious communities bringing to the reader's attention an area of cohabitation and multiculturalism, situated at the border between the Habsburg Empire (renamed the Austrian Empire in 1805) and the Ottoman Empire.

It is important to emphasise the content of the Italian edition, highlighting its similarities and differences with the German edition. While the latter includes twenty-one letters with eight recipients, the Italian version comprises twenty-six letters with fifteen recipients. Only six of the recipients are shared between the two editions, but what is important is that most of the letters/chapters include scientific content with analysis, experiment and argument stimulated by a diversity of fields such as physics, mineralogy, agronomy, cartography, history and linguistics. The Italian edition is of greater quality than the German one. It is richer in information, free from the official Habsburg constraints, and some themes – such as the Roman origin of Romania and the relationship between the Romanian and Latin languages – are discussed more extensively. All these are the result of curiosity and sensitivity displayed by the Enlightened author with his encyclopedic knowledge.

The intellectual value of Francesco Griselini's work derives not only from the method, ideas and practices typical of modern historiography, but also from his flair in identifying the region's specific traits: Romanian and Serbian communities sharing the same religion; colonists of different origins – German, Italian, French – brought by the imperial administration from Western and Central Europe; settlements erected by the House of Habsburg for colonisation; cohabitation of communities belonging to different religious faiths – Orthodox, Roman Catholic, Mosaic; the Europeanity of the geographical space and its inhabitants. The fact that the Venetian intellectual discusses the beginning of the Industrial Revolution in the Banat highlights the importance of the imperial reformist policies, while the preoccupation with how they can be extended by literacy is a sign of his attachment to the values of freedom and equality – not only with the theoretical principles of Freemasonry, but also with the pragmatic, Enlightened and mercantile doctrines of Austrian despotism. Besides, the description and the meaning offered to things and phenomena encountered during his travels would have had an impact upon the imperial functionaries, some of whom were members of the first Masonic lodge of Timișoara, the Three White Lilies. The new Banatian administration, the demographic experiments, the creation of bridges between regions, and particularly the economic progress achieved by modernising agriculture and industry would play an essential role for the House of Habsburg.

The history of the relationship between Freemasonry and Vienna's reformist policies in the research and writing of a monograph of a region then situated on the edges of Europe is fascinating. It shows how savant and Freemasonic societies played their part not only in imperial policies, but also in outlining 'the cultural corridors' between Western and Eastern Europe. On the other hand, as a border region between the Ottoman and Habsburg empires, eighteenth-century Banat has a rich history, containing multicultural experiments, attractive to the eyes of any visitor. This is evident from the content of each of the letters published by Griselini. In any case, the evidence – without being unique – is fascinating for the vastness of information and its rich content, presented in such a modern context. Concern for the identity of the region's old-established population was still non-existent. In conclusion, the contribution of the Venetian scholar is also important because it includes the first description of the Roman origin of the Romanian population, and discusses the similarities of its culture with the Italian and neighbouring Slavic ones.

It should also be mentioned that Freemasonry was among those institutions that have acted as a catalyst for change in the Central and East-Central European region. Its significant presence within diverse social segments (mostly urban) triggered the formation of new languages, and of sociocultural and institutional modernisation which is impossible to deny. Freemasons acted as a binding agent, being open to communication and association with pragmatic political and economic reforms. It is worth mentioning that they promoted relations between religion and civil society – especially during the eighteenth century – and brought into effect part of the reforms of the European imperial or royal houses. What we know for sure is that the Freemasons displayed a special predisposition towards association and the literary-academic culture – Francesco Griselini, Carlo Goldoni, Ignaz von Born and their congeners are bright examples – for the practice of multilingualism and the integration of spiritual experiments and scientific research within a framework of universal values. Many of these traits are found in the first Masonic lodge in Timișoara. We are talking about the fundamental links that generated the emancipation of the individual and the community, building at the same time the chain of civic, academic and economic institutions, formulating questions and solutions regarding the transition to modernity and changes in behaviour and mentality.

TIMIŞOARA AND LUGOJ: THE BEGINNINGS OF URBAN CULTURE IN THE BANAT

The territory of the Banat achieved its own status in the eighteenth century after it had become a new acquisition of the House of Habsburg. Starting in 1716, the region acquired administrative authority, having distinct economic and social responsibilities in relation to other regions of the Habsburg Empire. This involved management of a territory totally foreign to Vienna in which the fundamental institutions of local communities and their elites were either unknown to the new rulers or non-existent. Perhaps most important of all, the particularity of the region was a consequence of its strategic position at the south-eastern border of the empire, where the Ottomans still posed a threat to the Habsburgs.

The fields were very fertile, ensuring the extensive cultivation of wheat, corn and vines. The cities developed economically in close relation to the geographic features of the region and the riches of the soil and undersoil. The eighteenth-century Banat was situated between the rivers Mureş, Tisza and Danube.[22] Studying the works of past chroniclers of the region and using maps designed and drawn up by today's geographers, historian Lászlo Marjanucz has identified a 100,000-square-kilometre plain area as essential for the region. He divides it into three parts: one situated between the Danube and the Tisza, which was named Bácska; the second beyond the Tisza, known as the Banat of Timişoara; and the third named Srem (Szerémség).[23]

The Banat became a place where reforms and modernisation could be more easily promoted as compared with other regions that preserved their medieval structures. Having neither traditional institutions, such as diet, craftsmen guilds or commercial companies, nor the outlines of an urban culture, the Banat became a place of political, industrial, agrarian, demographic and cultural experiments. The emperor's intention was to establish here the first 'hereditary' province in the east of the Habsburg Empire.[24] Within a few decades, the region was particularised by economic dynamism; agriculture, mining and industry became important. This was possible due to the lack of a proper nobility and major social fractures, contrary to the case of Transylvania. The technical experiments, encouraged by the administrations of Timişoara and Vienna, generated open competition among the inhabitants of the region. The new history of the Banat in the eighteenth century would benefit from a project, a proper regional culture and a regional identity that had been absent in previous periods.[25]

The Banat was divided into the counties of Caraș-Severin, Timiș, Torontal and Arad. This organisation was imposed as a result of the interests of the Habsburgs. It took into consideration the multilingual and multicultural configuration of the region as it had existed before its inclusion within the empire. Adding the colonisations of the eighteenth century, the Banat became a true melting pot at the borders of the Habsburg and Ottoman empires. The main bridges between the different communities of the Banat were the Roman Catholic and the Greek Orthodox churches.[26] Having a rich soil, the land was densely populated. Following Turkish rule, the reconstruction of the region became important, and this was implemented by the will and imagination of Viennese administration.

Starting from this point, during the eighteenth and nineteenth centuries a regional plan of construction was outlined, with a different network of settlements than in the previous period and ensuring the necessary conditions for the sociopolitical and economic emancipation of every citizen. In the form of a square, limited by the rivers of the Danube, the Tisza and the Mureș and the Carpathian Mountains (demarcating it from Transylvania), the Banat benefited from urban competition in the eighteenth and nineteenth centuries between Timișoara, Arad and Szeged. Even if in most cases there had been tensions between Timișoara and Arad, the two towns managed to avoid conflicts. Arad, situated on the Mureș River, played the role of an open gate towards Transylvania. Rivalry also existed between Timișoara and Szeged,[27] but in this case more dominant were the partnerships in culture, trade and industry. Regarding relations with Lugoj, a generally active *comitatens* centre during the negotiations for regional political influence, they were mostly cooperative. The regional administration of Timișoara never ignored Lugoj's perspective, or that of Caraș-Severin County. There were many moments during the eighteenth century in which the cooperation between Timișoara and Lugoj was beneficial for politics, legislation and the coordination of multi-confessional congregations.

The eighteenth- and nineteenth-century Banat, which included Lugoj, was ruled directly from Vienna by an administrative body led by the emperor, and headed by the military or civil governor and president of the administration. The following personalities gained the rank of governor of the Banat: Claude Florimond de Mercy d'Argenteau (1716–34); Johann Andreas von Hamilton (1734–38); Wilhelm Reinhard von Neipperg (1738–39); August Jakob Heinrich von Succow (1739–40); and Franz Anton Leopold von Engelshofen (1740–51). Presidents of the Banatian administration were Franz Anton Leopold von Engelshofen (1751–53); Don Francesco Ramon de Vilana Perlas (1753–68); Karl Ignaz von Clary-Altringen (1769–74); Joseph Brigido von Bressowitz (1774–77); and Pompeo Brigido von Bressowitz (1778–79).[28]

The status of the region was in constant dispute between the House of Habsburg and the Hungarian aristocracy, which claimed its own administrative position and, after long conflicts (including armed ones), accepted a conditional subordination to the Habsburg and later the Austrian Empire. Among the conditions was that the emperor should accept the title of King of Hungary, and that Hungary should administer lands that had been owned by its nobility during the medieval kingdom. Such changes occurred gradually; for example, after long delays between 1750 and 1779, the Banat changed from a domain of the imperial crown to a region managed by the Hungarian State Council. This was far from simple, because the old Romanian and Serbian communities identified themselves with local traditions. On the other hand, the colonisation policies initiated by the Habsburg Empire generated a new demographic configuration of the region. Romanians and Serbians were joined by Swabian Germans, French, Italians, Spaniards, Czech, Slovaks, Bulgarians, Gypsies, Hungarians and Jews, all leading to the heterogeneous sociocultural condition of the region in the eighteenth century. The same concept of heterogeneity has contributed to the defining of a particular identity which has belonged to Central Europe for over three hundred years.

The existence of some distinguishing regional traits made the Banat hard to subordinate to any constraining governance from the religious, linguistic, ethnonational or political perspective. Thus, the change in regional status in the mid-eighteenth century was difficult for the dominant powers. The inhabitants were disappointed by the necessity for change at a time when the Viennese institutions had already established themselves as points of reference. The idea of administrative autonomy was very important for the people of the region. As for the religious congregations, they continued to play an essential role in the preservation of the multiple religious beliefs. The cases of the Orthodox Church with its metropolitan headquarters at Karlowitz and the Roman Catholic Church with Episcopalian centres at Timișoara and Vrsac are well known. During the second half of the eighteenth century, they were joined by the Greek Catholic churches and synagogues.

THE ADMINISTRATIVE RE-ESTABLISHMENT OF THE REGION

In 1777, Empress Maria Theresa agreed to the reorganisation of the Banat. The decision was preceded by a long political process. Until then, the region had directly depended upon the Viennese Aulic Chamber and the Imperial War Council. According to some nineteenth-century historians, among whom was Pesty Frigyes, there were many possible reasons for the imperial administrative re-establishment: the external relations of the House of Habsburg, the material benefit resulting from the Banat's territorial reorganisation and Maria Theresa's oath on her coronation as queen of Hungary, as well as Charles VI's coronation diploma and article 18 of the law adopted by the Hungarian diet in 1741, which provided for the integration of the Banat within the Hungarian administration. Frigyes regarded the issue from the prism of his time, which did not help him to understand the complex status of the region. He ignored the period of the Banat's direct subordination to the imperial administration, along with its geographical position at the intersection of religions, languages and cultures. It seems that he did not take into consideration the role of border defendants given by the imperial administration to the people of the region. Surely the Banat had established itself as an Austrian region, with an economy and a community and confessional life that conferred on it many peculiarities. This explains why local functionaries objected to the dissolution of the Banatian administration.

On the occasion of the regional political and administrative reorganisation, signed in 1779, the Hungarian nobility intended to gain extra power in relation to the House of Habsburg.[29] Maria Theresa needed the support of the Hungarian nobility in the external conflicts of the empire. What the Imperial Chancellery aimed for was the balanced preservation and development of the workforce and the establishment of some counties of similar size and status. According to Maria Theresa, schools should receive 'special attention'. The project pursued the multiplication of two types of schools: one for 'gentry' and other for 'commoners'. The aim was to educate the population to respect work rules and ethics. The particular condition of Timișoara and the region around it – as a border region to the Ottoman Empire, defined by the meeting place between two great Christian traditions – determined the Habsburg authorities to name Timișoara a royal free city. Maria Theresa formulated a new concept, different from the Hungarian practice, according to which people and communities belonging to different European religious faiths, with proven ability to work in agriculture and industry, crafts and trade, could settle in the Banat. In other words, the empress was no longer forced to take into account the old social and administrative structure of the Banat. As a land which had not become a possession of the nobility, but rather that of the empire, the Banat was a territory fit for colonisation.

In 1778, when the Banat was first included in the Hungarian administration, the local population did not react enthusiastically.[30] The bishops of Timișoara, Imre Christovich of the Roman Catholic Church and Moise Putnik of the Orthodox Church, had the task of informing the population about the new order of things. On 6 June 1778, Kristóf Niczky, president of the commission, presented the imperial-royal rescript addressed to the administration of Timișoara. This took place in the governor's residence, the Mercy palace, later the office of the Timiș County prefecture.[31] Even if the Banat was incorporated into a new administration, which in turn was subordinate to the empire, the experiences begun under the Viennese administration continued to be observed in the economic investments and development, demographic movement, and cohabitation of different 'confessional nations' – the Orthodox, Roman Catholic, Greek Catholic, Evangelical Lutheran, Reformed Calvin, Jewish and Mohammedan. Long after this change, the experiments initiated by the Habsburgs between the years 1718 and 1778 were proving their importance.[32]

This administrative re-establishment did not imply the Banat's total subordination to the Hungarian State Council. This is confirmed by the role given to the border regions in the following decades which were coordinated by the Viennese War Council. The Banat was divided into three counties: Timiș, Torontal and Caraș. Excepting the border regions, the counties represented free-standing administrative bodies. Becicherecul Mare (Nagybecskerek, Zrenjanin) was the residence of Torontal County, Timișoara that of Timiș, Lugoj that of Caraș. According to the Hungarian cameral archives, the administrative apparatus was located as follows: in Becicherecul Mare, the building of the public treasury (Remtamt); in Timișoara, the administrative building of the region; and in Lugoj, the building of the regional representatives. The prefects and sub-prefects represented the county officials and were appointed by the Hungarian Court Chancellery. András Semsey was appointed sub-prefect of Torontal County; Kristóf Niczky, prefect of Timiș, and Zsigmond Lovász sub-prefect. The position of prefect of Caraș was occupied by Count József Haller, while Ignác Madarász was sub-prefect. The officials were Hungarian- and German-speaking and came from either the Banat or Hungary.[33] The changes that occurred in 1779 did not trigger a new demographic situation, but only the promotion of officials originating from the new noble families who reached the top of the administration and often came from Hungarian counties.

EIGHTEENTH-CENTURY LUGOJ

Let us see what kind of city Lugoj was in the period immediately following its transformation into the residential city of Caraș-Severin County. With the aid of a document of the time – the Minorite journal, *Ephemerides sive Diarium Venerab. Conventus Logosiensis ordinis Minorum I. Francisci Conventualium* – we can better understand the status of the city, who ruled it, and what were the occupations of its people, the role of local churches and the new administrative formula of the city.[34] Some historians assert that the Hungarian nobility thus countered the decisions of the imperial court, according to whom the Banat was functioning as a free-standing region.

Situated at the crossroads between Vienna and Constantinople, between Karlowitz, Vrsac and Caransebeș, between the Banat and Wallachia, and the

Banat and Transylvania, Lugoj had hosted many visitors over a long period, among them the emperor, the bishops of Cenad-Timişoara and Karlowitz, the most important administrative bureaucrats of Vienna, Bratislava and Buda, diplomats and military men. The canonic sojourns of the Roman Catholic and Greek Orthodox bishops were a regular feature and were of great importance for the people of Lugoj, because the leaders of the two faiths had an essential role in the implementation of administrative reforms for the building of churches. The social life and the city culture of the people of Lugoj could only gain from the bishops' involvement, from the bureaucratic apparatus, but mostly from the traders, craftsmen, priests and teachers.

Lugoj owes a debt of gratitude to its traders and craftsmen, monks and priests, educators and teachers. The fact that they exist in quite large numbers shows that eighteenth-century Lugoj is a city; it has an urban economy, schools, churches and monasteries. Secondly, it is the residential town of Caraş County, which assumes the existence of an administrative and political elite, one connected to the imperial hierarchies of Timişoara and Vienna. Lugoj had an important religious life, since the Orthodox and Catholic bishops scheduled frequent canonical visits. The impressive Orthodox church of the Romanian community is proof of the organisation, the economic force and the religious identity of an important portion of the citizens. Like the Metropolitan and Patriarchal church of Karlowitz, its architecture is inspired by the Central European baroque, spread throughout the Danube regions, including the Banat, by the imperial Habsburgs in the eighteenth century. It was part of a whole current of cultural, artistic and literary ideas that started in Rome in the sixteenth century and had a long existence in the whole of Europe until the twentieth century. The Baroque style in which the main Orthodox church of Lugoj is built is free and generous, and was understood and appreciated by the citizens of the city. The Orthodox and Roman Catholic churches adopted it almost simultaneously. The foundations of the Orthodox church were laid in 1759 when a contract was signed with mason architect Johannes Breutter of Timişoara. The contract mentioned that the building of the church would be supported financially by 46 citizens of Lugoj.[35] The construction of the church, bearing the name of the Assumption and known to the locals as the church with two towers, was finalised in the year 1766.

To the aforementioned social categories we owe not only guild associations, but also civic and political partnerships, the citizens showing great interest in emancipation, which explains its later rise in the life of the county. Education, professions, modern ideas, constant interaction between religious and linguistic communities, cultivation of local and regional identity, all demonstrate the importance of the city. The management of political and religious conflicts was carried out by priests and bishops, with the help of cosmopolitan intellectuals. The Banat produced a series of scholars who were not only multilingual but also participated in a modernising culture. The bright examples of Paul Iorgovici and Constantin Diaconovici-Loga are not unique, but they are symptomatic of a very sinuous regional history in which the Western set of values was adopted earlier and more profoundly than in other East-Central European territories. Education was a fundamental component of this process. The bishoprics of Vrsac and of Timișoara-Cenad supported the extension of the school network, and were involved in the implementation of the imperial instructions and the drafting of regulations. From the journal of the Minorite order it appears that around 1,800 representatives of local linguistic and religious communities were elected as mayors. The mayor was a member of either the German Catholic or the Romanian Orthodox and Greek Catholic communities. At one point, a Romanian ruled the city of Lugoj for four years.[36]

Even if they did not originate from the region, the families of counts that settled there left their mark on urban life in Lugoj. On example is Count Soro, who offered 150 florins to the Roman Catholic church of Lugoj for painting an icon of St Nepomuk. As mentioned in the journal of the Minorite order, icons of St John Nepomuk and St Anthony were brought from Vienna and laid on the two altars of the church.[37] The greatest honour for the city was the visit of Emperor Joseph II: during one of the conflicts between Habsburgs and Turks, in 1788, he stopped at Lugoj, being hosted by the county house.[38] When the territories south of the Carpathians or Transylvania were the theatre of large social unrests, Lugoj was the preferred refuge or place of transition for priests, military men and bureaucrats—for example, the Roman Catholic bishop of Alba-Iulia, Ignác Batthyáni, during the revolt of Horea.[39]

Lugoj was not a marginal city of either the Habsburg Empire or of Europe. Visited by military men, diplomats and bishops, with its own intellectuals, traders and bureaucrats, it bore the mark of a city with no complexes.[40] The city sought – and often succeeded even without the strong involvement of its inhabitants – direct relations with the renowned centres of the time. The city reproduced significant parts of Viennese art and architecture, and cultivated classical music and artistic creation. For example, in 1790 the Roman Catholic church of the city bought an organ, whose maintenance was entrusted to its manufacturer, an organ maker from Timișoara.[41] In their journal, the Minorites mention that music and theatre stirred a real passion among the citizens of Lugoj and that there was no ceremony in the city without a musical band. This led the historian Valeriu Leu to assert that the people of Lugoj 'enjoyed beauty and refinement' and the population could 'cry with emotion before a new altar', while cult objects or merely those of good taste, incense boats, paintings and sculptures were prized, adorning churches and houses alike.[42]

There were occasions, especially during holidays, when the city was illuminated and plays were performed in the theatre. Educational, institutional and civic reforms contributed to modernisation. Between 1790 and 1810 Lugoj hosted sumptuous meetings of Church officials and of traders and military men travelling from South-East to Western Europe; it was the meeting place for Austrian or French diplomats who were going to or returning from Constantinople. From time to time, Lugoj also housed certain bandits or criminals. Periodically it dealt with floods and earthquakes, the poverty of marginalised people, violence and unfair decisions from the county leaders. It would not be wrong to state that at the end of the eighteenth century Lugoj was a place of amalgamation, situated at the border of Orient and Occident, with habits and behaviours borrowed from both. Under Vienna's imperial influence, the city had tended to absorb the Central and Western European set of behavioural values and habits. The policy became more and more open to the needs of the large population. The nobility, even the newly established one, was not the dominant social category. On the contrary, between 1760 and 1800, the middle class was born, aspiring to innovation and modern ideology. A national movement was yet to emerge from the traditions of the many religious communities. The people of the Banat were associating the idea of nation with that of religious faith. In the same way, later, the mother tongues or the multilingualism indicate the acknowledgement of diversity. This is one example from the period and the region which reveals unity in diversity. Lugoj at the end of the eighteenth century was opened to Europe; its leaders and its citizens, belonging to different religious cults, were striving for modernisation. Their intellectual horizon fused in the same manner as the other people of the Banat.

5
ADMINISTRATION, COLONISATION AND CULTURE

László Marjanucz

THE BANAT OF TEMES was founded by the Aulic rescript of November 1717. Between 1718 and 1779, it was directly administered from Vienna by the Imperial Banat Country Administration (*Kaiserliche Banater Landes Administration*), a name established by order of Governor Mercy on 23 September 1718. The Banat represented a stand-alone region with distinctive socio-economic relations in comparison to other parts of the Habsburg Empire.[1] Given these circumstances, the Banat benefited from its own development policies. During the eighteenth century, Vienna considered the implementation of a political and economic experiment within the region, with the intention of establishing the first 'hereditary province' in the eastern part of the empire.[2] This would include the territory situated between the Mureș, the Tisza and the Lower Danube. The region was characterised by a diverse and dynamic economy, in which an important role was played by agriculture, mining and industry. A fertile soil ensured the extensive cultivation of wheat, corn and grapevine, while the geographical position determined the profile of Timișoara's industrial development.

According to geographers, the Danube-Carpathian basin was divided into six large units. One of them represented the plain, which comprised the Danube-Tisza area and the so-called land beyond Tisza. Bácska was part of the first, the Banat of Temes part of the latter. There was also a third area situated in the same plain, which was named Srem (Szerémség).[3] By virtue of more administrative-territorial forms of organisation, Banat was split into four counties: Caraș-Severin, Timiș, Torontal and Arad. This establishment was dictated by the imperial interests of the House of Habsburg, and concerned the multilingual and multicultural experiment in the period of colonisation in the eighteenth century. In this context, the main bridges between the different communities were the Roman Catholic[4] and Greek Orthodox[5] churches. Banat was noted for the cultivation and production of food, having a rich soil and, as a consequence, being densely populated. Following Ottoman rule, reconstruction of the region was important, and this occurred according to the schedule of the imperial administration. Within the eighteenth and nineteenth centuries the region developed through a network of settlements totally different from the previous structure, which generated good conditions for its sociopolitical and economic emancipation. Spread over a square surface, bounded by the Danube, the Tisza, the Mureș and Carpathian Mountains (which separated it from Transylvania), between 1718 and 1918 the Banat witnessed a competition for urban primacy between the cities of Timișoara, Arad and Szeged.

Immediately after the departure of the Turks, Timișoara asserted itself as a regional centre, the disagreements with the neighbouring cities of Szeged and Arad being replaced by cultural, commercial or industrial partnerships.[6] We should stress that in the decades following the conquest of the Banat by the Habsburgs, Timișoara became the main regional centre, the newly appointed authorities investing in the process of urbanisation.[7] Arad, situated on the Mureș River, was seen as an open gate towards Transylvania and was also given an important role within the region.

THE HABSBURG COLONISATIONS

The Romanian-, Serbian- and Hungarian-language communities had a long tradition of cohabitation in the territory of the Banat, which predated its conquest by the Habsburgs. Therefore, it is important to understand the different historical periods in which the populations of Banat had formed and evolved, as well as emphasizising certain features. These periods personalise, by origin and cultural references, the new and old communities of the region as well as providing a sense of historical perspective on a region characterised by the succession of political regimes and the relation between past and present.

One of the special programmes of the House of Habsburg involved the colonisation of the Banat. This was effected by the transfer of part of the Catholic population from different regions of Europe: German, French, Spanish, Italian, Bohemian and Hungarian.[8] The programme was drafted by the Viennese court and its principles may be found in the central institution, the Commission of Acquired Territories (*Neoaquitica Comissio*) and also in the Facilities of the Kingdom of Hungary (*Einrichtungswerk des Königreichs Ungarn*). When in 1717 they defeated the Turkish army, the imperial troops occupied an extended territory, including 663 localities, populated with 21,289 houses. The inhabitants of the newly integrated region spoke Serbian and Romanian, and practised, on swampy soil, an agrarian economy of medieval type. The region was to be developed economically and culturally,[9] a project attended to by the House of Habsburg during the eighteenth century. For example, the so-called Mercy plan (named after the first imperial governor of Banat, Claude Florimond de Mercy) specified German colonisation. In 1722 the first 'Swabian march' (*Schwabenzug*) to the Banat took place; 15,000 people were colonised by agreement of the imperial administration. The second 'Swabian march' occurred between 1764 and 1771, when approximately 20,000 people were colonised. According to the public prescriptions, an owner possessed 22 acres of tillable land, 6 acres of hay and 3 acres of pastureland. Later, based on the rent roll (*urbarium*), the surface area of the households was extended.[10] The legal basis of migration was article 103 from the year 1723, which offered great amenities. In 1773, due to financial reasons, Empress Maria Theresa ceased the colonisation. It was resumed by Emperor Joseph II in 1782, based on the document entitled *Impopulacios patens*. Under its influence, the third 'Swabian march' took place (1782–87) and out of 7,600 families, 6,000 were colonised in the Banat (1,600 settled in Hungary). On this occasion, the colonists received substantial aid from the imperial administration: land, a house, two oxen, two horses, a cow, a carriage, plough, harrow, etc.

In the first stage of this process of population transfer, many colonists died of infectious diseases, poor crops and malnutrition. In the swampy lands of the Banat, typhoid fever created havoc among the population.[11] After 1817 the number of German colonists diminished. Between 1720 and 1740, other cultural linguistic groups arrived in Banat, for example, Spanish, Italian and French. Most of them adopted the German language. In the second half of the eighteenth century, the Slovak population settled in the southern part of Timiș and Torontal counties. A century later, when railways were constructed throughout the Austro-Hungarian monarchy, a Czech (Bohemian) population arrived in Banat and was colonised in Caraș County. The Czech villages became industrial parks, resembling to a great extent the Slovakian ones. The eighteenth-century colonists were mostly Catholics.

Following the same imperial demographic project, in the developing cities of the Banat (Timișoara, Becskerek, Vršac) a Hungarian-speaking population was settled. For example, in 1785, those from Heves County transferred to Medja (Párdány, Pardan, present-day Voivodina). In the 1780s the locality of Tormac (Végvár) was founded, hosting a small number of settlers of Reformed Calvinist confession. Those who had moved from Szeged, Csongrád and Cenad counties settled in the following localities: Sajan (Szaján, 1804), Gătaia (Gatálja, 1823) and Urmeniș (Ürményháza, 1840). All of them were tobacco farmers.[12]

The establishment of border regiments extended the duration of colonisation, especially in Caraș County where, within the border region, the geographical features of the localities played a decisive part. Sixty-seven per cent of the county area was mountainous, while agricultural land was found only along the banks of the rivers that emptied into the Danube. The colonisation continued in this county during the first half of the nineteenth century, some of the colonists arriving from the area of Bratislava, from the small villages of Trencsén and Turóc counties. They were peasants, serfs, craftsmen and lesser nobility. In the same period, approximately 1,000 people migrated to Caraș from northern Hungary, belonging to the Hungarian and Slovakian communities.[13] Research into the origins of the population of Banat has concluded that half of the Hungarian-speaking population of Timișoara and a third of Timiș County came from Szeged. They settled there due to the rich lands of the Banat, aspiring to a better life.[14]

Colonists for the most part were recruited voluntarily, but in some cases, as with the Lutherans, who were transported from Upper Austria to Transylvania and the Banat in the years 1734 and 1757, the colonisations were forced. Moreover, we should mention that instead of colonisation, in some instances there was deportation of certain social segments that fell afoul of the law. That happened between 1752 and 1768, with the so-called 'deportation to Timișoara by water'.[15] The third group of deportees, after the Peace of Hubertusburg of 1763, were war prisoners from Prussia, invalids and veterans of the imperial army. The colonisations during the reign of Maria Theresa were less numerous than those during the reign of her son, Joseph II. Under Maria Theresa, colonisation was motivated by the Habsburg policy of mercantilism. The policy was particularly costly – over 900,000 guilders – and the colonising population received uninhabitable homes while its cultural situation did not improve either. Joseph II did not agree with these methods, and when he inherited the throne he laid the basis of new colonisations. He offered twice the sum of money for intensifying the colonisation of the Banat. According to transport documents between 1743 and 1771, about 42,000 people – mostly from Vienna – arrived in Timișoara. In the imperial region of Bácska almost 10,000 people arrived. In 1763 the colonisation expanded, upon a more solid system. Between 1782 and 1788 around 12,000 persons settled in the Banat, contributing to the development of localities such as Nițchidorf (Nitzkydorf), Tormac (Rittberg) and Măureni (Moritzfeld), situated to the south-east of Timișoara. Between 1784 and 1787 Jamu Mare (Freudental), Aluniș (Traunau) and Orțișoara (Orczydorf) were founded.[16]

Even after the death of Emperor Joseph II, colonisation continued to be the key issue in the development of the Banat of Temes. Its social consequences were experienced until the nineteenth century. During the eighteenth century, colonisation had a great impact on southern Hungary – a region vastly destroyed by the Ottoman occupation – as well as on the Banat. In 1781 Banat was included as part of the Hungarian administration, under the coordination of the Hungarian State Council; this was nothing more than an attempt to decentralise the imperial power. Thus, colonisation became the main task of the Hungarian State Council,[17] which attended to the colonists' arrival, ensuring travel expenses, medical care, procurement of medical drugs, and also a financial allowance for daily necessities. The colonists also received land, seeds, animals, tools and equipment. For a period of ten years they were exempt from public duties. Many conventions regulated compulsory services in the community. Technical officials from the Hungarian State Council drafted engineering projects for the houses, schools and churches built in the colonised villages.

From 1788, the number of German colonists decreased, so that during the reign of Francis I it was necessary to increase the population, to spread it throughout the province, to cultivate the wild areas, to develop possessions of the new nobility and to encourage the production of goods. This meant the humanisation of the region, according to its features, and state integration. The private colonisation was different from the governmental one, the nobility pursuing the diversification of occupations, in the sense of multiplying the number of craftsmen and experienced farmers. The imperial measures also aimed at the deportation of people on religious, social and political grounds.

After 1800, in the context of the Napoleonic Wars, the Habsburgs reorganised themselves from an economic perspective. In order to cope with the increased number of inhabitants, they introduced taxation of the population, thus ensuring an additional source of income for the state. It was a time in which a disparity between demographic growth and the demand for food was felt in all Europe. The Austrian Empire slowed down the colonising activity in the first half of the nineteenth century. However, Francis I continued to colonise in the Banat subjects from Austria, the Tyrol, Baden, Württemberg, and Bohemia. The colonists were divided among the villages already inhabited by German-speaking communities. In 1829 the Hungarian State Council took measures to colonise people who already owned at least 300 florins (Ft.). They were exempt for taxation for a period of three years, also being stimulated to build their homes and arrange their households. Most of them settled in Caraș and Torontal counties, while a small part moved to Timiș County.[18]

THE REORGANISATION OF THE BANAT: THE COMITATENS (COUNTY) SYSTEM

In 1777 Maria Theresa agreed to a plan for reorganising the Banat. The decree was preceded by a long political process. At meetings of the Hungarian diet, the nobility discussed the issue of the re-establishment of territorial-administrative unity and analysed the border situation. Also in 1777, the problem of the reorganisation of the Banat was discussed. The province had directly depended until then on the Imperial Chamber and the Military Council in Vienna being separated from Hungary by a border post. Vienna agreed to release the Banat in exchange for certain compensations. The Hungarian councillors, along with the economic and political status of the empire, convinced the empress of the necessity to urgently resolve the issue.

In one of his books, Jenö Szentkláray depicts the Banat as part of southern Hungary. Hence, the partisan explanation of some authors according to whom the Banat should have been placed under Hungarian law. In reality, even when administered by the Hungarian State Council, the Banat region had its own status, its own demographic, linguistic and religious configuration, which did not overlap with Hungary's sociopolitical and cultural-confessional physiognomy. The reasons that convinced Maria Theresa to agree to the territorial reorganisation, offering an increased administrative role to Hungary. The possible causes are: (1) problems generated by the foreign relations of the House of Habsburg; (2) the material benefit that would result from the territorial reorganisation of the Banat; (3) the oath she took when she was crowned queen of Hungary; (4) the coronation diploma of Charles VI and article 18 of the law adopted by the Hungarian Diet in 1741, according to which the integration of the Banat within the Hungarian administration was compulsory. It is probable that, using this administrative, political issue, the Hungarian nobility tried to gain a power advantage vis-à-vis the House of Habsburg.

During the Seven Years War, the Habsburgs became excessively indebted to the Hungarian nobility. Given the detrimental effects of the Russo-Turkish War and the demands of the territorial expansion of Russia and Prussia, starting in 1772 the Empire was forced to strengthen its army. Vienna's involvement was so great that it decided to finance even the expenses regarding the division of Poland. It also financially supported the occupation and organisation of Bucovina, an expense that the treasury couldn't sustain. In the Banat, where Maria Theresa would have been able to raise taxes, government policy did not favour such a measure. On the other hand, the administrative apparatus of the Imperial Chamber was especially costly, thus the taxes could not be collected for several decades. All led to the burning need to increase state revenue. In 1776, by the retrocession of Fiume, the state managed to increase its revenues by trading.

A year later, Maria Theresa sent a letter to the governor of the Banat taking note of his inability to collect residual taxes and manage the mines and forests. At the same time, the clerks of the Court Chamber, the Hungarian Royal Chancellery and the Diet demanded the integration of the Banat into the Hungarian administration, reckoning that state revenues and possessions would increase. In 1778 a new Austro-Prussian war threatened to erupt because of the demands formulated by the Habsburgs upon Bavaria. In the same period, the Viennese court opposed the transfer of the Banat to Hungarian administration. There was also opposition from the German-speaking community towards the empire concerning Hungary's territorial expansion. On the other hand, Maria Theresa needed the support of Hungary in the external conflicts of the empire. Banat had identified itself as an Austrian province, with its own geographical, economic, confessional and community particularities. This was the reason why the officials strongly protested against the abolition of the Banatian administration.

When they founded the new counties, the Habsburgs took into consideration the population's living conditions and the territorial division. Vienna pursued regional unity and the well-being of the population living in the Banat. It concerned itself with territorial and administrative organisation in order to avoid regional division. The purpose of the Imperial Chancellery was to preserve and develop the workforce, and to establish several counties with similar size and status. According to Maria Theresa, schools should receive 'special attention'. The Imperial Chancellery's main task was to train the population according to the standards existing in the Kingdom of Hungary. The project aimed at the same time to develop two types of schooling, one for 'the nobility', the other for 'the common people', with the objective to prepare the population to respect work rules and ethics.

Timișoara's special condition determined the Habsburg authorities to name it a royal free city. Becicherecul Mare, itself aspiring to the rank of royal free city, was administered by Kristóf Niczky. The other privileged spots of the Banat, such as Kikinda Mare (Nagykikinda) and Vinga, had similar objectives. Maria Theresa issued new decrees and a new policy, differing from Hungarian practice, according to which persons and communities belonging to diverse European religious confessions who could prove their ability to perform agricultural and industrial work, crafts and commerce could settle on the estates of the Banat. In other words, the empress was no longer compelled to respect the old social and administrative structure of the Banat. Since it was a province that was owned not by the nobility but by the emperor, the Banat became a colonisable territory.[19]

The Banat region entered the Hungarian administration on 8 April 1778. The president of the integration committee was Count Kristóf Niczky, who was assisted by Count Ferenc Zichy, councillor of the Aulic Chamber, Antal Vörös, vice regent, Ádám Trajcsik, secretary of the Aulic Chamber, Zsigmond Lovász, subprefect of Arad. On 31 May 1778, the committee arrived in Timișoara. As reported by *Wienerisches Diarium* this news was not received with enthusiasm by the people, excepting some villages with a Hungarian population.[20] The bishops of Timişoara, Imre Christovich of the Roman Catholic Church and Moise Putnik of the Orthodox Church, were to inform the population of the new state of affairs.

On 6 June 1778, Kristóf Niczky, president of the committee, presented the imperial-royal rescript to the population of Timişoara. The event took place in the governor's palace (Mercy palace, later the headquarters of the Timiş County prefecture). The rescript was drafted by the Czech-Austrian Chancellery, which had been until then the central leading institution in the Banat. On behalf of the region, the administrative deputy of the Banat, Count Sauer Venczel, took note of the new decision. Kristóf Niczky took over the whole region from the old administration and delivered it to Antal Vörös, the Hungarian representative. That is how the legal procedure unfolded, according to which the chief commissary recorded that the Banat was integrated into the Hungarian administration. In fact, the regional organisation would continue, under multiple aspects, the experiments started under Viennese coordination: investments and economic development, demographic movement, cohabitation of different 'confessional nations' – Orthodox, Roman Catholic, Greek Catholic, Evangelical Lutheran, Reformed Calvin, Jewish and Muslim. The political experiences of the Banat, encountered at the time of its direct subordination to Vienna, cannot be underestimated. During the nineteenth century it became clear just how important the experiments initiated by the Habsburgs in the Banat between 1718 and 1778 were.

The administrative transformation did not assume the total subordination of the Banat to the Hungarian State Council, as a result of the continued activity of military formations of border control which were coordinated by the Viennese Military Council.[21] The first consequence of the territorial rearrangement was that 800 volunteers from Timiş County participated in July 1778 in the War of the Bavarian Succession, fighting against Prussia. The incomes of the Banat did not rise immediately but gradually, by changing the taxation system, by selling real estate to the treasury, and by increasing the number of inhabitants and their ability to pay tax. From the financial perspective, one of the advantages was a decrease in the number of officials. The selling of real estate to the treasury had a double advantage: on one hand, the state increased its income; on the other, a new social segment could develop: the nobility.

The Banat was divided into three counties: Timiş, Torontal and Caraş. Geographically, the region was situated between the Tisza, Mureş and Danube rivers, on the edges of Transylvania and Oltenia. With the exception of the border regions, the counties represented free-standing administrative structures. Becicherecul Mare (Nagybecskerek, Zrenjanin) was the residential city of Torontal County, Timişoara of Timiş, and Lugoj of Caraş. The administrative apparatus of Torontal County was established at Becicherecul Mare, in the state treasury building (Remtamt), that of Timişoara in the administrative building of the region, and that of Lugoj in the zonal office building. The prefects and subprefects were the county's authorities. They were appointed by the Hungarian Court Chancellery. András Semsey was named subprefect of Torontal, Kristóf Niczky prefect of Timiș and Zsigmond Lovász subprefect. In Caraș County, József Haller was prefect and Ignác Madarász subprefect. The functionaries were either Hungarian- or German-speaking and came from the Banat or Hungary. The 're-ennoblement' of the Banat started with the recruitment of civil servants. For example, Kristóf Niczky, appointed prefect, was given the title of 'count of Timiș' by the imperial-royal authorities. All these changes did not assume the settlement of a great number of Hungarians in the region, but rather the organisation of a nobility at the top of the administration. By the certificate issued on 23 April 1779, Maria Theresa instituted the counties. On 22 June, Timiș County was inaugurated; on 13 July, Torontal; and on 5 August Caraș.[22]

Kristóf Niczky proposed several concessions for the Serbian-speaking population, which led to the preservation of the old sociopolitical order. These can be seen in the Banat's views upon nobility, social order and territorial organisation. In 1777 József Hajnóczy, councillor of the chancellery, recommended a democratic system for the Banat, based on the abolition of serfdom and on land allotment. While Kristóf Niczky did not want to change the demographic situation of the Banat, József Hajnóczy promoted the natural development of social and public life. Niczky started from an aristocratic ideology, aiming to underline the differences among different social categories, while József Hajnóczy proposed the preservation of the old social relations of the Banat and also their development. Taking into account the new territorial division and the formation of new elites, Hajnóczy expected a greater involvement of the nobility in the relationship with Vienna. Kristóf Niczky had influenced the Hungarian policy of his time, expecting results especially from nobles, not from the officials of the new administration that coordinated the counties. In other words, Hajnóczy initiated the social principle, and Niczky the state principle, of reorganising the Banat.

THE SALE OF LAND

The sale of land to the treasury was the last great step of colonisation. Thus were formed the property relations which continued until 1918. The House of Habsburg was interested in selling land in order to increase its income. Kristóf Niczky introduced the principles of selling the land to the treasury.[23] The selling of mines and settlements across the Mureș River was not planned. The rice fields were not sold (for example those from Omor, Gătaia (Gattája), Opatica (Opaticza) and Sfântu Gheorghe). Due to its closeness to Timișoara,

Vinga earned the similar status of royal free city. The districts Chichinda Mare and Becicherecul Mare did not sell their lands to the nobility, predicting their future development and the rise of their towns to the rank of royal free cities. The lands were divided into four distinct categories: the first included lands whose value was 300,000–400,000 Ft; the second, those whose value comprised between 150,000 and 300,000 Ft, among which twelve were destined for sale; the third, those which had a value smaller than 150,000 Ft; and the last category, which included cheaper land which the lesser nobility could afford. The rating of these lands assumed the drafting of principles that regulated the purchase agreements and also the presumed buyers. The most important element was the relationship between old and new property. Thus, Vienna intended to include a sufficient number of noblemen who could contribute to the organisation and functioning of county institutions.

Maria Theresa calculated the possible land requisitions based on historical right, according to laws that had been issued in the Middle Ages. Thus, some could appeal for a continuation of their ownership rights. Hungarian law opened such a possibility, trying to demonstrate that the former noble properties had become imperial goods, and the owners had not lost their rights.[24] The Hungarian nobility opposed cases when the former owners did not take possession of the lands and/or were not reimbursed for them. In their view, Maria Theresa should have resolved the issue of property according to Hungarian law. The empress had figured that selling land in the Banat would contribute to the objective of increasing public income. Whoever bought land would become its absolute owner. Once issued, the decree made impossible the requisition proceedings based on the inheritance of lands that belonged to the former nobility of the Banat. Thus, the old properties were lost.[25] At the end of 1779, the possessions of the Hungarian nobility, the estates (*praedium*), settlements, lands, meadows and forests belonging to the villagers were divided into separate properties. Instead, the great landed properties remained undivided. By acquiring land, the new owners received a donation certificate that granted them a noble title.

These new owners either sold the estate or divided it, bequeathing to their children. The owners could come from any religious group, the authorities' sole demand being that these lands should be used for agriculture, livestock breeding or manufacturing. The projects of Emperor Joseph II pursued, in the first place, the development of agriculture and free industry.[26] On 1 August 1781 the first auction for the sale of land was organised in Vienna and Timișoara. Among the estates available for purchase in Vienna (having an average value of 42,000 Ft) were Sânnicolau Mare (Nagyszentmiklós, Großsanktnikolaus), Periam (Perjámos, Perjamosch), Sanad (Szanád, Sanad), Novi Kneževac (Törökkanizsa, Torontáljózseffalva, Neu-Kanischa) and Čoka (Csóka). Among those put up for sale in Timișoara (most of them valued under 30,000 Ft) were Checheș (Lippakékes, Kékes), Sinersig (Szinérszeg, Szinerszeg), Hodoș (Hódos), Brestovăț (Bresztovác) and Petrovaselo (Petrovoszelo).

For example, Paschia Medve Hagzsi bought an estate valued at 42,000 Ft; Specht, a beer brewer from Bratislava (Pozsony, Pressburg) acquired the village Frumușeni (Schöndorf), valued at 43,000 Ft; Landerer Füstkút, a typographer from Bratislava (Pozsony, Pressburg), bought land with 42,000 Ft. During the auction in Timișoara, Ádám Trejcsik bought the locality of Nadăș (Duboki-Nádas), with 31,000 Ft; József Scolonics bought Hodoș (Hódos), with 33,000 Ft; Károly Rajkovics acquired Checheș (Lippakékes, Kékes), with 17,500 Ft; Kereszturi, a court agent, bought Sinersig (Szinérszeg, Szinerszeg), with 33,000 Ft.

The second auction in Timișoara took place on 15 September 1781, when the following transactions were made: Ege Kőszegi bought Remetea Mare (Temesremete, Grossremete) with 94,000 Ft; István Kyriák bought Moșnița (Mosnicza, Moschnitz) with 70,000 Ft; Bazil Damjanovics bought Zădăreni (Zádorlak, Saderlach) with 59,000 Ft; Șandor Mihai from Bratislava (Pozsony, Pressburg) bought Giarmata (Gyarmatha) with 90,000 Ft. On the occasion of the second auction in Vienna (10 December 1781), Eötvenesi Zsigmond Lovász, subprefect of Timiș County, bought Aradul Nou with 157,000 Ft.

The third auction in Timișoara was organised on 10 April 1782, when smaller properties were sold: for example, István Balás, subprefect of Timiș County, acquired the Altringen (Kisrékás) estate; Ferenc Szabó, magistrate of Timiș County, bought the Sintar (Bukhegy, Buchberg) estate, for the sum of 82,000 Ft; György Konszky, the secretary of Baron Orczy, bought the Vizma settlement with 23,950 Ft. Besides those auctions, the Greek Orthodox nun monasteries of Meszics, Sfântu Gheorghe (Szentgyörgy) and Bezdin received a number of estates.

Among those who received land in Timiș County, János Osztoics acquired Şemlacu Mare (Nagyszemlak) and Șemlacu Mic (Kisszemlak); Pál Jankovics acquired Lukarecz; Count Saurau acquired Carani (Mercyfalva, Mercydorf); Izdenczy, state councillor, received Mănăştiur (Bégamonostor, Monostor); Sebő Vukovics earned Beregsău Mare (Berekszo); Counts József Bernyákovics and Antal acquired Boldur (Boldor).[27] Those who could not pay the requested price in Vienna or Timișoara, or the value resulting from the auctions, had to give up the property in favour of the treasury. This was a process by which state property was privatised, the wealthy people being able to acquire important lands. Many of the new owners, who also received noble titles, came from diverse linguistic and religious communities: Serbian (Vukovics), Hungarian (Marczibányi, Dezewfy), Jewish (Specht, Ürményi, Rónai), Macedo-Romanian (Sina, Nacu-Nákó) and Turkish (Hadzsi Paschia).[28]

INTRODUCING THE RENT ROLL (URBARIUM)

The delimitation of the counties' administrative borders represented the condition for introducing the rent roll. This demarcation preceded the formation of private properties and resulted in the transformation of part of the Imperial Chamber's properties into rural property. Starting in 1780, a land registry was instituted, whereby a record of real estate was kept for the properties across the three counties of the Banat. They numbered 29,000 lands. The land surface was calculated in acres (*pogoane*), being considerably larger in the Banat than in Hungary. The method of taxation for the counties was drafted by Kristóf Niczky and was known by the name of *Clavis Niczkyana*. Property-related issues were addressed by regulations used in Europe at that time. Timiș County had four networks: Timiș, Sânandrei (Szentandrás), Lipova (Lippa) and Vârşeţ (Versec); Caraș County five networks: Bulci (Bulcs), Căpâlnaș (Kápolnás), Lugoj, Caransebeș and Oravița; and Torontal County four networks: Sânnicolau Mare (Nagzsyentmiklos), Becicherecul Mare (Zrenjanin-Nagybecskerek), Szerbkanizsa and Peciu Nou (Ujpécs).[29] Most estates of Timiș were vast and belonged to wealthy people; the number of houses was large, like the total number of the population. In second place was Torontal County; in third, Caraș County. Unlike in Hungary, the villagers' lands were large enough to include grazing grounds.

The sources of different regulations were complex. For example, livestock breeding did not have a tradition similar to that of the neighbouring regions. In the Banat, there was a special type of so-called industrial lands, a concept launched by the imperial treasury immediately after colonisation. Vienna encouraged the exploitation of land, no matter what its type, sometimes motivating the population to work its own lands. This procedure continued even after the land repartition to the benefit of the colonists. The authorities stimulated the cultivation of industrial plants, one of the objectives being the drainage of the swampy lands existing in the northern part of the Banat.[30]

Taxation was lower for land owned by villagers. This can be explained by the intention of the authorities to appeal to the population from different parts of Europe. In most cases, the lands of wealthy landlords were not recorded in the rent roll (*urbarium*), and were thus excluded from taxes. The grist milling and the production and selling of alcoholic beverages were possible on large properties, but that did not mean they were sufficient for the survival of the inhabitants. The situation would change at the end of the eighteenth century and the beginning of the nineteenth, along with the development of agricultural goods production. The increasing number of sharecroppers and the multiplication of the real estate belonging to free farmers also contributed to the improvement of quality of life in the Banat.[31]

AGRICULTURE AND INDUSTRY

Agricultural crops were determined by the authorities. Among the first and most important crops were rice and tobacco. Rice was cultivated mostly in Timiș County, where a large production was attained with the help of specialised staff. Vienna was concerned to protect this branch of the economy for a better and more reliable supply of food. The tobacco plantations of Sânandrei, Denta and Covaci et al. were widespread;[32] factories at Timișoara, Szeged and Debrecen processed the tobacco cultivated all over the Banat. Silkworm cultivation had an appreciable share. Furthermore, certain industrial plants, such as flax, hemp, hops, rapeseed, sugar beet and cotton were acclimatised, with different degrees of success. Cotton, not being sufficient, was also imported on a large scale in order to balance local and regional necessities. Already by the end of the eighteenth century at Sânicolau Mare, on Kristóf Nákó's estates, cotton of a very good quality was being cultivated, and was sometimes exported to Vienna. Unfortunately, cultivation was abandoned because of the climate.[33] Among the crops that adapted very well to the conditions existing in the Banat were grain, corn and oats. There were many instances when farmers preferred to harvest clover, mainly in the areas where livestock breeding was dominant. The production of honey also expanded, and after 1840 the farmers adopted the procedure of crop rotation, which stimulated the modernisation of agriculture, multilateral production and the well-being of the land and its inhabitants.[34] The existence in the Banat plain of agricultural land totalling 100,000 hectares and grassland of 12,000 hectares was a distinct advantage.[35]

With regard to industry, this was developed on public properties and inside the cities. The people of the Banat were involved in the manufacture of silk and cloth and the preparation of charcoal. Many specialised in the wood industry, gold washing, pottery and mining. For example, in the given period, iron mining and ore processing were intensified in Caraș County. Coal mines were opened in Gârliște, Domani and Agadici.[36] The mines of Caraș County made possible the extraction of raw materials necessary for the development of the Banat's industry. On the other hand, numerous forests encouraged the exploitation and storing of wood, using modern methods of manufacturing (mechanical saw).[37] The most industrialised areas were Panciova, Timișoara, Becicherecul Mare, Arad and Szeged. The manufactures and guilds were remarkable, especially the silk and cotton weaving mills, oil presses, textile, wire, medicinal alcohol, beer and hat factories, paper mills and printing houses.[38] Since the period 1779–1849, the city of Timișoara has had the major, coordinating role of industrial production. This was due to the fact that the city was a node of water and land transportation (the railway network there was prioritised in comparison to other regions of the empire, and had been very well developed, starting in 1850). The proposal to construct the Danube–Tisza Channel was intended to move the centre of the Banat from Timișoara to Szeged, which meant that open competition began between the two cities for regional economic and administrative authority.

PROPERTIES AND POPULATION

In 1780 the counties of the Banat were part of the so-called district beyond Tisza. From a legal perspective, they were subordinate to the district court of appeal of Debrecen.[39] The difference was that, after 1780, political issues and trials would enter the counties' jurisdiction. Joseph II influenced that system, his administrative reforms dissolving their authority and subordinating them to the royal commissary of some larger districts. Among the ten newly created districts, Timișoara District was the sixth, and included the counties of Caraș, Torontal and Bács. After the union of the chamber and local council, legal issues were settled by the local council. The cameral administration of the Banat, established at the time of Joseph II, would deal with the management of public domains. The exceptional case of the Banatian administration derives from the fact that it had ten administrative chambers, which meant a larger area and numerous sociopolitical issues. Furthermore, it should be remembered that the region's particularity derived from the necessity of regulating the colonisations, the water supply, the complexity of leasing, and the management of land and goods. Following Joseph II's death, eight administrative chambers were dissolved. Only those from Timișoara and Zombor remained.

The reasons for which the cameral administrations of Timișoara and Zombor continued their activity were (1) the responsibility to manage territories situated far from the governing centre; (2) the relatively large area administered by the state; (3) the special importance of the region with regard to colonisation, while the social and religious configuration was totally changed from the period before Habsburg domination. Until the local cameral administration took over its attributes, the governor retained responsibility for the management of public possessions. After 1790, the issue of the public lands of Banat was settled by the Hungarian cameral administration.

Based on the census of 1786, the estates were divided as shown in Table 5.1.

Table 5.1
Number and type of dwelling

APPELLATION		NUMBER			
County	Network	Free Royal City	Cities	Village	Estates (Praedium)
Caraș	Bulci (Bulcs)	–	–	41	–
	Căpâlnaș (Kápolnás)	–	1	54	–
	Caransebeș (Karánsyebes)	–	2	39	–
	Lugoj (Lugos)	–	1	45	–
	Oravița (Oravica)	–	3	45	–
	TOTAL	–	7	224	–
Timiș	Timișoara	1	–	48	–
	Sânandrei (Szentandrás)	–	2	40	–
	Lipova (Lippa)	–	1	45	–
	Vrsac (Versec)	–	2	46	–
	TOTAL	1	5	179	–
Torontal	Sânicolau Mare (Nagysezentmiklós)	–	1	24	2
	Cănicea (Kanjiža, Kanizsa)	–	2	33	5
	Peciu Nou (Ujpécs)	–	–	33	2
	Becicherecul Mare (Zrenjanin, Nagybecskerek)	–	1	21	5
	TOTAL	–	4	111	14

Source: Dezső Dányi (ed.), Történeti Statisztikai Tanulmányok 2 (Historical and Statistical Studies 2), edition issued on the occasion of the first Hungarian census (Budapest, 1975), p. 4

The only royal free city of the region was Timișoara. Within the region there were many cities and market towns. For example, the Banat numbered 16 cities and market towns, among which Caransebeș and Becicherecul Mare stand out as administrative and economic centres. There were numerous rural setttlements, the region comprising 514 villages, including colonists' settlements. The only county that possessed deserted lands was Torontal, because the main economic activity of its inhabitants was livestock breeding. On the other hand, the best valued properties used for the benefit of the economy were in Timiș County, where the lands were intensively cultivated with industrial plants. The most 'urban' county was Timiș, even if Caraș had more cities.

The counties and the royal free cities had already gained an independent judicial authority, which allowed the development of a form of self-government. Table 5.2 shows the land surfaces that were included under the direct judicial authority of the Banat, and also their evolution during 1806 and 1861.

Table 5.2
The area included in the judicial authority of Banat

COUNTIES	SURFACE AREA (SQUARE MILES)	
	1806	1861
Caraș	108.9	95
Timiș	116.5	107.67
Torontal	132.1	214.66

Source: 'Számok és történelem' ('Numbers and History'), in Benda Gyula, *Statisztikai adatok a magyar mezőgazdaság történetéhez 1767–1867* (*Statistical Data in the History of Hungarian Agriculture 1767–1867*) (Budapest, 1983), pp. 58–59.

In 1849 Voivodina and the Banat of Temes were spread over a surface of 29,988 square kilometres.[40] Torontal County was the largest, having a large share of tillable and grazing land. In Caraș, due to the mountainous area not being favourable to agriculture, the judicial authority was narrower. Larger villages developed within the plain areas; smaller ones in hilly or mountainous areas. The villages from Timișoara Plain, designed by engineers, were built in the form of a chess table. They had their own status, not being annexed to larger cities.[41]

On the rich farmlands of the Banat and Bácska, some relatively developed towns were formed. That was the case with Senta (Zenta), Sombor (Zombor), Becicherecul Mare (Nagybecskerek, Zrenjanin) and Panciova (Pancsova). Since 1781, Timișoara had been a royal free city, and from 1876 it received the right of judicial authority. This status provided the opportunity for rapid and important development. Between the medieval Timișoara and the reconstructed and modernised Timișoara there were social, political, administrative, religious and cultural differences.[42]

The areas between Mureș and Criș, Bácska and Timișoara Plain flourished immediately after colonisation. Sándor Bálint's research indicates that the Hungarian population of Timiș County came from the Szeged area and was mainly involved in tobacco farming. This population was colonised during the first half of the nineteenth century, gaining the status of free peasantry, whose activity unfolded according to the contracts with landowners. In the Banat serfdom could not be re-established.[43] The most important settlement of the whole region in the eighteenth and nineteenth centuries was Timișoara, which gained increased significance after the Bega Canal became navigable, after the

Banat Plain started to be exploited and capitalised, and industrialisation began. The city was elevated to the rank of military, economic and administrative centre and became the city of reference of the Banat, shaping the activity of Timiș, Torontal and Caransebeș counties.

With regard to the multiple functions that had been already achieved during the eighteenth century, but especially during the nineteenth century, Timișoara was able both to satisfy the demands of the local population and to manage the neighbouring area by addressing the specific issues of the region. Among its basic functions was also to maintain a continuous supply for the inhabitants of the city. In the period before 1848, the level of urban development was mirrored by the existence of numerous offices and cultural and administrative-political institutions: prefecture, post office, savings bank, food stores, schools, high schools, seminaries, etc.[44]

The increase of population in the Banat was one of the priorities of Habsburg policy. Demography was a precious tool for doubling the workforce and increasing taxes. Organised colonisation, as well as spontaneous migrations, did not unfold on the basis of nationality, the colonists being often selected depending on religion, which preceded the mercantile concern regarding the capitalisation of the newly integrated territory.[45] The multicultural aspect of the region was generated by the diversity of languages spoken by the local and colonising population.

The highest density of population was in Timiș County. During the Napoleonic age, agricultural production and processing increased. The well-being of the population was owed to the development of trading, building of roads and channels, drainage of swamps, and exploitation of natural resources. All these appealed to the colonists settled on public domains. Between 1720 and 1820 population growth was moderate; between 1821 and 1830, an annual increase of 0.74 per cent was recorded; between 1841 and 1850, 1.25 per cent. The most accelerated rate of population growth was recorded in the Timișoara Plain in the mid-nineteenth century. The first modern population census of Hungary was carried out in 1869, being preceded by numerous conscriptions dating from the eighteenth century and from the first half of the nineteenth, all accomplished by Vienna. The population register from the period prior to the modern census can be traced in the demographic documents issued in 1786 and 1828.[46]

The most conclusive imperial census was initiated and conducted by Joseph II. His data reflects the situation of the Banat of Temes after the termination of the status of common law. The results of the census indicate the social structure under the conditions of the new administrative organisation. The number of noblemen in Caraș was 108, in Timiș 200 and in Torontal 129. The number of officials was 99 in Caraș, 210 in Timiș and 62 in Torontal; the number of peasants with land was 25,414 in Caraș, 28,029 in Timiș and 16,943 in Torontal; the number of peasants with no land (*jeleri*) was 14,833 in Caraș, 19,056 in

Timiş and 15,610 in Torontal.[47] These statistics highlight the social particularities of the Banat, underlining both the imperial economic interests regarding the population and the fact that community delimitation based on language, religion or history was not relevant to the authorities. The issue of religious identity and of nationality was not included in the census, a fact that can be understood by the observation that imperial policy was in accordance with the enlightened, cosmopolitan direction typical of the eighteenth century, with mercantilism and control over any type of collective ego.[48]

CULTURE

According to Maria Theresa's decree *Ratio Educationis*, six elementary schools functioned in the Banat with tuition in several languages. They were managed by the Church and functioned according to the curriculum drafted by the Habsburg Empire. The schools were strongly connected to the landowner in each village: he was responsible for the building and maintaining of schools and churches, appointment of teachers and priests, supply and support of monks, and control of the entire schooling process. It is true that this related only to the Catholic schools. The patronage right was not valid in the Protestant or Orthodox villages, their religious life being based on the autonomy of religious institutions. For example, during the eighteenth century and the first half of the nineteenth, the Orthodox popular schools of the Banat were placed under the jurisdiction of the metropolitan of Karlowitz (Sremski-Karlowci). Due to the fact that the imperial Orthodox hierarchy belonged to the Slavic-Serbian community, both the educational system and cultural life were coordinated by that metropolitan and its subordinate churches. The schools were under the control of the two Orthodox linguistic communities, the Slavic-Serbian and the Romanian. The schoolbooks used by the Bishopric of Timişoara, written in Slavic-Serbian and Romanian, were edited in Vienna, where the teachers were also trained. The Slavic-Serbian culture attained remarkable results. Teodor Jankovic-Mirijevski, one of the most active of the Banatian intelligentsia, was the promoter of some modern teaching methods practised in the empire during the second half of the eighteenth century. In 1785 within the Orthodox Bishopric of Timişoara there were 262 parishes, while in the Bishopric of Caransebeş there were 144. They were capable of opening and maintaining the popular schools, some of which developed an education of the highest class, such as those in Bezdin, Sângeorge (Szentgyörgy), Voilovitza and Hodoş (Hodos).[49] The first secular schools from the Banat were established in 1850: Panciova, Vršac, Chichinda Mare. In 1837 the gymnasium at Lugoj was founded, followed by those of Timişoara, Zrenjanin and Arad in 1859. All of them were German schools. The Piarist gymnasium of Timişoara taught the German language until 1861, and after that, Hungarian. More gymnasiums changed their curriculums according to the imperial administration and to the official language. In the Banat during the nineteenth century, the high schools became Hungarian-language institutions.[50] School life developed in Timișoara in competition with the schools from Szeged. In the nineteenth century, young people of the Banat often attended the schools from Szeged, both at the level of middle- and high-school education and at the level of elite training. Regardless of this orientation, Timișoara had a dominant German-language culture.[51]

The churches and religion had an important role in the affirmation of diverse cultural environments. Mother tongues were especially promoted by the churches. Timișoara's central geographical position favoured the city in this aspect. During the age of reform, the episcopal palace, the Piarist church and monastery, the Orthodox bishopric and the synagogue were erected, all contributing to the outlining of common values and practices. Social institutions also contributed to cultural life. That was the case with hospitals, pharmacies, theatres and restaurants. The refinement of society contributed not only to the promotion of rational thinking and science, but also to the improvement of life, noticeable in the number of houses built and the extension of communal facilities. In Timișoara in the 1850s the water was potable, being provided by 197 public fountains. Starting in 1857, necessary energy was supported by gas plants, and from 1887 by electric plants. After 1893, one of the most modern electrical networks of Europe was created in Timișoara. Electric trams were introduced. In the last decade of the nineteenth century, the sewage system was created.[52] Regarding mother tongues, there were voices in the middle of the nineteenth century who demanded the continuation of the good habit of learning and using more than one language. For example, Tobias Gottfried Schröder, a teacher at the evangelical high school, opposed the nationalist tendencies of imposing the Hungarian language to the detriment of others.

Civic-mindednesss had an important role in the education of citizens in the main towns of the region. Timișoara has benefited from a German theatre since 1776. Moreover, the city was visited by European theatre companies, and renowned composers and performers, the Banat having an exceptional status in music. For example, the first choir in Timișoara was founded in 1845; in Lugoj in 1841; in Panciova in 1853; in Biserica Albă in 1854; in Orșova in 1859; in Vrsac in 1861; and in Oravița in 1863. A point of reference was the foundation of the Philharmonic Society of Timișoara in 1871. Concern for book editing and publishing was no less important. In the domain of historiography, works by Johann Nepomuk Preyer (*Monographie der Königlichen Freistadt Temesvár*, 1853), Johann Heinrich Schwicker (*Geschichte des Temescher Banats*, 1861), Karl Wilhelm Martini (*Pflanzen und Schlacht. Bilder und Gestalten aus dem Banate*, 1854) and others stood out. The settlements of the Banat that were considered worthy of attention by the imperial-royal administration gained from the construction of houses, churches, schools, roads, transportation and postal services. Moreover, the judicial, social and civic issues of the rural and urban communities were answered thanks to the same administration.[53]

CONCLUSIONS

The most important feature of society in the Banat in the eighteenth and nineteenth centuries was its cultural and religious pluralism. This was the consequence of the largest European migration during the eighteenth century, due to Habsburg imperial policy. In conclusion, Banat was formed in the modern European spirit, which was more important than the promotion of languages, religions or community origins. Vienna regarded economic development and social emancipation as relevant issues, thus justifying the opportunity of colonisation. In just a few decades, the Banat outlined not only its administration, but also its own identity. The multi- and intercultural characteristics of its inhabitants contributed to the first Europeanisation of a region situated on the outskirts of the Ottoman Empire. In 1780 the situation of the inhabitants of the Banat, according to the existing cultural-linguistic communities, was as shown in Table 5.3.[54]

Table 5.3

CULTURAL-LINGUISTIC COMMUNITY	RESIDENTS	
	Number	%
Romanian	181,639	57.5
Serbian	78,780	24.5
German, Italian, Spanish	43,201	13.6
Bulgarian	8,683	2.7
Gypsy	5,272	1.6
Jewish	353	0.1
TOTAL	317,928	100

Source: Franz Griselini, Versuch einer politischen und natürlichen Geschichte des temeswarer Banats in Briefen an Standespersonen und Gelehrte (1780) (Vienna, 1780), pp. 195–96. Griselini himself underlines the fact that the data was uncertain. The population of the 11th district (which included Timişoara) numbered 317,938, among which 181,639 were Romanians, 78,780 Serbian, 8,683 Bulgarians, 5,272 Gypsies, 43,201 German, Italian and Spanish colonists, and 353 Jews.

This is a general image of the demographic movement within the region, not mentioning the existence of communities according to smaller territorial units. The Romanian community represented the majority, with 57.5 per cent, followed by the Serbian community, with 24.5 per cent.

The situation of the Banatian population according to religious faith is shown in Table 5.4, based on a census made in 1784–85.

Table 5.4

County/ City	Roman Catholic	Evangelical Lutheran	Reformed Calvinist	Greek Orthodox	Jewish	TOTAL
	No.	No.	No.	No.	No.	No.
Caraş	15,076	50	30	173,000	44	188,200
Timiş	40,227	2,000	1,200	172,000	118	215,545
Torontal	46,019	1,500	1,500	103,000	64	153,08
Timişoara	4,476	60	20	4,300	386	9,242
TOTAL	105,798	3,610	2,750	452,300	612	566,070

Source: Danyi Dezső and Dávid Zoltán, Az első magyarországi népszámlálás 1774–1784 (The First Hungarian Census 1784–1787) (Budapest, 1960).

For the imperial administration at the time of Joseph II, the census based on religion was more important than the one referring to the languages spoken. Besides, the census from 1785 does not include questions regarding linguistic and community affiliation, and even less concerning nationality and ethnicity, notions that would influence the cultural and sociopolitical vocabularies of Central and Eastern Europe (including the Banat), starting in the first half of the nineteenth century.[54] During the following decades, some religious communities would become politicised, militating for their acknowledgement as ethnocultural identities. That was the case with Romanian and Serbian Orthodoxy, which comprised 80 per cent of the population within the three Banatian counties. The smallest percentage of the Orthodox population was in Torontal County: 67.3. This was due to the administrative changes from 1779, when a displacement of the Hungarian population of Roman Catholic and Reformed Calvinist religion from north to south took place. Timişoara represents a self-contained religious phenomenon, and the numbers confirm this. Of the total 9,242 inhabitants, 4,476 were Roman Catholic, 4,300 Orthodox, and the rest Jewish, Evangelical Lutheran or Reformed Calvinists. The proportions mirror Timişoara's plural demographic structure and the attractiveness exerted by the city for people of different religious affiliations.

The last censuses allow an overview of the identity configuration. For example, in the year 1840, during the Hungarian nobility administration, the State Council initiated a county census. A second one was organised by the Austrian neo-absolutist regime, when the region became autonomous under the name of the Banat of Temes and Serbian Voivodina. The dissemination of the diverse cultural and linguistic communities of nineteenth-century Banat is registered, in numbers and percentages, in Table 5.5.

This statistic reveals an increase in the Hungarian population, although its share is still small in comparison with the Romanian people. The Serbian population registered a decrease between 1775 and 1840, its share representing only 18.7 per cent in 1840. A large number of soldiers are included in this percentage, specifically 28.03 per cent of the total number of population that ensured the military service in the border regiments of the empire (250,485). The military vocation of Serbians was officially acknowledged, offering them certain privileges. The Romanian population involved in the border regiments numbered 145,106 people (58 per cent), while the Germans numbered 26,155 (10.5 per cent).

Table 5.5

CULTURAL-LINGUISTIC COMMUNITY	CIVIL BANAT/COUNTIES					
	Caraş	Timiş	Torontal	Military Border	Total (nos.)	Total (%)
German	15,252	85,449	80,864	26,155	207,720	19.2
Romanian	191,158	183,228	46,738	145,106	566,230	52.3
Hungarian	1,200	4,560	50,332	3,250	59,347	5.5
Serbian	–	18,320	113,660	70,230	202,210	18.7
Slovakian	–	2,954	2,500	5,386	10,840	1.0
Croatian	7,714	1,698	700	–	10,112	1.0
Bulgarian	–	3,000	9,000	–	12,000	1.1
Montenegrin	–	2,830	–	–	2,830	0.26
Greek	–	400	200	200	800	0.04
French	–	150	6,000	–	6,150	0.6
Jewish	308	1,898	2,252	158	4,316	0.4
TOTAL	215,632	304,187	312,246	250,485	1,082,550	100

Source: Elek Fényes (ed.), *Magyarország geographiai szótára (The Geographical Dictionary of Hungary)* (Pesta, 1851), pp. 194–95.

All the other cultural-linguistic groups – regardless of their occupation – represented 4.4 per cent; it was not their number that was important, but their contribution to economic development and to the establishment of a creative sociocultural environment capable of promoting individual values and a multi- and intercultural public spirit.

The demographical situation of the Banat in 1851 is shown in Table 5.6.

Table 5.6

CULTURAL-LINGUISTIC COMMUNITY	POPULATION OF CIVIL BANAT	
	No.	%
Hungarian	56,329	7.6
German	148,740	20.1
Romanian	380,926	51.4
Serbian	123,687	16.7
Slovakian	3,177	0.4
Bulgarian	7,256	1.1
Croatian	9,743	1.3
French	5,992	0.8
Jewish	3,066	0.4
Montenegrin	762	0.1
Gypsy	152	0.02
TOTAL	740,485	100

Source: Elek Fényes, *Magyarország leírása* (*The Description of Hungary*), pt. 1 (Pesta, 1851), pp. 332–38.

Beyond the changing numbers, a civilisational evolution is observed, in the European sense of the notion. This is due not only to the demographic movements, but also to the improvement of living standards, fertility, health, education and interaction among the communities. Table 5.7 depicts the population structure of Timişoara between 1840 and 1910.

Table 5.7

Year	Hungarian	German	Romanian	Serbian	Ruthenian	Slovakian	Croatian	Others
1840 (%)	11	26	17	24	–	–	–	22
1880 (no.)	7,289	18,539	3,279	1,719	28	397	–	1,510
1880 (%)	21,63	55,02	9,73	5,10	–	1,18	–	–
1910 (no.)	28,552	31,644	7,566	3,482	4	341	148	818
1910 (%)	39,35	43,64	10,43	4,80	–	–	–	–

Source: Deák, *Ausgewählte Materialien*, vol. ii, p. 313.

The reference to 'other' communities is interesting, addressing the process of building regional identity by the emergence of mixed families, of multiple, multilingual cultural identities. This process was especially visible in the cities, outlining the phenomenon called the Banatian 'melting pot' by the historian Victor Neumann.[56]

6

THE POLITICAL STRATEGIES OF THE HOUSE OF HABSBURG IN THE SECOND HALF OF THE EIGHTEENTH CENTURY

László Marjanucz

AFTER 1718, THE BANAT OF TEMES was perceived as a new Austrian military province (*peculium austriacum*). The administration consisted of mixed governmental offices (military, civil, cameral), military coordination being considered the most important during the first stage. The change occurred during Maria Theresa's reign, when the administration became civil.[1] The activity of the Viennese court authorities was coordinated by the State Council, functioning as a consultative organ. For the centralised administration of the Banat, Vienna founded more governmental agencies, all subordinate to the court. Among those, in the period researched here, the Hofkammer (Aulic Chamber), Hofdeputation in Banaticis (the Imperial Deputation of the Banat) and Hofkammer Department in Banaticis und Domänen-Wesen (the Aulic Chamber's Department of Banatian Affairs and Domanial Issues) had special importance.[2] The most important statements were submitted by Councillor Clary, an expert on Banatian affairs and by Count Hatzfeld, president of the Aulic Chamber. Reports and accounts of the situation in the Banat also were drafted by the Hofkriesgrat (Imperial Military Council) and the Hofkanzley (Aulic Chancellery). The reports addressed to Empress Maria Theresa were drawn up by the Staatsrat (State Council), based on specialised notes, and included personal views and decisions.

This study was elaborated from the minutes of the State Council examined at the Vienna Archive (Hof- und Staatarchiv). It should be pointed out that the Banat appears indirectly in the documents, within a broader approach to the different aspects considered by the authorities of the State Council, the information concerning the empress's decisions not being directly reproduced, but resulting from the councillors' speeches. The documents prove that the Austrian administration was highly professional, a fact that determined the establishment in 1745 of a superior commission named 'Hofkomission in Banaticis, Transylvanicics und Illyricis' (High Commission on Banat, Transylvania and Illyria).[3] Moreover, a study of the State Council minutes – informative reports, summarised notes and votes – reveals the diversity of issues presented to the sovereign. From the legal and political perspective, the empress's responses come in different forms: a decision, writing, a warning or a confidential letter for the trusted person. Using the sources mentioned earlier, I examined the documents from 1770 to 1772, which facilitated identification of the most important issues referred by the regional administration. These were economic policy, the condition of the Church and the colonising of different populations.

CAMERALISM IN THE BANAT

The Banat of Temes, as an imperial region, formed a distinctive territory, separated by borders from the kingdoms of Hungary and Transylvania. These circumstances determined that commerce was of primordial interest for the court, the profits directly enriching Vienna. In this sense, cameralism represented the ideological background. This economic doctrine was practised within the German-language regions of the Habsburg Empire, promoted by Leopold I's policies and by Maria Theresa's reforms, becoming a science of the governmental budget, typical of the time. Cameralism was formulated by Viennese specialists who dealt with financial and administrative science. This represented a form of guidance for the monarch, putting into effect the economic doctrine of the empire.[4]

With regard to the Banat of Temes, the shared border with the Ottoman Empire had special importance, not only because of territorial disputes but also because a portion of the consumer goods came from the Orient. For example, Turkish or Indian coffee was distributed in all the regions of the Habsburg Empire. Another important product, with a great share of customs revenues, was sugar. In order to encourage local production, the importation of sugar was limited and possible only when demand was higher than internal supply.[5] These situations are analysed by the Aulic Chancellery, as can be seen in a document issued in 1770 regarding the sugar trade. According to the information provided there, sugar could be imported through Trieste and Nikolsburg, but it had to be declared at the customs and the established net weight had to be respected. The empress entrusted the authorities with the control and strict tracing of this product. They noticed that the transportation of sugar bypassed the city of Nikolsburg in order to escape the control. Most of the time, sugar passed through the imperial regions as transit goods, thus reaching the Banat and Transylvania. Sugar trade for internal use was justified only in the case of unsatisfactory 'internal production' and only within the limits authorised by a customs order. The Decree of the Aulic Chancellery impacted on sugar distribution in the Banat.[6] The regulation was born of the desire to gain economic independence from foreign goods and maximise local production. The action demonstrates the importance of shared borders with the Ottoman Empire, not only from the military perspective but also commercially, with Vienna also regarding relations with Turkey in the context of customs income.

In a system built upon monopolies, approvals and interdictions, importation directly impacted by inflating prices, resulting in an increase in income for the Treasury, in accordance with the cameral approach. Among monopolies, special attention was given to mining and salt, the improvement of the latter in the Banat requiring the continuous intervention of the Aulic Chamber. Attention was concentrated especially upon the functioning of the main headquarters of salt administration in Lipova (Lippa),[7] public profit being dependent on this point of purchase. Maria Theresa reckoned that a raise of income could be attained by an increase in the salt chambers, proposing that the regional administration 'from now on . . . amplify the salt chambers with no prior consultation'. With regard to production, 'the greatest economy'[8] was proposed. The system monitored the conditions for preserving and storing salt, so that trade could unfold with no obstructions. The clerk who weighed out the salt kept a record of the materials based on 'coupon-bills' of the administrative personnel and calculated the anticipated revenues. The accountancy in Timișoara sent monthly reports about the revenues, while the regional administration issued 'warrants' for accomplishment of tasks.[9]

Drafting reports concerning the development of imperial customs revenues, the state of internal production and especially the use of revenues, were permanent responsibilities of the chamber, and the empress was kept constantly informed. Total revenues included the money received from the Banat, the administration of Timișoara drafting a monthly report. The different reports concerning the revenues from the Banat were presented to the empress, who then made decisions concerning the use of the excess money from the customs treasury. These decisions ended with the specification 'and until then [the decision concerning the use of money], in every such thing [the money received from customs], all revenues must be highlighted for financial justification'.

This decision of the empress was valid over all the regions with one exception – the border area – which, due to its geographical position – was like an El Dorado for the circulation of secret goods. The empress brought to the authorities' attention the need to avoid the introduction of smuggled 'consumer goods' (coffee, cigarettes and spices from the Orient), because they, due to their features (durability and demand), should be treated 'in similar manner', meaning compliance with customs taxes. The border guards were not exempt from taxes, being forbidden to abuse their military situation and status.[10]

The empress argued in favour of the local economic policy based on customs protection, which was viewed as more important from the perspective of public revenue than indirect taxation. Contraband presented great problems in some of the regions within the empire, spreading in Hungary and the Banat by selling smuggled goods from Bohemia, Moravia and Silesia. Besides, this was perceived by the Viennese power as a problem of public safety rather than a financial one. The Banat of Temes was considered to be the land with the largest consumer market for smuggled goods, and thus received special attention.[11]

Other fiscal measures were taken for the increase of public revenue at all costs. Often, property belonging to the treasury was sold in order to cover expenses. For example, the Aulic Chamber advised the selling of Rheinfels beer factory. The price offered, 750 Ft, was a great business deal for the state. The empress accepted the advice and approved the transaction.[12] The cameral ideas were carried out and directed in the Banat by the Viennese authorities. For this, several public servants were carefully selected. Within the Habsburg Empire, the transfer of specialised bureaucratic personnel was common practice. It is noteworthy that a large portion of the officials of the Banat were Czech. The reason for this was first of all a material one, because they received better payment in the Banat, among other facilities. The human resources policy was backed by a special fund, which offered, for example, material support for moving from one part of the empire to the other. It happened that even officials of the Viennese Aulic Chamber apparatus accepted a position as councillor in the administration of the Banat of Temes.[13]

In 1770, a newly appointed tax inspector at the Regional Chamber of Taxation demanded money for his transfer and integration in the workplace. His request was accepted by the empress because the position in the Banat had special importance. Nevertheless, it must be noted that the central administration tried to maintain a normal financial framework for human resources policies. Hence, the reports referring to financial aspects of personnel (salaries, allowances, different benefits) were also made by the Council of Commerce, indicating that the transfer of officials was also evaluated from the perspective of the general financial flux (balance).[14] The job application for the position of deputy director in the Banat of a lieutenant major of the army was rejected by the Ministerial Banking Commission, which at the time was the main financial body of the Banat. The reason for the rejection was that in the army, the solicitor could not have acquired the necessary knowledge for the office work and the requested position. The professional training of the retired military man was considered unsuitable for the position within public administration. This was highlighted by the financial specialists who correlated the necessary expenses for the job with the anticipated benefits, concluding that the position in question was unprofitable.[15]

Within the state economy, an important area was connected with the subjects' standard of living. The data shows, in the majority of instances, that the authorities regulated agricultural production and tried to settle work obligations. Vienna supported the colonists with state allowances, considering that the centralised guarantee of their supply with the necessary means for practising agriculture was the most effective method. However, the Aulic Chamber was often forced to study local reports concerning insufficient cereal stocks. The problem was not the market, but the fault of management. Vienna encouraged the supervised administration in the Banat, and the centralised cameral economic policy was two-pronged: stimulation of land cultivation to the detriment of livestock breeding and enforcement by the authorities to eliminate potential obstacles.

Hence, for example, the growing of beets and cabbage was solicited in the Banat. The Court Petition of 1771 published the price list for the procurement of beets and cabbage seeds, and for the seeds necessary for the production of oils. Both were considered of great importance to Vienna, so the empress demanded – 'if possible' – the immediate start of the process.[16] The costs were analysed in order to stimulate vegetable production, but also to sustain the creation of agricultural industry (production of plant seed oil). The production of cereal crops was considered by the authorities a branch of the highest significance, representing the foundation for the necessary food supplies for the population. The support given to the peasant farmers is noted in a protocol of the Aulic Chamber issued on 9 January 1770 which mentions the necessity of distributing 'seeds to the needy'. On 24 January 1770, Count Hatzfeld reported to the empress the exceptional situation of agriculture within the empire.[17]

The empress reiterated: 'I expect you, according to the issued decision, to do your best to provide farmers with the necessary means for the summer production [year 1770] and to accelerate the payment of taxes.' The authorities ensured that people received enough seeds and bread in order to accelerate taxation. Taking into account Count Hatzfeld's exposition, attached to the minutes of the chamber meeting,[18] the empress decided to supplement cereal stocks.[19] Maria Theresa requested the assumption of responsibility for the seed and bread supply to the subjects, stipulating hard sanctions for the officials who did not follow the demand. Considering the promotion of the well-being of the population to be one of the duties of officials, the empress decided to ensure the necessary seeds and bread to her subjects in all domains of the chamber 'with no delay and with adequate care'.

In fact, the storage of cereals for bread reveals the great famine in Bohemia (1769), but also influenced the Banat since this region produced an important quantity of the grain necessary for the imperial population. The weak cereal production was characteristic of the estates of Bohemia, while in the Banat it was less felt, even if some supply problems had arisen there, too. A letter of 1771 sent to Councillor Raab of the Aulic Chamber states that 'Her Majesty wants to buy cereals from the Banat', the region being regarded as one of the important cereal producers and 'the greatest hindrance to the empress's will is the state of the waterways'.[20]

Influenced by the problems arising from supplies to the empire, the empress formulated the famous reprimand: 'The main offices already exist, and that is the reason why they swore to work for the benefit of the country and the well-being of the subjects. For this, given the existing circumstances, the supreme power invested the offices with the necessary freedom. The key to settle the current issues is to find solutions for every problem.'[21] In 1771, the Department of the Banat's administration for affairs and real estate issues regarded the region with the same eyes as other crown domains. The issues were similar to those existent in the old regions of the crown. There were many documents referring to the Bohemia, others to Austria, the only absentee being Hungary. With regard to the functioning of the Aulic Chamber Department, it was symptomatic that a problem from Pardubitz (in Bohemia) had to be answered by a clerk from Timișoara.[22] In practice, administration of problems by different authorities explains the shift of officials within the empire. The positions of those transferred from the Banat were taken by those arriving from other regions. The resolution to the empire's problems was global, as is apparent from the method of treating the livestock epidemics – the one which broke out in 1771 was not an isolated incident. Similar measures were taken against the general animal epidemics in Austria, and in the cases of Moravia and Hungary. According to the same administrative strategy, the methods were extended to the Banat of Temes.[23]

The issues regarding work obligations derived from the fact that, although land area diminished, the local power demanded the same quantity of work. Following the report presented by Hoyer, speaker for the Aulic Chamber, Maria Theresa commanded the settlement of complaints, taking into account that for a smaller land area one could not claim an identical performance with a larger one.[24] Nevertheless, the process of redeeming the tithe was functioning well. Therefore, the estimates of the Aulic Chamber show that 'the redeeming of tithe', encouraged from the year 1770, meaning the payment in money instead of in kind, was 85,737 Ft. in 1772. Maria Theresa was informed of this, expressed her agreement for the practice, and demanded its continuation.[25]

RELIGIOUS LIFE

Religious life and vitality of the churches signified two things for Vienna. First, the guarantee of religious life for the Roman Catholic colonists, most of whom were German-speaking, by sending Catholic priests and teachers to be alongside them in the Banat. Secondly, the acceptance of the Orthodox spiritual world of people already living there, which entailed administrative support. There was political agreement on this, the only problem being the financing. The most frequent issue was church building. Vienna decided that the administration should deal with the religious and schooling necessities of the Catholic people. Support had to be provided by the treasury and the revenue came from the monopoly tax on the gambling game Loto di Geneva, established in 1770.

According to one of Count Hatzfeld's reports, even with the help of the sums mentioned earlier, the issue of human resources was problematic. Maria Theresa requested the identification of the reasons that had led to the shortage of priests in the Banat. Given the circumstances, it was demanded that 'for many parishes, common priests, ordained in Austria, should be sent'.[26] In turn, the Orthodox Church benefited from public support as a privileged institution. For its financial autonomy, taxation of believers, setting up taxes and prices for managing church estates, the right of the Church to inherit the fortunes of those members who died without heirs, was permitted. Orthodox bishops did not benefit from tax rights, but collected conventional taxes from the faithful. The tax value was determined by the Church, but the manner of collection was decided by the local administration. The money for Orthodox bishops was collected differently. In the border area, the Serbian officers and under-officers collected the tax. In the Banat of Temes, the same tax was collected by local officials. In Hungary, the empress accepted the so-called Györ proposition by which the issue was resolved with the help of the local council.[27] The village priests also derived their living from the conventional tax.

Ioan Tusnu, the Orthodox priest of Sânicolau Mare (Nagyszentmiklos), 'refused to take possession of the parcels promised to him' because the assurance of conventional income was uncertain. The households could not support the existence of the priest because some of their assets were missing, since they did not have enough animals or the necessary tools for farming. In order to avoid support for the Church in the future, the Aulic Chamber of Vienna suggested giving earnest money for the Orthodox peasants who worked the parcels. According to a decision issued by Maria Theresa, 'the loan is given with the same interest as in the case of colonists'.[28] Vienna regarded Romanians and Serbians as local residents and not colonists; for them, the deductions and advantages did not apply.

The Chamber report presents the privileged position and material support granted to the Catholic Church. The central financial authority of the empire approved the sum of 839 Ft, coming from a private inheritance, instead of the state allowance proposed for building the church of Becicherecul Mare (Nagybecskerek; today, Zrenjianin). The empress reckoned that the reimbursement for building the church should be the task of the treasury, using public money.[29] The protection of the Catholic religion was a priority, which is obvious from more examples provided by the specialist literature. However, relatively little is known of the religious life of Orthodox believers in the Banat and the situation of the Orthodox Church during the second half of the eighteenth century. One reason is the focus of public interest on the Roman Catholics, while another is the special attention given to the colonists.

Due to the large number of believers, the activity of the Orthodox Church was tolerated. At that time, the imperial foreign policy stimulated a more attentive approach towards the Orthodox interests, bearing in mind that Russia viewed the Orthodox subjects of the Habsburgs as its supporters. Therefore, Vienna banned the use of religious books that had been illegally introduced from the regions beyond the south and east Carpathians.[30] The interdiction referred to the Orthodox population of the Banat and Transylvania. Only books printed under imperial control could be used legally. With the help of the renowned typographer Kurzböck, Vienna opened a printing house in Blaj to edit the books destined for the Orthodox Church and its followers. The aim was to restrict relations with Moldavia and Wallachia. Moreover, the imperial administration wanted to establish a distribution centre in order to cover the book necessities for the Greek Catholic believers.[31] This reveals the relations between the Habsburg authority and the Orthodox subjects. Even if the printing house was part of the Greek Catholic episcopal centre, it also attended to the Orthodox community. Both the Romanian and Serbian Orthodox from the Banat and Transylvania were assigned to the Slavic-Serbian metropolitan church of Sremski-Karlovci (Karlowitz).

In 1745, the Banatian Deputation of the Aulic Court was founded. After the death of President Franz von Kollowratnak, the Aulic Court was subject to changes. The most important transformation was the establishment of the Illyrian Deputation that functioned until 1777 and dealt exclusively with Orthodox issues. From the religious perspective, the foundation of the deputation meant the consolidation of the Orthodox Church and its hierarchy in Karlowitz. In that sense, the cases of the Orthodox population from Transylvania and the Banat and of the Romanian Greek Catholics from Transylvania were debated together, Vienna judging Romanians as one and the same cultural-linguistic community, regardless of differences of belief.[32]

The separate existence of the Orthodox religious authority is interesting due to the fact that in the Banat there were numerous authorities of the Viennese court, as well as a regional administration. It seemed that Vienna preferred a centralised coordination of the Orthodox believers, in order to preserve social peace. A different problem was represented by priests arriving from abroad. A large number of documents mention them. The cases from Transylvania were most frequent, because there were 'many [Orthodox] subjects coming from Turkey'. Several reports of the time concluded that Maria Theresa was informed of this phenomenon and demanded that the authorities 'should pay the greatest attention to Romanians, especially with regard to church issues'.[33] The experience related by Governor Auersperg is remarkable. In a report to the empress, he refers to a segment of society from Brașov and Sibiu (companies), not subordinated to the Transylvanian Greek Catholic bishop but instead bringing spiritual guides from Wallachia (at that time, subordinate to the Ottoman Empire). Even if a future appointment of the Romanian Orthodox metropolitan bishop of Transylvania by the empress was accepted, some groups of believers followed the old practices, wishing to be dependent on the church hierarchy from the Danubian Principalities.

Wallachian priests constantly came to Transylvania, and the believers followed their advice. Thus, in a confidential letter sent to Samuel von Brukenthal, the empress demanded that 'this state of disorder must be stopped immediately', proposing a 'moderate' approach, acting in accordance with the prescriptions of the regulations introduced in the Banat, too. Regarding the Banat of Temes, the empress decided that 'foreign priests should not be hired for the spiritual life' and that Orthodox priests should not be appointed without her approval.[34]

According to this principle, measures were taken when a Banatian priest who had been active in Transylvania was transferred back. This was the case of Ioan Pepa, an Orthodox priest and native of the Banat, who returned home after a period spent in Transylvania. The empress's resolution provided that 'a complete lot of land should be given for him in the Banat, and after that, he should be closely watched'.[35] It was a sign of caution towards a representative of a cult that was different from the Catholic one. For a totally different reason, the empress limited the area of influence of the Orthodox episcopal priest of Arad. A report of the Illyrian Committee from 1770 drew attention to the increasing sphere of influence of this priest, who had extended geographically his spiritual activity. This matter was assessed by the deputation following the episcopal priest's activity in Transylvania and Partium. In reaction, the empress forbade the priest to practise in Transylvania, on the grounds that in that region a distinct episcopal priest would be appointed, the one from Arad having no rights beyond his circumscription.[36]

In 1770, Maria Theresa named Sofronie Chirilovici the Orthodox episcopal priest of Transylvania. Chirilovici had arrived from the Danubian Principalities and was consecrated in Karlowitz.[37] The event was important for two reasons: on one hand, because there had not been any Romanian episcopal priest in the Banat and Hungary; on the other hand, Vienna only acknowledged the

Karlowitz Orthodox spiritual centre, meaning the Serbian church hierarchy. The involvement of the state in the religious life of the Orthodox population from Transylvania and the Banat draws attention to the correspondence between religion and linguistic community and, later, between religion and nationality. For example, the concepts of 'Illyrian', 'Romanian' and 'Serbian' are interesting, as they are used to define the communitarian particularities of religious life. As mentioned, Vienna founded the Illyrian publishing house in Blaj for the spiritual necessities of all Orthodox believers within the empire. It also intended to appoint a Greek Catholic and an Orthodox inspector. Maria Theresa underlined that both should speak not only the Illyrian language, but also 'the Wallachian and Greek languages'. In other words, for a proper functioning of Orthodox religious life, the Austrian authorities introduced the requirement to know all three languages.[38] Vienna associated Illyrian with the Serbian language. Regarding Romanian, it used the concept of 'Wallachian', religious affiliation being identified by the concept of 'unitus' (Greek Catholic), and 'Orthodox'. Count Auersberg's note of 1771 concerning the books revised by the Blaj publishing house highlights the 'Wallachian policy' (*Wallachisch-Politischen*), which only an expert of the Wallachian (Romanian) language could control. The linguistic component, as well as religious fragmentation, also influenced the administrative services. In the Banat, the basic principle was that in the administrative institutions, only Roman Catholic clerks should be hired. Thus, a large number of Romanians and Serbians were excluded from public administration. However, because of issues concerning human resources (in some places, there were insufficient candidates or suitable persons), the regional administration disregarded this rule. Count Hatzfeld submitted a request to the empress in which he made possible the employment of Orthodox people in postal offices. Even if, as a general rule, the employment of Roman Catholics in public administrative institutions remained in use, out of necessity, the Orthodox population was also accepted. This was the case with the postal office of Nagykikinda (Kikinda Mare).[39]

Because Serbians had many case files in the Timișoara regional courthouse, the superior judicial court of Vienna placed a permanent Serbian interpreter at regional level, for the proper functioning of justice in the Banat. An example of this is the act appointing Demetrio Paulovich as interpreter at the Timișoara courthouse. There is no indication of a Romanian interpreter, though.[40] What is clear from the documentary sources is that the court regularly solicited new interpreters, because justice in the German language was cumbersome, since the majority of people in the region spoke Romanian or Serbian. The Viennese Supreme Court supported the request of hiring interpreters, and the empress allowed it, along with the creation of new positions necessary for the smooth functioning of the regional courthouse.[41]

The situation in Transylvania was different: all public institutions and courthouses hired Greek Catholics on equal terms with Roman Catholics. It is true that the Romanian stipendiaries of imperial foundations and episcopal churches were expected to speak German fluently.[42] Equality of opportunity between Roman Catholics and Greek Catholics was not visible in the Banat, where the training was simply not sufficient; the most important condition was the unavailability of qualified Catholic personnel. What particularised the Banat was the access of public services to the Romanian Orthodox population, too. The Illyrian Regulation drafted by the empress in 1771 granted the Orthodox believers citizenship status, lessening the Church's governing authority over them. When the document was published, the empress completed it with a Memento, against which the Hungarian Chancellery raised objections.[43] The content of the Memento, attached to the Illyrian Regulation, was written in Latin and Serbian and had to reach all interested parties, offering information about the conditions for giving up the judicial authority of the Orthodox Church. According to the empress's will, 'the governmental document should publish the necessary documents in the same language they had been published before'. Maria Theresa made possible the duplication of the documents in the Romanian language, too.

THE COLONISATION

The fundamental principle of Austrian cameralism sounded like this: 'the table of well-fed people is the country's main treasure'.[44] To this effect, conditions for economic development and population enrichment were created. Hence the aim to recover the population lost during the period of Ottoman occupation of the Banat. This was accomplished by systematic colonisation that took place until the beginning of the nineteenth century, strongly affecting the public treasury. That explains why, at a given moment, the rules of colonisation changed. There was a contradiction between the demographic needs and the public programme of reorganisation of colonists due to its high cost, a contradiction reflected in the Viennese court documents. The material contribution of the empire to the successful repopulation of the Banat in the last third of the eighteenth century was partially stalled by budgetary problems. Continuity of colonisation was made by favouring those coming from the German Empire, even if the generosity displayed during the first half of the century decreased;[45] now, the contribution of every individual was expected.

The Aulic Chamber welcomed immigrants that settled at their own expense. At the same time, in the 1770s, the State Council regarded settlement in the Banat of the population coming from inherited territories as being opposed to Austria's interests. Steiermark, the regional commissary of commerce, analysing the methods used for colonising the Banat, talked about an inefficient, costly and unnecessary financing.[46] The report of the Upper Austria Chancellery draws attention to the 'nature' of those who immigrated to the Banat. The meaning of the term 'nature' is not explained in the documents, but probably refers to social condition. In any case, the population transfer from one region to another was considered a loss. At certain moments – for example in the decision of 8 September 1769 – the empress suggested that her subjects should stay put.[47]

The official court documents named the act of populating the Banat the 'repopulation affair' (*das Impopulation-Geschäft*).[48] This was not perceived in the modern sense of the word – as a commercial affair – but as a mission in the interest of the state. For the economic and financial exploitation of the Banat, the settlement of colonists was necessary. This did not always correspond to the view of the treasury. From another perspective, the sending of specialists to the region in order to take possession of its natural resources was necessary. The Aulic Chamber, based on the opinion of the Regional Administration of the Banat of Temes, suggested the creation of special jobs destined for administrative functionaries, their financing and payment being decided by the empress alone.

The colonisation was made in consideration with the economic and natural conditions of the region, as well as the state's own opportunities. This fact implied the strengthening of the corps of officials, in order to dispose the necessary human resources and to solve the 'repopulation affair' of the Banat. The labour participation of colonists was a state duty. The aim was to activate different areas of the economy (agriculture, industry, trade), not with the help of the market, but with the involvement of bureaucrats. Officials from all round the empire were sent to the Banat, qualified in all areas, in order to put into practice the administrative measures destined for mining, forest exploitation, seed production, salt exploitation, etc.[49]

Land surveying was a priority and would be the foundation of the land registry (*urbarium*). The proposal of scientist P. Lisgaing regarding the training of young engineers in 'the art of land survey' determined Maria Theresa to provide the learning of new, more efficient, trigonometric operations. Her confidential notification addressed to Count Lacy, president of the Military Council, shows that at that specific time, land surveys were conducted by military authorities. The Military Council asked Lieutenant Major d'Avrauge, the manager of the engineering school, to 'choose the most talented persons who would diligently learn the theoretical and practical part of geometry and trigonometry'. Because the empress expected an immediate result, she asked the Military Council to 'indicate among the employees several young engineers who could make up for the falling behind'.[50]

The arrival and settlement of the colonists created problems. To resolve them, the Aulic Chamber elaborated monthly individual records for those settled in the Banat of Temes. At first, centralised lists regarding the colonists were compiled, but the State Council, following the advice of the Aulic Chamber, demanded individual lists. The minutes of the State Council from 1770 keep the individual lists from September until December. The empress regularly received the monthly lists of colonists for approval, and formally acknowledged these documents – for example, the list of individuals settled in the Banat of Temes in December 1770[51] and the lists regarding the individual situation of the people during the first half of the following year.[52]

The minutes of the Timişoara regional administration drafted on the occasion of the colonists' arrival were sent to Vienna together with the reports of the imperial officials. The professional control of the 'repopulation affair' was assigned to Neumann von Bucholt, who was appointed to this position following a report sent to the empress, as requested by the Aulic Chamber. In this case, the former president of the Commercial Company (Commercien Compagnie) and Maria Theresa accepted the suggestion that von Bucholt be employed.[53] The sources show how he regularly and professionally evaluated and reported upon the state of colonisation during the year 1771.[54]

In several cases, the life of colonists before their arrival in the Banat had not been impeccable. The empress had to decide, in special cases, the circumstances in which people expelled from the Austrian or German Empire could settle in the Banat. One of those expelled from Austria was Bender Mallenovith. In his case, the Aulic Chamber offered a favourable review: 'due to his pardon and forgiveness, he has the right to live in the Banat and thus, he can provide for his wife and children honourably'. Maria Theresa accepted the proposal, but cautioned the locals to be alert to any small problems he might cause.

In various documents, the Banat at the end of the eighteenth century was mentioned as some kind of a 'colony for the condemned'. The documentary sources do not reveal such things; they never mention the criminals expelled to Banat. The legends have given the impression that those who opposed both the German Empire and the administrations from the inherited territories, were gathered up and sent to the Banat by water. It is true that some people were expelled from Austria as a punishment, but they were not 'criminals'. An example is the request addressed to the empress's legal service regarding the permit to send eight disobedient subjects, who were living on Geföll (Haupt-Radlführer) estate, to the Banat. The request was submitted by the government of Lower Austria. For the insubordinate subjects the empress imposed, alongside the expulsion, a period of detention.[55] The councillor, Count Seilern, asked the empress for their 'forgiveness', extending this pardon to other similar delinquents. The empress decided on 'their immediate departure to the Banat', together with their families.[56]

Vienna wanted to be informed about the issue of colonisation, individual data included. That is why the lists (*Colonisten-Verzeichnis*), drafted and sent to 'the highest consultation' (for approval), were accompanied by different proposals. There were deliberations regarding the place in which the colonists would settle, based on analysis and proposals. Maria Theresa declared: 'we have to be careful to build new villages in places less inhabited and not to extend already existing communities of more than 100 homes'. The empress preferred the establishment of smaller villages to directing the population towards settlements with a large population, which contradicted the former practice of settling colonists. To avoid any problems regarding the colonists' instalment, she asked the Deputation of the Banat to provide 'faster support' for this issue.[57]

The documentary research reveals that, alongside many officials, Count Hatzfeld, president of the chamber, and Neumann von Bucholt, the royal agent responsible for the repopulation, had the greatest influence on the repopulation of the Banat. The Deputation of the Banat drafted a detailed report about the situation of the population on 5 January 1771, together with a separate report (*Begleitungs-Vortrag*) from Count Hatzfeld, both of which were presented to the empress. These documents show the reasons for the temporary suspension of colonisation, such choices needing proper motivation. Hatzfeld's point of view was accepted by the empress, with the comment: 'it wasn't foolishness, but it was compulsory to clarify the reasons why colonisation should be suspended'. It is interesting that the empress was expecting the report from the Deputation of Mountainous Banat and claimed 'some of its copies from the Chancellery'. The name of Mining Deputation of Mountainous Banat (*Hofdeputation in Montis et Montanus*) is mentioned in the issue of colonisation, because the start of mining in the Banat was one of the prerequisites for settling people, the mission of recruitment being from the start entrusted to a specialised administration. One of the objectives that initiated the repopulation was the Hechengartisch mine owned by the Banat treasury. The Mining Deputation of Mountainous Banat offered a detailed report about the situation of the mine.[58]

The regional administration offices had another perspective upon the suspension of colonisation. For example, the Deputation of Banat and of the Court questioned the reasons that led to the issue of that order, and also why it had been 'extend[ed] to those who wish to settle there [in the Banat] without support or attendance'.[59] The answer of court councillor Welsperg was that the order stood, but for emigrants with their own resources it was permitted 'to get an adequate land and household after a proper evaluation'. In other places 'those – who have their own resources – can temporarily receive the necessary means of subsistence'. Those who possessed state capital, received land (a plot for building a house and extra land), this 'allocated resource' serving as a basis for subsistence. Their personal resources (money) and the allocated resource (land) allow that 'on the allocated land, they [the colonists] can build households, with the provided necessary tools'. The execution of these measures shows the changes that occurred in the regulations concerning the building of colonist houses.

Many uniform houses were built in the Banat, standard buildings with similar roof and configurations. After 1770, the number of people who erected their homes by their own means increased. The resulting buildings were different from the conventional ones. The former regulations imposed by Baron Kempelen for the homesteads, barnyards, stables or roofs built on the colonists' land were no longer obeyed. People reckoned that if 'an individual builds a house with his own money, he has the freedom to design the roof as he sees fit'. This point of view was considered fair and was supported by the regional authority. Thus, those who built by their own means received a derogation from the general construction regulations.[60] The colonising of the Banat was not stopped completely, but organised in a more selective manner.

Although Count Hatzfeld and Neumann von Bucholt's proposals aimed at stopping the colonisation of the Banat, Maria Theresa decided on its continuation with a caution. The 'caution' referred to the 'clarification of colonists', a task for the chamber officials (Sartori and Ried). Thus, the people willing to settle in the Banat were informed that they had to provide the necessary means to arrange the land they were going to receive. For example, the colonists arriving from the German Empire had to pay for their trip to Vienna. The vast majority of the 1771 statistics include information about colonists who travelled and settled at their own expense, financing their trip and arranging the land they received. Unfortunately, the data refer only to the number of those who arrived, but not to their origin. Thus, there is no information regarding how many came from the inherited territories and how many from the German Empire.[61] Data referring to colonists can be traced up to December 1771. In most cases, the authorities mentioned the decision that colonists who wished to change countries must support themselves.

The information regarding the following year, 1772, comes from a different source. According to the documents of the Austro-Czech Chancellery, by 1 April 1772, 313 families had arrived in the Banat in order to settle here.[62] This is the quarterly total, but later data is missing, thus a comparison between numbers is not possible. The complex nature of the Habsburg Empire considered the colonisation of Banat as part of the repopulation programme. Austria treated the demographic inheritance from the Ottomans in Hungary and the Banat globally. A series of documents deal with the situation existing in Transylvania and refer, directly or indirectly, to colonising the Banat. In Transylvania, too, small-scale colonisation took place, and its problems were similar to those in the Banat. The authorities analysed the situation and used the expression 'emigrants of the Empire' (*Reichs-Emigranten*) when referring to German colonists, mentioning how difficult it was to supply them.[63]

Maria Theresa urged the Chancellery of Transylvania and the Aulic Chamber to take the necessary measures for the colonists' accommodation and financial support. The empress was afraid to repeat the situation in the Banat, and for that reason she strongly warned the authorities that the 'allowed surplus' to the capacity of absorption should not result in an unbearable cost. The colonists from Transylvania settled mainly on the imperial estates with the approval of a committee established by them.

A very important aspect was the support given to the colonists who were financially ruined. The biggest problem was that the old colonists could not repay the advance they had received for settling. In 1771, the Aulic Chamber discovered that no documents had been drafted in regard to advance payments to colonists. As a result, the State Council urged the drafting of a credible report concerning the repayment of advances to the treasury.[64] The Aulic Chamber demanded to know 'the causes that led to the lack of documents regarding the state of repayment of the support given to the colonists a few years earlier', but these causes were still not known. In this context, the empress issued a warning: 'in due time, I expect a fair report about the stage you have reached concerning the regulation of the material support given to the colonists' – precisely how much of the loan had been repaid. Moreover, she notes in the margin of minutes received from Hatzfeld and presented by State Councilor Stupan: 'then, you have to explain what the proposal referring to a better and more wisely supply of the colonists means in practice and why it wasn't implemented earlier by the regional administration'.[65] The regional government had to administer the local debt; the empress expected the Banatian administration to draw up a project using imperial resources rationally.

Minutes of the Aulic Chamber from 30 October 1771, referred to in the report of State Councilor Stupan,[66] mentions the same issue. Maria Theresa acknowledged and confirmed the report regarding the accumulation of large debts by some colonists. She reckoned that, given general conditions of the economy and incomes of colonists, the debt issue could be closed, but such a situation must be prevented in the future. Moreover, the regional administration must 'try to continuously collect the debts for the treasury'. The impoverishment of colonists created other problems, too. For example, 56 families of Guttenbrunn had reached poverty. The case was pointed out by the local priest who threatened to stop a religious service because he had not received the appropriate allowance. Neumann von Buchold's advice that the government should help the needy families was accepted by Maria Theresa, who issued a personal directive to support those families in kind. The condition was that the colonists 'should immediately start work' in order to generate income. The directive also stated that the priest who refused the divine service 'should be punished', the episcopal bishop having to take the necessary measures for 'the accomplishment of spiritual assistance and religious comfort for the colonists'. The empress's decision can be considered a trait of the *Aufklärung*,[67] the top-down imperial policy. Thus, not only was the allocation of priests from public resources ensured, but also the church obligation regarding the assistance of spiritual life according to state regulations.

In some ways, the colonisation of the Banat is similar to that of America, as the region received a diversity of populations. German was the official language, the language of the Austrian administration. Later, the Hungarian language acquired the same status, also because of administration. In the eighteenth century, the Banat functioned as a capsule in which regional identity was strengthened by virtue of assuming a multiple cultural code.[68] The heterogeneity structured a real multi- and intercultural phenomenon that results from multilingualism, from the existence of more religious cults and from ecumenical practice. The cultural diversity, along with Vienna's mercantilist economic policies, meant the Banat had a unique place in the eighteenth-century history of the Habsburg Empire.[69]

7

THE ARCHITECTURE OF THE ROYAL FREE CITIES OF TIMIȘOARA AND ARAD

Gabriel Szekely

THE SPIRITUAL AND SCIENTIFIC accomplishments of the Enlightenment found their expression rather late in the Banat and quite differently from their original form. This was due to the different social and historical background, the peripheral position of the region within the Austro-Hungarian Dual Monarchy, and the manner in which European cultural production was understood and approached by the people of the Banat. With regard to architecture, it is noteworthy that almost all currents that reached the region retained their essential features, even when the original models had disappeared. The urban development of the settlements in the Banat was consciously planned. The streets and buildings that had been preserved from the Ottoman occupation were systematically demolished and rebuilt in order to facilitate the flow of traffic, to give a modern appearance to the dwellings, and for strategic reasons. Unlike cities in the Banat, those in Transylvania have retained the legacy of the medieval age up to the present day.

THE ARCHITECTURE OF TIMIȘOARA AND ARAD BETWEEN 1700 AND 1780

Following the arrival of the troops of Eugene of Savoy in Arad (1669) and Timișoara (1716), a re-establishment of the two urban centres was initiated. Timișoara's perimeter was defined by star-shaped defensive walls, within which the whole inner area was arranged. Arad was defended on all sides by the Mureș River. Following the expansion of the city around 1750, a moat was built on the northern side.

The urban areas of Timișoara and Arad, as outlined in the eighteenth century, were fundamentally different. Timișoara was designed as a city on the drawing board, with defensive walls, straight streets and squares. Arad developed spontaneously, because the town and the citadel were considered different architectural units. For that reason, Arad did not benefit from a predetermined street plan. This phenomenon is typical of the new Central European cities of that time. Some, like Timișoara, were partially or totally designed by Austrian engineers, while others, like Arad, retained their medieval structure.

Authorities favoured the option of pre-planned cities where financially possible. Some cities, which could not be reconstructed in this way after 1700, were rebuilt later. During the reign of Maria Theresa, there were plans to demolish and rebuild Arad according to a prior design. The restructuring was determined by the spontaneous and chaotic development of the city, lack of straight streets, and agglomeration of the space around the citadel, which had to be used as a defensive esplanade. However, Joseph II abandoned the idea of demolishing the city and decided to move the citadel to the opposite side of the Mureș River.

The reconstruction plan for Timișoara's inner city was approved in 1725[1] and provided for the complete demolition of the old city, with the exception of the Hunyadi castle and some of the churches. Bleyer, the first architect to write a monograph on Timișoara, claims that the model for the fortification was Neufbrisach citadel, designed by Vauban. Fortified Vauban-type cities originated in the designs for ideal cities that had preoccupied architects since the Renaissance.

Eighteenth-century Timișoara was a garrison, and many of its buildings were designed for army use.[2] Geometric space and straight streets were important features of the cities created during the Baroque period. In Timișoara, the main streets had to provide transport and communication between the barracks as efficiently as possible and facilitate access to different bastions. Timișoara also was an important symbol of imperial power and, implicitly, of all those serving the emperor. Thus, military parades, so fashionable at the time, were one of the main reasons for building straight streets.

Another innovation of the Baroque age, from the urban point of view, was the *corso*. The desire to go out into society and to have an exterior space of style and distinction was a feature of all Baroque cities. At that time, there were two main squares in Timișoara. Today, they are named Unirii (Union) Square and Libertății (Freedom) Square. The first was designed for parades; the second hosted the cathedral and the governor's palace and also functioned as a *corso*. Although situated on the outskirts of the Baroque area of influence, Timișoara remained true to the urban principles of similar European cities in its reconstruction. The speed with which the city was built, its size and complexity, and the beauty of its buildings, prove Timișoara's importance to the Viennese administration.

In Baroque Timişoara, the unbuilt public space became, as in all the cities of the age, an important component for displaying absolute power in its urban expression. Although modestly decorated, its eighteenth-century façades represented not only the boundaries of the building itself, but also that of the unbuilt open space beyond, which had its own significance.[3]

In contrast to the rest of the inner city, Timişoara's squares are generous. It could be said that there was a polarisation of the representative buildings around the two important squares. The third, St George's Square, hosted a Jesuit seminary and was more a space resulting from the placement of a church. If Union Square has been very little transformed from its eighteenth-century appearance, the area around Freedom Square (Parade-Platz) has suffered a lot from the demolition of some buildings that were initially erected here. The Jesuit and the Franciscan churches placed there, and also the Transylvanian Barracks, represented important landmarks. Each of these three edifices had a Baroque decorated tower rising above neighbouring buildings. Along with these buildings, the most important structures in eighteenth-century Timişoara were the cathedral and governor's palace in Union Square, and city hall and the general's house in Freedom Square.

The streets of Timişoara had a broad and bright appearance. Access from public to private space was made through arched entrances, usually situated at the median bay of the houses. The continuous frontage of the buildings formed a clear demarcation line between the two types of space. Due to the small size of the parcels of land in the city, inner courtyards were narrow in the eighteenth century. They were usually paved and surrounded by balconies on three or four sides. The continuous frontage of houses and their inner courtyards were characteristic of eighteenth-century Baroque cities. This urban space was perpetuated during the next century, even though house decoration changed.

Because of the limited space inside the city, starting in the eighteenth century, a number of suburbs developed: the Fabric, Josefin and Mehala districts. In the centres of the Orthodox suburbs Mehala and the Fabric, a large rectangular square, dominated by an Orthodox church, was designed. According to Mihai Opriş, 'initially, the Fabric had neither a central square nor a church. The absence of a church can be explained by the fact that the Catholic churches already built in the city were considered sufficient. However, the absence of a square is inexplicable.'[4] The squares in the suburbs are similar in size to those in Union Square, but the buildings around them are not of great aesthetic value. Generally, they are one- or two-storey houses, some with commercial areas on the ground floor. The rectangular designs of the suburbs resemble the plans for villages in the Banat built in the same period.

In Arad, urban configuration in the eighteenth-century is displayed on maps by the engineer De Sully and an anonymous cartographer (both in 1752) and Imre Ruttkay (1755). Three areas of the city are clearly notable. The first is a meander of the Mureș River, where the citadel with its four bastions and the strategic open space is located. The second zone, south of a present-day vanished arm of the river (Mureșul Mic), hosted the medieval quarter of the Serbian border guards (Reitzen Stadt), who defended the moat and external fortifications. On the outskirts of this quarter, a Serbian church was erected on the estate of border guard Captain Tököly, as seen on the maps. The area has retained its character to this day: small, medieval guild houses, with high roofs. The old main street of this area bears the name of Tribune Axente. The third zone visible on these maps is the German quarter, a district to the north of the vanished river arm. It is the starting point of the large boulevard which today represents the city's main street. On each side of the German quarter, there was a small Romanian community: one facing the riverbank, around the former Orthodox Bishopric, and the other to the west.

In 1763 construction of a new Vauban-style citadel began, on a natural bend of the Mureș River, on the opposite bank. Three years later the old citadel was entirely demolished. The old Serbian quarter expanded up to this area, in time taking up the space which had formerly been the citadel's latrine. The centre of this area, which emerged after 1752, was named the Old Square, or 'Fish Market', and acquired its present-day appearance in 1865.

By analysing Ruttkay's map, the conclusion is that Arad had 32 streets and six squares in 1755, and by 1783 had registered 84 streets. The expansion mainly developed to the north and the west, along today's main streets, but also to the south, on territory vacated by the demolition of the old citadel. The German district extended west over an area of land occupied by the Romanians – Wallachia – and over the Romanian cemetery, demolished in 1781 by an imperial decree which stated that cemeteries should be placed outside cities. Between 1725 and 1783, the German zone expanded to the north, from the city hall to today's Podgoria (Vineyard) Square, thus outlining the second half of the main street of the city. At that time, the city's salt bureau stood on the site of the Court of Justice, while Avram Iancu Square still hosted the old city hall of the German quarter, which was later demolished.[5]

The Serbian district preserved the appearance of a rural settlement, with mainly one-storey houses. It seems that most of the houses were built in rows, presenting a continuous street front since the eighteenth century. This area of the city lacked the possibility of expansion because it was physically bordered by the Mureș River and by the German district to the north. The only notable building in this area was an Orthodox church, built between 1698 and 1702, which can be considered representative of the small Baroque churches built circa 1700 in the Habsburg Empire. In contrast to the Serbian district, buildings in the German neighbourhood were mostly two-storey in the eighteenth century. Even though no street line was planned, houses were built according to the strict urban rules of Central European cities designed after 1700. The one- and two-storey buildings were arranged so as to respect the continuous frontage of the façades. Building isolated houses on the lot was not allowed.

Buildings with landmark status were few but include the Minorite church with its single corner tower (on the site of a Catholic church today) and the old German city hall. The latter was a small building with one floor, a façade with Baroque decoration, a pronounced central arch and a small tower above the entrance. The only urban space with a rectangular form and a more orderly appearance was Avram Iancu Square. To the north, the square continued into today's main boulevard. At an earlier time, this square was the only large one in the city, the others being very small, practically larger crossroads or areas free of buildings.

Buildings of eighteenth-century Central European cities were characterised by the unity and rhythm of their façades. Although buildings of that epoch strongly resembled those constructed in Timișoara and complied with the rules of continuous frontage of the façades, the urban space of Arad was very different from that of Timișoara. The lack of rectangular geometrical routes, of right-angled crossroads, and the somewhat random perspectives made Arad look different from its neighbouring city. The lack of a pre-established urban plan, and also of public buildings, shows that the Habsburgs gave less importance to rebuilding Arad than Timișoara.

FAÇADES, DECORATION, MONUMENTS

During the Baroque age, art acquired a new role in society. Interiors were completely decorated by artists, thus no detail could be randomly placed. Artistic compositions became complex, and behind them were creators aware of their role in society and their value as craftsmen. During the Thirty Years War (1618–48), Baroque art became part of Catholic ideology designed to banish Protestantism from Central Europe. During this early period of the Central European Baroque, buildings decorated in this style were simultaneously erected in Bohemia, Austria and western Hungary, which were under Habsburg domination. There were cultural links with southern Germany and northern Italy. The Church and Baroque art emerged as supra-state entities in the seventeenth and eighteenth centuries. Craftsmen could move freely throughout the Dual Monarchy. In Slovakia and Transylvania, the local traditional Renaissance style blended with imported Baroque elements, while in areas such as the Banat with no previous local tradition, the Central European Baroque was fully accepted as a new style. The families of Italian craftsmen who had been working in Central Europe since the 1600s carried an important role in spreading the Baroque. They were employed by noblemen as engineers, painters and architects, or contracted work in different cities as 'master builders'. Families like the del Bianco or Spazzo had worked from generation to generation in Vienna, Prague or Hungarian cities. The façades of the buildings in Timișoara and Arad were decorated, during the Baroque period, on principles used by German architects. The expression is that of the Renaissance and Italian Baroque, modified and blended to the concepts, needs and material means of the time. Columns with Corinthian or Ionic capitals, fake columns, plaster embossing and window platbands were all part of the decoration.

Ordinary dwellings were plainly decorated, with platbands, round windows and eventually some plaster embossing. In some cases, entrances were outlined by platbands, fake columns, etc. By contrast, the palaces and public buildings were very ornately decorated. While in the nineteenth century practically all buildings were richly decorated, during the eighteenth century there was a clear distinction between the decoration of important and ordinary buildings. The county palace in Union Square in Timișoara, built in 1754, has rich Baroque decoration, with distinctive architectural elements, such as fake embossing, platbands and tympanums. This imposing building is considered equal in importance to other Western European palaces of the time. The two-storey Episcopal palace is typical of the eighteenth-century Central European Baroque with fronts facing two different streets, a roof with skylights and platbands on the ground floor, windows and fake pillars on the first floor. The entrance is defined by a beautiful stone portal, decorated with geometrical and floral motifs. The façades of the eighteenth-century palaces of Timișoara are defined by harmony, equilibrium and a more restrained, less exaggerated decoration. Along with the common tympanums, embossment and platbands, on certain façades there are geometrical or vegetal motifs, or sculpted heads, included in the general composition. Many windows, especially on the ground floor, are finished with semicircles or fragments of arches. Iron cast lattices are also part of the stylistic ensemble, even if they did not reach the abundance of those used in the following century.

The most richly decorated buildings are churches. Unlike other buildings, their main fronts are composed of curves and broken lines, giving a characteristic flow to the Baroque architecture. Most of the churches are relatively small, having only one tower above the entrance. They are usually separate from neighbouring buildings, unlike those built in the next century. The towers are slim and end in a pointed roof, forming complicated designs, distinctive of the time. The façades, especially the main ones, are richly decorated with common Baroque motifs. The Catholic cathedral in Timișoara is a fine example, with its imposing front and rich decoration but with one notable exception: it has two towers. Interestingly, the Catholic and Orthodox churches were both decorated in the same manner at that time, and the designs were made by the same architects and engineers. In Arad, the largest church was built inside the new citadel and still exists today. It was the focal point of the buildings inside the citadel, to which civilians did not have access.

The barracks were usually simply decorated, with the exception of 'Generalalthaus' and the commander's house in Freedom Square, Timişoara. The Transylvanian Barracks (a building which has disappeared today) could be added to these, with its large Baroque tower and monumental portal. The stylish building in Freedom Square known as the Military Casino was decorated in Rococo style during the eighteenth century. It is the only Rococo building in Timişoara, although fragments of that style may be found on other buildings. In some cases the barracks had no decoration at all. This supports Hans Sedlmayr's comment that in the 1700s within the Habsburg Empire, many buildings with a functional role were practically devoid of decoration.[6] These large buildings, of which there were many inside the city, conferred a monotonous look on many streets. However, the justifiable difference between barracks, ordinary houses and palaces in the eighteenth century should be noted. In the eclectic nineteenth century, the significance of decoration in relation to social status fundamentally changed and, unlike the previous age, there were no more hierarchies.

The monuments and statues placed in public spaces in eighteenth-century European cities were almost exclusively creations with religious themes. One example is the statue of St Nepomuk in Arad, placed initially in 1729 where today's city hall now stands, and moved in 1870 to a small square on Battyány Street. This typical Baroque statue, representing a saint in large garments with rich embroidery and lace, was created in Vienna by an anonymous craftsman. Beside saints, there were statues depicting the Virgin Mary and the Holy Trinity. There were also monuments erected in gratitude for the end of plague epidemics that were much feared at the time. In Timişoara, some religious monuments for public use are preserved from this period. The statue of St John Nepomuk, by an unknown artist, is at No. 13, Dragalina Boulevard. The Holy Trinity monument (the Plague Monument), created in 1740 in Vienna, can be found in Union Square. The Virgin Mary and St Nepomuk Monument, the work of Viennese artists Blim and Wasserburger, dates from 1756 and is located in Freedom Square.

The monuments were erected in the city squares, usually in the centre, but the most privileged spots were in front of the churches. The theme and placement of the statues within the public space display the strong support given by the Habsburgs to the Catholic Church and its importance in cultural life at the time. These statues complete the image of a community attached to eighteenth-century tradition, which would be perpetuated in the following era, regardless of progress and the changes that had occurred in the meantime. They represent the expression of the collective spirit of a specific human community.[7] The eighteenth-century statues are suggestive and dynamic, and are perfectly matched with the Baroque church façades. Stylistically, all the statues follow the pattern of some Austrian and Central European workshops which, at the time, produced Baroque art with particular features.

THE NEW CONTEXT (1780–1900)

Contrary to the idea that during the nineteenth century urban centres would have a decor lacking in personality, the cities of the Banat are marked by eclectic façades. Unlike other cities of Central Europe or Italy, Timișoara and Arad had lost their identity during the Ottoman domination and were later totally rebuilt. The short duration of the Baroque age (from 1700 to 1780) allowed for the reconstruction of significant elements of the urban space alone. Palaces, barracks, churches and city halls were all ordered and built by the government. Bourgeois houses were few and small in scale. During the nineteenth century, the local bourgeoisie and aristocracy had the means to build, on their own initiative, larger buildings, which were designed and decorated according to their wishes. For them, after centuries of war and occupation, the time for reunification with the European space and the opportunity to import Western values had arrived. Unlike Italy, in the Banat these eclectic houses did not seem like imitations of neighbouring Renaissance houses even if the models were copied: they were buildings with personality and cultural identity. By constructing these buildings, the ruling class of the empire proved its allegiance to European cultural values. The foundations of the new order, in which private initiative achieves a new meaning, were laid as a result of the reforms of the end of the eighteenth century. It was then that private property was consolidated according to legislation, being defined by cadastral planning.[8]

During the nineteenth century, the changes that took place in the urban structure of Timișoara and Arad were stimulated not by initiatives from the authorities, but by a continuous and beneficial process by which the bourgeoisie, along with a portion of the nobility, invested in construction. While in Western Europe authors such as Balzac, Hugo and Dickens criticised the modern city and appreciated the confused, mysterious, though coherent appearance of the traditional town, Central European intellectuals supported urban reconstruction upon Western models, regarding them as progress towards integration into European culture.

THE LIMITS OF URBAN SPACE IN TIMIȘOARA AND ARAD DURING THE NINETEENTH CENTURY

During the nineteenth century, Timișoara and Arad considerably expanded their boundaries. Due to its defensive walls, the actual city of Timișoara could not extend its area; instead, its suburbs grew significantly. The development was made on a pre-established street line, completed over time. Outside the centre that was formed by the citadel, three areas developed during the nineteenth century: the Fabric quarter and on the opposite side, the Josefin and Elisabetin districts. Separating the three exterior areas was free land, partially used for agriculture. The Fabric and Josefin quarters were delineated with straight streets and their expansion was controlled by the authorities. The existence of a secondary arm of the Bega River in Fabric, near Trajan Square, had initially hindered expansion in that area but following drainage of the small canal, the street line was completed. Development of the three districts outside the city of Timişoara was regulated by the authorities. Later, their expansion outwards was permitted without restrictions but their advance towards the centre was prohibited, because the strategic approach demanded an area of free land around the defensive walls.

After 1780, Arad exceeded its initial limits. The canals that defended the city were drained and it expanded to the north, its southern and western development still being blocked by the Mureş River. The central square extended to the north until it formed the street that is the city's main thoroughfare, known today as Revolution Boulevard. This street has earned, over time, an unusual importance for such a relatively small city, having a large width and a length that finally justified the label of boulevard. After 1848, when the city was partially reconstructed, all the new streets had to be parallel or perpendicular to the boulevard. Even though it was impossible to impose an orthogonal plan on a street line that had spontaneously developed until then, from the mid-nineteenth century crossroads were built at right angles, if possible, while the streets were straight and as long as possible.

Both in Timişoara and Arad, the rule of the continuous frontage of façades, attentively tracked by authorities, was translated into a compact and orderly manner of building, which limited expansion. Consequently, until the end of the nineteenth century, there were few green spaces in either city.

STREETS AND SQUARES

An important feature of the nineteenth-century urban landscape in Timişoara and Arad was the relatively small height of the buildings. Before 1880, there were few three-storey and even fewer four-storey buildings there. Timişoara and Arad had no more than ten such buildings. In Arad, most of the taller buildings were placed on the boulevard, while in Timişoara they were built on the more important streets of the Josefin and Fabric quarters. In Josefin, the most important buildings were placed on the two main avenues, now named Tinereţii and 16 December 1989. The investors' preference for important streets was natural because they were starting to become important arteries for traffic. Inside the city of Timișoara, space was limited, although after 1848, when the city was bombarded during the siege, some buildings were destroyed and the resulting free area was quickly reconstructed. After 1880, some of the older buildings were demolished and taller ones were constructed. Inside all the cities of the empire, regulations permitted the construction of taller buildings depending on the district and the width of the street,[9] and, starting in the mid-nineteenth century, the government established commissions, coordinated by the city hall, which approved the façades of the new buildings. Generally, after 1860, buildings within the central areas of the cities had to follow the rule of continuous frontage and use only bricks or stone for construction materials.

For the corridor type of street, an important element was the commercial space on the ground floor of the buildings. They were grouped inside the so-called commercial areas, on the main streets, in the squares or on busy streets usually linking two important landmarks of the city. In Arad, most of the commercial areas were laid out on the primary boulevard. The only other street that hosted a large number of shops was what is today called Mețianu, which links the city's two important avenues. Thus, the integrated thinking of authorities and designers is clearly visible in the rational and correct differentiation of urban space and in the ranking of streets according to their importance within it. Order and coherence are typical features of Central European cities in the nineteenth century.

Inner courtyards constitute another architectural element that contributes to the shaping of the urban space. Some of these became passageways linking two streets or hosting workshops or storage areas and the like. Open all day towards the street line, these spaces were in direct relation to the public areas, which thus lost their rigidity. The historic centre of Arad was formed during the nineteenth century. The square which is named today the Romanian–Hungarian Reconciliation Park and the boulevard are urban spaces typical of Central European cities. Defined by perfectly aligned façades, they are richly decorated and of a remarkable unity. The buildings on the main streets and squares usually have commercial spaces on the ground floor, unlike those placed on the smaller streets. The squares and boulevards are quite large for a provincial city of that period. Some squares, such as Arad's Fish Market, resulted from the intersection of a number of streets during the eighteenth century but acquired their present style in the nineteenth century. In Timișoara, one such space is the intersection of the boulevards Tinereții and 16 December 1989. During the nineteenth century, urban spaces were characterised by symmetry, order and a specific rhythm due to distinctive decorations.

FROM BAROQUE TO ROCOCO AND ROMANTICISM

While the Baroque represented an artistic style imposed by the Habsburgs on their newly conquered territories, the eclecticism of nineteenth-century art emerged spontaneously, through the initiative of the artists and their patrons. Baroque style lasted in the Banat until the rule of Joseph II, whose administration promoted simple buildings, plainly decorated but appropriate to the purpose for which they were built.[10]

The architect Gheorghe Bleyer noted the penetration of the *zopfstil* in Timişoara between 1780 and 1790. This was a more sober style derived from Rococo.[11] He also mentions that, in the 1810s in Timişoara, Master Anton Schmidt designed palaces that bear the mark of classicism. According to Nikolaus Pevsner, 'Architects believed that anything created by the pre-industrial centuries must of necessity be better than anything made to express the character of their own era.'[12] Patrons appreciated faithful copies of works from other periods, attributing to them various meanings. Gheorghe Bleyer also reminds us that during the 1848 Revolution many buildings lost their original decoration and were redecorated in the spirit of the age. Between 1848 and 1867, many Viennese architects worked in Timişoara and Arad; their designs were characterised by a sober neoclassical style.

Romantic architecture was expressed in Timişoara by quiet volumes, a lack of decoration, simple lines, and low-sloping tiled roofs. Various decorative elements are sometimes used on the floors, in descending order: Romanesque, Gothic and Italian Renaissance. Most of the time, the top-floor windows had semicircular shape, while those on the ground floor had the shape of a circle segment in their upper part. The main cornice was supported by many consoles. The façades had decorations made of plaster imitating stone.[13] In Bleyer's view, the architecture of Timişoara in the nineteenth century had a provincial style, even though many Viennese architects were working in the city.

In some cases, decorations of the façade were designed to accord with those of existing buildings, especially neighbouring ones. When several buildings were erected at the same time, the problem of harmonising them was debated. In the Banat cities there is a remarkable unity in the façades. It could be said that the eclectic façades had a unifying value, both in the adjustment of the street front and from the social perspective, taking into account that both noblemen and bourgeoisie lived inside these buildings. The façades of blocks of flats, although often distinguished by their massive neo-Renaissance style, are harmonised by the rustic element and by the line and scale of the windows, in order to attain a homogeneous street appearance and a line that guides the perspective to the desired direction.

THE VIENNA RING AND THE NEW ARCHITECTURAL PROGRAMMES

The reconstruction campaign after 1848 in Timişoara and Arad embraced the predilection for the Renaissance and Baroque. More than in previous centuries, the architectural language was imbued with ideological meaning, whether political or artistic. The Romantics' veneration for past ages and for Greek and Roman culture influenced both the creators and their patrons. Artists went to Italy to study historical styles. In his monograph on Timişoara, Bleyer writes about Master Anton Schmidt who, having earned a considerable fortune, often travelled to Italy to study his favourite Renaissance monuments. This means that a direct link with Italy existed, and that artists did not just use the catalogues with drawings that circulated at the time. Precision of imitation was one of the major issues for artists in the Romantic period. Renaissance style took the palace as the reference point for urban dwelling, as can be seen in Italian cities of the fourteenth and fifteenth centuries. These were known in the nineteenth century and prompted interest in the architectural ideas and principles of the past. The imitation of historical styles also was criticised at the time for the discord between style and function.

Architecture in nineteenth-century Timişoara and Arad faithfully accepted the models of the capital city, as far as material means allowed. The wealth of investors was considerably smaller in Timişoara and Arad than in Budapest or Vienna. After 1870, the number of three- and four-storey buildings substantially increased. For aristocratic or bourgeois investors of the Romantic period, cultural self-projection was more important than functional concerns. The term most used for the urban transformation that took place was *Verschönerung des Stadtbildes* (the beautifying of city buildings). The cityscape had to mirror the image of an ideal society. For the different social strata, which in this specific period pursued the culture of aristocracy by borrowing its architectural styles, the image of their city was a source of pride. In the eastern part of the Dual Monarchy, where ethnocultural ideology was perceived as compensation for a past lost because of Ottoman domination, the new urban architecture represented the desire to reintegrate with Western culture and civilisation.

After 1860, in both Vienna and cities of the provinces, the triumph of constitutional law over imperial power and of laic culture over religious belief were celebrated. 'Not palaces, garrisons and churches, but centres of constitutional governance and cultural buildings are now dominating the [Vienna] Ring [as well as the main streets of Timişoara and Arad].'[14] Unlike Baroque concepts of the centre, and a perspective oriented to that unique point, in the nineteenth century the central area became a complex ensemble, a street built with a continuous front of façades. Inside this front, important public buildings were inserted without looking for symmetry in the design of an integrated ensemble. The victory of the bourgeois initiative democratised the concept of city design compared with the previous age. Unlike industrial buildings or installations for which no decoration was required, taste required city buildings to be covered by a façade that recalled the historical past.

The choice of style for each important building in the city was an important issue at the time. With regard to religious buildings, Timișoara preferred the Romanesque and Gothic styles, to the detriment of the neo-Renaissance and Baroque. The two great Catholic churches built in Timișoara circa 1900 are like basilicas, one Gothic and the other Romanesque. In Arad, the Lutheran church was also neo-Gothic, while the Catholic one was decorated in Baroque style with neoclassical elements. This preference for Gothic and Romanesque was common to church building in nineteenth-century German and English spaces. For synagogues, Moorish style was preferred. The synagogue in Timișoara, built between 1863 and 1865, was designed by the Viennese architect Karl Schuman and inaugurated in the presence of Franz Joseph.[15] The synagogues of the time, almost all done in Moorish style, are considered by architectural historiography to be classic examples of Romantic taste.

Unlike the city hall of Vienna, decorated in neo-Gothic style, in Arad the new city hall, built in 1877, is in Flemish neo-Renaissance style. For the Arad high school for boys and for the economics school, Renaissance style was preferred. In Timișoara the boys' high school (today Constantin Diaconovici Loga) was built in neo-Baroque style; the girls' high school in neo-Gothic style. In Vienna, the style chosen for the university was neo-Renaissance.

Theatres were another very important project for nineteenth-century cities. Almost all theatres in Central Europe, including the one in Timișoara, were built in that period by the renowned architects Helmer and Fellner. At the time, the construction of a theatre was a guarantee that the city would be classified as being part of European culture. Theatres were built in privileged spots and were granted substantial funding. The style chosen for the theatre of Timișoara was neo-Renaissance, while in Arad neoclassicism was preferred. The Arad theatre was built in the middle of the boulevard separating Avram Iancu Square from the rest of the centre. In Timișoara, the theatre was erected on a free parcel of land inside the city (its most privileged area), and after the walls were demolished, its façade faced the main esplanade. The important role of cultural buildings and material investment were characteristic of liberal Austro-Hungary after 1867.

Railway stations represented a category of construction that transformed urban architecture after 1848. Both in Timișoara and in Arad, they were placed on the outskirts of the city, on the edge of an important boulevard, encouraging the development of the city in that direction. The most utilised style for housing in the second half of the nineteenth century was Italian neo-Renaissance. Pilasters, cornices, windows with arches, and embossing remained the most widespread decorations. Neo-Gothic or neo-Baroque decorations appeared only accidentally on façades, but on some Renaissance-style façades there might be motifs borrowed from the Baroque or from the French or Flemish Renaissance. The reason for such a large expansion of classic styles may be explained by the great respect for classical culture at that time. In a society which used the values of antiquity as standard, regarded Latin as the supreme language of culture and science, based its legislation on Roman law, and admired the heroes of antique writers, it is no wonder that for the façades of buildings, a language derived from the classical was preferred.

Statues were also distinctive elements of the urban landscape. Apart from the new religious monuments, whose tradition dated from the previous century (for example the Holy Trinity monument in front of the Catholic church in Arad, or the Virgin Mary monument in Timișoara), statues on other themes appeared in this period. In Arad, on the spot of the Hungarian officers' execution of 1848, two memorials were erected. Liberty Statue was built in Freedom Square (today Avram Iancu Square). The statue of Lajos Kossuth, also on a patriotic theme, was placed in the middle of the boulevard near the city hall. There were other politically themed statues, such as the bust of Emperor Franz Joseph. In nineteenth-century Timișoara, almost all the statues were religious. Through their expression and the attention given to their placement, these monuments contributed to the outline of the urban space of Timișoara and Arad. They were complementary to the eclectic façades of the buildings, for example, the Austrian military monument constructed in 1853 by sculptor Joseph Max and architect Josef Kranner, today situated inside the Cemetery of Heroes on Lipovei Avenue.

Although the intervention of the authorities in outlining the urban space was reduced (only the maximum height of the façades and, sometimes, the size of the parcels of land were regulated), the cityscape had a remarkable unity. The desire of the architects and their patrons to conform to some common values is obvious. This direction was preserved until the 1900s, when the new European artistic trends would change tastes and views on tradition.

ARCHITECTURE IN THE PERIOD 1900–14

The period 1900–14 did not bring major transformations in the structure of the city of Arad. The two new quarters, Gai and Pârneava, which were established around 1900, were almost exclusively inhabited by workers. They had a regular street line, with straight and parallel streets. Two-storey buildings were still built inside the historic centre, in areas that remained unoccupied or had been freed up by the demolition of older buildings.

For the urban development of Timișoara, the period between 1900 and 1914 was very important. After 1900, the city expanded, following the demolition of the city walls, and the area between the citadel and the outer districts was gradually taken up by real estate. The most important achievements of this period are the central square and the boulevards that link the inner city to the Fabric and Josefin quarters. The construction of buildings on the boulevards started simultaneously in the inner city and the outer districts. Taking into consideration the technical means of the time, the development occurred at a very fast pace, transforming a provincial town into a large city with broad avenues. Boulevards and new urban spaces essentially changed the structure of the city. They were designed on another scale to the existing urban elements.

The buildings constructed in the central area during the first years of the twentieth century were different from those constructed before, especially in terms of size, because on the important arteries only houses of three or more storeys could be built. The façades, inspired by Secession style, no longer complied with the tradition of neo-Renaissance decoration of the previous period. However, the rule of continuous façades, which had been perpetuated since the eighteenth century, still stood, thus retaining some unity in the city.

The volumes of the new buildings on the boulevards were not as unitary as those of the previous period. Buildings with corner towers, bay windows and balconies, which provided more complex forms, were common. Large churches, such as those in the Fabric or Elisabetin districts, became local centres of interest in the urban landscape. Around 1900, at least five large churches, belonging to different denominations, were built in Timișoara.

Industrial buildings became more numerous and more important. The red-brick walls of industrial halls were now commonplace in many areas of the city. Many industrial buildings had pleasant façades with Secession-style elements. Allegorical figures, representing some of the guilds, were in fashion. Bas-reliefs depicting women and men carrying the tools of the trade adorned the façades of factories, train stations, etc.

The Bega Canal was an important element of the urban landscape, and its image was outlined by new parks and bridges. At the time there was consensus regarding the development of the city, coordinated by the chief architect László Székely. He designed entire complexes, such as buildings and the Piarist church in the central area, and the park, bridge and houses on 3 August 1919 Boulevard. Such complex compositions reshaped entire areas of the city, introducing the Secession and new spatial concepts as dominant elements of the urban image. Freedom of composition for the façades, an interest in all kinds of exterior spaces, traffic solutions, rethinking the function and role of the centre – all these were accomplished in Timișoara between 1900 and 1914.

The commercial areas, the banks and offices, were concentrated in the central square and on certain boulevards. By these measures, the new urban spaces became the main areas of the city, attracting pedestrian traffic as well as most vehicles. The central square was initially planned as a great esplanade, which would be continued with a boulevard linking it to the Josefin quarter. The closing of the esplanade by the Orthodox Church happened later, after the Second World War. The buildings of the central square form a valuable ensemble of Secession architecture practically unique in Europe. The numerous richly decorated houses became points of interest for the arteries or streets on which they were placed. Instead of the unity previously dominating the streets of Timişoara, a strong individualism emerges in the façades, each trying to capture attention. The wide, fluent traffic routes, the new bridges, numerous green spaces, and varied possibilities of using large areas of open space in the centre profoundly changed the image of Timişoara at the beginning of the twentieth century.

Among the most important public monuments built in Timişoara at the time, the Virgin Mary chapel should be mentioned. Made of Carrara marble and situated in Virgin Mary Square, it was designed by László Székely in 1906, with sculptures made by György Kiss.

THE SECESSION IN TIMIŞOARA AND ARAD

The Secession, or the stylistic rupture that took place at the end of the nineteenth century and the beginning of the twentieth, was a conscious phenomenon encompassing all the visual arts. Although there is some evidence for different origins of the style, it was propagated by the winds of change felt by contemporary society. The essence of these decisions is clearly expressed by the Austrian name of the movement: Secession – a conscious break with the past. The desire for change was not directed against the eclectic method of borrowing different decorative elements, because that tradition was perpetuated, but against the academic language which enforced historical, and especially classical, styles. On the social stage, the aim of the bourgeoisie to legitimise itself by using styles considered aristocratic lost importance after 1890. At the level of society in general, the desire to prevail over outdated structures was manifest. The social ideal was no longer to aspire to the rank of nobility, but to affirm some democratic ideas which had been in circulation in European culture since the eighteenth century. Demolition of obsolete dogmas was favoured over adapting to their outdated demands. After Secession, the second artistic objective was the search for novelty – the Art Nouveau style. It is no accident that this new style is often associated with youth, with Jugendstil, and a desire for life with freedom.

Specific elements of the art of the 1900s in architecture – plastic and decorative art – can be seen on the façades of buildings in Timişoara. These are the abandonment of dogma and denial of academicism; monumentality; decorativism; irony and playful images; richness of motifs and theme; eroticism and sensuality; cultivation of detail; use of historical references (in decorations); optimism; the search for light and brightness; depth of thought and power of synthesis; the search for truth in art; a concern to create an international art; celebration of work; use of historical and mythological motifs; and a special relationship with the sacred and the mystical.

In Timişoara, as in other cities of the eastern Austro-Hungarian Empire, Secession brought in large buildings, situated on important arteries or in the central square. The entrepreneurs were rich people, sometimes from outside Timişoara, who were investing there due to the advantages the real estate market of the city offered at that time. The designers were renowned architects, graduates of the universities of Budapest and Vienna. Most of them were disciples of Lechner Ödön or Otto Wagner. The patrons wanted to be in tune with the times and demanded that the architects favour the new style, Secession. Out of this cooperation, a cult architecture developed, made by reputable architects with solid backgrounds. Quite another situation was represented by the small buildings of one or two storeys. Here, Art Nouveau was only sporadically used, an eclectic style remaining dominant. An interesting example of this is the series of one-storey houses with continuous street fronts, built along Badea Cârţan Square around 1909–12. Of the eight houses, only one is decorated in Secession style, while the others faithfully follow the eclectic decorative tradition. For these buildings, the neo-Renaissance decoration of previous periods was considered most appropriate.

A very different situation existed in Arad, where Secession emerged at the periphery of the city on the façades of some simple houses.[16] This phenomenon, which was popular before 1900, is even more interesting because in this city Secession arrived only gradually and incrementally; nobody built whole ensembles decorated in this style, as they did in Timişoara. In truth, we cannot talk about an entirely new style that emerged at the beginning of the twentieth century. However, the refusal of academicism, an innovative spirit, the manner of using volume, and particular ways of using decorative elements are common traits of the buildings constructed between 1900 and 1914. Some façades still preserve elements from the ways of previous ages. The partition of apartments and the technique used are in any case the same inside these buildings. The apartments accessed from corridors oriented towards the inner courtyard respect the traditional type of dwelling which had been used in all the imperial cities starting in the Baroque age.

The buildings from the beginning of the twentieth century no longer all have flat façades, but are differentiated only by decorative elements. One common technique was using bay windows, which break up the monotony of the façades. The vertical silhouette of these architectural elements adds to the suppleness of the building, especially if supported by tall roofs or towers. Excepting the plastic effect, bay windows enlarge the surface of the floors, which was another reason for their use. There were no differences in height between the different parts of the building. Sometimes, mimicry of such effects was attempted in the case of high attics. The dimensions of the model style of the buildings are robust and sometimes even monumental. This probably reflected the will of the patrons, who were investing large sums of money in their buildings. The buildings constructed in the so-called gingerbread style all have rounded edges.

The roofs were usually tall, in order to extend and emphasise the vertical lines of the façade. They were covered, in some cases, by polychrome tiles for decorative effects. Attics played an important compositional role. Hungarian Secession buildings often had attics decorated with ceramic elements and might have triangular, semicircular or undulating forms – a common effect in the work of Lechner and his disciples. The attic windows created compositions with decorative elements and formed the crown of the façade. The roofs were often fragmented and interrupted at the corners by vertical elements acting as a visual sign.

The windows of this reference model, from which much was constructed, usually had an elongated rectangular form, like the older buildings. The height of the rooms probably contributed to this. The frames of the doors and windows are sometimes geometrical, at other times they imitate the decoration of traditional houses. In some cases, when the plastic effect demands, the windows end in an arch on their upper side. For the same reason, large windows are sometimes replaced by narrower vertical niches. Unlike in the eclectic period, decorations are treated with much more freedom, even if they belong to the repertoire of the previous century. Neo-Gothic and neo-Romanesque elements now emerged, rarely seen before in Arad and Timișoara, used in free combination with decorations in other styles. All the elements were slightly altered from the traditional versions to better integrate into the composition and to deliver individuality to the building. Fake columns, capitals and tympanums are used in many versions. Often, the capitals are stylised and used as elements in vast geometrical compositions. Historical references are used in a similar manner to postmodernism, but with the intention of providing a Romantic tone to the composition. In some cases, some registries of the façade are treated in a common neo-Renaissance style, but only to create contrast with others decorated in a different manner.

The floral motifs of Art Nouveau are quite rare in Timișoara and Arad. They are present, though, on some façades, sometimes in combination with folk motifs. Unlike Oradea or Târgu-Mureș, the folk and floral motifs characteristic of the Hungarian Secession were used in Timișoara and Arad only to a small extent. Historical or geometric compositions are much more widespread. Folk motifs usually emerged when the architect came from Budapest. However, on smaller surfaces floral ornaments were used, even in more modest houses.

Masks, busts, statues and bas-reliefs were part of the artists' repertoire around 1900. The possibilities of combinations for realising compositions on façades were freely used. Decorative elements, sometimes numerous, were built around the centres of interest which might be geometric contours, masks (sometimes stylised) or human shapes. Women's heads, human silhouettes or medieval sculptures representing monsters were always key elements of the composition. Through the use of these symbols, the artists expressed their allegiance to the Secession movement, which celebrated the beauty of the human body in an idealised form. Human shapes and women's heads always had a privileged position on the façades, being placed where they could be seen to best advantage and subordinating the elements around them. By their grace and perfection, these decorations, treated in a special way, delivered an air of harmony, stability and optimism which is so typical of Viennese houses of the last years of the Austro-Hungarian Empire. For the bourgeoisie living in these homes, the façade had to express not only their wealth and optimism, but also their attitude towards the favoured art of the time – proof that they belonged to the 'good society'. With their aesthetic and maybe even slightly erotic air, Secession artists kept a sense of measure and equilibrium. Bas-reliefs were usually used to draw attention to the function of the building. Often, the characters held in their hands the typical tools of a specific trade or an image representing the protective god of some craft.

The metal fittings preserve the Central European tradition. The high-end houses have beautifully crafted fittings. These might be similar to those of previous periods or simplified to the taste of modernists, who were starting to spread their ideas for the first time. The railings of terraces or balconies received the greatest attention, but there are even windows and doors with nice fittings. It should be mentioned that in Timișoara after 1912, the reference model called for houses to be built with simply decorated façades. The creations of Adolf Loos, a very successful Viennese artist who persistently opposed the aesthetics of the time, must be mentioned, along with the first attempts at modernist architecture in Budapest.

VARIANTS OF SECESSION STYLE

The large buildings constructed between 1900 and 1920 can be categorised according to the artistic expression of their façades. The transition from eclecticism to Secession decoration was not abrupt. In fact, most of the buildings from this period bear the mark of both styles, to a greater or lesser extent. During their studies, architects remained attached to the academic style cultivated in schools, but following their graduation, they embraced Art Nouveau style, either through personal conviction or according to the wishes of their patrons. It should be stressed that most graduates in architecture who were working in Central Europe after 1900 were willing to use any style as required. The most interesting example of this is László Székely who, during the course of his career, attempted virtually every style, regardless of the building programme, whether in schools, houses or industrial structures. The adherence of these buildings to Secession with elements of eclectic style is relative. The common elements of these constructions were the handling of volumes, in relation to the street, and distribution of interiors. However, Secession had a broader sense for many artists and can encompass all buildings that have any elements belonging to the style.

With regard to houses, connections with the new style are easy to spot; but in the case of schools, public buildings or churches, where decisions were made by the state authorities, the domination of historical styles could not be removed so easily. The boys' high school in Timișoara was constructed by architect Alpár Ignác in 1910 in neo-Baroque style, while Baumhorn Lipót decorated the façade of the girls' high school in neo-Gothic style. Almost at the same time, around 1900, two large Catholic churches were built in Timișoara, in neo-Gothic and neo-Romanesque style. The neo-Romanesque church, erected in the Roman Square in the Fabric quarter and designed by the architect Ybl Lajos, is a composition that faithfully borrows elements from authentic Romanesque churches. The new Post Office, built in Timișoara by Alpár Ignác (1911–13), an architect from Budapest, is considered by some to be a Secession building, but all its decorations are borrowed from eclectic language, with embossing on the first floor and a colossal order that marks the entrance.

In 1909–10, a reference model of large dimensions was built, based on Székely's sketches, with fronts facing both Trajan Square and Roman Square – the Municipal House – with money invested by the pension authority. The building has massive volumes that seem supple due to the large prismatic corner towers. The architect used medieval elements, with statues representing bears and monkeys, and in the corner, at roof level, a life-size human figure, representing a warrior with mail armour and helm. Female mascarons, entangled in stems – typical of the Secession – and small ceramic plates, resembling chess tables with yellow and blue squares, were added. The composition is free and the architect used different stylistic references to send the desired message. The only rules governing the choice of symbols and their composition were harmony and the artist's imagination.

Another important group of large buildings constructed in the same period in Timișoara are located at No. 9, May Street, in the city's inner quarter. The buildings house apartments and offices. The dominant style here is the neo-Renaissance. The strong embossing at ground-floor level, the tympanums above the windows and the rounded arches are typical of the Florentine Renaissance. In this case, the relationship to Art Nouveau is hard to find. Another example where historical references clearly appear is a building with fronts facing Union Square and Mercy Street: Bruck House (1910–12). This four-storey building displays on the first floor motifs from German Romantic medievalist architecture, built in the Jugendstil manner, while on the upper levels Székely conceived strong, simple forms, underlined by bay windows and an undulating cornice inspired by Ödön Lechner. This combination of folk elements with other decorations is not unique to Timişoara, being used in other Central European cities. Székely also used this combination in the city's slaughterhouse building (1904–5) and the Serbian episcopal palace, where he reshaped the façades.

A building constructed after 1910, also designed by Székely, has two fronts, one facing Freedom Square, the other oriented towards Ungureanu Street. The language used also comes from the previous period: embossing at ground- and first-floor levels, fake pillars with Ionic capitals, and tall and narrow windows. However, the high corner tower and the framework built in the style of Lechner, with undulating forms of the cornice above the entrance, all belong to the Secession. Also faithful to the Secession are the stone-carved bas-reliefs depicting strong athletic male figures holding the tools of various trades, which are placed on the first floor. With regard to the imposing Piarist high school (1907–11) Székely incorporated folk and Romanesque elements. The motif of the attic used there is reproduced by the architect on the façade of the Folea castle and also on a number of smaller buildings. Even though Romanesque elements are used, the ensemble has nothing resembling the atmosphere characteristic of this style, and the relationship with folklore, although visible, is intellectualised and subordinated to Székely's own ideas. The Bochus palace, built in Arad in 1912 by architect Lajos Szántay, with one façade facing the main street, stands out for its large size compared with the much smaller neighbouring buildings. The corner of the four-storey building is marked by a tower and by balconies supported by columns. The decorative elements of the building are mixed: geometric figures, classical capitals and iron fittings.

Buildings decorated in Hungarian Secession style with folk elements are rare in Timişoara and Arad and were designed by a few architects from Budapest who were working there at the beginning of the twentieth century. The most beautiful example is the bank building in Timişoara situated at the corner of Gheorghe Lazăr and Vasile Alecsandri streets, seen from Union Square. Built between 1906 and 1908, it was designed by architects Komor Marcell and Jakab Dezső, who also designed the city hall and the House of Culture in Târgu-Mureş and the 'Black Eagle' complex in Oradea. The gingerbread style with rounded corners gives the building a distinctive air. The ceramic elements made by the Zsolnay Company in Pécs and the sculpted door frames reproduce themes from Hungarian folklore. The simplicity of form and meticulous details create a harmonious contrast. Another building conceived in the gingerbread style, dotted with decorative elements, is Merbl palace in Timișoara's Central Square. The architectural repertoire is similar to that of the bank building described earlier: rounded corners, Hungarian Secession attics with undulating cornices and massive bay windows. The difference lies in the lack of ceramic details and elaborate fittings. The architect, Arnold Merbl, was the editor of a magazine that promoted Secession style and a specialist in this new current.[17] The neighbouring building, Nuehausz palace (1910–12), was built at the beginning of the century, to designs by Székely. The relatively simple volumes are dominated by a large-sized bay window, placed centrally on the façade. Above, there is a monumental attic, which gives equilibrium to the composition. The fine decorations are subordinated to the whole and are inspired by Art Nouveau repertoire, but also recall folk elements. The Piarist gymnasium chapel in Timișoara, designed by Székely and finished in 1914, is part of the ensemble's general composition, being enriched with a slim tower to compensate for the massiveness of the other façades. Romanesque style is referenced in the succession of pilaster found on this tower and on the two smaller ones that surround it.[18] At the same time, the well-pronounced undulating cornice is reminiscent of traditional wooden architecture from Transylvania, a motif sometimes used by other architects of the period and also featuring in the palace building (1911–12) designed by the same architect in Timișoara.

Secession style with geometrical decorations appears in Timișoara, especially on the façades designed by Lipót Baumhorn, an architect from Budapest who worked in the area between the rivers Danube, Mureș and Tisa. His designs for schools and synagogues bear the mark of eclecticism. For synagogues, he used the Moorish style, while for schools, his preferred style was neo-Gothic. After 1900, Baumhorn chose Art Nouveau style for office buildings. His geometrical style was, at that time, original and unique. In his creations, he combined forms of Viennese Secession with original geometrical compositions.[19] In Szeged, Baumhorn created the most beautiful synagogue in Europe and several houses.

In Timișoara, three large palaces were built to Baumhorn's designs. The first is the building of the Timiș–Bega Hydro-Amelioration Society, constructed between 1900 and 1902 on Tinereții Boulevard, on a corner area near the Bega riverbank. On the façade, there are Secession and eclectic elements. The Ionic columns that mark the entrance are eclectic. The Jewish community palace was built between 1905 and 1907. Here, Baumhorn renounced eclectic elements in favour of Secession decoration. The building has well-articulated volumes, with bay windows, attics and towers that mark the entrance and the corner. The typical Baumhorn decoration is plain and geometric, dominated by stylised geometric capitals and mascarons. The Lloyd palace in Central Square was built between 1910 and 1912 and was one of the most imposing buildings in the city at that time. The façade drawn by Baumhorn creates a true kaleidoscope of plain geometric forms, reserved but very interesting and diverse. This composition demonstrates the architect's great knowledge of Art Nouveau language. It is conceived on registries that become more and more decorated, culminating with the monumental attic which is taller than an entire floor. Here, the capitals, columns and window panels are all abstract and transformed into geometrical shapes. The few sculpted human heads are key pieces of the façade, contrasting with the other elements. This desire for abstraction and the search for pure geometric games is unprecedented in Timișoara's architecture. It represents a first step towards total abstraction, which materialised in Timișoara in the following years in buildings lacking decorations.

A particular category is represented by the buildings decorated in floral Secession style. Gheorghe Lanevschi observes that in Arad, unlike in other cities, Art Nouveau made its debut in small buildings, even before 1900. On the two corners of Cloșca Street with the main street, two single-storey buildings appeared between 1903 and 1907, each decorated with artistic floral ornaments. They are distinguished by their elegant simplicity, by the beauty of the decorations and by the harmony of the façades. The direct influence of the Viennese Secession is clearly visible.

Another building with beautiful floral decorations was designed by Emil Tabakovits on the corner of Eminescu Street, in 1899.[20] The floral decorations were carefully made and the iron fittings provided sophistication. Anthropomorphic elements were dotted around the façade. The corner of the building was marked by a tower with expressive roof. Another two buildings raised in the first years of the twentieth century, with Art Nouveau floral decorations, lie in Arad, in Avram Iancu Square. In Timișoara, Secession façades are rare. One is the apartment house situated in front of the monument to Gheorghe Doja on Tinereții Boulevard. According to some researchers, this three-storey house was designed around 1910 by architect Martin Gemeinhardt. He is also the author of 'Peacock House', a building constructed in 1905 in Plevna Square. The façade renders the peacock tail motif repeatedly, along with other geometrical curvilinear elements.

In Arad, floral Secession style is used in Arthur Kovács's house, facing General Milea and Nicolae Iorga streets. The building was designed in 1905 by architect István Babocs and built under the supervision of Lajos Szántay. The composition of the façade is divided on horizontal registries. Its dynamism is ensured by the existence of some bay windows, a corner tower and some spectacular attics. The tops of the pillars are decorated with symbolistic vegetal elements, mascarons surrounded by leaves and sinuous branches. The plaster-shaped window frames are different on each floor. A conical tower is placed on one of the corners of the roof, richly decorated and flanked by two attics, themselves lavishly decorated.[21]

Buildings with anthropomorphic and sculptural decoration are close in conception to those with floral decorations, although they form a different category. The most representative example is the row of three-storey buildings on 3 August 1919 Boulevard, which links the central area to the Fabric quarter. These buildings have plain façades, decorated in the spirit of Viennese Secession. Few motifs are used but they are selected with great refinement. The front of the houses was built from Trajan Square towards Bega River. On the other side of the street lies the Coronini Park (today, People's Park), designed in the same period by Székely. He thought up the whole ensemble, formed of the park, the bridge on the Bega Canal and the neighboring houses, which were partially designed by him, too. The building at No. 7 is richly decorated in a delicate floral style. On the ground floor, the embossing evokes the Italian Renaissance, while on the upper level the decoration is formed of floral motifs. The strong pediments at the corner of the building and above the main entrance each have in the middle a ship's prow bulging from the façade. Some pediments are supported by caryatids, while others, which contain two characters leaning against them, sit on massive lion heads. This building, commissioned by businessman Steiner Miksa, resembles the building of the Hungarian river administration in Budapest, at No. 11 Apáczai Csere János Street, constructed between 1910 and 1911 by architects Karman and Ulmann.[22] The composition expresses symmetry and harmony, while the decorations are more pronounced than in other buildings with floral ornaments. The next house, at No. 5, has a pure Secession 'winged muses' frieze. The feminine silhouettes, together with the floral window frame, form a composition full of finesse and grace. The Steiner house has well-delimited volumes, emphasised by strong pilasters which underline the verticality of the façades and the massive brickwork balconies. The decoration consists of intertwined ribbons and feminine mascarons instead of capitals. The composition of the façade has a lot of vigour, but also refinement.

Another building with anthropomorphic and floral decorations is the former Chamber of Commerce and Industry in Arad, facing Gheorghe Lazăr Street and Dragalina Boulevard. The construction achieved its current form by reconstructing an older building decorated in eclectic style in 1918. The plans were laid by Rudolf Szömörkény, and the bas-reliefs by sculptor Géza Rubletzky from Arad. The building has massive yet simple forms that recall Adolf Loos's houses. However, as a compromise to the taste of the age, decorative vertical strips separate the windows. Apart from these, the only decorations are the bas-reliefs which depict six allegorical athletic male figures, each embodying a different trade affiliated to the Chamber of Commerce and Industry. The façade made from light-coloured plywood is both plastic and expressive. The six bas-relief figures seem to sit, two by two, on plywood pedestals of darker colours. The building represents a moment of transition between Art Nouveau and modernism. Façades of this sort are more expressive than the common Secession fronts of houses in Timișoara and Arad and seem to be inspired by the finest creations of Viennese or Budapest Art Nouveau. The association with the Secession style present in other arts at the time, especially painting and sculpture, is more evident here.

The silhouette of the building is drawn by high roofs, corner towers and large balconies (open or closed), which break up the monotony of the façade. These touches have little connection with either nineteenth-century eclectic style or Secession. Common decorations are window frames, plaster panels, different geometric forms, stylised balusters, bas-reliefs, anthropomorphic or zoomorphic (usually stylised) figures, stylised capitals, statues representing different characters. The repertoire of decorative elements is vast, and the resulting compositions cannot be integrated within a certain style. Many of the buildings designed by Székely in Timișoara fall into this category: the Hilt, Széchenyi, Weiss and Löffler palaces in Opera Square; the Hungarian Baths on 3 August 1919 Street; the little palace situated on the banks of the River Bega (Tudor Vladimirescu Street); the houses on 9 May Street. The most expressive elements on these façades are the bas-reliefs, statues and sculpted female heads.

Buildings without decorations form a special category of houses erected at the beginning of the twentieth century in Timișoara. The most illustrative are those built between 1911 and 1914 by Székely on an island which is surrounded today by Galați and B. Linția Streets and 3 August 1919 Boulevard. With the exception of the Hungarian Baths, all the others are free of decoration, although the window shape is similar to that of other houses of the time. The simplicity of these façades represents one of the first attempts to impose an incipient version of modernism. Their designs were made by architects from Adolf Loos's family in Vienna. The attics are the only elements which break up the monotony of the façades, but even they were not decorated.

There are more houses devoid of decoration on Kogalniceanu Street in the Fabric quarter. These three- or four storey-buildings were raised in the last years before the First World War. It is possible that the lack of decoration could be due to financial constrictions, but it is more probable that it reflects a conscious adjustment to the concepts of the new style that was just emerging in Western Europe. The Secession style entered Timișoara and Arad after 1900, although there is evidence of Secession decorative elements on the façades of some modest buildings in Arad before 1900. Later, Secession became a distinctive sign of houses built after 1900 in the two cities. At first, the options of floral or geometric figures (promoted mainly by Baumhorn) seem to be prevalent. Also, the few examples of buildings whose decorations are inspired by folklore also come from that period (1900–7). The floral style is used both by local architects (Martin Gemeinhardt in Timișoara, Emil Tabakovits in Arad) and by Hungarian architects from Budapest who were working there. Even though it is hard to determine the exact limits between the stages of Secession in the Banat, we can argue that after 1908 purely floral and geometric versions were abandoned. From then until the beginning of the First World War in 1914, architects preferred solutions related to eclecticism. Mixed façades with Secessionist and eclectic elements were created throughout the period when this was trendy in the Banat. Along with eclectic solutions, façades without decoration – in anticipation of modernism – appeared after 1911 as a novelty.

The ornamented versions belonging to different periods are hard to analyse or place in a certain category. They start to lose importance in favour of the more varied and complex volumes which were trying to break the canon, while urban regulations were still demanding the perfect fit for the street front. Pure, unitary façades, having only one type of ornament, seem more refined and have a superior artistic value. The Chamber of Commerce and Industry built in 1918, possibly the last building decorated in Secession style in Arad, displays the change in preference at that time. There is a clear choice from the artistic point of view. On one hand, the forms are simplified and purified, closer to modernism; on the other hand expressive sculptural representations can be appreciated in the presence of the six male figures in the bas-relief. Apart from houses, interesting industrial buildings with Secession façades are worth mentioning. Among the most remarkable were those designed by Székely: the slaughterhouse in Timișoara and the city's hydroelectric plant. The Art Nouveau buildings in Timișoara are today the most representative of the city. Their façades possess great artistic expressivity, and have come to define to a great extent the character of the urban space in this city.

CONCLUSION

The architecture of the Banat between 1700 and 1918 is, on the whole, a cultural architecture inspired by the artistic styles and buildings of the western part of the Habsburg Monarchy. At first, the models were accepted mostly with no changes, but eventually slightly adapted to the space destined for construction. After some decades, European models were more selectively adopted. The transition from Austrian Baroque, provincial architecture, towards eclectic architecture, much more diverse in form and method of expression, greatly favoured this attitude. The stylistic variety seen on the streets of Timișoara and in other cities of the province is characterised, however, by a remarkable harmony. This is because the decorations (Renaissance, Baroque, Rococo) have a common origin and because the urban regulations relating to streets, the shape and alignment of buildings, were strictly respected.

In the 1900s, the styles used for public buildings in Timișoara and Arad were chosen from traditional ones, according to the function of the construction. These were usually classic styles; the Secession was hardly accepted for public buildings. There was a significant unity in eighteenth- and nineteenth-century architecture within the area comprised by Vienna, the Carpathian Mountains to the east and north, and the Danube River to the south. In rural areas, as well as on the outskirts of the cities, Baroque and eclecticism gave birth to a spontaneous classic style created by local artisans by approximately copying the decorations of public buildings. This style was perpetuated until the interwar period in different forms.

The Secession current brought a new approach to the arts in general and to architecture in particular. Alongside common floral and geometric patterns, on the newly built façades decorative elements materialised, inspired by folklore, popular architecture, and sometimes medieval European architecture. Some years after 1920, the neo-Romanesque would become the quasi-official style for new public buildings.

If the village Baroque combined with eclectic influences perpetuated on the façades of rural areas and in the periphery of cities, after 1900 buildings designed by architects became more and more influenced by the ideas of modernist art and by the will to create a 'national' architecture. Interestingly, the cultural architecture of the two centuries of Habsburg domination generated a spontaneous art which endured until the Second World War, while architects tried to create an art inspired by folklore and tradition. Thus, a conflict between Central European culture (rooted in the Habsburg perspective), and the national tendencies of Central and Eastern European people emerged in the 1900s. Starting from 1930, modernism would increasingly dominate architecture in Romania – and in the Banat, too – slowly replacing all the other styles.

The Art Nouveau of the 1900s did not suppress the style of the historic centres of the Central European cities, but initiated a creative dialogue with the neo-Renaissance and neo-Baroque styles. In the Banat, the urban architecture of the eighteenth and nineteenth centuries embodied an image of society, of people's aspirations and their way of understanding culture. The multicultural, multilingual and multi-confessional character of the region, the different social groups that lived in this region, generated a local identity and a common, typically Central European, culture. Apart from social status and cultural allegiance, the buildings, furniture, art objects and other material elements of the urban culture are proof of the spiritual unity of the people from this European region.

8
THE RURAL HABITAT AND THE HABSBURG ADMINISTRATION

Teodor Octavian Gheorghiu

WHILE BEFORE THE INSTAURATION of the Habsburg administration in the Banat, settlements had developed spontaneously and organically, in strong relationship to the natural environment and to the particular characteristics of the respective population groups, after the colonisation and systematisation initiated by Vienna, centres of habitation were conceived upon new urban principles. The network of existing settlements was doubled and partially replaced by ones that were planned and developed according to models which sometimes did not correlate with the features of the particular area or population.

From the urban-administrative perspective, the placement of colonists and the construction of new settlements were combined with the restructuring of old ones. A few trends may be observed: the grouping of several settlements (mostly Romanian) into a single one, designed upon a geometric model; the 'alignment' of old settlements, especially compact ones, resulting in regular structures; the reconstruction, usually on the same site, of some settlements grouped together but with irregular structures; the foundation of new settlements adopting a particular geometric layout (mostly rectangular). There were many situations when mixed procedures were used.[1]

The first phase of colonisation in the Banat lasted from 1718 until 1740. The military governor of the new Habsburg region until 1733, Field Marshal Claudius Florimond de Mercy, divided his time between administration of the area and participation in military campaigns. Using the map of the region edited in Vienna in 1728, Mercy's concerns were to consolidate existing villages and establish new ones. Francesco Griselini, who wrote about the achievements of the time,[2] reported on the Swabian, Italian and Spanish colonists and the new villages of Sânpetru (1724), Zădărlac, Beșenova Nouă, Peciu Nou, Deta, Kudrić, Pișchia and Guttenbrunn (today Zăbrani).[3]

A relatively unique episode was the founding in 1723 of two settlements of Serbs (Nermet and Vodnik) in the Carașova region, drawn there by the existing concentration of Serbian and Croatian villages. Also in 1723, due to the activity of the Banat Superior Mining Office, the revitalisation of mining in the Banat Mountains began, by opening mines, setting up foundries and bringing in different ore-processing plants, as well as by the continuous improvement of the administrative-financial system and legislation, such as the Maximilian Mining Legislation, introduced into the region in 1727. Labour was provided by colonists (mining and metallurgical specialists) brought in from different parts of the Habsburg Empire.[4]

THE STRUCTURE AND MORPHOLOGY OF THE SETTLEMENTS IN THE EIGHTEENTH CENTURY

The old settlements in the Banat which predated the Habsburg administration continued to exist without significant alterations. Those which were colonised (Ciacova, Aradul Nou, Giarmata, etc.) are an exception, proving that important changes could occur as a consequence of colonisation. However, the modus operandi of the Habsburg administration during the first stage of colonisation is sketchily documented. Earlier works promote the idea that the villages founded in this period were not created upon clear urban principles.[5] Only in the seventh decade, during Maria Theresa's reign, were some standard elements for building dwellings and households imposed. However, there is also the possibility that those early urban principles are simply not known.

The relatively spontaneous character of some of the initial colonist settlements is attested in several cases (significant examples are the German villages of Guttenbrunn and Sânpetrul).[6] However, there are also numerous examples of urban configurations with an exact geometry of street grid and lots. The area occupied by the German colonists in Ciacova, who were brought in during 1722–34, and some of the villages mentioned by Griselini (for example, Deta, Peciu Nou, Beșenova and Giarmata) started their evolution with simple rectangular or linear networks of streets.

Regarding the colonists' habitations, a contemporary traveller[7] revealed in 1726 that the Germans arrived in the region after the banishment of Turks, settling in 30 or more colonies. Their two-room houses consist of one chamber and a kitchen. The entrance faces the street and the overhang of the ridged roof is a little enlarged at the front, serving as a protection roof for certain objects and tools. The walls are made of entwined twigs, branches or hemp sticks glued with clay.

Here we recognise building procedures similar to those used for the native population. There is proof that this technique was borrowed from the autochthonous environment, since the colonists 'were not happy to build their own homes, being often constrained to work alongside Romanians who specialised in those crafts'.[8] What we can see is the spreading of this technique to the colonised villages from the plains area, populated by German- and French-speaking people. Furthermore, it is possible that groups among the first colonists that landed in the Banat were temporarily living in reed houses (in areas where wood was scarce), or huts (in the Banat Plain, between the Danube and Mureș rivers).[9] This was the case in villages such as Lenauheim (Csatad) in 1767 and continued until the 1870s.[10]

The second phase of colonisation began in 1744 and ended in 1772, during the reign of Empress Maria Theresa. During this period, the first stage of urban planning continued, focused more on cities and fortifications, but with an acceleration in the rhythm of organising existing villages and establishing new ones. Following the discovery of new and important iron, brass, lead and silver ore deposits, the region of the Banat Mountains was organised into four mining offices and was colonised. Another development was the transformation of the Banat from a military zone to a civil, 'cameral' one in 1751. From then on, ten of the districts were governed by the civil administration and only the border areas (Panciova, Palanca Nouă, Mehadia, and a part of Caransebeș and Becicherecul Mare) retained a military administration. The first governor of the new civil imperial administration was Count Perlas who ruled the region until 1768. Because the area had been dramatically depopulated during the war with the Ottoman Empire, in 1764 recolonisation with Swabians, Serbians, Italians, French (from Lorraine), Bulgarians and Romanians began.

The few high officials who dealt with urban issues (Knoll, Laff, Hildebrand and Neumann) expanded the existing settlements (Sânpetru, Pișchia, Giarmata, Recaș, Cenad, Periam, Sânnicolau, Zăbrani, Aradul Nou and others) and established new villages (such as Biled, Săcălaz, Jimbolia, Iecea Mare,[11] Lenauheim, Neudorf, Frumușeni and Fântânele). Vinga (Theresianopol or Theresienstadt, according to the Viennese Imperial Chancellery) was granted urban status in 1740. The number of families living in the newly founded villages was between 40 and 200. In 1768, when Count Clary was appointed governor of the regional administration, the expansion of existing villages and establishment of new ones began. In 1770–71 20 new villages were created.[12] In parallel, allocation of land according to the number of families took place. Also, the first accurate map of the Banat was drafted, coordinated by Lieutenant Colonel Elmpt.

The third stage of the colonisation of the Banat and restructuration of rural settlements began after Joseph II's accession in 1782, with the founding of six new villages, and ended in 1787. According to the census ordered by Joseph II in 1784–87, there were 565,000 inhabitants in the Banat. Regarding the morphology of the settlements, during the second half of the eighteenth century the incidence of government-controlled enterprises, and clear, standardised geometry in urban planning became widespread. In 1762 the establishment of new villages controlled by the state was discussed, following depopulation during the war. Starting in 1764 (the year the 'Circular' reached the Banat), this generated an effective control over buildings. Both Cothnamm, member of the Hungarian Royal Chamber, and Wolfgang von Kempelen, Court councillor, enforced a technique for organising the colonised dwellings which later made history: house position relative to the lot and street, protected access to the house, etc.[13] According to the official instructions of 1764, it was obligatory to place the house at the edge of the plot of land,[14] perpendicular to the street, in a similar manner to the Franconian model seen in Transylvania.

The vast majority of residences from the researched area adopted this model, regardless of occupation or ethnicity. An imposing barn separates the front and back courtyards, being flanked by stables. In the evolution of the residence, a second house ('new house', *Haus*) is often present, parallel to the first ('old house', *Vorbehalt Haus*),[15] a practice used by Serbians and especially by Romanians. The imperial provisions of 1766[16] determined rules for the new colonised settlements, and were enforced in the Banat around 1770 by von Neumann. The new villages were conceived in rectangular form, having uniform or identical land to the old ones. Francesco Griselini offers important details (the first known) regarding the general plans of the villages, which were usually rectangular (even square in some cases) with one exception which was circular (Charlottenburg); the central area (with church, pub, etc.), the residences (with garden and annexes – stables and barn) and the houses (often having three rooms); and the materials used (especially vegetal knitting and clay used as a binder and plaster).[17]

Also very important was the systematisation (especially after 1770) of some of the villages that the Habsburgs had found in the region. Within the border areas, villages were merged and made into a standard geometric form for military purposes. This was achieved by either encouragement or force, according to the specific context. There were areas (Făget, Lugoj, Podgoria Aradului, the Mureș corridor, the Zărand basin or the Crișul Alb corridor) where the systematisation was delayed until the nineteenth century or only partially enforced. In general, the new rules were clearly not applied very quickly, since the 'Josephine Land Survey' (1769–72) records many villages which were spontaneously organised.

THE RURAL HABITAT OF THE BANAT, 1800–1914

The fourth stage of colonisation extended throughout the nineteenth century and was characterised by a combination of state-initiated and private colonisation. The arrival of some new groups of settlers (Germans, Czechs and Slovakians – all Roman Catholic) between 1823 and 1828, mainly in the Banat Mountains, for mining, ore processing and logging, was among the features of this stage. The first Czech (Pems) colonisation was initiated by the wood trader János Magyarly who founded the new villages of St Elisabeth and St Helena in 1823–25. In 1847, due to the lack of water, the inhabitants of St Elisabeth moved to St Helena, deserting the first village. Further waves of Czech colonisation led to the establishment of more new villages: Bigăr (Schnellersruhe), Eibenthal, Ravensca, Sumița, Ogradena Nouă and Clopodia (in the plains). The agrarian reform of 1854 did not bring about major changes. In the later nineteenth century Czechs settled in Moldova Nouă, Berzasca, Orșova, Caransebeș, Bocșa and Anina as well as in the main cities of the region.[18]

Other settlements were founded in the Banat in the first half of the nineteenth century by Germans: Gărâna, Brebu Nou, Lindenfeld and later Sadova, south of Caransebeș, on the Timiș Valley.[19] From the end of the eighteenth century, Hungarian colonists were brought in (Tormac, the first colony, was founded in 1791; Dorobanți and Mailat, to the north of the Mureș River, in 1819), and this phenomenon intensified in the next century, especially at its end. At that time, they settled in existing villages – Babșa, Bodo, Balinț, Târgoviște, Iosifalău, Tipari, Stanciova, Dumbrăvița, Fibiș, Dumbrava, Făget – where distinct Hungarian districts were organised,[20] while new villages such as Sânleani (1852) and Satu Mic (1866) were founded north of the Mureș River.[21] The Slovakian colonists settled in the Banat rather late: at Nădrag in 1803 and at Butin in 1813.[22] Other Slovakian waves of colonisation targeted the plain east of Timișoara (Vucova, Stanciova, Buziaș).[23] Before the First World War, some new villages emerged as an extension of the programme enforced during the previous century: Călugăreni (Ujvinga) and Variașu Mic (Kisvarjas) in 1910.

Regarding the planimetric conformation of the villages, geometric plans, which dominate the plains areas and the important corridors of traffic, were still used. However, there were also some innovations that contradicted this tendency. Following the building of geometrical settlements which were often indifferent to the realities of the terrain, consumed human energy and resources, and were hard to maintain, at the start of the nineteenth century new settlements, better adapted to the site, were founded. In the Banat Mountains, entire villages of colonists, such as Gărâna and especially Ravensca, were built with great attention to the environment.[24]

Within the same types of uneven land, some settlements were still built based on regular rectangular plans; for example, Brebu Nou, Vucova and Tormac.

However, following the abandonment in 1872 of the military border, followed by the termination of administrative control upon the process of construction, certain irregular conformations of villages were spontaneously generated.

Between 1800 and 1900, residences were still being built in the traditional manner (a mixture of medieval structuring and, to a greater extent, elements belonging to the Habsburg administration), with a tendency towards a compact household, a series of dwellings and annexes encasing and defining an interior space which was mostly or entirely closed. This phenomenon continued in certain areas until the beginning of the twentieth century. We can even speak of a certain normalisation of the types of households, starting in the eighteenth century, the resulting pattern being a rectangular or almost square courtyard (sometimes modified by circumstances) of roughly 400 square metres. The volumes and the materials varied.

The rural habitat in the Banat after 1850 emerges from the Habsburg *Second Military Land Survey* of 1806–69[25] and from the military topography of around 1880,[26] which supply very important evidence of all the settlements completely or partially systematised in the period between the Josephine Land Survey of 1769–72 and the twentieth century. We can conclude that the time limit for the adoption of some principles of traditional habitation is the 1770s (proven by numerous inscriptions on architectural elements of traditional buildings). One of the causes of the abandonment of this typology was collectivisation, combined with industrialisation, which resulted from the shift of population from villages to towns.

Globally assessing zonal realities, the opening idea can be reprised: the traditional rural habitation was a combination of older, medieval structuring and new principles that appeared during the eighteenth century. This mixture is apparent especially at the level of the whole settlement, and less at the level of the individual residences which borrowed more from the models proposed and imposed by the Habsburgs in the eighteenth and nineteenth centuries. The regular appearance of the residences, even within an irregular construction line, is one of the arguments in favour of this statement, the second being a comparison between the types of dwellings archaeologically discovered by Austrian topographers in the eighteenth century and the shape of residences built until the mid-twentieth century.

The beginning of the twentieth century perpetuated the use of zonal typologies, without any fundamental differences. Some new styles are extremely uncommon within domestic rural architecture. If the new settlements continued to favour geometric typologies with rectangular networks of streets, in the context of house configuration, the processes of changing construction materials, of closing the inner courtyards and of house orientation towards the street were accelerated. This is usually common in the plains or hilly areas, up to the valleys that rise to the lower mountain slopes. In the mountainous areas, inhabited by the Romanian population, the residence organised around an inner courtyard existed much earlier, as already mentioned. It is essential to note that these typologies of traditional organisation for the habitat persisted until the Second World War and, in a fragmentary way, until the 1970s.

BASIC PRINCIPLES OF THE RURAL HABITAT

Starting in the eighteenth century, the traditional method of selecting the habitation site in the Banat was augmented by the obligation to use locations imposed by the administration. Operating on a zonal scale, on a different level from that of traditional communities, the imperial engineers could not ignore basic principles; therefore, the network of settlements was naturally situated within the terrain. Moreover, due to the vast hydrographic operations within the western plain, sites that had been formerly impossible to inhabit were recovered; for example, swamps or arid land. New types of locations were tackled in mountainous areas, which were exploited for industrial logging, mining and metallurgical industry. In the Banat, the areas chosen for the establishment of new settlements can be divided into two groups, according to land formation: flat (in the plains areas) or uneven (valleys, slopes, ridges).

Villages in the plains were the most numerous and located mostly in the Banat and Arad (Mureș) plains. Flatlands were chosen for founding settlements in areas such as Lugoj, Lipova and the Mureș corridor. In the western plain, the villages represented 'nodes' of a relatively uniform rural network, created mostly by the Austrian process of colonisation. There were older settlements (Cenad, Ciacova, Recaș and Șag, for example) which were reactivated by the Habsburgs by modernising their general structure. In the rather flat plain north of Timișoara, land eminences were often selected, detached from the context by at least several tens of metres.

Villages in hilly and mountainous areas were placed within the site in a more complex manner. Villages organised in valleys emphasise many water-related systems, with communication paths towards the water or the slopes and at a certain distance from the valley line. Many examples of a single system can be found, as well as many that are mixed. The settlements located on slopes are arranged according to the contour line (there are also exceptions, with networks of streets of orthogonal geometrical structure), while those on the ridge either have regular planes (linear, orthogonal or circular), or adopt the line of the landform, or have an 'agglomerated' form (which I have named 'agglutinated', borrowing a term from biology).

According to the traditional method of organising a settlement in Romanian culture,[27] the village becomes the result of concentric growth from the family centre (the hearth, a centre established in almost all civilisations) to the village border. Thus, the settlement evolves into an intersection of all the concentric circles generated by households, which in the end form a 'wrapping' defining the village border. This model can explain the lack of consistency with regard to the centre in Romanian rural tradition (the settlement is frequently dispersed, spread, unfocused), by contrast with formulas established by the ancient Greek and Roman or the medieval Occidental civilisations: the square, the church, the meeting place, etc.

Another model is centred on the settlement as a whole, grouped around the sacred hearth of the community: 'The life of the community developed around the *Central Fire* of the settlement, in the hearth of the village – it was the place destined for meetings, rituals, or religious ceremonies.'[28] Such a model is commonplace in specialist interpretation. It becomes clear and very important that the traditional settlements, which developed spontaneously, oscillate between arrangements centred on the family home, on the one hand, and the village community, on the other. They often intersect or pass, over time, from one state to the other.

The urban model is another determinant, acting either alongside other factors (in an 'organic', 'spontaneous' type of development) or independently (in a 'controlled', 'enforced' type of development). The model might come from areas close by (from the sphere of influence of a local 'transmitter'), but might also be brought from far away, like most of the new actions of 'urbanisation' of a territory or of colonisation. The European Middle Ages – which in certain areas even extended into the nineteenth century – was a space in which the urban configuration was frequently influenced by such models.[29] The traditional conformation was doubled in the Banat and Crișana area by adopting plans imposed by the Habsburg administration, which were foreign to the area. They seldom correlated with the landform or other natural factors; in most cases the 'model' prevailed.

In the Banat, the relationship between the built-up area itself and what lies outside it (in other words, the way of defining the territory) is not uniform. Villages in the plains (usually compact and resulting from a controlled process, according to a plan) have firm boundaries, preserved up to the present day. Villages in hilly or mountainous areas (due to an organic process of gradual growth) have 'diffuse' and dynamic limits which evolve over time. In mountainous areas, some settlements are so dispersed that what actually constitutes the built-up area cannot be defined with any accuracy; the hearth of the village is confused with its boundary (the whole space being the property which is administered by the community). The dispersion is even more significant in areas with diverse economies (agriculture, cattle breeding, small village industries, etc.) where the settlement is doubled by a 'swarm' of small farms or installations (huts, shelters, strengthened enclosures, mills, sheepfolds etc.) that equip the whole area and make possible the control and the processing of all terrain as well as livestock breeding and some primitive industries.

The relationship between centre(s) and habitation area is important. If the first constitutes the heart of the establishment, the latter represents the rest of the settlement. The centre(s) brings together the essential spaces and community architecture, while the rural dwelling concentrates all the other functions. In this way the village is fundamentally different from the town, the latter separating out its components into economic, cultural, social and sportive functions. In the Banat, the relationship between the centre and the rest of the settlement is extremely diverse. In the plains villages systematised by the Habsburg administration at the end of the eighteenth century, the centre tends to be a space similar to that of the medieval settlements of the region. The marketplace (varying in shape), or the enlarged artery in which the major architecture is found (church/es, town hall, school), can be replaced by simple spaces defined as crossroads (almost always situated in the geometrical centre of the settlement), flanked by large lots on which major buildings are placed. If the first version represents the embodiment of social cohesion, the second is justified by the nature of the settlement and of the respective human group, far from forming a 'community'.

In the hilly and mountainous villages, given the two typologies (geometric and free, irregular), the centre is either the place defined as the geometrical centre of the settlement (similar to the plains villages), the place where directions of further development within the settlement intersect, the place occupied by the church (associated with a significant position vis-à-vis the landform), or the place of the round dance, religious ceremonies, meeting places, etc. Romanian settlements, in particular, do not have special arrangements regarding the centre, that being simply the area around the church (as in most of the villages in the valleys or on the slopes). The Habsburg interventions often aimed at the creation of new centres in a logical relationship with the new area of the settlement, furnished with buildings which formerly either did not exist or were dispersed (hall, school, church). Hence, the relationship between those centres and the rest of the establishment is varied, being determined by landform, history (how the settlement evolved), adopted model or local customs.

Structurally, the villages from the Banat can be divided into two types: discontinuous and continuous (dispersed and grouped-concentrated). Until the eighteenth century, both systems were preserved in the area in differing proportions according to the location. The Romanian settlements were usually discontinuous-dispersed (as perceived by travellers and marked by the topographical surveys of the late eighteenth century), and occasionally continuous-grouped (in a free manner, often leaning towards dispersion), while the Hungarian and German establishments were exclusively continuous-compact.

Beginning in the late eighteenth century, the number of discontinuous-dispersed villages decreased significantly, and eventually they ceased to exist. There are some fragments of such villages in the mountainous areas or in valleys (Bulza, Luncanii de Jos, Sichevița from Clisura Dunării, then Cornișorul and Preveciorul in the Bistra area, Cornereva, etc.). Otherwise, all the villages are continuous-compact (linear, grouped, tentacular), whether or not as a consequence of the Austrian systematisation. Regarding the use of some models (a controlled method of compliance and control), there are two types of settlements: (1) medieval and (2) modern Austrian. The first category is very difficult to determine, but its echoes may be detected in some settlements such as Cenad or Ciacova (with linear or rectangular-compact centres). The second generation of models originates from seventeenth- and eighteenth-century Central Europe. Here, too, there can be different options.

The first and most widespread model is the 'Cartesian': geometric-orthogonal, used after the second half of the eighteenth century. As Francesco Griselini[30] comments on the recent achievements of Habsburg planning, 'the plans of the two villages [Voiteni and Moravița] are not to be omitted, because they can serve as a model not only here, in the Banat, but in any other country'. A second model, the circular one, was only used once, at Charlottenburg, while the third is linear, used for some small settlements (close to Charlottenburg, for example). The last is that of 'lenticular piazza' with several variants (Aradul Nou, Reșița Germană, Bocșa), the consequence of the preservation of a pre-existing establishment partially conserved as a model by the Austrian systematisation.

Numerous villages, due to their location on different sites (horizontal or uneven) or to their evolution at different stages and in different ways, have mixed plans which are combinations of geometrical and free conformations. Similar blends are also observed when some parts of the establishment were compacted or 'aligned' during the eighteenth and nineteenth centuries, while others very likely preserved the older structures; considerable differences of morphology and density are observed between the parts situated along the main road and those on the vertical slopes.

Globally assessing the morphological and structural realities of the villages from the Banat, we can conclude that there are few cases incorporating a single typology. Most of them have mixed methods of organisation, due to ethnic factors, the diverse natural environment, or to historical evolution. There are some combinations of six or seven types (with reference only to those studied here) and frequent combinations of four or five types. Those of six or seven types belong mainly to the mountainous or pre-mountainous areas or, in a wider evaluation, to those with complex natural morphologies. To give an appropriate image, their variety can be expressed by calculating the mathematical formula of combinations of two, three or four types, which gives an impressive number of variants The same variety is observed by analysing the parcels and the structure of the household, the final conclusion confirming the initial impression of complexity and diversity.

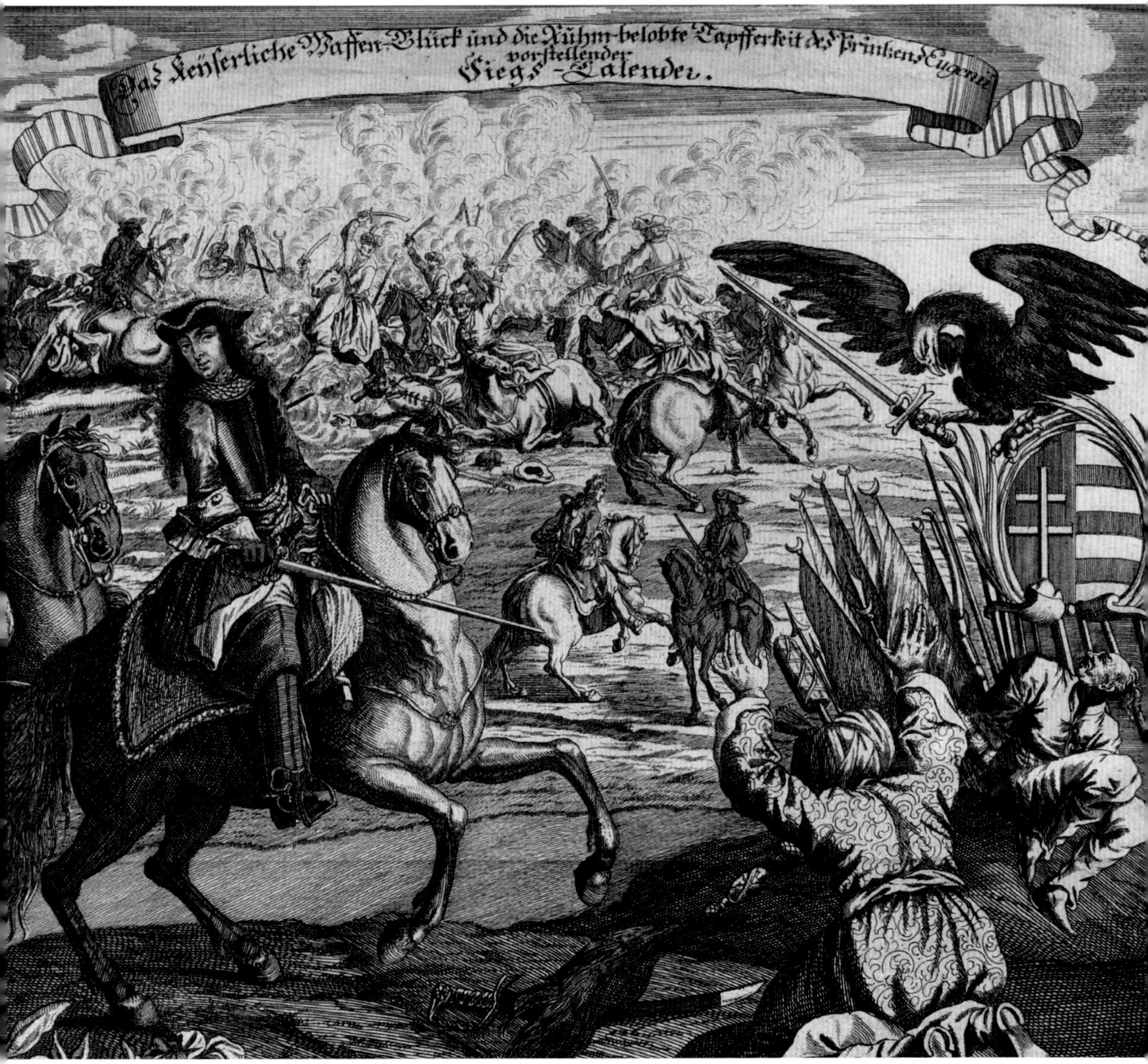

Plate 1
Prince Eugene of Savoy (1663–1736) on horseback, detail of engraving (*c*.1717). The German text reads: ‘The calendar of victory which represents the fortune of the imperial arms and the reputed bravery of Prince Eugene.’

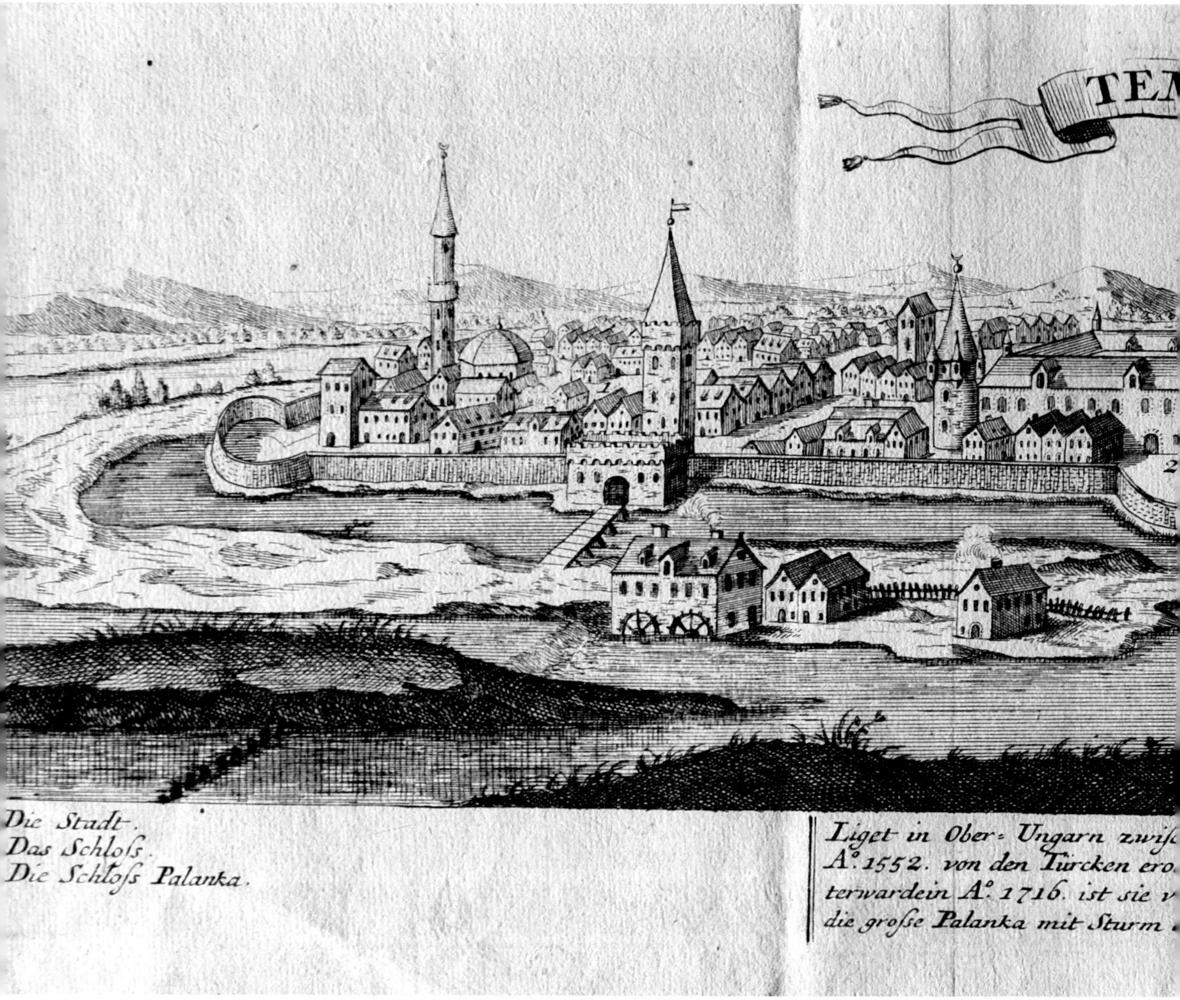

Plate 2 *(above)*
Temeswar (Timișoara), engraving (1721). The German text reads: 'Timișoara: in upper Hungary, between the Danube and the Transylvania Region. In 1552 it was conquered by the Turks, after the battle of Petrovaradin; in 1716 it was besieged by the (Austrian) imperial army and on 1 October the Great Palisade was conquered. On 12 October the city and the castle [were conquered] after an agreement.'

Plate 3 *(right)*
Medals by Georg Hautsch et al., commemorating the victories of the Habsburg Empire on the battlefields of Slankamen (1691) and Senta (1697)

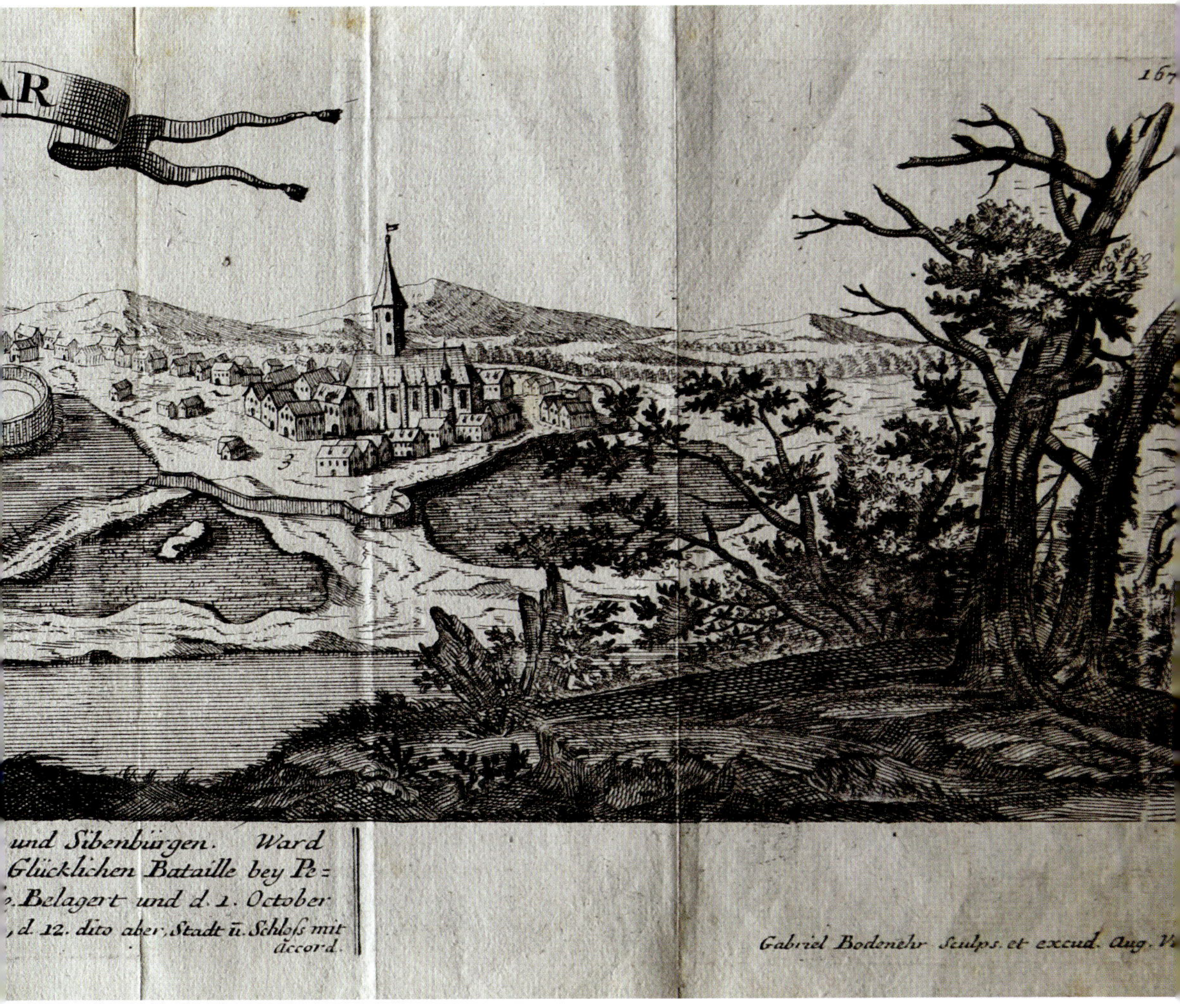
167
R
und Sibenbürgen. Ward
Glücklichen Bataille bey Pe=
. Belagert und d. 1. October
, d. 12. dito aber, Stadt ū. Schloss mit
accord.
Gabriel Bodenehr Sculps. et excud. Aug. V

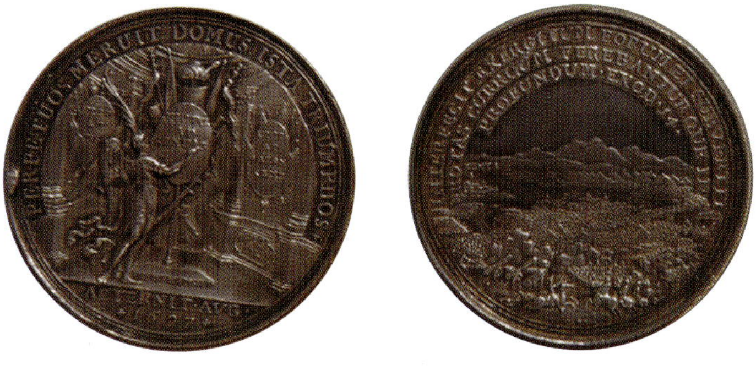

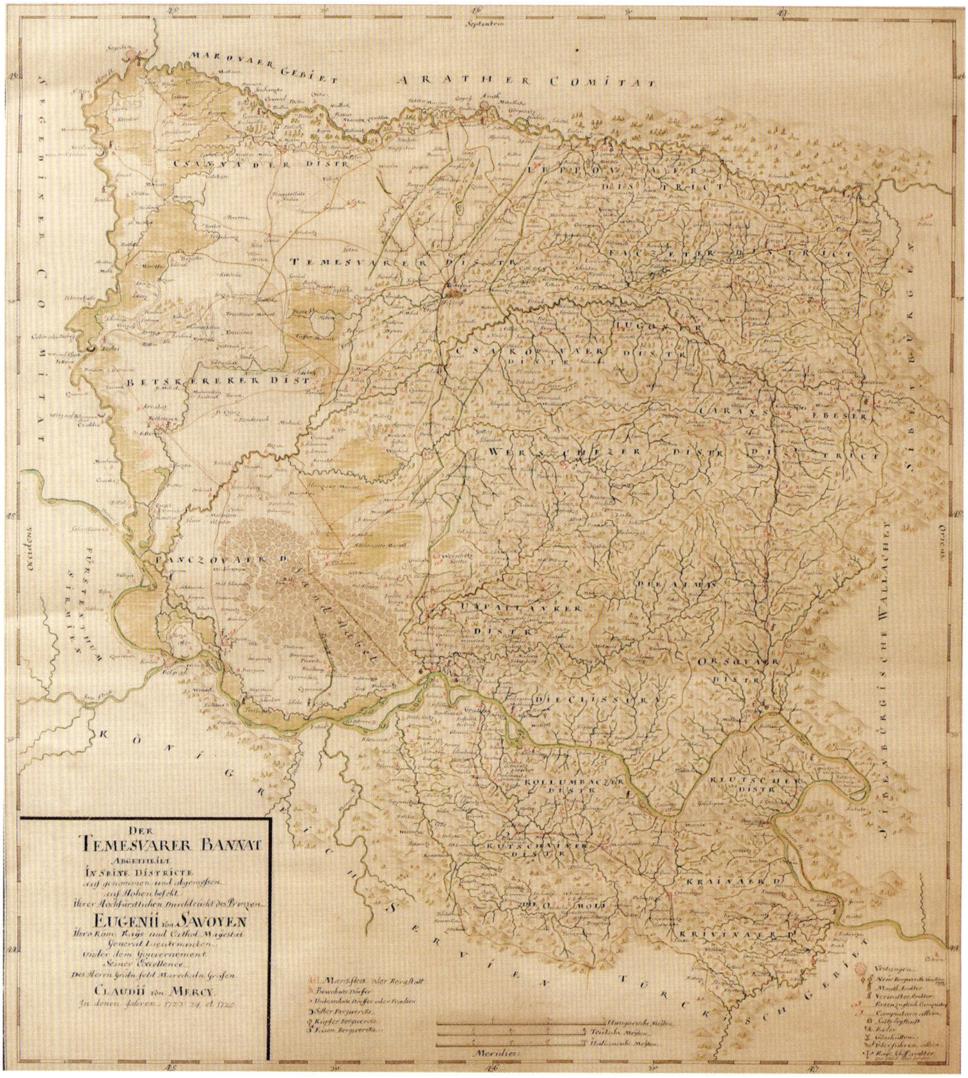

Plate 4 *(above)*
Map of the Banat of Timișoara (1723–5), comissioned by Eugene of Savoy and Claude Florimond de Mercy

Plate 5 *(right)*
Prince Eugene of Savoy after the battle of Belgrade on 16 August 1717, oil on canvas (1718), by Jacob van Schuppen (1670–1751)

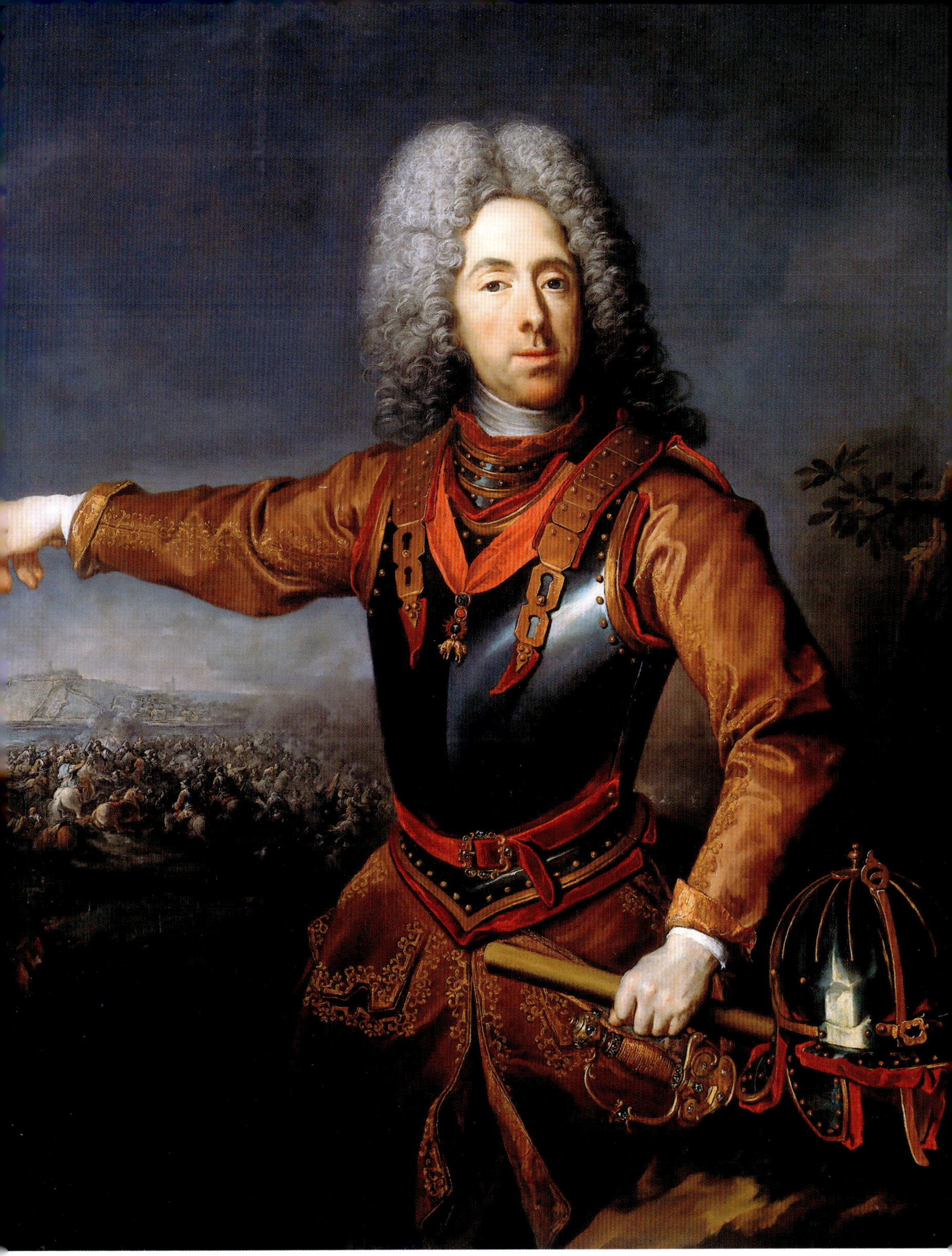

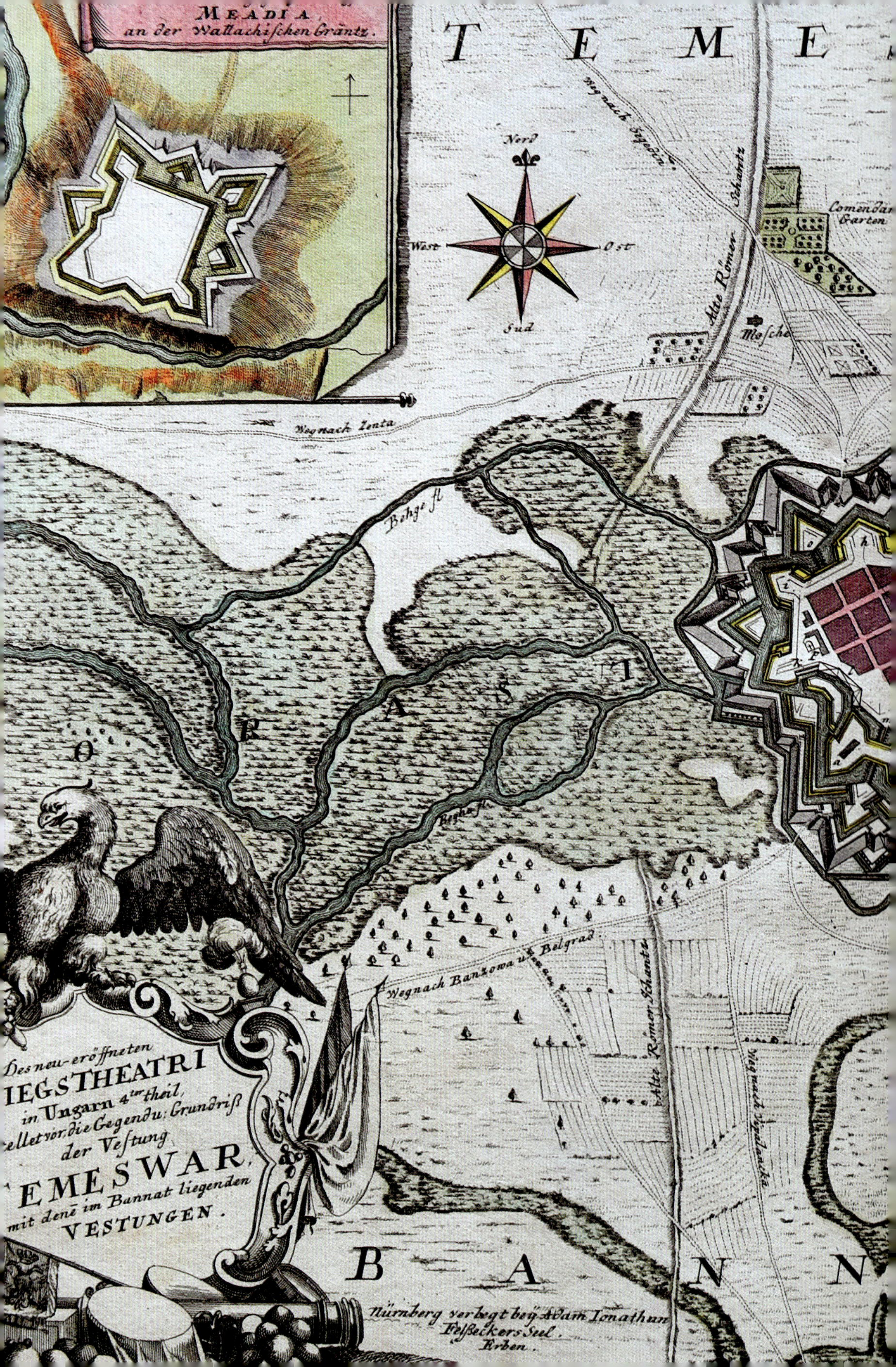
MEADIA
an der Wallachischen Grantz
TEMES
Nord
West
Ost
Sud
Comendant Garten
Alte Römer Schantz
Wegnach Segedin
Mosche
Wegnach Zonta
Behge fl.
BASTI
ORA
Begha fl.
Wegnach Banzowa u. Belgrad
Alte Römer Schantz
Wegnach Lipa
Des neu-eröffneten
IEGSTHEATRI
in Ungarn 4ter theil,
ellet vor, die Gegend u: Grundriß
der Vestung
EMESWAR,
mit denē im Bannat liegenden
VESTUNGEN.
BANN
Nürnberg verlegt bey Adam Jonathan Felßeckers seel. Erben

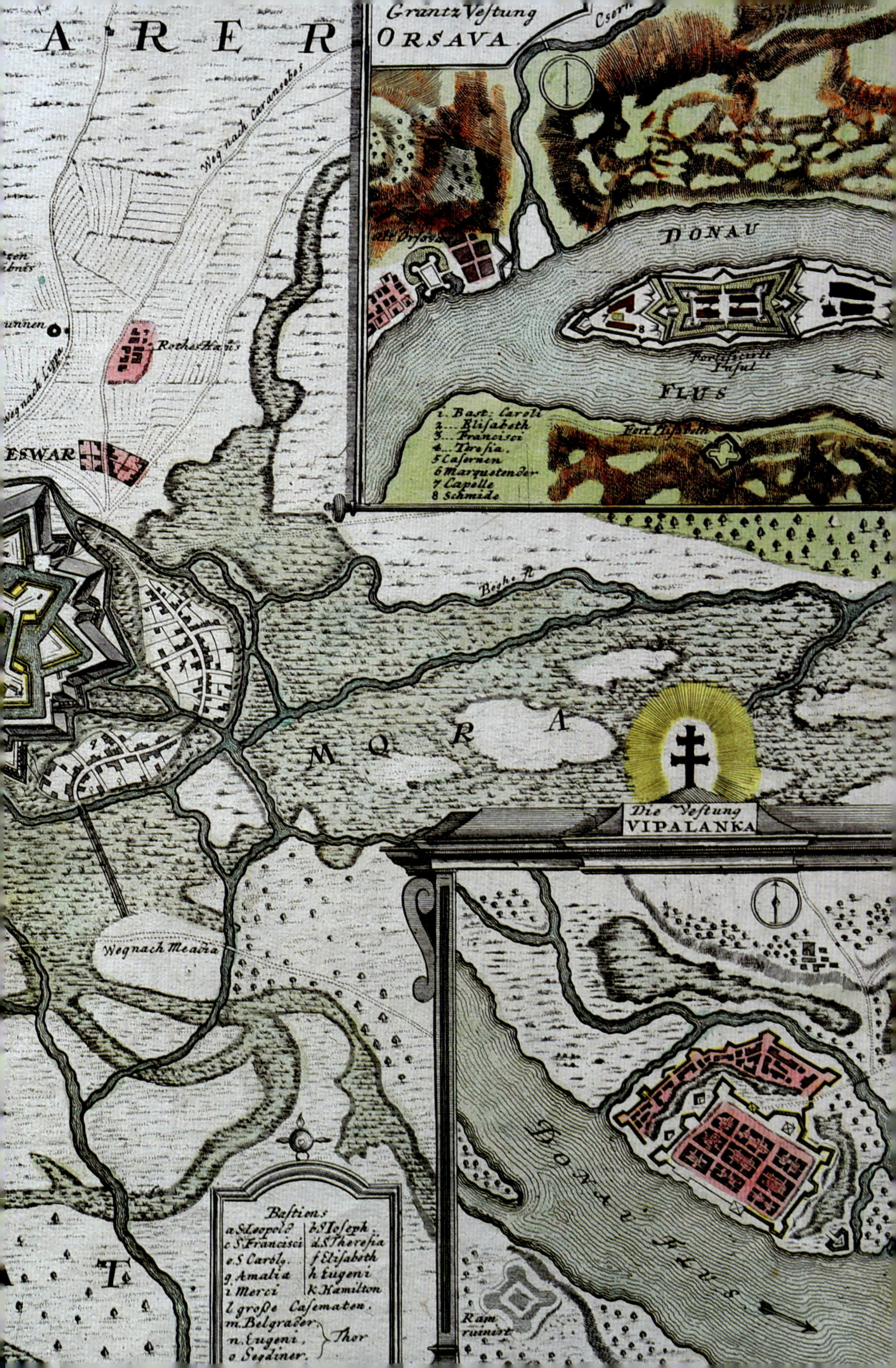
A R E R
Grantz Vestung
ORSAVA
DONAU
FLUS
1. Bast: Caroli
2. ... Elisabeth
3. ... Francisci
4. ... Teresia.
5 Casernen
6 Marquetender
7 Capelle
8 Schmide
Weg nach Caransebes
Rothes Haus
ESWAR
M O R A
Die Vestung
VIPALANKA
Weg nach Meadia
Bastions
a S. Leopold
b S. Ioseph
c S. Francisci
d. S. Theresia
e. S. Carol.
f Elisabeth
g. Amalia
h Eugeni
i Merci
K Hamilton
l große Casematen.
m. Belgrader
n. Eugeni,
o Segdiner.
Thor
DONAU FLUS

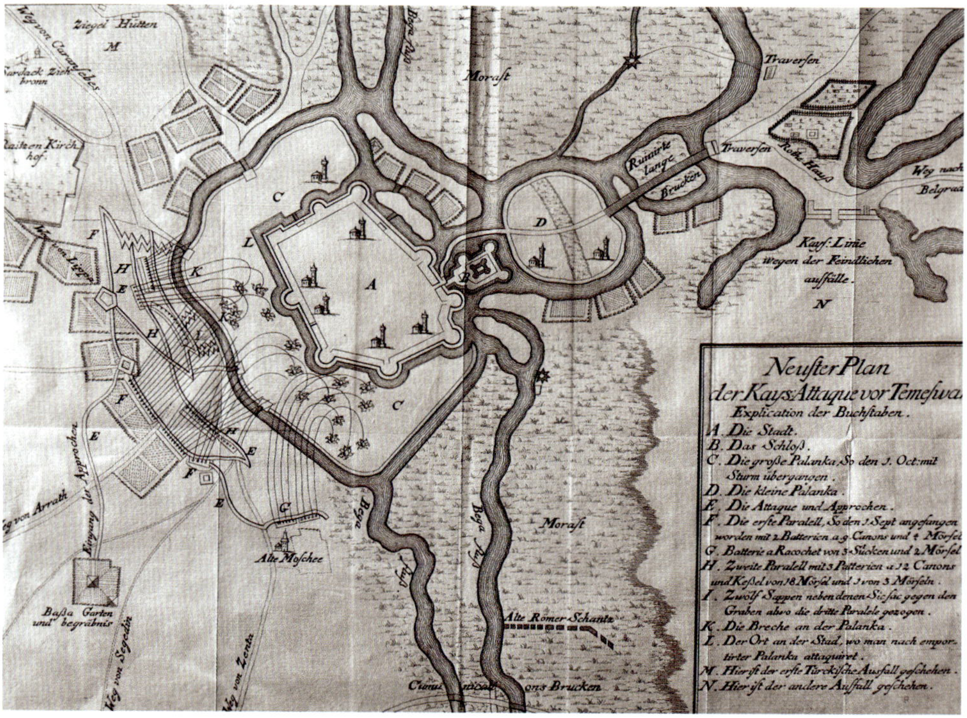
Ziegel Hütten
Raitzen Kirch hof
Morast
Traversen
Ruinirte lange Brucken
Traversen Roth Hauss
Belgrad
Kays: Linie wegen der Feindlichen ausfälle.
Alte Moschee
Bassa Garten und begräbnis
Alte Römer-Schantz
Weg von Segedin
Weg von Zenta
Weg von Arrath
Eingang der Approchen
Bega
Neuster Plan
der Kays: Attaque vor Temeswar
Explication der Buchstaben.
A. Die Stadt.
B. Das Schloß.
C. Die große Palanka, So den 1. Oct: mit Sturm übergangen.
D. Die kleine Palanka.
E. Die Attaque und Approchen.
F. Die erste Paralell, So den 1. Sept angefangen worden mit 2 Batterien a 9 Canons und 4 Mörsel
G. Batterie a Racochet von 3 Stücken und 2 Mörsel
H. Zweite Paralell mit 3 Batterien a 12 Canons und Keßel von 18 Mörsel und 1 von 3 Mörseln.
I. Zwölf Sappen neben denen Sie sich gegen den Graben alwo die dritte Paralele gezogen.
K. Die Breche an der Palanka.
L. Der Ort an der Stad, wo man nach emportirter Palanka attaquiret.
M. Hier ist der erste Türckische Ausfall geschehen.
N. Hier ist der andere Ausfall geschehen.

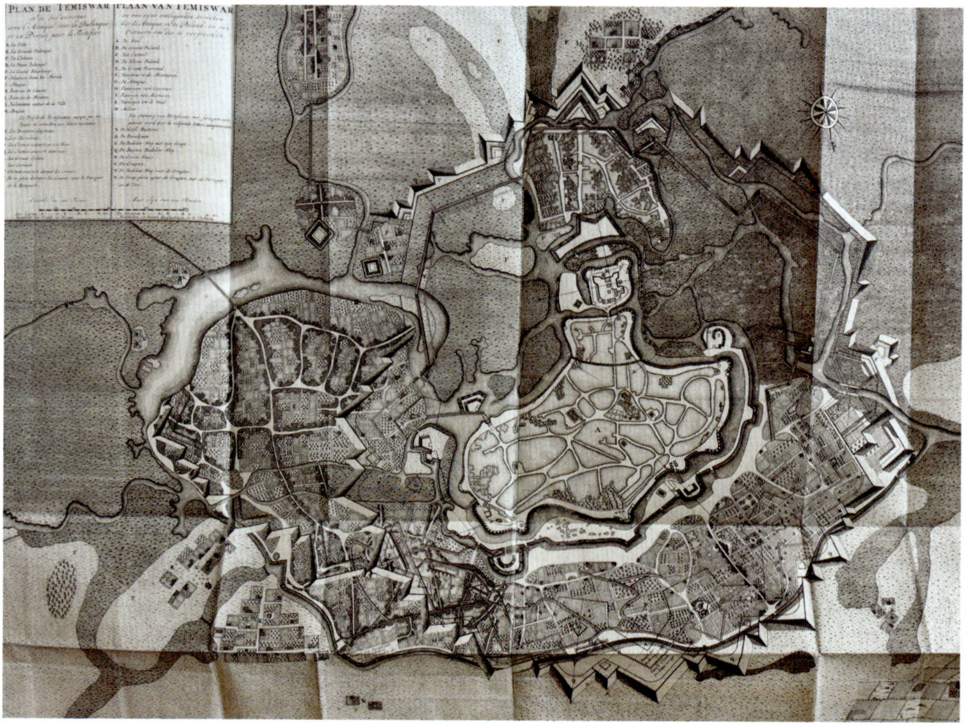
PLAN DE TEMISWAR
PLAAN VAN TEMISWAR

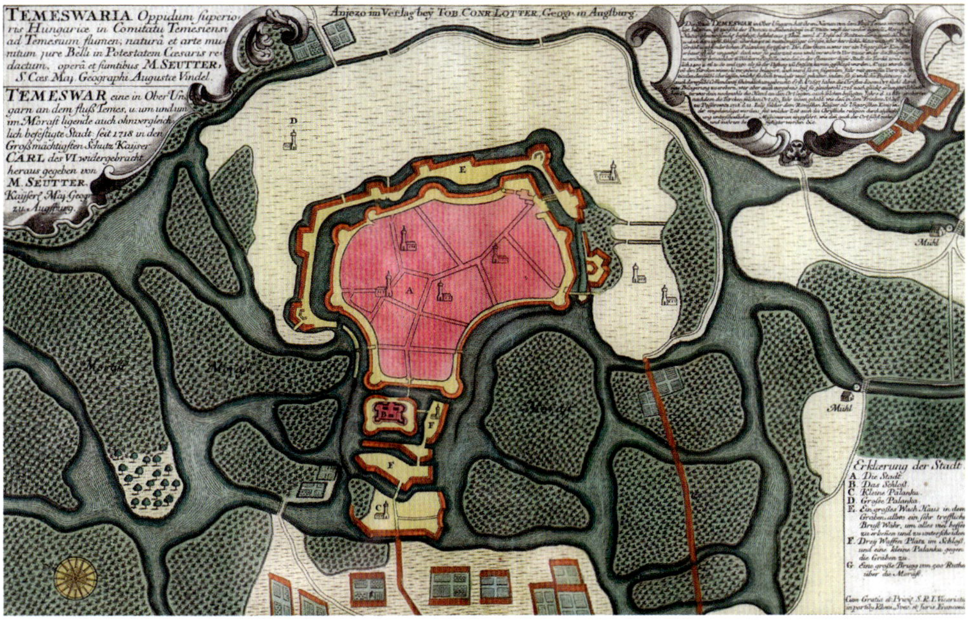

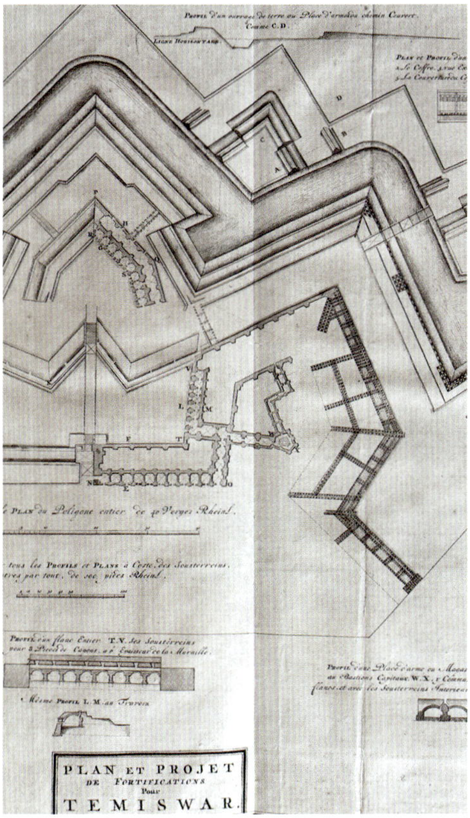

Plate 6 *(previous pages)*
Temeswarer Bannat (the Banat of Timișoara), engraving (*c.*1720), published in Nuremberg by Adam Ionathan Felßeckers Seel. Erben.

Plate 7 *(opposite, top)*
'The Latest Plan for the Attack on Timișoara', detail of engraving (1718)

Plate 8 *(opposite, bottom)*
City plan of Temiswar (Timișoara), engraving (1729)

Plate 9 *(above)*
Map and general view of the city of Temeswar (Timișoara), engraving (1729)

Plate 10 *(left)*
Plan and fortifications project/designs for Temiswar (Timișoara), engraving (1729)

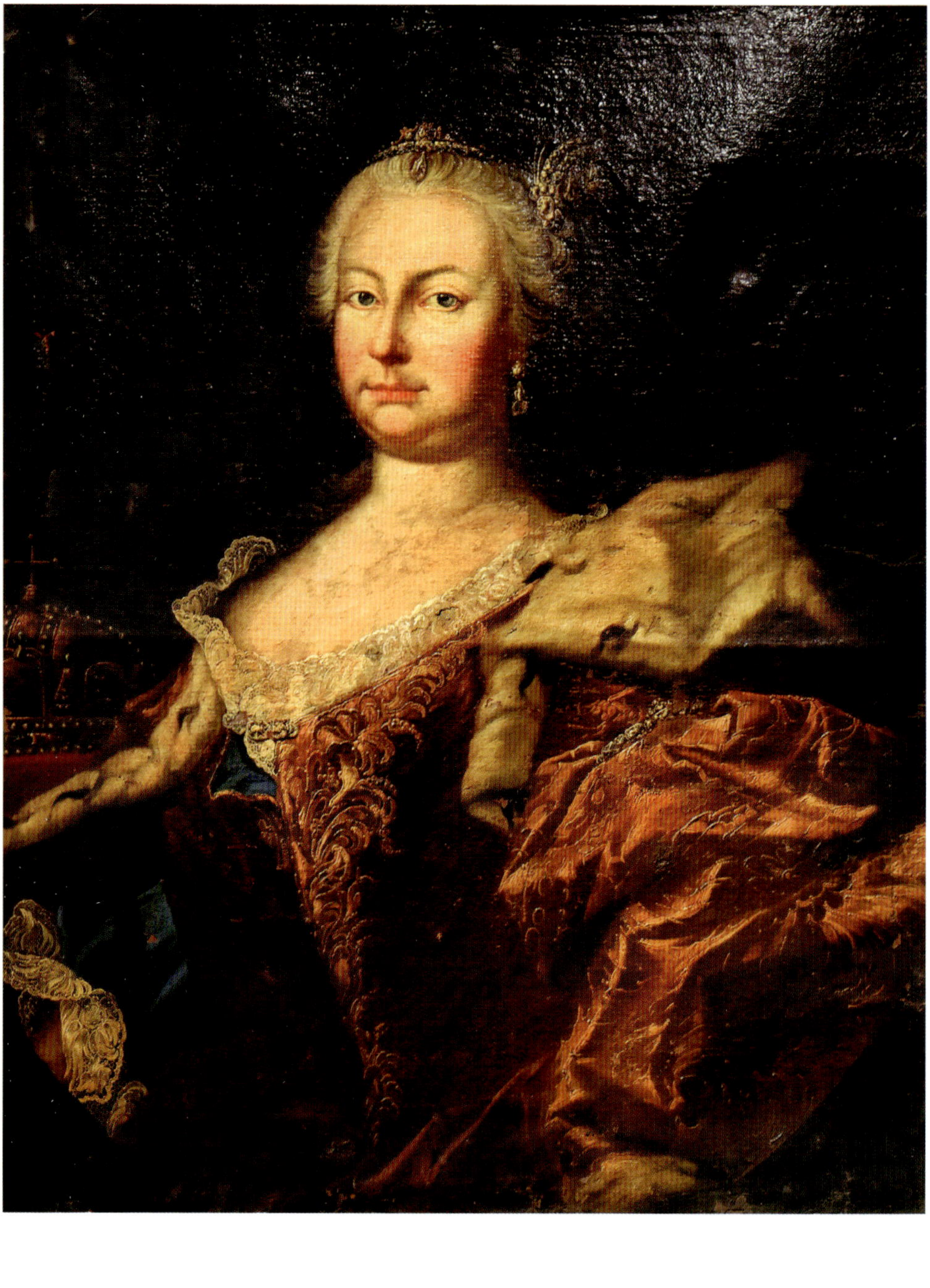

Plate 11 *(above)*
Portrait of Empress Maria Theresa (1717–80), oil on canvas, artist unknown

Plate 12 *(right)*
Portrait of Emperor Joseph II (1741–90), oil on canvas, artist unknown

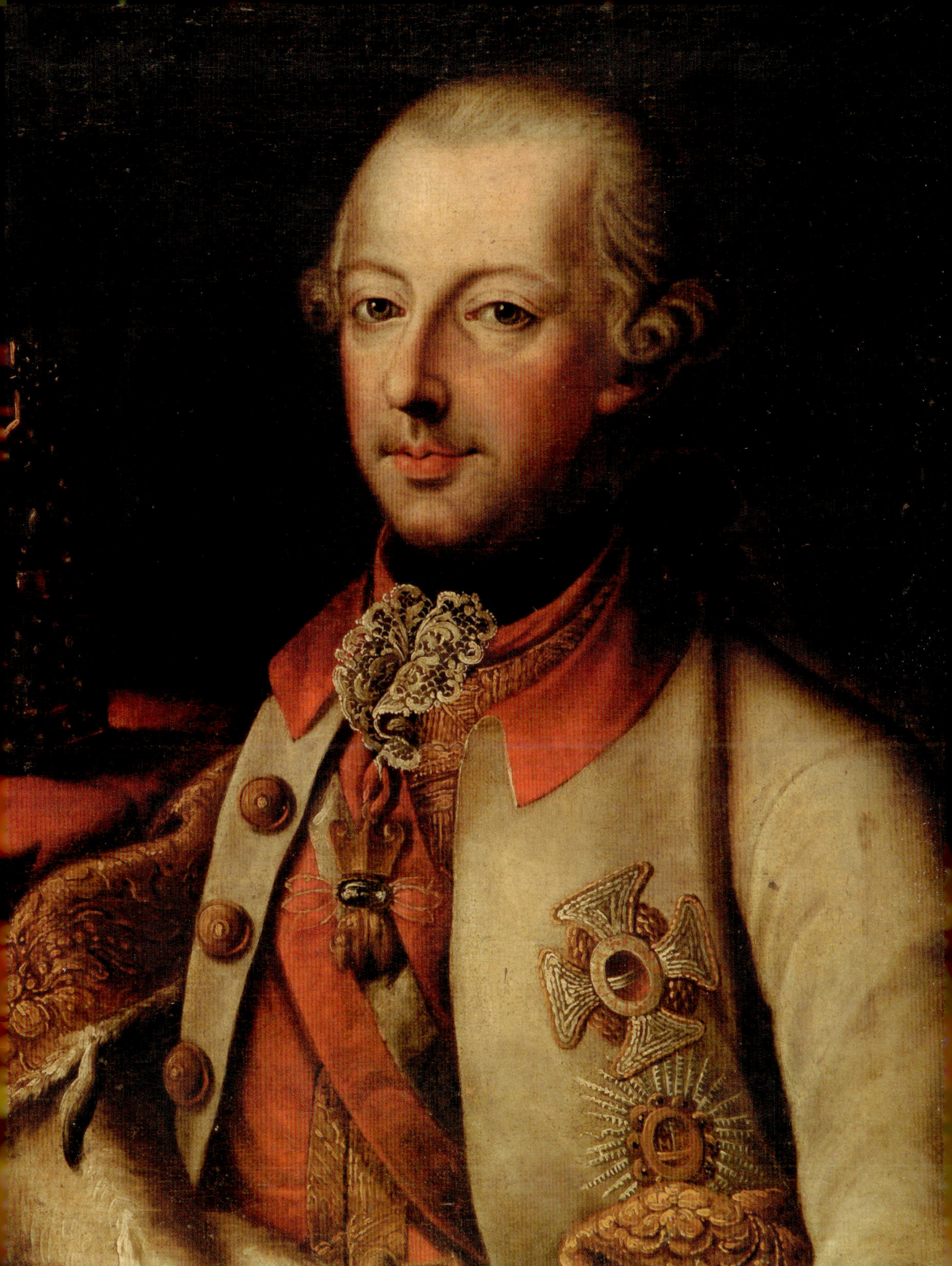

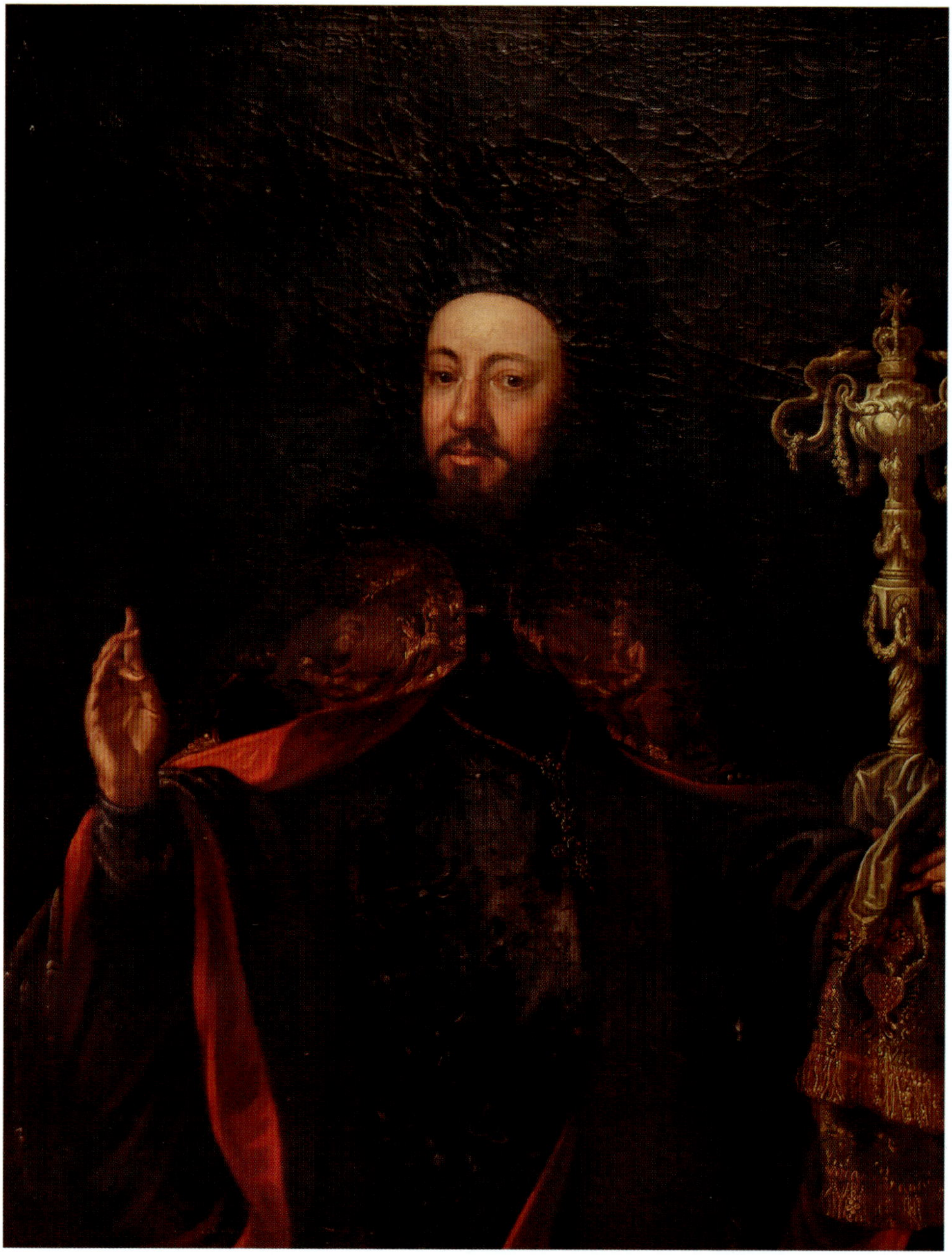

Plate 13 *(above)*
Portrait of Bishop Vikentije Iovanovici Vidak (1730–80) by Teodor Ilić Češljar (1746–93), oil on canvas

Plate 14 *(right)*
Portrait of Bishop Adalbert Eusebius von Falkenstein (1671–1739), artist unknown, oil on canvas

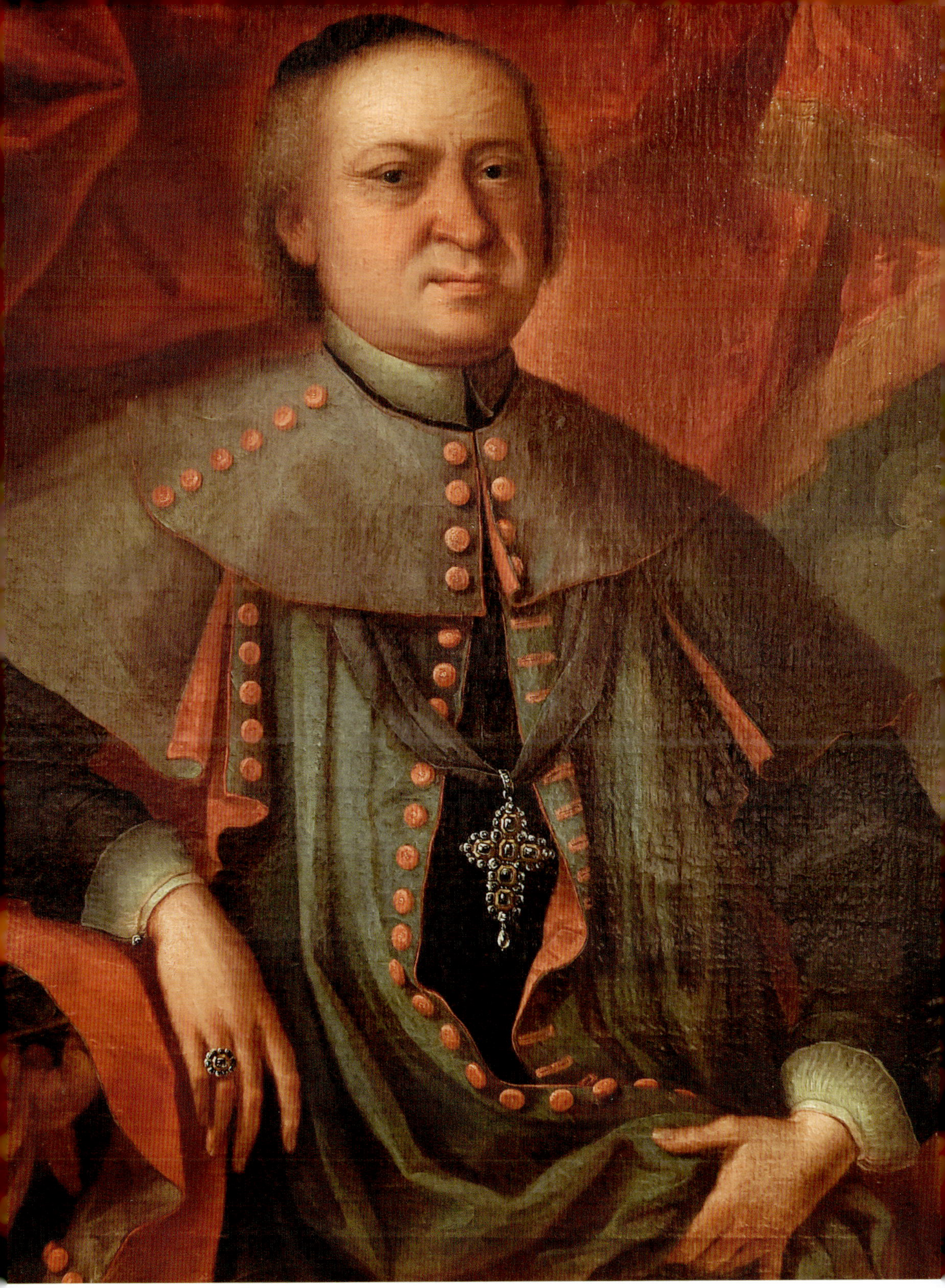

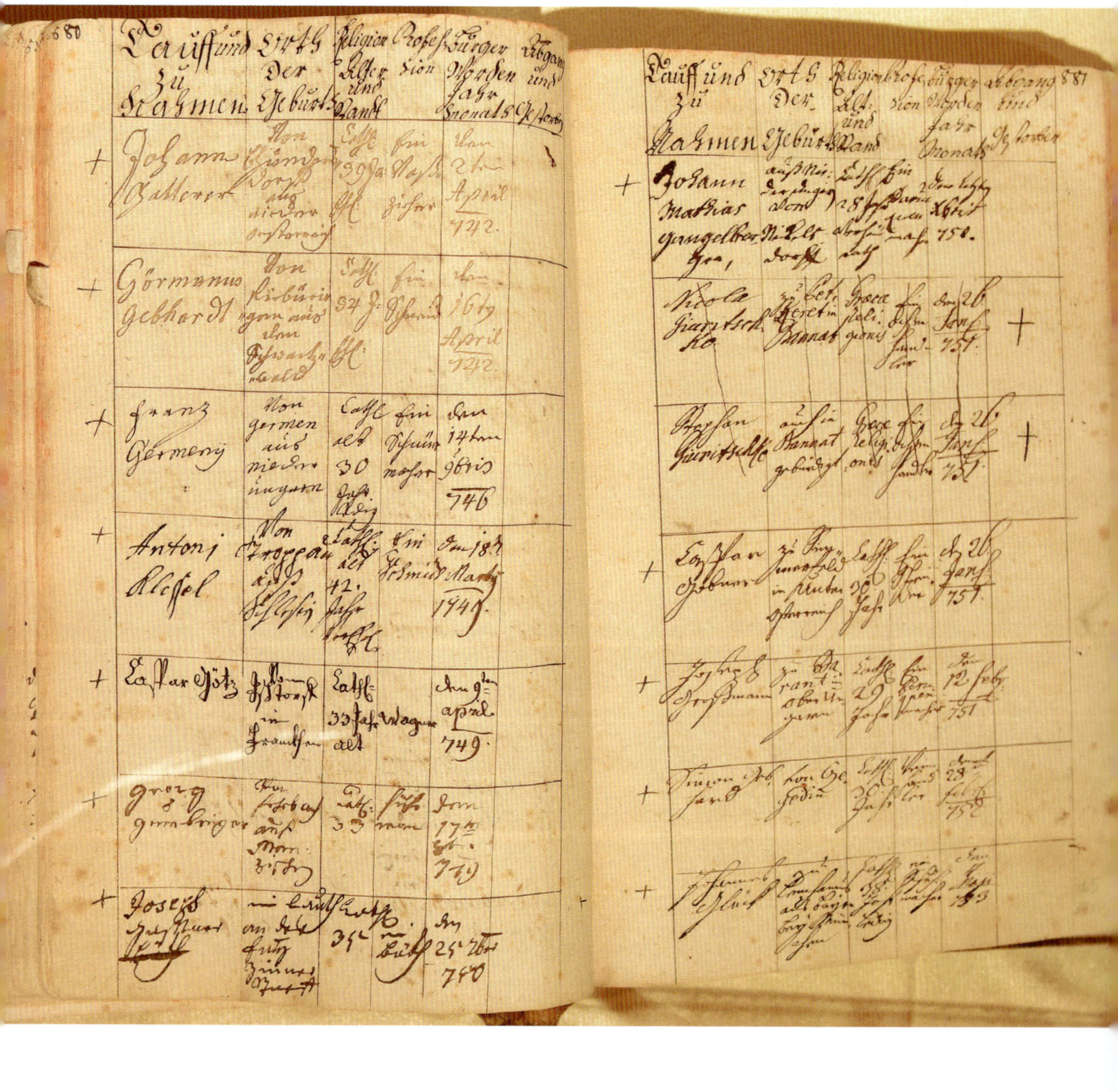

Plate 15 *(above)*
Catastrum Civium, the register book of all residents of Timișoara in the 18th century

Plate 16 *(right)*
The Battle of Petrovaradin (now Novi Sad), 5 August 1716, engraving by C. Benoist, with chisel and needle

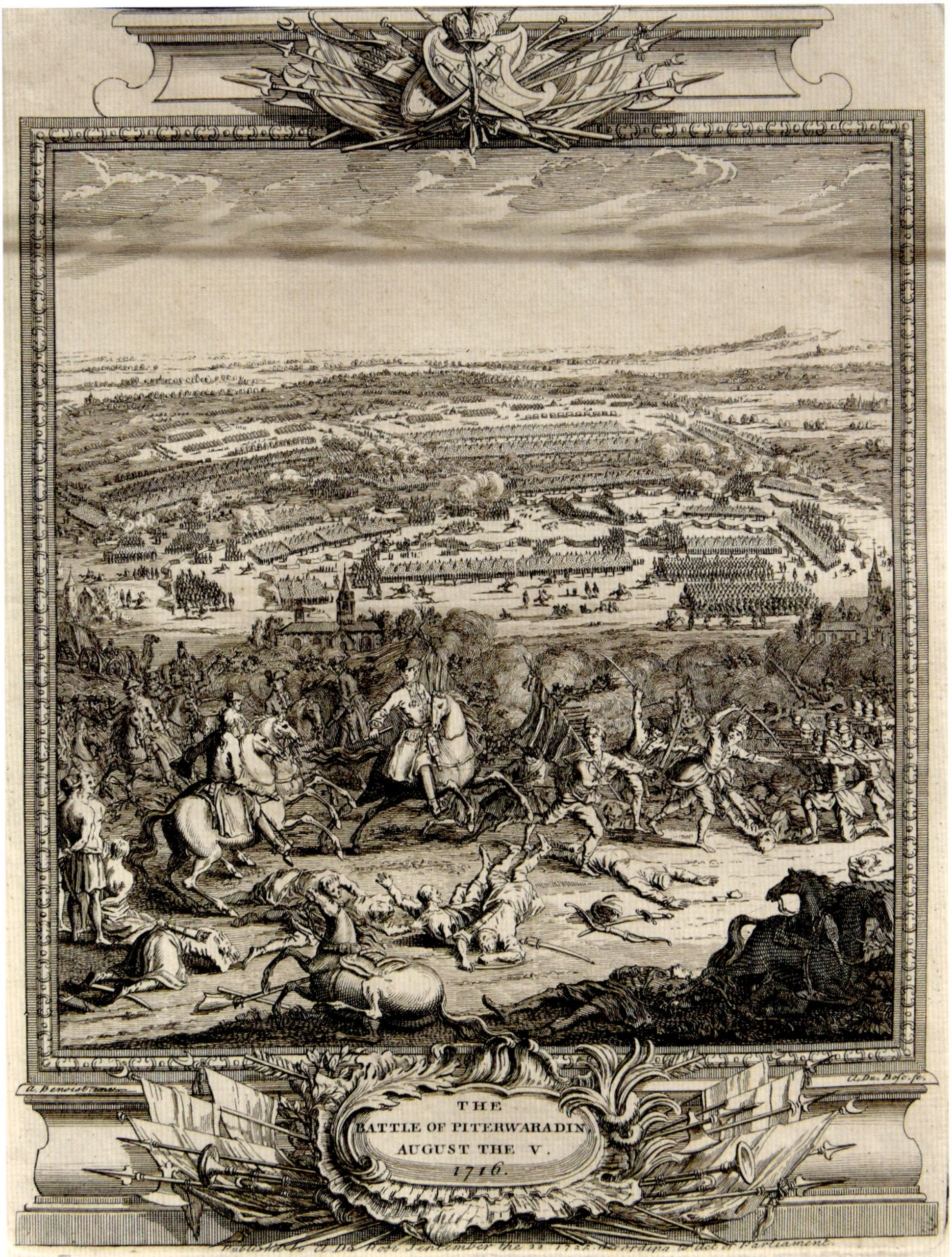
A. Benoist
A. Du Bosc fe.
THE
BATTLE OF PITERWARADIN
AUGUST THE V.
1716.

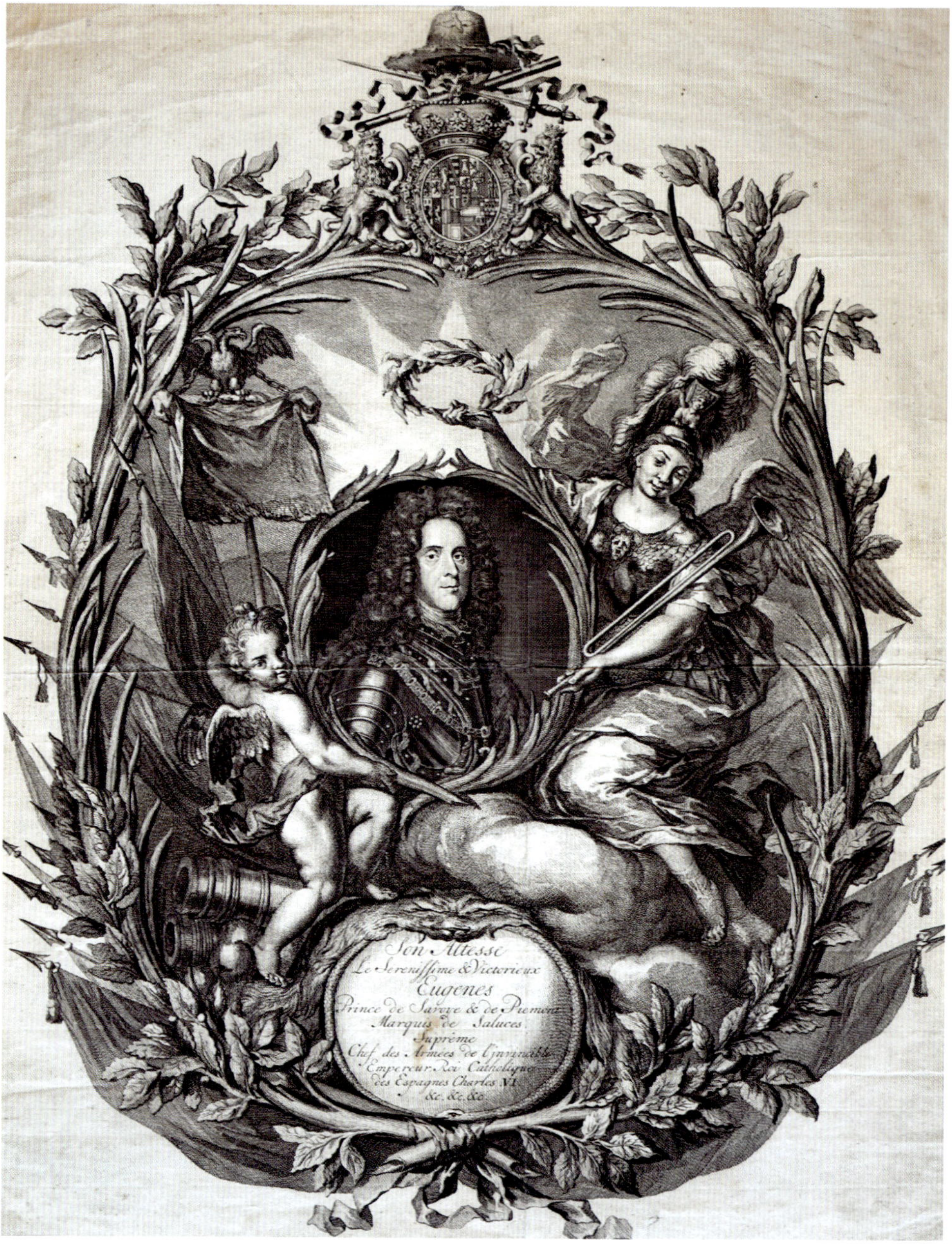

Plate 17
His Serene Highness, Eugene, Prince of Savoy (1663–1736), engraving, artist unknown

9

REGIONAL CHARACTERISTICS OF BAROQUE ART IN THE BANAT[1]

Mihaela Vlăsceanu

CHARACTERISTICS OF THE EUROPEAN BAROQUE

The Baroque may be considered one of Europe's first cultural movements. It is an artistic expression of the profound changes that occurred – in mentalities and in political and social life – following the Age of Discovery and the Scientific Revolution. A defining feature of the eighteenth century, from an artistic perspective, is the diversity of styles. Different stylistic concepts, from Baroque to Neoclassical, realist and academicist, were blended within an artistic universe in which the collective imaginary was fundamental. The visual and formal accents of the Baroque, traditional topics such as mythology, portraiture and ecclesiastical art, acquired new artistic values as a result of the naturalist vision introduced by this style. The human emotional registry was enriched by a new spiritual feeling, from the exaltation of religiosity and acceptance of the arbitrary nature of divine power to the re-evaluation of the ancient phrases *carpe diem* and *memento mori*. According to Jean-Baptiste Dubos, art became a medium of communication and persuasion, for 'out of all the talents that allow us to influence other people, the greatest is not superiority of mind and knowledge, but the talent to emotionally affect them as we desire'.[2]

According to Jan Bialostocki,[3] it is not that the Baroque was European, but that the entire eighteenth century was Baroque in the way in which it manifested itself in different styles through the evolution of art and architecture which defined the general sociocultural phenomenon. It is a phenomenon which has shown its influence upon media beyond those from which it was born, overcoming its spatial and temporal limits.[4] John Rupert Martin observed, 'we must grant that a single baroque *style* does not exist: on the contrary, one is almost tempted to speak of the very diversity of styles as one of the distinguishing features'.[5] Through the demands it imposes, the Baroque recurs in different stylistic contexts of universal art, a 'historical constant', according to Jean-Philippe Minguet,[6] or the first modern European sensitivity, as stated by Alois Riegl.[7] The artistic expression of the European continent spanning two centuries, the Baroque defines a period of liberation of thought and creation[8] from the ideological landmarks of the previous era. Baroque art is closer to the soul of the believer, reflecting his/her religiosity. The symbolic values within which it operates transformed this style into a reaction to the secularisation of Renaissance art.

In historiography, the Baroque was viewed in both positive and negative terms, like other stylistic notions that have been born out of negative aesthetic definitions, such as Gothic or Mannerism. The decryption of the positive values of the Baroque belongs to Heinrich Wölfflin, who was the first to define an autonomous position for this style in history.[9] Among historians, there were also many critics of the Baroque. Jacob Burckhardt,[10] for example, contested the artistic value of the style that marked the eighteenth century, considered it a 'wild Renaissance': Baroque architecture speaking in the same language as that of the Renaissance, but with a wild dialect.[11]

As with the Renaissance and its local variants, in the case of Baroque style we can speak of *Baroque* and *Baroques*, with direct reference to its local variants and styles. As the art of the Counter-Reformation and of enlightened despotism, the Baroque could not be unitary, since these two phenomena were not present across the whole of Europe. We can speak of two different directions of the style: an opulent Baroque that celebrated the triumph of the Roman Catholic Church over Protestantism and a late Baroque, *Spätbarock*,[12] representing the transition to Neoclassicism. Alois Riegl separates local and provincial variants from the Italian Baroque, regarding the Viennese Baroque as a local, original branch of the Italian.[13] The Baroque of the Banat can be expressed as an emanation of the Viennese Baroque of the early eighteenth century, a period in which the balance of power in Eastern Europe changed in favour of the Habsburg monarchy.

THE ARRIVAL OF BAROQUE ART IN THE BANAT

The theory of 'cultural corridors', formulated by Răzvan Theodorescu[14] for the area of South-East Europe, has been developed and applied by Victor Neumann[15] to Central Europe, and has created the necessary framework for a complex understanding of the history of the Banat, starting in the Middle Ages and continuing to the threshold of the modern age. Its geographical setting was along the 'Occidental cultural corridor', in which ideas and cultural facts easily penetrated, initially from Byzantine-Balkan centres and later from those of Central Europe. Interregional traffic added to this, for instance relationships with Bohemia, Dalmatia, Transylvania, Partium, Bucovina and Wallachia. This explains why the Banat could boast a true 'synthesis of civilisation',[16] integrating different but convergent cultural codes. Baroque art in the Banat, as a collection of forms and contents, evolved into a unique experience, a late expression of emancipation from previous artistic dogmas.

In the eighteenth century, following the integration of the Banat within the Habsburg monarchy, Viennese policies, aimed at reducing gaps in development between the periphery and the centre, also were applied to this province. These strategies complied with the ideas of French absolutism, which were absorbed by most European monarchies.[17] The Banat became part of the Austrian state in 1718, when the Treaty of Passarowitz established the new form of autonomous organisation as an imperial possession (*Kronland*), having its capital at Timișoara. This situation differentiated the Banat from Transylvania and Hungary, because here conditions of privilege and lands owned by the nobility did not exist and the Habsburgs were free to reorganise the province from scratch.

In the Banat, the Baroque arrived only in the third decade of the eighteenth century, shaping itself as a late version of the European style, with academicist values. The Baroque in the Banat is an expression of the Enlightenment and not of the Counter-Reformation, defined by an unprecedented general renewal, and by opposition to the dogmas, superstitions and biases typical of the Middle Ages. Reason took precedence in the new form of organisation for the province, generating a social, political, economic and cultural-artistic order that mirrored the Central European model. In Baroque art, the form was modified and adapted to an interpretation that becomes, in the eighteenth century, a *sensus allegoricus*. This concept can be observed from the beginning of the province's transformation into an imperial possession, with all the reforms enforced by the new Christian power in full territorial expansion. Right after the conquest, 'building mania' (*Bauwut*) would change the appearance of the province; genuine architectural programmes were launched, modeled on the imperial capital of Vienna.

Interested in attracting a greater number of believers, Catholic religious orders entered the new imperial province. Jesuits, Bosnian Franciscans, Piarists and Misericordians founded new monasteries and schools for their respective orders. The central model was largely reproduced, in all areas, on a scale appropriate to the province of the Banat. With regard to spiritual life, the Catholic orders had the task of enforcing new norms and forms. Politically and economically motivated, the measures undertaken in 'the Crown domain' with its capital in Timișoara were embodied in a complete official urban programme, developed in military and religious architecture, in sculpture and painting.

In the Banat, the first resolutions relating to architecture were aimed at the refortification of the city, which is why the first manifestation of Baroque style in the region is evident in military buildings. In 1719, the Transylvanian Barracks were built on the foundation of the old fortifications dating from Huniade's time.[18] The year 1723 witnessed the beginning of expansion for the city of Timişoara,[19] in accordance with the principles of European military architecture. The new Vauban-type city,[20] intended to correspond to eighteenth-century military technique so as to resist artillery attacks, was equipped with four gates. Of these, the Vienna gate was embellished with figurative plastic ornaments reminiscent of the Roman triumphal arch. The gates were arranged at intervals of three bastions inside the fortified belt formed of nine bastions.[21] The military architecture of the time was analysed in the 'Aedificia Bellica',[22] the fifth chapter of the treaty written by the Jesuit Anton Holler and published in 1733 by Johann Peter von Ghelen, entitled *Augusta carolinae Virtutis Monumenta seu Aedificia a Carolo VI. Imp. Max P(ater) P(atriae): Per orbem Austriacum Publico Bono posita*. Inside the citadel, urban elements of the Baroque appear in the new rectangular street configuration and in the demarcation of some open spaces with specific functions. Situated in front of the oldest church of the city, dedicated to St George, which had been a mosque during the Ottoman occupation and later became a Jesuit church after the Habsburg conquest of the province, the Jesuit Square became the intellectual hub of the city. The second square, delimited by the general's house, was called Parade Square (today, Freedom Square), while the largest was Prinz Eugen Square (today, Union Square). Following construction of the Catholic church, the seat of the Bishopric of Cenad moved to Timişoara in 1731 and became the city's religious centre. The new urban scheme of the Baroque city placed the square at its centre, focusing objectively on quotidian life.

The second sphere of penetration of Baroque art was that of religious architecture, the decisive role belonging to the Catholic orders who arrived in the province immediately after the Habsburg conquest. The Jesuits were the first, transforming St George's church and reconstructing its façade, which had been destroyed between 1754 and 1759, under Master Anton Platel's direction.[23] Franciscans from the province of Bosnia founded a church and a monastery in 1733 and 1736, the latter being ceded in 1788 to the Piarist college that moved from Sântana (Arad County) to Timişoara.[24] The Salvadoran Franciscans built their church and monastery in 1754–55,[25] while the Minorites of the same order founded a church dedicated to St John Nepomuk in 1732. We owe the construction of the Misericordia hospital and its church[26] between 1748 and 1753 to the brothers of St John Nepomuk.

Catholic religious orders spread throughout the Banat: in Lugoj, the Minorite brothers of the Franciscan order built a church in 1733–35; in Caransebeș, the Franciscan order built the Holy Virgin church between 1725 and 1730.[27] As the center of mining and heavy industry, Oravița, Bocșa and Reșița were endowed with Catholic churches during the same century. The Baroque style of these constructions was not ostentatious like those typical of Central Europe, being purged of excessive decoration and having its own rhetoric. The churches built by the Catholic orders all over the Banat in the eighteenth century were monumental constructions derived from the prototype created by Anton Pilgram. Specific to this was the plan of the basilica with two towers on the façade, a large choir and grandiose interior, and main and side altars as compulsory elements of Baroque scenography. The former church of the Bosnian Franciscans of Timișoara, St John Nepomuk, and the church of the Salvadoran Franciscans, St Catherine's – with its single-tower façade designed by Theodor Kostka – constituted models that would inspire church building in rural areas, both Orthodox and Catholic.

The new idea of the urban Baroque was inspired by Pope Sixtus V's construction programme, according to which the heart of the city should be 'the parish church, the essential cell of urban traffic, the centre of communication between the common man and the representative of the divine power'.[28] Of the imperial churches of the Banat, the most important is the Roman Catholic cathedral in Timișoara in what is today Union Square (formerly Dom Platz/Dome Square and earlier Prinz Eugen Square).[29] Among official models[30] the cathedral was begun in 1736 and finished in 1774, when the interior decoration was completed. This construction represented the model to follow in the architectural evolution of the Banat. The plans from Viennese archives reveal the typological complexity and rich exterior decoration, which in the end were not realised for economic reasons. The building[31] was attributed to the celebrated architect Johann Fischer von Erlach, who drafted an interpretation of the Viennese *Hoffbauamt*, similar to other edifices he had designed. Following in his father's footsteps, Emanuel Bernhardt Fischer von Erlach[32] contributed to the cathedral's construction plan, which was finalised in 1723 and considered an ideal design.[33] The construction began in 1736, a decade after the architect's death.[34] The initial plan was simplified by Johann Theodor Kostka, *aedificator operis*. He abandoned the plastic decoration of the façade depicting St George, and the side pedestals. The economic situation of the Banat in Maria Theresa's time contributed to the simplification of construction, especially the more modest composition of the façade and interior decor.

The Catholic church of Lenauheim is the second imperial religious construction[35] of the Banat, designed by two local masters, Abbé Gruber and J.G. Muller. The plan of the church was drafted by Carl Alexander Steinlein, who had created other churches in the Banat, such as Iecea Mare and Săcălaz in Timiș County, and Neudorf, Sefdin and Frumușeni in Arad County. Its initial elliptic cupola collapsed in 1823 and was later replaced by a ceiling. The cathedral and the church in Lenauheim are imperial buildings, both of which established certain formal norms of Baroque architecture in the Banat. For economic reasons, the plans were not applied, but only used as simplified models, adjusted to the urban and rural realities of the Banat. This was a common phenomenon in other provinces of the Habsburg monarchy, too. Late in expression and displaying classic features, the Baroque of the eighteenth century in the Banat passed through a period of experimentation, of adapting norms and forms to provincial conditions.

The stylistic features of the architectural Baroque in the Banat highlight the central motif by a strong jutty or aedicule on the façade (e.g., Catholic cathedral of Timișoara, built between 1736 and 1774), a canopy supported by columns (e.g., Serbian episcopal church of Timișoara) or varied decorative elements placed on the portal entablature, on the column heads which alternate and give rhythm to the façade, or on the window frames. They are buildings limited to the plan, balanced with well-exploited spaces which, with the exception of those which have collapsed, preserve the authenticity of late Baroque style, corresponding to Enlightenment ideology, to the rational and profoundly deist spirit of the time.

Eighteenth-century architecture in the Banat becomes a mirror of the different multinational mindsets[36] in the process of Europeanisation. From an urban perspective, the colonising phenomenon, no matter when it happens, has an interest in the rapid and uniform enforcement of official models. The manner in which those models are formed and spread, their relationship with local tradition, and their subsequent evolution are important. This is the case of the hall church, often used by the Orthodox population, with its clearly articulated elevation, traditional direction and compartmentalisation, the unitary interior space which, with the help of the roofing system (framing, curving), offered a large space for the iconographic programme. Among monumental works of the Baroque, the portal of the Timișoara episcopal palace presents a combination of phytomorphic and anthropomorphic decorative elements, analogous to the Salzburg episcopal palace[37] (a bas-relief displays a character whose physiognomic features are underlined by stylised vines and *Ohrmuschel* motifs).

In the Banat, Baroque art becomes a phenomenon of European culture and civilisation, overlapping with traditions existing before the Ottoman occupation. The art possesses a missionary element, aiming to express the triumph of Christianity and Western spiritual and material values. Imperial sculpture from the Banat preserves the illusion of power within an age perceived as the richest in formal expression, the eighteenth century being a period of heightened sentiment. The way in which Baroque art was transformed during the eighteenth century into a norm (*tehné*) may be observed in the established models of religious-themed figurative representations. Monumental sculpture depicts an iconographic repertoire specific to the Baroque in all the provinces of the Habsburg Empire. This is the plastic representation of some characters, highlighted for their strength of faith and martyrdom, who become mediators of the Divine through symbolic gestures and didactic eloquence.

The space of Baroque art is festive, educating with the help of gestures, hence the concept of theatrical art applied to the style. In the urban configuration of the Baroque, the arts compete to create an image of *total art*, the architecture being sculptural while the sculpture gains architectural value through its monumental character. The placement of commemorative or religious monuments in the centre of the urban squares is a peculiarity of the dominant religion, but it is also a meeting place and a means of creating community spirit. Reference to the two most important moments of existence is frequent, death being suggested as a performance for life, and life as a memento mori, a reminder of death.[38] The Baroque expresses a world of forms that embraces the peculiarities of the environments of its creators and is loaded with political, social and cultural significance. These forms are embodied in the spaces of everyday life, evoking a sensitivity specific to the Baroque, in which man was 'invited' to participate in religious processions whose visual support equaled monuments of sculpture and architecture.

ORTHODOX BAROQUE ARCHITECTURE IN THE BANAT

Typologically, the model of the church constitutes the mark of evolution during the eighteenth century in the Banat. The approved form of religious constructions, with unitary and longitudinally structured planimetrics, would also gain a monumental aspect by placing a bell tower on the façade. Exceptions with two towers on the façade include the cathedrals representative of the eighteenth-century Orthodox world in the Banat: the Metropolitan church of Sremski Karlovač (1758–1862), the Serbian church of Timișoara (1744–48) and the Romanian church of the Assumption in Lugoj (1759–66).

Although limited by the planimetric typology and by the system of vaulting and decoration, Orthodox architecture interpreted the Illyrian privileges addressed de facto to the 'racial nation' as a means of breaking away from the constraints imposed by the Ottoman occupation, which had limited church construction to less durable materials such as wood. The Illyrian privileges, granted by Leopold I on 21 August 1690 for the help offered by Serbs against the Turks, were a true constitution for the Banat, reinforced during the eighteenth century by many other imperial acts. They are considered to be the basis for the expansion of the spiritual authority of the Serbian Church over the Orthodox people of the empire.[39] Under the protection of these privileges, the Slavic/Serbian-language metropolitan church took over religious leadership in the region, churches built in the eighteenth century often being shared by Serbian and Romanian Orthodox believers. Through its affiliation to the Serbian Church under the trusteeship of the patriarchate of Sremski Karlovač, the situation of the Orthodox Church in the Banat up to the second half of the nineteenth century was special and reflected in its architecture. The stylistic innovations that emerged from the arrival of the Baroque in the Banat may be observed in planimetrics, the constructions being single-nave halls, longitudinal, with a bell tower on the façade, the interior partition being imposed by the Eastern rite. This official model was supervised by the Civil and Military Construction Service, which functioned here until 1751 when it was divided in two distinct departments. A series of memoranda issued thereafter referred to the requirement for Orthodox communities to submit projects and estimates of work to be done in order to receive imperial approval for construction.[40] Churches built on Hungarian territory with respect to the imposed model include those in Szentendre (1741), Csobánka[41] (1746), Budakalász (1752), Beremend (1755) and Arad (1764), where large Serbian communities lived. The authors of these constructions had mostly completed their training in the artistic surroundings of Central Europe. In other Orthodox artistic fields, like painting or decoration, Serbs are the most numerous.[42]

A common phenomenon of the Habsburg Empire, which includes the province of the Banat, is the redecoration of some Orthodox buildings according to Central European models. The tower on the façade (Mesič and Hodoș-Bodrog monasteries), the Baroque portal at the entrance (Krušedol monastery), and the adaptation of Baroque-style ornamentation (Fruška Gora monastery) are excellent examples of this. Most of the Baroque churches built in the eighteenth century respect the longitudinal grouping of masses, as opposed to the preferred centred articulation of the Renaissance.[43]

The Edict of Toleration promulgated in 1781 by Joseph II, while not referring directly to the rules of Orthodox architecture, included criteria for ecclesiastical building with regard to the orientation of the church: façades should face a direction other than the main street. It was stipulated that decoration should not be abundant, that the building should not exceed the height of its neighbours; the suggested plan was that there should be a longitudinal and balanced grouping of masses, covered with a roof and with a tower on the façade. This became the approved model in the Banat, used in rural areas by both Catholics and Orthodox. The complex plans of imperial religious buildings in the Banat (e.g., the Catholic cathedral of Timișoara, erected by Charles VI in 1736, and the church in Lenauheim in 1777), were not examples to follow, especially for financial reasons, with their complex structures and rich architectural decoration. For both secular and religious architecture, there is evidence of the presence in the Banat of some technicians and builders who had qualified in Central Europe: Carl Alexander Steinlein, Theodor Kostka, Kaspar Dissl, Johann Lechner, Johann Georg Herle and Frederick Cadusch. With regard to Orthodox buildings, qualified masters familiar with the stylistic morphology were rare, most of them being colonist artisans.

The Orthodox church of the Annunciation in Lugoj is a special case. Johannes Breutter from Timişoara, who participated in its construction, introduced a typology specific to Orthodoxy after the Middle Ages, namely, the hall church with three-cusped apse, reminiscent of the traditional tri-conical style.[44] The façade with two towers was inspired by the plans of the Catholic cathedral in Timişoara. Documents mention that the initiative for building this church in Lugoj, the most important Orthodox building of the eighteenth century, came from local landowners and administrators Gavril Guran, Alisandru Petraşcu and Mihail Faur 'along with the whole town'.[45]

Religious Orthodox art in the Banat strengthened its position in relation to Catholic art. The renewal of art started early, along with initiatives to restore the rural wooden churches, while the stone ones were subject to the Aulic Council, which had to approve the plan.[46] This was stipulated in a directive issued by the bishop of Timişoara on 12 August 1785, addressed to priests in rural areas, according to which 'building churches required approval from the authorities and to this end they must annex the church designs'.[47] The imperial administration enforced the building of standard churches, in order to shape the rural settlements according to Central European ones, the imposed model applying to the entire settlement. Thus, they complied with the concept of Baroque urbanism. According to this, the newly colonised villages were organised upon Cartesian and linear patterns, with the prevalence of the former.[48] There were also exceptions in some settlements dating from the previous period.

RELIGIOUS PLASTIC ART

In religious iconography, the symbols of Christian permanence in the history of Europe take priority, for example, the anti-plague saints (Sebastian, Roche and Charles Borromeo), each referring, with eloquent gestures, to their martyrdom in the name of the faith. They become symbolical intermediaries between life and death, a posture typical in most representations designated as a plague column.

A structural element in architecture, the column is the symbol of force and support in Baroque style, an essential principle in troubled times. The idea of a pyramidal monument that floats over clouds, erected in a large space, evolved from Bernini's work in Rome in the Piazza Navona and the Chair of St Peter in St Peter's Basilica. Lodovico Burnacini had the idea of placing a similar monument in Vienna, within a free space (*Graben*), so that it could be easily observed by passers-by. The Viennese prototype of the plague column was erected by command of Leopold I between 1682 and 1694, as an ex-voto following the plague epidemics of 1697.[49] Designed by Mathias Rauchmiller, the monument was continued after his death by Johann Bernhhard Fischer von Erlach.

The obelisk or Holy Trinity column, erected in Timișoara in 1741, is an ex-voto given by the cameral councillor Jean Deschan of Montcassel (Lotharingia), which bears the imperial insignia in the form of a heraldic element. The imperial crown is placed in an ascending line of clouds, a symbol of the Banat's particular status as a province of the Habsburg crown. The repertoire of anti-plague saints is located on the profiled base of the obelisk. St John Nepomuk, St Barbara and the prophet David encompass the allegorical meaning of the representation, while the top of the column refers to the Virgin Mary as intercessor. Monuments in Linz (Austria), and Pécs, Vác and Kesckemét (Hungary) can be considered stylistic analogies of the same type. Portrayals of the Holy Trinity in provincial style, with a simplified iconography, were built throughout the Banat in the eighteenth and nineteenth centuries, such as those in Teremia Mare, Vinga, Arad, Neudorf, Mașloc and Tisa Nouă.

An abstract concept of Baroque art is the idea of the Immaculate Conception/Righteousness floating over the Moon and stepping over the snake of heresy. In the Banat, this theme is depicted on the monument devoted to St John Nepomuk. The approved Mariological symbols – the lily and the starry halo – invoke the Virgin's traits. The representation refers to the triumph of the Christian Church over the Infidel, Islam, symbolised by the snake. Dating from 1756 and ascribed to the Viennese sculptors E. Wasserburger and F. Blim, the monument presents aspects of provincial religiosity, with the help of the iconographic repertoire. Dedicated to St John Nepomuk,[50] the monument is highlighted by a presentation of saints martyred for the faith: John Nepomuk (keeping the secrets of the confessional), Sebastian, Roche and Charles Borromeo (anti-plague saints), culminating with Mary in the Immaculate hypostasis. The depiction lacks the compositional pathos of similar monuments across the Empire, especially those built in the capital city but, by the eloquence of its gestures and symbols, it forms a visual support for faith in an era dominated by vicissitudes.

From 1722, most plastic representations were devoted to St John Nepomuk. Following his canonisation by Pope Boniface XII, the cult of this bishop from Prague quickly spread throughout Central and South-East Europe. The numerous portrayals depicting him attired in a surplice, holding the cross in his hand, are proof of the admiration for his cult. He is frequently accompanied by putti who bear his signs (the table of ex-votos) or refer to the secrets of the confessional by putting their finger to their lips. The saint is embodied in similar style in representations of the eighteenth and nineteenth centuries. In the Banat, the most successful plastic images are those in Sânnicolaul Mare (1757), Arad (1731), Tudor Vladimirescu, Periam, Pecica (1773), Fântânele, Neudorf, Bocşa Montană, Darova, Dudeştii Vechi, Lipova, Kiszombor, Magyarcsernye and Biserica Albă.[51] The provincial spirit and language follow Central European patterns, based on one of the oldest portrayals of the saint, on the Charles Bridge in Prague, executed after a model by Mathias Rauchmiller and Ferdinand Brokoff. The engravings of Johann Andreas Pfeffel, who illustrated J. Balbin's book *Vita Santi Nepomuceni*,[52] published in Augsburg in 1725, inspired the manner in which Nepomuk was graphically portrayed.

The group of patron saints and thaumaturges refers to the concept of *Gloria Mundi, Gloria Dei*, in fashion during the century of transition to the values that define European civilisation, the plastic representations being perceived as Baroque reactions in synchronicity with the West. In order to get closer to the faithful, Baroque art from the Banat evades stringent norms of representation. The persistence of norms can be sensed in official orders, dogmatic rigour and certain composition rules surviving even into the late nineteenth century.

The church of St John Nepomuk in Timișoara (1733–36) conferred an articulation of masses typical of the style and an interior that evokes, through visual rhetoric, its formal landmarks. In the collection of religious art of the Roman Catholic Bishopric of Timișoara, fragments of altars from the churches built by Catholics on Banatian territory during the eighteenth century are preserved and catalogued, with no documentary reference as to their affiliation. This is the case with some fragments that were attributed to the church in Vinga, destroyed by fire and rebuilt in neo-Gothic style.

In 1911, the church of St John Nepomuk was demolished, but not before Karol Baitz, a student of the Piarist School, had taken detailed photographs of the interior.[53] The images allow us to identify the structure of the altar, the decorative elements and characters illustrated: fragments of the altar preserved in the collection of the Roman Catholic Bishopric of Timișoara, rampant puttis, a decorative element, fragments of the cornice, statues of the main altar (St Teresa of Ávila and St Clare of Assisi, both stored today in the Misericordia church in '700' Square), even the two funeral stones of David von Hübner and Johannes de Soro[54] (today built into the wall of Calea Lipovei cemetery), all providing a testament to a period of Baroque style as practised in the architecture of Timișoara.

The sculpture of the main altar of the first imperial religious building in Timișoara – the Roman Catholic cathedral – is the most expressive accomplishment of the Banatian Baroque. The importance of the construction lies in the interest of the authorities to endow it with works of art created by known artists coming from the academicist scene or from Central European workshops (Johann Joseph Resler).

In addition to political instability, economic reasons determined that the furnishing of the cathedral with particular liturgical furniture was done in two stages: the first between 1736 and 1754, by which time services could be officiated inside, and the second between 1755 and 1774, when the construction and its interior decoration was finished. The first stage involved artists from Vienna who were educated at the Viennese Academy of Arts, while the second had contributions from local Timișoara citizens. The collaboration of the city administration with those artists is underlined by numerous contracts signed by some of them and by the designs sent for approval. Johann Joseph Resler[55] (1700–72) is known to be author of the tabernacle and of the monumental statues that depict the spiritual correspondences of Charles VI and Maria Theresa: St Charles Borromeo and St Teresa of Ávila, founder of the Discalced Carmelite order, depicted in a penitential state, with arms holding to her chest the pierced heart, a symbol of charity – both flanking the main altar.[56] Educated at the Viennese Academy of Arts as the student of Georg Raphael Donner, and influenced by Lorenzo Mattielli, Resler had already designed and constructed many altars for Central European churches.[57] Ilse Schultz,[58] who dedicated a study to Resler, declared the cherubim framing the tabernacle to be 'the most fragile of all his works devoted to this subject'. Analogies can be found in the Pilgrimage church in Vienna, the church in Jaszo (Bohemia) and the former Jesuit church in Györ.[59]

The main altar is based on the formal typology, with two registers and ample fronton, decorated with statues of the Holy Trinity: God the Father, with a flowing cloak, Jesus depicted as a bearded youth, signalling with his right hand a gesture of profound devotion, the Holy Spirit depicted as a dove. God the Father and God the Son are placed on the cornice of the altar to create a dynamic effect amplified by the tumult of stucco clouds and the foreshortened puttis. The Baroque scenery is completed by the heads of cherubim. To his left, Jesus is flanked by an angel, two kneeled cherubim are in the corners, one in adoration and the other in praying posture, while in the background the Holy Spirit is surrounded by rays of light. The plumage of the wings is only suggested for the fronton cherubim, and more detailed for the tabernacle one.[60] In depicting this composition, Resler uses similar patterns to his teacher Donner.[61] The main altar's median part is dominated by architectural elements: columns and pilasters, equally fluted, adorned by Corinthian chapters flanking the votive painting *St George Killing the Dragon* by Michael Angelo Unterberger, director of the Viennese Academy of Arts and Piazzetta's student; above, a strongly profiled entablature, articulated with cornice, presents Neoclassical decorative elements.

Even if the Baroque had entered its decorative Rococo or 'Theresian' stage in the second half of the eighteenth century, the altar sculpture was made accordingly to late Baroque stylistic tendencies, which were followed at the end of the century by the more austere Josephine style. This phase in the evolution of Baroque sculpture in Timişoara is represented by a stylistic transfer encouraged by the import of artists and materials from the imperial capital. The fact that these artists settled in the province and became citizens of Timişoara proves that the Banat, although a border area subject to constant instability, was attracting a workforce specialised in taking up official orders, which were completed upon contractual bases.

The pulpit of the Catholic cathedral was executed in 1766 by Georg Wittman.[62] Its main body is shaped in the form of a suspended cup, while the parapet is flanked by the statues of two prophets: Moses holding the Tables of the Law (left) and Aaron (right). On the sides of the main body, there are three panels in bas-relief: *The Good Samaritan* (frontal), *St John the Baptist* (left) and *The Temptation* (right), encased in frames decorated on the edges with rocailles; on the seat of the pulpit the scene *Jesus Preaching in the Desert* is depicted. The canopy of the pulpit has a profiled cornice, decorated with a 'wave crest' motif and rocailles and crowned by statues of puttis holding in their hands the characteristic symbols of the cross and the anchor. This model of altar decoration was utilised and adapted throughout the Banat in churches built during the late eighteenth century.

The interior decoration of the Franciscan monastery in Radna-Lipova preserves marks of the Rococo, but also of the late classical Baroque, on its three eighteenth-century altars. The main altar, by Master Fr. Joachim Eisenhut who is registered in the monastery's archive as 'faber arcularius', was executed between 1758 and 1767.[63] Following the specified plan, the Franciscan monk produced a unitary composition, an altar aligned according to a semicircular section with the fronton filling the conch of the apse to its half-height. The altar, which unfolds in two registers, has smooth columns with composite capitals starting directly from the pavement, marking the plastic votive painting. Its flanks are splayed. Above, an entablature with heavily profiled cornice and a fronton made of facing volutes on which two puttis displaying devotional attitude are placed, frames the window that emerges out of a circle of rays and the *Ohrmuschel* motif flanked by the statues of God the Father with the globe and Jesus carrying the cross. Joachim Einsenhut signs the altar: 'Ef[factuator] F[rater] M[uratorium] M[a]g[ister] Radnam, 1763.'[64] Around this date, Juniper Stilp (or Stelpp), sculptor and Franciscan monk, arrived in Radna to help finish the side altars: his work is mentioned in other neighbouring churches.[65]

The side altars are executed to Eisenhut's designs, but due to budget limitations were finished only at the end of the eighteenth century, when Matthäus von Salbeck (a salt merchant from Arad)[66] donated the necessary funds. The two altars have identical shapes, the votive painting of the second, illustrating the *Marriage of the Virgin*, was executed in 1781 by Franz Wagenschön.[67] During Charles VI's reign, churches were built in locations in the southern Banat that had become headquarters of mining offices: Bocșa Montană (1723),[68] Oravița (1722–27),[69] Ciclova Montană (a chapel named 'Mary of the Cliff' in 1727)[70] and Dognecea (1740).[71]

In the second half of the eighteenth century, beginning in Maria Theresa's reign (1740–80), models pertaining to the Rococo were introduced in the Banat. 'The Theresian Baroque' is defined in this area by a number of decorative elements that underline the architectural scenery of the altars built in this period. While the architectural scheme of these altars still is Baroque, Rococo style can be seen in the interior ambience of the churches, in their decorative repertoire, highlighting the triumphant atmosphere. Miners from Stiria, Craina, Tirol, Hungary and Wallachia were brought to Sasca Montană, a village built between 1730 and 1740.[72] The Neoclassical phase of the style is represented by Johann Georg Dorfmeister's presence in Sasca Montană, where he sculpted the altars of the Catholic church. Pertaining to the formal, three-register style – masonry that supports the median part and a simple fronton developed along a plane section in the width of the apse – the altar presents the most classical representations of St Teresa of Ávila and St Francis of Assisi, flanking the central composition of the Crucifixion. The physiognomy of St Francis has hard features, the carefully handled surface, the long expressive arms, the harmony, proportion and stylistic language that mark the passage from Baroque to Neoclassical – all these elements lead to the conclusion that the artist was the Viennese Johann Georg Dorfmeister, an assumption supported by the registration of his death certificate in 1786 in the village of Sasca Montană (present-day Caraș-Severin County) and by stylistic and formal analogies to his works in Central and South-East Europe: the altar sculpture in the Mariahilferkirche, Vienna, 1770–71; the parish church in Gumpendorfer, 1780–82; the altar sculptures for the pilgrimage churches of Sonnatagberg, 1767 and Maria Taferl, 1777–81 in southern Austria, all of which have Baroque features, while after the construction of Count Grassalkovich's funeral monument (1781) at Besnyö, near Gödöllö, Hungary, Neoclassical influences can be seen.

In terms of formal and stylistic language, this creation can be attributed to Johann Georg Dorfmeister,[73] who for unknown reasons arrived in the Banat towards the end of his life and was buried at Sasca Montană.[74] This attribution is possible due to the restrained pathos, but with real rhetorical accents, the detailed handling of the surface and the tendency to classicise the formal aspects, only the contrapposto recalling the European Baroque.

The altars of the Catholic churches built in the eighteenth-century Banat are registered in a typology with forms defined by the architectural ensemble, composing the interior scenery, along with the painting. In general, the main altars are built along the width of the apse, borrowing its slightly concave shape, with an elevation on three registers, comprising the mensa, the median part with votive painting and statues of saints according to its theme, and the fronton elaborated with architectural shapes and elements of figurative and decorative art (usually decorative urns). Most representative of this type are the church altars in Iecea Mare, Grabaț, Lennauheim, Sânandrei, Neudorf, Bocșa Montană, Guduriča and Varšac from the second part of the eighteenth century, and those that replaced, at the beginning of the nineteenth century, altars that had been destroyed in Giarmata, Carani, Oravița, Ciclova and Moldova Nouă.

BAROQUE PAINTING IN THE BANAT

Baroque painting completes the field of artistic expression of Banatian society. In the eighteenth century, the central authority was represented by portraits, while inside churches, the images evoked the transcendental realm using formal methods established by artists from Central Europe and among the colonists. In this area, too, there was a desire to be aligned with the Western current through the formal values that highlighted the Baroque. The dynamic style is particular to Baroque painting, with an open composition that gives the impression of space, lighting from multiple sources, and *trompe l'œil*. Baroque painting also brought new genres into evidence and exploited earlier ones, such as the portrait, perhaps the most incisive means of presentation. In the collection at the Roman Catholic Bishopric, there are many portraits of authorities who left their mark on the province's development (Maria Theresa, Joseph II, and others, most of whom were painted in professional workshops in Vienna) and even of cameral chancellors (such as Jean Deschan, donor of the Holy Trinity monument in Timișoara), along with a gallery of portraits of Catholic bishops (Ladislau Nádasdy, Adalbert von Falkenstein and Nicolaus Stanislavici).

The movement of artists was favoured by the large number of commissions in the Banat, both official and private, for buildings that were to be constructed throughout the province. The official phase is underlined by imported artisans who provided a European presence on the Banatian artistic stage. That is the case with the imperial commission for the painting of the altar of the Roman Catholic cathedral in Timișoara, and other Catholic churches of the city, involving a number of artists. One of them was Michael Angelo Unterberger, who painted the *St George Killing the Dragon* composition on the main altar and the *St John Nepomuk* composition for the eponymous Franciscan church, taken over by Piarists in 1788. The author of the cathedral's side altars is Johann Nepomuk Schöpf, who executed six compositions in a very dynamic and dramatic pictorial style, among which *The Last Supper*, *St Joseph's Death*, *St John Nepomuk* and *The Visitation* (1772) can be mentioned. Ferdinand Schiessl, who painted the altars of St Catherine's church, was a colonist who settled in Timișoara in

1753, where a painting school was founded in 1786.[75] The first secular painter from the Banat, also from the group of colonists, was Anselm Wagner. He renounced religious themes, becoming an important exponent of easel painting: he mostly did portraits (for example, that of Elisabeth Kessler-Koppauer, wife of the mayor of Timișoara) and adopted new techniques, besides painting in oils, using watercolours, gouache and crayon.

The 'Baroquisation' of the art of the Orthodox communities began in the sixth decade of the eighteenth century.[76] The revival of Banatian painting may be noted in the stylistic language and the iconographic types.[77] Baroque painting introduced new artistic values in the Orthodox environment which, along with Western influence, would constitute the two landmarks in the evolution of religious artistic expression. Regarding Orthodox painting, Francesco Griselini[78] noted that 'Romanians engage in plastic arts by painting in the Byzantine manner, and by carving in wood and sculpting in stone'. The *a vela* vaulting system, used inside Orthodox churches, offers a large space for painting. The values of the new European style may be observed in the thematic distribution in separate cartouches, abandoning the narrative style and respecting the Byzantine iconography, sometimes adapted to the new Western iconographic formulas. The asymmetrical compositions are horizontally aligned, the spatial depth being amplified by landscape and architectural composition, the principle of coextensive space being clearly expressed through these pictorial arts. The painting is enriched with didactic and moralising aspects typical of the Enlightenment, the preferred themes being those that present the triumphal aspects of Jesus's divinity, such as Eucharistic miracles. The paintings in the monasteries of Bezdin, Șemlac (Săraca), Vojlovica and Mesić[79] have been preserved from the first half of the eighteenth century. Their iconostases were replaced at the beginning of the nineteenth century.[80]

The iconostasis retains its function, the Western spirit of innovation operating at the level of thematic repertoire and dimensions. There is an enrichment of the iconographic and stylistic content with new elements. This becomes, along with mural painting and liturgical furniture, a typical setting for the Baroque ceremonial atmosphere.[81] Beginning in the nineteenth century, the iconostasis was formulated according to local character, due to the multilingual and multicultural nature of the Orthodox communities and the way in which they related to their own traditions and new influences. Sculpture has a secondary role in the iconostasis decorative repertoire, by reinforcing the painting with its stylistic values. According to Pavel Florenski, the iconostasis represents 'the boundary between the seen and the unseen world'.[82]

Here, Western Baroque influence, manifested in painting and decorative art, was added, starting in the last decades of the eighteenth century, to Byzantine tradition. The church iconostases built in the eighteenth century were either stylistically oriented to the Brâncovenesc style (Wallachian Renaissance), also known as intermediary or transitional iconostases, such as St John's church in Caransebeș (1878) and the church of the Holy Apostles Peter and Paul, Goruia (1818),[83] or those of obvious Western influence, especially from an architectural and decorative perspective. The influence of the southern Carpathian Brâncovenesc style is also present in an area in which there had existed early monastic life, the first Orthodox churches built of wood dating from the twelfth century.[84]

The Brâncovenesc influence penetrated the Banat along with the migration of a skilled workforce (painter families from Wallachia and Transylvania) in the period of urban development from the mid-eighteenth century. The case of the painter Vasile Diaconu, who arrived in the Banat from the region of Tismana, along with 50 other families, is well known.[85] He was the first to establish a school of church painting in the village of Sredіștea.[86] The Romanian iconostases' decorative repertoire was enriched with new models of Western influence. Vegetal and floral motifs are most frequent: pumpkin flower, acanthus leaf, vines with leaves and grapes, as seen in the church of the Assumption in Oravița (finished in 1784). The church is considered to be a 'provincial Baroque monument, with simplified elements',[87] highlighting the influence of the Baroque style both in architecture (in the tower with two bulbs) and in painting and sculpture. Having a composite ornamental repertoire, the Orthodox church of the Assumption in Ciacova (Timiș County) was painted by Dimitrie Popovici (1738–96) in 1771.[88]

CONCLUSIONS

Among the metamorphoses of the Baroque, the Banat version is a distant projection that shapes space in accordance with the new mentality. During an age of renewal in Banatian society, eighteenth-century art synthesises the entire evolution of Central European art in this local variety of the Baroque. Manifested as votive art in the first half of the eighteenth century, it gradually became decorative, tending to universality, comprising all domains and being adapted to Orthodox art. The first level of penetration of Baroque influence was that of the imperial religious buildings, which imprinted a natural evolution to the process, being assimilated by the Catholic rural environment. A second level of penetration was the Orthodox environment, influenced by tradition through its permanent contact with neighbouring Romanian provinces.

Monumental sculpture, in its initial 'imported' phase, may be observed in the case of the St John Nepomuk monument (1722) in Timișoara, the Holy Trinity monument (1740) and the Plague column (1756). St John Nepomuk, whose hagiography is connected to the settlers' places of origin (Bohemia), found more and more followers due to his role as protector against the plague, most disastrous of diseases, at the same time consecrated as keeper of the secret of the confessional (the episode is linked to the appearance of the new devotion, encouraged by the emergence of confessionals as liturgical furniture, by closeness to the common man, and by the individual's active involvement in the work of salvation, a manifestation of the unchanging nature of the sacred).

The official nature of Baroque art at the beginning of the eighteenth century is underlined by creations in the capital of the Habsburg Empire, based on models which had already been developed, with a relevant iconography and appealing to specialist workshops, sometimes using designs made by well-known artists. This is the case of the St John Nepomuk monument in Timișoara, made using the archetype created by Mathias Rauchmiller. The common concern for Christians had become the celebration of the most important moments of existence – life and death – and of the power and glory of God. Furthermore, the propensity for religious themes resulted from the principle according to which 'heaven is anticipated on earth, because on earth any space is a celebratory space'.[89]

The expression of sainthood acquires rhetorical accents in Baroque sculpture, illustrated by the gestures and imitations of the characters, the saint of the Baroque age being a witness of faith, attesting it by word, martyrdom or ecstasy.[90] The fashion of the time, namely the celebration of military triumphs with pomp, the glorification of the conqueror and his placement near his spiritual correspondent, was also adopted in the Banat, following the model of its neighbouring province Transylvania, albeit on a smaller scale. Also, the Baroque artistic phenomenon was perceived differently in the Banat, the investors' mindset playing a decisive role in forming new typologies. If, during the first phase, the orders for religious art, sculpture or painting had been economically supported by religious congregations,[91] the second phase highlighted some individuals among the colonists who had the necessary wealth to acquire monuments from Central European centres or by making them locally. The Baroque is the least homogeneous of European styles, local features being what distinguishes it zonally but also chronologically.[92] According to Lorenz Dittmann,[93] 'we can speak of the formation of a style when a specific language emerges, no longer imitation of a model, and the very agreement between the individual manner or the conception and the faithful imitation becomes the style'.

In the Banat, the Baroque, as a totality of forms, became an efficient instrument of multiplying Central European cultural and civilisational values, based on a theological philosophy common to all countries that were part of the Habsburg Empire. This style was not forcefully imposed by the authorities, but emanated from the colonists' common desire to recreate the image of the society to which they had been accustomed in their native lands. The provincial version of the Banatian Baroque, through its multiplication of forms and quality of representations, of suggested tactile values, became integrated into the Central European phenomenon, its evolution suggesting the different phases of Baroque style, but with a different chronology.

10
PAINTING WORKSHOPS

Adrian Negru

THE RAPID ECONOMIC TRANSFORMATION of the Banat during the eighteenth century generated profound transformations in social life and in the mentality of the population. Through innovation, modernity and openness, the Viennese administration's reformist policies conferred a dynamic effect on local traditional culture. The Banatian plastic creation was suggestive in that sense. During the Enlightenment age, art from the Banat managed to surpass the traditional, obsolete style and join the innovating artistic currents from centres such as Venice, Vienna, Graz and Bratislava.

The mutual relations and influences between Christian Orthodox churches regarding religious painting and architecture are relevant for two reasons. From the aesthetic and artistic aspect, they indicate the cultural transfer, the exchange of ideas and the multiculturalism that distinguished the Banat within the Habsburg monarchy. At the same time, the Romanian-Serbian cultural dialogue regarding religious art creation is the mark of an identity based on common Orthodox religion, and not on a certain linguistic or ethnical community, as a great part of the historiography on the subject states.

During the eighteenth and nineteenth centuries, the Banat represented a region rich in cultural life and artistic production. The Orthodox patriarchs' and metropolitan bishops' residences in Sremski Krlovci and Novi Sad were the spiritual and cultural centres that brought forth the most renowned artists. Moreover, religious authorities, politicians, writers, architects and painters were working in Arad, Becicherecul Mare, Kikinda, Panciova, Vârșeț, Lugoj, Caransebeș, Oravița, Biserica Albă and Timișoara. The Banatian visual arts comprised, in this period, Western artistic elements as well as Russian, Ukrainian, Wallachian, Moldavian, Transylvanian, and even more, influences from the Balkans and the Ionian Sea islands.[1]

Artists such as Dimitrie Popovici, Mihailo Bukurovici and Nikola Popovici were the representatives of the regional version of Baroque painting. In addition to Dimitrie Popovici, Dimitrie Bacevici is another outstanding representative of Baroque painting.[2] During the 1770s, Bacevici painted the iconostases from Ciacova, Orlovat, Srpski Itebei and Megia (Serbian Banat).

A former student of the Viennese Art Academy, Arsenie Teodorovici evolved within the context of classicist aesthetics of the late eighteenth century. The largest part of his work (approximately 20 painted iconostases) is spread over a large area of the Habsburg Empire, from Karlovci in the west to Budim in the north and Zemun in the far south. He also painted the church iconostases in Vršac in 1806; Sânnicolaul Mare in 1811; and Saravale, Beiuș, Becicherecul Mare and Comloșul Mare in the early nineteenth century. His iconostases are on a large scale, the one from Sânnicolaul Mare including 70 icons, albeit the themes and iconographic innovations are modest. The pedestal scenes, such as *Church Festivals* or the *Passion of Jesus Christ* cycle, are typical elements of eighteenth-century religious art. Teodorovici also tackled a series of themes from the Old and New Testament, rarely painted before, thus supporting Serbian clergy's theological concerns of that time.

Pavel Giurkovici is another painter of the early nineteenth century.[3] Although he belonged to the Josephine Renaissance in pictorial rationalism, having a large collection of graphic models, as icon painter he never allowed form-relating issues to blur the colour irradiation. Although his place of studies has not been identified, one can easily observe Giurkovici's well-cultivated academic attachment to the discipline of drawing and form. The work of Arsenie Teodorovici and Pavel Giurkovici influenced Banatian painting over the nineteenth century. There are many works from this period that carry the same archaic character promoted by the two artists. An example of this is Danilo Ciolakovici's painting which decorated Tolvădia church in 1863. Also, the brothers Popovici from Oravița, active in the mid-nineteenth century, stayed true to the pictorial expression of the early part of the century. Mihailo Popovici's icons in Lescovița, from 1842 to 1850, were copied time and again. Dimitrie Popovici's mural painting in the St Nicholas Serbian church of Svinița was destroyed during the construction of the *Iron Gates* hydroelectric plant.

The name of Banatian painter Moise Jivoinovici is worth mentioning. A native of Ferdin (Ilancea, in present-day Serbian Banat), he was known only for the unusual composition *Moses's Finding*[4] placed on the throne of Virgin Mary from the Tolvădia (Livezile) Serbian church. Also, Marcu Acim, known for his *Crucifixion of Christ* in the cemetery chapel of Kikinda, was the author of the paintings belonging to the iconostasis of Satu Mare.

In the second half of the nineteenth century, the social and political transformations within the Austro-Hungarian Monarchy had direct consequences on the Banat. The revolutionary year 1848 caused not only the breakdown of monarchy, but also a division of population based on confessional and ethnic criteria. Serbian artists mostly opted for Bucharest, Budapest or Belgrade. The small number of icons they (Novak Radonâci, Pavel Simici and Aksentie Marodici) painted, is relevant in this case. The paintings made by Hungarian artists in the Banat were few. On the other hand, Romanian artists managed to exceed the standards of local workshops, as Timişoara and Arad were starting to assert themselves as important artistic centres.[5]

THE WORKSHOPS OF PAINTERS NEDELCU AND ŞERBAN POPOVICI

After a part of Andrei Andreovici's team had left Karlowitz/Sremski Karlovci, painters Nedelcu and Şerban Popovici[6] remained in the Banat as representatives of the Brâncovenesc (Wallachian) style. Working among them was Gheorghe Ranite, Grigore Ranite's brother and the son of Master Hranite or Aranit. In 1732 the Ranite brothers decorated Tismana monastery's nave and altar, overlaying the entire old paint from 1564, while in 1738, together with Mihai and Ioan, they painted the chapel of St Nicholas in Braşov. After completing his work in Braşov, Ioan moved to the Banat and took over the painting of the Assumption church in Lipova, aided by Nedelcu and Şerban Popovici, who were considered as the same person in the specialist literature.[7]

There are more arguments that lead to the conclusion that Nedelcu Popovici's activity starts with the painting of the Săraca monastery. The influence of the Brâncovenesc style is emphasised here, mostly by the distinct presentation of the benefactors, those who financed the restoration and painting of the monastery. Regarding the collective works of the mid-eighteenth-century churches, it is difficult to determine the author. In Săraca's case it is clear that the main role was credited to Master Andrei, while Iovan and Chiriac provided more than just technical support. It is possible that Iovan and Chiriac also participated in the Bălceşti church painting (1732). Like the resemblance of Chiriac's work at Bălceşti, in the case of Săraca it is Nedelcu Popovici, who had been the most distinguished member of the team that worked at Vracevşniţa and Lipova. This presumption is argued further by the fact that most of Nedelcu Popovici's icons were painted in Brâncovenesc style.[8]

It is important to state that Nedelcu and Şerban Popovici, together with Gheorghe Ranite, were colleagues for a long period of time, and some information recorded their presence at Vracievşniţa monastery (1737) as members of the Timişoara guild. However, their first common artistic project does not include the same features on the entire inner surface, which confirms past assumptions that the painting was created by more artists.[9] Meeting the modest needs of the village clientele, Nedelcu Popovici continued to paint in the same manner as at the beginning of his career. His efforts to improve are only observed in the case of the Ciacova church icons. Here, the old master, with the help of Ukrainian templates, tried to imitate Stefan Tenețchi's Baroque style, but, lacking systematical training, he could not satisfy ambitions that overcame possibilities.

There are some hypotheses regarding Șerban Popovici's origins, which, missing material proof, have to be accepted as possible. Thus, some believe that Șerban came from the east, where he had learned the profession. Later, he moved to Serbia, where he was a member of Andrei Andreovici's team for the interior decoration of Vracevșnița monastery, and finally he moved to the Banat, where he decided to settle. The theory according to which he was of Macedo-Romanian origin and was later 'adopted' as Serbian, due to the environment in which he worked, is also possible, but also the version that he was of Serbo-Romanian origin is plausible.[10] His first religious art project was the painting of Ecica church (Serbia), in 1744, and between 1752 and 1755, together with Nedelcu Popovici and Gheorghe Diaconovici's group, he decorated the interior of Modoș church (Jașa Tomici, Serbia).[11]

Gheorghe Ranite, probably Romanian from Tismana monastery, was, at the beginning of his career, Nedelcu Popovici's constant partner and later, member of the painters' guild of Timișoara. Together with the members of the Diaconovici family, he promoted the Romanian specific art decoration. His name is mentioned for the first time in the specialist literature in relation to Tismana's nave and altar painting. Gheorghe Ranite is also mentioned in a letter sent by the guild of Timișoara, attesting that he is the author of the Szenendre iconostasis. Later, Gheorghe Ranite's iconographic creations were no longer identified on the Banatian art scene.[12]

At the end of the eighteenth century, more crafty apprentices, instructed in artistic workshops or members of certain groups of painters, arrived in the Banat. They took over works that exceeded their competences, thus becoming unfair competition for the established artists. Thereby, the guild of artists from Timișoara was founded in 1750, an organisation that disapproved of travelling painters with no proven artistic abilities.

Overall, we can conclude that the permanent circulation from the Wallachian territory favoured the activity of traditional painters, associated in family groups, by origin or on the duration of completing church projects.[13] Once the artistic taste changed by the sudden orientation to the Slavic Baroque, Nedelcu's and Șerban Popovici's activity slowly fades.[14] Șerban Popovici's initial approach was more authentic but, by attempting stylistic transformation, some pictorial values were lost and there were no others to replace them.

Şerban and Nedelcu Popovici belonged to the time of artistic changes of the early eighteenth century, when the icon painters were forced to compete with more educated artists.

THE SREDIŞTEA MARE SCHOOL OF PAINTING

One of Nedelcu Popovici's contemporaries was Vasile Alexievici (Vasile Diaconu), who arrived in the vicinity of Vrsac along with 50 families of emigrants from Little Wallachia, settling in Sredişţea Mare (Serbian Banat) in 1736.[15] Before his arrival in the Banat, he had been the deacon of Tismana monastery. At Sredişţea Mare he established a type of school, an artistic workshop that was attended, among others, by his sons – Eustahie, who became a priest, Gheorghe, Dimitrie and Petru – who continued their father's activity, adjusting, according to the demands of the time, to religious painting.[16] It should be mentioned that at that time there was no painter named either Dimitrie or Petru, who would have painted the inside of Fabrik-Timişoara church. Gheorghe Diaconovici, born in 1736 at Sredişţea Mare, was an important figure of the religious art of eighteenth-century Banat because, unlike other short-lived local workshops,[17] he managed to stylistically address the future concepts of Baroque art. The influence of the Wallachian artistic climate determined the preservation of traditional artistic methods of painting of those artists who were working within family or local groups.[18] In such associations, the craft passed, most of the time, from father to son. This was the case of Deacon Vasile, who decorated the interior of the former Clopodia church in the diocese of Timişoara, the two throne icons from 1762, attributed to the father and his son, Gheorghe Diaconovici,[19] being proof. Other members of the group, Stancu Raicu of Vrsac and painters Ioan Popovici and Radu Lazăr from Caransebeş,[20] also contributed to the painting of Clopodia church.

Gheorghe Diaconovici worked along his father on the Clopodia church iconostasis, and a year later he created the imperial doors for the same church. In 1762, he painted the Caransebeş skinners' flag, together with Radu Lazarevici, who was trained at Diaconovici's workshop in Sredişţea Mare. Painter Gheorghe is registered as the author of the guild banner, and also of the icons composing the *Royal Church Festivals* series from the Assumption Church of Lugoj (1777), although the stylistic analysis nominates Gheorghe Diaconovici as their author.[21] An inscription from the Povergina wooden church informs us that the same painter established his home in Bocşa in 1756, and together with his father and his brother Dimitrie, set up an artistic workshop.

During the second half of the eighteenth century, Gheorghe Diaconovici and Dimitrie created representative works in the church of St George in Caransebeş. They also painted in the wooden churches in Băteşti and Povârgina, both situated in the Făget area, in the first of which they were helped by Vasile Ștefan Popovici from Vasiova, and in the second they worked along Petru from Fabrik, Timișoara. It is supposed to be the same Petru Diaconovici who, in the family genealogy, is mentioned as Deacon Vasile's third son.

Petru, the most important member of the Diaconovici family, had a fruitful activity. His painting from the Povârgina wooden church deserves special attention. It portrays Ioan Medescu, its peasant founder, displayed on the western wall of narthex. The value of this portrait, painted in 1785, lies in the precise depiction of clothes, which constitutes a starting point for the recovery of Banatian Romanian costume. Nedelcu Popovici's role in the activity of the Srediștea Mare workshop must be emphasised: having vast artistic knowledge, he participated, alongside Andrei, in the decoration of Vracevșnița church interior. Led by Nedelcu Popovici, Deacon Vasile and Gheorghe Ranite from Craiova painted the interior of Modoș church.[22]

Following Deacon Vasile's guidance, some local painters were trained at Srediștea Mare, among them Stancu Raicu from Vršac and Ioan Popovici and Radu Lazarevici,[23] both from Caransebeș. Another student of the workshop was Iovan, a travelling painter. He was criticised by the religious authorities from Timișoara for decorating some churches with no authorisation. Documents show that he had been trained by Master Vasile for four years, and later, as travelling painter, he collaborated with painter Toma.[24]

Gheorghe Diaconovici's artistic activity and that of the workshops from Srediștea Mare and Bocșa was developing some conservative iconographic concepts. For the Banatian painters, the work of Nikola Neșcovici, one of the most famous artists of the time, served as a model for a long period.

THE PAINTING WORKSHOPS FROM BOCȘA

Including three neighbouring villages (Vasiova, Bocșa Română and Bocșa Montană), Bocșa experienced a thriving economic period during the eighteenth century, due to mining exploitation followed by massive colonisation. Understanding the economic potential of the settlement and the need of local people for religious art, the Diaconovici family moved from Srediștea Mare to Bocșa. Nikola Neșkovici, Pavel Giurkovici and Arsa Teodorovici[25] worked there.

There is no precise information regarding the founding of the first artistic workshop in Bocșa, established by Deacon Vasile. For this purpose, we can take into consideration the year Gheorghe Diaconovici married a local girl, and also the information related to his generations of descendants born in Bocșa, among whom was Constantin Diaconovici Loga. The short-lived nature of this workshop, starting with Deacon Vasile's arrival and continuing with his son Gheorghe, who often changed his domicile looking for work, could not provide an advanced level of training. That is the reason why, in the late eighteenth and early nineteenth centuries, patterns and model books of local painters were used.[26]

At Bocșa, Gheorghe Diaconovici, along with his father Vasile, and other painters, apprentices and collaborators, decorated a number of churches from the neighbouring area. Dimitrie, an obscure painter, is mentioned as apprentice, but his accomplishments have been lost. It is possible that he may be Dimitrie Mihailovici, born in Bocșa, summoned to paint the interior of St George's church in Caransebeș in traditional fashion. Later, Mihailovici is mentioned as Mihail Velceleanu's collaborator, the latter being considered the first Banatian academic painter.[27]

In all likelihood, Mihail Velceleanu arrived in Banat around 1824, when he painted the church in Cuptoarele Secu. He was probably a member of the group of painters that, under Gheorghe Diaconovici's guidance, created the painting in the church of the Bocșa. It is possible that Velceleanu understood the limited artistic capabilities of Diaconovici's workshop and he decided to go to Munich, one of Europe's most important artistic centres. Velceleanu's training in Munich results from an enquiry made by all Banatian churches with the purpose of completing an artistic topography of the region. The fact that young Velceleanu left for Munich with a German friend is mentioned there.

Although he had access to much more evolved models, Velceleanu remained true to the tradition. The manner in which he painted the interior of Cornea church, a unique complex that has been preserved in its initial form, is relevant. A self-portrait considered to be the first work of this kind made in the local workshops from the area Bocșa-Lugoj-Caransebeș-Oravița is worth mentioning.[28] Besides the quality of his works, Velceleanu managed to establish at Bocșa one of the most representative artistic workshops in the Banat, actively taking part in the evolution of Banatian art in the first three decades of the nineteenth century. Velceleanu's workshop trained Nicolae Popescu, the most renowned Romanian painter of the second half of the nineteenth century, Matei Popovici and Filip Matei, the latter being the author of over 60 iconostases and himself founder of an artistic workshop.[29]

Born into a family of poor peasants, Filip Matei headed initially to Oravița, where he began his training at the workshop owned by the Popovici family. At Bocșa, he married Gheorghe Diaconovici's daughter, establishing an artistic workshop with the aim to train future apprentices. Filip Matei is mentioned as contributor to the interior painting and the mural compositions of Seleuș church (now a village in the area of Serbian Banat), along with Matei Popovici and Master Nicolae Popescu.

Filip Matei's house in Bocșa was a meeting place for priests, painters and top intellectuals of the Banat.[30] However, his achievements in religious art, similar to Matei Popovici's works and those of other contemporaries he had worked with, were based on imitating the patterns of his predecessors.[31] At the end of the eighteenth and the beginning of the nineteenth century, painters Dimitrie Mihailovici, Nicolae Săiman and Ioan Ionescu were mentioned as apprentices of the workshops in Bocșa. It is possible that other painters were also trained here, among whom Nicolae Mărișescu, a modest painter, and Ioan Ionescu, the author of the iconostasis of the church from Bărbosu village.[32]

THE WORKSHOPS FROM LUGOJ

In Lugoj, administrative restructuring stimulated urban development, materialised by a series of public buildings, offices and churches, all built in the style enforced by the Habsburg Empire. For the town, this period is characterised by development and prosperity, due to commercial activities. On the spot of the former monastery of St Nicholas, the church of the Ascension was erected. Built in the Baroque style, the church has a similar plan to that of Săraca monastery.[33] The artists who worked at Lugoj in the first half of the nineteenth century were Moalăr Nicolae of Lugoj (1808), Igna the Painter (1824), Ioan Lazăr (1832–44) and Ioan Ștefanovici (1833).[34] The works made by these painters were underappreciated in the specialist literature, and they were considered as belonging to the village schools. This is also the case with the Diaconovici family.[35]

Instead, there is more information regarding Atanasie, the painter whose presence in Lugoj was mentioned at the end of the eighteenth century. The decoration of Zolt church is illustrative for his artistic style. Apart from his particular technique, the painter signed the wall which separates the nave from the narthex and which is part of the old church decoration. Answering the demands of benefactors and donors, Atanasie painted the portrait of the local prince, Obadă. The work is considered one of the first Banatian art portraits. Having limited financial possibilities, the benefactors and donors wished to be immortalised on the church walls, sometimes together with their families. Among the few portraits preserved in the churches from the Lugoj area, the painting depicting the peasant Medescu in Povârgina church is worth mentioning. Here, Gheorghe Diaconovici demonstrated the skills achieved during his training at the workshop in Vršac, along with Nikola Nescović.

A large number of works made by painters from Lugoj at the end of the eighteenth century were influenced by Ștefan Tenecki.[36] His apprentices and collaborators had participated in the creation of the pictorial complexes in the churches of Dubești and Groși. Within the Banatian painting of the late eighteenth century, these ensembles belong to the influence of Western artistic direction, much more advanced than the local traditional art, which was conservative and dominant by the Brâncovenesc style. Although the local painters adopted some novel elements, the traditional artistic approaches were still present throughout the nineteenth century.

Petru Nicolici, an artist trained in Gheorghe Diaconovici's workshop, had a significant role in the religious painting of the area. His works exist in many churches from Srediștea Mare, Bocșa, Lugoj and Caransebeș.[37] Petru Nicolici's presence at Lugoj is attested in 1801. His most renowned works are those from the churches of Curtea, painted between 1804 and 1806, Poieni (1911) and, partially, Topla.[38]

One of the artists who took part at the interior decoration of the church of the Ascension in Lugoj, finished in 1764, was Ștefan the Painter (Ștefan Tenecki). Among his works, *The Portrait of Benefactor Gavrilă Gurean*, *The Portrait of Vrsac an Caransebeș*, *Bishop Iovan Gheorghevici* and *The Portrait of Father Superior Gavrilă* have been preserved. Amidst the benefactors who contributed to the construction of the church, Prince Gavrilă Guran is notable and his portrait is placed on the opposite wall of the lectern.[39]

The people of Lugoj decided to replace the old church iconostasis, and the execution of the painting was assigned to Pavel Giurkovici, the most important and requested artist of the time. He is the author of the pictorial ensembles from Vršac, Biserica Albă and Oradea. Pavel Giurkovici's activity in the Banat had an important impact on local painters, many of whom used his models.[40] His collaboration with Lazar Gerdanovici and his son's with Pavel Giurkovici influenced the technical and stylistic training of the artists from Lugoj.[41] Natives of Vršac, the two Gerdanovics participated, in the early nineteenth century, as Giurkovici's assistants, in the painting of the iconostasis of the Lugoj church. In the year 1818, when the contract was signed by Pavel Giurkovici, it was mentioned that Lazar Gerdanovici had to take part, too. With one condition: the church inscription must be written in the Romanian language.[42] Influenced by Pavel Giurkovici, George Gerdanovici reached artistic maturity, his main work being the Denta Orthodox church iconostasis painting.[43]

After the repainting and the restoration of the iconostasis, Giurkovici's original works have been preserved only on the lecterns and pulpit. The icon technique was well considered and adapted to the liturgical demands. On the north wall, there is *Doubting Thomas* and *Let the Little Children Come to Me*, along with the mandatory presence of the icon of St John *Damascene*. Opposite the lecterns there are three compositions: *Healing of the Blind Man*, *The Parable of the Pharisee and Tax Collector* and St *Anatolius Oriental*.[44] The original parts of Giurkovici's icons in the church of the Ascension are an expression of thematic and iconographic traditionalism in eighteenth-century Banatian religious art, exploring elements of Central European influence.

Lazar Gerdanovici's activity in Lugoj is mentioned in 1793.[45] Like other painters, he had acquired his artistic skills outside Lugoj. He collaborated in creating the painting in the St John Orthodox church from Caransebeș where, upon a tin oval frame, he painted *Virgin Mary*. Its fine modelling, in dominant ochre tones, is similar to the interpretation of other figures from related icons, especially those that highlight the mix between local traditionalism and Western influences. The blue coloured clothes are accentuated with golden frames, in the distinct manner of Banatian local workshops from the late eighteenth and early nineteenth centuries.

At the demand of some rich merchants from Caransebeș, Lazar Gerdanovici painted the guild flag in the church of St John, which he signed *Moloval Lazar Gerdanovič*. Although he mastered the necessary technique, Gerdanovici could not submit to the requested criteria of the civil portrait when he painted the portrait of *Lady Ilka*. The almost flat face shows a lack of anatomical knowledge, a problem for most artists of his group. Trying to compensate for these shortcomings, the painter drew a rich decoration, depicting floral motives down to the smallest details, in the manner used for church interiors. Around her neck there is a necklace of gold coins, a mark of the wealthy.[46] The particular characteristics of Western painting were increasingly imposed upon the Banatian masters, an aspect revealed by the frequent use of illustrations from calendars and gravures, and of Baroque-style religious scenes as models.

During the eighteenth and nineteenth centuries, within Banatian art, a series of important paintings are linked to the name of Ioan Capețianu. This is another artist whose work was influenced by Gerdanovici's painting. *Portrait of Ion Nica* (1868), for example, is in many ways similar to the works of the artist from Vršac. In the church of the Descent of the Holy Ghost in Lugoj there is a work attributed to Ion Capețianu, given the author's signature.

During the nineteenth century Lugoj became an important urban centre with a rich cultural and artistic life. After more journeys to Rome, Nicolae Popescu settled in Lugoj in 1876. In the same year, he painted the imperial doors of the church of the Ascension and the portrait of the Greek Catholic bishop Victor Mihali Apșa. In the last decades of the nineteenth century, Banatian religious art is characterised by the contrast between the refined taste of the urban customers and the demands of the less privileged rural environment. Upon the influence of artistic traditionalism, cheap works made by painters trained in local workshops were preferred. In such conditions, the interest for technique and repertoire renewal diminished, and the painters who were decorating village churches repeat, in a traditional manner, the same conservative composition, resistant to iconographic novelties.

THE POPOVICI FAMILY WORKSHOP IN ORAVIȚA

The personality of the artist Ioan Popovici is connected to the beginnings of the painting workshops in Oravița.[47] Ștefan Popovici, Dimitrie Popovici,

Mihai Popovici and Dimitrie Turcu worked there. They would accept the artistic demands of village churches,[48] under the strong influence of Gheorghe Diaconovici's style in Sredistea Mare.[49]

The first painter from Oravița of whom there is information was Ioan Popovici, whose activity can be traced between 1762 and 1789. Founder of the local workshop, he collaborated, in 1762, with Gheorghe Diaconovici[50] at the interior decoration of the Clopodia church.[51] He worked, along Radu Lazarevici and Stancu Raicu,[52] as Diaconovici's assistant, and made his artistic debut in the workshops of Sredistea Mare and Bocșa,[53] owned by the Diaconovici family.

Ștefan Popovici painted a large number of religious icons for modest employers. In 1823 he engaged in the interior painting of the churches in Eftimie Murgu, Iablanița and Crușovăț.[54] It was he who introduced the landscape within Banatian art. The painters from Oravița and its neighbouring areas, which had started their activity in Ștefan Popovici's time, continued to be influenced by the old master, only rarely accepting the tardy echoes of Western art that reached them due to the artists who had trained in the European artistic centres.

From the third generation of the Popovici family, at the end of the nineteenth century, the most important artists were Dimitrie Popovici and Mihai Popovici.[55] While the works of the latter display significant artistic contradictions, Dimitrie Popovici lacked skill in representing the human body. However, his works differ from those of his contemporaries Nicolae Hașca, Matei Popovici or Iosif Matei, which suggests the possibility of collaborating with a workshop that used a more advanced technique.[56] Dimitrie Popovici's large-scale mural compositions are found in the churches of Domașnea and Sălcița (in present-day Serbian Banat), proving his good knowledge of frescoes. Together with his mentor Ștefan Popovici, he created the mural compositions, while in 1834 he decorated the iconostasis togther with Dimitrie Turcu.

The Popovici family workshops in Oravița established themselves as important painting centres in nineteenth-century Banat. Although trained according to the demands of religious painting, the artists who worked at Oravița were interested to improve their manner of work and enrich their themes by depicting some historic subjects.

THE WORKSHOPS OF CARANSEBEȘ, BISERICA ALBĂ AND BECICHERECUL MARE

The increasing number of architectural works and religious paintings reflected the rapid socio-economic development of Caransebeș in the second half of the nineteenth century.[57] First painting requests[58] came from the skinners' guild, in 1762. Gheorghe Diaconovici and Radu Lazarevici, both members of the Sredиștea Mare School of painting, decorated the guild flag. Five decades later, in 1807, Lazar Derdanović, founder of the artistic workshop from Lugoj, painted the town craftsmen flag. Stancović family from Caransebeș funded a number of requests and also paid for the renovation of paintings in St John's and the murals in St George's.[59]

The auspicious economic situation of Caransebeș led Nicolae Popescu,[60] one of the most renowned Banatian painters, to suggest the founding of the Academy of Fine Arts. The idea coincided with the establishment of the Romanian Orthodox Bishopric of Caransebeș, in the year 1865.[61] The art historian Carlo D. Ormeville wrote on 30 June 1867 about Nicolae Popescu's talent in *Eptacordo*, the journal dedicated to arts.

The long addiction to traditional art and the association with Wallachia's monasteries of Hurezi and Tismana, from which travelling groups of painters were arriving, were traits of the art from the mountainous Banat. Those were the artists who decorated the monastery of Caransebeș. The collaboration was continued in the second part of the nineteenth century, when Banatian artists Zaharie Achimescu and Nicolae Popescu painted the church of Târgu Jiu.

In the eighteenth century, some artists from Europe were summoned to the Banat to adorn the houses of wealthy families. In 1866, the Viennese painter Karl Gutsch, Jovan Popović's friend since the time of his studies at the Viennese Art Academy, was invited to finish the interior of St George's church, honouring the benefactors' requests to paint in a new manner. Karl Gutsch's activity in the church is confirmed by the inscription on the icon of Jesus on the southern doors. Dimitrie Turcu, who signed the composition *Jesus Entering the Church*,[62] also participated in the mural painting. The presence of Western painters in Caransebeș and its neighbouring area facilitated the emergence of laic artistic and technical innovations in the religious art production of Banat.[63]

Painters Vasile Teodorovici, Gheorghe Zugravul and Trifon Achimescu, the last being the founder of the workshop where Zaharia Achimescu was trained, worked in Caransebeș during the first half of the nineteenth century. Trifon Achimescu's artistic activity between 1833 and 1861 can be traced based on his works and on archive documents. The artist decorated the church interiors of Obreja (1834), Valea Bolvașniței (1834), Goleț (1842) and Plugova (1861). The southern lateral doors and the icon of *St Barbara*[64] from St John's church of Caransebeș have been preserved to this day.

Zaharia Achimescu, along with the Italian artist Bartolomeu Dellomini, did the painting of the Lugoj traders' guild flag. Due to the attempts at renewing and modernising the pictorial manner and technique, the centre for painting in Caransebeș can be considered an important precursor of Banatian contemporary art.

The founder of the first artistic workshop in Biserica Albă, Simeon Iakșici, is mentioned for the first time in 1796, when he paints the built-in iconostasis of the Râtișor (Serbian Banat) Orthodox church.[65] Iakșici's work suggests the low level of artistic technique, especially regarding proportions and physiognomies. From the stylistic analysis of his mural compositions we can observe that the accentuated contours of the physiognomies were drawn by moulding the material with half-tones and contrasts of light and shadow. On the damaged wall painting, we can discern the initial colouration in which the dominant palette was pink, ochre and green, used in all the landscapes.[66] Between 1801 and 1802, Simeon Iakșici decorated the interior of the Sasca church, a work which, due to unknown reasons, was finalised by his son, Arsenije Iakșici.[67]

The signature of Axentie Mărișescu is frequently mentioned in the churches from Banat. He painted mostly in Southern Banat and the Danube Gorge between 1850 and 1884. He decorated the churches in Măcești, Radimna and Moldova Nouă, as well as the iconostases in Divici (1877) and Zlatița (1884).[68] The analysis of his work indicates a high-class technique, this being the reason why his icons are so easily distinguishable. Following requests from the people from Biserica Albă,[69] he made the portraits of *Aca and His Wife*, *Maca Nedeljković*,[70] *Mateja Davidov*, *Priest Kosta Vujić*, *The Girl in Green Clothes* and *Romanian Villager from Grebenaț in Traditional Costume*.

Gioca Putnic is another artist who worked in the workshops in Biserica Albă. Together with his son, Iovan, he painted mobile icons for numerous churches throughout Banat. Among those, we can mention the pedestal, throne icons and lateral doors of Sts Michael and Gabriel the Archangels' church in Izbiște.[71] Gioca Putnic also decorated a large dimension structure in the same church. The Iakșici family had an important role within the workshops of Biserica Albă. The paintings made by the members of this family in the first decades of the nineteenth century, under Pavel Giurović's influence, alongside the creations of the Mărișescu and Putnic families, represent a significant chapter in Banatian art history.[72]

We can state that the workshops from Biserica Albă did not function in unity, according to common artistic and iconographic concepts, but as distinct ateliers, adjusted to the demands of the time.[73]

Becicherecu Mare School of painting was founded by Dimitrie Popović, or Popov, as he signed his own icons. The work *Virgin Mary* in the Orlovat church, dated 1756, represents the painter's debut.[74] His artistic activity is concentrated between 1770 and 1779, when he decorated the iconostases and the mural compositions from the churches in Titel, Orlovat, Meda, Srpski Itebej (all part of the present-day Serbian Banat) and Ciacova.[75] In 1774 Popović painted the Srpski Itebei iconostasis, visibly influenced by Western Baroque iconography. Dimitrije Popovici's compositions from the *Passion of Christ* series were at the time a novelty in Banatian religious painting.

Similar to the painters of the Jakšić family from Biserica Albă, Dimitrije Popovici's accomplishments belong to Banatian transition art. The works made in this period have a distinctive style which combines traditional elements with Ukrainian and Central European Baroque. The influence of Slavic Baroque, which Popovici had known from intermediaries, is evident in his work. Among the iconostases painted by Popovici and preserved in their original form, the one from Ciacova exhibits a slight influence of Russian realist art, especially in depicting saints' figures. Dimitrije Bačević's influence upon Popovici's works is obvious, even if the latter couldn't reach the ability of his master.

In the 1830s Constantin Daniel was trained at the Viennese Academy of Arts. Born in Lugoj, he started his career in Arsa Teodorović's workshop in Timișoara during 1812–15.[76] Constantin Daniel and his school decorated the Ascension church iconostasis in Panciova between 1833 and 1836.[77] Constantin Daniel's school activity is attached to the Uzdin (today in Serbian Banat) Romanian Orthodox church iconostasis (1833–36), the Serbian church in Timișoara (1838–43),[78] the Orthodox church in Dobrița (Serbian Banat) and Jarkovac church (Serbian Banat), between 1858 and 1861.[79] After he had finished the Timișoara church iconostases he painted the iconostasis of the Serbian and Romanian church of Dobrica (Serbian Banat).

THE PAINTING CENTRES FROM TIMIȘOARA AND ARAD

Within the generous art collection of Arad-Gai monastery, art historians from Banat have identified the works of some renowned painters. For example, the priest Simion painted in a traditional manner the icons of *St Nicholas*, *St John the Baptist* and *Deisis*. Mihai Popa's rustic painting can be traced in the icons of *St Nicholas* and the *Virgin Mary with Jesus* from 1763. Painter Iovan, contemporary of Nedelcu Popovici, made the same icons of *St Nicholas*, *Virgin Mary with Jesus* and *Deisis*, while in 1783 Constantin painted the imperial doors.[80]

Ștefan Tenețchi's painting, cherished by bishops Isaia Antonovici, Sinesie Jivanovici and Pahomie Knejevici, is an example of the local interpretation of Baroque, which was starting to penetrate Banat.[81] Having a privileged status, Ștefan Tenețchi was in great demand in Arad and its neighbouring areas. In 1767 the artist painted the iconostasis of the Arad-Gai church,[82] at that time Bishop Sinesie Jivanovici's residence, currently the Romanian monastery of St Simeon Stâlpnicul. The decoration of the Greek Catholic church of Blaj reflects not only Tenețchi's artistic prowess, but also his solid theological education which allowed him to illustrate uncommon religious themes.[83] Another important painter from Arad was Nikola Aleksici. Upon finishing his painting studies at the Viennese Academy, he returned to Arad and made iconostases and mural paintings in Sânnicolaul Mare, Cuvin, Sânpetru Mare and Arad.[84] Nikola Aleksici painted the mural compositions of Sânnicolaul Mare and Tekelia church of Arad.

Between 1830 and 1840, Banatian art came under the influence of new programmes and pictorial aesthetics, mostly Viennese, which represented the artistic model to follow in this part of the monarchy. As a Central European style, the Biedermeier inspired a whole generation of painters and sculptors. The new style brought changes in the thematics of mural painting, with moralising scenes and medieval history gaining a special place. Banatian painters who adjusted to the new artistic evolution were Dimitrie Avramovici, Pavle Simici and Nikola Aleksici.

A representative artist of Banatian painting is Stevan Aleksici, Nika's grandson. Trained in Munich, he worked in the Banat before settling at Modoš. He painted mural compositions, such as the one in Lugovet. At the church of Ciacova, he tried to merge the Baroque image of iconostasis with his own realistic dramatism. The large-scale mural compositions in Ciacova depict typical themes for Banatian religious painting. On the lateral walls of the church nave, Stefan Aleksici painted the compositions *Crucifixion* and *The Descent from the Cross* using an accentuated dramatism, the artist being a gifted advocate for historical subjects.[85]

The first painters' guild of Timișoara was founded around 1750 with the aim of supporting the rights of established painters in relation to anonymous travelling artists.[86] During that period, the acknowledged associations of painters were those of Nedelcu and Șerban Popovici.[87] Țešljar, Nikola Neškoviš and Arsenije Teodoroviš[88] worked here too, while Constantin Daniel started his activity in Nesentaler's workshop,[89] also in Timișoara.

Painting in Timișoara during the first half of the nineteenth century was strongly influenced by Arsenije Teodorović, master of Serbian classicism. The artist's relation with his students is described in Nickola Aleksić's biography, where he was also named 'painter Nica from Arad'. In his workshop artists such as Nikola Aleksić, Constantin Pantelić and Sava Petrović studied, and his style influenced Dimitrije Dimšić, Lazar Milić, Gheorghe Boieru and Petar Šortanović.

Arsenije Teodorović's impact upon Sava Petrović is obvious in the icon *Coronation of the Virgin Mary* from the Serbian church of Fabric quarter in Timișoara and also in the composition *Agara Points Towards the Life-Giving Spring*,[90] painted on a medallion. Sava Petrović also made the painting *Coronation of Virgin Mary*. Such works led to his professional consecration, so that in 1819 he was assigned to do the painting of Mehala church, near Timișoara. The inscription above the iconostasis mentions the painter alongside the goldsmith Emanuil Antonović, who did the gold works for the iconostasis, as Petrović's collaborator. The two artists continued to work together on the restoration of the iconostasis icons from Parța, south of Timișoara. The portraits of Bishop Iosif Putnic, made by Sava Petrović, prove the painter's recognition as portraitist of church officials.

The artistic activity of Pavel Pavela Petrović, Sava Petrović's son, started in his father's workshop from Timișoara, in line with the tradition of many Banatian families. Pavel's academic education was at the Viennese Academy, in Professor Kupelvizer's class.[91] Upon finishing his studies, the painter settled in the Banatian village of Modoș, where he created four icons for the local church.[92] In creating these works, he repeated the compositional scheme of Daniel's icons from the church of Uzdin.[93] Pavel Petrović's successor in the artistic life of the early nineteenth century was Constantin Daniel.[94] In 1843 he painted the iconostasis of Timișoara cathedral, one of the most appreciated works of nineteenth-century Banatian art.[95]

The brothers Imre and Béla Vizkelety, born in Arad, worked for several years in Timișoara, when Dőme Szikora, D. Jägermann, Endre Makő, Adalbert Schäffer, Isidor Neugas, Laios Csillagi and Janos Kővary were also painting.[96] With the money they earned from painting portraits of wealthy customers, Imre and Béla Vizkelety financed their studies at the Viennese Academy. Béla Vizkelety returned to the Banat, in the village of Baziaș, where, in 1856, he painted two portraits acquired by Ormosh Szigmund for his private collection.[97]

Among the Banatian painters, Anton Bissingen and Ludwig von Bersuder were of special importance. Anton Bissingen supported the talented apprentices of his workshop, being a real Maecenas for young talents. One of the painters who had benefited from Bissingen's protection was Gheorghe Baba, Corneliu Baba's father. A few watercolour paintings attributed to Bissingen, among them *The Victory Scene*, made in the Romantic manner, are preserved at the Timișoara Museum of Art.

Ludwig von Bersuder was one of the most important supporters of the artistic creations in Timișoara.[98] He studied at the Vienna Academy of Plastic Arts, when Waldmüler's work was influencing the painting of the Austro-Hungarian Monarchy's capital city. Upon finishing his studies, Bersuder opened a workshop in Timișoara, where lots of future artists acquired their knowledge of painting. Among those worth mentioning are Gheorghe Baba, Ferdinand Gallas, Stefan Szőnyi and Julius Podlipny. One of the most outstanding works painted by Ludwig von Bersuder is *The Parade*. Another important artist of nineteenth-century Timișoara was Franz Komlossy.[99] A student of Ferdinand Waldmüler, he painted idyllic landscapes and still lifes, especially flowers. His romanticist manner is noticeable in *Soldier's Portrait*, a recurrent motif in nineteenth-century Banatian painting.

Within Banatian painting, Adolf Humborg and Johann Wälders are worth mentioning. The first was distinguished by his depiction of children's portraits and scenes of their lives. A frequent theme was inspired by the life of monks, an example being *Monks in Conversation*. As drawing teacher, Johann Wälders marked the artistic direction of his pupils by instilling in them the love for portraits, his favourite[100] genre.

Josef Ferenczy is also part of the Banatian painters' gallery. After he graduated from the Budapest Academy, he opened a painting school in Timișoara.[101] Ferenczy published an important work, *Theoretische Studie über die Malerei*, a small treatise on painting, which was used by students as theoretical material for artistic studies. In numerous drawings and paintings, he used the impressionist technique to depict the colourful richness of Hungarian traditional costume. *Girl in Traditional Costume* and *Hungarian Folk Dance* are just two of Ferenczy's paintings from his period in the Banat and Transylvania. He was a faithful historian of traditional customs and a portraitist of his contemporaries. The social theme is illustrated in *Reșița Founders*, a work painted in almost expressionist manner.

Many less-known artists worked in Timișoara. Among them was Petru Diaconovici from the Fabric quarter, mentioned in the church of Povârgina, who was possibly a member of the renowned intellectual Diaconovici family. On the *St John the Baptist* icon, preserved in the Orthodox Episcopate of Caransebeș, is the signature of Jancović, another painter from the Fabric neighbourhood. Caius Giorgevici, a mural painter trained in Massi Tonelli's and Alberto Franchetti's workshop, painted in 1826 the interior of St Elijah's church in Fabric, having among his collaborators a certain Ion Negrea from Sibiu. Ion Chioreanu, whose presence is mentioned in the contract of the Sculia church, also originated in the Fabric quarter. Pavel Murgu from Izvin decorated in the mid-nineteenth century a number of churches from villages around Timișoara: Chișoda, Recaș and Budinți.

CONCLUSIONS

A series of observations arise from the presentation of the emergence, evolution and transformation of the painting workshops within travelling groups, guilds and family studios in the Banat during the period of study. In the eighteenth and nineteenth centuries, the Banatian artistic workshops served, generally, the demands of religious art, in which the main master, owner or leader of the workshop, had a decisive didactic role. More or less qualified teachers initiated, in their own workshops, improvised schools of unknown duration, having a structure often deprived of rigour. The artistic training presents features emphasised by specialised books, which remind us that this form of training often had a quasi-familial character. The apprentices gathered around the unique master were frequently his close relatives, thus leading to dynasties of painters.

At the end of the eighteenth century and particularly in the nineteenth century, Banatian artists assembled in the most important centres of the region. In these workshops a large number of students could be trained for a longer period of time. The artistic education promoted by these workshops continued the tradition based upon the assimilation of knowledge from consecrated artists. The imposed models were transmitted by painters' workbooks from one generation to another. Sometimes they were completed with other drawings or, in the modern age, even with gravures, which facilitated the emergence of western iconographic themes among the Banatian painters' repertoires. Gradually, the accepted models were altered by adding new elements. At the mid- and late eighteenth century, Baroque influences become more and more significant. Also, modelling of figures and clothing are increased, landscapes become more numerous and diverse, so that the traditional Orthodox iconography representations had to adapt to the influence and spirit of Western art.

Parallel to Baroque painting, the Byzantine art tradition was also promoted within the workshops of the eighteenth century. Before accepting Baroque as a dominant model at the end of the eighteenth century, the rebirth of the Banatian art had greatly benefited from the Wallachian painters. They were travelling painters and bearers of change. Frequently requested, with their enterprising spirit, the Wallachian painters or those coming from the artistic area of Kiev Monastery of the Caves propagated their manner of work on the territory of the Banat.

Following research on the activity of Banatian workshops, we can conclude that they served the needs of society, whose orders were placed according to economic wealth and the artistic taste. Often talented, open to innovation and novelty, Banatian painters from 1718 to 1918 were financially dependent on their benefactors, and for that reason could not overcome the artistic models imposed on them.

11
THE GERMAN-LANGUAGE PRESS AND THE IMPERIAL IDEOLOGY

Victor Neumann

UNDER THE COORDINATION OF VIENNA, the Roman Catholic Diocese of the Banat of Timişoara was re-established; the Swabians, an important segment of the population of German origin, were colonised; and basic administrative and economic institutions were founded. The Catholics coordinated the religious life of the region, representing the main bridge to the Austrian Empire. As soon as German was imposed as the official language of Timişoara and its neighbouring area, as well as a language for communicating and popularising information, the German-language press became an effective tool. During both the eighteenth and nineteenth centuries, it was in tune with the conqueror's ideology and with the direction of the imperial authority in Vienna. The two German-language publications, *Temeswarer Nachrichten* and *Temeswarer Zeitung*, are among the best examples of the scale of Austrian reforms in the Banat during the eighteenth and nineteenth centuries, and of their role in promoting and establishing European modernity within the East-Central regions of the continent.

THE FIRST REGIONAL NEWSPAPER: TEMESWARER NACHRICHTEN (TIMIŞOARA NEWS)

Following the recommendations of Maria Theresa and Joseph II in 1768 to establish a German-language press in the region (along with one in Serbian and one in Romanian), Mathäus Joseph Heimerl established the newspaper *Temeswarer Nachrichten* (*Timişoara News*), the first of its kind in the Banat. As a result of the goodwill of Count Clary und Altringen, president of the city administration of Timişoara and governor of the Banat, the first issue of the newspaper appeared on 18 April 1771, modelled on papers printed at Vienna, Bratislava and Pest.[1] Through transmission of the news, and also through the content of some of its articles, the newspaper created a vibrant intellectual climate.

Its first issue popularised information from the Viennese Court,[2] reproducing passages from *Diarium*,[3] one of the best-known contemporary Austrian publications, about the actions of Maria Theresa, the audiences granted, the imperial orders regarding the official currency and its circulation, and the mourning gatherings organised on the death of political personalities or members of the imperial family. Along with such news, the editor Mathäus Joseph Heimerl advertised the new orders of Count Clary und Altringen relating to regional economy and trade through which state control over the exchange of goods and transportation was to be effected. This followed the centralist model, of French origin, which had been assimilated by the imperial administration.

In the third issue of the newspaper, published on 2 May 1771, Mathäus Joseph Heimerl published an article in which, after inserting some news regarding Austro-Prussian relations, he assessed the political situation of the Romanian principalities of Moldavia and Wallachia, the unification tendencies of the Tsarist Russian maritime forces, and Poland's precarious political and economic situation:

> It seems that the Russians hope to keep Moldavia and Wallachia under their domination. They seek to combine the cameral works [*Cameralwesen*, relating to finance and administration] within a good constitution [*gute Verfassung*] and in this regard Field Marshal Ruminatsev summoned Baron Gartenberg from Warsaw . . . A fleet from Azov will act at sea to attempt the unification of Russia's maritime power in the archipelago. Beside all this, there is still talk of peace . . . At the same time, Poland suffers the most. And if the war continues, the country will be deprived of people and cattle.[4]

THE CULTURAL AND EDUCATIONAL ASPECTS OF THE PUBLICATION

During the last decades of the eighteenth century, the Banat was not only a region in which craft and trades prospered, but also one which was concerned with education and with intellectual emancipation. Close contacts had been established with Central and South-Eastern Europe through some of Timişoara's intellectuals. Supported by the imperial administration, schools were founded and textbooks published. In a report submitted to Maria Theresa in

1879, the lawyer Daniel Lazarini of Caransebeș (commissioned to investigate the possibility of improving the educational process in the Romanian school network in the Banat) stressed the necessity for the authorities to provide an appropriate number of textbooks in the Romanian language.[5] Mathäus Joseph Heimerl's contribution was to publish and sell textbooks and children's books: *Spelling Book, ABC and Multiplication Tables, Magazine Full of Lessons for Children with Multiplication Tables,*[6] *Magazine Full of Lessons for Children, for the Correct Training of Mind and Heart, Magazine Full of Lessons for Young People, especially Young Women, Handbook for Young People, Poor People,*[7] etc. These were reprints of Viennese editions intended for use in normal schools (those intended for training teachers).

Many works of literature and history were popularised through *Temeswarer Nachrichten*: Diderot, *Theatre*; Friedrich Hagedorn, *Complete Works*; Friedrich Gottlieb Klopstock, *Writings* (including the poems *Messiah*, *Solomon* and *Adam's Death*); Ossian, *Poems*; Samuel von Pufendorf, *Introduction to the History of Europe's Best Known Empires and States*; Ludwig Muratori, *The Happy Christians of Paraguay*; eight different works by Caraccioli; and Friedrich Lauterbach's chronicle on the lives of Polish princes and kings.[8] Mathäus Joseph Heimerl understood the importance of works written by literary celebrities and historians of his time, and that is the reason he disseminated them. His printed editions could not meet demand or satisfy the population's cultural aspirations. A sizeable importation of books printed in Vienna, Paris and Berlin was needed. It is telling that Diderot's dramatic work was known in Timișoara in the years 1770–80 and that among teachers, doctors, public servants, traders and officers there were people with serious cultural baggage, some making an effort to understand the Gaelic poetry of Ossian. Gottfried von Brettschneider, one of the scholars of the time, affirmed that Timișoara was a true cultural centre in which the followers of Goethe confronted those of Wieland.[9] The activity of other intellectuals – Wolfgang von Kempelen, councillor of the imperial administration; Clemens von Rossi, first canon and vicar of the Roman Catholic cathedral and former priest of the Italians colonised at Orțișoara; and Johann Jakob Ehrler, senior bureaucrat of the imperial administration – showed the existence of an environment that cultivated the humanities.

THE HISTORY AND GEOGRAPHY OF THE BANAT OF TIMIȘOARA DURING THE ENLIGHTENMENT

Temeswarer Nachrichten stood out by publishing a well-documented study on the history of the Banat. The imperial authorities of Vienna took a constant interest in the history of the region, and the paper tried to satisfy their curiosity. In the appendix to the second issue of 25 April 1771, Mathäus Joseph Heimerl announced that he would print a 'Historical Description of the Banat of Timişoara' ('Historische Beschreibung des Banats Temeswar'). The study was addressed to readers from Timişoara and the neighbouring area as well as foreign subscribers (*auswärtige Pränumeranten*).[10] Starting with the third issue, the 'Historische Beschreibung des Banats Temeswar' was published in instalments with no signature. The information was carefully selected, the author having insisted upon significant facts. A geographical description of the Banat was followed by a short historical overview from antiquity to the eighteenth century and then a presentation of demographic movement and the socio-economic situation. The descriptions – and the interpretations of them – were constrained by the limits of contemporary knowledge.

In the introduction to the 'Historische Beschreibung', the borders of Dacia from the time of the kingdom of Decebal are indicated, comprising the land between the Danube, the Tisza, the Carpathian Mountains, the Nistru and the Prut. The Banat of Timişoara was considered to be part of old Dacia. The same paragraph also states that Dacia was conquered by Emperor Ulpius Traianus and transformed into a Roman province, while Sarmisegetusa, the old capital, became a Roman colony.[11] As proof of this, the texts of two Roman inscriptions discovered during the first half of the eighteenth century and preserved at the administrative office in Caransebeş are reproduced.[12] Regarding the indigenous population, the study mentions its military force and the desire to remain autonomous and continue in the same territory.

This perspective indicates the overlapping of ancient and modern views and is particular to Enlightenment and Romantic historical literature. The proof of origins, of continuity of habitat, and of the language peculiarities of a specific community coincides with the debut of the national idea. In the case of the Germans, this idea – in the absence of statehood, or an administrative and judicial system – facilitated the formulation and promotion of identity as based on history and ethnoculture.[13] Influenced by the new orientation of his time, the author is interested in identity in the ethnonational sense in an area in which at that time (the 1770s and 1780s) communities did not define themselves in that way. They had been shaped by religion and the Church, the confessional nation being their main reference for identity in the eighteenth century. The article we discuss must be placed in the context of the intellectual and political life of the late eighteenth century.

The narration of the facts in this article shows that the author takes an interest in defining the moral and spiritual profile of the Romanian and Serbian population of the region. The author affirms that Romanians in the Banat represent the largest portion of the population and call themselves Romanian, being considered as the descendants of colonists placed in the region by Emperor Ulpius Traianus. The author also observes that the Romanian language has profound roots in Latin and that the Roman origins of the Romanians can be demonstrated in their clothing, traditions and food.[14] Speaking of the relations between the different cultural-linguistic communities,[15] he underlines that all the people of the Banat – among whom, alongside Romanians, were Germans, Serbians, Hungarians, Bulgarians and Jews – were able to live together under good conditions, They often lived in mixed neighbourhoods, working together, while retaining their own language and religion.[16] Regarding Romanians and Serbians, who shared the same Orthodox religion, it was mentioned that they 'are slim, tall, strong and handsome by nature'. While the staple diet of the Romanian population was some sort of polenta, prepared in the same manner as bread, from 'Turkish wheat' (corn), home-made bread was the food of the Serbians. Both communities enjoyed eating raw ham, smoked in the open air, their preferred alcoholic drink being *răchia* (a boiled liquid of plums and cherry plums). The desire to coexist in a civilised manner with the neighbours – writes the author of the article – was due to the education of the old village sages. Thus, the Habsburg experiment was not new to the population of the Banat. The promotion of healthy cohabitation had been a constant of local culture, and the discipline and education promoted by the imperial administration meshed with one of the region's traditional character traits.

For a better understanding of its past, Heimerl's columnist noted, in approximately chronological order, the successive military occupations of the Banat in the medieval and early modern periods: Hungarian, Turkish and Habsburg.[17] In the same context, he showed, based on official imperial documents, that the Banat became (after the Habsburg conquest) a new acquisition, occupied after war, thus any private right issued before 1716 could not be acknowledged or taken into consideration. The region was placed under the direct authority of Viennese central institutions (the Aulic Chamber, the so-called Commission of New Acquisitions and the Aulic War Council), and was not incorporated within Hungary. It was a domain of Crown and Chamber, being entrusted to an administration (*Landesadministration*) led by a military governor.[18] These observations match subsequent historical studies and indicate why the eighteenth-century Banat was a different region from Transylvania. On the one hand, Ottoman domination interrupted the continuity of religious institutions, guilds, and sociopolitical and economic relations patronised by the nobility. On the other hand, under the same Ottoman domination, local elites were weakened and local structures neglected. Cohabitation with the Turkish population left marks on the local habitat. Unlike in Transylvania, the conquest of the Banat by the Habsburgs did not meet social and political opposition. The region was not obliged to take into account the legislation of local institutions which pre-existed its integration among the Austrian territories. Since it was an area where most of the administrative and political structures had been destroyed or abandoned by the Ottomans, the Banat became a place of real experiment for the Habsburgs.

The 'Historische Beschreibung des Banats Temeswar' was written by J.J. Ehler. He provides information worthy of consideration in a historiographical perspective,[19] and his preoccupations precede those of the Italian historian Francesco Griselini, who, two years later in 1773, introduced his ample synthesis upon the Banat's past, publishing in *Giornale d'Italia* a concise narration of the economic and social demographic issues of the region from the date of the Habsburg conquest until 1773.[20]

Who was Ehrler and what lay behind his concern with the past of the region? As a senior official of the imperial administration of the Banat during the reign of Empress Maria Theresa, he had gained experience at gathering information and offering clear solutions to achieve the administrative reforms advocated by the Habsburgs. He was appointed to this role by Count Clary und Altringen, the regional governor. The fact that he published a fragment of his work in *Temeswarer Nachrichten* without giving his name is probably explained as a precaution against possible criticism from both his colleagues and the Viennese authorities, for making public the contractual obligations with the imperial administration.

What is interesting is that J.J. Ehrler's writing distinguishes itself from other examples by the diversity of the sources he appeals to, based on his own discoveries during his travels through the Banat. Compared to the 1771 article from *Temeswarer Nachrichten*, his work of 1774, *Banatul de la origini până în prezent* (*The Banat from its Origins up to the Present Day*), included details about the material and spiritual life of the inhabitants of the region. Reconstruction of the domestic economy, the livelihoods of the population, the incomes and obligations of officials, human curiosities, useful data regarding the land, people and cattle of the Banat are just a few examples of the subjects discussed in his important monograph. Its role was to fill in the gaps regarding the geography and history of the Banat. It is clear that his article stimulated the intellectual curiosity of his congeners, the first and most important result being the travel diary and interpretation of the Venetian historian Francesco Griselini.

TEMESWARER NACHRICHTEN AS AN INSTRUMENT OF POPULARISATION

Temeswarer Nachrichten includes many other pieces of information from the medical, economic and administrative fields which, through their content, reveal the intellectual preoccupations of the time, especially those concerning the emancipation of the population in the sense of acquiring the reflexes of modern civilisation. For example, in Appendix 3 of 2 May (*Anhang zu den Temeswarer Nachrichten*), there are comments on a book of medicine entitled *Dispensatorium*, which included recipes for healing illnesses and an enumeration of the medicines in circulation. The editor underlined the usefulness of the book for any citizen, also stating that the price of 3 florins and 6 kreutzers was affordable for anyone who wanted to buy the book. In the same issue of the newspaper, special interest was given to an essential book of medicine, Plattner's *Surgery*.[21] For the farmers, there was news about animal breeding and the cultivation of cereals and industrial plants. Works published recently in Vienna, dealing with tobacco cultivation, the techniques of cultivating land depending on the landform, the price of animal and vegetal products, and sheep breeding, were popularised. The new educational programmes, drafted by the Viennese Imperial Chancellery, were also published for the peasants. This kind of information implied literacy, a process started in the Banat in the mid-eighteenth century, when within church or secular schools, students learned in parallel in German, Romanian, Serbian and Hungarian.

Special attention was given to administrative issues. Since Timișoara at that time (and later) attracted people of different cultural-linguistic, religious and professional categories who travelled between Constantinople and Vienna, Hamburg and Trieste, Thessaloniki and Buda, Belgrade and Moscow, Ragusa (Dubrovnik) and Lemberg, Pressburg (Bratislava) and Arad, it was natural for the imperial administration to consider a more accurate record of the population. Mathäus Joseph Heimerl informed the public of the regulations that were to be put in place. By order of the police commander, his publishing house printed 'tables of evidence' that the citizens were obliged to buy for the sum of 4 kreutzers and fill in with the first and last names of homeowners, tenants and employees, along with their age, religion, place of birth and occupation.[22] As with those before the year 1771, the measures taken by the imperial administration had a restrictive character that took into consideration the applicant's ability to build a house, to pay the annual compulsory taxes to the administration, and to be employed in a profession or to do commercial work that was useful for the local community. The term 'restrictive' also refers to the fact that a portion of the inhabitants placed within the City walls (for example, Jews, Macedo-Romanians, Armenians and Greeks) were considered only as tolerated – the military and officials of the *Banater Landesadministration* being an exception. In Timișoara, the German colonists received land for building houses beyond the walls of the city, in the Elisabetin quarter. In the same manner, the Serbian, Romanian and Jewish communities lived in the Fabric, Josefin and Mehala neighbourhoods respectively.[23]

The aspirations of certain people belonging to these groups to enter the City had been preceded by a long evaluation. For some of the new inhabitants admitted inside the City, the so-called *Toleranztax* was applied. The lack of privileges of these communities made it difficult for them to have access to the city, in the first place. But, regardless of this, it is clear that the control system was designed first for protection. Fear of the plague that had descended upon

Timişoara during 1738 and 1740 obliged the imperial officials to introduce measures to prevent a new tragedy. *Temeswarer Nachrichten* offered the necessary guidance to prevent the plague, popularising scientific papers on the subject.

It is clear that this eighteenth-century German newspaper contributed to the creation of a modern cultural climate within the region. It proves not only the existence of a local intellectual elite, but also the desire to inform and shape the different social segments, including the future bourgeoisie, which began to appear during the nineteenth century. *Temeswarer Nachrichten* proves the point of community meetings and suggests how it was possible to create a multiple cultural code. Today's concerns regarding the intercultural phenomenon of the Banat and those relating to intercultural education are well supported in studies on the evolution of the multilingual press. There are numerous examples similar to that offered by *Temeswarer Nachrichten*, in publications printed in all the languages of the region – German, Hungarian, Romanian and Serbian.

The newspapers edited in the second half of the eighteenth century promoted the imperial idea of intellectual and social emancipation. The institutional mechanism on which the cultural life from the Crown territories was built depended on the goodwill of the Viennese administration, the education and the emancipation of population coming about as a result of the emperor's will and reforms. Centralism on the one hand, and censorship on the other, indicate two of the major means of coercion encountered by followers of the Enlightenment ideal within the regions and cities of Central Europe. The progress made in the formation of the intellectual class suggested by the presence of *Temeswarer Nachrichten* is confined within the limits imposed by the Habsburgs and must be understood in that specific state and political context. The descriptions contained in the newspaper serve as documents of the time; they provide information useful for the knowledge of European history and geography. This debut of the press in Timişoara in 1771 is an unmistakable testimony of its contribution to the first modernity of the region.

TEMESWARER ZEITUNG AND CENTRAL EUROPEAN CIVICISM

When we discuss the history of Central and East European cities, the retrieval of history depends on the understanding of regional, social and political characteristics, and on the analysis of confessional, linguistic and cultural diversities as manifested in the former Austro-Hungarian Monarchy. The decoding of dominant cultural models in the period before the First World War shows the existence of some cosmopolitan societies whose origin and traits were outlined during the Enlightenment.

Starting in 1718, Timişoara became a strategic city for the Habsburg Empire, and later, during the nineteenth century, an important economic and commercial city within the Austro-Hungarian Monarchy. In each of these two stages, Timișoara defined itself as multi-confessional, multilingual, civic-bourgeois and cosmopolitan; a cross-border city, promoting the model of the modern European burg. Thanks to the influence of the Viennese administration, and also to the locals' pursuits and ingenuity, Timișoara had a distinct personality. Its advantages were: (1) its geographical position, the basin of Cerna-Timiș-Bega rivers, under the influence of the Mediterranean climate, which facilitated the meeting of different cultures; (2) numerous colonists, German, Hungarian, Slovakian, Czech, Croatian, originating from all corners of Europe and the empire; (3) Jews, allowed inside the city after the payment of tolerance tax, who asserted themselves as good craftsman and traders, and also doctors, teachers, artists and journalists; (4) the Romanian Orthodox, Slavic Orthodox and Turkish Muslim neighbourhoods; (5) the spiritual and cultural patronage of the Roman Catholic Church. Therefore, the city defined itself as a society of many languages, cultures and religious confessions, without identifying wholly with one or other of them. Despite the fact that the nineteenth century is considered to be one of nationalities, Timișoara can hardly be defined by the notion of nationality, or by the predominance of a single ethnocultural group. Like Cernăuți, Timișoara was a successful experiment in social, cultural, economic and political terms.

THE CONTINUITY OF MULTI- AND INTERCULTURAL TRADITIONS

Temeswarer Zeitung (*The Newspaper of Timișoara*) resumed and developed the multi- and intercultural tradition started in the eighteenth century. It contributed to social pedagogy, to the cultivation of diversity, and to the promotion of a lifestyle that was in harmony with the inhabitants of Timișoara and the Banat. Even if, during the last decades of the nineteenth century, the intention of the Budapest government to Magyarise the population from the east of the monarchy was obvious, the German press stayed alive. This demonstrates the survival of multilinguism and the cultural landmarks of the Banat built in the previous century by the Viennese administration. The concern of Timișoara's inhabitants then turned to social emancipation, professional training and economic competition. The use of Hungarian as official language did not cause problems for the people of Timișoara and the Banat. Civicism was of prime importance and explains the absence of ethnonational confrontation.

Beyond politics, the liberalism represented by *Temeswarer Zeitung* was a human postulate, presupposing tolerance and understanding of individual aspirations. The development of commerce, finance and transport made civicism strong in Timișoara and the neighbouring area, being a true philosophy of life. The concern for civicism equated to the interest in modernity and Europeanism. It was expressed in most Central European cities, symbolising urban behavioural culture. Civicism was the messenger and defender of liberalism. The well-known Hungarian politician Franz Deák asserted himself as the supporter of emancipation of the different sociocultural and religious segments that populated the Austro-Hungarian Monarchy. Among others, this attitude led to the recognition and broad integration of Jews from Transleithania (east of the monarchy) into socio-economic life and also state institutions. Most Jews joined the civic movement, promoting multilingual culture and defining their identity by a transnational culture that was consonant with the political direction of the imperial house. The Jews represented the modern version of aristocracy. Contemporary publications hired them, affirming their fight for individual and civic rights.[24]

Alexander Krischan – one of the researchers into the history of *Temeswarer Zeitung* – claims that Jewish journalists from Austro-Hungary contributed to the development of the German-language press.[25] On the one hand, they played the role of intermediary of the Austrian cultural legacy; on the other, they promoted bilingualism in German and Hungarian, the two official languages of the monarchy. Thus, they contributed to the preservation of the ambivalent cultural code of Central Europe. Their significant involvement in the press was accelerated by their knowledge of German culture, Jews studying at the universities of Vienna and Prague.[26] Timișoara profited from this manner of manifestation of Jewish intellectuals, their fruitful activity being visible not only in the economy, but also in science, technology, education and the press.[27]

During the last decade of the nineteenth century, when Budapest was making visible efforts to promote literacy among the lower segments of population, Hungarian policy was not aimed at suppressing the multi- and intercultural profile of Timișoara. The number of German publications proves this fact. As for *Temeswarer Zeitung*, it really had a golden age. Managed for two decades by Armin Barát, it transformed itself from a provincial into an imperial newspaper. Barát employed many young journalists from all over the Banat and also other regions of the monarchy, being concerned with their training and acknowledging their performance. Together with several colleagues from Arad, Györ and Szeged, he founded the Eastern Monarchy Journalists' Association. Some of the journalists trained by Barát made brilliant careers in Vienna and Budapest. His multilingual knowledge overlapped with that of the local culture. He wrote in three languages: German, Hungarian and French. He translated literary works from German to Hungarian and vice versa. He had a decisive role in founding the Arany János Society, in organising numerous cultural and humanitarian activities, and also contributed to the affirmation of civicism in Timișoara.[28]

CENTRAL EUROPEAN CIVICISM

How can one explain the success of Barát's *Temeswarer Zeitung*, a German newspaper in a city under Hungarian administration? As already mentioned, the identity of the Dual Monarchy was not built on the idea of a single language and culture. In the first stage of its history, 1867–90, the idea of nation was not similar to that of the *Voelkische Nation*. The Germans belonged to the same state entity as the Romanians, Serbians and Slovaks from the eastern part of Austro-Hungary. A notion used at the time to define this entity was nationality. Budapest's policies ensured school education in the languages mentioned above as well as the practice of different religious cults and the functioning of cultural associations and foundations belonging to the nationalities. Along with acknowledgement of this type of plurality, each nationality had the right to send representatives to parliament. As the idea of *Voelkischekultur* (ethnolinguistic culture) overlapped with that of nation, the controversies on themes and theories of identity grew, becoming more radical during the First World War.[29]

The German-language press of the second half of the nineteenth century was not in conflict with the Hungarian state. As director of *Temeswarer Zeitung*, Armin Barát was a recognised personality within the Hungarian cultural and political environment. The situation was similar to that of *Preßburger Zeitung*, the German-language newspaper from Pozsony (Preßburg, Bratislava). The will of the majority for peaceful cohabitation was obvious; local concern was with preserving a spiritual environment without an ethnonationalist direction. Even if some articles had been written for the benefit of Hungarian propaganda, Armin Barát and *Temeswarer Zeitung* promoted ideas that were equally directed towards all of Timișoara's citizens, without favouring specific ethnic origins, mother tongues or religious traditions, and opposing any idea of segregation. In the years 1890–1900, *Temeswarer Zeitung* was a German-language newspaper that corresponded to Central Europe's multicultural profile – supported by Emperor Franz Joseph.[30] Filtered through the grid of collective egoism, this ideal was minimised or neglected by ethnonationalist orientations.

Beyond these realities, visible in many regions of the monarchy, *Temeswarer Zeitung* was a modern newspaper, concerned with educating the population in the spirit of a Central European city. It was inspired by the liberal idea that 'We respect and love the German nation, but we don't belong to it.'[31] These words imply more than the acknowledgement of a state identity; they evoke, at the same time, the idea of *Mitteleuropa*, having a multiple cultural code, impossible to sum up as a *Kulturnation* or a *Volksgeist*, as the most popular contemporary ideologues were thinking.[32] Except for the concessions necessary for survival, Timișoara was following its own multilingual and multicultural policy destined to ensure its status as a city open to all.

Armin Barát wrote about water supply, sewerage and management of the Bega River, about building railways and regularising city streets. He gave special attention to the theatre movement, the activity of scientific associations, art and literature, pedagogy. According to *Temeswarer Zeitung*, the popularity of the theatre was growing between 1890 and 1900, and this could benefit the entire society. The annual general meeting of the association for supporting the theatre mentioned that the number of spectators had risen in those years by 50 per cent, a portion of Timişoara's citizens being attracted to Hungarian language and culture.[33] In terms of native language, Hungarian increased by 4.9 per cent in the decade 1890–1900. *Temeswarer Zeitung* mentions that the number of German speakers decreased by 1.7 per cent and Romanian and Serbian speakers by 1.4 per cent.[34] For the year 1890, statistics regarding the inhabitants of the city were as follows: 55.91 per cent German, 26.72 per cent Hungarian, 3.87 per cent Serbian and 9.6 per cent Romanian.[35]

According to statistics, the Germans and Hungarians were Roman Catholics; some Romanians were Greek Catholic, while the majority was Orthodox, as were the Serbians. There were many cases of Jews who declared themselves to be either German or Hungarian. In some statistics they appeared as either Hungarians or Germans of the Jewish religion; other statistics simply mentioned them as Jews.[36] What has always been omitted in this misleading proportion are the mutual exchange of values, mixed families and the sense of modern urban life in which the norm of cohabitation became the main point of reference, rather than ethnicity or religion. This was similar to many Central European cities.

EDUCATION AND REGIONAL ADMINISTRATION IN THE AGE OF THE NEW GOVERNING CLASS: THE VIEW OF TEMESWARER ZEITUNG

The laws of Magyarisation of elementary (1879) and middle education (1883), along with the law of changing the names of localities (1898), were part of an assimilationist policy that could not change the cosmopolitan identity of Timişoara. Despite pressure from the Hungarian authorities, many local peculiarities were preserved. For example, the German language continued to be used in the administration of the majority of German villages from the Banat, bilingualism and multilingualism being present in the different social environments of the city and region.[37]

In 1897 *Temeswarer Zeitung* underlined the importance of founding associations for promoting and spreading language and culture, motivated by the existence of illiteracy among a segment of the population within the counties of the Banat.[38] The central and local administrations were concerned with training the population for integration into industry. The expression of civic sentiment was the result of an extensive process of emancipation in schools. In 1896, according to *Temeswarer Zeitung*, there were 33 educational institutions in Timişoara, of which four were state, eight municipal, 11 Roman Catholic, three Romanian Greek Orthodox, three Serbian Greek Orthodox, and four private schools. Moreover, there were 19 elementary schools, three vocational schools, one lower commercial school, one up-to-date trade school, two civil schools (*Bürgerschule*) – one for boys and one for girls – a commercial middle school and two teacher-training schools. The total number of teachers and instructors was 144.[39] Elementary and middle schools had seen a steady growth, and after Cluj and Oradea, Timişoara had the most educational establishments in 1896 with 58.[40] Training the population was viewed as extremely important and in tune with the policies promoted by the administration of the Dual Monarchy.

In February 1899 the school inspector Karl Sebeßtka visited a number of municipal schools, emphasising the activity of vocational schools (*Wiederholungsschulen*) for girls aged between 12 and 15 who had graduated from popular school. These schools were for those who did not intend to attend a higher education institution. In the Cetate quarter of Timişoara, there was a class with 73 girls; in Fabric, one with 94 girls. The students attended classes on Wednesday afternoons between two and five o'clock. The inspection noted that there were 5,182 students attending classes in at least one school, and 4,819 attended day schools. Of the latter, 549 were in Cetate quarter; 1,836 in Fabric; 1,818 in Josefin; and 616 in Elisabetin. The paper also notes that the schools from the Josefin and Fabric quarters had been renovated.[41]

Along with the administration, the private institutions and the bourgeoisie of Timişoara had made plans for economic expansion, so the training of technicians had to go hand in hand with that of businessmen. In an issue of 1897, *Temeswarer Zeitung* observed the need for trained traders, with knowledge of the languages of Eastern Europe, who could adapt to the expansion in the Balkan Peninsula. Their role would be to multiply ties with neighbouring states and develop exports of goods from Timişoara. This is the reason why a commercial high school and an academy of commerce were established: to develop trade with the Orient.[42]

Between 1890 and 1900, the city had its features imprinted by a solid bourgeoisie who bore the mark of the new governing class of Budapest and Vienna, or even the coats of arms accorded under the social policies of the two imperial capitals.[43] This was less visible in the cities of Transylvania, where the new governing class – often represented by Jews – was not accepted by the communities of Saxons and Romanians, being only present among the Hungarians.[44] *Temeswarer Zeitung* notes that the population of Timişoara was inclined to respect the rules of the political game when they were not absurd. Generally, interpersonal relations and respect for the city prevented the population from turning to extreme ideologies.[45]

THE EUROPEAN IMAGE OF THE CITY

The development of all types of associations had been a convincing sign that society was interested in the technical, scientific, cultural and sporting fields, without being attracted to ephemeral political ideas. An instinct of emancipation and openness allowed 1,469 cultural institutions to flourish in Timișoara in the year 1891. The liberal professions of lawyers and doctors were very much sought-after and appreciated. For example, in 1900 there were 60 lawyers and 41 doctors, most of whom were graduates from the universities of Budapest, Vienna and Graz. There were 41 scientific, cultural and sportive associations with 4,183 members; 31 humanitarian associations with 6,806 members; small associations of craftsmen and agricultural associations with 5,286 members; cultural foundations with a budget of a quarter of a million guilders; institutions that promoted the art of the theatre. The Association of the History and Archaeology Museum was founded in 1885 by merging two other associations, with 172 members, among whom were five honorary members and 67 founding members.[46] An exceptional role in this association was played by Zsigmond Ormos, a leading figure of the city, prefect of Timiș County. He laid the basis for the Museum of Banat in Timișoara which holds the historical, archaeological and art collections of the region.

An example of an association reflecting important scientific and civic matters was the South Hungarian Association of Natural Sciences, led by Professor Franz Rieß. On the occasion of its silver anniversary, *Temeswarer Zeitung* published an article on its merits. The association was founded on 25 March 1874, from an idea of the state high school. Among its founders, there were some notorious figures of the time: Julius Szalkay, Ludwig Buko, Michael Kriesch and Eduard Themak. The association's activities included meteorological observations; observations on plant development; the analysis of drinking water from Timișoara and artesian water from Union Square; the analysis of land in Timiș County; the exploration of unknown caves from the Banat; mineralogy studies; the cataloguing of birds of prey within the region; ethnographic studies, especially regarding the Swabian and Bulgarian communities in the region; and geographical studies on the Banat Mountains. The association owned a natural science museum; a library containing 1,506 specialised books, including 643 on medicine, 170 on physics, 152 on chemistry, 140 on natural science and 85 on mathematics. It also published a magazine. The South Hungarian Association of Natural Sciences registered 248 members, among whom there were 93 medics, 41 pharmacists, 27 professors and teachers, 18 lawyers and judges, 17 officials, 16 manufacturers and traders.[47]

During the years 1860–1900, the interests of society were focused on the introduction of technical experiments that could be accomplished relatively easily in Timișoara. The town and county dignitaries were receptive to renewal and invited prestigious Western societies to put into practice the experiments of local technicians and scientists. As innovations at regional or European scale, Timișoara promoted gas lighting, electrical street lighting, an urban telephone network and electric trams.[48]

Small industries and craftsmen only satisfied local needs. Agriculture had technical and production problems in all the villages of the Banat. There was a crisis of capital, and the general situation was not encouraging. A way out of this situation was specialised industrial education, offering the chance of urbanising a segment of the peasantry, as well as the possibility of industrial development.[49] There were fields of small craftsmen that disappeared or declined at the end of the nineteenth century. The craftsmen's guild of Timișoara and Pancevo tried to work through craftsmen production cooperatives, but could not succeed because of competition from big business.

Renewal in the life of the economy triggered important social change. On the occasion of celebrating the millennium of the founding of the Kingdom of Hungary in 896, Timișoara organised a great international fair. Among the participants, there were workshops and small businesses from Timișoara and all over the Austro-Hungarian Monarchy: the Anton Petrof piano factory, displaying all types of pianos, with Viennese and English mechanics; small factories of carpentry and furniture production; Armin Krauß's upholstery workshop; Kolarits's textiles workshop; Ulrich Hinterfeer glove factory; Ignaz Spizer's hat workshop; Johann Tedeschi & Co's machinery factory; Stefan Farkas and Michael Ludwig's hardware workshop. For Timișoara, this marked an unprecedented development. Events such as this, as well as the involvement of the city's inhabitants, are admirably depicted by *Temeswarer Zeitung*.[50] The newspaper also mentioned, at the end of the nineteenth century, the processes of transforming the city through the integration of its peripheral districts. The example of the Mehala quarter illustrates how the number of inhabitants had risen in Timișoara, the city becoming the fifth largest of the eastern area of the Dual Monarchy.

CONCLUSIONS

What does all this prove? *Temeswarer Zeitung* shows that between 1890 and 1900 Timișoara was an urban centre with a spirit of initiative, new institutions, a modern society eager to learn, multilingual and multi-confessional, adaptable to capitalist policy. *Temeswarer Zeitung* confirms the conclusions of Jenő Lendvai, secretary of Timișoara's Chamber of Commerce and Industry, that the city was connected to the contemporary European economy by producing goods that were in demand with the German, English, French, Russian and Balkan markets.[51] The information in *Temeswarer Zeitung* about civic and scientific associations, about the bourgeoisie and its programme in the years 1890–1900, about education and culture for the population shows that the social component was the most important link in the political-administrative construction and the city's economic development. The rapid integration of the inhabitants into industrial activities, the transportation facilitated by the trains that connected Vienna to Bucharest and London to Constantinople, linking Western to South-Eastern Europe, the regularisation of the Bega Canal, had been possible due to a well-trained and progressive professional elite, and also to a cooperative society, open to communication and competition. The civicism of Timișoara and the Banat asserted itself as the process of emancipation developed.

Although it was often considered a German city, nineteenth-century Timișoara can be mainly identified with the cosmopolitan direction taken by Vienna and Austria during the Enlightenment. Timișoara had rejected the idea of both German identity (the *Volksgeist*) and Hungarian identity (*a Magyar nép*). In the same way, in the later interwar period, it opposed the Romanian national-organicist idea. Timișoara's shift of status from a city that was subordinate to Vienna to one subordinate to Budapest, and later to Bucharest, could not alter its freedom of conscience. For a long time, Timișoara had assumed a social culture in which the main values were cohabitation, communication, understanding and reciprocity – all of which stimulated competition, creativity and innovation.

In the late nineteenth century, *Temeswarer Zeitung* highlighted the plural culture, confessional diversity and dominant social characteristics of the inhabitants of the Banat. Despite having shifted from one language to another, from one administrative status to another, and from one political system to another, Timișoara and the Banat had preserved their cross-border urban and regional peculiarities.

12
THE EDUCATIONAL SYSTEM IN THE BANAT UNDER HABSBURG ADMINISTRATION

Grozdanka Gojkov

SEEN AS A WHOLE, THE ENLIGHTENMENT PERIOD, encompassing the years between the Assembly of Timișoara and the Hungarian Revolution (1701–1848), was characterised by important changes within the Austrian provinces, including the consolidation of a young intellectual group, along with the decline of feudalism and the advance of modernity. Education became part of the modern conception of the state, its ultimate purpose being the transformation of subjects into loyal citizens and a productive workforce.

The first Serbian-language schools in the Banat date from the eighteenth century in Mesici in the southern Banat, Petrovo Selo (present-day Vladimirovac) and Stara Palanka (on the Danube River).[1] Historical records also mention a German school in Vršac which was inaugurated in 1727, linked to the city's Catholic parish and situated near the Catholic church. Josif Mihajlo Servati was the school's first head, and after 1735 Christoff Redl[2] taught there.

The condition of Serbian-language schools was debated in 1769 at the Karlowitz Assembly. On that occasion, the so-called 'trivial school' of Vršac was mentioned. It seems that the school had been founded two decades earlier and the initial teachers, both Serbs and Germans, were clerics. The Serbian-language school of Vršac was situated behind St Nicholas church (the episcopal cathedral), on Zmaj Jovina[3] street.

School activity was coordinated by church and school councils, which appointed teachers, determined their salaries, and also had supervisory authority. At the beginning of school life, Teofan Prokopovic's alphabet book was used (brought from Russia in 1726 by a teacher named Suvorov), along with the Book of Psalms and other religious textbooks. Writing, religious chanting and calculus were not compulsory, being taught only where there were well-prepared tutors. Thus, neither the school subjects nor the didactic methods benefited from a syllabus.

During the Late Englightenment period – last decades of the eighteenth century leading into early nineteenth century – the school system was managed by clerics, inheriting many traits from medieval education; this continued until the second half of the eighteenth century. The clergy ensured that the youngsters were taught prayer and church regulations using the catechetical method. Until 1773 clerical influence was accentuated in the case of the Jesuits and Piarists. Piarist high schools were well known in all regions under Habsburg dominion. One such school was established in Timișoara and attended by children of wealthier families from diverse communities and religious denominations. The classes were taught mostly in German and partly in Serbian. Dimitrie Tirol, a close friend and collaborator of the renowned scholar Vuk Karadzic,[4] taught there. The reforms carried out during Maria Theresa's reign were appreciated by the Germans of Vršac in their attempts to enforce Johann Ignaz von Felbiger's school regulations (he initiated the eighteenth-century educational reforms in the Habsburg Empire).

For the Austrian administration, the role of the educational system was to ensure political and social stability and cultivate loyalty towards the imperial house. Maria Theresa decided that the imperial authorities should manage the schools, thus limiting the clergy's influence. Apart from political interests, there were also economic arguments in favour of enforcing such measures. The economic development promoted by the empress and her son, Joseph II, carried the expectation of production on a larger scale, and, implicitly, of a new and better trained workforce.

The imperial authorities decided that secular school textbooks should be written in the Latin alphabet and the printed rulebook forbade the celebration of certain Serbian holidays. The Serbs protested, seeing these changes as dissociation from Orthodox learning norms, and although Bishop Vicentije Jovanovic tried to settle things down, his efforts were in vain. Finally, the reforms were accepted, but, in the Church's opinion, the Orthodox spirit should have been preserved in schools. This situation remained up to the mid-nineteenth century when, alongside the banishment of absolutism, liberal ideas regarding political and social activity emerged.

However, although the clergy's influence was now limited, Maria Theresa and Joseph II continued to gain important support from the Orthodox Church, which was consulted with regard to printing textbooks, designing the school curriculum and syllabus, and selecting the teachers – the bishops and their representatives having an important role in these decisions. The Serbian and Romanian schools, which still belonged to the same metropolitan church, were left under religious supervision, thus educational issues were often debated in the metropolitan or episcopal assemblies. Within two decades, more regulations, laws and decrees were published, such as the *Illyrian Law* (1770), *Normal – Patent* (1771), *Regulae directivae, Allgemeine Schulordnung* (1774), *Educational Constitution* (1776), *Ratio declaratorium educationis publicae* (1777) and *Rescriptum declaratorium* (1779), which related to the regulation of Romanian and Serbian schools. One of the basic rules was that a school for both sexes was to be established in each settlement that had an Orthodox church and a parish priest: religion, prayer, psalms, religious chanting, reading, writing and calculus were to be included as compulsory subjects.[5]

The building and maintenance of schools was the task of city hall in each jurisdiction. The cantor teachers also worked as general teachers and were rewarded with money and goods. In many cases, their lodgings were provided by the local mayoralty, who also paid shepherds for local necessities in order to release children from duties such as tending flocks.[6]

During the mid-eighteenth century a large population was colonised in the Banat – especially Germans, but also people of Hungarian, Romanian, Greek, Jewish or Gypsy origin. Under the Protestant German influences some towns witnessed an ethnic polarisation. Vršac, for example, was divided into two entities, each with its own mayor and other distinctive administrative structures. The Serbian community was pushed out to the suburbs, which were named for a few families living there.

By the 1780s, there were 218 Serbian schools in the Banat and almost the same number of schoolmasters attending Teodor Jankovic Mirijevski's courses in Timișoara. In Vršac, the Serbian school had 150 pupils, divided into three classes, based on the model of similar schools in Hungary. From the 1794 examination report of teacher Grigorije Zosimovic, we discover that the school had further classes: a beginners' class, an elementary class, an advanced class, a class for learning psalms and a spelling class. From the first to the third grade, the pupils learnt reading, school regulations, an introduction to Christianity, biblical history, the Gospels, calculus, German, and Christian studies. Among those specifically mentioned on the staff were Grigorie Zosimovic, from the school behind the episcopal church; Sava Stefanovic, second-grade teacher; Jovan Teodorovici, third-grade teacher; and Gregorije Botak, first-grade teacher.[7]

VRŠAC GRAMMAR SCHOOL (1790–1819)

At the end of the eighteenth century and the beginning of the nineteenth, the city of Vršac was one of the important educational centres in the south-east region of the Dual Monarchy. The headquarters of the bishopric, which included six districts (Vršac, Biserica Albă, Mehadia, Lugoj, Caransebeș and

Vărădia), was here. The city of Vršac had 1,125 households, a community made up of 8,121 Orthodox Christians and the same number of Catholics who spoke German as a mother tongue. There were four Romanian and Serbian schools, two Serbian-Slavonic schools, one middle school and one Latin grammar school. The classes for pupils from poor families were held at the episcopal residence.[8] Vršac was already an important educational centre within the Bishopric of Karlowitz, due especially to the existence of the Latin grammar school, founded by Vršac city hall in 1790, following the efforts of Bishop Josif Jovanovic Şakabent.

In 1799 the so-called 'alumni' were instituted.[9] As a result of this, two young people from each district, hard-working pupils with exemplary behaviour, were financially supported. There were 12 in total, plus a further 12 from other dioceses and other youngsters who were training to continue their studies at Karlowitz. Two teachers were hired, one for each section. Vršac grammar school and Karlowitz high school, founded in 1791, were at the time the only Serbian middle schools in Hungary.

The school in Vršac was different from other high schools, including the one in Karlowitz, because four rather than six courses were held each year. In the first grade (grammar) the following subjects were taught: syntax, classics, Hungarian history, geography, mineralogy and religion. In the second grade (humanist), stylistic theory, classics, experimental physics, ancient history and universal geography were taught and the pupils were called humanists. The courses were taught in Latin, but Romanian and Serbian[10] were also used. In 1805 the grammar school accommodated 80 students and two teachers.[11]

After graduation, the youngsters could continue their studies, becoming priests or teachers. Those with excellent results could become members of Karlowitz's alumni, with a scholarship of 20 florins per year, thus being able to graduate to the subjects of the upper high school: syntax, poetry and rhetoric. Among the professors, the following are mentioned: Sobek, Loyen and Krestić until 1794; then Samoilo Martini, supported, between 1796 and 1797, by his students Konstantin Jovanović and Aleksije Djakovic. Jovan Radovanović, Uros Volić and Jovan Balaicki are also mentioned. Romanian-language courses were held between 1802 and 1808 by Paul Iorgovici, author of a well-known grammar and representative of the Transylvanian School (Şcoala Ardeleană).[12] Many famous people from Vršac studied at this school, among them Jovan Sterija Popović, who attended classes until 1819, continuing his studies in Karlowitz and Timişoara. After graduation, he returned to Vršac to teach Latin for five years. The grammar school ceased activity in 1819 following a decision issued at Buda, due to lack of financial support.[13]

THE ROMANIAN AND SERBIAN CLERICAL SCHOOLS OF THE AUSTRIAN EMPIRE

By an imperial decree of 12 February 1810, the metropolitan bishop Stevan Stratimirović was asked to express his opinion on the possibility of creating a general theological seminary which would benefit from public financial support to supply the needs of the Orthodox population. By the same decree, the emperor commanded that Stratimirović consult the school inspector Uros Nestorović regarding the regulation of education for the Orthodox population within the Dual Monarchy. The bishop believed that religious education should start in middle school because, in his opinion, the formation of personality and moral characteristics developed at that time. He recommended the establishment of more high schools, in which future clerics would acquire necessary knowledge. Later, the students could deepen their theological knowledge in academies.

Hungarian authorities approved the founding of the general seminary in 1785 during Bishop Mojsije Putnik's period of office. It was envisaged that the seminary would be located in Timișoara, and decisions were made on details such as the construction plan, curriculum and finances. Some 120 alumni were to take classes there. However, after the bishop had been transferred to Karlowitz, he demanded that the seminary be established there. Various circumstances, including lack of financial support and the small number of high schools and academies capable of preparing students for seminary, favoured the idea of creating one general seminary, but the thinking evolved over time. For example, the metropolitan bishop Stefan Stratimirović and his predecessor Mojsije Putnik reckoned that, rather than one or at most two Orthodox general seminaries – one for Serbians in Karlowitz and one for Romanians in Timișoara – every diocese across the region should have one. The proposition was accepted at the Assembly of Timișoara in 1790 and seminaries were founded in the dioceses of Pakrac, Arad, Timișoara, Vršac, Backa and Budim. The smaller dioceses created a single seminary at Novi Sad.[14]

The oldest written evidence about the existence of a theological course at Vršac comes from the archpriest of Mehadia, Nicolae Stoica of Hațeg. In the 1773 edition of the *Banatian Chronicle*, he wrote about classes of religious chanting and biblical canons for young priests, held by the bishop of Vršac at his residence. There is no information regarding the duration of these classes, but it is known that they were instituted by Josif Jovanovic Šakabent immediately after he became bishop in 1786. Some data about the respective courses was provided by the bishop himself and were included in the plan he sent to the imperial court, based on the decree of 30 December 1791. It is possible that the courses were not intended to offer the pupils instruction that was pretentious, but rather to support them in their daily religious practice.

According to Bishop Stratimirović's plan, the following disciplines were agreed: religious chanting, reading of religious books, catechesis, writing and calculus. The first two were taught by Dean Teodor Ilic, the others by notary Vasilije Mihailović. The courses were held for two semesters (the first from 1 November to 31 December and the second from 1 March to 30 April). Following a demand from the Illyrian Chancellery of 26 March 1791, Bishop Šakabent filed a report on 18 May regarding the educational situation in the diocese of Vršac, including his private confessional school. In order to verify the information included in the report, the chancellery sent a commission to Vršac, led by Stefan Marcović. Marcović's report was discussed at the chancellery meeting on 15 December, which determined that the emperor approved of the methods of appointing teachers, since they were proficient and dedicated to their task of guiding the pupils.[15]

Bishop Petar Jovanovic Vidak founded the second clerical school at Vršac. Like Šakabent, he set up classes at the episcopal palace, starting in 1806, immediately after taking over the bishopric. The school had two teachers, Dean Arsenije Jovanovic Šakabent and cleric Sofronie Ivackovic, who did not benefit from a fixed salary, instead being periodically remunerated by the bishop. The school functioned upon the model of the Karlowitz seminary. Because most of the pupils were Romanians who did not speak Serbian, the classes were held in Romanian. Among the disciplines taught were Molnar's grammar, Plato's dogmatic and general theology, and Rajic's catechetics. In order to combat pupils' superstition, the bishop asked that, when they taught about the Creation during the course in symbols of belief, the teachers should accentuate the scientific approach of natural phenomena (existence of celestial bodies, cloud formation, thunder, rain, wind, etc.). Among the other disciplines were geography, Avram Mrazovic's arithmetic, religious chanting and church rules, and on Sundays and holidays the examination of evangelical pericopes. During the second year, theology and Serbian catechetics upon Plato were taught, together with the history of the Church translated by Vujanovski. These disciplines were studied in the period between 1 November and 30 April, after which the pupils were allowed to go home for agricultural work. In 1814 the school numbered 30 pupils.[16]

The graduates were usually assigned as cantors either in the city or in their place of origin, or as teachers in other schools. The best were appointed clerks in European chancelleries. Many of them worked as teachers even after their ordination. After the authorities had decided that nobody could teach without graduating from the teacher-training college, some deans were unable to exercise their function as teachers. Bishop Vidak persuaded the general inspector Uros Nestorovic not to dismiss those deans who had no other financial means. This situation was maintained for two years (1815–16), after which the courses were suspended. Following the bishop's death, the administrative position was occupied by archimandrite Sinesije Radivojević of Mesic monastery. Not knowing how long he would stay at the head of the bishopric, Radivojević did not take any measures regarding classes, leaving this to his successor.

The procedures for establishing a permanent clerical school were initiated by Bishop Stratimirović. This functioned as a diocesan school between 1822 and 1867, training priests for the two episcopacies of Vršac and Timișoara and therefore the whole of the Banat. From the beginning, the school had two departments, one for the Serbian language and the other for Romanian. At first the duration of the school was two years and from 1827 three years, with two semesters per year.

The school curriculum focused on teaching the knowledge and skills required to become a priest. The disciplines taught were the Slavonic and Romanian languages, with grammar and exercises; dogmatic theology; rhetoric; moral and pastoral theology; catechetics; history of the Church; interpretation of evangelical pericopes; religious chanting; pedagogy; teaching method; religious style and writing. Among the didactical materials were Russian and Romanian religious books, as well as courses devised by teachers. Between 1822 and 1865, 1,216 Romanian students attended the courses and from 1876 until the Second World War, 737 Serbian students.[17]

Regarding qualifications of students before attending the clerical school in Vršac, the majority, especially Romanians, had graduated from the Serbian, Romanian, German or Hungarian teacher-training colleges. Some were high school graduates from Becicherecul Mare, Lugoj and Oravița, while others were educated at the Piarist high school of Timișoara. A smaller number were graduates of the Oradea and Szeged high schools. The students of Vršac were, in large part, graduates of the grammar school or teacher-training college.

THE GERMAN SECONDARY SCHOOL (UNTER REAL SCHULE) AND ITS TRANSFORMATION INTO THE ROYAL HUNGARIAN SECONDARY SCHOOL

The *Unter Real Schule*, the predecessor of the town's secondary school, was founded by the city hall of Vršac. From the report sent by the school board to the Viennese Ministry of Culture and Public Education on 23 December 1852 regarding the founding of the school, we find that the seal of approval was issued by a ministerial directive of 9 July 1852, and on 3 November the school was opened. Since it had no proper headquarters, the school was situated in the Concordia building, provided by the city hall, behind the German teacher-training college.

A commission from Pančevo examined its method and initiated a procedure for bringing in teachers. Because not all positions were filled, the provincial authorities appointed some substitute teachers. These were Jovan Neisidler (natural sciences), Ludwig Vodecki (technical disciplines) and Paul Hudi (grammar). On the recommendation of the bishopric and city administration, the provincial authorities named Jovan Stenzer, teacher of religion and Hungarian language, as director of the school. With the exception of the Serbian-language teacher, who was appointed in November, all other teaching staff were presented to the local authorities on 29 September.[18] Their task was to implement Austrian schooling principles, which implied, among others, a pronounced German influence, but also some degree of emancipation. The objective of the school was to offer basic instruction to young people, especially regarding craftsmanship and trade. This objective was clearly stated by the school inspector Bondac Landov at the opening ceremony on 15 October 1852.[19]

Analysing the facilities (the various didactic methods, the mineral collection, the insectariums, the geographical maps, etc.), along with the teachers' qualifications and the sums of money destined for school functioning, we can conclude that it was well organised. Apart from Hungarian, Serbian was also taught in the school, the German pupils being free to choose one of those two languages. Among the 18 candidates from Austria, Bohemia and other regions, two were chosen to teach at one of the secondary schools. In that year, the school had 66 students, of whom one-third were Serbians, the rest being Romanians or Germans. The institution operated according to an approved curriculum, hence the authorities determined that the school satisfied the conditions required for it to be acknowledged as an institution of public education, and thus to be included in the public education system. Between 1858 and 1859, the school was attended by 155 students (84 Germans, 42 Serbians, 12 Hungarians, 8 Romanians, 2 Bulgarians and 7 Jews).[20]

The same situation obtained at the teacher-training college in Vršac, which began in 1854, two years after the founding of the secondary school. Although it was an independent institution, it had a strong connection with the secondary school until 1871 when it was moved to Szeged. At the beginning, the same teachers taught at both schools, each of which was supported by the city administration. The director of the teacher-training college was also remunerated by the provincial authorities with 500 florins for teaching Hungarian-language classes.

During the Dual Monarchy from 1867 to 1918, great attention was given to middle schools and, with the adoption of the middle-school law in 1868, these became schools of six grades. In addition, a school inspector was appointed for Voivodina. Even in 1861, there were intentions to dissolve this school and instead found a lower secondary school. The idea was approved by the Ministry of Education on 1 December 1868.[21] The secondary school used the curriculum valid in all Hungarian similar schools. In 1868 the first grade was opened and in the next year the second grade. However, this led to the end of the institution, because the people of Vršac were not content with the changes, and the local authorities decided at a meeting on 5 September 1870 that it should be converted into a municipal school.[22] During the 1871–72 academic year, the fourth grade of the school was inaugurated, with classes taught in German. August Trefor, Minister of Education, arrived in Vršac on 17 April 1873. Along with the parson and the school inspector, he visited the municipal school and expressed satisfaction at the way it functioned, the existing facilities and the textbooks used.[23]

The idea of founding an upper secondary school in Vršac was delayed a couple of times by the Ministry of Education. At a school council meeting on 12 October 1878, it was decided to forward an application requesting the founding of the school to the ministry, who responded by incessantly demanding that Hungarian should be the language used in the school. Because of this, the idea of opening a general secondary school was discarded until 1882. The president of the school council at that time was Jovan Semeier, who was also the town mayor. One of his priorities was the enlargement of the Concordia building, in order to respond to the needs of a general secondary school. Unfortunately, the idea of founding a new school did not get the expected answer because young people of wealthy families were already being educated in the Hungarian style, both in language and culture, thus the opening of the school was not a priority. The German nature of the municipal school was preserved until its transformation into an upper secondary school in 1888.

Many members of the teacher-training college asked that German should be the teaching language at the newly founded secondary school. The demand was only partially answered by the ministry, in the sense that manuals written in the native language were allowed for the lower grades – a right revoked shortly after.[24] Therefore, the classes at the upper secondary school of Vršac were taught in German and Hungarian, and later only in Hungarian, the Serbian and Romanian languages being optional. Religion was taught by Herzeg Ferenc from the Bishopric of Cenad; Milutin Trbić, a Serbian Orthodox priest; and Isidor Adolf, rabbi of Vršac. A quality teaching staff was provided, supported by the Hungarian Minister of Education. The best teachers were appointed, some of whom were PhDs, other scientific researchers.[25] The very well-equipped school library had particular importance, numbering over 10,000 books in its four halls. Among its volumes, the sixteenth-century books, printed in Latin and Greek in different European centres, were of particular interest. The teachers' activity was supervised by Inspector Ferenc Petrovic from his headquarters in Oradea. Between 1892 and 1897 school inspections were carried out by Nalafalussy Koruc, together with the Oradea Canonical who continued the medieval tradition of a cleric inspecting the civil schools.

During the years 1892–1903, the school in Vršac became an institution following a contract signed by Klamarik Iosef, ministerial councillor, and Sender Janos, the town prefect and representative of the local administration.[26] The contract mentioned a series of obligations for the local administration, among which was the construction of a building on land approved by the ministry, with the city hall to handle its equipment and maintenance. Thus, the city took the responsibility of paying 6,000 florins each year to the Hungarian state. The salaries and pensions were covered by the state.

The city managed to provide financial means sufficient to ensure that the institution was adequately equipped. The courses were held in laboratories that were equipped as follows: the physics laboratory, 397 didactical instruments; the chemistry laboratory, 592; the natural sciences laboratory, 492 books and 798 mineral collections; the geography laboratory, 157; the drawing laboratory, 1,380 examples, 70 sculptures and 30 other necessary instruments. The sports hall was equipped with 204 pieces of apparatus made by Oboroli János, a craftsman from Budapest.[27]

As a sign of appreciation for the role of the school in their education, its graduates supported it financially. The largest sum was donated by the cavalry major Karlo Trenbolski and his wife: 4,000 florins in total. Every year, two students (one Catholic and one Orthodox) were given a grant.[28] Later, the city treasury provided the underprivileged students with a total sum of 25,000–30,000 florins. The Romanian metropolitan church opened a grant fund to support future Romanian priests and teachers.

During the following years, the number of students rose constantly, later even doubling, eventually reaching 7,000. Most of them were Germans, followed by Hungarians, Serbians and Romanians; the majority came from the Vršac area, but there were also students from the Timișoara region and even from outside Voivodina (Hungary, Serbia and Croatia). According to reports, 310 students graduated from the secondary school. Most of the teachers were Hungarian, some German, and a small number Serbian. The secondary school was closed at the end of the First World War.

THE TEACHER-TRAINING COLLEGES OF CARANSEBEȘ AND BISERICA ALBĂ

At the beginning of the nineteenth century in the Habsburg Empire, there were no institutions for training teachers, thus different courses of qualifications were organised. In 1805 the School Constitution provided that three-month courses for training teachers should be supplied in the most important schools of the region. After that period, students had to pass an examination in the presence of the district school director. Graduates were given a certificate, granted by the district director, the school director and the teacher who taught the classes, bearing the seal of the school, which allowed them to work as substitute teachers.[29] Candidates who did not pass were re-examined or fired.[30] The following disciplines were taught: basic teaching principles, religion, German language, calculus, reading method, reading, calligraphy, grammar and writing to dictation.[31]

In order to register for the teacher-training courses, the candidates had to have completed at least three years of middle school and have exemplary behaviour. Graduation allowed the candidates to work as substitute teachers for a year, and after the age of 20 they could take the examination for a permanent position. Permanent teachers were exempt from military service, while substitutes were only temporarily exempt. Those that came from more important schools were trained according to a different curriculum over a period of six months.

After 1812, with Uros Nestorović's appointment as inspector of all Serbian, Romanian and Greek schools of the Dual Monarchy, two teacher-training colleges were opened. The Serbian one was established at Szentendre and later moved to Sombor, while the Romanian one was at Arad. The two schools mostly trained young people who came from the wealthier families of border policemen. That is why the classes had to be held at the middle schools situated within the border territory, as regulated by the School Constitution of 1805.[32]

In the border territory of the Illyricum-Wallachian Regiment, Ioan Tomic, the archpriest of Caransebeș, was granted approval by the authorities to hold an annual three-month course in Caransebeș over three years, with the objective of training substitute teachers for the middle schools in the region. A special fund was opened in order to pay the teachers' salaries and grant allowances for underprivileged students. The idea and management of these courses (including supervision by a special commission) was inspired by the model of the teacher-training schools in Sombor and Arad.[33] The first course started in the summer of 1820, led by the director of the national schools of the regiment, and among its teachers were Ioan Tomic and George Andrejevic. In 1924, due to lack of financing, the position of director of national schools of the regiment was abolished, and the metropolitan church of Sremski Karovci assumed management of the courses. At Caransebeș, they were conducted by Dean Arsenije Jovanovic Šakabent, and after 1930 the directorial position was re-established and was held by Constantin Diaconovici Loga, instructor at the teacher-training college in Arad. By order of the authorities, the headquarters of the school directorship was moved to Biserica Albă, and the teachers' courses were also held there. Loga continued his lectures until 1852, because the existing teacher-training schools were not equipped with what was necessary.[34]

SCHOOLS IN VRŠAC DURING SERBIAN VOIVODINA AND THE BANAT OF TEMES

Following the Austrian emperor's decree of November 1849, Serbian Voivodina and the Banat of Temes was established as a distinct administrative region, autonomous from Hungary and directly subordinate to Vienna. The capital of the region was Timișoara. In 1851, the administration of the territory was reorganised. Vršac belonged administratively to Timișoara, and its official language was Serbian for a short period, then German.

The teacher-training college of Vršac opened in November 1854, its layout being determined by the authorities of Timișoara. The lower secondary school and the teacher-training college represented models of organisation, the training period for teachers being four to five years. Graduates were granted the right to teach at the three-grade city schools. The compulsory disciplines were religion and biblical history, basic notions of educational activities, linguistics, calculus, calligraphy, drawing, voice and organ. The teacher-training college of Vršac operated within the secondary school. In the first grade, 39 students were registered, among whom was a Jewish student who took religion and Hebrew-language classes at the Jewish school. The school director, Iosef Stenzer, taught religion, while Johann Paul Hudi was the German-language teacher.[35] The school year started on 1 October and ended on 15 August. Obligations regarding school maintenance were usually covered by the local authorities.[36]

Many permanent and substitute teachers working in the territory of Serbian Voivodina and the Banat of Temes lacked adequate qualifications. As a result, the Ministry of Education in Vienna decided to introduce a compulsory public examination for teachers from 2 November 1854. Thus, teachers were obliged to attend the five- to six-month summer courses at the teacher-training college of Vršac (1855). Upon graduation, they received a certificate. The candidates had to display impeccable behaviour, too. Johann Benis was the course coordinator, and among the disciplines taught were German language and its methodology, calligraphy, grammar and stylistics, calculus, and general educational practice.

After the Dual Monarchy was created in 1867, the tendency was to separate schools from the influence of the Church. The Hungarian authorities decided to move the German teacher-training college of Vršac to Szeged, where it merged with the already existing school. The teachers' college didactic staff also left, which meant the end of the German teacher-training school.[37] A few words must be said regarding the institutionalised schooling system for the children and families of Russian refugees. The system included the general and middle school, based on the model of the Russian educational system, with a cadet corps, girls' institute, high schools and universities. In

Serbia, there were five educational centres for Russians – in Vršac, Bela Crkva, Kikinda, Novi Sad and Belgrade – but such centres functioned in Serbian and Croatian towns. The system was coordinated by Russian emigrés, officers, professors, medical doctors, artists and church representatives who were forced to flee the Bolshevik Revolution; at the time (of Russian influence before and during the First World War) there were approximately 75,000 emigrants living in the Kingdom.

In 1921 at Sremski Karlovci (formerly Karlowitz) the Holy Synod of the Russian Orthodox Church outside Russia was founded and a metropolitan was appointed, this city being an important centre for Russians living outside their homeland. In the Serbian, Croatian and Slovenian territories, the Russians had eight parochial centres, under the jurisdiction of the Synod of Karlovci. One of these centres was in the small town of Biserica Albă, where around 1,000 Russians had made their home.[38] The whole Crimean cadet corps was transferred to Biserica Albă, and in 1923 the total number of cadets was 579, distributed in 20 classes and five platoons. In the buildings granted by the authorities, the young Russians were taught humanist studies in a Christian and patriotic spirit. This institution was a model of activity, tidiness and performance, being among the first in the country. The students and didactic staff of the Girls' Marine Institute and Harkov Girls' Institute, who had left the town of Novorosijk in 1920, arrived in the Banat, in Biserica Albă but in the end, only 74 students and seven teachers from the Marine Institute settled here. The institution bore the name of the Russian Girls' Institute 'Empress Maria Fyodorovna', after the name of its benefactor. In fact, it was a Russian girls' high school, where students attended eight grades followed by a final bachelor exam. The pupils were girls of Russian and also Serbian nationality. Along with the arrival of Russian refugees in the Banat, especially in the south, Russian colonies were being formed. They cohabited with the locals, leaving marks on their culture.

CONCLUSIONS

In the nineteenth century the educational system of the Banat, like other regions of the Habsburg Empire, transitioned from a religious system (1790–1810) to a secular one (1810–48). During the process of development and modernisation of the Banatian schooling system, an important role was played by the political, economical and administrative elites, and later, by the citizens themselves. The citizens, elites among them, were respected by the Serbs of the Habsburg Empire. The citizens were quite active within intellectual circles, their influence growing larger and larger. The development of the educational system facilitated cultural interactions in the Banat. Great care was given to teacher-training. Teachers were considered pillars of education and literacy, capable of elevating the general knowledge of the population. The role of the teacher-training college in Sombor has already been mentioned. In southern areas populated by Serbs, other necessary schooling institutions were founded. Later, due to the tenacity of the German population, this region was also granted a teacher-training college. The changes were major, and here, unlike the southern area (across the Danube), cultural and educational development occurred.

PART IV

13

THE REVOLUTIONARY MOVEMENTS OF 1848

Miodrag Milin

SERBS IN THE BANAT BEFORE THE 1848 REVOLUTION

For the Serbian political elite in the Banat, discourse on identity became central in the years before the 1848 Revolution. The theme of social, linguistic and religious differentiation began to be omnipresent in the regions of East Central Europe, and the Serbian elites were no exception. Their dispute aimed to identify the distinctions between Serbs and Southern Slavs,[1] according to the Nacertanije project (1844). Attributed to the Belgrade politician Ilija Garašanin, Nacertanije was the political option of the Forty-Eighter generation.[2] The fact that the idea of national awakening was equally present within the whole of the Southern Slavic world made the delineation of the Slavic population a provocative issue for any of them. Given their background of long-term coexistence, the demarcation between Serbs and Croats was a real problem. When the ideas of the Nacertanije project were conceived in Ilija Garašanin's ministerial chancellery, the Croats had already developed their own programme and were looking for cultural and political support from the other Slavs and especially from the Serbs. In fact, this was the main objective of the so-called Illyrian movement of the 1840s.

The Croatian representatives also reflected on the construction of a joint Serbo-Croat state. One of Garašanin's advisers, the Czech František Zach, defined the concept of a common Southern Slavic state, following consultation with the initiator of the Illyrian movement, Ljudevit Gaj,[3] and his close collaborators.[4] They had convergent ideals, which were highlighted in Garašanin's project. In the political programme drafted by Zach, the words 'Serb',

'Serbian' and 'Serbia' appear instead of the terms Yugoslav and Yugoslavia; however, Zach remained in support of a broad Yugoslavian policy, intended to unite all Southern Slavs under a common state. He seemed to have been aware that Serbia would not be able to build a powerful independent state alone, without cooperation from the other Slavic communities in the Balkans.

In the clerical and academic circles of the Serbs of Pest, Novi Sad, Arad, Vršac and Timișoara, the Orthodox view was dominant. The reformation of language and writing, initiated by Vuk Karadžić (promoter of the Serbo-Croatian idiom), had long been fought, as had the Illyrian ideas, which were perceived as an instrument of Roman Catholic proselytism. Even Karadžić had to curb his enthușiasm for the promotion of linguistic nationalism, saying: 'whoever obeys the Greek or Eastern law, wherever he may live, will never reject the Serbian name; while whoever obeys the Roman law may call themselves Croatian if they wish'.[5] In Garašanin's Nacetanije project, there are no references to a union with Croatia, the Serbian orientation towards Srem (Sirmiu), the Banat and Bacica, later Voivodina, being preferred.

Nacertanije was drafted as a building programme for a Serbian nation-state while expressing the option of uniting all Serbs under the authority of the Ottoman Empire. As a second stage, the project foresaw union with Serbs from the Austrian Empire, and then the integration of Croats, and eventually Bulgarians, in the same nation state.

TENSIONS WITHIN THE AUSTRIAN EMPIRE: RELATIONS BETWEEN SERBS AND HUNGARIANS

The Viennese insurrection of 13 March 1848, along with the cessation of the activities of Metternich, the imperial chancellor, the formation of the National Guard and the proclamation of constitutional freedoms in Austria, had a strong echo within the social environment, also stimulating revolutionary events in Pest. The Hungarian revolutionary programme had 12 points, claiming citizen freedoms and judicial equality, general taxation and the elimination of feudal constraints. The Hungarian Diet adopted the 'March laws',[6] and on 17 March 1848 the imperial court recognised the independent Hungarian government with Count Lajos Batthyány (1807–49) as prime minister and Lajos Kossuth (1802–94) as finance minister.

Born of revolution, this government had shown a propensity for compromise, formalising its position and taking the first steps towards protecting the privileged status and supremacy of the nobility, discouraging social movements and communities of any language other than Hungarian. Kossuth believed that the supremacy of the nobility and the continuation of the old political administration should be the basis for the new state order. At the same time, Hungarian national autonomy was put in the shade as Hungary was perceived as representing 'unitary and indivisible' statehood.[7] From the early days of the revolution, Serbs had joined Hungarians, believing they would identify their proper place within the new state organisation promoted by the Pest revolutionaries. One of the advocates of this direction was the lawyer Pavle Radovanović. Influenced by the revolutionary ideas, he edited the paper *Sojedinimo se* (*Let's Unite Together*) which was also published in Hungarian (*Egyesülünk*) and even in German (*Vereinigen wir uns*).[8] The Serbian pupils and students hosted by the 'Tekelianum' alumni foundation in Pest reacted, along with the members of Matica srspka, the academic society that had been operating since 1826 in the Hungarian capital.

Serbian student action started as a demonstration against the inspector-censor of Serbian schools, a certain Giurcović. Things soon escalated and on 17–19 March the demonstrators formed a national assembly, adopting the first Serbian revolutionary programme. Drafted by the Budapest writer Jakob Ignjatović, it had 17 points. The Serbs recognised the new Hungarian authority, but they also demanded collective rights and the freedom to officially use their native tongue, freedom of conscience and religion, their own schools, representation in the Diet, and regulation of the military border 'on the principles of freedom and nationality'.[9]

The Serbian claims, also translated into Hungarian, did not yet refer to the autonomy of Voivodina. However, they soon became a source of discontent and a public topic. The political movements of the Serbian-language communities began in those days of euphoria in the city of Novi Sad, an important Serbian and multicultural centre. The urban magistrate set himself up as the main representative of political militancy. The senators of the city soon realised the change Vienna had made regarding all state authority and concluded that 'the opposition must not be pushed to its limits; there is a need for accommodation and even, as far as possible, understanding with the new government'.[10] By mutual agreement, they decided to send a delegation of their city to the Diet of Bratislava with a petition on Serbian national rights. These included the young lieutenant Djordje Stratimirović, nephew of the metropolitan,[11] Senator Alaxandar Kostić, spokesman for the delegation, and Jovan Polit.[12] Senator Kostić's speech was enthusiastically received by the Diet, and the delegates were then introduced to the ministers Batthyány and Kossuth. This was the context in which a dispute broke out between young Stratimirović and Kossuth, the Hungarian revolutionary, which would affect the course of Serbo-Hungarian relations.[13]

On the other hand, on 23 March the young Romanians in Pest declared themselves against the Serbian programme and formulated a programme of the Romanian community in the Banat, with seven demands:

1. Administrative separation of the Banat of Timișoara (the counties of Caraș, Timiș and Torontal and the Banatian border);
2. Separation of the three episcopal dioceses (Arad, Timișoara and Vršac) from the Serbian metropolitan church and their union with Transylvania, under the authority of a Romanian bishop;
3. Election of Romanian high hierarchs by priest and lay deputies;
4. Establishment of a fund to support education of Romanian clerics;
5. Use of the Romanian language in schools of Romanian communities;
6. An annual church synod;
7. Election of bishops from among anointed priests.[14]

Although the Serbian revolutionary population wanted an association with Romanians as part of their anti-Hungarian approach, Romanians focused their attention only on the development of administrative and religious institutions for the Romanian-speaking population of the Banat.[15]

GARAŠANIN'S SERBIA: ACTION FOR SERBIAN VOIVODINA AND THE PATRIARCHATE

From the first days of revolution, the involvement of the Belgrade government and its emissaries in Voivodina was obvious. Serbs in Hungary were urged to ally themselves with the Croats and adopt an intransigent attitude towards the Hungarians. Deliberately pursuing the Nacertanije objectives, Serbs loyal to Prince Alexandar Karadjordjević and his prime minister, Garašanin, intended to take control of Serbian armed resistance in Hungary, obstructing the consolidation of Hungarian authority in the border areas, without affecting relations with Russia and the Ottoman Empire.[16]

Prior to the outbreak of Serbo-Hungarian armed conflict, the Belgrade emissary, the Croat Matia Ban, advised Colonel Knićanin, the prime minister's military councillor, to be ready to intervene in time to support the Serbian community beyond the Danube and the Sava, and recommend the political programme they should follow. Ban observed: 'now is the time for Serbians to regain their autonomy . . . led by the voivode and the patriarch'. As envoy of the Serbian government, Ban was sent to Zemun, Karlowitz and Novi Sad. He met the metropolitan Rajaćić, persuading him to conclude an agreement with the Croats if Serbia would honour its pledges. In Zagreb, he informed Prince Jelacic and Gaj that Serbia wanted the unification of all Croatian lands and their alliance with the Serbs in Hungary, being ready to offer military support for this initiative. Travelling to Zemun, Prime Minister Garašanin made caustic comments, criticising flag and cockade parades, and urging Serbs to prepare their guns to defend their nationality 'about which they make so much noise'.[17]

THE ECHO OF THE HUNGARIAN REVOLUTION IN TIMIȘOARA

Following the events in Pest, on 18 March a movement started in Timișoara with the aim of implementing the revolutionary programme. Aside from the Hungarian civil servants, the bourgeoisie of the city mostly consisted of Germans, Jews, Romanians (including Macedonian Romanians) and Serbs. The language of the bourgeoisie in the city was German,[18] Romanian being more prevalent in the suburbs and Serbian in clerical circles. Since, both in 1848 and over the following decades, the demographic situation indicated the existence of a multicultural and multilingual world, the representatives of the revolution in the Banat of Timișoara (Timiș County) identified only to a small extent with the aspirations of the revolutionaries from Hungary or their Hungarian sympathisers in the Banat. Petar Čarnojević and Sava Vuković were Serbs; Kulterer Ignàcz was Swabian, and Gorove Istvàn, Armenian.

On the initiative of the Timiș County administration, a 12-point *Revolutionary Programme* was printed and disseminated in Pest[19] and Gorove Istvàn advised the population to adopt it. Decisions were taken to solve current problems: freedom of the press and the establishment of a committee of nine members (the Committee for Public Good), to which the National Guard was subordinate for the maintenance of public authority. The assembly requested that the military headquarters of the city should not be involved in the public life of the town. Signatures for a petition addressed to the Diet and for enlisting in the National Guard were gathered. Prime Minister Batthyány's memorandum regarding the enactment of new democratic laws was publicly read. The following day, 19 March, Sava Vuković addressed a crowd which had spontaneously gathered at the city hall, and was interrupted by cheers for the revolutionary programme. It was decided that Parade Square in front of the city hall would be renamed Freedom Square[20] in honour of the events.

Over the next few days, following news of the official confirmation of the revolutionary government, at the city hall, in front of the commandant's office and the new guard, four altars were built where religious services were conducted, giving thanks and promising support for the new government. It was here that the idea of liberty emerged, an aspiration to which all Timișoara's citizens subscribed. The events were attended by Catholics, Protestants, Orthodox and Jews. Although this seemed like an indication of good relations within the urban community regardless of religious affiliation, there were nevertheless some tensions between Christians and Jews.[21]

NATIONAL ASSEMBLIES

On 19 April 1848 the leader of the Serbian delegation from Bratislava, Aleksandar Kostić, made an extensive report on the issues discussed in the Diet and during the meeting with Kossuth. To the young nationalists in Novi Sad, it appeared that the Hungarian government was opposed to the convocation of the Serbian national assembly, and furthermore was considering the Pest government's intention to Magyarise the Serbs by introducing the Hungarian language, including in church administration. The crowd entered the Episcopal church, setting fire to the Hungarian registers. From there, regrouping in front of the city hall, holding national flags and wearing cockades symbolising the identity of the Serbian community, they went to Karlowitz, demanding that the metropolitan convene a representative assembly of the Serbian community (*skupstina*).

The metropolitan was concerned about the rebel demonstrations in Novi Sad. As a figure with public responsibilities, he tried to 'calm' things down, assessing the demonstrations as the actions of some 'prodigal sons'. At the insistence of the crowd, he suggested first holding a preparatory conference of the assembly, but was interrupted by vehement shouting for a *skupstina*. Finally, on 13 May he agreed to convene the great national assembly at Karlowitz.[22]

THE SERBIAN RELIGIOUS AND POLITICAL COMMUNITY: THE KARLOWITZ ASSEMBLY (MAJSKA SKUPSTINA)

Count Čarnojević was assigned to oversee the synod that the government approved on 15 May, not as a national assembly but only as a church congress[23] of Orthodox subjects, similar to those summoned for the election of bishops or other important events in the life of the Church. In Novi Sad, he met Jovan Hadžic-Svetić, the most esteemed Serbian authority in the city at that time,[24] and the metropolitan Josif Rajačić. There was a heated dispute, during which the delegates were surprised to find that Josef Hrabowski, the commander of the Petrovaradin fortress, had pro-monarchist beliefs. 'You want to be acknowledged as a distinct people. Show me – here is the map – where in our Monarchy is the land on which the Serbs can be considered a political people?', he asked.[25]

On 13 May the Serbian metropolitan inaugurated the *skupstina* with a speech in which he stated that 'Serbs must receive back (and benefit from) all the natural, political and legal rights which they have lost or had taken from them'.[26] The *skupstina* answered by acclaiming Rajačić as patriarch and Colonel Stevan Šupljikac as voivode.

On 15 May, the *skupstina* adopted the following decisions:

1. The Serbian people proclaims itself 'politically free and self-governing under the authority of the House of Austria and the Crown of Hungary'.
2. It proclaims itself 'Serbian Voivodina', in which are included Srem (Sirmiu) with border, Barania, Bacica with Cecej district and *șaike* (boat) battalion, the Banat with border and the Kikinda district.
3. Serbian Voivodina enters into a 'political alliance on the basis of liberty and full equality' with the United Kingdom of Croatia, Slavonia and Dalmatia.
4. The Permanent National Council is established as executive body of the *skupstina* and its members are appointed.
5. 'Wallachian [Romanian] National Self-Determination' is recognised.
6. A body of representatives is appointed to deliver the decisions of the *skupstina* to the monarch and the Croatian synod.
7. A delegation is appointed to attend the pan-Slavic congress in Prague.[27]

After the elation of the first days, some reserved and even critical opinions on the decisions of the *skuptina* began to circulate. Jakov Ignjatovic, the Romantic writer and revolutionary who had drafted the programme of the Serbs of Pest, believed that further action must be taken, abandoning the idea of Voivodina and pressing for union with Serbia, following Ștefan Dușan's model. A more reserved opinion was expressed by the conservative Jovan Hadžic-Svetić who, opposing separation from the Hungarians, deposited his mandate as a delegate.

In Zagreb, opinion was divided, although the democratic majority welcomed the accord with the Serbs. In Innsbruck, Emperor Ferdinand agreed to receive the Serbian delegation led by Patriarch Rajačić in a private audience and in the presence of Prince Esterházy as representative of the legitimate Hungarian government. The sovereign informed them that the only decrees he could recognise were those issued by the Diet or the government. On that occasion, Archduchess Sofia, mother of the future emperor Franz Joseph, displayed ribbons in Serbian colours, while Archduke Franz-Karl told the Serbs: 'We have to admit that both We [the Court] and you are unhappy and we need to help each other. Continue on your chosen path, because it leads to the deliverance of Us and you.'[28] This was a useful gesture for calming spirits. Later, in the second half of the nineteenth century, competition between national and imperial ideas took centre stage in the disputes regarding the Dual Monarchy.

ROMANIAN REACTIONS: THE ASSEMBLY-CONSULTATION IN PEST

At first, Romanians in the Banat tried to distance themselves from the radicalism of the Serbian movement, demarcating their own options in line with the policy of the Hungarian government. On Emanoil Gojdu's initiative, 39 Romanian deputies from the Banat (Caraş, Timiş and Torontal counties) and from Partium (Arad, Bihor, Bichiş) and from the city of Pest gathered in the Hungarian capital between 15 and 21 May.

This assembly, or rather meeting, of the Romanian leaders in Hungary had two objectives. The first was to define Romanian demands and the delimitation of the Serbs of Karlowitz, with whom they still shared the same Orthodox faith. The second was to attract the Romanian national body to the legitimacy of the church congresses under governmental authority. With regard to collaboration with the Hungarians, Petru Cremena[29] from Timişoara judged that, due to the knitting-together of a national conscience, Romanians would be able to preserve their own distinctiveness.

The main interest of the debates was, however, the Karlowitz decisions, one of which directly concerned Romanians: encouragement of the 'self-determination' of the national body in the Kingdom of Hungary. From the beginning, the Romanians rejected any possible collaboration with the metropolitan of Karlowitz. The historian I. D. Suciu reckons that the moderate Emanoil Gojdu, who had summoned the meeting in Pest, leaned towards a more rigorous demarcation of the hierarchic and functional structures of the common Church rather than full separation. The 'independence' initiatives towards the Serbs, he continued, were in fact taken by the delegates from Lugoj.

For Romanians, the feeling of linguistic community and political aspiration prevailed over membership of the Orthodox Church. The intelligentsia assembled in Pest protested against the appointment of Josif Rajačić as patriarch of the common Church, taking over the governmental arguments that regarded this act as illegal according to civil and canon law. The deputies declared allegiance to the emperor, demonstrating that the Empire had a special symbolism for Romanians in the Banat. In *The Petition of the Romanian People in Hungary and the Banat*, a document addressed to the Hungarian government under whose jurisdiction the Banat was at that time, they called for the cessation of affiliation to the Serbian hierarchy and the establishment of their own religious and educational institutions.

The people gathered in Pest assumed the spirit of the letter and subsequent decree of the minister of religious affairs, József Eötvös, to summon a new church congress, under governmental authority, in Timişoara on 25 June 'to consult together for the common good'.[30] The stated desiderata were, as Suciu noted, 'of religious, political and national interest'.[31] They included a Romanian metropolitan (a metropolitan vicar for the time being); a mixed commission for the Romanian separation from the Serbian church and the Serbian school; free use of the Romanian language in church and school and 'in all affairs of the nation'; Hungarian as official language; and the improvement of conditions for Romanians in the administration, justice and the military.

TIMIȘOARA AND THE ANTI-SERBIAN CONGRESS

On 12 April the new county dignitaries were elected in Timișoara. Magnate Petar Čarnojević was appointed supreme administrative commissioner, assisted by Sava Vuković and Kulterer Ignácz. On 25 May, the Timiș County Assembly issued a proclamation informing citizens about the latest reforms and events. In order to prevent any disturbance, the assembly requested the citizens of Timiș to listen only to the government in Pest. Citizens were also asked to donate objects, precious metals, clothes, animals, and young people to join the army of volunteers (Honvéds).[32] On 23 May, Szemere, minister of the interior, informed the recently appointed royal commissioner Čarnojević that the government had outlawed the Serbian decisions, and that the proclamation of Voivodina 'contravenes the Constitution' and 'destroys the unity of the country'. The minister asked the commissioner to keep a strict watch so as to prevent the infiltration of ammunition and printed matter from Serbia, to control the printing houses, and to warn the Belgrade government to control its subjects. In order to facilitate his task, Sava Vuković was appointed vice commissioner.[33] The delay in fulfilling the promises made to Romanians at Pest generated the first signs of mistrust towards Hungarian authority, and at the same time contributed to the radicalisation of the demands expressed by the Romanian assembly in Lugoj.[34]

THE SERBO-HUNGARIAN CIVIL WAR

Following the decisions taken at Karlowitz, the Serbian Central Council assumed the mission to defend in face of the danger that the revolutionary Serbs might represent. Squads of the Hungarian National Guard were patrolling the Hungarian villages of the Banat and Bacica, and Serbs were being disarmed, arrested and submitted to military justice. In Szeged and other centres of the Banat, newly erected military camps were threatening the Serbs from Voivodina. The president of the Serbian Council, the young officer Djordje Stratimirović, tried to draw the border guards to his revolutionary movement. The decision of the imperial court, issued on 7 May 1848, supported him by advocating the subordination of the regiments of the military border to the Hungarian government.

In the early days of June, when a Hungarian attack upon Karlowitz and Novi Sad seemed imminent, the border communities rose to arms. On 21 June Commissioner Čarnojević informed the ministry that 16,000 'insurgents' with eight cannons had seized positions in Karlowitz and around the 'Roman earthworks' of Novi Sad. They hoped for support from the Croats. At the same time the Petrovaradin incident took place between Commander Hrabowski and the Serbian officers who wanted to establish a new region under the name of Voivodina. The border guard delegation returned to Karlowitz where they drafted an appeal to the emperor against Hraboski, expressing disagreement with the Hungarian revolutionary policy towards a government that disregarded the decisions of the *skupstina* by enlisting 'mobile guards' and terrorising the whole population with military justice. The same delegates demanded the replacement of the general. They also wanted the metropolitan Jelačić and voivode Šupljikac to be sent to Voivodina to prevent civil war. The imperial administration had already ruled against the initiative of the Serbian-language community: in a telegram of 20 June 1848, the emperor informed the Hungarian minister of war, L. Mészáros, that he was transferring to him authority over the whole border army of Hungary, Transylvania and 'the annexed territories'.[35] Civil war began on the morning of 24 June, when the commander of Petrovaradin dispatched a subunit to conquer Karlowitz and dissolve the Serbian Council. Stratimirović mobilised his fellow citizens and, with the support of a volunteer squad and the guard of Vule of Montenegro, repelled the attack.[36]

THE POPULAR ASSEMBLY OF THE ROMANIANS OF LUGOJ

At the beginning of June, Eftimie Murgu left Pest for the Banat. Before leaving, he launched a manifesto approved by Szemere, minister of the interior, in which he praised the Hungarian revolutionaries who had contributed by their demands to the liberation of Romanian peasants from feudal dependencies. Murgu obtained the minister's consent to convene a Romanian assembly at Lugoj 'in which only desires would be expressed, without taking decisions'. However, Jakabffy, vice commissioner of Caraş, regarded this as dangerous for the local authorities. Using his popularity, Murgu tried to attract the support of the Caransebeş border regiment. General Commander Appel isolated him by asking them to leave the city.

The main Romanian revolutionary action took place in Lugoj where, on 27 June, a large popular gathering took place on Liberty Field. One historian has estimated the number of participants at 10,000. The desiderata of the assembly were:

1. Establishment of a Romanian army by providing the people with arms within six days;
2. Appointments of Eftimie Murgu as supreme captain of this army and of one captain for each of the three counties of the Banat (Timiș, Caraș, Torontal);
3. Use of Romanian as the language of command of the popular army;
4. Recognition of Romanian as official language throughout the Banat;
5. Hungarian to be used only in correspondence with the Hungarian government;
6. Independence of the Romanian Orthodox Church.

According to Sava Vucović, Eftimie Murgu wanted similar things to the Serbian revolutionaries.[37] He demanded the establishment of a Romanian army with himself as supreme commander.[38] He promoted Romanian, rather than Hungarian, as the official language of the Banat, showing that he had taken into consideration the demographic condition of the region, according to which Romanians represented the majority. Vucović's attitude foreshadowed the distrust regarding both Murgu's future activity as a politician and the expectations of the Romanian-Hungarian association for achieving the objectives of the revolution, among which the most important seemed, for a short time, to be the overthrow of the imperial administration.[39]

WAR OPERATIONS IN VOIVODINA AND THE BANAT

Following the failed attack upon the city of Karlowitz, both parties – Hungarians and Serbs – began military preparations, building fortified camps and storing ammunition. Moreover, they accused each other in front of the emperor. On 28 June the Court sent a message urging peace and obedience, demanding the abandonment of 'rebel' fortifications and the return of cannons and ammunition appropriated from the army's arsenal. Commissioner Čarnojević tried to achieve a ten-day ceasefire between the conflicting parties based on the imperial peace manifesto.

In Novi Sad, elections for the Hungarian Diet were held, resulting in incidents, bloodshed and military terror against Serbian citizens. The population was only saved from massacre due to the intervention of the high commissioner. On 5 August the president of the District Council of the Banat and the supreme commander Djordje Stratimirović addressed a proclamation to the minorities, informing them of the suspension of border institutions and their replacement by national councils subordinate to the District Authority in Pancevo and the Central Council in Karlowitz. The officers of the 12th German-Banatian Regiment refused to obey, and were consequently arrested, along with the disobedient members of the magistracy.

The Serbs finalised their objectives: the absolute separation of Voivodina, along with the preservation of community privileges and church and Serbian-language institutions which had already taken ideological and political form. Minister Szemere of revolutionary Hungary was similarly decisive, declaring to the commissioners from the territory:

> We regard the [Serbian] border movement as treason and there is no place for either peace or negotiation. The annihilation of this movement must be achieved by means of arms or by Serbian surrender; otherwise we would have to surrender the southern part of our homeland, something Hungarians cannot and will not do.

Such radical revolutionary sentences were also formulated in the Diet. On 11 July, Lajos Kossuth called the Serbs insurgents and rebels because of their decision to establish the region of Voivodina – a decision that had been taken by the assembly of the Serbian community that refused to obey Hungarian governmental officials. As expected, the insurgent Serbs put their hopes in the lands beyond the Sava and the Danube. Stevan Knicanin, the Belgrade councillor, continued to be in direct contact with Stratimirović's general headquarters. Prince Aleksander, Karagheorghe's son, seemed delighted by the 'good start' of the Serbs across the river. Fighting resumed with the attack of the Hungarian guard upon the Serbian positions of Vlaicovăț in the Banat. The following day, 23 July, 3,000 Serbs from the Alibunar camp started to march towards Vršac. At the entrance to the city they encountered Colonel Blomberg's imperial army and Major Esterházy's hussars, who scattered the Serbs and captured their two commanders, Council Commissioner Stanimirović and Major Naum Kojić.

After the victory at Vršac, Hungarians decided to destroy the advanced positions of the Serbs from Sentomaș (renamed *Srbobran*, 'the Serbian Bastion') in Bacica. Losses were great on both sides, as well as for the Serbian population from the neighbouring villages. The Serbian war council decided that the troops from Perlas should start an offensive towards Becicherecul Mare, under the command of Colonel Jovan Drakulić, a former imperial officer. They aimed to meet the border guards from Kikinda Mare district (comprising 11 villages and the city itself). Drakulić's army clashed at Ecika with the infantry, squadron and cannons of the commander of Becicherecul, Kiss Ernö. The Hungarians retreated, hiding inside the city.[40]

Although the Romanian villages from the territory did their duty towards the Karlowitz authority,[41] there were incidents between Serbs and Romanians, some associated with former conflicts, for example in Biserica Albă.[42] Following Croatia's entry into the war on 23 September, and the aggravation of relations with Austria, the position of the Hungarian government became more problematic. Pest decided that, given the new conditions, it was necessary to neutralise the Serbian nucleus in Bacica. Command of the army was taken over by none other than Mészáros, minister of war. On 3 October he ordered the deployment of 25,000 Honvéds to attack the fortification defended by 5,000 border guards and volunteers led by Captain Petar Biga. Despite the infantry attacks and hussar charges, the defenders managed to resist, supported by a troop of 3,000 border guards who attacked the besiegers. In the end, the Hungarians retreated. Neither side had achieved its objectives. The Serbs repelled the attack upon Bacica, while the Hungarians successfully defended the Banat. This equilibrium was maintained until the House of Habsburg revised its position towards the Hungarian government, declaring war on revolutionary Hungary.[43]

TIMIȘOARA UNDER SIEGE

The launch of open hostilities between the Hungarian revolutionaries and the imperial troops determined the establishment of a stage of siege in Timișoara on 10 October 1848. The Hungarian government's request that, within seven days, the commanders of the country's cities should display the Hungarian flag and express loyalty to Hungary was refused by the garrison of Timișoara:

> The garrison feels obliged to issue the following declaration: the Manifesto of His Majesty, the constitutional emperor and king of the Schönbrunn on 3 of the current month . . . has put Hungary, Croatia and Slovenia [broadly speaking, Voivodina] under martial law. Therefore, the city of Timișoara has been placed in a state of siege by its commander. According to the same very important Manifesto, the military are unwilling to listen to the Hungarian Ministry [Government] which has been dissolved; former minister Kossuth is labelled an instigator of the people.[44]

At the municipal elections held in the summer, the 'conservative' elements (followers of Hungarian government) won. The life of civil authorities was nevertheless curtailed by the imposed state of siege:

> With reference to the most important decision issued by His Majesty, on 3 October at the Schönbrunn, according to which the entire Kingdom of Hungary is subject to martial law, the city of Timișoara, with all its suburbs, is under siege from now on and, as such, martial law is proclaimed.
>
> According to point 3 of the most important royal decision, the National Guard here is placed under the direct command of the city commander.
>
> Whoever incites revolt, opposes the troops or illegally arms himself

will be treated according to martial law.

All meetings of more than six persons are prohibited.

As long as peace and order are not broken, the state of siege will not affect industry or passenger transport.

All weapons in the hands of the National Guard must be delivered within 24 hours to the artillery arsenal, in exchange for a receipt.

Timişoara, 10 October 1848

Baron Rukavina, field marshal lieutenant and commander of the city.[45]

At the same time it was declared that, as long as turmoil in the country continued and until a legal government was established, the garrison would neither hand over the city nor take orders from anyone, meaning that the garrison was in a state of war with the Hungarian government. On 24 October the disarmament of the Hungarian guards in Timişoara began. The military authorities, summoning the municipality with cannons, seized the city treasury, confiscating all existing money for the benefit of the entire army. The city gates were shut and the whole army was deployed inside. Cannons were directed on the city hall and the prefecture. On 28 October all anti-Hungarian political prisoners were released, most of them loyal citizens, former prisoners from the Serbo-Hungarian battle of Vršac. At the end of the disarmament operation, imperial troops occupied the main centres of the Banat. Lugoj was occupied on 8 November 1848, Lipova on 13 November, and Bocşa on 5 January.[46]

The remainder of the civilian population, numbering approximately 3,000,[47] was encouraged to gather the necessary food supplies for three months. The magistrate provided 250 cattle, along with reserves of hay and corn necessary to feed them. War operations changed in the spring of 1849. After the reconquest of Transylvania, the Hungarian army led by General Iosif Bem headed for the Banat. Faced by the Hungarian forces, the border guards of Caransebeş fled to Wallachia, which exposed the Banat, the city of Timişoara remaining the only hope of the imperial resistance. At the end of April 1849, the Hungarian military forces gathered around the city, which was considered a decisive target. On 25 April/6 May, its gates were closed for 107 days of siege.[48]

THE CONCLUSION OF THE SERBO-HUNGARIAN WAR

Following the appointment of the voivode by the Court, the most dramatic events in the Austro-Serbo-Hungarian war took place in the Banat. The Hungarian army aimed to take control of the area around the city of Pancevo, while the Serbs sought to conquer Becicherecul Mare and Kikinda in order to meet the imperial forces at Timişoara.[49] On 13 October, after a series of hard-fought battles, the Serbs occupied Becicherecul, and on the following day, Kikinda.

They were forced to abandon their positions under pressure from the new units led by generals Peter Antal and Jovan Damianić.

As a professional soldier, Voivode Supljikac was aware that he needed discipline and constant support from the cavalry to mount an offensive against the brave and well-equipped Hungarian army. That is why, by appealing for imperial support with special officers and weapons, he forced the troops under his command to 'be faithful to the imperial flag', and the Serbian national councils to 'work for the Emperor, people and country'. Thus, gradually, the Serbian army was integrated into the imperial one, a process implemented by General Ferdinand Mayerhofer, former imperial consul at Belgrade.

Violent battles for the fortified positions of the south-western Banat continued, and on 21 November 1848 the Hungarians defeated the resistance at Straja, near Vršac. Five days later, General Damjanic (who had left the garrison of Timișoara as a rebel officer[50]) attacked the Tomaševac camp which was defending the city of Pancevo. Other battles were fought at Banatski Karlovac and Alibunar. Meyerhofer's Serbo-Austrian units, backed up by Knicacin's volunteers, expelled the Hungarian general's cavalry.[51] In Vienna, Ferdinand abdicated in favour of Franz Joseph, son of Archduchess Sophia. Generals Windisch-Graetz and Jelačić were active factors in the new policy which envisaged a tougher attitude towards Kossuth's Hungary[52] and at the same time more understanding of the Serbian cause. By the imperial act of 27 November 1848, Emperor Ferdinand confirmed the decisions of the Serbian *skupstina* to restore the old dignities at the end of the war. Within the Serbian leadership, there were tensions between young Stratimirović and the venerable Rajačić. Taking control of the Central Council in Karlowitz, Rajačić delegated Stratimirović to Vienna to discuss the future of the province.

During a new enthusiastic offensive, a joint meeting of Serbs was organised in Timișoara on 9–10 February 1849, when the members of the Central Council took up the patriarch's position and the accusations addressed to Stratimirović. On that occasion, a reorganisation of the movement took place. The members of the council would in future be appointed (and dismissed from office) by Josif Rajačić, who was confirmed as supreme leader (*upravitelj*) of Voivodina.[53]

THE HUNGARIAN RESTORATION OF THE BANAT

At the same time, Bem's army entered the Banat through the Bistra Valley. After the first clashes in the border villages of Voislova and Marga, arson and abusive requisition took place. A large portion of the army continued its march to Caransebeș. In the manifesto issued on 14 April, the revolutionary general summoned the Banatian border guards to join him: 'If you work against us, punishment, death and devastation await you, but if you work alongside us, you will be granted forgiveness, life and freedom.' The border guards refused and retreated to Orșova and later to Wallachia. On 17 April, the Hungarians reached Caransebeș and a day later, Lugoj. There they joined the rest of the army, which had arrived from Făget. All the other important cities in the Banat – Vršac, Biserica Albă, Oravița and Orșova were conquered and controlled by the Hungarian army with the exception of Timișoara and the network of Serbian fortifications in the west and south. In Lugoj, the important governmental fief, Bem and his soldiers were welcomed enthusiastically by the Hungarian population, as mentioned in the journal of the Minorites: 'In the evening, around seven o'clock, General Bem arrived and was saluted . . . by the town leaders . . . The happiness of the people cannot be described. All were speaking Hungarian.'[54] In that period, when Hungarian independence was being celebrated,[55] the press reported the euphoria of Lugoj.

During the few months of their authority over the Banat, the Hungarians began to reorganise political and administrative life. Lipót Fülöpp was appointed governmental commissioner in Caraș. Among the county's high officials there were Romanian dignitaries, too: Vice Commissioner Gheorghe Ioanovic of Duleu, district dignitaries, commissioners and jurors. On 30 May the official newspaper *Közlöny* confirmed the appointment of Archpriest Ignatie Vuia of Vărădia as episcopal administrator of Vršac. Vicențiu Babeș was named director of the Orthodox schools of Caransebeș. In Timiș County, because of their failure to conquer the city of Timișoara, the Hungarian authority established headquarters at Sânicolau Mare, and the Orthodox archpriest of Lipova, Dimitrie Petrovici-Stoicescu was invested vicar of Timișoara.

RESTAURATIO AUSTRIAE

In January and February 1849, Knićanin's volunteers reached Sombor and were approaching Szeged. The border guards' troops led by General Todorović joined the imperial units driven by Bem from Transylvania, and those stationed in the southern Banat. Under Mayerhofer's command, this Austro-Serbian military structure managed to occupy Becicherecul Mare, and later Vršac and Kikinda, thus re-establishing connection with Timișoara.

Windisch-Graetz's Austria intended to restore the system of the *Vormärz* period before the revolution. Decisions were taken against the Serbian councils and against the restoration of the military border. In this new context, disputes arose between Patriarch Rajačić and General Djuro Rukavina, the military commander of the Banat, the latter having reservations about the new state structure designed by the Orthodox patriarch of Karlowitz.[56] It was obvious that the Serbian revolutionary movement around the patriarchate was evolving towards a dynastic, pro-Habsburg entity which intended to establish its headquarters in Timișoara, the symbolic fortress of the Austrian Empire.

The so-called Stadion Constitution, after Count Stadion, minister of the interior, was issued on 4 March 1849 by Emperor Franz Joseph. It dealt a fatal blow to the expectations of the people from the Austrian Empire, since the promises made at Innsbruck to the patriarch and to the Serbian population were not included in the text of the law. Voivodina was separated from the military border and acquired an uncertain status, annexation by Croatia, Hungary or Transylvania becoming a real possibility. Later, on 14 April 1849, Hungary was newly organised into military districts, of which Voivodina became one, and military command was given to General Mayerhofer, assisted by the patriarch, as 'imperial commissioner for the civil province'.[57]

THE BATTLE FOR TIMIȘOARA AND THE CONCLUSION OF EVENTS IN VOIVODINA

From the end of April 1849, all the military forces of revolutionary Hungary stationed in the Banat were focused around the city of Timișoara. Given the successes and high reputation of General Iosif Bem, the garrison of Timișoara was prepared for a long siege. The city army was led by four generals – Rukavina, von Glaeser, Leiningen and Wernhardt – and its personnel numbered 8,847, of whom 4,494 were recruits from the villages around Timișoara. Moreover, the fortress was in good condition; between it and the Bega Canal there was a depth of 100 feet (approximately 30 metres) and a width of 300–400 feet (100–20 metres), surrounded by earthworks.

The siege started in the Josefin quarter, an attempt at clearance taking place on 12 May.[58] The Hungarians were pushed back as far as the Freidorf quarter but this was followed by a comeback and, two days later, the occupation of the Fabric quarter. After the water supply of the fortress was cut off, the wells became the sole source of water. On 18 May the city was bombarded for the first time. The batteries were fired from different quarters: one in Josefin, the second in Maiere (later Elisabethin) and the third in Fabric, near the beer factory. On the night of 19–20 May, other cannon balls fell upon the city, one over the 'Illyrian' church (the Serbian Episcopal church in the Great Square or Dome Square, today Union Square). On 27 and 28 May, during two repeated attacks, the imperial forces tried unsuccessfully to regain the Fabric quarter. On 31 May, approximately 400 people, who had exhausted their food supplies, were allowed to leave the city.

On the morning of 11 June cannon fire was unleashed on both sides, which was prolonged for six days. Destruction within the city was great, imprinting the marks of the battle on almost every building. The population sought refuge inside bunkers and in the cellars of the destroyed houses. On the night of 13–14 June, a cannon ball penetrated the canopy of the Roman Catholic dome, where over 100 people were seeking refuge. Between 4 and 9 July, the city was again heavily bombarded. After another successful attack on 16 July, the Hungarian emissary demanded capitulation, but this was rejected. In the meantime, the Hungarian army had finalised its siege set-up, preparing for the conclusion of the battle. The number of siege troops was increased to 11,000 soldiers and 68 cannons. On the night of 18–19 July, a general attack was unleashed, but it was repulsed. The Hungarian governor himself took part in the attack, demanding that the besiegers conquer Timişoara at any cost.

On 29 June, the Hungarian army demanded the evacuation of the population from the city, a proposition appropriated by the council of war in the city. On 1 July, 80 carriages, some of them pulled by men, left the city carrying between 800 and 1,000 people, among whom were Mayor Johann Nepomuk Preyer, Chief Rabbi Oppenheimer and other important citizens. The Hungarian troops hurried their preparations for the final attack, while the imperial forces responded with raids in the besieger's battle camp. Heavy battles were fought; the artillery fire intensified and lasted for almost two weeks. A fire began at the Minorites monastery, which endangered the whole city, especially the powder tower and the military hospital. Although the fate of the city seemed sealed, the firemen managed to localise and neutralise the fire.[59] On 20 July the Huniade castle was completely destroyed, and General Glaeser died four days later.[60]

The general assault started on 4 August. After evaluating the increasingly critical situation, General Count Dembinsky ordered retreat; command of the city was given to General Bem. He fought alongside the imperial troops sent to free the city and deployed his people on the Sânandrei–Săcălaz alignment. The Hungarian army capitulated, and Colonel Blomberg, with six cavalry squadrons and two infantry divisions, emerged from the city and gave pursuit, pushing it away from the road towards Giarmata and Sânandrei. On 9 August, the winning general Haynau entered Timişoara through the Vienna Gate. The head of the army, Field Marshal Lieutenant Baron (Djuro) Rukavina, was awarded Austrian high orders.

ROMANIAN DILEMMAS

The Romanians within the empire were confronted with a double identity dilemma. In Transylvania, by decreeing union[61] with Hungary at Cluj, imperial-dynastic loyalism was reactivated under the slogan 'unitary territory, independent nationalities'. While the Serbs demanded almost the same thing at the outset and were then pushed by the exclusive nature of Hungarian project (and the effective support of the Serbian Principality) to more radical solutions, the Romanian dilemma was much more complex. The Romanians of Transylvania did not follow an integrated national pattern; on the contrary, the two Romanian Trans-Carpathian principalities had their own objectives: they were open to the revolution but vigilant towards their imperial neighbours. This would generate a remodelling of identity by the symbiosis between nationalism and dynasticism, in a 'pro-imperial affiliation' and a 'limitation of the Romanian revolutionary approach'.[62]

There was a predisposition towards Romanian action in the Banat. The emulation of nationalism, generated by the ever more pressing need for the Orthodox body's emancipation from the Serbian hierarchy,[63] could stimulate the intelligentsia[64] in the direction of revolutionary activism. But this activism was triggered late, having a rather passive connotation of reaction to the immediate and peremptory actions of the Serbian border guards.[65] Moreover, we must observe that the demands of 23 March from Pest, regarding the necessity for complete separation of the Romanian ethnic group from the Banat, were passively handled by the Transylvanian Romanians, who were still opting for autonomy by petition.[66]

Ferdinand's abdication in favour of his nephew, Franz Joseph, at the end of 1848, rekindled Romanian hopes. Hence the prospect of establishing a Romanian 'dukedom' within the Austrian borders with a national voivode and a national 'church leader' was outlined. According to historian Liviu Maior, this petition was the result of the cooperation of the Transylvanians (I. Maiorscu, A. Treboniu Laurian and Bishop Andrei Şaguna) with the people of the Banat (Ioan and Lucian Mocsonyi, Ioan Dobran) and Bukovina (Eudoxiu of Hurmuzaki and Mihail Botnar). It was forwarded to the emperor at Olmutz, on 25 February 1849.[67] He assured the Romanian delegates that he would 'resolve it' in the shortest time 'to their satisfaction'. However, by that time things had been already definitively 'settled' by the Stadion Constitution issued on 4 March.

SERBIAN VOIVODINA AND THE BANAT OF TEMES

In November 1849 Patriarch Rajačić and the bishops of the metropolitan church of Karlowitz arrived at the imperial court in Vienna to discuss the implementation of the Serbian decisions of May 1848 (the *skupstina* of Karlowitz). The imperial act establishing the Serbian voivodeship and the Banat of Temes was issued on 18 November 1849. The new entity was separate from Hungary and directly subordinate to the Viennese Ministry of the Interior. The option for this voivodeship was based on the contents of the imperial manifesto delivered to the Serbs on 15 December 1848, at the same time promising 'the establishment of an internal national authority on the basis of equal rights for all'.

Article 72 of the Stadion Constitution stated that 'the Serbian voivodeship and the Banat of Temes will be organised in such a way as to guarantee the protection of the Church and its nationality on the basis of the old imperial privileges and edicts'. Further, the delimitation of territory within the counties of Bodrog, Torontal, Timiș and Caraș and the Ruma and Ilok districts from Srem County (Voivodina)[68] was made clear.

Moreover, the same document refers to the proposed internal reorganisation of the new territory:

> Taking into consideration the special merits of the different peoples living in these lands, we dispose that the territory will be defined by three administrative perimeters, according to the interests of the three main populations that live here (Serbs, Germans and Romanians). Regarding the leadership of the Serbian voivodeship and the Banat of Temes, we have decided, along with our imperial title, to add that of great voivode of the Serbian voivodeship and Banat of Temes, and the administrative leader, whom We will appoint from time to time, will be granted the title of vice voivode.

At the same moment as the new state entity was established, the duties of the Central Council and its president, Josef Rajačić, ceased. At the head of the new administration which had its headquarters in Timișoara, General Ferdinand Mayerhofer was appointed as provisional leader (*nacelnik*). The voivodeship was then separated into two administrative areas: Bacica-Torontal and Timiș-Caraș. Leading each of them was a great administrative ruler (*jupan*), seconded by imperial and vice commissioners. Hungarian officials and the use of the Hungarian language were eliminated from the administration. The official terminology was adapted into Serbian and later into German. The military border with a majority Serbian population was left outside the boundaries of the new country. Instead, the voivodeship included the whole provincial Banat, which had a Romanian majority. The military border was reorganised. The Petrovaradin regiment, the *șaike* batallion from Titel, the regiments of the Banat (from Pancevo, Biserica Albă and Caransebeș) and the district of Kikinda Mare were regrouped within the Serbian-Banatian territorial military command, with headquarters in Timișoara. Field Marshal Lieutenant Johann Coronini was appointed leader. According to the 1850 census, the population of the country comprised 1,525,214 inhabitants, consisting of 414,947 Romanians, 396,156 Germans, 309,885 Serbs, 256,164 Hungarians, 73,642 Croatians, 25,982 Slovaks, 23,014 Bulgarians and 12,596 Jews.

The administrative organisation was completed in 1851, when the voivodeship was divided into five districts (prefectures): Timișoara, Lugoj, Torontal, Sombor and Novi Sad. These were subdivided into sub-prefectures and then into communes. The Supreme Court of Justice was in Timișoara, and courts of appeal existed in Timișoara, Lugoj and Sombor. Most of the public offices were owned by Germans or German-speaking Slavs (Czechs), and the number of Serbian officials, albeit higher than previously, remained small.

The Germanisation of the administration was explained by the desire to make the state apparatus more efficient, the unity of the Empire presupposing that all people had knowledge of the German language as well as their own. Bureaucracy was the factor in Germanisation in this case: mastering the official language of the empire, but 'practising, at the same time, bi(multi) lingualism'. Service in the state represented certainty, accreditation and social advancement, generating attachment to the model of a united and centralised Austria. The industrial bourgeoisie and all the other active forces of capitalism appreciated this return to order 'and especially the remarkable prosperity' of Count Alexander von Bach's neo-absolutist system.

With regard to both the different aspirations of the three regions of the same administration – Transylvania, Banat and Voivodina – and the relations between the Romanians and Serbs of the Banat, it is necessary to understand the different perceptions of the concept of freedom. Thus, while Romanians in Transylvania wanted liberation from Hungarian domination, Romanians in the Banat wanted liberation from the administration of the Serbian Church. On the other hand, the relationship between Romanians and Serbs in the Banat reflects two different options, Serbs having the upper hand from the point of view of political preparation and wanting release from the servitude of the Hungarian State Council. Unlike them, Romanians in the Banat wanted the establishment of their own institutional structures, those of the Church being the most accessible, which would permit the beginnings of a sociopolitical life.

14

FROM HABSBURG CENTRALISM TO AUSTRO-HUNGARIAN MONARCHY

Victor Neumann

THE AMBIVALENCE IN HUNGARIAN POLITICAL ATTITUDES

This chapter discusses changes within the Austrian (later Austro-Hungarian) Empire in the nineteenth century and assesses their impact upon the re-establishment of sociocultural life and regional policy. From this perspective, the Banat is contextualised within the administrative and political space that evolves throughout the period.

Understanding the evolution of political thought in East Central Europe requires exploration of the cultural diversity that underlies the formation of ideologies and political expression. There are many states which support the idea that the formation of the modern nation is a more or less accurate replication of medieval traditions and that the transfer of a set of values from one era to the next is perfectly legitimate. Within the regions of the Austrian Empire – more than any other part of Europe – people believed in a perfect or near-perfect analogy between the ancient, modern and contemporary worlds. The idea of 'national specificity', of distinguishing the character of a community group based on ethnic origins, and defining it with the help of the term 'people', had a long history in the past of East Central Europe. The social dimension could not play its proper part in the structuring of political thought.

Let us start with Hungary, the eastern part of what became the Austro-Hungarian or Dual Monarchy. This is revealing for the current analysis, and elucidates the role of the intelligentsia in political decisions in the area. Also, Budapest in 1848 was an important reference point for the political thought of Central Europe and would remain so for the remainder of the century. Another argument is suggested by the fact that the area of the Banat, Bukovina, Galicia, Silesia and the Tyrol) – under Hungarian administration from 1867 – was inhabited by a diverse range of people, who spoke several languages, practised different religions, and had a wide variety of traditions. The nationalities were Serbo-Croat, Romanian, German, Slovak, Ukrainian and Ruthenian, and their cultural and civilsational landmarks had multiple origins: Austrian, German, Italian, Hungarian, Russian, Greek and Turkish.

The features of nationalism in the different countries of East Central Europe have always been close, sometimes identical, as a result of the absence of differentiation between segments of society across the region. At the time of the 1848 Revolution, the majority of the inhabitants of the area were peasants at an early phase of literacy. They were easily manipulated by an intelligentsia of aristocratic-feudal origin (or with a behavioural culture borrowed from the nobility) whose aspirations towards innovation went hand in hand with a desire for power.

The historian Peter Sugar has a different opinion. He believes that, since political aspirations were not identical throughout the area, forms of nationalist expression could not be identical either. Sugar also claims that in nineteenth-century Hungary an aristocratic nationalism was born which was similar to that of Poland. He distinguishes between the expressions of nationalism in the area: Czech nationalism is considered bourgeois; Serbian and Bulgarian nationalism is called peasant-populist; Romanian and Greek nationalism is bureaucratic.[1] However, what emerges from the applied research of the history of the region does not seem to correspond to Sugar's scheme. (The same differences reported in the mid-nineteenth century can be transferred – with some nuances – to the interwar period.)

During the Romantic age, in the regions of East-Central Europe develops a messianic nationalism of German/Prussian inspiration developed in the regions of East Central Europe. Even Czech nationalism may be called less 'bourgeois' and more ethnic, in the German Romantic sense. The distinctions mentioned by Sugar – whose works have become a point of reference within the literature on nationalism in East Central Europe – do not take sufficient account of the social reality of the area. The concept of nation has different connotations in this area than in Western Europe. The analysis of facts from the perspective of social history highlights a relatively homogeneous world which related in the same way to collective identity: soil, culture, language and race. The terms *nép*, *narod* and *popor*, like the German *Volk* or 'ethnic group', indicate a relationship due not only to common origins, but also to similar mindsets.[2] The Hungarian example is distinguishable from others by the temptation to assimilate the cultural-linguistic and religious communities in its immediate neighbourhood. Moreover, the Hungarian intelligentsia was the only one that dared to challenge the status of the Empire, opposing monarchical absolutism and the laws of the Viennese administration.

The revolutionaries of 1848 were dominated for a time by Parisian ideas, and drafted utopian projects. They met in parliament, granted freedom of the press, abolished medieval serfdom, and discussed community interests and democratic ideals. It was not only the Hungarian revolutionaries who did this, but also those in other regions within the Austrian Empire: the Romanians of Transylvania and the Banat, the Swabian Germans of Voivodina and Timișoara, the Saxons of Transylvania, and the Czechs of Prague. However, taking advantage of popular unrest, the leaders of the Hungarian Jacobin movement wished to go further and establish a state independent of the Habsburgs: a free republic based on equality. Through this bold manoeuvre, they placed themselves in the vanguard of the Forty-Eighter movements of East Central Europe: none of the emerging nations besides Hungary expressed a desire to break with the imperial administration.

All this took place against a background in which the non-Hungarian population under Habsburg jurisdiction was strongly affected by the myth of paternalism. Reverence to the capital of Vienna, the emperor and the imperial administration was encouraged by all religious faiths – Catholic, Orthodox, Greek Catholic, Jewish and Protestant. Even the non-Hungarian notables of the Austrian Empire envisaged the emancipation of their linguistic communities as being possible through the protection and stimulus offered by the House of Habsburg. In Hungary, evolution, in the sense of the formation of national consciousness and the creation of the nation state at the beginning of the twentieth century, took society in another political direction. However, while the Hungarian intelligentsia may no longer have supported the old paternalism, it does not mean that that reflex had disappeared altogether.

The models embraced by the Forty-Eighter generation were not only of French, but also of American inspiration. The book *Journey to North America* (1835) by the Translyvanian author Alexandru Farkas Bölöni became widely known in the Hungarian community and was enthusiastically greeted by Count István Széchenyi (1791–1860).[3] It would inspire the democratic reforms proposed by the Hungarian intelligentsia in 1848. Among these, the idea of the republic deserves special attention and its treatment in Bölöni's book was particularly noted by Széchenyi. Bölöni identified America as the country of fast development, unlimited social development and political freedom. What he appreciated in Americans, first and foremost, was a republican society whose legislative system offered all its citizens equal access to the ballot box. *Journey to North America* became a true manual of democracy for the Hungarian Forty-Eighters.

The idea of the republic was also invoked by the Hungarian poet and revolutionary Sándor Petőfi (1823–49). In his *Journal*, Petőfi referred directly to the possibility of establishing a Hungarian republic and was certain that it would be victorious in the not-too-distant future. 'I am a republican, heart and soul. I have been from my very first breath and I will remain so until my last.' Elsewhere, he declared with the same conviction: 'Monarchy in Europe is at its end and not even Almighty God can save it.' However, the ambivalence of his position is clear from the following fragment in the journal: 'Monarchy is the flower, and republic is the fruit.' Does this amount to a real intellectual controversy, or simply ignorance of the differences that separated the two forms of government? Aware that the Austrian Empire was not in decline, Petőfi admitted that his intention was to provoke debate in order to familiarise the public with an idea that would at some time return to the foreground.

In this debate Lajos Kossuth (1802–94) seems the most interesting voice. Kossuth greatly contributed to the spread of dissatisfaction with the Habsburg authorities. Although he was among the most feared of the Jacobins of the Hungarian revolution, Kossuth respected the law in everything he did. Following the French model, he and his radical colleagues understood that the aim of the revolution must be to gain independence from Austria and proclaim a Hungarian republic. This was what happened on 15 March 1848, although anti-monarchism started to gain popular support only from September. The Diet of Bratislava was in charge of implementing the transition to a form of constitutional government. In Kossuth's opinion, it was up to a parliament elected by the free will of its citizens to decide the form of government for the country. The Forty-Eighter leader was a convinced anti-monarchist, but that did not prevent him from seeing the situation of his country in an international context.[4] He displayed some caution in refusing to link the declaration of independence with the proclamation of the republic. Even though he was at the head of a republican government, Kossuth thought that the right moment for confronting the Empire had not yet come. Later, when he emigrated to the United States, Kossuth was regarded as the leader of the first Hungarian republic.[5]

Among the Hungarian intelligentsia there were also more cautious attitudes, often inspired by the privileged social condition of the elites. Széchenyi, a supporter of the reforms, and familiar with the evolution of European political thought like his colleagues from the barricades, was in doubt about a clear theoretical position: 'Saint Stephen [the founder of the medieval Kingdom of Hungary] or the republic.'[6] He was fully aware of the need for political change, although he believed that the voice of the revolutionaries had to be silenced. The radical nature of the gestures and declarations of the Forty-Eighters had caused great unease inside the circles he frequented. The attitude of Széchenyi, who was also the founder of the Hungarian Academy of Science, reflects that of the Hungarian aristocracy. As he saw it, no matter what name was given to the new state configuration, the nobility must preserve political power. This ideological attitude was far from that of Kossuth, and reflects the ambivalence of the political phenomenon in this area of East Central Europe: on one hand, the Jacobinist discourse, which tried, like Robespierre, to impose democratic norms by force; on the other hand, the reformism of the new aristocratic generation trying to adapt to the new situation in order to preserve the power that it had inherited from the great medieval families.

ETHNOCULTURE: THE FAILURE OF A PEACEFUL TRANSITION FROM ABSOLUTISM TO CONSTITUTIONALISM

What happened in 1848 in Hungary was not confined to the anti-Habsburg approach. The political representatives ignored the fact that the emancipation of people from neighbouring regions was also taking place in parallel with its own. Romanian and Slovak nationalism was born under the same auspices as Hungarian nationalism. Hence the difficulty to impose a monolingual policy and a new independent state – or at least autonomous – in relation to Vienna. The subordination of the national-linguistic communities within the perimeters of the former medieval kingdom of Hungary was not possible in the absence of a modern administrative structure. The civil war of 1848–49 between Romanians and Hungarians was a consequence of the ideological radicalism of the Forty-Eighter Hungarian intelligentsia and politicians. In place of democratic revolutionary demands they substituted the Romantic understanding of national options. They added the idea – which was counterproductive – of reconstructing the medieval kingdom, which triggered anti-Hungarian, anti-Magyar and counter-revolutionary attitudes among Romanians, Croats and Slovakians. The tendency towards ethnonational disintegration could not be averted by the brightest revolutionary minds and pens. The idea of collective identity, formulated as early as the years of reform of 1800–40, was adopted by the entire intelligentsia of the region, not only the Hungarians. Thus, competition on the fragile terrain of searching for and identifying origins arose, enflaming spirits in 1848. 'Taking advantage' of the cultivation of their own language and history to define difference or specificity in relation to an alterity, the Forty-Eighters of East Central Europe did not follow the example of their fellow revolutionaries in the West either in the content of their ideas, or in their social and political objectives. Here we see that the role of identity imprinted by the Romantic current was more powerful than that of cosmopolitanism. While in the decade preceding 1848, the influence of the French Revolutionary model of social emancipation and differentiation of professional categories was stronger, eventually the German *Volk* model won out. The so-called national propaganda was the first moment when the aspirations cultivated by the cosmopolitan Enlightenment were stifled. Irrational collectivist discourse took the place of the multiple convergences that had marked harmonious cohabitation and mutual recognition through the mediation of Austrian state identity. Once again, progress towards the emancipation of society had been interrupted for the benefit of a dominant minority, which now claimed the idea of belonging to the same tribe.

The defeat of the revolutions hindered the evolution that had been anticipated by the Jacobin intelligentsia but it generated a series of other controversies regarding Hungarian policy on the one hand and imperial policy on the other. It also encouraged the preservation of feudal institutions which dominated the social, economic and political spheres. The year 1848 demonstrated that the imperial structure was not as solid as had been thought. The aristocracy in Vienna was overtaken by the will of bourgeois intellectual circles within the city and at the same time challenged by the Hungarian and Czech aristocracies. Consequently, the monopoly of power could be preserved in Vienna only if the dominant social class was able to impose strict administrative order. The sociopolitical force of the great noble families of the Austrian Empire was responsible for the proclamation of Viennese neo-absolutism, a precautionary measure that caused great tension between old and new, between different segments of society and opposing ideologies. Neo-absolutism had annexed the most generous of the Forty-Eighter aspirations for the good of the Empire, stimulating economic growth, legislative reform, modernisation of administrative institutions and the formation of the bourgeoisie as a distinct social category.

Despite an obvious conservatism – highlighted by exaggerated bureaucratic control – the imperial administration encouraged the liberal orientation of politics in order to preserve political normality. In doing so, they temporarily halted the development of the ideology of ethnonationalism which ignored the cohabitation of different linguistic communities. The monarchy had become the only regional administration capable of avoiding the overexertion of collectivist pride and the tragedy of civil war. The situation is even clearer if we follow it from the perspective of the historical *longue durée*.

The Hungarian-born French historian and political scientist François Fejtő has a different opinion. Inspired by Jean-Michel Leclercq's observation that nationalism represents the failure of a peaceful transition from absolutism to constitutionalism, Fejtő believes that in the later nineteenth century, the Austro-Hungarian Empire was strongly affected by just such a failure. He points out that the situation of Switzerland cannot be compared to that of the Empire. In his book *Requiem pour un empire défunt: Histoire de la destruction de l'Autriche-Hongrie*,[7] Fejtő asserts that a double oppression – absolutist and national – gave birth to a nationalist ideology that defined man not only by his nature as a human, but also by his ethnicity and his roots. This situation would lead to an initiative to reorganise the Austro-Hungarian Monarchy on ethnic principles and not on a universalist constitution.

This point of view would be worthy of consideration only if we could say that the societies of East Central Europe at that time were entirely emancipated from feudal servitude and no longer oppressed by the nobility. What can we discover by analysing the region's social components? First of all, that the process of literacy had been much delayed by comparison with Western Europe, even when evolution towards modernity was evident, as was the case with the Hungarian and Czech communities. Secondly, that the interests of the nobility coincided up to a point with those of the revolutionaries, hence the cooperation or tacit acceptance of the privileged social group in a revolt against the Empire. This results in an overlapping of interests which generates confusion in the understanding of the Forty-Eighter historical phenomenon. Lastly, a more complex analysis cannot ignore the relationship between the social dimension and political thought, nor can it ignore the backward economic status – premodern in its quasi-totality – in the area under discussion. Without such a retrospective we cannot answer the question of who the Forty-Eighters were speaking to.

What attracts the attention of the researcher interested in decoding the Forty-Eighters of East Central Europe is their modest concern with the acquisition of modern politic culture, promoted in England and France. This can be found only in small circles, usually within families of the nobility whose children had had the opportunity to study in Western schools. (Here we can observe a real cult of local elites, an exaggerated admiration for the scholars of all communities in the area, as well as a superiority complex often displayed ostentatiously vis-à-vis the masses.) Fejtő's interpretation can be taken into consideration if we equate it to the role of ethnonationalism or if we admit that the abandonment of liberal theses was accomplished in favour of nationalist ones. There is evidence for such a point of view in documentary research which highlights the hundreds of monocultural variables, the aspirations and radical ideas of the intelligentsia, which multiplied after the events of 1848.[8]

However, Fejtő's schematic interpretation becomes vulnerable when he places absolutism and nationalism on the same level. His intention was to confer an extremely negative image on the imperial administration. Still, despite its minus points – among which were the preservation of some exaggerated class privileges, centralism, and the absence of modern economic institutions – the House of Habsburg made a decisive contribution to the process of literacy within the population of the Empire, built the first interregional communications, developed existing cities and built new ones, and encouraged the formation of the bourgeois elite without which the emancipation and formulation of liberal ideas could not have been achieved. Even against the background of the propagation of ethnonationalist ideologies at the end of the nineteenth century, the imperial administration played an important role in the development of modern values, by creating local administrative structures and by the civic education of an impressive number of people.[9] Monarchical absolutism was not unique in this, but the delay in providing administrative reform in such a system was a mistake. One aspect that was overlooked throughout the monarchy was the establishment of common cultural landmarks, thus understanding education in a cosmopolitan paradigm and the use of German as a language of inter-community communication for the masses. Operetta (for example *Die Fledermaus* by Johann Strauss the Younger) and literature played an important role in establishing common cultural references for the inhabitants of the Dual Monarchy, but this was not always enough. My hypothesis is that the Prussian model became more attractive to the intelligentsia within the imperial provinces, not only competing with the Austrian model, but defeating and excluding it. While during the Enlightenment, representatives of the countries of East Central Europe had been inspired or influenced by Vienna, from 1848 Berlin would gradually gain their sympathy. What determined this shift in direction? The transition from a cosmopolitan ideology, where the temptation to form the Austrian citizen had been visible during the more relaxed periods of imperial history, was dominated by the exaggerated search for ethnic identity, in the sense promoted by Treitschke's histories and Herder and Hegel's speculations on political philosophy.

Many of the literary, historiographic and philosophical works of the age were characterised by the subordination of individual problems to the collective ideal. This explains not only the ideological partisanship but also the confusion generated among an insufficiently educated public. In East Central Europe, there are numerous examples of the distortion of the past for the purposes of propaganda, some of which incited prejudices which have had harmful consequences for political thought over the last century and a half. In Czech culture, for example, men like the historian František Palacký and the politician and philosopher Tomáš Masaryk depicted the Hussite movement as the first substantial manifestation of nationalism. The same interpretative registry is found within Hungarian Romantic culture, which described Imre Thököly and Francis Rákóczi II's anti-absolutist feudal revolts as true nationalist revolutions. In Romanian historiography, many historians portrayed the revolt of Horea and Cloșca as a national uprising, while in reality it was no more than a social rebellion against the feudal system.[10]

Against an ideological background that substantially reduced the chances of looking at the past in a rational way, cultural life in the communities became tense, and this in turn generated an unpredictable evolution of political thought. However, it should be mentioned that in parallel with ethnonationalistic options, in urban environments civic culture produced a modern way of thinking and a tendency to create a middle class which then expanded. Moreover, the temptation to build a federal system, which appealed to a considerable portion of cultured people, was not insignificant. These tendencies make the regions of East Central Europe unique in relation to South East Europe. The set of values of Western civilisation was assimilated – gradually and not always with the same meaning – in many of the regions dominated by the Austro-Hungarian Monarchy. This explains why, even after the establishment of nation states, a significant portion of the intelligentsia invoked the role of the monarchy's administrative structures in economic development, in generating chances for the formation of regional communities in the European sense, and in the multiplication and modernisation of towns.

A comparative retrospective of the two great tendencies of the age characterising the Austrian Empire prompts us to ask whether the process of emancipation started too late amid the contradictions stirred up by the Romantic current. Based on the documentary studies and analysis of the dynamics of ideas by historians, sociologists and political thinkers, it must be admitted that the overlap of Enlightenment and Romantic principles produced much confusion in a region where reception of the French and English experiments was not only delayed but also dominated by the inaccurate translation into German culture.[11] It is also worth mentioning that in this region exaggeration of ethnonational feelings alternated with transnationality. On one hand, writers, plastic artists and musicians were made spokespersons of the *Volksgeist*: what else was Chopin's and Liszt's music if not the result of Polish and Hungarian popular cultures? What of the warlike songs composed in France and the German Confederation during the Rhine crisis of 1840? Or the paintings reproducing the world of the soldier that fed the French Napoleonic legend?[12] On the other hand, one feels the presence of the cosmopolitan aspiration that allows for acknowledgement of alterity and transcends the narrow frame of a single identity. The multiplicity of community-linguistic membership was characteristic of the so-called Republic of Letters during the Enlightenment. It was an aspiration which reappeared from time to time during the nineteenth century in the foreground of intellectual and political concerns.

The Forty-Eighter political elite in Hungary perceived the issue of establishing modern Hungary as a problem of state sovereignty outside the Austrian Empire. After the Revolution of 1848, the issue became completely inseparable from the relationship to Vienna. During the period when the Habsburgs were ruling by the decrees of the minister of the interior Baron Alexander von Bach (1813–93) and with the help of the army, the Hungarians had already rethought their own political strategy. The propensity of the political groups to adapt during the years 1860–67, as revealed in the debates led by József Eötvös and Ferenc Deák, is proof of this. Compromise (*Ausgleich*) with Austria seemed to be the solution to satisfy both the ethnonational and the aristocratic-statal options: the Dual Monarchy which came into being in 1867 was the result. It assumed a two-headed leadership with two governments, two capital cities and two territorial administrations, while defence and foreign policy were under a single centre of command. The architect of the Austro-Hungarian compromise was Ferenc Deák. He acknowledged Hungary's vulnerability, reckoning that the Hungarian nation was too small and exposed to stand alone. He believed that the reality ignored by his Forty-Eighter predecessors had to be taken into consideration, namely that the Danube Basin was inhabited by many linguistic and religious communities, each of whom was claiming its political rights. Therefore, an administration in which his co-nationals were given a major role could only be conceived in cooperation with Vienna.

The illusion of historical Hungary proved counterproductive, because in 1848, when the Hungarian nation fought for independence from the Habsburgs, it faced confrontation with the evolving nations within the Empire: Serbo-Croat, Slovak and Romanian.[13] While Austria had understood since the end of the eighteenth century that the Empire could only endure as long as it accepted the plural development of communitarian religions and cultures, the Hungarian elite rushed to institute a series of rules that favoured the idea of a single national identity. This tendency did not disappear with the signing of the *Ausgleich*. The assimilationism practised without discrimination between 1867 and 1914 would turn against not only Hungary, but the whole of the Empire. This cannot be attributed solely to Hungarian political ambitions. In any case, it seems plausible that the attempt at assimilation contributed to the weakening of the monarchy's political system during the nineteenth century. In 1848 the Empire saved itself due to some favourable circumstances, while in 1867 Vienna was forced to accept compromise with Budapest in the context in which Prussia had already earned pre-eminence in the Germanic world after victory in the Austro-Prussian War the previous year.

Baron József Eötvös (1813–71), one of the most important political thinkers of the time, was not deceived by the incomplete programmes or the provocative actions towards the nationalities of the Empire by the Pest Forty-Eighters. Sensing the moment of radicalisation of the Revolution and the misguided attitude of his comrades, Eötvös resigned from the first constitutional government formed in April 1848 by Count Iuliu Batthyány. A few years before the events of 1848, Eötvös had written a brochure on Jewish emancipation, which he printed at Pest in Hungarian and Italian, surprising the European world by the maturity of his political work. While in exile in Munich in the 1850s Eötvös wrote *The Influence of the Dominant Ideas of the 19th Century on the State*,[14] and *The Equality of Rights of the Austrian Nationalities*. Returning to Hungary in 1860, he participated in the negotiations with Austria, along with Ferenc Deák. Following the establishment of the Dual Monarchy in 1867, he was appointed minister of education, a position that allowed him to propose extremely liberal reform. However, this was sabotaged by the reactionary administration of other departments and was never implemented.[15] Eötvös wanted to find solutions to the dilemmas of liberty and equality for every citizen. He militated against the discriminatory treatment of religious and cultural minorities and truly believed in the fulfilment of the great rational ideas of the Enlightenment. But it was too late; the propaganda of his colleagues in favour of a simple and apparently efficient fiction had already won.

DIVERGENCE AND COMPROMISE: FEDERALISATION PROJECTS

In a comparative analysis on the evolution of political thought in East Central Europe, István Bibó showed that Hungarian politicians reached two conclusions in the period immediately following 1848, which had important long-term consequences: first, that Hungary had been abandoned by Europe during the struggle for independence, and second, that non-Hungarians would use their democratic freedom – once they had acquired it – to create their own political and administrative body. The decisions of the Hungarians, which did not correspond to the lesson learned from the catastrophe of 1848–49, consisted in forming the Dual Monarchy with Austria and constraining those who had reached their own historical and communitarian consciousness. That is why the reforms proposed by Eötvös were unsuccessful, the result being an upsurge in national movements in all the eastern regions of the Austro-Hungarian Monarchy. In regions such as Transylvania, the relatively autonomous status preserved under the Austrians was lost. The situation was similar in the Banat and Voivodina, which formed an administrative and political unit, the Voivodeship of Serbia and the Banat of Temeswar (Timișoara), under the direct coordination of Vienna.

The problem of establishing an independent state is absent from Hungarian consciousness, from the concept of nationalism circulated by the political culture of the late nineteenth and early twentieth centuries. The process of structural modernisation generated great debates involving front-rank political thinkers such as Széchenyi, Eötvös and Deák who saw, for the first time in the history of East Central Europe, the need to revolutionise the institutional system. While Széchenyi emphasised the social sphere, Eötvös focused upon the role of the state, both preferring the modification of structures and neither professing authoritarianism. Many contemporaries were not yet ready to absorb such political ideas. Their aspirations were resumed during the twentieth century by some brilliant thinkers: Endre Ady, Oszkár Jászi, József Atilla, Imre Csecsy and István Bibó.

Ferenc Deák's political liberalism was important, but not decisive, at a moment when Hungarian political life needed it the most. Strongly linked to Herder and Fichte's autopoietic Romantic nationalism, the phrase 'national ideology', developed by Sándor Petöfi and Lajos Kossuth, often won the day rather than notions of democratic equality and freedom. It is true that the nationalist propaganda based on the *Volksgeist* also included some dynamic elements that predicted modernisation. However, it contained, first and foremost, the attributes of 'closed nationalism'[16] (M. Winock), which can be found in the policy of the defensive state nationalism in Hungary during the government of István Tisza (1861–1918). The Tiszaeszlár Trial of 1882–3, which reflected the anti-Semitism of some political circles, and the collective narcissism demonstrated in the Millennial Celebration of 1896, are just two examples of a series of attitudes demonstrating a manner of thinking still influenced by feudal reflexes.[17]

'The holy cause' which had been embraced by Prime Minister Tisza from his youth was actually nationalism. For three decades, his political career was marked by this ideal, which inevitably diminished the objective perception of political phenomena and the clarity of his strategic options (even in the short term). His self-assurance convinced many to follow his political thinking and actions. His passionate nationalism also included a profound attachment to Hungarian liberal traditions.[18] From his perspective, the reasoning against cultural and linguistic pluralism was obvious. The ideological option of *Volksgeist* promoted in Budapest by Tisza's government – and renewed in various forms and under diverse pretexts during the twentieth century – can be explained as a reaction to the international context which was unfavourable to national emancipation. Once again it incited the ethnonationalism of the non-Hungarian half of the population under Hungarian administration. The superiority complex cultivated by Tisza was assumed by most of the Hungarian intelligentsia at the end of the nineteenth and beginning of the twentieth century. Endre Ady (1877–1919), a well-known writer whose literary and journalistic work reveals a spirit of openness and tolerance, had been impressed by Tisza's nationalist discourse in his youth.

The Treaty of Trianon, signed by the victorious Allied powers at the end of the First World War during the Paris Peace Conference, meant losing territories that had belonged for hundreds of years to Hungary. The collective pain which was felt by Hungarians as a result of this became known as the 'Trianon Syndrome'. The politicians of the new state of Hungary became resentful in relations both with their neighbours and with the great powers. It was impossible for Hungarians to accept that there had been mistakes under the Dual Monarchy with regard to the policy on nationalities. On the other hand – as emphasised by István Bibó – they were incapable of drawing a distinction between the emergence of new ethnonational states through the territorial separation of the non-Hungarian population and the injustice suffered by losing Hungarian-language regions.

Let us look at this in more detail, in order to determine more exactly the doctrines that inspired Hungarian policy at that time. Serious economic problems and defeats at the front were accompanied by unrealistic political programmes. Controversy over reconciliation with the nationalities under the administration of Budapest took up a lot of space in the press and thus stole precious time from the political class who faced difficulties in taking radical decisions. Against this background, an accentuated idea of ethnonationalism arose which was to become more successful than that of federalism. Unlike the case of Czech intellectuals, the Hungarian nationalist delirium did not take into consideration the establishment of an independent state. For the majority of the political groups in the Hungarian parliament, there was no question of dismantling the Dual Monarchy. That is why on 22 October 1918 the Hungarian parliamentarians voted against the declaration of independence formulated by Mihály Károly. At that time there was only one method of calming the fury of the crowd: the installation of a popular government and the proclamation of necessary measures for urgent and serious national reform. The left wing of public opinion supported Károly. If this had been put into practice, Oskár Jászi wrote, Hungarian history would have taken another course.[19]

Jászi was writing not just as a political thinker, but also as someone involved in the actions preceding the collapse of the Dual Monarchy. He was a supporter of federalism, later of a fundamental change in relations with the nationalities under Hungarian domination. At the beginning of the century and particularly during the First World War, he understood not only that the Empire would die, but also that, if political change led to democratic government, regional populations would promote the national idea. When he nostalgically invoked Kossuth and the Forty-Eighter idea of a confederation of Hungarians, Serbs and Romanians, Jászi was considering the survival of a political force that was capable of balancing power between Germany and Russia.[20] The distrust of the poorest segments in society upset all the predictions of the intelligentsia and politicians and instilled a strong revolutionary spirit in all spheres of human relations in the years 1918–19. The population of Budapest had been exasperated by the suffering and the injustice of war, and as a consequence it supported some radical reforms.

The Bolshevik assault and the proletarian dictatorship installed under the influence of the October Revolution in Russia was the first serious consequence of the conflict of ideas which had confused Hungary. The second harmful direction of Hungary's policy was ethnicism. This explains the anti-liberal option, the exaltation of Hungarian Christianity in contempt of the Jewish religion and the cultivation of pure ethnicity as an alternative to capitalist corruption. This tendency was outlined in the 1920s and would dominate the public scene during the interwar period, supported by some of the most popular historians and novelists of the time, for example Gyula Szekfü and Dezsö Szabó. What was the origin of this racist orientation? The historian Vera Ránki believes that, despite the Nazi terminology used by the future Fascist leaders Gombos and Szálasi, there was no indigenous racism. She seems convinced that the mindset of the Hungarian middle class was the legacy of education during the Dual Monarchy, which held a different set of values, perceptions and articulation of social and ideological issues.[21] However, I believe that the role of the middle class – important for social emancipation at the end of the nineteenth and the beginning of the twentieth century – was still relatively minor in the 1920s and 1930s, while the intelligentsia of rural origin was obviously on the rise. The examples of the advancement of Szekfü and Szabó are just two in a long line. Books such as Szekfü's *Harom nemzedék* (*Three Generations*) prove an interest in nationalism, an interest that dominated Hungarian cultural and political thought during the interwar years. This kind of book appealed to an audience of the first literate generation (this was the case with the majority of the peasant population). A specific social framework existed which encouraged the appearance of extremist ideologies. The discussed *Völkische Kultur* of populist nationalism which had been inspired by German Romanticism created the basis for the pro-Nazi direction.[22] If the political ideas of interwar Hungary had coalesced due to the contributions of the middle class and its values, as Vera Ránki claims, the unpardonable drift to the right would have never existed. The role of the middle classes would be felt after the Second World War, when the new generation of intellectuals was appearing on the public stage, and the old radical Marxists were reaching a mature stage in their political discourse.

As there was never a single direction within the Dual Monarchy, it is appropriate to consider the rival ideas. In the mid-nineteenth century, Vienna's concept of centralisation relied on the army and the emperor, seen as a bridge between different regions inhabited by the great mosaic of linguistic communities. Two decades later imperial political thought turned to a 'trial solution' towards ultimate acceptance of the Austro-Hungarian Dual Monarchy. The way in which political ideas were shaped within the Empire led to compromise and divergence. What we know for certain is that nineteenth-century politics was left contaminated by the idea of separatism on ethnonational criteria and that was why it tried to base the administrative structure solely on convergent interests. The projects of federalisation of the Dual Monarchy must not be underestimated, much less ignored, particularly since they seemed to be among the viable forms of gradually dissolving divergence and making a transition towards coexistence based on mutual respect for the values of each community. These projects were formulated by Czech, Romanian, Austrian and Hungarian intellectuals alike. When the issue of federalisation of the Empire was discussed, the contradictory opinions expressed by Austrian Renner, Czech Pekar, Hungarians Károly and Jászi, or Romanian A.C. Popovici were a feature of political debate over a long period.

Archduke Franz Ferdinand, heir to the Austro-Hungarian throne from 1896 until his death in 1914, encouraged a similar view in his office, which acted in parallel to the official one and included Austrian military men (Karl Freiher von Bardolf and Conrad von Hötzendorf), Czech aristocrats (Count Ottokar Czernin, Heinrich Clam-Martinitz, Jaroslav Thun, Silva Tarona, the two Schwarzenberg princes), Romanian politicians (members of parliament Alexandru Vaida-Voevod and Iuliu Maniu, writer A.C. Popovici) and some pro-Habsburg representatives of Hungarian origin (Bishop Lányi, József Kristóffy and Count János Zichy). The nationalist accents of some of them – for example, Aurel Popovici, well known after the publication of *The United States of Greater Austria*[23] – were overlooked in the context in which Franz Ferdinand was disavowing Hungarian policy on the one hand and German tendencies of supremacy in East Central Europe on the other. The fact that Romanian, Czech and Serbian relations with Vienna were often auspicious from a formative point of view explains the existence of federalist ideologies within each group: a large portion of people of culture claimed allegiance to Vienna as the main cultural and university centre of Central Europe and were inspired by liberal culture and by the Empire's social and ethical ideals.

It is no accident that many intellectuals within the region praised the Empire, not only in good times, but also in bad. On the emperor's death in 1900 – when the Dual Monarchy's chances of surviving were much diminished – the Czech historian Joseph Pekar did not hesitate to review the unprecedented progress of his own nation under Franz Josef's rule: 'The difference between what we were in 1848 and what we are today is remarkable. Most of the things which we are proud of today as a civilised people were created during this period, including consciousness of our great past and our national ideas.'[24] His comrades Beneš and Masaryk had already reached agreement with Great Britain to proclaim the Czechoslovak nation state. According to Masaryk, the Czechoslovak Declaration of Independence in October 1918 opposed the Empire's attempt at federalisation. Instead, it conformed with the declaration of Czech representatives on 8 January 1918. Masaryk thought that recognition of the provisional state government and the Czech nation by the Allies would settle things once and for all. It was about the nineteenth-century concept that every nation had the right to pursue its own destiny and aspirations. Masaryk saw evolution of things in the light of his theory, which was transferred to the understanding of the whole social body. Hence the idea of nation, in which he included both Czechs and Slovaks.[25]

Judging not only on historical facts, but also on the political configurations of the present, researchers are often tempted to reveal only the positive aspect of the idea of the nation state. They reproduce politicians' speeches uncritically to reflect a reality that seems natural to them because it resembles that of today. The examples of J. Kalvoda and R. Portal are not unique, but are suggestive for this manner of understanding the past. When he refers to the formation of Czechoslovakia after 1918, Kalvoda speaks through Tomáš Masaryk, without seeing that his colleagues did not think similarly to that philosopher and political leader. Education in a cosmopolitan environment in Prague – where the German, Czech and Jewish communities disputed cultural and civic supremacy between 1867 and 1914 – encouraged a series of political positions different from Masaryk's. If in the case of the scholar Josef Pekar we noted that even ethnonationalists could respect what they called the chance Austria had offered for the development of Czech identity, writers such as Jaroslav Vrchlichky, Jules Zeijer and Franz Kafka placed themselves on the other side of the barricade. Pro-Western orientation and indifference to national folklore or to the ideas of separation from the Empire and creation of an independent state indicate a distinct type of political thought. What is certain is that the Viennese experiments during the Dual Monarchy appealed to them and influenced both their education and creations.[26]

It should be said that the political evolution of Czech nationalism was not considered as linear: in the understanding of some of its representatives, *Volk* ideology could match Austrian federalism under protection of the Habsburgs. Therefore, only a determinist interpretation – the case of Portal – can highlight a single ideological aspect. As we noted before, both segments in society and political allegiances diversify. The doctrine of Austro-Slavism, which conceived of an Austrian Empire composed of a federation of eight national regions with equal rights, was proposed by František Palacký in 1848 in Prague during a congress that reunited members of the whole Slavic world. As a political concept, Austro-Slavism continued until the First World War. It was adopted by a series of Czech, Slovene, Croatian and Serbian intellectuals and politicians and became one of the preferred doctrines of Slavs within the Empire, signaling its differentiation from the Eastern Slavic world and the abandonment of pan-Slavism which was promoted mainly by Russian Tsarist theorists.

On the other hand, the doctrine of Austro-Slavism is proof that some of the politicians of East Central Europe intended to gain proportional representation for Slavic-language speakers within the administrative bodies of the Austrian Empire and the Dual Monarchy. For a long time, the aristocracy, the liberal bourgeoisie and the Slavic peasantry had been supported, morally and economically, by the emperor in their struggle to gain sociopolitical emancipation. Austro-Slavism intended to contribute to Slavic unity without assuming separation from the Empire. As with Hungarians, in Slavic communities the aristocracy was the first social category to modernise. That explains why the bourgeoisie was more cautious than in the West. All the social classes had gained from Austro-Slavism in the development of civil society, urban industry and trade. The appearance of Serbian national radicalism, for example, would be delayed until the beginning of the twentieth century, breaking out only after the occupation of Bosnia-Herzegovina by Austria-Hungary. Until then, the 900,000 Serbians living within the Dual Monarchy (under Hungarian administration) had tended to integrate with imperial structures, with special emphasis on trade, bureaucratic and military activities.

The federalist options, as well as the separatist choices that would lead to the collapse of the Dual Monarchy, cannot be sufficiently understood without correlating them with the discontent generated by Austro-Hungarian policies in relation to the other cultural-linguistic, self-styled national, communities. The anti-Hungarian and anti-Austrian attitudes were triggered by other factors, too. It would be better to admit – which seems closer to the truth – that the nation states which emerged after the First World War in East Central Europe echo the relatively backward position of the people living in that region. The fact that the majority was (and continued to be during the interwar period) of rural origin, that evolution of the elites took place in a hurried fashion over a very short time, made possible another interpretation of nation states from the area of the former Dual Monarchy. Until the mid-nineteenth century, imperial absolutism contributed to the preservation of typical federalist traits at the expense of constitutionalism. This is a more credible explanation for the long persistence of confusion in political language. This appears when affirming the rights of nationalities and in the circumstances in which the idea of the nation state is propagated.

The cohesion of the state in the modern sense used in the Western part of the continent was impossible in Central Europe due to the absence of cultural landmarks that could have contributed to the development of a pragmatic judicial system, but mostly because of a weak tradition of civic solidarity. The experience of Western Europe in the nineteenth century – according to which 'the nation . . . is the sociopolitical group corresponding to the ideology of the individual'[27] – replicated without judgement, only generated the emergence of hybrid entities, of administrative patterns in which the principles of the medieval communities coexisted with those of the modern world. The dissolution of the Dual Monarchy did not lead to pluralist democracy and modernisation in the true sense of these terms. Instead, it produced a series of social, cultural and political convulsions and, in some instances, true crises of conscience that descended into extremist movements. The two types of nation state that emerged after the peace of Versailles are represented by Czechoslovakia on the one hand and Romania on the other. The first symbolises a federalist entity that was pluralist, built upon a civil society slightly more articulated than in the eastern part of the former monarchy; the second indicates the opposite pole, the centralist, authoritarian state, based on the collective identity of the majority ethnic group, which did not understand or plainly ignored the economic, administrative and socio-civic advantages offered by the regions that had been under Austro-Hungarian domination. The example of the Banat of Timișoara – partitioned on ethnonational criteria among three states newly created after the First World War – is suggestive of this second type.

The delay in the profound emancipation of the communities inhabiting the space under discussion of the former Austro-Hungarian Empire made possible the existence of social groups located at opposite poles with regard to intellectual aspirations, living conditions and behaviour. Czechoslovakia was one of the few exceptions: the Czechoslovakian state exploited the set of Western values promoted by the Empire and the important economic gains ensured during the Viennese administration. Unfortunately, many of the new nation states deliberately refused to take over the experience of the Dual Monarchy; this was the situation in parts of Poland and Yugoslavia and in Romania as a whole. In our current historical analysis, what is striking is that instead of being founded on laws, the state was based on traditional linguistic subcultures; instead of being made up of citizens, it was based on the concept of ethnicity. Lastly, cultural pluralism, permitted not without difficulties in the Empire, was replaced by a monoculturalism that allowed the foundation of a new authoritarian centralism. Was it a radical variant of Prussian political thought that triggered the awakening of consciousness in only a single direction? After a century and a half of history one can see that the individual was given a tiny role in relation to the idea of subordination to the community. Hence, the acceptance of nation as 'collective individual', as the exaltation of 'us' in contempt of others. A metaphysics of nationity resulted, which decreased the chances of profound modernisation of social and institutional bodies on principles similar to those of West European civilisation.

15

RELIGIOUS REFORM AND THE POLITICAL EMANCIPATION OF THE JEWS IN THE BANAT[1]

Victor Neumann

THE METAMORPHOSIS OF JEWISH SOCIETY in the Banat, by which I mean the voluntary cultivation of links outside their own community – prominence in cultural and scientific fields, intense engagement in economic life, and ample involvement in the political realm – cannot be fully understood without describing and analysing the phenomenon known as Jewish emancipation, a century-long struggle (first within the Habsburg Empire and later in the Austro-Hungarian Dual Monarchy) to acquire civil rights. The struggle did not unfold in just one province, so it is useful to make reference of their emancipation as a whole in East Central Europe. Emancipation would encompass changes in lifestyle, important shifts in mentality, religious reforms, and the renunciation of Hebrew and Yiddish as the main means of communication and their gradual replacement with German and Hungarian languages. The theme was exhaustively debated within the community, in political circles, and among the intelligentsia – both Jewish and non-Jewish.

Can this be viewed as an echo of Enlightenment debates on the ideas of Moses Mendelssohn, embodied in his reforming works? We know that in the libraries of Jewish communities, Mendelssohn's books were forbidden; however, his books were acquired in Catholic and Protestant circles and particularly by the public libraries founded in Transylvania at the end of the eighteenth century and the beginning of the nineteenth, such as the Central University Library at Cluj and the Brukenthal Library in Sibiu. These works included *Jerusalem oder über Religiöse Macht und Judentum*;[2] *Morgenstunden oder Vorlesungen über das Dassein Gottes*;[3] *Philosophische Schriften*;[4] *Philosophische Gespräche*;[5] *An die Freunde Lessings . . . ein Anhang zu Herrn Jacob: Briefwechsel über die Lehre des*

Spinoza;[6] *Phaedon oder über Unsterblichkeit der Seele in drei Gesprächen*;[7] *Lettres juives du célèbre Mendelssohn*.[8] The ideas of this scholar of the Berlin Enlightenment had an impact upon the Hungarian, Saxon and Swabian scholars in Hungary, Transylvania and the Banat and would contribute, to a certain extent, to the content and amplification of discussions on Jewish emancipation. For example, when István Szécheny and Józef Eötvös wrote or participated in debates on this theme, they already had been trained in the school of the French Enlightenment and German *Aufklärung*, where the issue of emancipation had in some way been resolved. It is interesting to consider when and to what extent Jews, and their religious and administrative authorities, became involved. How did rabbis and scholars of the communities of East Central Europe – in this case, the Banat – understand participation in a dialogue on reform – especially since they had not been interested in Mendelssohn's works, and had rejected reading his books and, consequently, his concepts from the beginning? Our task is to describe and explain the double aspect of Jewish life at the beginning of the modern age: religious reform and, by correlation, the background to its cultural, social and political emancipation.

Historical analysis shows the linear aspects of the past of the Jews of the Banat, especially the spectacular differences in orientation between the positions of the rabbis and the communities, often in spite of their proximity. We will therefore reveal another side (benefiting from a lengthy and dense rabbinical controversy) of the religious reform that started in Hamburg and spread to Prague, Buda, Szeged, Arad and Timișoara. This is the movement with which Aron Chorin, rabbi of Arad, became perfectly integrated. I call it another reformist movement, taking into consideration its scale and proportion, but also its nuances in relation to the rebirth proposed by Moses Mendelssohn.

Many analysts consider that eighteenth-century Jewish literature ends with Aron Chorin's work. In a short history of the Jewish community of Arad, Chorin's activity is acknowledged as extremely important from a religious point of view for the history of the communities of this region. It is recognised for its impact on the congregation and placed among those enterprising reforms that provoked great disputes at the heart of Judaism. Rabbi Chorin was regarded as the most prominent figure in the Arad community,[9] and a source of justifiable pride, if only because he made the community famous. Through his work, the Arad Jews attracted the attention of the entire Jewish population of Central and Northern Europe. Löw Lipot, rabbi of Szeged, is the most likely inspiration for Chorin's reforms, although he is not the only one. Reassessment of this well-known scholar and exegete of the Torah was among Chorin's concerns, at least at the beginning of his career, and some of Löw's ideas challenged Chorin's thinking.

In a recent monograph on the Jewish past in Transylvania, Chorin is named as initiator of the movement for religious reform in the Banat and Transylvania. Moreover, he is considered an innovator in Modern Hebrew language and science, a disciple of the famous Ezekiel Landau,[10] rabbi of Prague. Deeply involved in the great disputes with the rabbinical authorities of the nineteenth century who opposed the spread of reform,[11] Chorin proposed and introduced sensational innovations for the time regarding religious ritual: playing organ music; praying with an uncovered head; reduction of the mourning week; travelling on Saturdays; merging religious and philosophical meditation (for him, the most important laws were those that regulated behaviour among people); changes in the order of service; tolerance of eating starlet, or small sturgeon, which corresponded to biblical demands because it had scales and flippers (eating Kosher, or conforming with Jewish dietary regulations, meant fish had to have fins and scales).[12]

Documentary sources[13] reveal that in 1819, at one of the meetings of the Arad community, a discussion was held on building the first reformed synagogue. A decision on this was made in 1828, building began three years later, and the synagogue was completed in 1834. It appears that an important number of believers adhered to the reformist movement. The echo of Chorin's pleas was also felt at Pest, the Hungarian capital. His correspondence and meetings with Ullmann Gábor, the president of the Pest community, laid the basis for a lasting relationship and demonstrated the existence of mutual influences. The Jewish community of Pest was the first to assume new religious practices proposed by the chief rabbi of Arad; others followed.

How important was Chorin's role as mediator? According to some claims in Moshe Carmilly-Weinberger's book on the history of the Jews of Arad, the rabbi had direct links with the imperial administration in Vienna. Evidently, Metternich himself offered Chorin support during his period as rabbi. This seems a probable explanation of Chorin's attachment to the Empire and to the emperor himself. In 1827, he became the first rabbi to pray in the synagogue for the emperor. Later, he set the tone for the new encyclopedic education (in the sense of integration within the imperial structures), being careful to consider learning of the rites as the prime objective. His steps towards a *schola universalis* started in the 1830s. The rather large Jewish congregation of his rabbinate included people who were prepared to establish such an institution. The sources mention his son, Henric Chorin, and the teachers Jacob Steinitzer, Joseph Leopold and Francisc Steinbach.[14]

Many of Chorin's initiatives coincided with imperial political trends. For example, the Jewish Hebrew–German *Real-Haupt-Schule*,[15] proposed in 1829, fits almost exactly within the principles of the Viennese Chancellery. This is just one of the cases in which we can compare the imperial edicts with the measures of the chief rabbi of Arad in order to understand the local Jewish community's tendency towards assimilation and its particular way of obeying propositions at the centre of government. It is equally true that the types of communities created here and their activities demonstrate the complexity of Jewish life. Evolution was similar in Lugoj, Timișoara, Reșița, Jimbolia, Vršac and Buziaș due to the very strong ties in the area. Communities from the Banat and the plain of Arad communicated well with each other. Their statutes were almost identical, as was their subordination to the Empire.[16] The rites performed were conducted by rabbis with great influence. It so happened that these Neologs (a faction of Hungarian Jews at the time) were the main points of reference for both religious life and communication with authorities. Therefore, the main societies in Arad organised by the Jewish community embraced the ideas expressed by Chorin, I am thinking of their extraordinary involvement in the life of the city and issues faced by the community as a whole. Against this backdrop was a mutual intention: the establishment of *bürgerliche Gesellschaft*, a type of civil society promoted during the eighteenth and nineteenth centuries in the Central European cities. The main objective of Habsburg policy was to ensure a decent administrative body, multiple forms of social communication, and the necessary convergences for the cohabitation of the great communitarian, linguistic and religious diversity within the Empire. Such a role was also played by the small Jewish institutions of Arad: Heilige Brüderschaft, Humanitäts Verein and Frauen Verein.[17] Over time, they would become important players in an urban social structure in which mutual assistance had to prevail.

The fact that a more liberal evolution of the Jewish communities of the Banat was possible meant the absence of the classical form of the ghetto. Thus, a network of possibilities was created. Chorin exemplifies this remarkably through the complex of ideas he formulates. However, all of these presumed inevitable compromises. One of these – to which he subscribed – was the introduction of Hungarian as a language of service in the synagogue. The use of Hungarian in cultural life was expressly demanded by the administrative leadership. In a document issued in 1833, conceived by the magistrate of Arad County, Hungarian was recommended alongside Hebrew for religious services on the grounds that 'most of the Jewish population doesn't speak this language [Hungarian] well'.[18] Chorin exchanged letters on this delicate issue on behalf of the community. In one letter addressed to the administrative leadership, the rabbi gives a formal reply (more to justify the situation), invoking not only his lack of Hungarian, but also his weak mastery of Hebrew. What is certain is that the Jews of Arad had to quickly start using Hungarian. Chorin's contribution would prove important, like that of one of his followers, Rabbi Jakab Steinhardt.

In 1844, the rabbi of Șimand,[19] Abraham Friedman, published a book in Hungarian, entitled *Az Izraelita Nemzetnek Védelmezése* (*Defending the Jewish Nation*). He preached in Hungarian in 1845 and his discourse was printed in Arad under the title *Egyházi Beszéd* (*Confessional Lecture*).[20] If we mention that Abraham Friedman became chief rabbi of Transylvania by 1879, we can understand why learning and practising the cult in Hungarian was essential. We can perceive more exactly the geographical and historical contours of the politics of identity in the century of nationalities, and understand that there was always cooperation between Jewish representatives and officials, without which the very existence of the community, not just its religious identity, was endangered. There was also a certain benevolence that is exemplified in the reformism of Chorin and his followers. In conclusion, if during Joseph II's time the German language was compulsory in all administrative activities and dealings with the Habsburg authorities – and in middle- and secondary-school education – a second fundamental change for the Jews of the Banat came about in the mid-nineteenth century, requiring the compulsory acceptance of Hungarian as both a language of communication and a language of worship. Thus, can we deduce that Jews renounced once and for all the Yiddish and Hebrew languages, and that the German learned during the previous historical periods was abandoned?

In certain regions of the Habsburg Empire a new phenomenon emerges, that of multilingualism and interculturalism, which would profoundly mark the Jewish people. Within East Central Europe, the Banat is especially representative in this respect. This phenomenon defines the German, Swabian, Hungarian, Romanian, Serbian, Slovak and Bulgarian environments. The cultural context, the cohabitation of multilingual and multi-confessional communities, favoured an evolution in which Jewish families usually spoke two or three languages. Hebrew remained the language of worship, but the rabbis of Arad, Timișoara and Lugoj often held sermons in regional languages. For example, between 1870 and 1918, Hungarian became the dominant language. Following the unification of the Banat and Transylvania with the Old Kingdom of Romania, the Jews also adopted the Romanian language, along with German and Hungarian. Regardless of this reform and the contradictions it raised, rabbis from the Banat and across East Central Europe did not ignore (then or later) studies in Hebrew. All spoke and wrote in Hebrew, too. Aron Chorin himself, when expounding his theses, used more than one language, both written and spoken, and among them was Hebrew. He was an excellent interpreter of the Torah, which assumed a strong mastery of the language of fundamental religious texts. It is understandable that neither he, nor his colleagues, ever denied the traditions.

In the booklet entitled *The Letter of an African Rabbi to His European Colleagues* (*Igeret Elassaf oder Sendschreiben eines Afrikanischen Rabbi an seinen Collegen in Europa mit einem Vorworte*), published in Prague in 1826, Chorin explains his intentions very clearly: as an exponent of reform, he wanted to open both religious schools and professional schools for training in various cultural and scientific disciplines, so as to integrate parishioners into everyday life, in the professions of light industry of that time, or to re-educate them in farming. He never went as far as denying the traditional Sabbath or moving it to Sunday (from Saturday).[21] The main critique of his arguments was formulated by the contemporary leader of Orthodox Judaism, Rabbi Moshe Sofer.[22] Sofer affirmed that any reformist movement was dangerous because many Jews were in exile at the time. He did not agree with the removal of the Hebrew language from the holy books, nor with the moral instruction of Jewish children based on the books translated and with commentary by Moses Mendelssohn. However, history could not be stopped; these arguments illustrate a state of affairs that the historian is bound to relate.

What we should remember is that alongside the emergence of reformist ideas, modernisation of community life began. On the other hand, the increasing presence of the Hungarian language in Jewish intellectual circles may be observed. During the Enlightenment period, the prayer books had been translated into German. In the years of the Austro-Hungarian Dual Monarchy they were changed into Hungarian. Consequently, linguistically and culturally, there was a mutation. The well-known rabbi and historian Moshe Carmilly-Weinberger states that a large number of the graduates of the Rabbinical Seminary of Budapest strengthened the religious life of the communities from the Banat and Transylvania as well as contributing to the enrichment of the Hungarian language and culture by their lectures.[23] Their movement towards emancipation was often echoed by the literati, artists and scientists, as well as by the liberal bourgeoisie. I emphasise the elements relating to language and culture because emancipation, like the conservation of identity, was linked to the double situation that characterised the modern Jew: civic and religious. The first was about the fight for equal rights. The second was to ensure through reform a connection to the new European political paradigm, and the revival of its own spirituality.

In the Banat in the nineteenth century, the issue of emancipation was intertwined with that of Hungary. There are also particular aspects which deserve consideration. Debates, like solutions, are often alike. The aristocracy in Hungary (with few exceptions), like those in Central and East Central Europe, was hostile to Jewish emancipation. Things did not differ much in South-Eastern Europe, where intellectuals from wealthy families in the mid-nineteenth century were in the process of formulating their own theory of national identity. However, the very group we are referring to did not have always the same opinions. Social origin, on the one hand, and Western liberal influences, on the other, made possible differences in their discourse on emancipation. Absorbing the ideas of the great French Revolution, scholars and politicians such as József Eötvös in Hungary; Döbrentei Gábor, Stephan Ludwig Roth, Anton Kurz and Gheorghe Barițiu in Transylvania; Nicolae Bălcescu and C.D. Rosenthal in Wallachia; and Eftimie Murgu in the Banat were drawn to the idea of the general emancipation of the peoples from this area. Hence, their plea for the equality of cultural-linguistic and religious groups and communities.

The period of formation of national consciousness does not coincide with one of categorical refusal to come into contact with others, which explains the presence of several Jews in the culture and politics of the time. An example of this is the involvement of some of them in the 1848 Revolutions in Poland, Hungary, Transylvania, the Banat and Wallachia. Distortions in relations between the majority and the Jews arose when the first big difficulties appeared on the road towards national and state emancipation. As a result, the programmes of the Revolution could not be implemented, nor did they conflict with nationalism shortly after their formulation. In a certain context, a portion of the intelligentsia (especially nostalgic aristocrats) became the main author of the exacerbation of nationalism.[24] Generally speaking, the intellectual environment was one in which, in addition to the national idea, nationalist deformities, either Hungarian or Romanian, germinated and developed, sometimes slipping into xenophobia and anti-Semitism.[25] The emancipation of Jews from the Banat was primarily linked to Magyarisation. That was the thinking within the radical circles of the Forty-Eighters. As we observed earlier, rabbis like Aron Chorin and Jakab Steinhardt accepted Magyarisation without offering any resistance. The Jewish community of Arad is an exception, in the sense that in that area there were no repeated acts of revolt. In Timișoara – although there was no explicit opposition – the rabbis delayed the introduction of the Hungarian language in the synagogue.

In an article published in 1844 in *Pesti Hirlap*, Lajos Kossuth expressed the revolutionaries' point of view. He demanded total reform from the Orthodox Jews, considering it to be a prerequisite for emancipation.[26] The liberals in Hungary called for the reformation of the social-administrative institutions of the Orthodox Jews, meaning those communitary bodies that had resolved, up to then, not only issues of internal order, but also the religious and civic status of every Jew.[27] In fact, they asked the Jews to renounce their old names (the same thing had been requested some decades before by the Habsburgs), adopting this time Hungarian names instead of German ones and replacing Yiddish with the Hungarian language. What did these positions mean? Did they cover the ideological interests of the moment or did they express the opinion of the scholars, the thinking and the mentality of the population? A value judgement presupposes questioning the sociopolitical phenomenon. The moment was tough, and I mentioned that not only external but also internal pressure indicated a crisis of conscience.

The xenophobic and anti-Semitic accents seen for the first time in their modern version in the small East Central European regions in the mid-nineteenth century, may be explained by the intellectual inability to formulate a national ideology without denying those who bore the marks of cultural and religious difference. This is one of the great tragedies that have fuelled for more than a century, including today, exclusive theories, doctrines of extremist parties, radical options of a few (sometimes) significant social segments. Let us resume the facts. In its sessions of 1839–40 and 1847–48, the Hungarian Diet declined the requests for emancipation. However, a manifesto drafted on 17 March 1848 by the Jewish committee of Hungary and Transylvania shows enthusiastic support for the causes of revolution. Among the signatories was a Jew from the Banat (Torontal County): S.D. Adler.[28] The issue of the emancipation of the Jews from Hungary, the Banat and Transylvania was presented to the Hungarian Parliament by Deputy Lajos Schnel. Kossuth dismissed it, maintaining that it was not possible given existing political circumstances.[29]

In order to support the standpoint of a portion of the Jews, especially those who were socially, culturally and linguistically integrated within city life, I. Einhorn's newspaper *Der ungarisher Israelit* was published. It militated in favour of emancipation. From the first issue, dated 15 April 1848, we discover that there were also Jews among the young people who freed Eftimie Murgu (the main leader of the Banatian Romanian revolutionaries) from the Neugebäude prison in Pest.[30] The moment reflects the existence of similar objectives in the Revolution of 1848, questioning the social and political structures of the Empire. Eftimie Murgu's release from prison indicates a peak in the fight of the Forty-Eighters: the liberation of political convicts. It is no accident that it produced enthusiasm among the young revolutionaries, whether Hungarian, Romanian, Jewish or Italian. Progressive journals increased in number. Some of them resumed the cause of the Jews in Hungary and the Banat with even more arguments: for example, *Der Südungar*, which was issued in Timișoara and whose editor was the Jewish medical doctor Davin Wachtel; or *Der Patriot*, a journal edited and printed in Arad under the guidance of the teacher Leopold Jeiteles. Articles and petitions on the issue of emancipation increased significantly. The climate was tense within the Jewish environments in Arad, Timișoara and Lugoj. The officials preferred a conservative position. They perceived things differently to the Jews, despite the fact that intellectual debates on the theme had had a certain resonance. Instead, it is supposed they related to the typical *forma mentis* of the dominant class. In that sense, the attitude of the Minister of Internal Affairs, Bertalan Szemere, is suggestive: stating that the Parliament and the Government did not have the necessary time to draft and adopt such a law. He also said that Hungarian politicians had argued that a precondition for Jewish emancipation would be the modification of their religious cult.[31] Concerns about the situation of the Jews in general,[32] but mostly about the Jews from Hungary and the Banat,[33] had not offered until 1848 solutions that were acceptable on both sides. If for some Jewish intellectuals resumption of the Enlightenment theses drafted and formulated by Moses Mendelssohn represented a maximum possible in establishing connecting bridges, for Orthodox Jews they symbolised the great danger of assimilation, the loss of religious identity.

In Arad, as a consequence of Chorin's activity, a large number of Jews were inclined to give up part of their religious prescriptions. They made their choice public on 24 April 1848.[34] On 8 July of the same year, the Reformist Association of Hungarian Jews (Ungarischer Israelitische Central Reformverein) was set up in Pest to coordinate religious reform in the Banat, too. In the last meeting of the Diet, held at Szeged on 28 July 1849 (when the Revolution had reached its dramatic phase and when conflict increased, nearly becoming civil war), a law on Jewish emancipation was issued, including, nevertheless, the condition of the Kossuth wing: 'Jewish religious reform according to the requirements of the time'.[35] The more moderate ideas and Széchenyi's diplomacy seemed closer to the state of mind of the Jewish intellectuals and the reformist rabbis. Gathering around him some of the most illustrious scholars, Széchenyi aimed at securing the independence of Hungary by establishing a modern European culture and civilisation. The ideals of the Enlightenment may be found in his political writings and actions. He predicted a happy future for his country if scholars and politicians could understand how to cultivate the particularities of the language, tradition, religion and habits of each people, how to develop flexible relations, convergence of ideas with all their neighbours. 'It is a great art', Széchenyi observed, 'to know how to win hearts . . . If you wish to be respected, respect others first.'[36]

For the Forty-Eighter scholar, the new age had to overcome all limits, to assume the image of an ideal national family:

> Let us imagine a national family comprised of no more than a million members, in which so much intellectual weight, civic virtue, pleasing habits, good taste, evolved science, life wisdom, practical experience, tact and more such primordial features are accumulated that they could all lend a helping hand, honest guidance, wise advice . . . in short, starting from its intellectual superiority, we could call it the people of reason. And we have to admit, if we don't want to question the very desire for progress and perfection of humankind, that such an ideal people would be slowly merged with all those with whom they had closer contact.[37]

I reproduce this long passage from the famous speech held by Széchenyi at the Hungarian Academy of Science in 1842 to highlight the thinking of some of the intellectuals of the time. Conceptually, Széchenyi relied on law, on social relations based on justice. Even though he bore the mark of nobility, he had become a conciliatory spirit with a reformist attitude that inspired the avant-garde scientific and cultural circles of the time. The ideal Széchenyi fought for was understood by a relatively small group of his colleagues. His pleas for a general emancipation of nations and regions within the Empire did not envisage specific analysis of the Jewish issue. Széchenyi was overlooked by the liberal wing of the Forty-Eighter revolutionaries, who distinguished themselves by the attitude they assumed towards the Jewish religion.

While Széchenyi had been the moderate promoter of modern ideas, Jósef Eötvös is linked to the explicitly contrarian position of the intellectuals from small nations (under Habsburg domination) towards the centralisation of the Austrian Empire and its conservative legislation, which prolonged the backward mentalities of the Middle Ages. In his book *Das Nationalitäten Problem in der Habsburger Monarhie*, historian Robert Kann evaluated some of the many views expressed by Eötvös, considering them even more worthy of mention as they grew distant from the ideology of the aristocracy out of which the publicist and Forty-Eighter politician sprung. Eötvös stands out for his totally unique position on Jewish emancipation. The work entitled *A zsidók emancipátiója* (*Jewish Emancipation*), also printed in Italian as *Dissertazione sulla emancipazione degli Ebrei* (Pest, 1842),[38] reflects a real concern about the condition of Jews from the regions of East Central Europe. What does this essay comprise and how did it stimulate cultural and political debate in intellectual circles in the mid-nineteenth century? What were the main arguments of the author when he presented for the first time to public opinion in this part of the continent, the issue of equal rights for the Jews, like those of the civilised countries in the world?

Eötvös begins by declaring:

> The people who, instead of surrendering, survived the war of discrimination; the people who, deprived of its own land or whose towns were ruined and totally seized by others, is considered forever to be an enemy and a stranger in the place where it lives . . .; the people who find nothing but the adversity of others and all that is most miserable throughout written history, that people is Israel.[39]

He discloses the prejudices that persisted among the vast majority of the Hungarian population at that time, who continued to identify the Jew with 'the stranger with a strong heart who doesn't usually attach himself to the collectivity in which he lives, unless he has an interest [in it]'.

False theories about the Jews, resulting from unfounded interpretations of religious texts, lead the author to ask: 'Can a religion be sacred while it endorses degeneration and cruelty?' God did not ordain the destruction, answers Eötvös, while also observing that an understanding of the unfortunate people of Israel depends upon access to contemporary ideas. 'We have reason to hope that the true religious idea assumes acceptance of all diversity, because the God that is worshipped at the altar is the God of benediction; we hope that a time will come when people will find better doctrines than those from our holy books, doctrines that will be closer to God's will to end lack of understanding with the help of love and compassion.'[40]

The scholar does not blame the Christian religion itself, but rather the practice of it, for making possible the formulation and proliferation of unjust offences towards Jews in the Middle Ages. Religion cannot be the reason why the small linguistic and religious communities of East Central Europe persist in denying human rights to Jews. Eötvös believed the problem could only be solved in a rational manner and that politicians, turning their backs on invective, would be able to draft a law on Jewish emancipation. He justifies his position by the heartfelt desire to see his Jewish peers as citizens with equal rights. It is about behaviour directed towards the recognition of others; in fact, acceptance of the existence of a plurality in society that can and must take action together. Besides, the idea of competition that emerges from this essay points to liberal activism, the acquisition of a new political idiom, an echo of Enlightenment cosmopolitanism.

Eötvös asked, Why not offer land to Jews? Why not reward them for work? Why not allow them into the guilds of craftsmen and artists, thus stimulating competition?[41] The invitation to debate, expressed in this manner, generated countless ideological confrontations, causing delays in adopting the law, but also the possibility of finding less passionate arguments. Even if the Jews were to be exclusively engaged in trade, Eötvös writes, this is not an argument for denying them their human rights. It should not be necessary to see danger everywhere and persecute an entire population because of some individuals who deal with trade, the author concludes, not without reason. It cannot be denied that Jews practised trade because they had been forbidden access to any other profession for a long time. The aptitude for trafficking in goods, perceived by some as a basis for so-called corruption, was not typical of them. There is no such inclination in the religious books. However, if the trade practised by Jews might be harmful to morals, why not try to rectify the situation by drafting and adopting the law of emancipation?[42] Eötvös poses many questions, believing that reason would prevail and that medieval mental conventions and reflexes would be overcome. For him, improvement in all problems regarding Jewish civil existence would produce a general improvement of social relations. The examples of Holland, France, the United States and England were invoked often in assessing the importance of a law on emancipation.

If we investigate more and more deeply the moral qualities of this people – concludes the author – there will be only elements that deserve the consideration of humanity. A religious community that resisted intimidation, facing the bloodiest persecutions in order to keep its faith intact, is a community worthy of respect. The fact that Eötvös develops a historical, theoretical and political point of view in accordance with that of Western democratic intellectualism is remarkable. His approach is all the more commendable – despite numerous objections and, later on, virulent anti-Semitism – since it contributed for the first time to the understanding and acknowledgement of Jews in East Central Europe as a component of regional culture and civilisation. Eötvös's analysis indicates research and knowledge of the essential books of Judaism, consultation of a special bibliography upon the subject, all designed to control the veracity of claims expressed by other authors. The relationship between Judaism and Christianity that he develops is not based on simple speculation or common-sense criteria.[43] It starts from the comments of medieval exegesis or the parables offered in the books of the renowned philosopher, Moise Maimonide.

Why did Eötvös publish an essay that was so provocative and difficult for the intellectual circles of Central and East Central Europe to assimilate in the mid-nineteenth century? Why did he think it useful to expose the causes of anti-Semitism, the malicious comments in Parliament, and in books and brochures published in Hungarian in the early nineteenth century? Eötvös was militating for a non-discriminatory treatment; he believed in the enunciation of great ideas that would contribute to the ennoblement of humankind.[44] Privately, he hoped his country would not be the last in Europe to give equal rights to the Jewish population. His dissertation contains an admirable intellectual plea in favour of Jewish emancipation, which introduces a new understanding of the theme, a clever way of thinking about the alterities that cohabited with the Hungarians and from which one can conclude that the rewriting of history in moments of transition involves a change of the cultural paradigm. With regard to the Forty-Eighter generation, the overcoming of prejudices seemed possible, and at the same time the fundamental values of society would be brought back, generating a mentality in accordance with the progress of ideas and science promoted by the Enlightenment.

While Széchenyi's ideas regarding zonal cooperation were partially accepted by the politicians of the nineteenth century, Eötvös's arguments in favour of granting civil rights to Jews did not receive acceptance from many of his compatriots. The majority of Hungarians viewed assimilation as a *sine qua non* of emancipation. Without exaggeration, we can say that East Central and Eastern European ethnonationalist Romanticism opposed the true acknowledgement of others in terms of linguistic, cultural and religious diversity. Despite the fact that the law of emancipation was to be adopted by the Hungarian parliament two and a half decades after the publication of Eötvös's work, a non-partisan analysis and theoretical interpretation would be delayed for another century. Only after the Holocaust was the theme clearly resumed in István Bibó's study, entitled *A zsidókérdés Magyarországon 1944 után* (*The Jewish Issue in Hungary After 1944*). The ethnic state as substitute for the national one was a hindrance to the more rapid development of political life in the regions east of Vienna. Under the influence of German Romantic literature, this aspect manifested itself as an identity formula on which the state construction of Central and Eastern European regions was based and contributed decisively to the genesis and affirmation of totalitarian political systems of the twentieth century.[45] Against that background, the Banat in the nineteenth century found internal intellectual resources to ensure balanced social behaviour and peaceful cohabitation of the peoples within the region. Even if Eötvös's ideal was not possible with regard to the Jews, compared to other regions of the former Austrian empire, administrative structures in the Banat created greater individual freedom of expression and better communication between leaders of the cultural and religious groups.

Following the defeat in the 1848 Revolution, Jews from the Banat were accused by the authorities of active participation in support of their demands. As a consequence, they were obliged to pay collective fines totalling 500,000 guilders. In 1859, Emperor Franz Joseph I reopened the debate on Jewish emancipation in Hungary, the Banat and Transylvania, summoning Parliament on 2 April 1861. The early dissolution of the legislature postponed things again. In 1866, representatives of the Jews in Transylvania gathered at Cluj to analyse the juridical status of the regional communities. Disagreements with the authorities concerning issues of religious practice were obvious. A year later, the Union for the Defence of Religion – an association of Jews who regarded emancipation at the cost of abandoning Jewish precepts as unacceptable – founded the newspaper *Magyar Zsidó (Hungarian Jews)* to defend Jewish interests.[46] On 25 November 1867, Prime Minister Gyula Andrássy presented to the Hungarian parliament the draft of the law on Jewish emancipation. On 22 and 23 December 1867, the two chambers of the Hungarian legislature of Pest adopted Law XVII regarding Jewish emancipation. With 64 votes for and 4 against, the law came into force as soon as the emperor signed it.

Enforcement of the law led to other controversies, this time especially at the heart of communities. Some Jews agreed with the provisions of emancipation; they formed part of the Neolog group of religious reformists, as referenced earlier. Others, faithful to tradition and called Orthodox Jews, objected. Procedures to enforce the law were agreed upon at a congress of Jewish representatives from Hungary and Transylvania.[47] The leader of the Neolog community of Pest, Ignác Hirschler, was one of the main advocates of Magyarisation. On governmental advice, he accepted limiting discussion so as to prevent arguments on religious grounds, which the official view considered uninteresting and lacking in purpose. The Congress (December 1868–February 1869) adopted the statute of communities according to the Neolog perspective. By royal decree on 14 June 1869, the new statute received official approval. According to this, one city could only accommodate a single community: the Neolog-reformist one. As was to be expected, this decision was not satisfactory to Orthodox Jews. They did not submit to the regulation and, after years of pressure, finally obtained the right to form their own communities. Thus in 1871 there were four types of religious communities: (1) based on the statute adopted by Congress, known as status quo; (2) Orthodox, those focused on tradition; (3) based on the organisation prior to the Congress, named status quo ante; (4) independent, unaffiliated to any of the other three types. The division of the Jewish population in the Banat is easy to spot in Timișoara and Arad, where sources indicate the existence of all four types of community.[48] The same aspect of fragmentation in Jewish life can be seen in the fact that in Timișoara there was a subsidiary of the Alliance Israélite universelle, led by Rabbi Dr Moritz Hirschfeld.[49] On the other hand, the rapid connection of Jews in the Banat to the international bodies designed to support their rights, promote their material and cultural interests, and defend against the anti-Semitic denigrations visible within the Austro-Hungarian Empire during the late nineteenth century, is remarkable.

There were reasons for concern because widespread recognition of emancipation did not occur soon after the enforcement of the law. This was, first and foremost, because the mentalities of the population could not change from one year to the next, the backward behavioural complexes (of medieval origin) still being very much present in the Central and Eastern Europe; and secondly, because the authorities (following the segmentation of power between Austria and Hungary) had promoted a nationalist policy, in which myth, irrationality, traditional wisdom and modern discourse would meet. In the period under discussion, anti-Semitic movements intensified within the whole Dual Monarchy, supported by a media who upheld the same doctrine and by representatives meeting periodically in self-proclaimed anti-Semitic international congresses which provoked scandal.

Between 1882 and 1902 there were many trials on the theme of so-called ritual murder. One which had strong echoes in Transylvania and the Banat took place in Tiszaeszlár in 1882–83 and provides an insight into the relations between the Jews and Christians of East Central Europe after the official recognition of emancipation.[50] The Tiszaeszlár inquiry on the disappearance and presumed death of 14-year-old Eszter Solymosi, lasted 14 months, from April 1882 to June 1883, and was followed by a criminal trial in which 15 Jews from the neighbouring village, Nyiregyháza, stood accused. During this trial, the Public Ministry, represented by Ede Szeyffert, adopted an unusual position, recommending that the suspects accused of ritual murder should be acquitted. On 3 August 1883, the judges pronounced their verdict: 'They were innocent.' According to the historian Hilel J. Kieval, 'the confrontations between the Jews and their accusers collided, in an unpredictable manner, with the political and cultural configuration, ruining the balance of Jewish social and community life; the disputes reveal a significant level of misunderstanding and suspicion, calling into question the very premises of Jewish emancipation:

their belonging to humanity, their status as Europeans and their fundamental similarity with non-Jews'.[51]

Viewed across more than a century of history, reform and emancipation remain two of the most resounding events in the Jewish diaspora, sparking much controversy within Jewish communities and beyond. Complementary points of view were rarely visible, and emotions have dominated many of the historiographical studies and religious debates. That is why this chapter has tried to bring the two phenomena of reform and emancipation face to face, trying not to overlook religious renewal and the adaptation of *homo religiosus* to modern times – an adaptation suggested by Aron Chorin, rabbi of Arad. On the other hand, I have sought to understand the issue of identifying the Jew with the social and political experiences of Central and East Central Europe. In the first case, I observed that efforts started with the local rabbinate and extended to regional level and beyond, triggering a diversity of religious directions and adopting a new status of communities. This did not impact the profound relations of the Jewish world. In the second case, I observed that assimilation was not the dominant choice of communities from the Banat. Jewish families did not break up. Religion was not abandoned or replaced by another. It is true that a percentage of the Jewish population chose to create mixed families, an issue that I researched and presented for the cities of Arad and Timișoara in the period between 1895 and 1940.[52] There was a Jewish minority identifiable in the marriage registers in the municipal archives. This phenomenon within a border culture created bridges between the different families and groups, generating a civic myth which post-Enlightenment Europe did not know how to cultivate.

What conclusions can be drawn from the Jewish emancipation movement in the Banat? A concept such as that of multiple identities is well illustrated by the Jews of this area. Multicultural and multi-confessional cohabitation, along with multilingualism, generated a civil society which was at home with pluralism. If we consider that the experience started in 1716 and continued until 1850, the Banat was one of the few successful cultural and political experiments of the Habsburgs. It provides an excellent example of an area of convergence not divergence, of interculturalism and not just a certain ethnic or religious culture. That is why I believe that here we must see emancipation and reform differently. For such regions, privileged by the game of historical events, geographical placement or a mentality formed over a long period, we can highlight the positive side of the two phenomena – even less, or perhaps never, the tragic consequences of such options.

An identical interpretation is not possible for Transylvania, although the phenomenon of emancipation also relates to the Jews of that region. Things are much more complicated when evaluating the Jewish past in this area, because there the Orthodox Jewish community was predominant. In other regions of the Dual Monarchy, things are complicated because we are talking about other cultural-linguistic and religious configurations. Finally, in some towns the multiple identity of citizens was acquired rather than evolving naturally. In those circumstances, one of the self-constructed ethnocultural groups tried to impose supremacy using theories of historical right and superiority of civilisation, or demographic statistics indicating numerical superiority. In those disputes, Jews always were placed in the space reserved for the minority, in all respects. Hence, the necessity for options according to political, linguistic and social circumstances – rarely, according to their own reflections and feelings. This is essential background for understanding the phenomenon of emancipation as it appeared in the Banat and neighbouring regions.

Mutual tolerance is self-evident in the Banat. The multi- and intercultural, multi- and inter-religious melting pot of this region explains why reform had first-rate representatives among the Jewish communities of Arad and Timișoara. It also explains why Timișoara was home to one of the strongest Zionist movements of the region. It was a primarily political movement, seen by Jews as an answer to nationalism in Central and Eastern Europe and easier to assert in a multilingual social environment and within a cross-border and cross-cultural region. The history of Jews in the Banat in the nineteenth century presents an unusual picture, one in which the condition of the Jews overlaps with the historical process of modernisation of the peoples in this part of the continent. Looked at in depth, but also linearly, the religious reform and political emancipation of Jews in the Banat offers a great opportunity to reflect on and evaluate an important fragment of the history of the diaspora, and of Jewish political thought in the modern era.

16
THE EDUCATION SYSTEM IN THE BANAT DURING THE AUSTRO-HUNGARIAN MONARCHY

Áron Kovács

THE ECONOMIC AND SOCIAL REFORMS initiated within the Kingdom of Hungary from 1830 generated significant transformations that can also be seen in the educational system. The law on state education, given assent by the monarchy in December 1868, is popularly known as 'Eötvös's law', after József Eötvös, minister of religion and public education, and author of studies on state structure, minorities and educational policy, whose ideas were at its core. The law was unique in Europe because of its provision for compulsory elementary education.[1] For the Hungarian administration, education was a priority, along with reformation of the common law. However, although Eötvös's ideas resonated with European liberalism, they were greeted with reservation in Hungary and in the German-speaking area of the Austro-Hungarian Empire.[2]

According to István Fenyö, Eötvös's political thought, as it appears in his main work, *The Influence of Nineteenth-Century Dominant Ideas upon the State*, can be synthetised into four principles: (1) progress but not revolution; (2) a state that is strong but does not limit individual freedom; (3) equality of opportunity; and (4) resolution of the problems of minorities within a unified state. Eötvös's concept, based on local autonomy, was designed to prevent national movements and revolutionary outbreaks of any kind.[3] With minor changes, this organisation of education was constant throughout the period discussed in this chapter. The idea of a federal state, promoted by Eötvös, was gradually dismissed by the ethnonationalist movements that were becoming increasingly evident within the Austro-Hungarian Monarchy.[4] Due to the role that those movements attributed to education, the organisation of the school network became an important indicator for the functioning of society in general.

In Romanian historiography, there is no comprehensive work on this particular theme. Studies up to now have concentrated on describing particular schools or have approached the history of education as part of the Romanian national movement, sometimes with no regard for the social and historical context of the time. The present study aims to describe and explain the educational system within the Kingdom of Hungary in the period 1867 to 1914, in order to highlight the legislative framework that regulated education and identify possible local peculiarities. Our research is mainly based on statistic sources and the almanacs edited by schools.

KINDERGARTENS AND CHILD SHELTERS

The first kindergartens were founded in the Banat in 1840 on private initiatives, as parochial institutions or associations, but were not regulated until 1891, when Law XV was issued. The law stipulated that the education of young children could be carried out in two types of institution: a kindergarten, with the help of a specialist teacher, or a child shelter, managed by a nurse who had proved her ability to tend small children in the presence of an inspector. Besides differences in staff, the two types of institutions also differed as to purpose. Although the main responsibility of both was looking after children between three and six years of age in the absence of their parents, the kindergartens assisted in child development through learning prayers, conversation and songs, physical education, and manual work.

Unlike elementary schools, the establishment of kindergartens was compulsory only in cities with municipal rights, in county centres, and in communes which registered annual taxes of more than 15,000 florins (Ft) and which numbered at least 40 children of an appropriate age. Settlements that paid an annual tax of between 10,000 and 15,000 Ft had to organise shelters for 40 children; those that paid less than 10,000 Ft had to organise a summer shelter for at least 15 children. For these expenses, a supplementary tax of 3 per cent was provided.[5] As well as the state, any commune, church, individual or legal entity had the right to establish a kindergarten.[6]

The setting-up and operation of kindergartens was subject to compliance with health and fire safety regulations. The maximum number of children allowed in a hall was 80, thus every child had a personal space of at least 0.8 square metre. The building had to be spacious, with a minimum of 64 square metres, well-lit and with adequate ventilation, and preferably located in the middle of a playground with trees. Controlling these provisions was the task of a supervision committee of at least five people. Along with elected members, it included the local doctor and women with a reputation for childcare. This supervision committee managed the kindergartens and ensured that parents sent their children there; if they did not, they were subject to a fine.[7]

The organisation of the kindergarten network in the Banat began in the 1890s. Thereafter kindergartens appeared in each county and city of the region; some areas show a rapid growth in numbers, probably closely linked to the degree of urbanisation.[8] In Arad County, for example, the number of institutions for childcare rose from 17 to 42; in Caraș-Severin from 8 to 31; in Torontal from 75 to 151; in Timiș from 39 to 100. The period between 1895 and 1914 was marked by a rise in the number of institutions and, moreover, a qualitative development of the kindergarten network across the Banat. In several counties, instead of summer shelters, normal kindergartens were set up.[9] Between 1895 and 1898, most of the kindergartens in the Banat used Hungarian as either the sole language or as one of two languages, this being mandatory according to article 8 of Law XV of 1891. Each linguistic group could establish kindergartens in its mother tongue.[10]

POPULAR ELEMENTARY SCHOOLS

Eötvös's law provided for compulsory elementary education for children aged between 6 and 15: children aged 6 to 12 had to go to school every day, those aged 12 to 15 only at weekends in schools which used rote learning. Alongside the popular elementary schools that had functioned until then around the churches, a state school network was established.[11] The basis of the new system was represented by popular schools alongside faith schools, the churches having the right to manage schools within the communities of believers. The law required the foundation of communal popular schools where there were no confessional schools, or where, apart from church followers, there were at least 30 children of school age. Where the number did not exceed 30, education was provided by faith schools, along with specific religious education. The state founded schools only when churches and communes were not able to maintain popular schools.[12]

Initially, the popular school network could not reach the density level required by law. According to the data of the Statistics Office of the Kingdom of Hungary, for the school year 1869–70, in Hungary and Transylvania, there was generally only one popular school for every 20 square kilometres.[13] In Caraș-Severin County, the ratio was one school to 43 square kilometres, but by the school year 1911–12 the density of popular schools had doubled.

With regard to the number of teachers, in the school year 1870–71 in Hungary, the ratio was one teacher for every 135 children who were legally required to attend compulsory education and for every 70 pupils who actually attended. In Transylvania during the same period, the ratio was one teacher for every 104 and 44 pupils, respectively. In the counties of the Banat, the ratios were as shown in Table 16.1.[14]

Table 16.1

County	Number of children required to attend compulsory education per teacher	Number of children actually attending school per teacher
Arad	191,54	64,01
Caraş-Severin	139,23	48,88
Torontal	242,17	11,41
Timiş	105,19	77,37

Source: Magyar Statistikai Évkönyv (1872), pp. 482–83

From Table 16.1 we can see that, with the exception of Torontal County, in all counties the number of pupils attending schools was below the limit of 80 per teacher stipulated by law. Furthermore, out of the total number of children required to attend school by law, only 33 per cent from Arad County, 35 per cent from Caraş-Severin County and 46 per cent from Torontal County actually attended. (The only exception was Timiş County where 73 per cent of children attended school.) Eötvös remarked on the situation in cities, where school attendance was equally low. In Arad, out of 7,071 children only 30 per cent attended school, while in Timişoara, out of 6,099, around 41 per cent attended.[15] The situation improved in the 1890s when, with some exceptions, in all administrative units attendance reached over 80 per cent.[16]

According to Victor Ţârcovnicu, low attendance was due to the pupils' lack of discipline. The statistics above demonstrate that attendance throughout the school year was practically impossible in village schools. Peasant families, no matter what their financial status, needed a workforce for agriculture. That is why the school year usually ended before the official date. With regard to children from poor families, judges did not comply with their duty to impose penalties on parents who avoided sending their children to school or attending classes. These aspects significantly distort the data.[17]

In his report to Parliament, Eötvös pointed out that compulsory education could not be made a general rule because of the insufficient number of teachers and classrooms. If we consider strictly the provisions of the education law on the maximum number of 80 pupils per teacher and 60 pupils in a classroom, then, in the counties of the Banat, in the school year 1870–71, the situation was as shown in Table 16.2.

Table 16.2

County	Number of pupils	Number of teachers				Number of classrooms			
		Existing	Required	Shortfall (nos.)	Shortfall (%)	Existing	Required	Shortfall (nos.)	Shortfall (%)
Arad	53,440	279	668	389	58.23	268	891	623	69.92
Caraș-Severin	42,885	308	546	228	42.54	301	715	414	57.90
Torontal	79,432	328	992	664	66.93	295	1324	1029	77.71
Timiș	47,128	448	589	141	23.94	429	785	356	45.35
TOTAL	222,885	1,363	2,795	1,422	51.59	1293	3715	2422	65.19

Source: Magyar Statistikai Évkönyv (Hungarian Annual Statistics) (1872), pp. 482–83

As demonstrated in Table 16.2, over the entire territory of the Banat there was just under half the required number of teachers. For classrooms, there was just over one-third of the required number, and even those which existed were often substandard. With regard to the ratio between the numbers of pupils and teachers, we can see an improvement over the following years. In Arad County, for example, the number of teachers increased from 227 in the 1869–70 school year to 627 in the 1911–12 school year; in Timiș County from 401 to 861; in Caraș-Severin County from 303 to 675; in Torontal County from 350 to 1,105.[18]

During the 1869–70 school year, the largest network of popular schools in the Banat belonged to the Romanian Orthodox Church. The bishoprics of Arad and Caransebeș together supported 700 popular schools with 717 teachers and 30,636 pupils. In next place was the Roman Catholic Bishopric of Cenad, with 360 schools, 680 teachers and 66,666 pupils. The 104 schools of the Greek Catholic Bishopric of Lugoj, which had 106 teachers and 7,759 pupils, can also be counted as part of the Romanian school system. Information regarding the Serbian school network is incomplete.[19]

Research on those who maintained elementary schools reveals the development of the state school network after 1890. In Arad County, between 1892 and 1914, the number of these schools increased from 5 to 91, in Caraș-Severin from 20 to 84, in Timiș from 26 to 84, and in Torontal from 19 to 110. In the same period, the number of institutions managed by churches and communes was decreasing.[20] With regard to the language used for teaching, an increase in Hungarian-language schools may be observed. In Arad County, the number increased from 93 in 1892 to 145 in 1914, in Caraș-Severin from 12 to 147, in Timiș from 22 to 145 and in Torontal from 100 to 214. It is clear that a portion of the existing elementary school network, especially the German-language popular schools, were transformed into Hungarian-language schools.[21] This evolution occurred mainly while Baron Bánffy was prime minister, between

1895 and 1899. Since Gyula Wlassics, minister of religion and public education, was also a member of successive cabinets, the Magyarisation of education continued up to 1903, although the policy became more moderate after the fall of Bánffy's administration in 1899.[22]

In the Banat, alongside the Hungarian school network, there were also German, Serbian and Romanian schools. The German population – a large portion of which consisted of craftsmen, public servants or factory workers – was a special case. They contributed to the increase in population in the cities and were willing to absorb Hungarian language and culture. The peasantry from German villages were also open to Hungarian schooling for their children; thus, this segment of the population was later named *deutsch-magyaren* (German-Hungarian).[23] By 1910, a large portion of the German school network passed its authority of the state, and the German language was replaced by Hungarian. Eighteen other educational institutions were taken over by the Roman Catholic Bishopric of Cenad, preserving German as the teaching language in accordance with the bishopric's policy regarding mother tongue.[24]

The number of Serbian schools also decreased, but at a lower rate than the German ones, the degree of urbanisation of the Romanians and Serbs being less than that of the Germans. The number of Romanian schools within Arad County declined from 222 in 1892 to 142 in 1914. In Caraș-Severin the number of Romanian schools decreased from 314 to 248 while the number of Serbian schools decreased from 23 to 8. In Timiș County, the number of elementary Romanian schools decreased from 160 to 125, while the Serbian schools decreased from 55 to 43; in Torontal, Serbian schools were reduced from 89 to 75, while the number of Romanian schools maintained constant at 40.

Law XXVI of 1893 regarding the 'income of teachers who serve in elementary schools owned by churches and communes' determined the salary of 300 Ft for ordinary teachers and 200 Ft for assistant teachers. In many instances, these remunerations could not be made without the help of the Ministry of Religion and Public Education who had the permanent right to intervene in the organisation and management of these schools. This phenomenon probably explains the sudden increase in the number of bilingual Romanian–Hungarian and Serbian–Hungarian schools in the Banat between 1893 and 1908. Following the laws of 1907, drafted by Count Albert Apponyi, minister of religion and public education, bilingual schools gave up state support and returned to the status of single-language schools.[25] Graphs 16.1, 16.2 and 16.3 show comparisons in the number of monolingual and bilingual schools within the Banat between 1892 and 1914.

Graph 16.1

Numbers of monolingual (Romanian) and bilingual (Romanian–Hungarian) schools in the Banat between 1892–93 and 1913–14

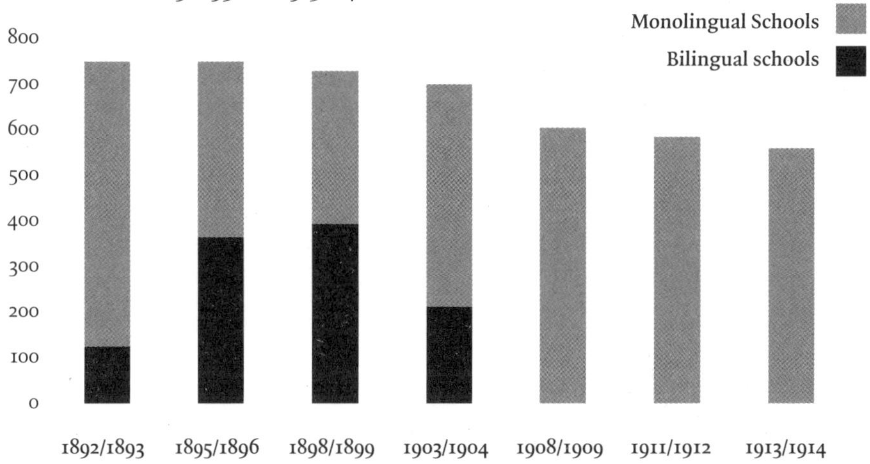

Source: Magyar Statisztikai Évkönyv. 1893. (Új folyam I). (Hungarian Annual Statistics, 1893, number 1), Magyar Kir. Központi Statisztikai Hivatal (Center for Former Hungarian Kingdom, Statistics), Budapest, 1893. pp. 308–309.; Magyar Statisztikai Évkönyv. 1896. (Új folyam IV). Magyar Kir. Központi Statisztikai Hivatal, Budapest, 1897. pp. 412–413; Magyar Statisztikai Évkönyv. 1898. (Új folyam VI). Magyar Kir. Központi Statisztikai Hivatal, Budapest, 1899. pp. 298–299; Magyar Statisztikai Évkönyv. 1904. (Új folyam XII). Magyar Kir. Központi Statisztikai Hivatal, Budapest, 1904. pp. 356–357; Magyar Statisztikai Évkönyv. 1909. (Új folyam XVII.) Athenaeum, Budapest, 1910. pp. 344–345; Magyar Statisztikai Évkönyv. (Új folyam XX). 1912. Magyar Kir. Központi Statisztikai Hivatal, Budapest, 1914 pp. 368–369; Magyar Statisztikai Évkönyv. (Új folyam XXII). 1914. Magyar Kir. Központi Statisztikai Hivatal, Budapest, 1916 p. 251.

Graph 16.2

Numbers of monolingual (Serbian) and bilingual (Serbian–Hungarian) schools in the Banat between 1892–93 and 1913–14

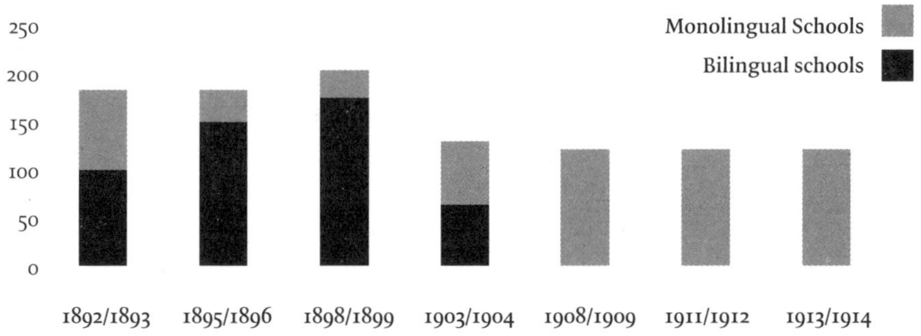

Source: Magyar Statisztikai Évkönyv. 1893. (Új folyam I). (Hungarian Annual Statistics, 1893, number 1), Magyar Kir. Központi Statisztikai Hivatal (Center for Former Hungarian Kingdom,

Statistics), Budapest, 1893. pp. 308–309; Magyar Statisztikai Évkönyv. 1896. (Új folyam IV). Magyar Kir. Központi Statisztikai Hivatal, Budapest, 1897. pp. 412–413; Magyar Statisztikai Évkönyv. 1898. (Új folyam VI). Magyar Kir. Központi Statisztikai Hivatal, Budapest, 1899. pp. 298–299; Magyar Statisztikai Évkönyv. 1904. (Új folyam XII). Magyar Kir. Központi Statisztikai Hivatal, Budapest, 1904. pp. 356–357; Magyar Statisztikai Évkönyv. 1909. (Új folyam XVII.) Athenaeum, Budapest, 1910. pp. 344–345; Magyar Statisztikai Évkönyv. (Új folyam XX). 1912. Magyar Kir. Központi Statisztikai Hivatal, Budapest, 1914 pp. 368–369; Magyar Statisztikai Évkönyv. (Új folyam XXII). 1914. Magyar Kir. Központi Statisztikai Hivatal, Budapest, 1916 p. 251.

Graph 16.3

Numbers of monolingual (German) and bilingual (German-Hungarian) schools in the Banat between 1892–93 and 1913–14

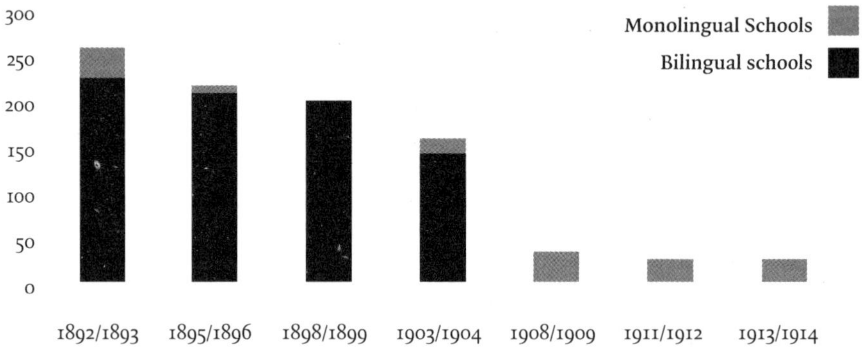

Source: Magyar Statisztikai Évkönyv. 1893. (Új folyam I). (Hungarian Annual Statistics, 1893, number 1), Magyar Kir. Központi Statisztikai Hivatal (Center for Former Hungarian Kingdom, Statistics), Budapest, 1893. pp. 308–309; Magyar Statisztikai Évkönyv. 1896. (Új folyam IV). Magyar Kir. Központi Statisztikai Hivatal, Budapest, 1897. pp. 412–413; Magyar Statisztikai Évkönyv. 1898. (Új folyam VI). Magyar Kir. Központi Statisztikai Hivatal, Budapest, 1899. pp. 298–299; Magyar Statisztikai Évkönyv. 1904. (Új folyam XII). Magyar Kir. Központi Statisztikai Hivatal, Budapest, 1904. pp. 356–357; Magyar Statisztikai Évkönyv. 1909. (Új folyam XVII.) Athenaeum, Budapest, 1910. pp. 344–345; Magyar Statisztikai Évkönyv. (Új folyam XX). 1912. Magyar Kir. Központi Statisztikai Hivatal, Budapest, 1914 pp. 368–369; Magyar Statisztikai Évkönyv. (Új folyam XXII). 1914. Magyar Kir. Központi Statisztikai Hivatal, Budapest, 1916 p. 251.

Eötvös's law made clear stipulations regarding the building of new schools. They had to be located in a healthy environment, the building was to be dry and well ventilated, and in each class the maximum number of pupils was not to exceed 60. Alongside the building of new schools, the law provided for the modernisation of classrooms in already-existing buildings. In 1870 in a report addressed to Parliament, Eötvös wrote: 'I can truly say, from personal observation, that a large portion of the classrooms existing in our country are built in such a way that children who spend half the day inside them suffer greater losses to their health and development than they gain from the education provided.'[26] The state of popular schools was no better in the Banat. Although there were some well-equipped schools in modern buildings (such as, in Timișoara, the communal school in the Josefin quarter or the schools of the Sisters of the Virgin Mary established in 1858), the village schools, which represented the great majority of educational institutions, operated in modest conditions. Victor Țârcovnicu has identified many schools that operated under difficult circumstances. For example, the schools of the Bishopric of Caransebeș had small, dark and insanitary buildings; were not provided with the necessary books; and, in some cases, did not have sufficient desks and chairs for pupils.

For elementary schools, the number of classes per week was regulated by law with a minimum of 20 and a maximum of 25 hours per week. The annual study period was eight months in villages and nine months in cities.[27] The autonomy of the educational system designed by Eötvös allowed churches to schedule the hours of study and to decide upon the school textbooks and agendas, on the basis of state requirements.[28] The legal provisions on these issues were not altered later, although autonomy in making decisions was significantly limited. Eötvös's objective of educating loyal citizens of the state without making a distinction based on ethnic criteria, was abandoned with Apponyi's laws of 1907, which considered education to be the main instrument of assimilation.

With regard to the teaching language in elementary schools, Eötvös's law had supported schooling in the native language when that language was spoken in the respective commune and he did not impose Hungarian as compulsory. Teachers or assistant teachers who spoke the language of the community were hired in popular schools.[29] However, by Law XVIII of 1879 Hungarian became compulsory in elementary schools as the language of the state, and teachers had to be competent to teach this language, which is why the law provided for four years of preparation.[30] Apponyi's laws of 1907 preserved the right of the Church to decide upon the teaching language, but, by a series of provisions, gave priority to Hungarian: if one-fifth of the total number of children demanded to learn Hungarian, the school was compelled to offer such courses; if more than half the pupils opted for Hungarian, it would become the official teaching language for the school.

Besides the educational policy of the government, which was designed to encourage the assimilation of different populations and the attenuation of nationalist tendencies, there were phenomena that can be ascribed to the multiculturalism of the population of the Banat and the social arrangement of its inhabitants. In fact, a significant portion of children from different cultural-linguistic groups only took the minor classes of elementary school in their own language. Frequently, higher studies were held in Hungarian schools, based on the conviction that a better knowledge of that language would contribute to professional training.[31]

The classes taught in schools were faith and ethics, reading and writing, arithmetic and geometry, speaking and logic, geography and history, natural sciences, agriculture and gardening, civil rights and duties, singing, and physical education. In schools of the nationalities, the mother tongue was added.[32] The curriculum of a typical elementary school run by the Orthodox Church in 1874 is shown in Table 16.3.

Table 16.3

SUBJECT		NUMBER OF HOURS PER WEEK			
		Grade I	Grade II	Grade III	
				Group 1	Group 2
Religion		6	7	5	3
Mother tongue	Spoken	4	2	–	–
	Reading & writing	9	7	5	5
	Grammar	–	3	3	3
Arithmetic		5	3	3	3
Geography		–	2	2	2
History		–	–	2	2
Natural sciences		–	–	2	2
Physics		–	–	–	2
Civil rights and duties		–	–	–	2
Singing		1.5	1.5	1.5	1.5
Church hymns[a]		1	1	1	1
National hymns		0.5	0.5	0.5	0.5
Physical education (in 2 groups)		0.5	0.5	0.5	0.5

[a] Church hymns were studied in two lessons of half an hour each per week.
Source: Ţârcovnicu, *Contribuţii*, p. 177.

It is unlikely that this curriculum was followed in the rural environment. The teaching of physics and natural sciences was hampered by a lack of didactic materials, and was based on oral explanation. Many schools did not have a garden necessary to practise agricultural knowledge, and where one did exist, it was usually used by the leaders of the community for their own benefit. There was also a lack of adequate space for physical education.[33]

Until 1873, elementary schools in the border region held a special status. These institutions, divided into two classes with a schooling period of four years, did not differ much from popular elementary schools, but were under the authority of the border guards. During public examinations, along with the school inspector and the leader of the commune or village, the officer of the regiment commissioned with control of the school also attended.[34] By §§24–25 of Law XXVII of 1879, the border region became civil, and the schools then passed under the control of the Ministry of Religion and Public Education, entering the state school network. From then on, these schools could only hire teachers who were able to teach in Hungarian.[35]

SECONDARY EDUCATION

Between 1867 and 1914, the secondary education was less concerned with the pupils' training pupils for life, and more so with preparing them for higher education. On the basis of legal provisions, the interval 1867–1914 can be divided in two distinct periods: (1) between 1867 and 1883 when the secondary education system functioned upon the curriculum of the Austrian *Gymnasium* and *Realschule*, (2) between 1883 and 1913, when Law XXX 'regarding secondary schools and the training of their teachers', was in force, approved while Ágoston Trefort was minister of religion and public education. Changes in common law occurred after 1867 but these reforms did not affect the sphere of secondary education which continued to be based on the *Entwurf der Organisation der Gymnasien und Realschulen in Oesterreich*, approved by Emperor Franz Joseph on 15 September 1849. The minister of religion and public education at that time, Count Leo von Thun-Hohenstein, appointed Franz Exner, professor of philosophy at Prague University, and Hermann Bonitz, professor of Latin and Greek at Vienna University, to draft this document.[36]

The law required that secondary education should not be limited to the passive acquisition of knowledge, but should pursue the practical acquisition of skills. Historians Béla Pukánszky and András Német consider that this idea was strongly influenced by neo-humanism and Herbartianism. Alongside literature and history, which had been the usual subjects up to that time, the new formula for secondary education gave an important role to mathematics and natural sciences. Following the Austrian model, the project introduced two types of secondary school: the *Gymnasium* and the *Realschule*. The difference between the two lay in their objectives. The *Gymnasium* ensured entrance to all types of higher education, while the *Realschule* allowed entrance to technical institutions only. Education in *Gymnasien* can be divided in two types: the minor *Gymnasium*, with classes from I to IV, and the major *Gymnasium*, with classes from V to VIII. Training in the *Realschulen* provided a cycle of 3+3 years – also divided into minor and major.

A new measure introduced in the *Entwurf der Organisation der Gymnasien und Realschulen in Oesterreich* required appropriate training for those who taught in secondary schools. Furthermore, the language of the settlement where the school was located became the official language of the school. To facilitate learning natural sciences, the law provided for the setting up of laboratories.[37]

The timetable of the major *Gymnasium* in the Kingdom of Hungary after the changes of September 1871 is shown in Table 16.4.

Table 16.4

SUBJECT	NUMBER OF HOURS STUDIED PER WEEK (BY GRADE)							
	I	II	III	IV	V	VI	VII	VIII
Religion	2	22	2	2	2	2	2	2
Hungarian	3	3	3	3	3	3	3	3
Latin	6	6	5	6	6	5	5	5
Greek	–	–	–	–	5	5	4	4
German	–	–	2	2	2	2	2	2
Geography	2	2	2	–	–	–	–	–
History	-	-	2	2	3	3	3	4
Mathematics	4	4	3	3	4	4	3	2
Mathematical geography	–	–	–	–	–	–	–	2
Natural history	2	2	–	–	3	2	–	–
Physics	–	–	·3	4	–	–	4	3
Chemistry	–	–	–	0/4[a]	–	2	–	–
Drawing	4	4	4	4	–	–	–	–
Philosophy	–	–	–	–	–	–	2	2
Physical education	2	2	2	2	2	2	2	2
Calligraphy	1	1	–	–	–	–	–	–

[a] Four hours in the second semester of the year.

Source: Endre Zibolen, 'Az Organisationsentwurf és a nyolcosztályosmagyar gimnázium' ('Design Organisation and the Eight-Year *Gymnasium*'), in *A tantervelmélet forrásai 12. Az ausztriai gimnáziumok és reáliskolák szervezeti terve* (*Sources of Educational Theory 12. The Organisation Plan of Austrian* Gymnasien *and* Realschulen), ed. Nándor Horánszky (Budapest, 1990), p. 19

Law XXX of 1883 preserved the two types of secondary schools, the purpose of both of which was to teach higher culture and prepare for higher education. The *Gymnasium* continued to emphasise humanist subjects and classical languages, while the *Realschule* concentrated upon modern languages and natural sciences.[38] In an important development, the duration of the *Realschule* was extended from six to eight years.

The curriculum of state and communal schools was drawn up centrally by the ministry, but could be modified at the request of the teaching staff. The ultimate goal of the confessional schools was learning Hungarian and subjects of the baccalaureate.[39] The duration of each term was 10 months, both in the *Gymnasium* and the *Realschule*. The law determined the weekly number of hours in class at a maximum of 26 for the four lower grades and 28 for the four upper grades. It also allowed four so-called extraordinary hours. Thus, pupils spent between 30 and 32 hours weekly in school.[40] Secondary schools admitted pupils who had graduated from popular elementary school with a certificate rated 'good' or better, and those who had passed an entrance exam.[41]

THE GYMNASIUM

Between 1867 and 1914 there were eight *Gymnasien* in the Banat. The most important education centre of the province was Timişoara, with two major *Gymnasien*. The oldest was the Piarist *Gymnasium*, established in the 1750s by Jakab Bibics from Deva, in Sfânta Ana, Arad County. In 1788, the *Gymnasium* moved to Timişoara. In 1806, it had six grades, in the school year 1850–51 seven, and in 1851–52 eight.[42] The Piarist *Gymnasium* played an important role in the cultural life of Timişoara and the Banat. Among its teachers was the historian Jenő Szentkláray, member of the Hungarian Science Academy; Albin Körösi, a specialist in Spanish literature and member of Spanish Academy of Madrid; the historian György Számek; and Antal Pfeiffer, professor of foreign languages and natural science. Among its graduates, the composer György Kurtág and writer Ioan Slavici are worthy of mention.[43] From the mid-nineteenth century, the Piarist *Gymansium* suffered constantly from lack of space. From the time of its move to Timişoara, the question of erecting a new school building and a parochial house had been raised but the project was not accomplished until 1867–70, while Eötvös was minister. The new building did not resolve the problem of space, however, and the school was moved again, sharing a building with the crafts school.[44]

Secretary of State Ágost Pulszky considered that the space-related problems of the Piarist *Gymnasium* could be solved by establishing a new state *Gymnasium*, which would improve the existing situation for a time. The number of pupils dropped from 550 in the school year 1896–97 to 426 by 1908–09. Finally in September 1909 the building complex based on László Székely's designs was completed. Built on the site of the city's fortress, it cost 1 million crowns and included a boarding school, monastery and church. The city paid 600,000 crowns of the cost, in exchange for which it received the Piarists' old building with related land.[45]

After moving to new buildings, the number of pupils at the Piarist major *Gymnasium* increased significantly from 426 in 1909 to 625 in 1914.[46] The quality of teaching resources also greatly increased. The new building included rooms for drawing, a hall for physical education with locker rooms and showers, a theatre, a space for festive occasions that could accommodate several hundred people, a philological and geological museum, and laboratories for physics and natural sciences; 14 apartments for teachers, a monastery library, music hall, common room, dining room and servants' rooms.[47] The school endowment contributed to the purchase of teaching materials and the young pupils of the school collected donations for the same purpose.

Although Hungarian was the official language of the school, and it was managed by the Catholic parish, the pupils had diverse origins. Data regarding the number of pupils in the school year 1871–72 is shown in Table 16.5.

Table 16.5

NATIONALITY	NO.	%	RELIGION	NO.	%
Hungarian	259	58.7	Roman Catholic	250	56.5
German	37	8.29	Greek Catholic	4	0.89
Romanian	87	19.50	Orthodox	138	30.94
Slovakian	2	0.44	Lutheran	11	2.45
Croatian	4	0.89	Calvinist	5	1.12
Serbian	57	12.78	Jewish	38	8.52
TOTAL	446	100	TOTAL	446	100

Source: Center for Annual Statistics of the former Hungarian Kingdom, 1872, pp. 594–595.

After Imre Réty's report, the Roman Catholic parish of Cenad took a particular position on teaching the mother tongue, which may have contributed to its popularity among non-Hungarian pupils. Starting in 1850, the *Gymnasium* hired Orthodox teachers for Romanian and Serbian students, so that they could learn religion in their native languages. Moreover, non-Hungarian pupils could benefit from exemption from tuition fees in Catholic schools and could opt, like their Catholic colleagues, for free care in the parish.[48] Alongside the Piarist *Gymnasium* of Timișoara, there was also the Catholic major *Gymnasium* of Arad, founded in 1745 by the Minorite order. At first, its main teaching language was Hungarian, with German and Romanian as secondary languages.[49]

Starting in 1870, the administrative power of Arad expressed its intention to establish a state civil *Gymnasium*. This was inaugurated in 1873 by restructuring the Minorite school.[50] In parallel, a new building was constructed which housed, in addition to the *Gymnasium*, the major *Realschule* and teacher-training college. In 1891, the *Gymnasium* and the major *Realschule* were managed by two directors, which made for a difficult relationship between the two institutions who shared the same building.[51] As with the major *Gymnasium* of Timișoara, the students of the *Realschule* were of different nationalities and religions. That situation started to change in the 1910s, and by 1914 most of the students were Hungarian.[52]

Orczy-Vásárhelyi Library was an important asset for the school in Arad. In the school year 1894–95, it had 22,483 volumes and nine incunabula, including the Bible edited in 1475 by György Rákóczi and a copy of János Thuróczy's *Chronicle*.[53] Among the teaching staff of the *Gymnasium* in Arad we find an important number of researchers: Benedek Jancsó, Lajos Mangold şi Sándor Márki and the linguist Ioan Goldiş.[54] As well as the two major *Gymnasien*, there were also some minor *Gymnasien* in the Banat: in Lugoj, Kikinda, Pančevo, Zrenjanin and, for a short period, in Vršac.[55]

The minor *Gymnasium* in Lugoj was founded in 1823 as a Hungarian and German state school. It was later transferred to county management and transformed into a major *Gymnasium*.[56] The *Gymnasium* in Lugoj had an important role even when it was a minor school, because until the school year 1907–08 it was the only secondary school in Caraș-Severin County. Like the other schools of the Banat, this was also heterogeneous in terms of the ethnicity and religious faith of its pupils; for example, in the school year 1893–94 the students included 58 Hungarians, 70 Germans, 87 Romanians, and 1 Serbian, and besides German and Hungarian, teaching was also done in Romanian. In the first four years of the eight-year curriculum the accent was on learning grammar, while from the fifth year the history of literature was the main area of study.[57] Most of the students came from neighbouring areas: out of 131 students, 57 were from Lugoj, 46 from Caraș-Severin County and 28 from other counties. Its pupils were the children of intellectuals, craftsmen and landlords. The origin of the 3 private students are not detailed in the yearbook.[58]

Another Banatian minor *Gymnasium* during the Dual Monarchy was the Piarist school of Zrenjanin, founded in 1846 near Lugoj, with instruction in Hungarian and German.[59] The major *Gymnasium* of Kikinda was established in 1869 by transforming the three-grade minor *Realschule* which had public status. Because this status was withdrawn in 1869, the institution functioned until 1876–77 with temporary licences, as a private minor *Realschule*. In 1877 Trefort approved the opening of the first grade of the *Gymnasium* as a minor *Realschule*.

The major *Gymnasium* of Pančevo was formed with the structure of an imperial royal *Unterrealschule*. It was a German school, with Serbian as a second language. Until the border region passed to civil administration, it was under the authority of the Imperial and Royal Ministry of Military Affairs. At its own request, the school became a *Gymnasium* of six grades in 1863 and of seven grades in 1871. The Hungarian Ministry of Religion and Public Education imposed compulsory teaching of Hungarian for three hours a week in all seven grades. In the school year 1888–89, the institution became an eight-grade major *Gymnasium*. Gradually, the *Gymnasium* lost its German character in favour of Hungarian.[60]

With regard to the origins of its students, the Pančevo *Gymnasium* was the most interesting in the Banat. Statistics show that, during the school year 1884–85, 26 Hungarians, 25 Germans, 47 Serbs, 9 Romanians and 2 Croatians studied here. Regarding their native languages, for one it was Hungarian, for 5 German, 28 German-Hungarian, 8 German-Serbian, 40 Hungarian-German-Serbian, 6 Hungarian-German-Romanian, and 11 Hungarian-German-Serbian-Romanian.[61]

On 30 May 1895 the Bánffy government and the administration of Timișoara agreed to establish a state major *Gymnasium* in the city. The city's contribution to the founding and management of this school consisted in securing the land, covering a portion of the construction costs and contributing 50,000 florins to the annual budget of the institution.[62] On 1 September 1897 its first classroom was inaugurated in a temporary building.

The most recent Banatian secondary school was the state major *Gymnasium* in Caransebeș, founded in 1907. In 1881, the border-guard general Traian Doda, supported by the Orthodox Church, initiated procedures for founding a Romanian *Gymnasium*. The plan was abandoned after the establishment of a civil six-grade school.[63] The subsequent establishment of the *Gymnasium* was completed thanks to Constantin Burdia, a member of parliament, who convinced the minister of religion and public education of its necessity. The school was temporarily located in the building of the boys' civil school, and its dorms in the old building of the wealth administration fund.[64] A new building was planned for 1909, but was completed only in the school year 1914–15.[65]

THE REALSCHULE

The *Realschule* represented another type of secondary education. According to the *Entwurf der Organisation der Gymnasien und Realschulen in Oesterreich*, its objective was to train professionals for economic activities. Students at minor *Realschulen* achieved practical training so that after graduation they could immediately be hired. Major *Realschulen* trained specialists for superior technical institutions.

There were minor *Realschulen* with four, three and two years of study, the last year of each being allocated to practical education. The four-year minor *Realschule* offered the possibility of continuing studies at a higher *Realschule*. If there were classical languages among the subjects studied, a new type of school could be created – a combination between minor *Realschule* and minor *Gymnasium*, which offered the possibility of continuing studies at a major *Gymansium*. Before Trefort's law of 1883, the school curriculum of minor *Realschulen* was as shown in Table 16.6.

Table 16.6

SUBJECT	NO. OF HOURS STUDIED PER WEEK (BY GRADE)			
	I	II	III	IV (practical)
Religion	2	2	2	2
Main language	4	4	4	5
Second modern language	4	4	3	3
Geography and history	3	3	4	–
Mathematics	4	4	4	–
Applied mathematics	–	–	–	3
Natural sciences	3	3	3	–
Technology	–	–	–	5
Knowledge about merchandise	–	–	–	2 in second term
Drawing	6	6	6	6 in first term; 8 in second
Calligraphy	2	2	2	–

Source: *A tantervelmélet forrásai* 12 (*The Sources of the Theory of School Syllabuses*), p. 189

The school curriculum of the major *Realschule* was, during the first three years, similar to that of the minor *Realschule*. In major *Realschule*, it had the structure shown in Table 16.7.

Table 16.7

SUBJECT	NO. OF HOURS STUDIED PER WEEK (BY GRADE)		
	IV	V	VI
Religion	2	2	2
Main language	5	5	5
Second modern language	5	5	5
Geography and history	3	3	3
Mathematics	5	4	4
Natural sciences	4	2	–
Physics	–	4	5
Drawing	6	6	6
Calligraphy	2	2	2

Source: *A tantervelmélet forrásai* 12 (*The Sources of the Theory of School Syllabuses*), p. 201.

There were three minor *Realschulen* in the Banat: the Jewish *Realschule* with teaching in Hungarian and German, founded in 1832, and the *Realschule* founded by János Rotter in 1848, with teaching in Hungarian (both in Arad) and the Weisner private minor *Realschule*, founded in 1863 with teaching in German (in Timișoara).[66]

The three schools were heterogeneous with regard to ethnicity and religious faith. Among the pupils of the Jewish school in Arad, there were also Roman Catholics, while at Timișoara minor *Realschule* almost half of the students were of the Jewish and Orthodox religions. Regarding mother tongue, during the school year 1870–71, of the total number of students, 20 spoke Hungarian, 38 German, 10 Romanian and 19 Serbian.[67] Weisner's minor *Realschule* in Timișoara was transformed into a four-grade civil school and three-year commercial secondary school. After the founding of the state *Realschule*, the Jewish minor *Realschule* in Arad was converted into a four-year school for girls and a five-year school for boys.[68] Between 1867 and 1914, three major *Realschulen* maintained by the state were founded in the Banat, in the cities of Arad, Timișoara and Vršac.

The largest of the three institutions was in Timișoara, becoming a six-grade school in 1870 and an eight-grade one in 1876. During its first nine years, the school was located inside a wing of the central hospital, which caused problems. During a smallpox epidemic in January 1874, the school was forced to temporarily cease activity, because the smallpox patients were placed in the immediate vicinity of the classrooms. According to management reports, the classrooms were insufficient, lighting was inadequate, drinking water could only be found in the neighbouring building, and the number of toilets was below what was required.[69] The government intervened to settle the problem, and a new building was provided in 1879,[70] with 11 classrooms, 9 halls for teaching different professions, libraries, laboratories, halls for the teaching staff, and a hall for festive occasions.[71]

In setting the school curriculum and the timetable of the major *Realschule*, the school plan of the major *Realschule* in Buda was taken into consideration along with the provisions of the *Entwurf*. During the first school year, 1892–93, classes were held as shown in Table 16.8.

Table 16.8

SUBJECT	NUMBER OF HOURS PER WEEK (BY GRADE)					
	I	II	III	IV	V	VI
Religion	2	2	2	2	2	2
Hungarian	6	4	4	4	4	4
German	6	2	3	3	3	3
Geography	3	3	3	–	–	–
History	–	–	–	4	4	4
Mathematics	4	4	3	7	4	3
Construction	–	–	4	–	–	–
Natural sciences	–	3	–	–	4	4
Physics	3	–	–	2	2	2
Chemistry	–	–	5	2	2	2
Applied geometry	6	6	–	4	–	–
Descriptive geometry	–	–	–	–	4	5
Free drawing	–	4	4	4	4	4
Calligraphy	2	2	2	–	–	–
Physical education	2	2	2	2	2	2

Source: Berkeszi, *A temesvári Magyar Királyi Állami Főreáliskola története*, p. 144.

The management of the school stressed the importance of learning Hungarian and German, especially for students who wished to continue their studies at higher institutions.[72] Due to the efforts of the teaching staff and the methods used, the school became one of the best Romanian educational institutions.[73] The high level of education it provided is attested by István Berkeszi's list of the subsequent occupation of its graduates, among whom a large portion became engineers, higher officials, architects or military officers.[74]

The history of the major *Realschule* in Arad is linked to the history of the major *Gymnasien* there. Two years after the building was finished in 1875, the school opened with grades I to IV, common to major *Gymnasien*.[75] The two schools were separated in 1891, the major *Realschule* functioning from then on independently, with eight classrooms, two rooms for drawing and a chemistry hall, while the physics, natural sciences and physical education halls were used jointly with the major *Gymnasium*.[76]

The *Realschule* in Vršac operated in place of the minor *Realschule*, and was founded by the state in 1851. By decrees of the minister of religion and public education, it went through various transformations until the early 1890s.[77] The school was later taken over by the city administration, which promised to build it a new headquarters and support its activity with 6,000 florins each year.[78] In the twentieth century, the major *Realschule* in Vršac surpassed the one in Arad in size and came close to the number of students of the one in Timişoara. More than 60 per cent of the students did not have Hungarian as mother tongue.[79]

The data presented earlier shows the lack of a secondary school network for the minorities. In our opinion, this was not because of the restrictive legislation, but because learning in languages other than Hungarian negatively impacted on the graduates' careers. Moreover, a high level of proficiency in Hungarian was one of the conditions for accessing superior institutions. The ratio of non-Hungarian students was quite large in all Banatian secondary schools and no examples have been found of differentiation on ethnic or religious criteria. It should be emphasised that choosing a secondary school was a personal decision. Pupils enlisted in Hungarian schools, even if this involved their families in substantial expense and even if in some cases there was the possibility of attending a school in their mother tongue. The high ratio of students of different nationalities does not represent the success of assimilation policies, but rather the wish of young people to acquire the necessary skills for a rapid integration into society.[80]

GIRLS' SCHOOLS

The establishment of the Dual Monarchy was followed by a transformation in the system of schooling for girls and women. Social evolution in the period 1848–67 and an increase in the level of civilisation redefined the role of women within the family and society. Besides the classic role of mother, within the less wealthy middle class the need for professional training arose, especially among girls lacking a dowry. In parallel, the women's movement and the female press intensified, for example the weekly literary paper *Családi Kör* (*The Family Circle*), edited by Szegfiné Emilia Kánya.[81]

The most significant educational institutions for women in the period before the Dual Monarchy had been primary schools run by nuns, most of them training young girls for motherhood. In this context, Eötvös's law regarding popular schools created the possibility of establishing civil girls' schools which would ensure four years of schooling based on the curriculum he decreed.[82]

However, the civil schools established by Eötvös did not meet the expectations of the middle class regarding girls' education. Therefore, a new type of school was founded, with a superior level of instruction, structured around four or six grades. This institution gave equivalent qualifications to those issued by the secondary schools for boys, and its curriculum was adapted to the educational needs of women. In 1910 Rozina Mársits, headmistress of the girls' high school of the Kingdom of Hungary in Timişoara, summed up the educational objectives of these institutions: 'the establishment of girls' high schools was made in order to provide necessary cultural education to middle-class girls'.[83] Upon graduation, the girls could continue their studies in order to become teachers in professional trade schools.[84] The curriculum of the girls' high school of the Kingdom of Hungary, the oldest school of its type in Timişoara, was as shown in Table 16.9.

Table 16.9

SUBJECT	WEEKLY LESSONS (BY GRADE)[a]					
	I	II	III	IV	V	VI
Psychology				X		
Housekeeping				X		
History		X	X	X	X	X
Geography	X	X	X			
Astronomy				X		
Hungarian	X	X	X	X	X	X
Manual work	X	X	X		X	X
Calligraphy	X					
French		X	X	X	X	X
Drawing		X	X			
Arithmetic	X	X	X	X	X	X
Natural sciences	X	X			X	X
Physical education	X		X	X	X	X
Chemistry			X			
Piano					X	X
German	X	X	X	X	X	X
Physics					X	X
Economy			X	X		
Singing	X	X	X	X	X	X

[a]The source does not specify the number of hours per week; X indicates that the subject was studied in that particular grade.

Source: Mársits, *A temesvári háztartási tanfolyammal és bentlakással egybekapcsolt Magyar Királyi Állami Felsőbb Leányiskola Értesítője az 1909–10. tanévről*, pp. 16–18.

Because there were no *Gymnasien* for girls, the young girls had to be examined in the boys' *Gymnasien*. The idea of founding girls' *Gymnasien* first appeared in 1890, and five years later, after women had earned the right to enter the philology, medicine and pharmacy faculties, the girls' *Gymnasium* of the National Association for Training Women in Budapest was founded.[85] The education of women from the Banat followed, largely, the national trend. Civil schools for girls were founded in 1870, and high schools for girls in the 1880s. By 1912, 12 civil schools for girls and three high schools for girls had been founded.[86] There were also state civil schools for girls in Bela Crkva, Caransebeș and Pancevo. In Arad and Timișoara, there were schools operated by the city administration; in Lugoj and Timișoara, schools managed by the Roman Catholic Church (in the Central, Fabric and Josefin quarters); in Arad, by the Romanian Orthodox Church; in Pančevo, by the Serbian Orthodox Church. Finally, in Lugoj there was a private school for girls' education.[87]

Between 100 and 200 girls per year studied in these institutions. At Arad and Pančevo, the proportion of Hungarian-language girls was larger, given that civil schools for girls of Orthodox religion also operated in these cities. The Roman Catholic girls' schools in Lugoj and Timișoara managed by the Poor Sisters of the Mother of God were usually attended by pupils who spoke languages other than Hungarian.[88] Regarding mother tongue and religious faith, in the school year 1909–10, Timișoara (state) high school for girls was composed of students as shown in Table 16.10.

Table 16.10

MOTHER TONGUE	%	FAITH	%
Hungarian	85.6	Jewish	60.6
German	10.2	Roman Catholic	25.6
Romanian	2.8	Evangelical	4.4
Serbian	1.4	Reformed	3.4
		Romanian Orthodox	3
		Serbian Orthodox	1.5
		Greek Catholic	1
		Unitarian	0.5

Source: Mársits, 'Magyar Királyi Állami Felsőbb Leányiskola Értesítője az 1909–10. tanévről', p. 52

This data confirms Victor Karady's observation that within the Austro-Hungarian Monarchy, the percentage of the Jewish population in school was very high as compared to other populations.[89]

Most of the students were from Timișoara; the rest came from Arad, Caraș-Severin, Timis, and Torontal counties.[90] Each year, between four and eight girls from the Banat can be found among the students of the National Association for Training Women in Budapest.[91]

APPRENTICE TRAINING

The industrial law of 1872 abolished the guilds along with the existing system of apprentice training.[92] Eötvös's law took the first step towards the regulation of apprentice training. According to the provisions of Law VII, any boy over the age of 12 could be an apprentice. His master was obliged to teach him reading, writing and arithmetic and ensure he regularly attended school. The first statute of the apprentice school was drafted in 1877 and proposed introducing preparatory training and two- or three-year schools, with 11 classes, of which three were allocated to drawing.[93]

The next change was instituted alongside the industrial law of 1884, which obliged localities that had at least 50 apprentices to establish a separate school for them. For this, they had the right to use the buildings and the teaching staff of local elementary or civil schools.[94] This decision generated substantial growth in the number of apprentice schools, which rose from 49 in 1884 to 215 in 1889 and 535 in 1893.[95]

The Banat was included in this development. At the beginning of the twentieth century, every county and municipality with full rights had apprentice schools. Until 1914 there were 95 apprentice schools in the Banat, 12 of which dealt with apprentice training for commerce, and the remaining 83 with training craftsmen.[96]

For example, in 1884, Timișoara organised four apprentice schools, which merged in 1892. In 1894, the building of the civil school of commerce hosted the apprentice school of commerce,[97] which took place on Sundays from 8 a.m. to 12 noon and twice during weekdays, from 6 to 8 a.m. The subjects taught were reading, practical disciplines, business notions, industrial arithmetic, accounting, drawing and religion.[98]

INDUSTRIAL SCHOOLS

Apprentice training, based on the system described above, encountered numerous problems. One of these was the fact that a good number of pupils reached the apprentice school without knowing how to read or write. For this reason, apprentice classes offered minimal knowledge, and the level of instruction of the apprentices suffered a significant delay. The system of apprentice education could not provide the quality required, while during evening classes the students were tired and frequently fell asleep.[99] At the end of the nineteenth century the basis was laid for a new type of institution for apprentices, in hostels, whose aim was to train homeless and orphaned children. In the Banat, between 1867 and 1914, three such hostels were founded.[100]

The first general industrial school was founded in Timișoara in 1879, integrating workshop practice within everyday training. Students preparing for a technical career, following a three-year school programme, did practical work in an atelier starting in the second year. Those who did technical training worked in a workshop only in the third year. The school operated initially in the building of the state major *Realschule*, and beginning in the school year 1895–96, in the building of the communal elementary school in the city centre.[101] In 1897, the institution was reorganised as the state industrial school of wood and metal of the Kingdom of Hungary.[102] In accordance with the agreement between the city and the government, the city received the requested land from the military treasury and finished construction in 1900.[103]

At Arad there was a special industrial school for woodwork and metalwork, while at Reșița, on the occasion of the establishment of the self-specialising workers' club, local miners requested the establishment of an industrial school of mining and metallurgy.[104] Another aspect of apprentice training was commercial education. Its basic level was equivalent to craft school. In the Banat, there were schools like this in Lugoj and Caransebeș, and two in Timișoara, which included a special one for waiters. The modernisation of apprentice education in commerce at national level started in 1879, along with the transformation of higher classes of civil schools into so-called higher commercial schools, one of which was in Arad.[105]

There was also a special agricultural school in the Banat in Sânicolau Mare, founded by Count Kristóf Nákó in 1799. The school ensured training and school materials, free of charge, for 12 local boys, in 24 acres of land. The graduates received 42 florins for their own households, and those who wished to continue their studies received an annual grant of 126 florins, up to the age of 24. In 1887, the institution was transferred to state maintenance and the practical grounds were extended to 100 acres. On its centennial, the school was named 'the Kristóf Institute Agricultural School of the Kingdom of Hungary', with the objective of training personnel to manage small and medium-sized estates. The teaching body, excluding the director, was comprised of three permanent teachers and two contract teachers, while the number of students varied from 45 to 50.[106]

SPECIAL SCHOOLS

There was a special branch of pedagogy for the blind, deaf-mutes and the mentally challenged. In Hungary, their education began in the first decades of the nineteenth century on private initiative.[107] Although Law XXVIII of 1868 provided for compulsory learning, the second and third paragraphs excluded handicapped children, which is why their education could only take place in private institutions.[108]

The history of deaf-mute education started with Károly Schäffer, a school director in the Josefin district of Timișoara, who arranged a public examination for three deaf-blind pupils in 1885. Their results encouraged the community, and in the following year a city school for 12 children was founded: Vác State Institute for Deaf-Mutes.[109] At its inauguration, Mayor Károly Telbisz declared that 'educated and trained deaf-mutes can become useful members of society'. Therefore, along with the eight normal grades, industrial classes were introduced for this special category.[110]

In 1885 József Roboz organised a deaf-mute institute in Arad, and, after a long trip through Europe, he returned to Arad and founded the first Speech Therapy Institution of the Kingdom of Hungary, which he also managed until 1894.[111] Additionally, the institutionalised education of the blind started in the Banat in 1894. The municipality of Timișoara used a legacy from Antal Saller to buy a building for the boarding school, which accepted students up to the age of 36.[112] The trainees learnt how to make baskets, chairs and mats, and could study typing. The institution was strongly involved in cultural life, with an eight-piece string orchestra and a choir. There was also a plan for a Braille library.[113]

TEACHER TRAINING

During the period of Eötvös's reforms, one of the strongest challenges faced by the new educational system was the lack of teachers and, in some instances, insufficient training. In order to change this situation, Eötvös's programme aimed to establish 20 teacher-training institutions.[114] In the report he presented to parliament, Eötvös declared that while there were many well-trained teachers active in the country, there were also many who seriously lacked pedagogical and didactical knowledge and were not capable of self-improvement. In many cases, the teachers did not know the subject they were teaching. Unprepared teaching staff were often hired, while sometimes the faith schools gave teachers religious, not pedagogical, training. Moreover, the salary was very often too small.

Eötvös's law introduced training schools for teachers which consisted of a director-teacher, two teachers and an assistant teacher, as well as an instructor for the practical school. During the three-year training, the future teachers were instructed in religion, ethics, pedagogy, didactics, geography, native language, Hungarian, German, natural sciences, economy, practical gardening, the constitution, mathematics, geometry, singing, music, drawing, calligraphy and physical education. They also took part in pedagogical practice. After training, there was a final exam in every discipline, no later than two years after graduation.[115] The students had to be at least 15 on graduation, physically healthy, and having completed at least four years at a *Gymnasium*,

Realschule or civil school. Training for female teachers was separate from that of males, and had different aims. Male teachers were especially trained for elementary schools, while women were trained for teaching girls after primary school classes at girls' high schools and girls' civic schools. Girls over the age of 14 were admitted if they had graduated from the three-year girl's high school. They learned religion, ethics, drawing, calligraphy, native language, grammar, Hungarian, German, geography, history, pedagogy, arithmetic, natural sciences, physics, gardening, food preparation, singing, household rules and women's work, and took part in pedagogical practice. There were internal exams and one final exam.[116] Unlike the boys' institutions, the girls did not pay school taxes, while the poor ones received free food and grants.[117]

In the Banat, there were four schools for male teachers and one for female teachers. The first school founded on the provisions of Eötvös's law was the Arad state school for teacher training, following Minister Trefort's decree of 21 June 1873. It held classes in the building of the Arad high school.[118] The students learned religion, methodology, grammar, the history of education, school management, stylistics, the science of education, poetics, the history of literature, Hungarian history, universal history, constitution, natural laws, mathematics, geometry, body and health, physics, chemistry, agricultural knowledge, German and geography, and attended classes in music, physical education and manual labour.[119] Most of the students came from modest families from Arad, Bács, Békés, Brașov, Caraș-Severin, Timiș and Torontal counties.[120] Students of the school year 1873–74 are classified by religion and nationality in Table 16.11.

Table 16.11

NATIONALITY	NO.	%	RELIGION	NO.	%
Hungarian	630	46.18	Roman Catholic	1058	77.62
German	588	43.11	Greek Catholic	11	0.80
Romanian	103	7.55	Orthodox	133	9.75
Serbian	20	2.20	Lutheran	38	2.79
Bulgarian	5	0.37	Calvinist	61	4.47
Slovakian	8	0.58	Jewish	63	4.62

Source: Szabó, *Az Aradi Áll*, p. 13

The other school for teachers was in Timișoara, founded by inspector Márton Mártonffy and inaugurated in 1893. The new building was completed in 1895 and included dorms and a six-grade practical school.[121]

In parallel with teacher training by the state, the Orthodox bishoprics of Arad and Caransebeș ran schools to train teachers in Romanian. In the Banat, the training of Romanian teachers was traditionally a task of the Church. In 1810, with the appointment of Uros Nestorovic as inspector for the Orthodox schools on Hungarian territory, a new age in teacher instruction began. In 1811, three Orthodox institutions for training teachers were founded, among which was the one for Romanians in Arad.[122] In the school year 1903–04, the school curriculum was as shown in Table 16.12.

Table 16.12

SUBJECT	NO. OF HOURS STUDIED PER WEEK (BY GRADE)			
	I	II	III	IV
Religion	2	2	2	2
Pedagogical studies	2	3	4	4
Pedagogical practice	–	–	2	6
Romanian language and literature	2	3	2	2
Hungarian language and literature	3	3	3	3
German language	1	1	1	1
Mathematics, algebra	3	3	3	1
Geography	2	2	2	–
History	3	3	2	–
Construction	–	–	–	2
Natural sciences, chemistry	2	2	2	–
Physics	–	–	2	2
Hygiene	1	2	-	-
Religious chanting	3	3	3	3
Singing and instrumental music				
Calligraphy	1	1	–	–
Drawing	2	2	2	–
Physical education	2	2	2	2
TOTAL	34	36	36	32

Source: Pârvulescu, *Şcoală şi societate*, pp. 98–99; Teodor Botiş, *Istoria şcoalii normale (Preparandiei) şi a Institutului Teologic Ortodox-Român din Arad (The History of Teacher Training and the Romanian Orthodox Theological Institute)* (Arad, 1922), p. 101

Due to the lack of teachers in Orthodox schools, the Bishopric of Oradea ensured free boarding for local students, on condition that, after graduation, they remained in the parish.

There was another Orthodox teaching school in Caransebeş, opened in 1876. The preparations to launch the school began in 1872, when the Bishop of

Caransebeş decided to send two students – the later professors of the school – abroad with grants given by the Gojdu Foundation.[123] In Vienna one of them studied philosophy, mathematics and physics, the other attended history courses. Later both of them went to Gotha to study pedagogy. The school finally opened in September 1876; there were 4 teachers, 12 boys, 3 girls and 13 listeners with no obligation to attend classes.[124]

The Orthodox Pedagogical Institute of Caransebeş was organised over a period of three years; its curriculum is shown in Table 16.13.

Table 16.13

SUBJECTS	NO. OF HOURS STUDIED PER WEEK (BY GRADE)		
	I	II	III
Religion	2	2	2
Romanian	3	3	3
Hungarian	4	4	4
German	1	1	1
Arithmetic	2	2	2
Geometry	2	2	2
Geography	2	2	2
History	2	2	2
Pedagogy and methodology	3	3	3
Constructions	–	–	2
Drawing and calligraphy	2	2	1
Hygiene	1	1	1
Singing	2	2	2
Violin and piano	2	2	2
Religious chanting	2	2	2
Mass	2	2	2
Agriculture	2	2	2
Physics	2	2	2
Natural sciences	2	2	2
Physical education	–	–	3
TOTAL	38	38	43

Source: Pârvulescu, *Şcoală şi societate*, p. 102

Later, the subjects included accounting, history, pedagogy and chemistry. In Arad and Caransebeş, the study programmes for teachers differed greatly from the state curriculums, excepting religious education.

In the Banat, the training of female teachers was carried out by the Roman Catholic Institution for Female Teachers of Timișoara, starting in 1881–82. The training of kindergarten teachers started in 1891, with the law regulating the operation of kindergartens. Girls over 14 years of age and boys over 16 could attend the school. They had to be physically healthy, to have an ear for music, to be graduates of four years of secondary schools, civil schools or girls' high schools, or of two years at higher schools.[125] During the two-year schooling period, the students learnt religion, ethics, Hungarian language and literature, hygiene, Hungarian history, constitution, geography, natural sciences, geometry, drawing, singing, violin, manual labour,[126] crafts and physical education. Learning Hungarian was compulsory in the training schools for female kindergarten teachers and the obligation to take a final exam was extended retroactively to those who had already finished their training.[127]

The studies ended with a qualification exam, taken in front of the school inspector or his delegate, and those who passed received a qualification diploma. Girls up to 18 and boys up to 20 worked under the supervision of an experienced instructor, and afterwards they received a definitive certificate.[128] The only institution for training female teachers in the Banat was in Timișoara. The school had 5–6 teachers and, until 1904, around 40 students. Their number decreased to 13 in the school year 1910–11.[129]

THE TRAINING OF PRIESTS

There were three institutions for the preparation of priests in the Banat: two Roman Catholic seminaries – one in Timișoara, founded in 1806, the other in Arad, established in 1822 – and the Romanian Orthodox Institute in Caransebeș. There was no centralised regulation regarding the training of priests. The Roman Catholic Church used the guidelines set down in the 1855 Concordat between the papacy and the Austro-Hungarian Empire, according to which the duration of theological education was set at four years, with four to six teachers. The compulsory disciplines were religion, dogmatics, morality, rhetoric, church history, canon law, knowledge of Old and New Testament, Hebrew and, if circumstances allowed, patristics as an auxiliary discipline. In March 1858, Leo von Thun, minister of religion and public education, made the law compulsory throughout the Empire. In parallel, in 1855 Bishop Sándor Csajághy drafted the organisational rules for the institute for the preparation of priests in Cenad.[130] The year 1867 saw the removal of the Church from the tutelage of the State. The purpose of these attempts at reform was for theological education to become more comprehensive, more modern and more practical. In Timișoara in 1878 the curriculum included philosophy, patristics, homiletics, pedagogy and religious art. The number of hours per week for each discipline is shown in Table 16.14.

Table 16.14

YEAR	SUBJECT	NUMBER OF LESSONS PER WEEK
I	Bible: Old Testament	5
	Biblical exegesis: Old Testament	4
	The History of the Church	4
	Homiletics	3
	Patristics	2
	Philosophy	5
II	Bible: New Testament	5
	Bible exegesis: New Testament	4
	The History of the Church	4
	Philosophy	5
	Patristics	2
	Religious education	3
III	Fundamental theology	8
	Moral theology	5
	Pastoral theology	3
	Canon law	5
	Religious stylistics	2
IV	Special dogma	8
	Moral theology	5
	Pastoral theology	3
	Canon law	5
	Christian art	2

Source: Kováts, *A csanádi papnevelde története 1806–1906*, pp. 443–44

The first two years of study represented the so-called small seminary, and the final two, the great seminary. The classes were held on weekdays, from 8 a.m. to 1 p.m. Thursdays were devoted to ceremonies, religious songs and choir practice. The language of most textbooks was Latin, although some were written in Hungarian.[131]

In 1869, with the outlining of the organisational rulebook of the Orthodox Church, the configuration of Orthodox theology was also regulated. The duration of theological studies was set at three years, and the didactic staff included two teachers and a chorister, who also held church positions.[132] The Roman Catholic seminary founded in 1822 preceded the Orthodox Theological Institute in Arad.[133] The parish council of 1870 decided to establish a central seminary aimed at raising moral training through higher education of theology students. New disciplines were introduced, and a highly qualified teacher staff was hired. In order to improve learning conditions, a new building was erected next to the school's headquarters.[134] The school curriculum remained unchanged from 1834–35 to 1875–76. In the school year 1875–76, there was a new curriculum as shown in Table 16.15.

Table 16.15

TIME	YEAR I	YEAR II	YEAR III
8–9 a.m.	Romanian grammar	Dogmatics	Pastoral theology
9–10 a.m.	Practical grammar	Rhetoric	Canon law
10–11 a.m.	Pedagogy	(left blank in original)	(left blank in original)
3–4 p.m.	Hermeneutics	The history of the Church	Moral theology
4–5 p.m.	Singing and ceremonial	Singing and ceremonial	Singing and ceremonial

Source: Botiș, *Istoria școalii normale*, pp. 577–78

After the examination held at the end of the school year 1886–87, Constantin Gurban and Ioan Damșa, representatives of the parish, requested a change of curriculum[135] in favour of a more detailed education of priests in secular disciplines, which would help them in their everyday activities.[136] The change was approved and put into practice in 1888.

The newest theological institute in the Banat was the Romanian Orthodox Diocesan Theological Institute of Caransebeș, which Bishop Ioan Popasu founded in November 1865 by moving the Romanian theology classes from Vršac to Caransebeș.[137] Between 1893 and 1927, the theological curriculum included the disciplines shown in Table 16.16.

Table 16.16

YEAR	SUBJECTS
I	Archaeology, logic, hermeneutics, the history of the Church, isagogics, Romanian, biblical exegesis, church songs, ceremony, instrumental music
II	Dogmatics, moral theology, canon law, pedagogy, architecture, hygiene, church songs, ceremony, instrumental music
III	Liturgy, religious education, biblical exegesis, canon law, Romanian grammar, rhetoric, agriculture, church songs, ceremony, instrumental music

Source: Petrica, *Institutului Teologic Diecezan Ortodox Român Caransebeș*, pp. 48–52

UNIVERSITIES

At the beginning of the twentieth century, the Hungarian government decided that there should be a third institution of higher education in addition to the 'Pázmány Péter' Science University of Budapest and 'Ferenc József' Science University of Cluj. On 6 March 1907 the city council of Timişoara sent a letter addressed to Prime Minister Sándor Wekerle and Apponyi, minister of religion and public education, explaining that, although Timişoara was the regional centre, it did not have an institution of higher education and establishing one would contribute to training of loyal citizens. However, Apponyi favoured Bratislava over Timişoara, although he promised to establish the next university there.[138] In January 1910, at the general assembly of the Timişoara construction engineers' club, the president of the society, Mihály Kajlinger, emphasised that it was necessary to establish a university because of the rich industrial activity of the city and the demand for specialists.[139]

THE INSPECTORATE OF EDUCATION

Along with the founding of popular school networks, according to Eötvös's law, inspectorates of education were organised to supervise the activity of schools.[140] The minor level of the inspectorate was represented by the so-called school boards, with members elected for three years from at least nine local schools. A place at this board was reserved for the local priest, and another one for the teacher of the popular school or (if there were several teachers) a representative elected by the teaching staff.[141] The duties of the board were appointing teachers, supervising communal schools on a weekly basis, overseeing absences, and eventually the application of sanctions. The institution mediated disputes between parents and teachers and resolved disciplinary issues. One or more administrators were appointed by the board with the task of managing school money.[142]

The next level of the inspectorate was the regional education board, created in each county and including, with the exception of Pest and Buda, every royal free city. The school inspectors who managed the regional boards were directly elected by the minister of religion and public education. Under their supervision was a school council of elected members or delegates. As officials appointed by the minister, the school inspectors received an annual salary and were obliged to make annual inspections of schools in the region and enforce the law. The regional education boards supervised the communal school boards and when there were disagreements or disciplinary problems, they adopted the role of a second-degree court of justice.[143]

Eötvös's inspectorate system lasted only for a short time. Law XXVIII of 1876 abolished the autonomy of the school boards and placed them under strict control of the minister of religion and public education and his apparatus. The regional board was dissolved, while the school inspector continued to act as a member of the county administrative council and as education councillor. Decisions of the administrative council relating to education could be adopted only when he was present.[144]

CONCLUSIONS

Based on this study we can conclude that, between 1867 and 1914, a new educational structure was created in the Banat. Its base was the state and communal school network, completed by the school networks of the Serbs, the Romanians and, more rarely, the Germans. We can observe a specific symbiosis within these networks. The minority school networks had no secondary schools, nor did they attempt to create them. This cannot be explained by the lack of material means of Romanian and Serbian communities or of the Orthodox Church: at the beginning of our period, the bishoprics of Caransebeș and Arad controlled the largest elementary school network in the region, which remained so until 1914. A more plausible explanation is that between 1867 and 1914 Romanian, Serbian and German students picked secondary schools according to the professional or intellectual opportunities they offered, frequently choosing a Hungarian school over native-language ones. Hungarian was the language of the two universities in Hungary and, moreover, any position in the administration required knowledge of that language. It is also true that there was government pressure for the linguistic and cultural assimilation of minorities within the Austro-Hungarian Monarchy.

The modernisation of the school network between 1867 and 1914 resulted from the need to raise the level of instruction and, against the background of economic development, the need for specialists in various spheres. In the Banat, with the exception of university studies, the educational system could meet local needs, from the elementary education of peasants' children to the claims of intellectuals. Analysis of the curricula shows that they were designed so that the graduates could meet the demands not only of their profession, but also of contemporary society.

PART V

17

THE BANAT AND ROMANIA AT THE END OF THE FIRST WORLD WAR

Vasile Dudaş

THE MILITARY DEFEATS of the Central Powers on the battlefronts were echoed in the Banat. Starting in the autumn of 1918, protests for the end of the war multiplied. The administrative authorities were forced to take preventative measures. The Timiş County leader inspected the southern part of the county and made reassuring statements.[1] On 6 and 20 October, demonstrations took place in Timişoara. On 27 October, the local branch of the Social Democratic Party organised a big rally in the centre of the city, demanding the end of the war and the establishment of a new government that would include representatives of the workers and the nationalities. Under street pressure, the city council met on 28 October 1918 under the chairmanship of county leader György Körössy and demanded the end of the war; a durable peace; demobilisation of enlisted soldiers; abolition of the Dual Monarchy; preservation of Hungarian territorial unity; legislation for universal suffrage and a secret ballot; abolition of censorship; the right to association and assembly.[2]

The anti-war mood permeated the entire population of Timişoara. The Social Democrat leaders Otto Róth and Leopold Somló spoke at one of the meetings, along with Jákobi Kálmán, representative of the local branch of the Radical Party. They asked the population of the Banat to take their fate into their own hands and negotiate directly with the powers of the Entente. The idea of transforming the region in an autonomous entity started to take shape.[3] On 30 October 1918, a number of meetings of the Social Democrat Party in Timişoara and the Banat took place. Dr Otto Róth and Dr Koloman Jákobi met the county leader György Körössy in the afternoon, and Lieutenant Colonel Albert Bartha, chief of the general staff of the local military command, in the evening. In order to protect the region from military confrontation, Róth, Jákobi and Bartha reached the conclusion that proclaiming autonomy within the Hungarian state would be a reasonable solution. Next day there was a new and substantial demonstration against the war; this was the context in which the idea of regional autonomy was presented[4] – 31 October 1918 was a particularly agitated day in Timişoara. County leader Körössy received a telegram from the Hungarian National Council, which had taken over power at Budapest, asking the local authorities to acknowledge this central forum and to create a similar one at county level. Körössy summoned the political leaders of Timişoara. Gathered in the office of the mayor, Josef Geml, they decided to create the Hungarian National Council of Timiş County, and agreed on the 20 members who would participate and represent the local political organisations.[5]

THE REPUBLIC OF THE BANAT

Baron Hordt, the military commander of the garrison, received a telegram from Vienna from the chief of the imperial general staff, regarding the establishment of military councils by nationality. (To maintain order, the emperor had made the decision to set up military councils by nationality.) Lieutenant Colonel Albert Bartha summoned all officers to the great hall of the military casino. The leaders of the Social Democrat Party, Otto Roth, Alfred Pinker and Leopold Somló, were also invited. In front of a few hundred participants, Baron Hordt read out the telegram announcing freedom of all those under arms to form national military councils. The news surprised the participants. Otto Roth took the podium and announced that Emperor Charles I had abdicated and that revolution had broken out everywhere. He also said that the local military forces would be led by Lieutenant Colonel Bartha, explaining the necessity of establishing a people's council that would include representatives of all nationalities from the region. He ended the speech with the words 'Long Live the Republic of the Banat!', proclaiming the autonomy of the region through his use of the word 'republic'. After applause, most of the officers removed the badge with the monarch's inscription from their berets.[6]

In the great hall, several Romanian officers were present for Otto Roth's speech, among them Dr Aurel Cosma. Taking the podium, he reported that Romanian soldiers from the garrison would comply with the orders received from the Romanian army and form a Romanian National Military Council. A few years later, in an interview for *Temeswarer Zeitung*, Otto Roth declared:

> Mr Aurel Cosma put the ideal of every Romanian politician at the forefront: Greater Romania. And he did this at a time and place that was

very risky. As far as I'm concerned, I gambled with my life by proclaiming the republic during that officers' conference on 31 October 1918 and only afterwards did I realise that, out of the 700 attending officers, no one drew his sword for the Habsburgs or for Count Tisza. They could have cut Cosma to pieces, too, because he was the only one who leapt to the stage in the military casino, ranting: 'Romanians, follow me, long live the Romanian National Council!'[7]

The small group of officers then withdrew to the small hall of the nearby 'Kronprints' restaurant, and formed the National Military Council. Contemporary records mention the names of Colonel Jivan of Caransebeș, Lieutenant Colonel Iosif Mustețiu, Captain Dr Aurel Cosma, Captain Dr Lucian Georgevici, and Lieutenant Dr Iustin Nemeth. Aware that without a good military organisation and the support of Romanians from the villages of the region, the council could not be imposed, they entrusted the military command to Lieutenant Colonel Miron Șerb. He had already held several important positions within the local units of the Austro-Hungarian army. As a lawyer in Recaș who knew many people from the surrounding villages, Captain Lucian Georgevici was appointed to organise the military formations. Dr Aurel Cosma was elected president of the council. The military councils of the nationalities and of the workers, which were in the process of being formed, were informed that

1. the Romanian soldiers and officers on the territory of the military command of the Timișoara garrison are the National Council of Romanian soldiers;
2. their attitude will be totally in accordance with the 'resolution of the Greater Romanian National Council, to which we submit with unaltered fidelity';
3. the Romanian military will contribute 'at any moment and with readiness to maintenance of internal order and calm'.[8]

The document was submitted to public opinion. Point 2 refers to the 'Greater Romanian National Council', about which those present seemed to have no information (the Central Romanian National Council had been established on the night of 30/31 October in Budapest).

The Romanian officers understood that their success depended on the activity of the national military councils that were being formed in areas with a Romanian population in Transylvania and the Banat. Hence, the desire to unite with them. Those present drafted a telegram and sent it to Teodor Mihali, president of the Romanian parliamentary club, underlining the fact that the 'Romanian officers and soldiers from the garrison of Timișoara and those on the territory of Timișoara's military command wish to inform you that these officers and soldiers are at the disposal of the Romanian National Military Council elected by our Romanian people'.[9]

After the reunion, the Social Democrats organised a meeting of their leaders, deciding that the forthcoming demonstration would be a good opportunity to proclaim the republic. According to the planned scenario, after work several thousand people in Timișoara went to Freedom Square to participate in the demonstration. Under street pressure, the Social Democrat leaders approved Franz Geistlinger's proposal to create the People's Council of the Banat (which did not make distinctions based on nationality, language or religion) and assumed leadership of the region. At the helm of the new authority were Otto Roth as civilian commissioner and Albert Bartha as military commissioner. The two of them addressed the crowd from the balcony of the city hall, communicating the latest decisions. Otto Roth declared: 'Revolution came, but it is now over. We have shown to the world and to our heirs that the people of the Banat and Timișoara know how to fight for the republic and for a better future without bloodshed.'[10] They spoke in the name of Timișoara and not of a particular community or nationality. For them, and for most people in the city, segregation was inconceivable.

Albert Bartha's speech was followed by the municipal general assembly in which the People's Council was presented as an exponent of the Hungarian National Council established at Budapest on 25 October and which had taken power on 31 October. Informed about the existence of the Romanian National Military Council, military commissioner Albert Bartha invited Aurel Cosma to a meeting during which Cosma said that the two councils could cooperate only on matters of public order. The Romanian National Military Council would act as the Romanian National Council of Timiș County.[11] Under the leadership of the Romanian National Council, large demonstrations took place in Timișoara along with marches of military guards, intoning the song 'Wake Up Romanians' and demanding the proclamation of Greater Romania.[12] The establishment of the Romanian militia was followed by that of the other communities from the Banat. The Hungarian militia formed the Hungarian National Military Council, the chosen president being Albert Bartha.[13] A Swabian (German) National Military Council was elected by officers and soldiers, in agreement with the Hungarian, Romanian and Serbian councils from the Banat, with Lieutenant Colonel Bela Fuchs at its head.[14] Its task was to lead the Swabians, and it had authority over all the councils of German communes. The proposal was accepted, those present writing an 'Appeal' to all Swabians to organise themselves in the communes of the Banat and Bacica.[15] These councils were established in most areas in the Banat which had a Swabian population.

On 31 October 1918 the Serbian National Military Council was established. Bishop Gheorghe Letić was elected honorary president[16] and stressed that the Banatian Serbs should act firmly in favour of their own interests.[17] Like the other national military councils, the Serbian Council also appointed delegates to the People's Council. The following day, the Serbian military and civilians suggested an appeal to the military forces of the Entente. A few days later on 10 November, the Serbs of Timişoara held a new meeting at which one of their leaders, Mladen Pilić, declared that the wish of the Banatian Serbs was to live in a Yugoslav state. He also stated that the Serbian soldiers, who had already crossed the Danube and were marching towards Timişoara, would be warmly welcomed not only by their co-nationals, but also by the Romanians of the Banat, as their allies.[18]

With regard to the formation of national military councils in the Banat, the Romanian-language newspaper *Drapelul* (*The Flag*) from Lugoj wrote that 'some [councils] already acclaim the Republic, others lean towards the consolidation of southern Hungary as a separate province, wishing to ensure the peace as soon as possible, so as to avoid making the territory on which the guns are already rattling, become the theatre of further terrible destruction at the end of the war'.[19] Concluding the evolution of events, *Volkswille*, the Social Democrat publication in Timişoara, noted that 'as if to quickly recover what had been lost, national and popular advisory councils were hurriedly created in order to strengthen their respective independence'.[20] Hungarians, Germans, Romanians and Serbs focused on the preservation of their linguistic community and demanded Western support to support their goals. It was a time when the identification of some leaders with a group or a nation could cause havoc, or at least divergent aspirations.

However, it should be noted that in the Banat, the very idea of nationality did not coincide with sociocultural realities, the inhabitants of the region having several roots. Identity was fluid, bi- and trilingualism being common in many of the cities and villages. Between 1848 and 1918, native German speakers tended to define themselves as citizens of the city and the state, and less – if ever – as people of German nationality.[21] The Jews pleaded for and obtained in 1868 social and political emancipation, integrating both with the state and with the Hungarian and German cultures. The distinction between Church and State had long been a reality accepted in the culture of the Jewish diaspora.[22] The native Bulgarian speakers were Catholic, their modernisation being directly related to the use of the German and Hungarian languages. The Romanian and Serbian inhabitants had not lived themselves in closed communities; in most villages in the Timişoara plain, cohabitation and interaction with people and families from other cultural-linguistic groups was the result of the successful experiments of the House of Habsburg in the eighteenth century.[23] It is true that for many Romanians, affiliation to the Orthodox Church and the retrieval of its autonomy on the criterion of language had become an important theme in the revolutionary year 1848 and would be extended in the second half of the nineteenth century.[24] The melting pot of the Banat was a reality, hence its fluid identity and also the complications deriving from the new tendencies of the time regarding defining or self-defining people according to the concept of *Völkischenation*. The trend was promoted by the Protestant intelligentsia in Prussia, who multiplied it and disseminated throughout Central and East Europe during the nineteenth century.[25] The pressure of this ethnonationalist ideology and the tragic interstate conflicts during the First World War explain the centrifugal movements we have referred to and to which we will return. The Banat of Timișoara was facing the first trend towards a split in its territory, as well as disagreements between the inhabitants that had lived, modernised and built together the region for over two hundred years.

On 1 November 1918, in the room in the city hall that was used for special festivities, the People's Council of the Banat was formed. Among its members were representatives of the former municipal council, the national military councils, the workers and the parties that were represented in Timișoara. An executive committee was elected, including 20 politicians, which was to hold daily meetings.[26] The county leader of Timiș regarded this political body as subordinate to the Hungarian National Council, while the Social Democrat Otto Roth wished for as much independence as possible. Faced with difficulties in attempting to control the whole of the Banat, subordination to Budapest was accepted. After a trip to the Hungarian capital on 8 November, Otto Roth obtained Albert Bartha's appointment as war minister in Mihály Károly's government, while the position of government commissioner was transferred to Otto Roth (21 November).

THE NATIONAL MILITARY AND POLITICAL CONTROVERSIES

Regardless of the military organisation and the measures taken, the situation in the localities of the region was out of control. Gangs of villains damaged the electrical plant, the city of Timișoara remaining in darkness. A few boarding houses, the post office and several public institutions were plundered. To restore order, cadets of the military school of non-commissioned officers were summoned. They fought real fights with bands of thieves.[27] Describing the atmosphere on the city streets, a witness noted:

> On the streets of Timișoara, an unusual sight greets the pedestrian. Army officers no longer wear the badge with the symbol of monarchy, but some three-coloured cockades after different national councils. The Romanian, Hungarian, Serbian and German national councils are vying for supremacy. For now, they are in a state of anticipation, because in the city revolts are breaking out which have to be stopped. A bunch of fugitive prisoners and tramps attacks the shops near the train station. The school of officers fights them and shots are fired. The city is in a state of alert, bullets whistling past the ears of the pedestrians.

Citizens are stopped on the street, forced to go to barracks where they are armed to fight against the bandits. There is feverish movement on the streets, officers who shout with their swords drawn and ready to shoot their pistols. People bound in ropes are brought in by the hundreds. Officers are degraded in the streets.[28]

The revolts spread over the whole region. After the break-up of the Austro-Hungarian military units, tens of thousands of soldiers and officers returned home. Many of them kept their weapons. From a letter sent by the Hungarian war minister at the beginning of November to the sub-prefects within the counties, it appears that, despite orders, many soldiers who returned home with weapons and ammunition, refused to hand them over. The minister demanded that the weapons be retrieved from the soldiers.[29] The leaders of the Romanians, Swabians, Hungarians, Serbs and other communities from the Banat urged the population to respect each other's possessions, calm their spirits and to restore order. The Romanians gathered in a meeting of the Central Romanian National Council and initiated a motion for Mihály Károlyi's government. Vasile Goldiş was authorised to draft a final diplomatic note demanding governance over the territories inhabited by Romanians. Among the counties mentioned were three from the Banat. In the event of a positive resolution, the Romanian leaders were prepared to guarantee public order and the safety of life and property; otherwise, that responsibility would revert to the Hungarian government. The manner of handing over power was to be established by a joint commission. Sibiu would become the headquarters of the Romanian government.

The answer of the Hungarian government to this political action was a 12-hour delay. Then, a delegation led by sociologist Oszkár Jászi, the minister of nationalities, was sent to Arad. The delegates for Timişoara were the government commissioner Dr Otto Roth, Lieutenant Colonel Dr Sebastian Brânduşa, the lawyers Dr Aurel Cosma and Dr Josef Gabriel, Prof. Josef Striegl and Dr Franz Neff. According to the *Temeswarer Zeitung*, before the talks, the three representatives of the Banatian Swabians met Jászi and asked him to consider the specific interests of the Swabians in delimiting administrative precincts.[30] The dialogue started in a tense atmosphere. Before setting up the agenda, Ştefan Cicio Pop, a Romanian political leader, informed the meeting that it was clear from information he had received at the Central Romanian National Council, that more and more villages of the Banat were the scene of mistreatment and killing of Romanian people. Jászi promised that the Hungarian authorities would investigate all reprehensible acts and that those found guilty would be punished.

After listening to the Romanian demands, the Hungarian minister of nationalities proposed the establishment, before the Paris Peace Conference, of some national blocs with their own governance in the Banat. They were to function within the Hungarian borders, and it was stressed that they could be a solution for holding off the Communist danger. The Romanian delegates delayed their answer until the following day. When discussions were resumed, Iuliu Maniu participated, along with representatives of the Banatian Swabians. The Romanians did not accept the proposed solution and the dialogue continued in the same tense atmosphere. Jászi made a new proposal, according to which his government agreed that Romanians could take over the administration of the cities and counties where they had a majority, on condition that the existing laws would be provisional and that the officials, with the exception of the prefects and governmental commisioners, would remain in their positions. This offer was dismissed too, and the Romanian leaders demanded the recognition of absolute sovereignty over the territories under discussion. At the end of the talks, the Hungarian delegation held a press conference, and the Romanians issued a press release through which the failure of the talks was announced to the public.

Parallel with the Arad talks, the Hungarian government was involved in negotiations with the representatives of the Entente in Belgrade. The documents of the armistice concluded on 3 November on the Italian front stipulated that the Allies had the right to occupy strategic positions throughout the Austro-Hungarian Monarchy. Following separation from Austria, the Hungarian government led by Mihály Károly was looking for the means to ensure his state's integrity. At the beginning of November, a Hungarian delegation went to Belgrade for talks with General Louis Frachet d'Esperey. After a number of meetings, a military convention was signed. If for the French general the document had only military importance, for the Hungarian government it was a political statement. The executive led by Mihály Károly regarded the convention as an armistice, signifying an international acknowledgement of the frontiers of its state.

As for the Serbs, their political leaders declared, even at the beginning of the war, that one of their main objectives was the union of the Serbs, Croats and Slovenes, currently under foreign domination, in a single state.[31] After the Bulgarian withdrawal from the war, the military units of the Serbian army, together with those of the French, advanced north, liberating in a short time the whole territory of Montenegro and Serbia. On 1 November 1918, they entered Belgrade. Their intention was to continue their advance across the Danube. On 5 November 1918, the Serbian General Headquarters decided that, given the favourable international context, commanders of the major Serbian units should continue their actions across the Danube, one of their objectives being the occupation of the Banat. This action started on 6 November 1918, through the Grădiștea Mare point. After occupying some villages on the left bank of the Danube, they headed to Kusici, Biserica Albă, Lugoj and then went on to Timișoara.[32] It was also stipulated that 'the civil administration will remain in the hands of the current government'.[33]

Taking advantage of the provisions of the military convention signed at Belgrade between the representatives of Hungary and the Entente, the Serbian army entered the Banat, and within a short time had gained control of the whole region.[34] The first Serbian military units entered Timişoara on 17 November 1918. Mayor Josef Geml asked the officers to be tolerant to the citizens. Aurel Cosma called for the protection of Romanians living in the Banat. Colonel Colović gave an assurance that all the inhabitants of the Banat would be treated humanely. In parallel, the civil guard was dissolved, responsibility for keeping order being handed over to the police, assisted by the soldiers of the Serbian army. Francisc Bee, as chief of police in Timişoara, announced to the population that, in agreement with the Serbian command, every citizen should wear the colours of the community he belonged to. A Serbian army circular stated that whoever insulted or hit a Serbian soldier would face capital punishment. By controlling the region, the Serbian authorities reached an agreement with those in Timişoara. According to this, the Serbian army would have military control, and the People's Council the civilian authority. A few days later, a delegation led by Jákobi Koloman went to Budapest, obtaining the approval of Count Mihály Károly's government to the agreement. Otto Roth was appointed governor of the Banat, and Emerik Tökes became prefect of Timiş County. On one hand, we can see the recognition of a cosmopolitan, autonomous and independent region – an idea supported mostly by Timişoara and its politicians. On the other hand, taking into account the nationalist views, a dispute between the Romanian, Serbian and Hungarian states emerged, each claiming the right to integrate and administrate the Banat of Timişoara.

In the meantime, the local Serbian national councils decided to subordinate themselves to the Central Serbian National Council in Novi Sad, which began its activities on 3 November 1918. The same council organised a large popular assembly of the Slavic people of the Banat, Bačka and Baranja. The Slavic people, both men and women, aged 20 and over, were to appoint their delegates in the city halls, each elected person representing 1,000 voters. Thirty-six localities from the Banat sent 72 delegates to the Serbian National Assembly which met on 25 November 1918. The Czech, Slovakian and Krashovani representatives (Slavic-language communities) refused to participate. The 757 delegates from 211 localities within the Banat decided to separate their territories from Hungary and unite with the Serbian kingdom. On 1 December in Belgrade, the Kingdom of Serbs, Croats and Slovenes was proclaimed. The Novi Sad Assembly elected a Grand National Council with legislative powers and an executive body named the People's Administration.[35]

On 30 December 1918, Otto Roth, the government commissioner, sent a letter to the commander of the French army, informing him that the commander of the Serbian occupation troops had asked him repeatedly to resign, in order to replace him and the mayor of Timişoara with officials appointed by the Serbian National Council in Novi Sad. In the event of refusal, the Serbian Council threatened the use of force. The two political leaders of Timişoara refused to leave their positions. They asked the French general to intervene with the Serbian authorities in order to respect the provisions of the Belgrade armistice. At the same time, they promised to do everything possible to maintain public order, and to supply provisions for the population and the occupying army.[36]

In order to strengthen his position, Otto Roth initiated a plan to reorganise the People's Council. It was to be transformed into a People's Parliament of the Banat, consisting of 150 deputies, one for every 10,000 citizens. As executive body, a council of 15 would be elected.[37] On 20 February 1919 the Serbian authorities intervened using force, the People's Council was dissolved, lawyer Marin Filipon was appointed prefect, engineer Reinhold Heegen as mayor, and Colonel Mihai Jivanovici as commander of police. At the same time, the national councils were dissolved. These measures violated the provisions of the Belgrade military convention and triggered an adverse reaction from the local population. On the morning of 21 February a general strike was launched. The trains stopped running. In order to overcome the stalemate, the Serbian authorities were forced to start negotiations and sign a protocol that provided for the observance of citizen rights and freedoms.

With the help of some French officers, Otto Roth managed to take refuge in Arad. He drafted a memorandum asking the French government to support the establishment of an independent Banat, so that intercommunity conflicts could be resolved and the partition of the region could be avoided. After analysing the proposal, the French authorities concluded that this was unachievable. At the same time, the new Serbian administration decided to take action in three directions: (1) attracting German inhabitants, (2) intimidating the Romanians and (3) displaying a tolerant attitude towards the Hungarians. A report of the 2nd Bureau of the Staff of the French 11th Colonial Division, recorded that the Serbian National Party, under the leadership of engineer Pilić who was responsible for propaganda, was aiming to create a shift of opinion favourable to Serbia.[38]

Historian Victor Neumann has revealed in several of his documentary and theoretical studies on the physiognomy of the region that ideas on politics and identity and on local and regional administration reflected not only the chaos of the Dual Monarchy, but also ignorance regarding the sociocultural realities of the Banat. Many of the citizens of Timişoara and the neighbouring region had been confused by the opinions expressed first by Vienna and Budapest and later by Belgrade and Bucharest. Not being segregated on the basis of language, nationality or religion, the people of Timişoara and a large portion of those of the Banat regarded their region as a European melting pot. Contradictions based on national criteria were not theirs. For them, identity was related to the peculiarities of the area, to the cross-border world by which the people had been shaped and expressed themselves. In any case, as far as the population of cities was concerned, it defined itself by multiple affiliations, by multilingualism and interculturality, by citizenship, and less (if ever) by the so-called specifics associated with the concept of nationality and/or nation. It was not by chance that Social Democrat orientation had a share in regional political life, by campaigning for peaceful cohabitation, for the integration of all inhabitants and against the war. The ideologies, interventions and decisions of external regions had no direct connection with the complex realities of this region. Starting from such a situation, rarely found in Europe, we see the political challenges of the time and the way in which the population reacted and adapted to them. Controversies over nationalist dogma had become accentuated during the Dual Monarchy at the end of the nineteenth century, questioning, for the first time, regional cosmopolitism and ecumenism. As for the Banat of Timișoara, even if this dogma did not create havoc as it did elsewhere, it was received here too, contributing to the disputes between the three states, Romanian, Serbian/Yugoslavian and Hungarian, and also to the partition of the region.

THE BANAT DURING THE DEBATES OF THE PARIS PEACE CONFERENCE

The occupation of the greater part of the Banat by the Serbian army led the government from Bucharest to launch a propaganda campaign against its former ally. The Romanian authorities accused Serbia of terrorising the Romanians in the Banat and of hampering the activity of the delegates who took part in the Great National Assembly at Alba Iulia. Romanian Prime Minister I.C. Brătianu demanded clarifications from the Belgrade government,[39] who answered that their country was not engaged by the alliance of 1916 and that their troops were occupying the Banat at the request of the French general staff. Faced with this situation that could degenerate into a military conflict, the Entente representatives called on their governments to send a military force to prevent the outbreak of a conflict between the two states and to ease tension among the nationalities that lived in the region. This explains the emergence, as early as December 1918, of the first French army detachments formed by colonial units from Morocco and Algeria. They were led by General Jouinot-Gambetta, who set up his command point at the Lloyd Palace, in the centre of Timișoara. Later, the 11th Colonial Division, under the command of General Léon Farret, was mobilised. The French military authorities stationed in the Banat received the order to replace the Serbian troops from the east of the region.

At the end of the war, there was a tense situation in the Banat. One option, which corresponded to the provisions of the international treaty signed in August 1916 by the Romanian government and the great Entente powers, envisaged the integration of the whole region within the Kingdom of Romania. A second view, that of the Kingdom of Serbs, Croats and Slovenes, claimed the entire Banat or at the very least a part of it. The third belonged to recently established German political and military formations that supported the organisation of the Banat as an autonomous entity.[40]

The Romanian delegation led by Brătianu made a short stop in the Serbian capital, the prime minster wishing to demonstrate that he did not want a deterioration of relations with the neighbouring country, but rather a rational understanding of the border delimitation. The Serbian claims upon a part of the Banat were conditioned by Belgrade's position and by the 250,000 Serbs who lived in the western part of the region. Brătianu took into account the fact that 300,000 Romanians lived within the Serbian state and he was willing to draw the border along the Danube River.

The negotiations failed. In Paris, taking note of the Romanian–Serbian dispute, the Supreme Council decided to invite the representatives of the two delegations to present their claims. Then, on 3 February 1919, eight experts were appointed to study territorial issues relating to Romania: Sir Eyre Crowe and Allen W.A. Leeper from Great Britain, André Tardieu and Jules Laroche from France, Giacomo de Martino and Count Vanutelli-Rey from Italy, Clive Day and Charles Seymour from the United States.

The president of the Territorial Commission, André Tardieu, informed the two delegations that the decision had been made to give the western part of the Banat, where the Serbian-speaking inhabitants were in the majority, to the Kingdom of Serbs, Croats and Slovenes, and the eastern part, where the Romanian speakers were in the majority, to the Kingdom of Romania. The Romanian delegation were not happy with this and submitted a new statement, arguing for the continuity of the Romanian element within the territory. The statement was supported by a speech from the leader of the Romanian delegation, insisting upon the fact that Banat was a region in its own right, one and indivisible.

Answering the intervention of the Romanian prime minister, the Territorial Commission suggested that the Supreme Council appoint a commission to visit the region and gather information based on which the Territorial Commission could make fair proposals regarding the border between the two states. Following this request, the Supreme Council appointed two American experts. On 19 February 1919, Goedwin and Davison arrived in Timișoara and met General Farret from France and the Serbs General Gruić and Bishop Letić. They also held discussions with the representatives of all the nationalities. The report drafted after the discussions describes the tense situation created by the presence of Serbian army.

The situation found by the American commission is supported by a telegram sent to the American delegation at the Peace Conference.

> The Serbian National Council of Novi Sad has enforced its total control upon Torontal County and part of Timiş County and continues to extend its authority upon the entire region ... The Serbian military patrols have committed more crimes against the inhabitants, illegally dispossessing them of material goods, without any effort from the superior authorities to calm down and punish the soldiers' excesses. For these reasons, there is a state of general discontent at Timişoara ... This explains Otto Roth's actions, supported by an important segment of citizens, intending the proclamation of the autonomous republic of Banat.[41]

The social and economic dissatisfaction had a partial connection with the presence of the Serbian army. It did not simply represent a reaction to the abuses of the Serbian soldiers stationed in the region but had several other causes. Otto Roth's actions showed an interest in social protection, in keeping the region under a single administrative unit, in the continuation of the multi- and intercultural life of the inhabitants of the region. There were aspirations that were opposed to regional partition, supported by most of the citizens of Timişoara and part of the population of the Banat.[42]

After repeated negotiations, on 23 May 1919 the Council of Foreign Ministers meeting in Paris received the report of the Territorial Commission on the demarcation of the Romanian–Serbian border according to the solution proposed by the French experts. The leader of the Romanian delegation, Brătianu, made it known that Romania was prepared to give to Bulgaria the area called Southern Dobruja in exchange for the western part of the Banat, while Serbia was to be compensated with Vidin.[43] Brătianu's proposal was not taken into consideration. Romanian public opinion was attentively following the debates of the Paris Peace Conference. The Supreme Council's decision of 21 June 1919 regarding the partition of the Banat was received with indignation in Romania, protests taking place in many cities. One of the largest protests took place on the Liberty Field of Lugoj, with 70,000 participants from the Banat. A similar manifestation took place in Timişoara at the beginning of August 1919.[44] In their turn, the Swabian representatives organised a gathering of over 1,000 Banatian Germans. The *Banatul* newspaper noted the debates and the objectives of a resolution drafted by Michael Kausch:

> In the name of all the Banatian Swabians we declare that only from an unpartitioned Banat can we hope for the good of each nation of the Banat, because a Banat divided into unnatural borders would mean economic ruin for all the people who live here, and would be cause for continual quarrels and dissatisfaction and a disturbance of the desired peace. In consequence, we wish for an undivided Banat.[45]

On 15 August 1919, a delegation of Swabian Banatians presented themselves in Sibiu to hand over to the Romanian Provisional Government the text of the resolution adopted on 10 August in Timișoara.

During the last days of July 1919, under pressure from international events and decisions, the Serbian troops withdrew from the eastern part of the Banat, which was returned to Romania. The proposed border had a temporary nature, the relations between the two countries continuing to be tense. On 10 August 1920, the Treaty of Sèvres was signed, the diplomatic act being accepted on 28 October 1920 by the Romanian government led by General Alexandru Averescu and sealed by the foreign minister, Take Ionescu. The demarcation line among the two states was to be finalised by a mixed commission comprised of seven members (five foreign and two local). Due to the persistence of French diplomacy, in the autumn of 1920 and the spring of 1921, more official meetings between the representatives of the two countries took place, a mixed commission having the task of finalising the frontier line. That happened only in 1924, after long debates and negotiations, when the common dynastic and political interests of the two states became a priority.

CONCLUSIONS

The end of the war was followed by the redrawing of the European map by the victorious powers. According to the principle of national self-determination formulated by President Woodrow Wilson, an American far from the European realities, the Austro-Hungarian Monarchy was to be split into nation states. The principle of division was ethnolinguistic. The language spoken by the majority of the population from a particular territory was considered a sufficient criterion for the delimitation of a new state. Local aspects, populations with double or multiple identities were ignored. Central Europe, more precisely the territory within the borders of the former Austria-Hungary which was dissolved at the end of the war, included a large number of linguistic and cultural groups that had to find a way to continue to live together in the same areas, but under different dominant cultures and policies.

The drawing-up of the new borders ignored the populations of multicultural areas. To further complicate the situation, often the historical principle was applied instead of the linguistic one. In other cases, a mixed formula of the two criteria was preferred. The example of Poland is relevant here, which invoked the linguistic right to the west, comprising territories from Germany which included numerous German people, and the historic right to the east, integrating Belarussians, Ukrainians and Russians. The result was the appearance of some nation states in form only. In reality, these included populations which had lived together for centuries and which, during the war, fought for opposing camps. They faced the situation of either being included within the borders of the state with whom they had been at war, or to live together within the borders of a new state, as was the case of Czechs and Germans in Czechoslovakia.

The reconfiguration of Europe's borders also affected the Banat. After the war, following the Paris talks, it was decided to partition the Banat upon linguistic, geographical and strategic criteria. As an imperial province, the Banat was demarcated by the Mureș, Tisza and Danube rivers and by the Carpathian Mountains and formed a single administrative unit with its own culture and identity. Some opinions within the Banat demanded the preservation of the province with its traditional borders, in an autonomous formula. Others demanded its integration in different proportions, on linguistic criteria, within Serbia, Romania and Hungary. The ethnonationalist ideology manifested in 1918 (and in the years before the war), against the background of President Wilson's Fourteen Points, stirred up frictions between Germans, Hungarians, Romanians and Serbs, even though their communities had lived peacefully together for centuries. The presence of the French troops in the region to mediate between Romanians and Serbs is relevant from the perspective of ending the military and civil conflicts.

Finally, the partition of the Banat among the three neighbouring countries ignored the regional peculiarities resulting from the synthesis of several linguistic groups, cultures, religions and traditions formed within the context of the Austrian civilisation.[46] Although subject to the centralising and Romanianising policies of the interwar governments in Bucharest, the part of the Banat included in Romania retained its local identity and multi- and intercultural footprint. An examination of the roots and an understanding of the facts presented here should not ignore the fact that we are talking about a historical time and about a geographical area where ethnic issues (*Völkischenation*), or, as it is called today, the cultural identity of the majority people (*Völkischekultur*), dominated understanding and political actions. Sadly, as we can see in the decades that followed the partition, and especially during Fascism and Communism, this way of understanding interhuman relations replaced individual aspirations, affirmation of individuality and an open society.[47]

18

THE PARTITION OF THE BANAT IN 1918–19

The Serbian Historiographical Perspective

Slobodan Bjelica

BETWEEN 1914 AND 1920, during the years of the First World War and the Paris Peace Conference which followed, the territory of the Banat was disputed by three emerging states –Hungary, Greater Romania and Serbia, and Greater Serbia – each of whom had a national outlook which started with the exclusion of the neighbouring countries. During that time, the Banat was populated by different communities: Serbian, Romanian, Hungarian, German, Jewish, Slovakian and others.[1] At the outbreak of the First World War, the Banat was part of Transleithania – the Hungarian part of the Austro-Hungarian Monarchy. All groups of the population were rallied to the Austro-Hungarian army and sent to the front. However, it was obvious to the Austro-Hungarian authorities that the war against Serbia was unpopular and they were suspicious of the intentions of Serbs living in the Banat, many of whom were arrested and imprisoned immediately after the outbreak of the conflict.

Following Austro-Hungarian reprisals in the Banat, the first year of the war produced casualties among civilians, too, for example during the battle of Cer in Serbia. In August 1914, after repelling the Austro-Hungarian troops from its territories, the Serbian army initiated the Srem campaign. A detachment of soldiers crossed the Banat at the village of Borcea, near Pancevo. The Serbian population of the village, which the Austro-Hungarian troops released without a fight, greeted the liberators enthusiastically. When the Serbian troops withdrew a few days later and the Austro-Hungarian units returned, ten of the Serbian villagers were shot and 19 arrested in retaliation.[2]

The victory at Cer and the operations in Kolubara in the autumn of 1914 against the Austro-Hungarian army, who were much better equipped and more numerous, gave heart to the Serbs. The development of the war motivated the Serbian government to explain its objectives in the Niš Declaration of December 1914: the release of all Serbs, Croats and Slovenes and their union with Serbia in a single state – a kind of Piedmont for Southern Slavs (Yugoslavs). This new state was designed to include the Banat, as highlighted by documents which the Serbian officials presented to the representatives of the Triple Entente. As early as December 1914, Prime Minister Nikola Pašić instructed Serbian diplomats in Allied countries to support the claims to Timișoara and the Banat. The historian Stanoje Stanojević presented arguments in favour in a pamphlet entitled *What Does Serbia Want?*.

At the same time, the geographer Jovan Cvijić, one of the most important Serbian savants of the first half of the twentieth century, submitted maps with details of the future Yugoslav state to the Russian representative in Serbia. With regard to the Banat, Cvijić drew the border with Romania along the Tisza River up to the confluence with the Mureș River, then along the Mureș to Lipova. From Lipova, the border would continue either towards the Carpathian Mountains to Orșova on the Danube (the maximum claim) or east to the 'Banatian Montenegro', Reșița and Oravița, towards Liupcova on the Danube (the minimum claim). (The Banatian Montenegro comprises, in Serbian historical memory, a series of villages around Recaș (Cralovac, Petrovaselo, Stanciova and Lucareț).) In May 1915 in London, Cvijić handed the Allies the map containing the Serbian claims to the Banat. In a statement submitted by the Serbian government to the Allied powers, these claims were backed up with ethnic, historical and economic arguments. It was asserted that, within Serbia, the Banat would become the country's green space as well as a territory fit for colonisation with population from other regions.[3]

The intensification of Serbian politics and diplomacy, and the involvement of scientists, was due to information that Romania was also claiming the same territory. As the war advanced, Romania's importance for both sides continued to grow. The Romanians were aware of this and on August 1914 declared their neutrality, even if King Carol I had already signed some secret conventions with the Central Powers before the war. Carol died in September 1914 and his successor, King Ferdinand I, along with politicians headed by Prime Minister Ionel Brătianu, leaned more towards the Triple Entente.

The Central Powers offered Romania Bessarabia (at that time part of the Tsarist Empire), along with the region of Timoc in Serbia, in return for an alliance. Because of Hungary's insistent refusal, Transylvania, which was the main Romanian claim, was not included in the offer. On their side, the powers of the Entente promised Romania territories which were part of Austria-Hungary. Obviously, expansion to the west was more faithful to the Romanian national programme, and this was clearly expressed by public opinion. For example, as early as 1914 Professor Vasile T. Nicolescu had printed a map of Greater Romania on a postcard, with a border extending to the Danube and the Tisza.[4]

This border was not motivated by the presence of a Romanian population between the two rivers, but by the need for the future Greater Romanian state – a potential force in the Balkans – to have natural boundaries. While Serbia was making known its own claims upon the Banat, in May 1915 Constantin Diamandi, the Romanian minister in Petrograd, issued a statement to Sozonov, the Russian minister of foreign affairs, regarding Romanian claims, together with a map that included Bukovina, Transylvania and the whole of the Banat. Sozonov expressed his reservations, especially regarding the claims to the Banat. Unlike him, the Western Allies – mainly the French and the Italians – were more than ready to take into consideration all the Romanian demands, and even pressured the Russians on these matters.[5]

Finally, in August 1916 in Bucharest, a secret military convention was signed between the Entente and Romania, guaranteeing Romania a border from the Tisza to the Danube, with a commitment not to place military sites near Belgrade. The war against Austria-Hungary was backed by the Romanian population. Even if this military convention was never advertised, public opinion openly discussed Romanian claims during the war. Transylvania, the Banat and Bukovina were mentioned not only in the newspapers, but also in speeches by members of the Romanian Academy involved in political debate. Aware of Romanian claims to the Banat, the Serbian government, which after the occupation of the country in autumn 1915 had retreated with the army on the Thessaloniki front, was watching Romania's entry into the war with concern. By contrast with the suspicious attitude of the Serbs, the powers of the Entente expected that Romanian involvement would bring about their supremacy over the Central Powers.

However, the Romanian performance on the front was modest. After a successful military incursion in Transylvania, the Romanian army was obliged in October to retreat from the Carpathian line. Reprisals followed for the Romanian civilians of Austria-Hungary who had enthusiastically welcomed the Romanian army, as had happened to the Serbs in Borcea. Banatians were among those arrested, imprisoned and executed.[6] Facing a strong two-pronged offensive from the German, Austro-Hungarian and Bulgarian armies, the Romanian army had to give up the capital and the greater part of the country and concentrate upon Moldavia. On the Dobruja front, a division of Serbian volunteers, consisting of former Austro-Hungarian prisoners (including a large number from the Banat),[7] fought alongside the Romanian and Russian units. The difficult military situation in Romania at the end of 1916 was the catalyst for strong diplomatic activity regarding the Banat issue at Iași, and also on the island of Corfu, to which the Serbian government had retreated.

Even though both countries and governments faced a precarious situation, neither would abandon their aspirations. Pašić repeatedly refused Brătianu's offers to discuss the Banat directly, to avoid acknowledging the secret military convention signed in Bucharest. Moreover, in spring 1917 the Serbian government tried to convince Russia's military representatives to demand the annulment of the convention in exchange for Russian support on the Romanian front. On Pašić's orders, the Serbian ministers in Iași (Pavle Marinković) and Petrograd (Miroslav Spalajković), and especially the military attachés from the two diplomatic missions, were involved. Brătianu himself went to Petrograd for discussions with the Serbian ministry, threatening them with Romanian claims to the Timoc if they did not give up their claims to the Banat.[8]

Shortly after Romania signed a separate peace, there was a sudden change of situation on the western front, followed by the breach of the Thessaloniki front in September 1918. The Serbian army had a decisive role in operations in Macedonia, which rushed the final outcome of the war. After Bulgaria had been taken off the fighting formations of the Central Powers, the Serbian and French units started the northern offensive, which ended on 1 November 1918 with the full liberation of Serbia. Only after that did Romania re-enter the conflict, with a new declaration of war on the Central Powers which were facing capitulation: on 3 November Austria-Hungary signed a truce with the Entente, followed on 11 November by Germany. Thus, the First World War ended. Another danger loomed: a confrontation between the former allies Serbia and Romania over the Banat region.

After the truce with Austria-Hungary, Pašić issued a document urging the Serbian army to advance on the Banat. Therefore, the supreme command of the Serbian army gave the order to occupy the Biserica Albă–Vršac–Timișoara alignment and a territory 10 kilometres east of this line. This was in accordance with the advice of the French general Franchet d'Espèrey. The Serbian army units crossed the Danube on 5 November at Biserica Albă and a day later at Veliko Gradište. The Danube Gorge was occupied on the 7th, Biserica Albă on the 8th, Pancevo on the 9th, Vršac on the 10th, Becicherecul Mare and Timișoara on the 17th, Kikinda on the 18th and Aradul Nou on the 21st. The Serbian army entered the Banat without any resistance, because the Austro-Hungarian army was demobilising and the German units were no longer able to fight.

While the Serbian army was entering the Banat and other Austro-Hungarian territories, the president of the Hungarian government, Mihály Károlyi, went to Belgrade. Together with General Franchet d'Espèrey, he discussed the main conditions for a separate truce between Hungary and the Entente. After prolonged hesitation and surprise that Hungary was considered by the Allied command to be a defeated party in the war, Károlyi signed the Armistice of Belgrade on 13 November. The line of demarcation between the Hungarian army and the Entente powers was established, following the course of the Mureș River. The area to be occupied by Serbian troops was defined by the Orșova–Lugoj–Arad line, while the eastern area was given to the Romanian army. On the day of the armistice, Serbian troops were camped near the Anina–Reșița–Moravița alignment. A week later, they took under their control the entire territory that had been designated for military administration.

French colonial troops soon appeared within the line of delimitation between Serbs and Romanians. They had been called to discourage a potential Romanian–Serbian conflict, which might have unpredictably impeded matters in this part of Europe. The situation was tense, as the Serbian army might face the Romanian army after taking the Banat, as well as the open hostility of the Romanian population. At the same time, the Romanians strongly protested against the arrest of a few hundred of their co-nationals from the Banat, incriminating the Serbian military authorities. Discontent among the Romanian population was also caused by the prohibition on public meetings and pressure for declarations of loyalty to Serbia.

In order to prevent a military conflict, in December 1918 the French demanded the withdrawal of Serbian troops from the Banat – a demand that was refused by Belgrade, even with the possibility of facing the Romanian army. The French insisted that their troops should replace the Serbian ones in a buffer zone along the alignment that followed the western side of the railway linking Timișoara and Vršac, stating that the operation would not impact the final border delimitation. The Serbian supreme command accepted French troops in the area, while refusing to withdraw its own units. Finally, in March 1919 the Serbian army agreed to withdrawal from the Orșova–Lugoj–Lipova alignment, situated 10 kilometres east of Timișoara. This disposition of the occupation zones, which allowed Romanians to administrate the Danube Gorge, Carașova lands and the Banatian Montenegro, remained in place until July.[9]

The threat of Romanian attack was not the only problem the Serbian army faced during its occupation of the Banat. In the autumn of 1918, the region was in a state of anarchy. In the cities, parallel authorities functioned, based on national interests, which had their own armed formations; these did not openly fight, but tried to stop any revolutionary tendency. A large number of deserters from the Austro-Hungarian army, the so-called 'green cadres', were wandering about and were not responsible to any authority. During the process of dissolving the state structures, pillaging, arson, murder and other infractions took place. In October, in the large industrial centres like Timișoara, Lugoj and Arad, workers' demonstrations ended in disarray. Institutions of authority disintegrated, and the discontents demanded 'bread' and 'peace'.[10] Those returning from detention in Russia also had a destabilising influence, having been exposed to revolutionary ideas. At Cusici and Zlatița, the (Serbian) villagers proclaimed a 'Soviet republic' to no effect.[11]

Consequently, the entry of the Entente units into the Banat as an organised military force was regarded favourably by all segments of the population. Social unrest diminished and order was restored.

The anarchy in the Banat which confronted the Serbian, French and Romanian armies was characteristic of the Austro-Hungarian space as a whole, which had disintegrated during the autumn of 1918. Poland, which also integrated the region of Western Galicia, was the first to gain independence. In Prague on 28 October, Czechoslovakia followed suit, and on the 29th in Zagreb, the State of Slovenes, Croats and Serbs came into being (an enlarged form of this became the Kingdom of Serbs, Croats and Slovenes on 1 December). In Budapest, on 31 October, the Hungarian National Council comprised of Social Democrats and Count Károlyi seized power, and 15 days later the Hungarian People's Republic was proclaimed.

The date 31 October 1918 is significant also in the history of the Banat as the day on which Romanians formed their Central National Council, based in Arad, which proclaimed the separation of the province from Hungary. The Serbians from Timişoara founded their own National Council (led by Bishop Gheorghe Letić and General Svetozar Davidov), set up their own national guard, and founded a newspaper. There were parallel councils on ethnic criteria throughout the Banat, aiming to take control of the power vacuum that followed the dissolution of the Austro-Hungarian army. When taking control was difficult, the Serbian army (or the Romanian one, in the case of Romanian councils) intervened. The Germans, Hungarians and other Slavs in the region acted in a similar fashion.

While the Serbs and Romanians from Timişoara were establishing their own councils, the Social Democrat Otto Roth initiated the People's Council and proclaimed the Banat as an independent republic. He was appointed civilian commissioner and Albert Bartha military commissioner. Even though all nationalities had been invited to join the People's Council, it was comprised mostly of Germans and Hungarians. Later on, a citizen guard was founded, as army formation of the Council. The Banat Republic lasted only a week until 7 November.

In spite of promises to institute national equality, social justice and universal suffrage, Otto Roth was unable to convince the Serbs and Romanians to support him. The Central Romanian National Council had been established in Arad, and the Central Serbian National Council, which had initially agreed – in order to keep peace and order – to delegate its own members to the Banat People's Council, on 10 November renounced any collaboration with the Hungarian staff, institutions and press. In parallel, it strengthened collaboration with the other Serbian councils that were forming on Austro-Hungarian territory, of which the Council of Novi Sad, led by the Banatian radical politician and Serbian national rights leader Jaša Tomić, was the most important.[12]

The Council of Novi Sad, the central political body for the territory of the whole of South Hungary, had as its main mission to prepare the Serbians and other Slavs from Hungary for political self-determination. After the elections, when women had the right to vote for the first time, the Great People's Assembly of Serbs, Bunjevci and Slavs from the Banat, Bačka and Baranja met at Novi Sad on 25 November 1918. Among the 757 delegates, there were 393 Banatian Serbians (including 73 from 35 localities in today's Romania).[13] The Council of Novi Sad decided on the separation of the regions it represented from Hungary and union with Serbia. At the same time, it agreed new structures of power: the Grand National Council for the Banat, Bačka and Baranja as the legislative body and the People's Administration with executive authority.

Greater Romania was proclaimed in a similar manner. According to the instructions of the Central National Council of Arad, elections were to be held for the Assembly of Alba Iulia on 1 December 1918. On that day, 1,228 delegates from all over Transylvania and the Banat convened. The Assembly decided on the union of this region with Romania. The Great National Council was elected, along with its executive body (the Directory Council), led by Iuliu Maniu. There were 321 Banatians in the Assembly, among whom were 52 from 20 localities of the future Yugoslav Banat. The Serbian troops from the Banat were unable to obstruct elections for deputies to the Romanian Assembly, but the Romanians complained that a significant number of delegates were not allowed to leave for Alba Iulia.

The organisation of the assemblies of Novi Sad and Alba Iulia, as well as the establishment of the Serbian and Romanian structures of power on Hungarian territory, were contrary to the Armistice of Belgrade, which stipulated that the civil administration should remain under Hungarian control. The takeover of power by Serbians in the western Banat had started before the signing of the armistice, and intensified after the entry of the Serbian divisions. At first, there were Serbian local councils, and from December 1918 the People's Administration for the Banat, Bačka and Baranja started to appoint their own candidates for local administration. The Hungarian government protested to the French against the violation of the provisions of the armistice, but to no avail. The Hungarian local councils from the Banat tried, by different means (for example, the hiding of communal cashier's offices), to stop or at least slow down the process.[14]

In the central area of the Banat, including the city of Timișoara, the situation was totally different.[15] Regardless of the presence of the Serbian army and the establishment of Serbian national councils, the civil administration remained under the authority of the Banatian People's Council, led by Otto Roth. As soon as the Serbian units entered Timișoara, Roth, an able politician, was ready to collaborate, even suggesting that Serbs should continue to advance into Romanian territory, so as to take over the coal mines from the mountainous area. Roth declared that his interest lay in preserving the unity of the Banat, even as a Serbian as opposed to a Romanian territory. The commander of the Serbian army in Timișoara, General Djordje Djordjević, was willing to cooperate with Otto Roth and the Banatian People's Council, hoping that it could bring supporters from the Hungarian, German and Jewish communities. The general was aware that the Banat's main competitors were the Kingdom of Serbs, Croats and Slovenes, and Romania, but not Hungary; consequently, goodwill towards Hungarians, Germans and Jews could decisively turn the odds in favour of the Serbs, in case of an election. General Djordjević's view was supported by the Belgrade government, but not by the People's Administration of Novi Sad for the Banat, Bačka and Baranja.

The administration of Novi Sad tried in December to extend its effective control upon western Banat as far as central Banat, by appointing the lawyer Martin Filipon, from Uljma, as supreme ruler of Caraș and Timiș counties and mayor of Timișoara. General Djordjević refrained from putting this decision into practice, indicating that one person should not hold so many offices. At the same time, he reckoned that it was unwise to exclude the Hungarians and Germans from exercising power, in the context of the Peace Conference and the decisions regarding the Banat. The French command was concerned at the possible turmoil provoked by disregarding the provisions of the Armistice of Belgrade. The People's Administration took note that the Károlyi government was generating continuous national and social propaganda, promising agrarian reform, a republic and so on. In the conflict between General Djordjević and the People's Administration, the Belgrade government supported its military commander, assessing that Novi Sad was promoting a nationalist and counterproductive policy.

The tensions between General Djordjević and the People's Administration became more acute at the end of December, when the general approved the arrangements for the new elections to the Banatian People's Council. Those from the People's Administration were expecting the military to end the existence of the council, not to be concerned for its future. Accusations mounted against Djordjević who was variously labelled as naïve, deceived by Otto Roth and 'Hungarian'. After many tense incidents, Roth successively presenting and retracting his resignation, the Supreme Command of the Serbian Army dismissed Djordjević at the beginning of February because of some older concerns relating to disregarding the provisions of the Armistice of Belgrade and tolerance towards the Hungarian administration.[16]

After this episode, adequate conditions for putting into practice the decisions of People's Administration were created: on 20 February, the new Serbian commander appointed Filipon as great governor,[17] the position of mayor of Timișoara being transferred to the German Reinhold Heegn. At the same time, all people's councils were dissolved, including that of the Banat which submitted a complaint to the French military authorities. The complaint was rejected and, as consequence, a general strike was organised by the Hungarian Social Democrat Party which broke out on the 21st, in Timişoara, Pécs, Subotica and Sombor simultaneously. Reckoning that the motivation was political and not social, the Serbian army interrupted the strike using violence. Thus, the attempt at preserving the Hungarian administration in Timişoara failed, and Otto Roth moved to Budapest. Local power was transferred to the Banatian Serbs, who believed that such a development would be a strong argument in favour of the Serbian delegation at the Peace Conference.[18]

Around the time when the conference convened in January 1919 at Versailles, there were some encounters between Serbian and Romanian diplomatic representatives regarding the fate of the Banat. Serbian Prime Minister Nikola Pašić, during his trip to London at the end of November 1918, met Take Ionescu, leader of the Romanian opposition. They reached a compromise whereby the western extremity of the Banat would be given to the Serbs and the eastern part to the Romanians, while the fate of Timişoara would be decided by the Allies' arbitration. At the same time, the Romanian government pleaded for the enforcement of the military convention signed in Bucharest, while Pašić sent his emissary, Pavle Marković, to Paris to combat the Romanian actions. On the eve of the Peace Conference, at the Serbian Embassy in Bucharest, Romanian offers arrived, asking Serbia to give up the Banat in exchange for the guarantee of a strong friendship between the two countries. Sometimes, these proposals were accompanied by open threats of armed force. Brătianu himself admitted to the Serbian diplomats that, according to the nationality principle, the Serbs had the right to a part of the Banat, but, based on the same logic, Romania also had a claim to the territories between the Timoc and the Morava, which were populated by the Wallachian people. On his way to Paris in January 1919, Brătianu stopped at Belgrade to meet Stojan Protić, the new prime minister of the Kingdom of Serbs, Croats and Slovenes, and the regent Alexander. They discussed the possibility of Romania giving up a small part of the Banat in Belgrade's hinterland, in order for the capital to be protected militarily.[19] Nevertheless, the new Kingdom of Serbs, Croats and Slovenes was not interested in making arrangements with the Romanian side before the Peace Conference. (Since the Kingdom of Serbs, Croats and Slovenes was officially acknowledged by the Allies only in June 1919, the delegation from the Peace Conference counted as a Serbian delegation, even if it included Croats and Slovenes.) They felt that their claims to a larger portion of the Banat were justified by Serbia's performance during the First World War and by the fact that the Serbian army was occupying the parts of the Banat which they claimed from Romania.[20] At the Paris Peace Conference, the Serbian delegation was counting on the concept developed during the war by the Serbian government with regard to the Banat. The more precise border delimitation between the Kingdom of Serbs, Croats and Slovenes and Romania with regard to the Banat was unveiled to the representatives of the great powers by General Petar Pešić, head of the Serbian military mission at the Peace Conference. According to this proposal, the border would be placed approximately 25 kilometres east of Biserica Albă, 30 kilometres east of Vršac, 10 kilometres west of Reșița, and 28 kilometres east of Timișoara, including Lipova up to to the river Mureș and downstream Mureș to the Tisza. General Pešić's reasons were not ethnographic by nature but strategic, aimed mostly at the military safety of Belgrade. At the same time, Romanians presented to the representatives of the victorious powers their maximum claims. This included the Banat in its entirety which, the Romanian delegation insisted, represented a single geographical and economic unit, while Serbians asserted that there was a natural barrier between the Banat of the mountains and of the plain. The British, French and American representatives, having different affinities with one or other, considered both the Romanian and the Serbian claims to be exaggerated.[21]

The Serbian savants who were part of the delegation – Jovan Cvijić, Aleksandar Belić, Jovan Radonić and Stanoje Stanojević – provided strong intellectual support in favour of the claims of the Kingdom of Serbs, Croats and Slovenes. At Pašić's personal request, the delegation included Mihailo Pupin, a well-known North American scientist who was born in the Banat. Due to his prestige among the Americans, he substantially contributed to the success of the Serbian programme. Historian Jovan Radonić was particularly involved in the Banat issue. In 1915 he had drafted an account in French on the region and during the Peace Conference he prepared a few more memoranda, with the intention of reinforcing the historiographic arguments supporting the claims of the Kingdom of Serbs, Croats and Slovenes. Although he did not deny that the present population of the Banat was ethnically diverse, Radonić claimed that the Serbs had been established for longer than the Romanians, who had immigrated later to the Banat. At the same time, he denied that the Romanian population was an ancient people of the region, since Romanians claimed themselves to be Roman descendants. Radonić supported the claims to the whole Banat not only on ethno-historical, geographical and economic grounds, but also on the grounds of the positioning of routes of communication. Another argument was the difference between the contributions of the Romanian and the Serbian militia to the victory of the Triple Entente. Regarding the suggested border, Radonić's ideas totally overlapped with those formulated by General Pešić.[22]

Nikola Pašić, the former Serbian prime minister, was also a member of the delegation of the Kingdom of Serbs, Croats and Slovenes at the Peace Conference. According to him, the eastern part of the Banat should be given to Romania, while the Kingdom of Serbs, Croats and Slovenes should take the western part. Reckoning that the separation should take into consideration not only the ethnic criterion of the time, but also the historical evolution of the area, Pašić referred to the strategic necessities of defending the terrestrial border. That is why he insisted that the Serbo-Romanian border should not pass the Banatian plain, but instead follow the line of the mountain range east of the Banat. Pašić declared in his notes:

> Our separation with Romania in the Banat must be established on such a solid base that it will remain forever unchanged. For as long as we have known each other, there has been no war between these neighbouring countries. At this moment of separation, we wish for this good neighbourliness to be preserved and remain forever immovable. For this reason, too, before deciding on the border between these two peoples, we have to consider the present and the future interest of both parties.[23]

It is interesting that the most ambitious project regarding the Banat border from the Yugoslav delegation was that of the historian Niko Županić, who drew a line starting from Orşova, including the 'Banatian Montenegro', the Caraşova region, passing between Lugoj and Timişoara, up to the Mureş River, thus including in the Yugoslav territory a large part of the mountainous Banat. Grgur Jakšić, a Serbian historian of international relations (although not included in the Yugoslav delegation, being only a member of the press section along with the only Banatian from the delegation, the historian Vasa Stajić), showed his own project for dividing the Banat, at the request of Cvijić,[24] who knew Jakšić's writings; in 1915 he had published the brochure *Le Banat* in Paris. The border proposed by Jakšić was the most modest and left Timişoara on the Romanian side.[25]

All these projects had to be agreed upon during the sessions of the Yugoslav delegation at the Peace Conference. The Croatian members of the delegation insisted that the principle of nationality should prevail over that of strategic interest. Thus, Smodlaka considered that the claims to the Banat had been exaggerated and outgrew the Serbian ethnic space. Nikola Pašić's authoritative opinion imposed itself. By contrast with the case of other disputed territories, he was not willing to revise his opinions about the Banat, declaring that the disputed part of the region was not, from the point of view of homogeneity, Romanian or Serbian; at the same time, German and Hungarian interests were ignored as being those of defeated nations. Pašić believed that the most equitable split would be to give the plain area to the Kingdom of Serbs, Croats and Slovenes, and the mountainous part to Romania. At the end of January 1919, with no great dissension, the Yugoslav delegation adopted Pašić's view.

Representing just one portion of the territorial issues which had to be settled at the Peace Conference, the Yugoslav–Romanian dispute regarding the Banat started to concern the victorious powers since it concerned two

Allied countries whose armies were ready to confront each other. For this reason, the Supreme Council of the Peace Conference decided that the two delegations should be invited to a meeting to express their views. Thus on 31 January 1919, Pašić and Brătianu, along with their supporters, appeared at the Supreme Council before the American President Woodrow Wilson, British Prime Minister Lloyd George, French Prime Minister Clemenceau, Italian Prime Minister Vittorio Emanuele Orlando and the Japanese delegates. It had been settled that each of the two parties were to present their arguments and then leave. The first to plead was Brătianu, presenting in a memorandum the Romanian views, which were based first on the authority of the military convention of Bucharest and then on ethnographic and geographic arguments in favour of his own thesis: that of the unity of the Banat which should not be divided. He also brought into discussion the 'Wallachian issue' as a counterweight to Serbian claims in the Banat; even though he demanded the entire territory between the Danube, the Mureș and the Tisza, he was open to the idea of a protected area around Belgrade.

The Yugoslav delegates followed, but did not present any previously prepared memorandum. Pašić, Trumbić and Milenko Vesnić (the Serbian minister in Paris) freely addressed the representatives of the Conference, highlighting that, unlike the Romanians, who signed secret agreements, with regard to the Banat they were exclusively invoking the principle of national self-determination, which struck a chord with the American delegates. Then they appealed to the historical links between the Banat and Serbia (comparing them to those between the Île-de-France and France, or between Tuscany and Italy), without ignoring the Banat's importance for the Morava Valley (the field of the last Serbian–French offensive (at the Salonica front), in the autumn of 1918, which left Bulgaria and Austria-Hungary out of the war, hastening the armistice). The memorandum of the Serbian delegation was drafted a few days later and presented to the delegates of the victorious powers. It comprised an ample elucidation of the known positions and claims, with the amendment that, alongside the nationality principle, the strategic principle was much accentuated. As proof of the modest demands of the Serbian delegation, it presented data suggesting that, based on the ethnical configuration of the Serbian and other Slavic populations, the Kingdom of the Serbs, Croats and Slovenes was entitled to demand the eastern Banat, too, but would abstain from this claim. The final line of the Serbian claims was more modest than previously and did not include Lipova and its neighbourhoods. Essentially, the proposed borderline went from the Danube, east from Moldova Veche, to the Mureș, south of Arad, including Biserica Albă, Vršac, Great Kikinda and Timișoara.

The arguments expressed to the Allies indicated the antagonism between the two delegations regarding the Banat, in all but one respect: both the Yugoslavs and the Romanians denied the possibility that the Hungarians, whom they regarded as a defeated nation, should be consulted in matters relating to the territory. (At the same time, it was considered that the Banatian Germans, geographically split from their country of origin, were in no position to make any demands. However, on the initiative of the Banatian Germans, in the spring of 1920 a proposal was made at the Conference, regarding the establishment of the independent Banatian Republic, which, alongside the Banat, would include Bačka, thus having 2,350,000 inhabitants. This idea was not successful, though.[26])

The next day, the Romanians presented to the Allied statesmen their claims to Dobruja, Transylvania, Bukovina and Bessarabia. The absence of Serbian representatives at this meeting was exploited by Brătianu who hoped to secure the withdrawal of Serbian troops from the Banat, accusing them of various abuses. However, Lloyd George rejected a discussion about the Banat in the absence of the Serbian delegates, so the issue was entrusted to a special commission which would analyse the issues arising from the new Romanian borders. In February the Romanian and Serbian representatives had further opportunities to express their arguments to this commission. The Serbian delegation formulated the idea of a plebiscite so that the population could decide which state should take the disputed central territory of the Banat (including the city of Timișoara). The Romanian arguments – the military convention of Bucharest and the Wallachian population of Serbia – had been disproved by the thesis that the secret convention had been cancelled by the Romanian capitulation, while the Wallachian population of Timoc 'never wanted to become a part of the Romanian nation'.[27]

In March 1919, in reaction to the alarming news that Romania was to get not only Timișoara but also Vršac, Kikinda and Biserica Albă, the Yugoslav representatives intensified their activity to convince their foreign colleagues to reject such a decision, arguing on the grounds of the large number of volunteers coming from this territory and enrolled in the Serbian army.[28] The Great People's Council for Banat, Bačka and Baranja also expressed its view, during the meetings of its second session on 27 February 1919, and issued a new request to the Paris Peace Conference, claiming the union of its regions with Serbia. A plebiscite in Timișoara was officially requested for 2 April.

The Territorial Commission of the Conference finally decided on 6 April that the Banat should be partitioned: Biserica Albă, Vršac and Kikinda being given to Serbia; Timișoara and western Banat to Romania; Szeged and its environs to Hungary. The Serbian delegation was finally content with this solution, taking into consideration that their losses in the Banat could have been greater. The plebiscite in Timișoara never took place. The Yugoslavs, concerned not to lose more in the context of Romanian armed intervention against Béla Kun's government,[29] were satisfied.

On 18 May the Serbian delegation tried, by an intervention to Clemenceau, the president of the Peace Conference, to reopen discussions regarding the border issues, among which was the dispute over the Banat. Then, it again addressed the Territorial Commission, demanding a correction of the demarcation line, in order to ensure the continuation of the railway line of Biserica Albă–Vršac–Great Kikinda. The Banat issue was brought into discussion with the eventual mutual compensations of Bulgaria, Romania and the Kingdom of Serbs, Croats and Slovenes. The representatives of the Allies intended to make concessions to Romanians in the Banat, and in return, Romania was to give Dobruja to Bulgaria, and Bulgaria deliver Vidin to the Kingdom of Serbs, Croats and Slovenes. On 23 May the meeting of the foreign ministers of the great powers accepted the border in the configuration which was unchanged from the initial proposal of the Territorial Commission.[30]

At the same time, a 'propaganda war' was developing in the Serbian, Romanian and even the Allied press. In May, more gatherings were held in Romania, which demanded, under the threat of war, the urgent withdrawal of the Serbian army from the Banat. The Romanian government issued an official protest to the Serbian legation in Bucharest, regarding gunshots on Romanian border guards presumed to come from the Serbian side of the Danube. The Kingdom of Serbs, Croats and Slovenes itself expected, if not an attack, at least a provocation from the Romanian army, and were in readiness to respond. In the Allied countries, there were rumours that Brătianu had decided on war, but also an assurance that the victorious powers would never allow such a conflict.

In the Banat, even during the dispute, there had been different incidents. On 19 June, the Romanian authority closed the dam on the channel near Lugoj (Coștei), which resulted in the interruption of water flow from Timiș to Bega and the cutting off of the electricity and water supply to Timișoara, which was still under Serbian authority.[31] Therefore, the Serbian delegation intervened on 1 July, requiring that the temporary authority from Lugoj should be transferred from the Romanian army to the French troops, in order to avoid similar incidents in the future. The potential participation of the Serbian army in the armed intervention in Hungary was discussed. Against the background of these discussions, the Serbian delegation again requested that the border in the Banat be corrected. In July 1919, the Romanian army intervened against the Hungarian Communists and in August occupied Budapest.

In the summer of 1919, petitionary activity intensified from the areas that, according to the Peace Conference, were not to be part of the Kingdom of the Serbs, Croats and Slovenes, but which desired to be. Ten Serbs from the Banat went to Paris, and presented the Peace Conference with the resolutions of the popular gatherings which demanded that the 'Banatian Montenegro', the Danube Gorge and the city of Timișoara should be attached to the Kingdom of Serbs, Croats and Slovenes. Among the petitions that were sent to Paris in 1919, apart from those of the Serbs, there were some signed by Slovakians or other Banatian Slavs. Counting on these documents and on the conviction that the Germans, Hungarians and even Romanians from Timișoara would vote for the union with the Kingdom of Serbs, Croats and Slovenes, on 11 July the Serbian delegation requested again that the Peace Conference agree to hold a plebiscite in Timișoara, mentioning the principle of national self-determination. The establishment of an international commission was proposed, to take into consideration the state of mind of the local population.[32]

Similar actions were organised by the Romanians. In the summer of 1919, a group of Slovaks sent a telegram to Eduard Beneš, the Czechoslovakian foreign minister and participant at the Peace Conference, demanding acknowledgement of the decisions in Alba Iulia. At the gathering of 10 August in Timișoara, the Banatian Germans adopted a declaration expressing their wish to live in Romania and brought it to the Peace Conference.[33] But Germans were among the participants at Serbian gatherings, too. Petitions were also formulated by Banatian Hungarians, who demanded a plebiscite in which the population of the Banat could freely express its membership to one or other of the states. This 'petitionary war' continued, with appeals arriving from the lands which were disputed at the Conference.

Despite all the efforts of the Serbian delegation in Paris, in mid-July Franchet d'Espèrey commanded the Serbian army to leave the Banat on the alignment decisively established by the Council at the Peace Conference. The Serbs delayed and protested, knowing that the withdrawal of the army would block any chance of revising the border. On the eve of retreat, the army took industrial installations, cattle and other goods – this was personally observed by d'Espèrey on the occasion of his visit to Timișoara. These practices generated discontent among the Allied powers and even more among the people of Timișoara. There were rumours about the dissatisfaction of the local Serbs, and of Serbian soldiers and officers, whose commander tried to appeal to the army to resist. At the assembly of Modoš, a resolution of Serbs and Croats was adopted, showing their desire to oppose the Romanians, again appealing to army resistance. Finally, though, on 28 July, the Serbian units evacuated Timișoara and its surroundings, being replaced first by the French and then by the Romanians.[34]

The Supreme Council of the Peace Conference issued the definitive decision regarding the Banat on 1 August 1919. The proposal of the Territorial Commission on 25 July ignored the Serbian claims to revise the border, excepting the northern extremity of the Banat. The Serbs claimed some villages around Szeged, arguing that Hungarian authorities were mistreating local Serbs. The Commission was to decide later upon this issue. With the adoption of the proposals of the Territorial Commission by the Supreme Council, the Serbian mission ended. It did not try to achieve any territorial rectification from the Romanians, for fear that the latter, after their successful intervention against the Hungarian Communists, might intervene in the Banat, too. The Romanian side firmly decided to take military action in the Banat, and this was confirmed by Take Ionescu to the Serbian diplomatic representative in Bucharest. The Kingdom of Serbs, Croats and Slovenes was afraid of a Romanian–Bulgarian joint attack and, in consequence, mentioned the involvement of Czechoslovakia and Greece in this scenario. At the same time the Serbs warned the Peace Conference of Romanian propaganda and the bellicose reactions from the Banat. The French became aware of the complexity of the situation. They reassured Belgrade that a possible Romanian attack would mean a revolt against the Peace Conference. During September, there were armed incidents on the line of demarcation. Reports of mistreatment of the Serbian population were issued. A concentration of troops was observed on both sides. The threat of war in the Banat was eliminated when Brătianu's government fell.[35]

The new government, led by Alexandru Vaida-Voievod, adopted a pacifist policy towards the Serbian government and in November showed its willingness to compromise regarding the Banat. Nevertheless, after all the trials and threats of armed conflict, the Serbian delegation was sufficiently pleased with the partition, giving up the Serbian villages of Sirig, Saint Ivan the New and Deska from the northern Banat, to Hungary. On 4 July 1920, the Treaty of Trianon was signed with Hungary. It finally closed the issue of the Banat, all three parties being left with unfulfilled ambitions. The Kingdom of the Serbs, Croats and Slovenes received a surface area of 9,000 kilometres, Romania received 18,000 kilometres, and Hungary 271 kilometres. With small rectifications made in the first half of the 1920s, the Banat preserves the same configuration today.

In conclusion, the period between 1914 and 1920 is decisive in the history of the Banat. The military operations, backstage diplomatic games and difficult negotiations during the Paris Peace Conference decided the future of this multinational region. The historiography – whether Serbian, Romanian or Hungarian – has tackled the issue of the Banat exclusively as a paradigm of nationality. Future generations of historians will have the task of overcoming these limitations in the interests of constructing a complete and plausible narrative of the past of the region. They are impeded by the mutual ignorance of the three historiographies, mirrored by the small number of translations of the most important works regarding this theme in the languages of the neighbours. The conviction of this author is that such study could contribute to a more detached understanding of the history of the Banat, from a position of dialogue among the historiographies of the neighbouring countries.

PART VI

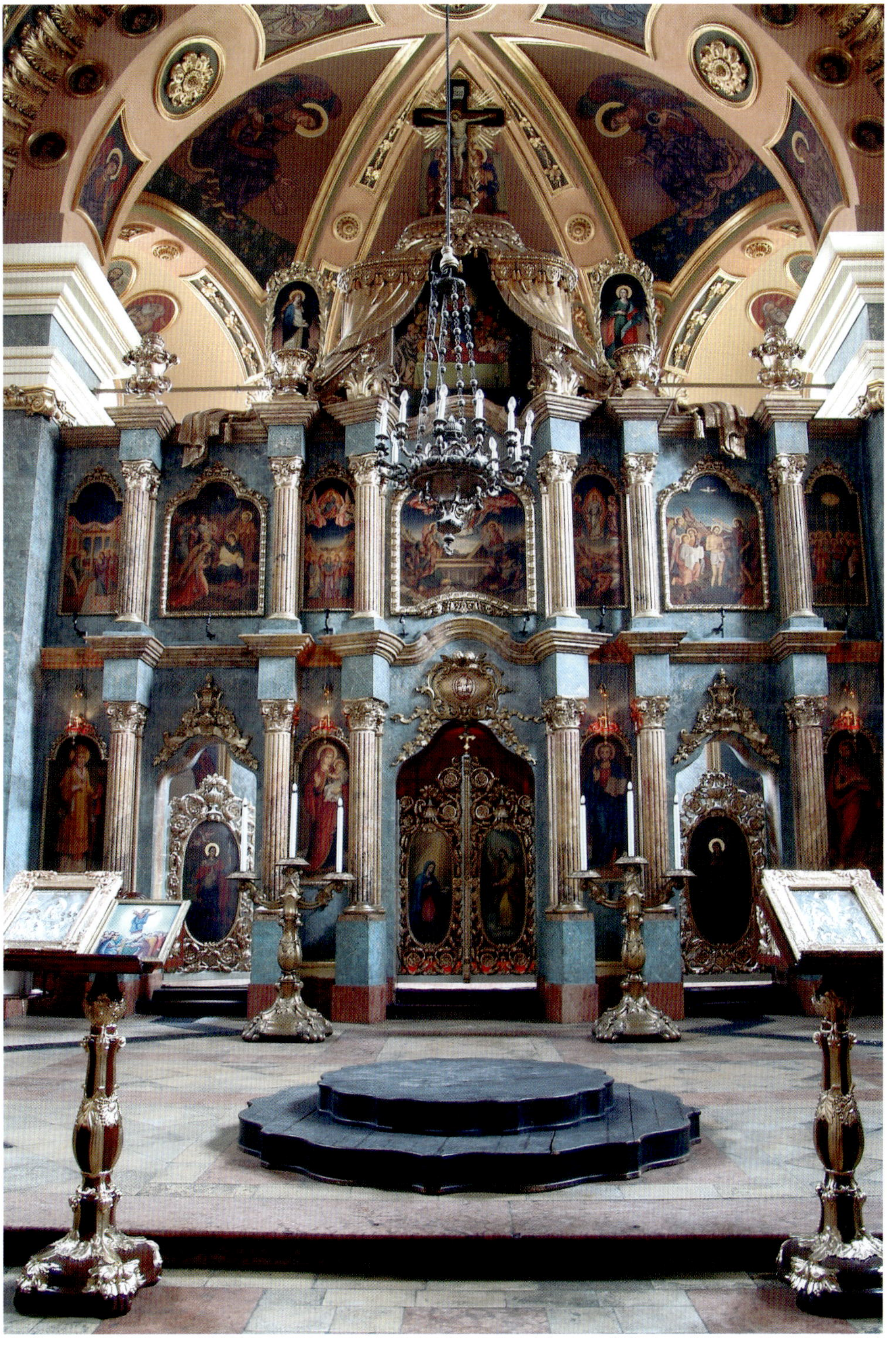

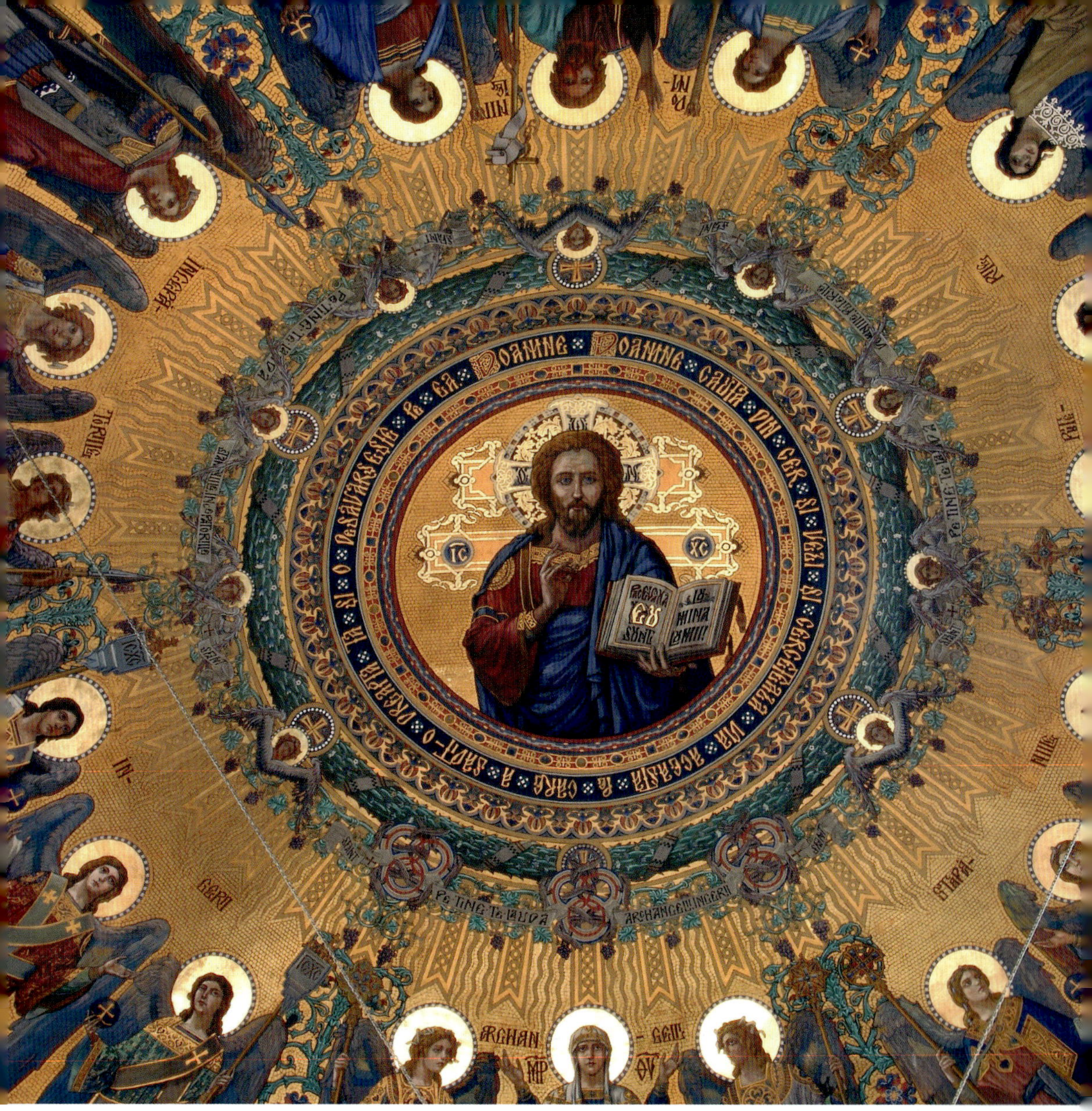

Plate 18 *(previous page)*
Iconostasis of the 'Adormirea Maicii Domnului' (Assumption of the Virgin Mary) Orthodox church of Lugoj, built 1759–66 by Knyaz (Prince) Gavril Gureanu in the Austrian Baroque style; doors painted 1819–21 by Pavel Giurcovici; oil paintings by Aurel Ciupe (1900–85); icon of the Assumption by Anastase Demian (1899–1977)

Plate 19 *(above)*
Dome of the neoclassical 'Pogorârea Sfântului Spirit' (Descent of the Holy Spirit) Greek Catholic church of Lugoj (architect: L. Oettinger; built 1843–54), showing Christus Pantocrator by Moritz Breyer (1868; restored 1929–34 by Virgil Simionescu)

Plate 20 *(opposite top)*
One of a cycle of four frescoes by Virgil Simionescu (1881–1941) in the 'Pogorârea Sfântului Spirit' church in Lugoj, depicting the Passion of Christ

Plate 21 *(opposite bottom)*
Overview of the central square of Lugoj

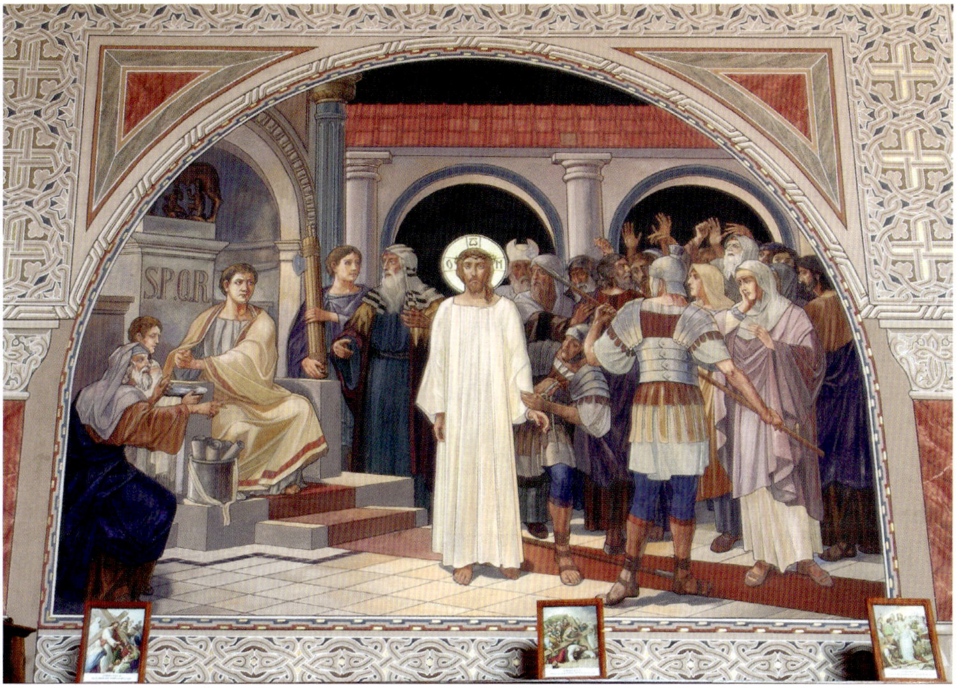
S.P.Q.R.

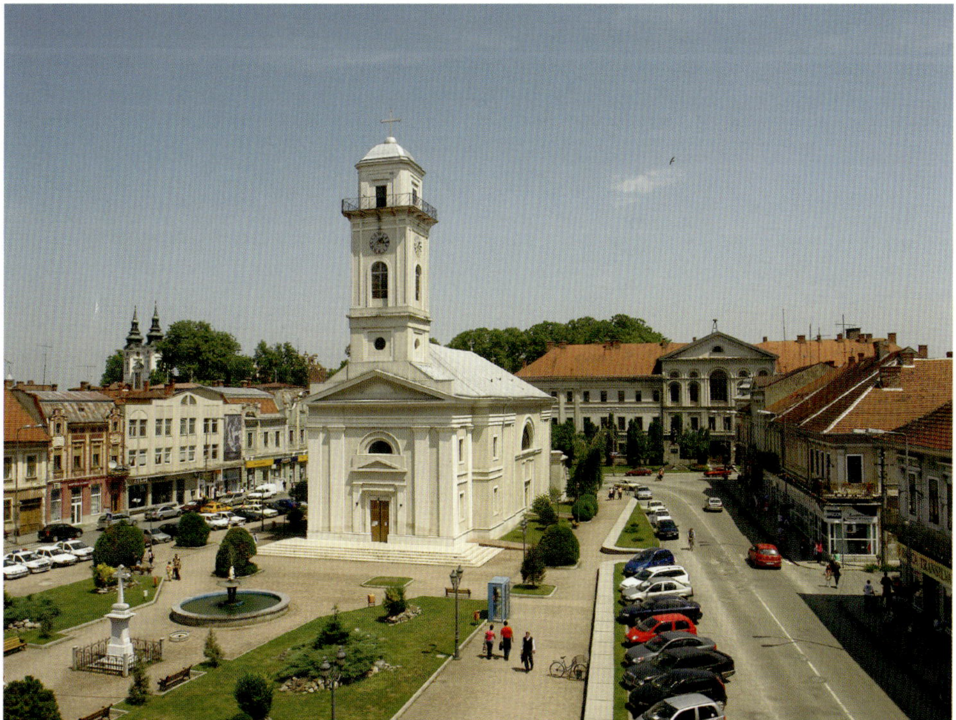

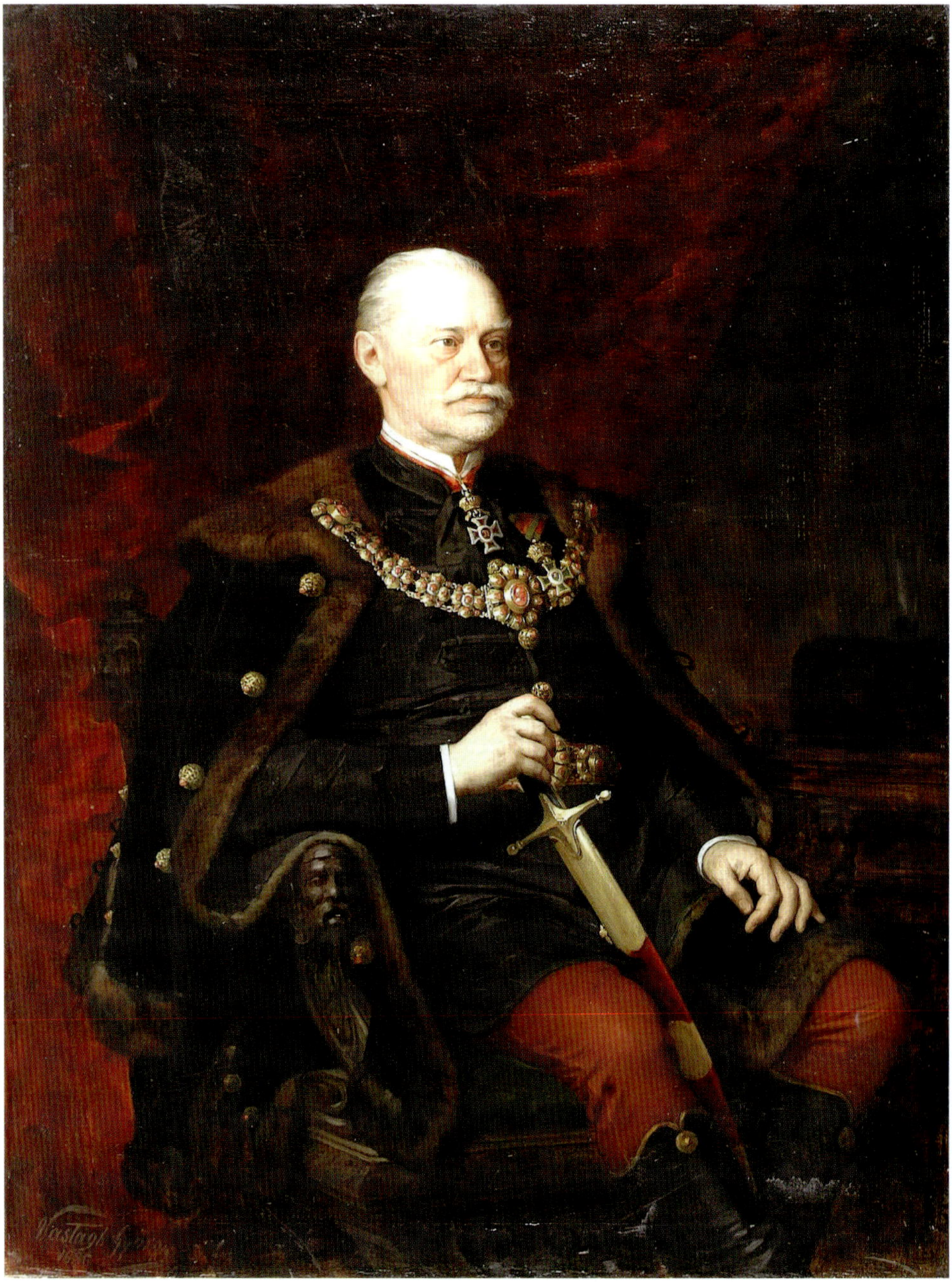

Plate 22
Portrait of Sigismund (Zsigmond) Ormós (1813–94), founder of the Timișoara Museum of History, Art and Archaeology, by George (György) Vastagh (1834–1922), oil on canvas (1889)

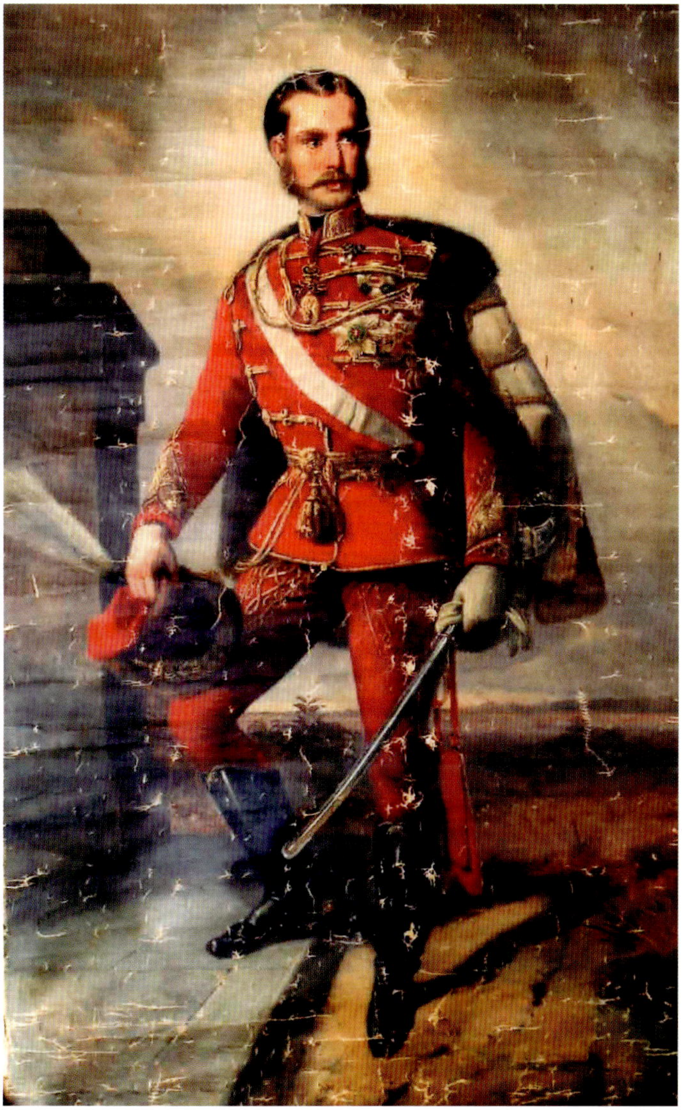

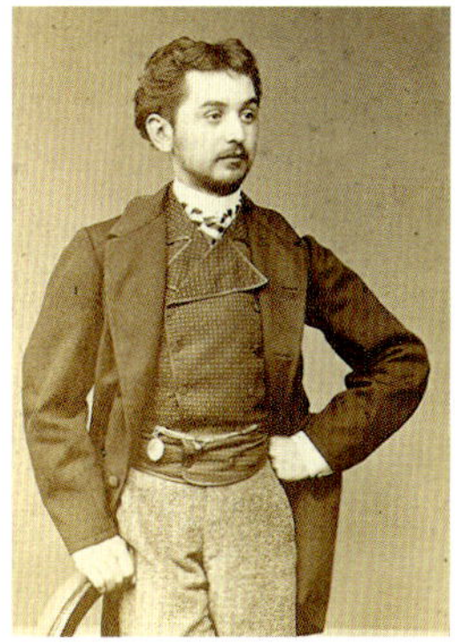

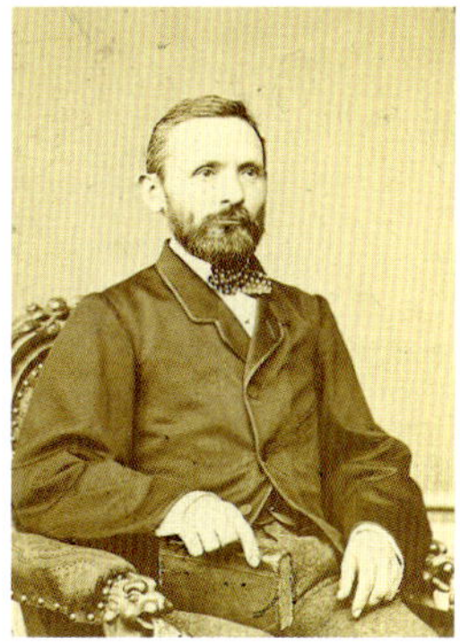

Plate 24 *(top right)*
Photograph of the Banatian politician Alexandru Mocsonyi (1841–1909), deputy in the Hungarian Parliament, and one of the founders and presidents of the Romanian National Party of the Banat and Crișana

Plate 25 *(bottom right)*
Photograph of Vincențiu Babes (1821–1907), Banatian lawyer, professor and journalist; one of the founders of the Romanian Academy of Sciences

Plate 23 *(above)*
Portrait of Emperor Franz Joseph (1859) by Friedrich Horschelt (1824–81), oil on canvas

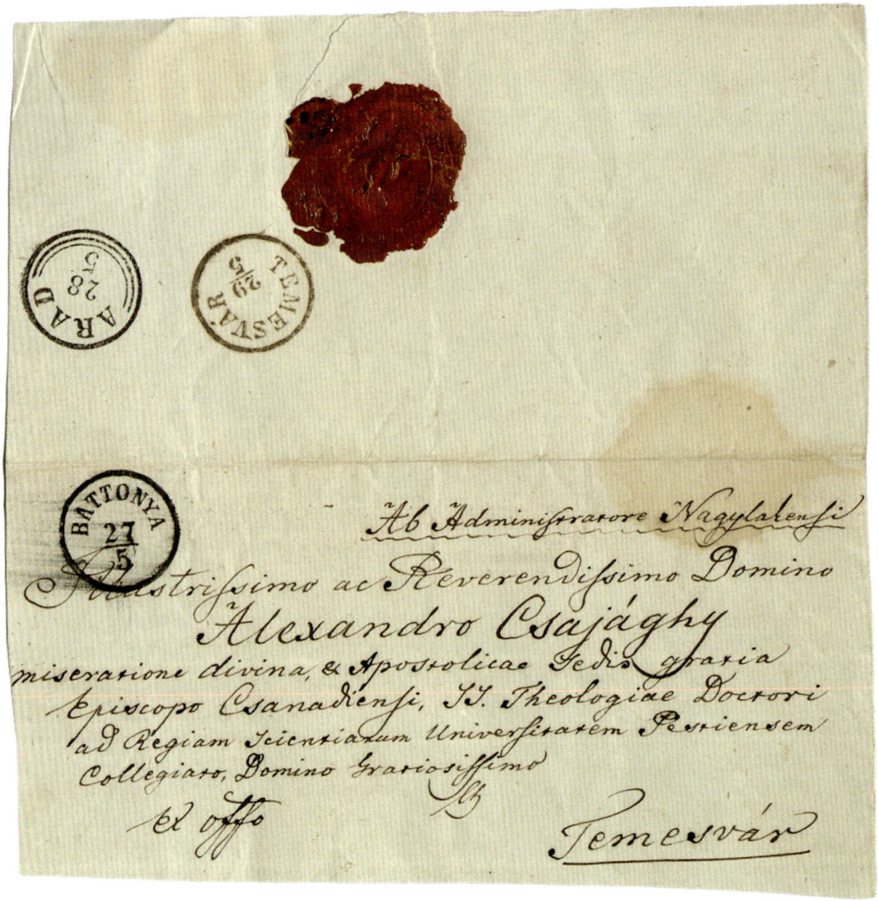

ARAD 28/5

TEMESVÁR 29/5

BATTONYA 27/5

Ab Administratore Nagylakensi

Illustrissimo ac Reverendissimo Domino

Alexandro Csajághy

miseratione divina, & Apostolicae Sedis gratia

Episcopo Csanadiensi, SS. Theologiae Doctori

ad Regiam Scientiarum Universitatem Pestiensem

Collegiato, Domino Gratiosissimo

Ex offo

Temesvár

Plate 26

Correspondence addressed to Alexandru Csajághy, Roman Catholic bishop of Timișoara-Cenad (1851–60)

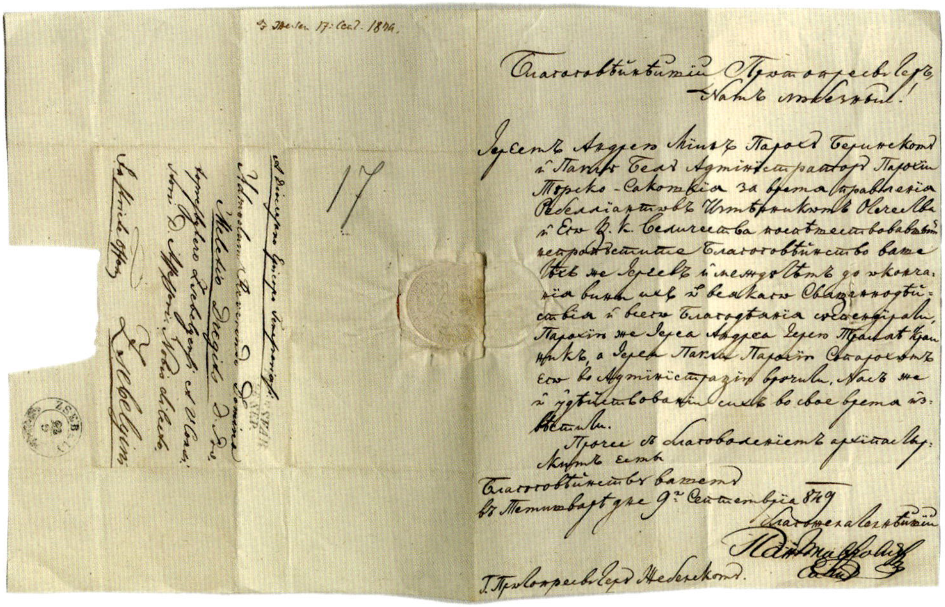

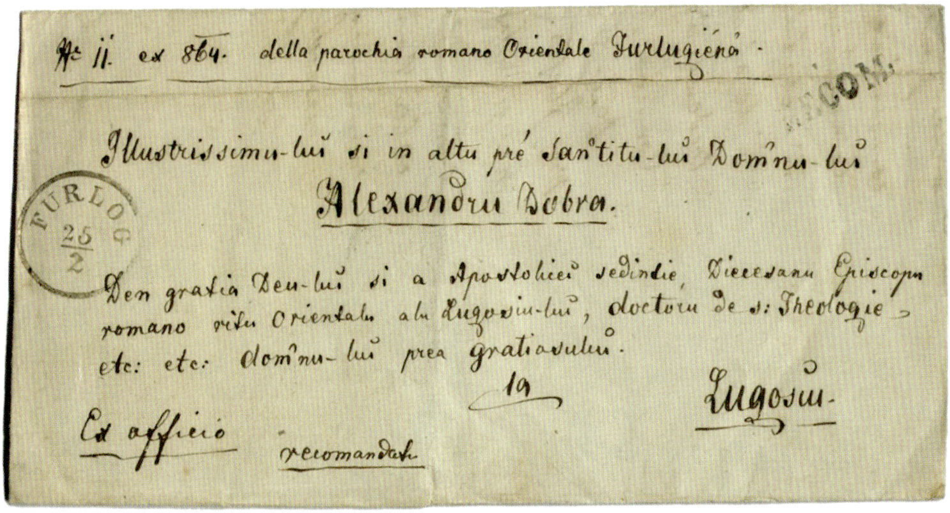

Nr. 11. ex 864. della parochia romano Orientale Furlugiena.

Illustrissimu-lui si in altu pré San^ti^tu-lui Domnu-lui

Alexandru Dobra.

Den gratia Deu-lui si a Apostolicei sedindie, Diecesanu Episcopu romano ritu Orientalu alu Lugosiu-lui, doctoru de s: Theologie etc: etc: domnu-lui prea gratiosului.

19

Lugosiu.

Ex officio

recomandat

Plate 27 (*top*)
Letter of 1849 sent by the Orthodox bishop of Timișoara to the Orthodox dean of Jebel, Meletie Drăghici, Banatian writer and politician

Plate 28 (*bottom*)
Letter (c.1864) from the Greek Catholic parish of Fârliug to the Greek Catholic bishop of Lugoj, Alexandru Dobra (1854–70)

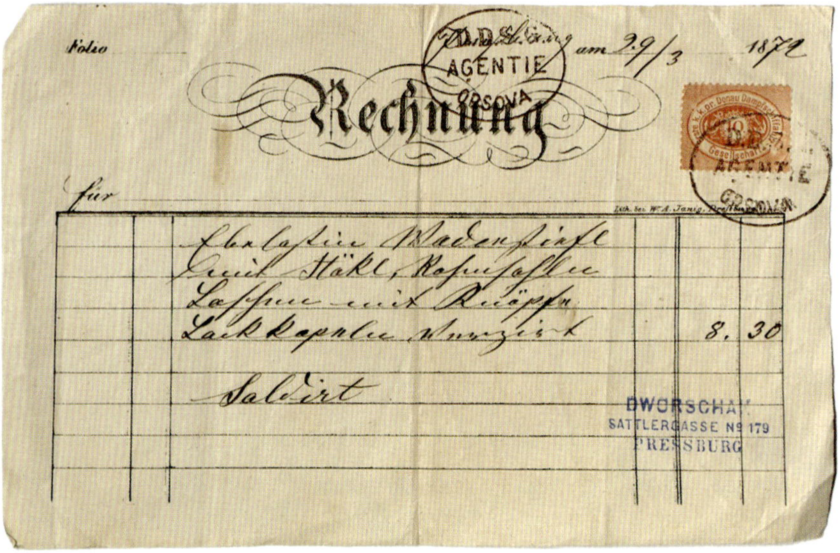

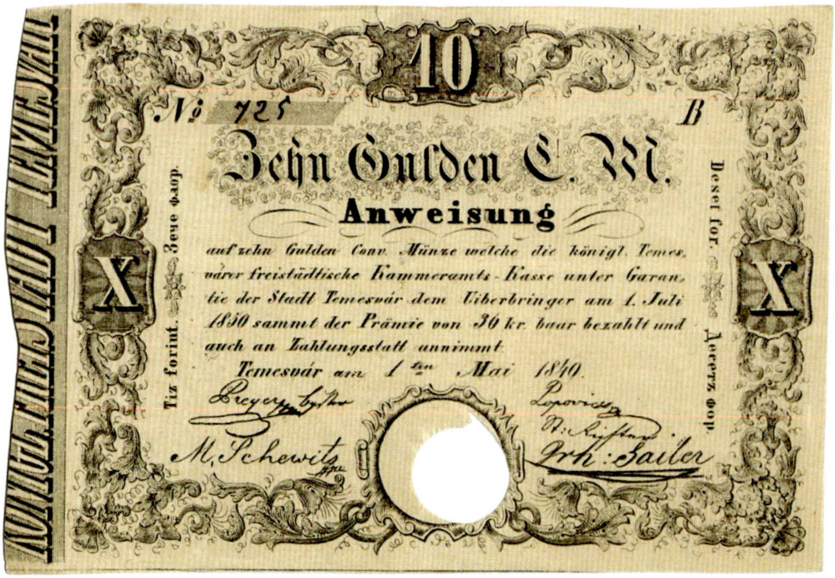

Plate 29 *(top)*
Invoice of 1872, attesting the first Austro-Hungarian (joint-stock) company of navigation on the Danube

Plate 30 *(bottom)*
Ten-gulden note issued on 1 May 1849 by the Austrian authorities during the siege of Timișoara by the Hungarian revolutionary troops; the signatories include J. N. Preyer, then mayor of Timișoara

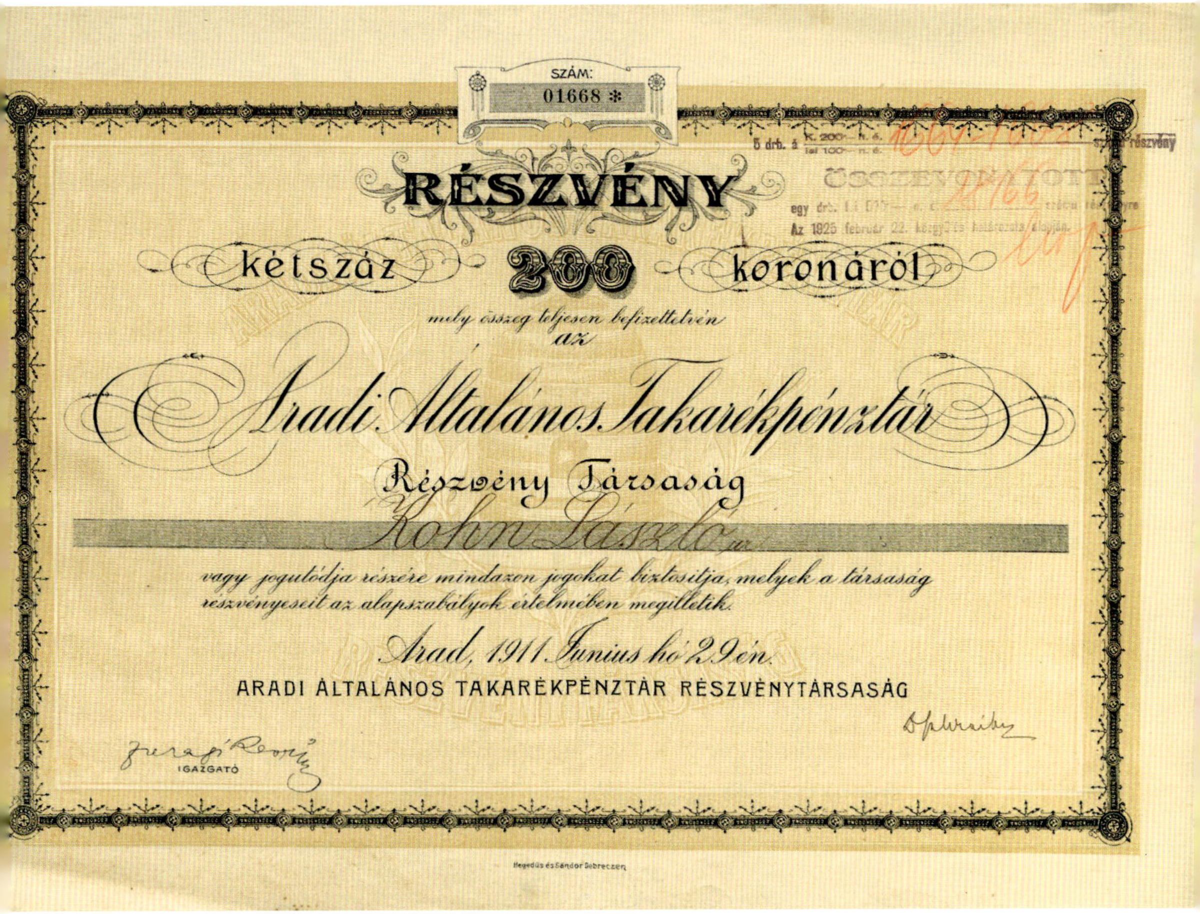

Plate 31
Share certificate for 200 crowns issued
by the General Savings Bank of Arad
(29 June 1911)

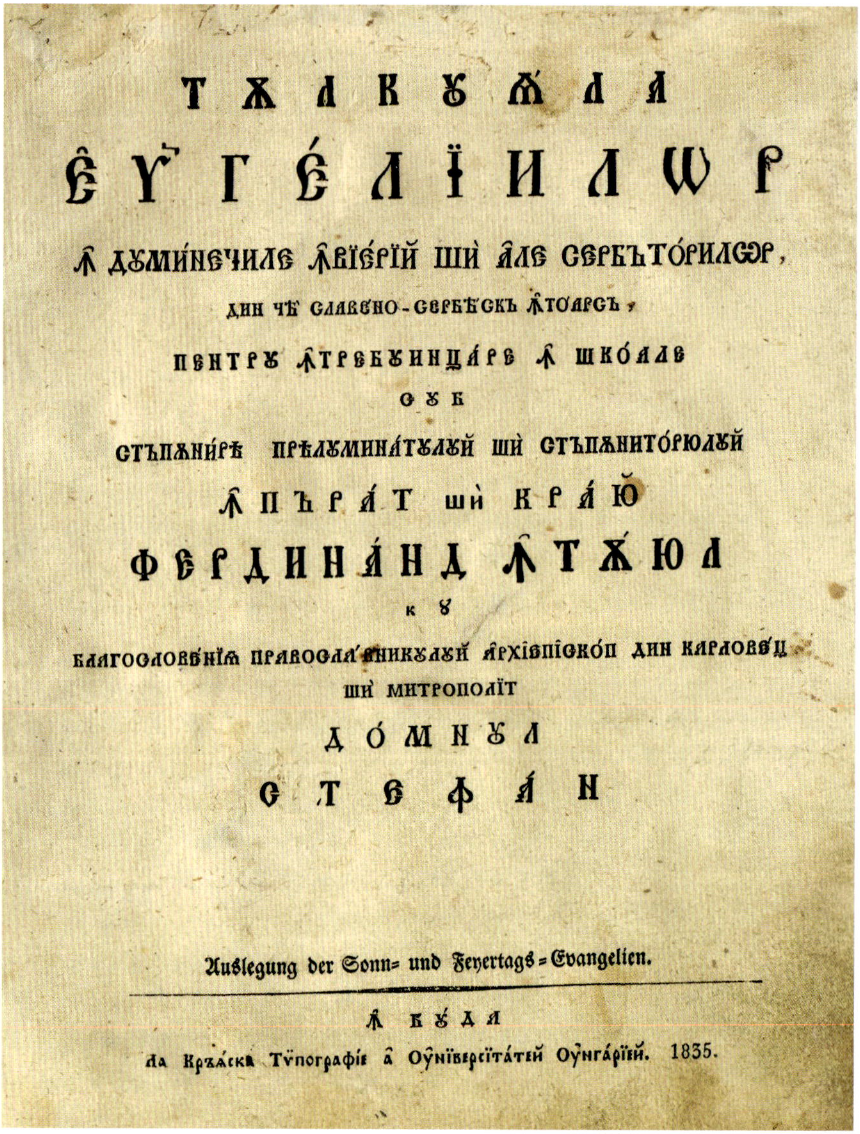

ТЖЛКУЖАЛА

ЕУГГЕЛІИЛѠР

ꙟ Думинечиле ꙟвіерїй ши але сербъторилѡр,

дин че Славено-Сербеск ꙟтоарсъ,

пентру ꙟтребуинцаре ꙟ школае

суб

стъпънире прелуминатулуй ши стъпънитoрюлуй

ꙟпърат ши краю

Фердинанд ꙟтжюл

ку

благословенїа православникулуй Архиепископ дин Карловец

ши митрополит

Домнул

Стефан

Auslegung der Sonn= und Feyertags=Evangelien.

ꙟ Буда

ла Кръѧска Тѷпографіе а Оунїверсїтатеи Оунгаріеи. 1835.

Plate 32
Textbook *Tâlcuiala Evangheliilor în Duminicile Învierii și ale serbătorilor (The Interpretation of the Gospels for Easter Sunday and Holy Days)* (Universitatis Hungaricae Budae, 1835) for use in schools; text edited by Bishop Ștefan Stratimirovici of Karlowitz and translated from Slovenian–Serbian to Romanian by C. Diaconovici-Loga

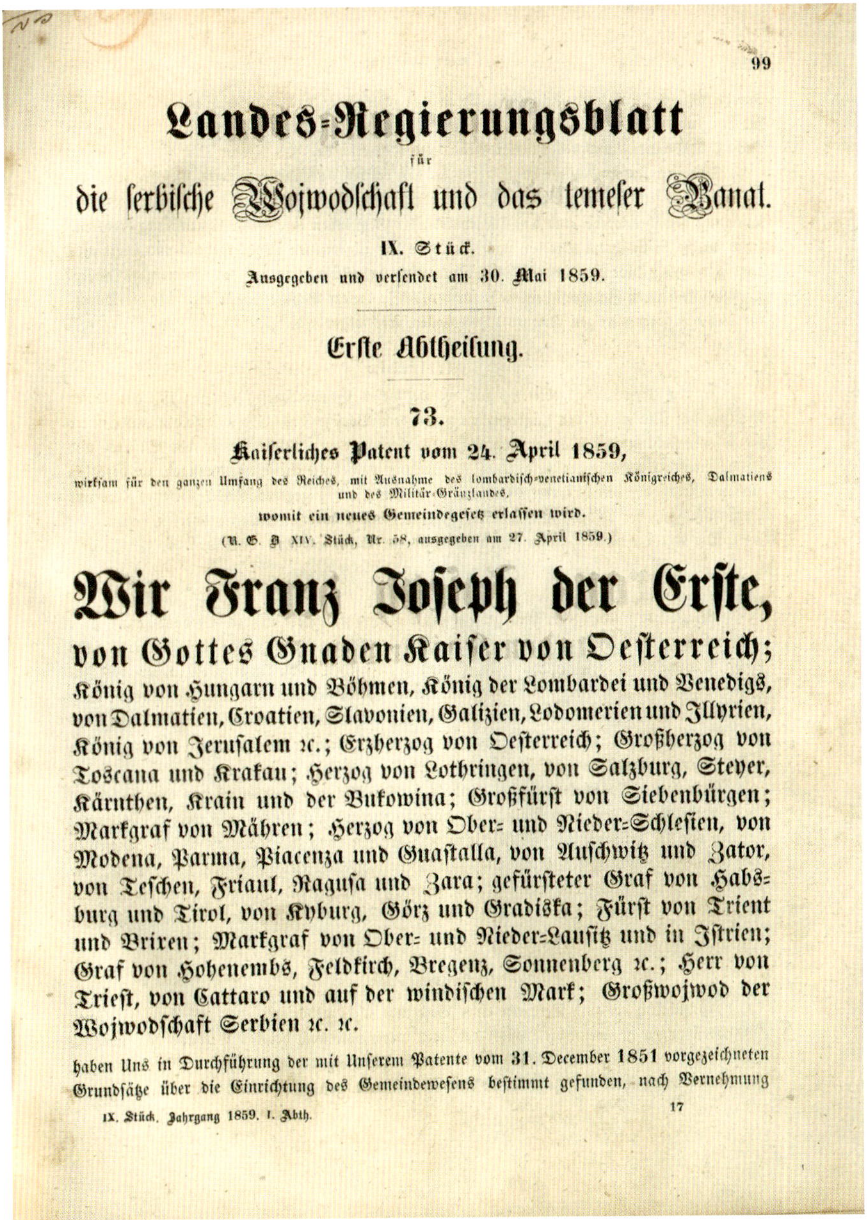

99

Landes-Regierungsblatt

für

die serbische Wojwodschaft und das temeser Banat.

IX. Stück.

Ausgegeben und versendet am 30. Mai 1859.

Erste Abtheilung.

73.

Kaiserliches Patent vom 24. April 1859,

wirksam für den ganzen Umfang des Reiches, mit Ausnahme des lombardisch-venetianischen Königreiches, Dalmatiens und des Militär-Gränzlandes,

womit ein neues Gemeindegesetz erlassen wird.

(R. G. B. XIV. Stück, Nr. 58, ausgegeben am 27. April 1859.)

Wir Franz Joseph der Erste,

von Gottes Gnaden Kaiser von Oesterreich;

König von Hungarn und Böhmen, König der Lombardei und Venedigs, von Dalmatien, Croatien, Slavonien, Galizien, Lodomerien und Illyrien, König von Jerusalem rc.; Erzherzog von Oesterreich; Großherzog von Toscana und Krakau; Herzog von Lothringen, von Salzburg, Steyer, Kärnthen, Krain und der Bukowina; Großfürst von Siebenbürgen; Markgraf von Mähren; Herzog von Ober- und Nieder-Schlesien, von Modena, Parma, Piacenza und Guastalla, von Auschwitz und Zator, von Teschen, Friaul, Ragusa und Zara; gefürsteter Graf von Habsburg und Tirol, von Kyburg, Görz und Gradiska; Fürst von Trient und Brixen; Markgraf von Ober- und Nieder-Lausitz und in Istrien; Graf von Hohenembs, Feldkirch, Bregenz, Sonnenberg rc.; Herr von Triest, von Cattaro und auf der windischen Mark; Großwojwod der Wojwodschaft Serbien rc. rc.

haben Uns in Durchführung der mit Unserem Patente vom 31. December 1851 vorgezeichneten Grundsätze über die Einrichtung des Gemeindewesens bestimmt gefunden, nach Vernehmung

IX. Stück. Jahrgang 1859. I. Abth. 17

Plate 33

Landes-Regierungsblatt für die serbische Wojwodschaft und das Temeser Banat (Bulletin of the Regional Administration of the Banat of Timișoara and Serbian Voivodina), Year Nine, 30 May 1853; the imperial patent enumerating Franz Joseph's titles ends with 'Great Voivode of Serbian Voivodina and the Banat of Temeswar (Timișoara)'

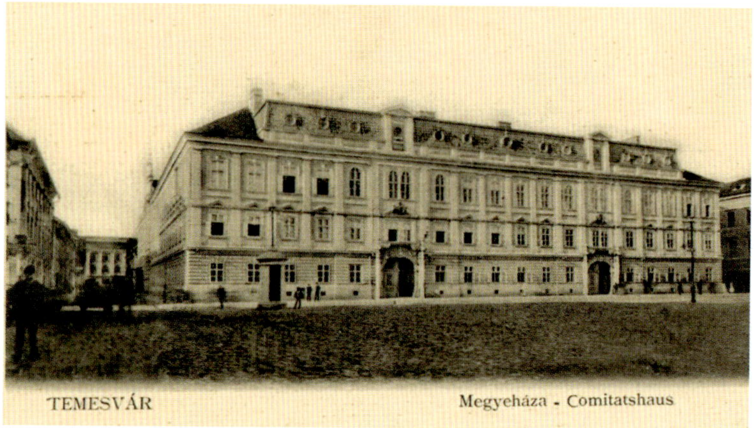

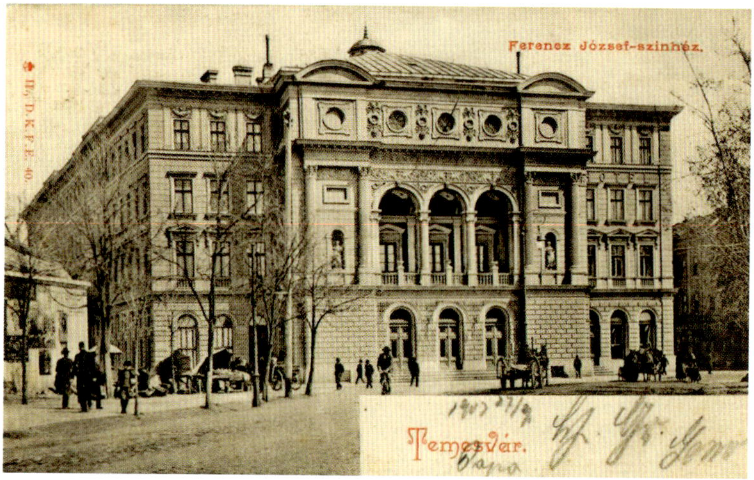

Plate 34 *(top)*
Postcard (c.1900) of the Baroque Palace or Governor's Palace in Dome Square (now Union Square). In the 18th century it was the headquarters of the civil governor of the Banat and is now home to the Art Museum Timișoara.

Plate 35 *(bottom)*
'Franz Joseph' Theatre of Timișoara (1903), today the home of the National Theatre, National Opera, 'Csiky Gergely' Hungarian State Theatre and German Theatre

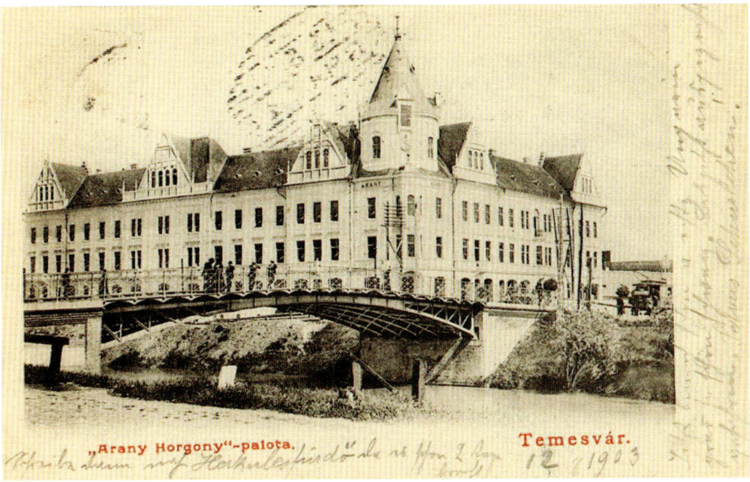

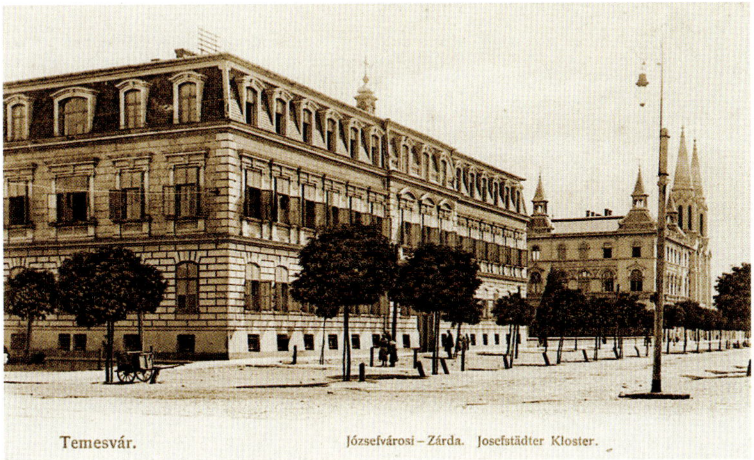

Plate 36 *(top)*
Postcard of 'Golden Anchor' Palace (1903), the headquarters of the former Harbour Master's Office in Timișoara

Plate 37 *(bottom)*
Postcard of the Girls' Superior School of the Sisters of Notre Dame, Timișoara (1900)

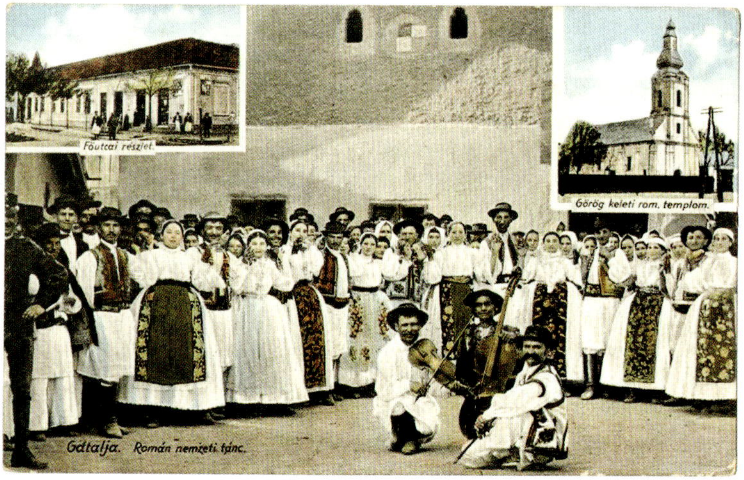

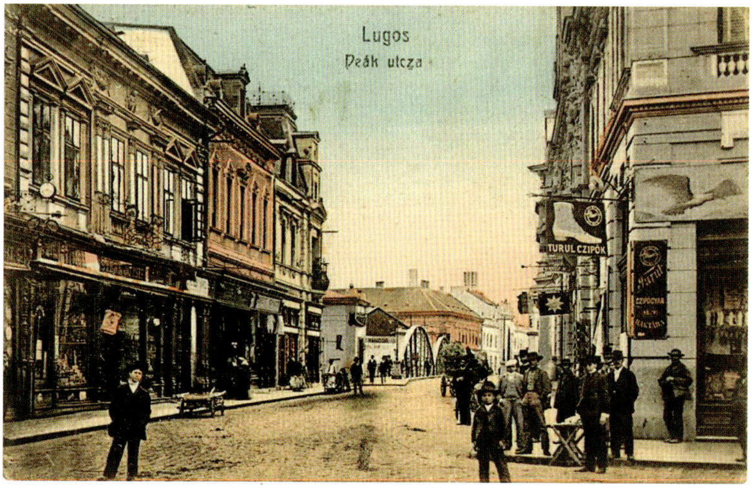

Plate 38 *(top)*
Postcard of Gătaia (*c.*1900) showing the main street, the Orthodox church and Romanian folk dancers

Plate 39 *(bottom)*
Postcard of Deák Street (now Union Street) in Lugoj (1910), one of the main commercial streets of the town; the Iron Bridge over Timis River can be seen in the background

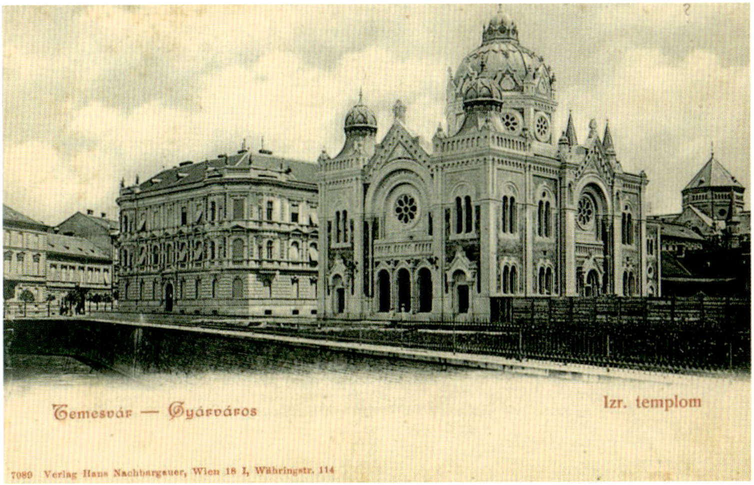

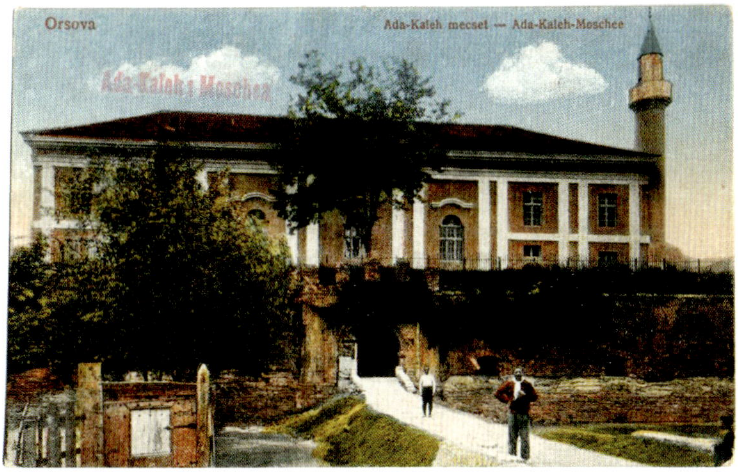

Plate 40 *(top)*
Postcard of the Neolog synagogue in the Fabric quarter of Timișoara (1900)

Plate 41 *(bottom)*
Postcard of the mosque on Ada-Kaleh ('Island Fortress') on the Danube (southern Banat) (1915) (the island was submerged in 1970)

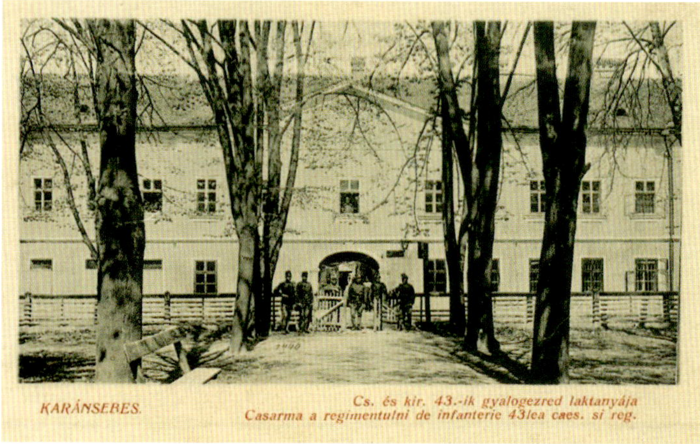
KARÁNSEBES.
Cs. és kir. 43.-ik gyalogezred laktanyája
Casarma a regimentulni de infanterie 43lea caes. si reg.

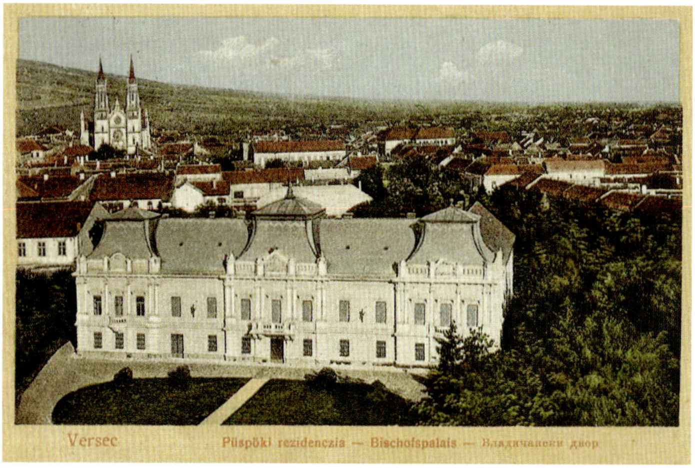
Versec
Püspöki rezidenczia — Bischofspalais — Владичански двор

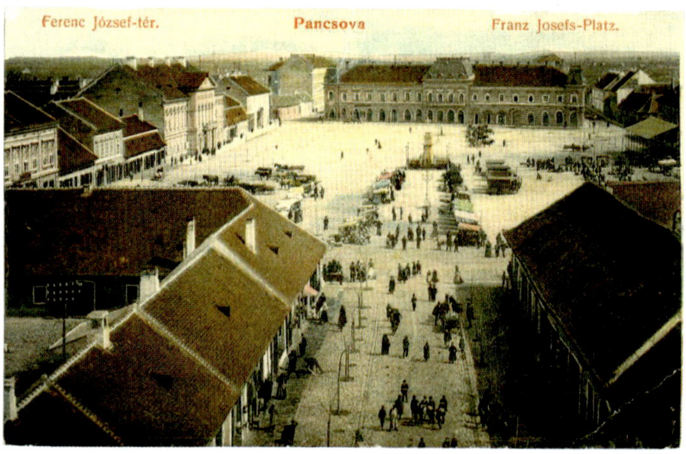
Ferenc József-tér.
Pancsova
Franz Josefs-Platz.

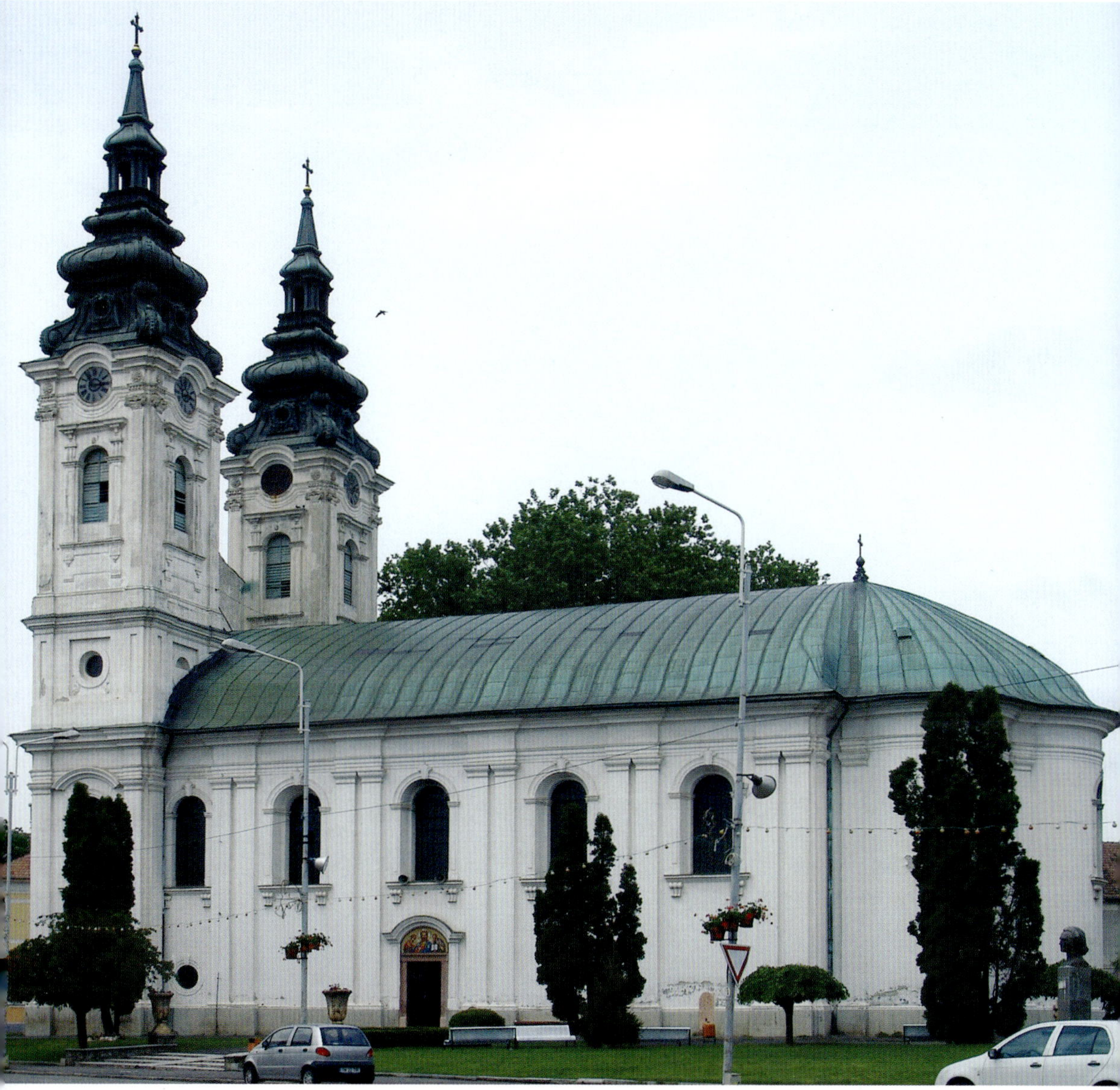

Plate 42 *(opposite top)*
Postcard of the garrison of the Austro-Hungarian 43rd Infantry Regiment of Caransebeș (1910)

Plate 43 *(opposite middle)*
Postcard of the palace of the Orthodox bishop of Vršac (1911)

Plate 44 *(opposite bottom)*
Postcard of Franz Joseph Square in Pančevo (1911)

Plate 45 *(above)*
The 'Adormirea Maicii Domnului' (Assumption of the Virgin Mary) Orthodox Cathedral of Lugoj

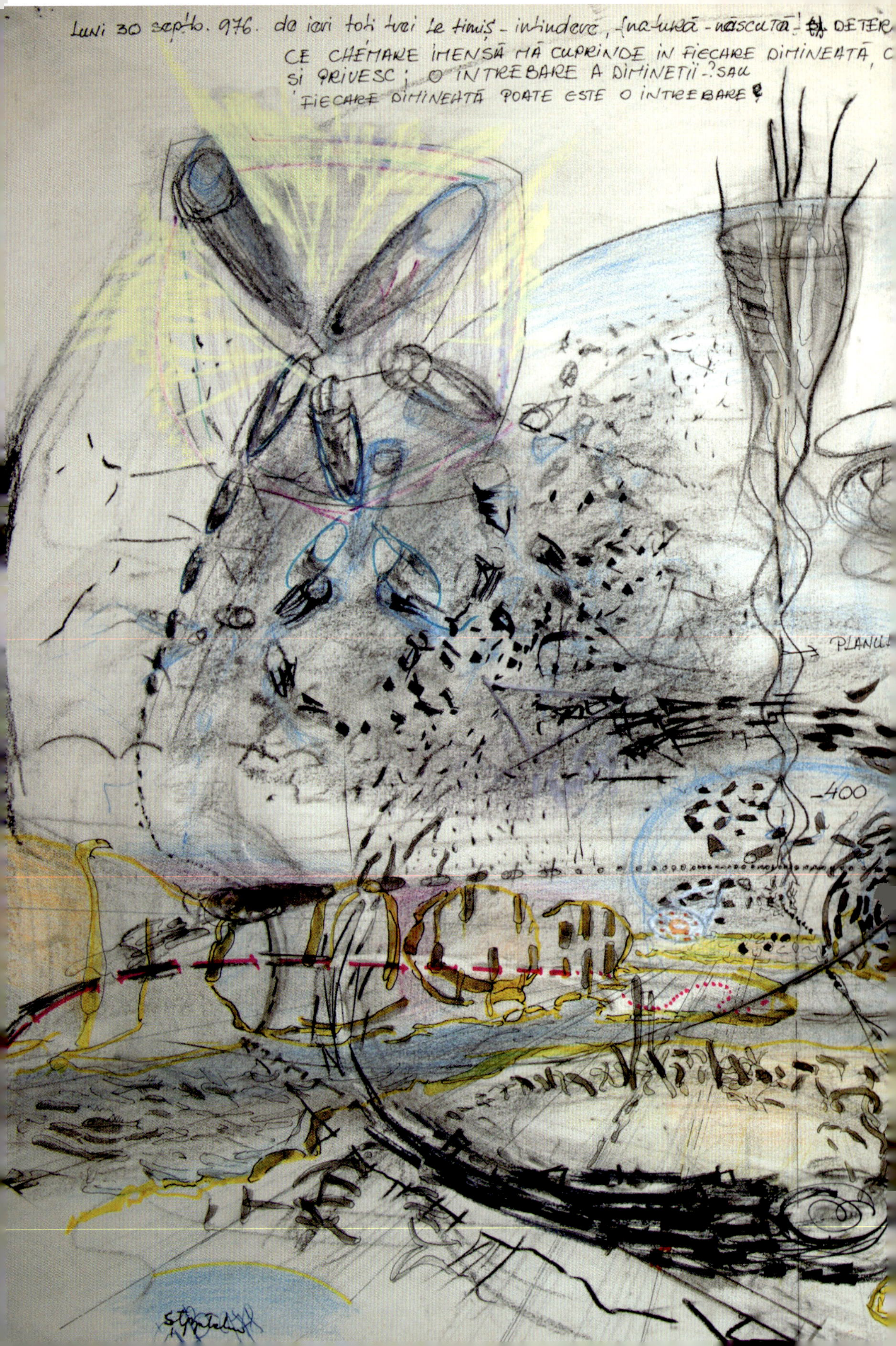
Luni 30 sept. 976. de ieri toți trei la timiș - intindere, natură - născută! DETER
CE CHEMARE IMENSĂ MĂ CUPRINDE IN FIECARE DIMINEAȚĂ, C
si PRIVESC; O INTREBARE A DIMINETII-? SAU
FIECARE DIMINEAȚĂ POATE ESTE O INTREBARE?
PLANU
400

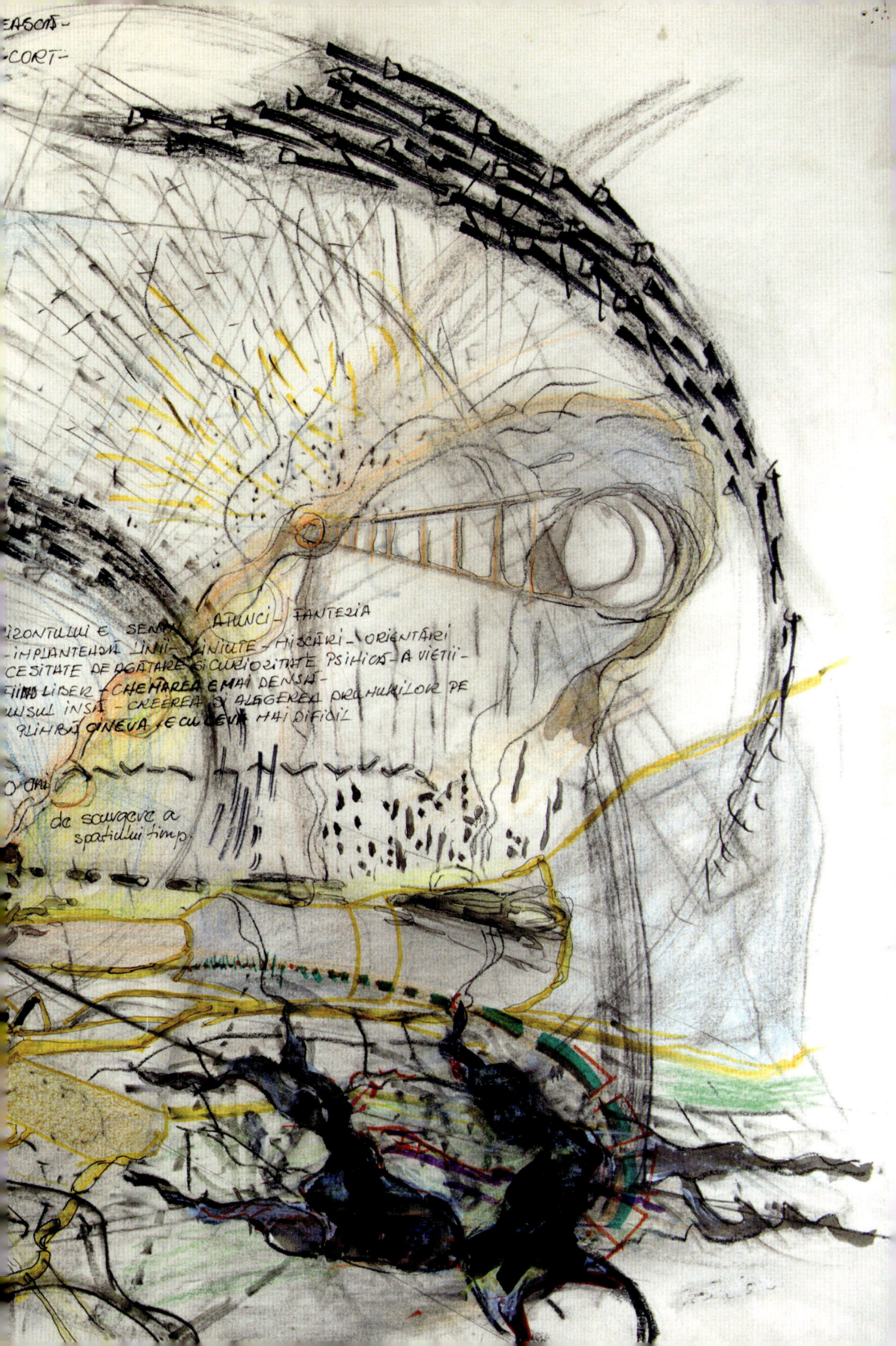
CORT
ATUNCI – FANTEZIA
MIŞCĂRI – ORIENTĂRI
CHEMAREA E MAI DENSĂ
CREEREA ŞI ALEGEREA
MAI DIFICIL
de scurgere a
spaţiului timp

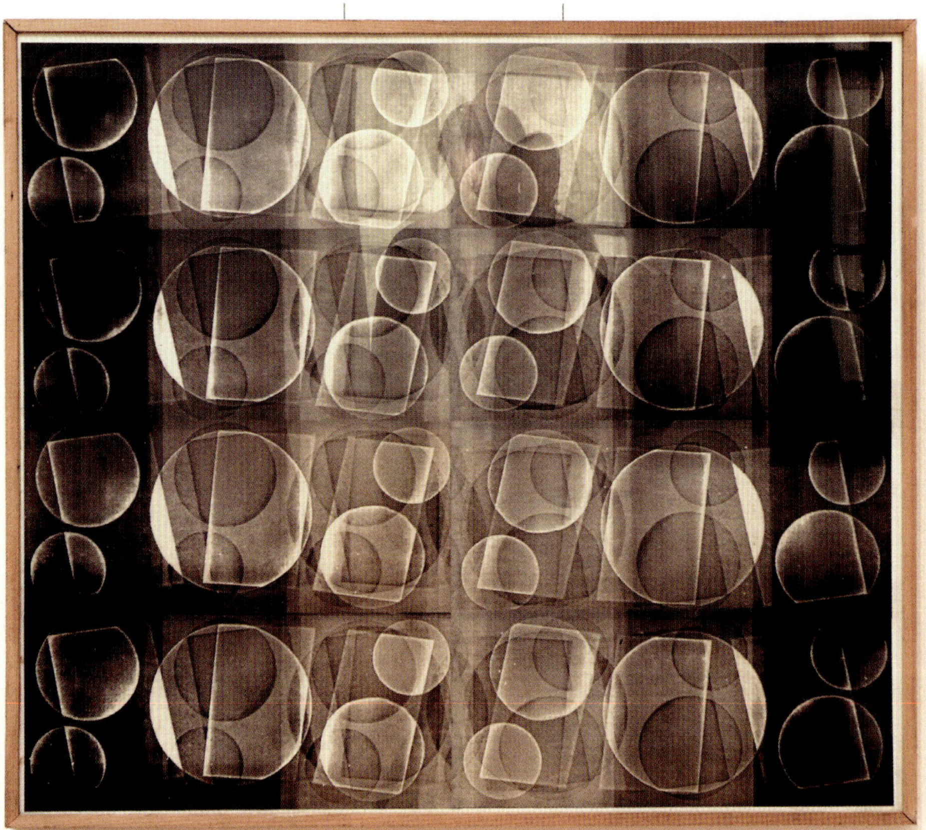

Plate 46 ***(previous pages)***
Memories from the River Timis (1977–78), by Ștefan Bertalan (1930–2014), charcoal, gouache and pastel on cardboard

Plate 47 ***(above)***
Visual Sequences, monotype/collage, from the cycle Kinetic Art Projects (1965), by Roman Cotoșman (1935–2006)

Plate 48 ***(opposite)***
Self-Portrait (detail), charcoal on paper, by Julius Podlipny (1898–1991)

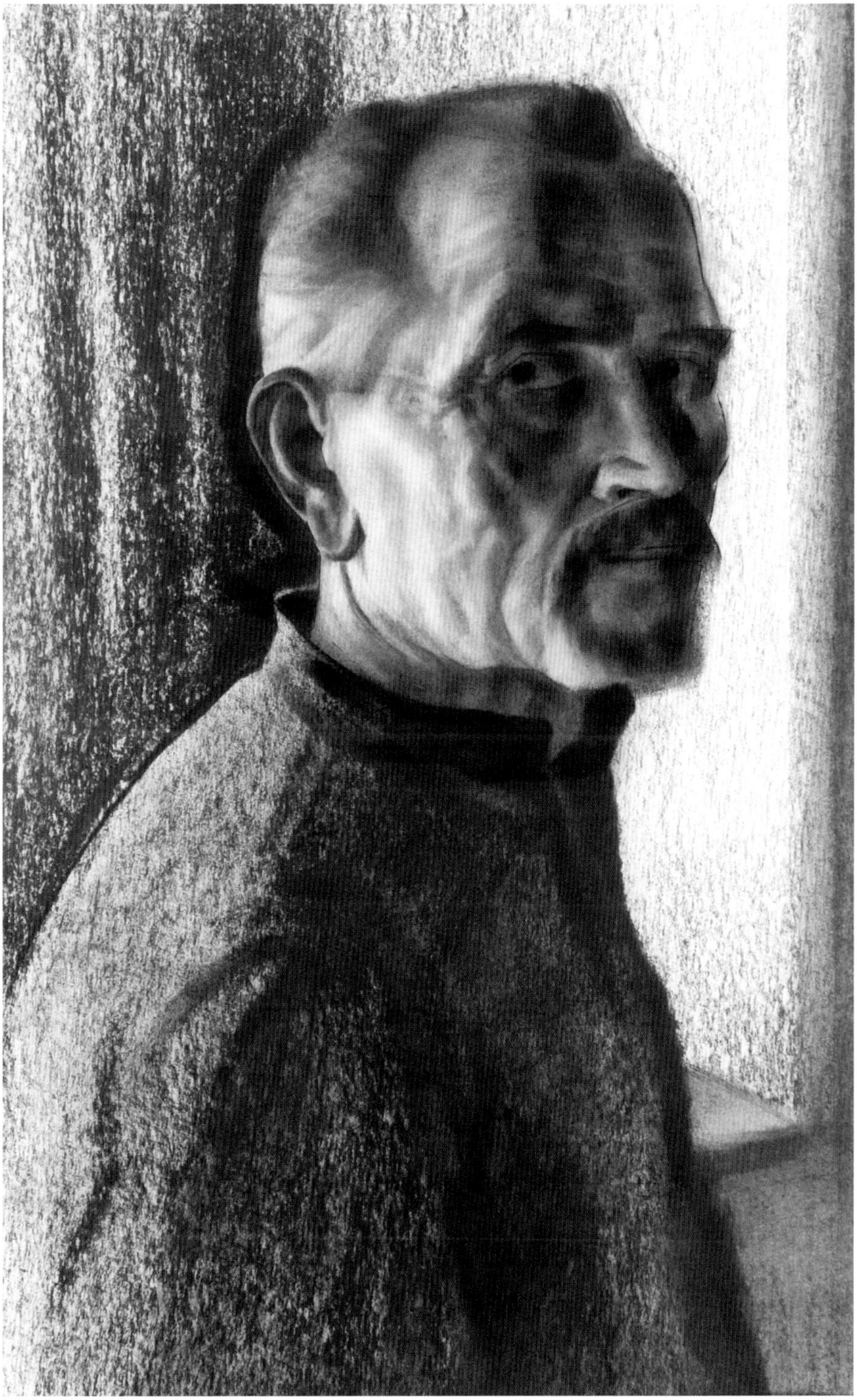

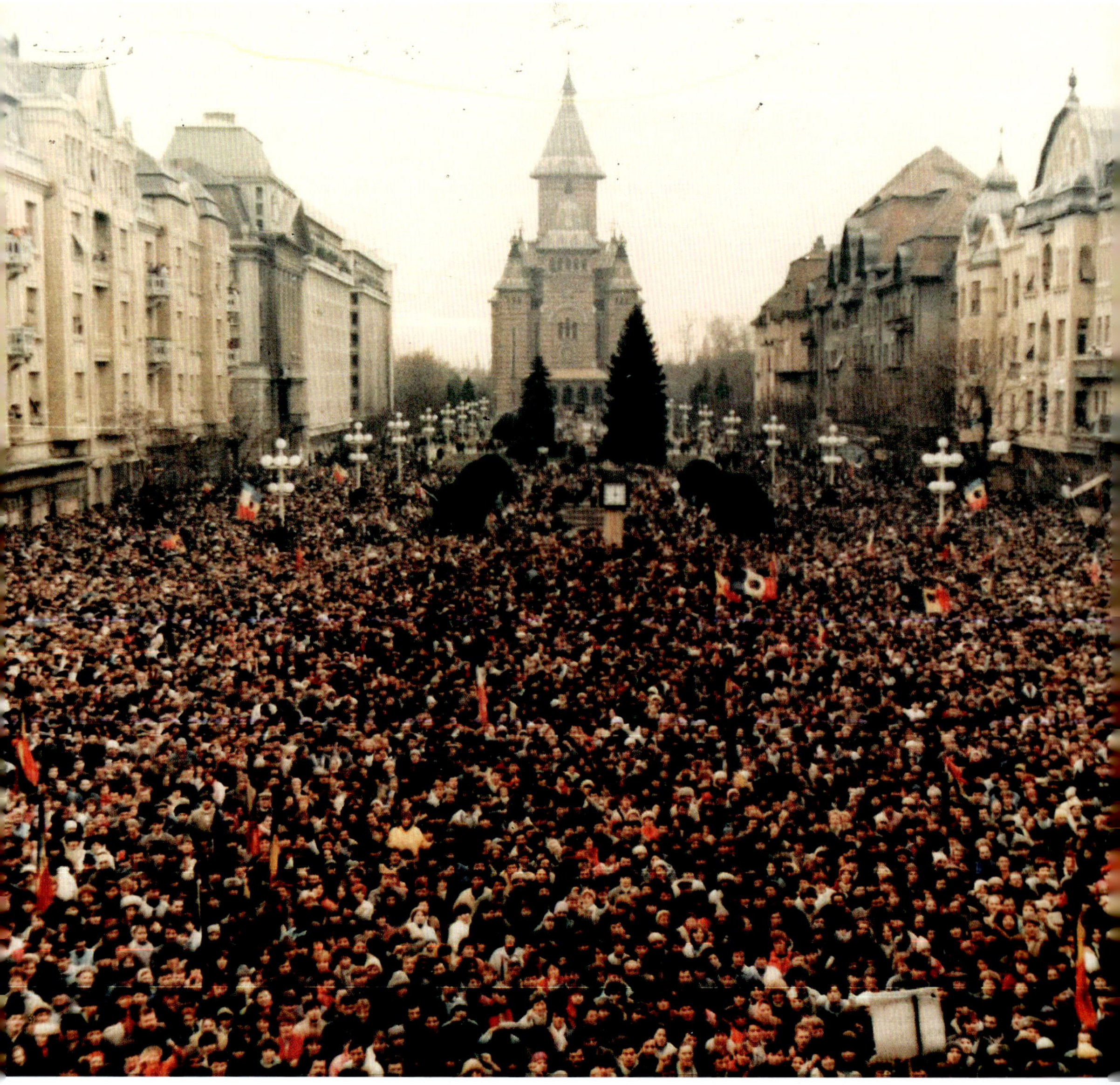

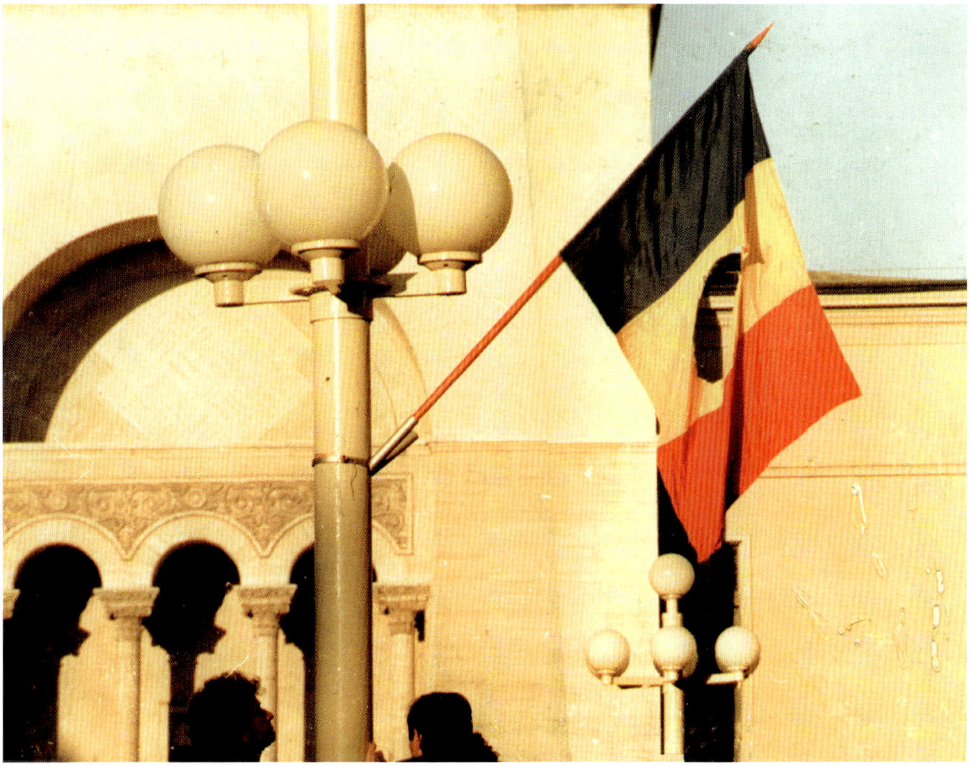

Plate 49 *(opposite)*
The great demonstration of 20 December 1989 in the Opera Square, Timișoara; 100,000 people claimed Timișoara as the first city free from Nicolae Ceaușescu's dictatorship

Plate 50 *(above)*
Symbols of the anti-communist Revolution of Timișoara in 1989: the flag of the Revolution, and the Opera Balcony where political rallies were held for citizens during the days and nights when they demonstrated against the Romanian communist system

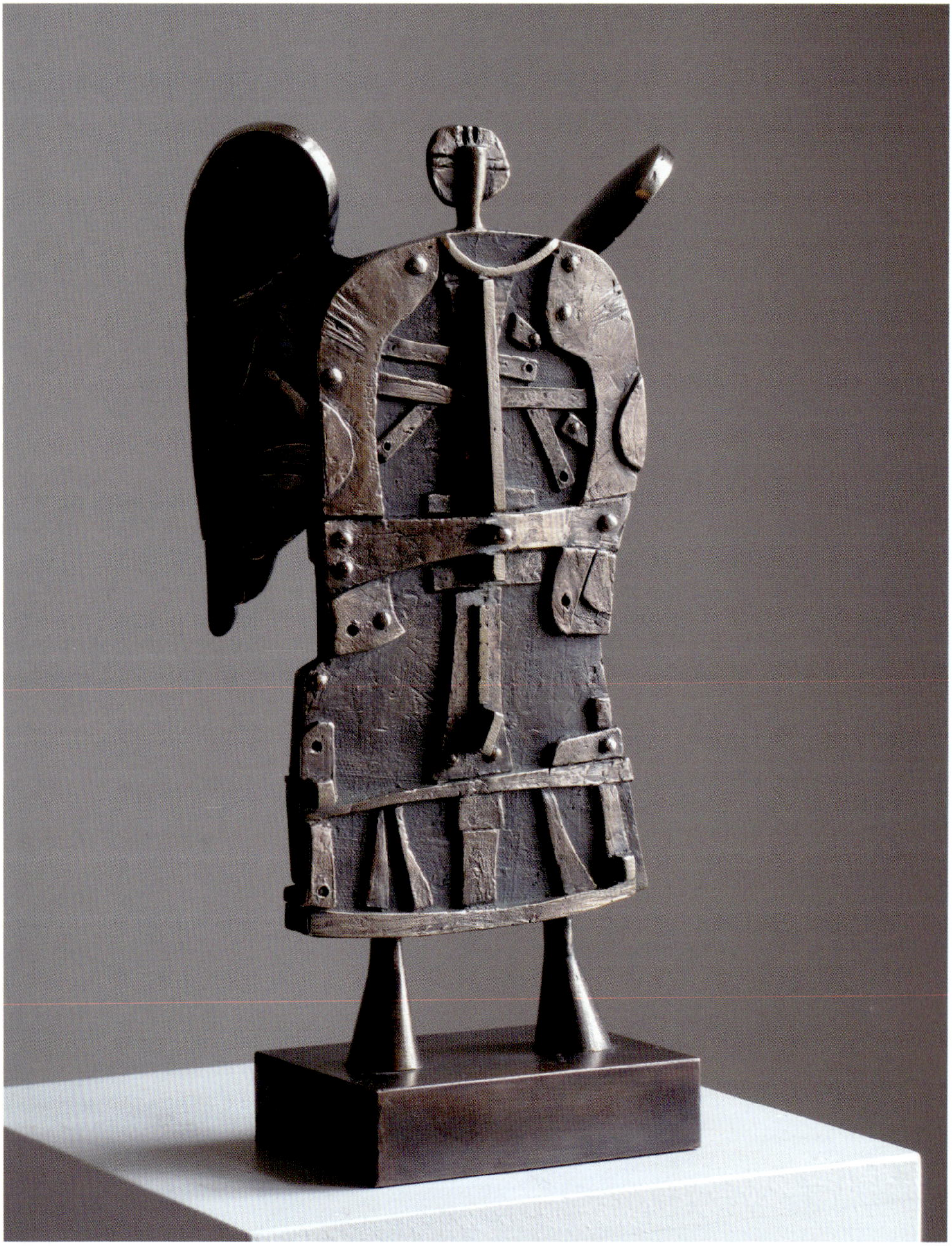

Plate 51
Archangel, bronze sculpture (2013)
by Béla Szakáts (*b*.1938)

19

INTERWAR TIMIȘOARA

The Multi- and Intercultural Capital of a Euro-Region

Victor Neumann

THIS CHAPTER SEEKS TO DRAW ATTENTION to the identitarian profile of Timișoara – a city situated at the crossroads of cultures and civilisations between Central and South Eastern Europe – during the interwar period. The post-1918 urban identity phenomenon will be considered, when the Banat region – of which Timișoara was the capital – was partitioned between Romania, Serbia and Hungary and when a long-standing debate was focused on how to preserve the various legacies of the Austro-Hungarian Empire and the Dual Monarchy. Numerous voices advocated keeping the Banat as an undivided region, relying on geographical, administrative and economic arguments. One of the documents presented to the Paris Peace Conference refers to the issue as follows:

> To partition the Banat would mean the economic, industrial and commercial ruin of this province and of its inhabitants. We know only vaguely about the strategic and ethnic reasons which could have spawned this idea of partitioning the Banat and we believe that nobody could ever affirm that partition could be made without exposing the province to total economic disaster. Its geographical and economic unity has been an uncontested fact over the years, [so] that never during its history did this province belong to more than a single country at once . . . This province has a regular rectangle shape, bordered by three large rivers – the Mureș, the Tisza and the Danube – and by the Carpathian Mountains. Within this rectangle there is a system of waterways, railways and roads which connect the province with the Tisza and the Danube.[1]

However, written under the pressure of nationalist ideologies and the consequences of war, documents like this failed to refer to the plurality of sociocultural and religious legacies of the region: the legacies of cohabitation between the Orthodox and Catholic Churches; the interactions between the Germans, Austrians, Romanians and Serbians; the association of the Yiddish-speaking German Jews with the Ladino-speaking Spanish Jews; and the assimilation of the emancipated Jews to other cultures such as German or Hungarian. All this symbolised a history which the inhabitants of Timișoara recognised as their own and which they wanted to continue. Interaction is the natural consequence of a mixed history in a border city, a fact which is reflected in its names in many languages – Timișoara (Romanian), Temeswar and Temeschburg (German), Temesvár (Hungarian) and Temisvaru (Serbian); by a multilingual press in German, Hungarian and Romanian; by non-discriminatory social behaviour; by individual and civic initiatives; by the cooperative attitude of administrative authorities.

Not only did partition of the region, agreed by the Treaty of Trianon as part of the Paris Peace Conference, create tensions among the three neighbouring countries – Romania, Serbia and Hungary – but it also ignited anxiety among the inhabitants regarding centralist policies and ethnonationalist ideologies. States formed on ethnographic criteria after the First World War experienced the real problem of recognising and integrating regions with a heritage of diverse origins. The new authorities faced challenges such as multi- and intercultural expression, the existence of many religions, and the recognition of plural histories. These did not correspond to identity formulated on the basis on a fictive ethnicity, as contemporary elites had imagined.

Romanian interwar political parties and governments – even the most tolerant – were not comfortable with admitting that society in Timișoara was the result of the intermingling of many languages and cultures, that it did not belong exclusively to a single religious denomination, and that it did not bear the signs of a so-called ethnonational specificity. Its plural cultures and histories did not correspond to the monolingual and monocultural orientations of the newly created nation state.

Imperialist and nationalist censuses served as a means for political hierarchies and centralised administrations to redraw the map of Europe in the nineteenth and twentieth centuries. The administration in Budapest compiled statistics on Timișoara's inhabitants in 1910, focusing on mother tongue (see Table 19.1) and religion (see Table 19.2).

Table 19.1
Timişoara's inhabitants in 1910 by mother tongue

DECLARED MOTHER TONGUE	NUMBER OF SPEAKERS
German	32,963
Hungarian	28,645
Romanian	7,593
Serbian	3,490
Slovakian	341
Croatian	149
Ruthenian	4
Other	818
TOTAL	74,003

Table 19.2
Timişoara's population in 1910 by religion

DECLARED RELIGION OR DENOMINATION	NUMBER OF FOLLOWERS
Roman Catholic	49,981
Orthodox	11,257
Jewish	6,729
Reformed Calvinist	3,554
Evangelical Lutheran	1,609
Greek Catholic	754
Unitarian	80
Other	39
TOTAL	74,003

Source: Rotariu, Semeniuc, and Mezei, *Recensământul din 1910: Transilvania*, pp. 548–50.

What conclusions may be drawn from the figures in Tables 19.1 and 2, as classified by the enumerator of the census? Firstly, that German speakers were the most numerous, representing 32,963 inhabitants or 44.5 per cent of the total population. An explanation may be useful here. Starting with the rule of Joseph II, the Habsburg authorities approved the use of German, without imposing it, as a means of communication with the population. The reason behind this was that Timişoara had been inhabited by colonists of German origin (Swabians) during the eighteenth century and most of them did not speak any language but German. Secondly, the Italian, Spanish and French settlers were assimilated by the Germans, so they also used German as the language of communication. Thirdly, during the process of emancipation and modernisation, German had been the language of instruction of the elites and of printed matter throughout the Austro-Hungarian Empire. Benedict Anderson's remark that the German language 'increasingly acquired a double status: "universal-imperial" and "particular national"'[2] – is perfectly valid in this case. At the end of the nineteenth century and the beginning of the twentieth, the German language represented a reference point not only for the civic and cultural code of the entire population but also for its ideology and ethnonational movements. It was a time when people and groups were increasingly identified on the basis of language and cultural differences.

As for the Hungarian speakers in Timişoara, their number – 28,645 – reflects an increase in the second half of the nineteenth century to account for 38.7 per cent of the total population. This was due to the political changes that occurred in the aftermath of the 1848 Revolution when the Hungarian language replaced Latin and/or German in the public administration, the Hungarian aristocracy preferring to use it since it was understood by the large mass of peasants. Classification based on language and religion, as shown in Tables 19.1 and 19.2, was only seldom in line with the social and intellectual aspirations of the majority of the population of Timişoara. In the decade 1900–10, the city continued to exist on its own coordinates, and cooperation among its citizens in the interests of the common good was a generally accepted way of life. The Budapest administration learnt with surprise that Timişoara was challenging the dominant ideological orientation of the time, namely linguistic nationalism. In this regard, the Hungarian regime observed that the German language continued to hold an appreciable share not only of interpersonal communication but also with regard to education, culture and the press. For instance, the most important local newspaper was the German-language *Temeswarer Zeitung*.[3] Despite the politics of Hungarian assimilation, 44.5 per cent of the total population continued to speak German as their mother tongue.[4] The Romanian speakers accounted for 10.2 per cent and the Serbian speakers, 4.7 per cent. There was a real distribution as far as social composition was concerned.

As for the religious denominations, even though Roman Catholics represented the majority, with 67.5 per cent of the total population,[5] freedom of conscience was not restricted. The population was free to practise the Orthodox, Jewish, Reformed Calvinist, Evangelic Lutheran and Greek Catholic faiths, churches and synagogues for each of these being spread across the cities' neighbourhoods.

All this cultural and religious variety was conducive to the organisation of the population in professional, technical and scientific associations. The bourgeoisie embarked on numerous liberal initiatives, with the support of the local administration, while a social democratic orientation formed part of the political culture of the majority of the population.

A NEW STATE AND THE REDEFINITION OF IDENTITY

The statistics of Timişoara's interwar population, carried out by the Romanian administration, show sociocultural transformations but also the continuity of the relationship between the majority and the minorities.[6] The category of identity has changed as compared with the earlier period, 'nationality' or ethnoculture becoming the main reference point for the census. Table 19.3 presents the situation inventoried in 1930.

Table 19.3
Timişoara's population in 1930 by nationality

DECLARED NATIONALITY	NUMBER OF PERSONS
German	27,807
Hungarian	27,652
Romanian	24,217
Jewish	7,171
Serbian, Croatian or Slovene	2,156
Russian	700
Czech or Slovak	597
Gypsy/Traveller/Roma	337
Bulgarian	257
Polish	101
Turkish	67
Ruthenian or Ukrainian	53
Albanian	10
Armenian	10
Hutsan[a]	7
Greek	8
Tatar	2
Other	179
Non-declared	249
TOTAL	91,580

[a] Small Orthodox community with origins in Galicia. From time to time part of this population moved from Galicia to Bucovina, Maramures, Transylvania and the Banat.

Source: Manuilă, *Recensământul*, vol. ii. *Neam, limbă maternă, religie* (*Kinship, Mother Tongue, Religion*), Central Institute of Statistics (Bucharest, 1938), pp. 468–69.

While the policy of Magyarisation was aimed at the linguistic and civic assimiliation of the inhabitants of the Hungarian part of the Dual Monarchy, Romanianisation, which began in 1918, introduced new criteria of differentiation based on ethnocultural origin and on the number of persons living in the respective community. For the enumerator of the census, the notion of 'nationality' was equivalent to kinship (*neam* in Romanian meaning tribe or race).[7] Thus the enumerator considered that it offered accurate and unambiguous data.[8] The former criteria of language and religion were not abandoned but acquired new meanings.

The statistics regarding Timișoara's inhabitants in 1930 suggest that the Romanian state was very concerned with the idea of nation and belonging to a nationality. This was a general trend in the states newly formed after the First World War and was reflected in the sociopolitical language that was used. Defining identity on the basis of 'ethnonational' affiliation generated uncertainty as until then the cities and regions where the majority and minorities coexisted involved an integration of the diverse cultures, religions and histories and had allowed for nuances when it came to defining personal or group identity. At that time, about 30 per cent of the Romanian population belonged to a different cultural group, or 'nationality', from the Romanian one. In the historical and sociological literature, and also in the Romanian press during the interwar period, the term 'foreigner' defined both a person coming from another country and someone belonging to a minority group within the borders of the same state. Such an approach was used by certain intellectuals in Timişoara at that time, an example being *Revista Institutului Social Banat–Crișana: Buletin Istoric* (*Journal of the Banat–Crişana Social Institute: Historical Bulletin*) (1933–46), published under the auspices of the Banat–Crişana Social Institute. The journal and the institute were led by Cornel Grofșorean, one of Timișoara's mayors in the 1930s, and the model was taken from the Romanian Social Institute of Bucharest and the Institute for Social Research of Romania. The institute in Timișoara had been subordinated to the centralist system and deeply influenced by ethnonationalist ideology, an orientation often visible in the articles of the journal's contributors: Cornel Grofşorean, Aurel Ciupe, Gh. Cotoşman, Anton Golopenţa, Romulus Ladea and Ioachim Miloia.[9] Consequently, the journal failed to reflect the local context and thus to serve the interests of all citizens.

Such an orientation was already visible in the years immediately following the First World War. During the process to set up the first institution of higher education in Timişoara, Mayor Stan Vidrighin spoke about the identity of the city:

> A higher school such as the Polytechnic . . . will prove the strength and superiority of the Romanian genius, will contribute – to a remarkable extent – to the consolidation of the Romanian element in Timișoara

and the Banat, and will bring with it the nationalisation of all the institutions which are today still foreign. The overwhelming majority of the Romanian element within the Banat will gain through this establishment those intellectual forces to which the majority of Hungarians and Swabians, who are today better armed, will be forced to surrender. And our particular inferiority in Timișoara, which is the regrettable result of our minority status in this city, will certainly be transformed here, too, into superiority.[10]

Onisifor Ghibu, director of the Ministry of Religion and Public Instruction in the Council of Directors (Consiliul Dirigent)[11] followed the same line. According to him, the establishment of the institution of higher education had as its main objective 'the fortification and nationalisation of this border city'.[12]

By examining the notion of 'nationality' used as the main criterion in the census of 1930, it can be asserted that Timișoara represented a challenge for the enumerator for the following reasons:

1. the city was inhabited by many groups, each speaking two or more languages;
2. nationality did not always coincide with the mother tongue used;
3. the identity of some of the inhabitants of the city – for example, the Jews – was in certain cases determined by religion rather than the mother tongue (the census introduces in this case the notion of 'Jewish nationality');
4. Timișoara's character as a melting pot made the identification of its citizens with one particular nationality often impossible, mixed marriages being numerous, indicating relationships between Roman Catholics and Protestants, Orthodox and Greek Catholics, Christians and Jews;
5. 'nationality' or ethnonation were very relative notions in a region where cultures and customs intertwined.

Timișoara's population in the 1930 census by mother tongue and by religion is shown in Tables 19.4 and 19.5 respectively.

Table 19.4
Timişoara's population in 1930 by mother tongue

DECLARED MOTHER TONGUE	NUMBER OF PERSONS
German	30,670
Hungarian	32,513
Romanian	24,088
Serbian, Croatian or Slovenian	1,820
Russian	688
Yiddish	442
Czech or Slovak	375
Gypsy/Traveller/Roma	167
Bulgarian	234
Polish	44
Turk or Tatar	53
Ruthenian or Ukrainian	30
Albanian	26
Armenian	3
Greek	7
Other	151
Undeclared	269
TOTAL	91,580

Source: Manuilă, *Recensământul general al populaţiei României din 29 decembrie 1930*, vol. ii. *Neam, limbă maternă, religie*, pp. 468–69.

Table 19.5
Timişoara's population in 1930 by religion

DECLARED RELIGION OR DENOMINATION	NUMBER OF ADHERENTS
Roman Catholic	48,136
Orthodox	24,307
Jewish	9,368
Reformed Calvinist	4,690
Evangelical Lutheran	2,279
Greek Catholic	2,056
Baptist	193
Muslim	84

Unitarian	66
Adventist	42
Armenian Gregorian	26
Lipovans	8
Other	14
Freethinkers	41
Undeclared	270
TOTAL	91,580

Source: Manuilă, *Recensământul general al populației României din 29 decembrie 1930*, vol. ii. *Neam, limbă maternă, religie*, p. 755.

As can be seen from Tables 19.4 and 19.5, the particularity of Timişoara lies in the preservation of a large number of multilingual citizens, among whom the Hungarian and German speakers disputed pre-eminence, closely followed by the Romanian speakers. From this viewpoint, the Hungarians, Germans and Romanians in the census represent respectively 35.5, 33.5 and 26.6 per cent of the total population.

As for freedom of conscience, the statistics suggest that the authorities had a tendency to impose affiliation to one faith or another, a fact illustrated by the very low number of those who declared themselves to be 'Freethinkers': 0.04 per cent. This is not surprising, however, because official statistics did not record any information about those who were bi- or trilingual, nor did they use the concept of citizen, nor did they record those who were assimilated to one of the dominant cultures and religions. The authorities imposed a specific identity on each member of the population, while in reality identity was fluid.

Despite these shortcomings and the tendency to create more categories of citizens, multilingual and multi-confessional Timișoara continued its existence, revealing its personality through its sociocultural model, its industrial and commercial contribution to Romania, its own resources, the openness of its society, and the impressive number of cultural, sports and civic associations. A few examples of this will illustrate the contradiction between the nationalist political orientation and the aspirations of the local society.

1. The very first professional club and the most popular football team of Romania in 1930–40 was Ripensia Timișoara, the result of admirable cooperation, reflecting intercultural harmony. The team included players with diverse cultural backgrounds – German, Romanian, Hungarian, Jewish and Serbian – reflecting the very nature of the city. Among the prominent players were Alexandru Schwartz, Gheorghe Ciolac, Nicolae Simatoc, Rudolf Burger, Rudolf Kotormany and Silviu Bindea. Between 1930 and 1940, Ripensia repeatedly won the national football championship and competed with the main football clubs of interwar Europe, thus becoming the undisputed legend of

Romanian football. The club conveyed one of the most credible messages about the spirit of integration of interwar Timișoara to the whole of Romania, the names of its players symbolising both the recognition of their talent in sport and the continuity of the pacifist values characterising most of the multi- and intercultural cities in East Central Europe, values which were inherited from previous generations.[13]

2. Another proof of this spirit is the impressive list of journals and newspapers,[14] as well as mono- and multilingual books and postcards, which appeared.[15] Some newspapers and journals were published simultaneously in Romanian, Hungarian and German during the interwar period. In 1922, there were 4 such trilingual publications; in 1925 there were 7; in 1926 there were 4; in 1930 there were 3; in 1932 there were 4; in 1933 there were 6; and finally in 1934 there were 7.[16]

3. A postcard inventory by the collector Thomas Mochnács reveals that the postcards depicting Timișoara had explanatory texts not just in one of three languages – Romanian, German or Hungarian – but in two or three of them. Out of a total of 480 postcards, 106 had explanatory text in Romanian and Hungarian; 50 in Romanian, Hungarian and German; 15 in Romanian and German; 15 in Hungarian and German; one in German and Hebrew; and one in Esperanto.[17] Not only were many of them rarities, but they also testify to a state of mind in which the interest and preoccupation of citizens with the particular features of the city as compared with those of other towns in Romania or Europe in the interwar period prevailed.

4. Much of the elite had taken over and capitalised on this spirit in the population. This was the case with some of the cosmopolitan writers who translated poetry and prose[18] from one language to another by experimenting with new literary genres. Among them were Ion Stoia-Udrea, Nicolae Ivan and Mircea Șerbănescu.[19]

5. The same orientation can be found in the circle of fine artists of Timișoara represented by the painters Franz Ferch, Ioan Isac, Albert Krausz, Corneliu Liuba and Ioan Eminet, as well as by the sculptors Andrei Gál, Ferdinand Gallas, Romul Ladea, Sebastian Rotschingk and Géza Rubletzky.[20]

6. A particular emphasis was generated by the musical milieu, especially by the Conservatory of Timișoara which managed to capitalise more than any other institution on the richness of the folkloric traditions of the Banat. Among those who gave substance to its creative and formative programmes were the cellist Nicolae Papazoglu, the violin professor Maximilian Costin, violinists Béla Tomm and Josef Brandeis,[21] composers Guido von Pogatschnigg, Sabin Drăgoi, Tiberiu Brediceanu, Filaret Barbu, Alma Cornea-Ionescu, Filaret Barbu, Zeno Vancea, Hermann Klee and Richard Carol Oschanitzky.[22]

These arguments support the idea that Timișoara in the 1930s was the result of cohabitation and intermingling rather than a city with separate linguistic communities living parallel lives. Both nationalist and National Communist historiography of the interwar period declined to take note of this fact or maybe failed to understand it.[23] Intercultural harmony among different communities rather than conflict prevailed during that time.

Later, in 1941, the statistics once more referred to the population in Timişoara based on 'nationalities', precisely requesting each citizen to declare his or her affiliation in this sense (see Table 19.6).

Table 19.6
Timişoara's population in 1941 by nationality

DECLARED NATIONALITY	NUMBER OF PERSONS
Romanian	46,466
German	37,611
Hungarian	24,891
Other	16,084
TOTAL	125,052

Source: Traian Rotariu, Maria Semeniuc and Elemér Mezei, *Recensământul din 1941: Transilvania* (*The Census of 1941: Transylvania*) (Cluj-Napoca, 2002), p. 107.

Table 19.6 suggests the slow but sure incarnation of attachment to a particular 'nationality', ethnic group or an ethnonation. It is worth mentioning that counting and classifying the population according to the 'nationality',[24] language or religion of the inhabitants was also embraced by some of those who were part of a minority community. This type of quantification was adopted not only by the Romanian institutes who were subordinate to the central administration, such as the Banat–Crişana Social Institute, but also by the administration of each linguistic or religious group. Special attention was even directed towards the protection of minority groups in the region, the main voice being *A Magyar Kisebbség: Nemzetpolitikai Szemle* (*The Hungarian Minority: National Political Leaflet*), a bimonthly publication which appeared from June 1923 to June 1942, totalling 480 issues. The editors were István Sulyok and Elemér Jakabffy. It is clear from the title that the Hungarians considered themselves not only as a minority, but also as belonging to a different nation from the Romanian. From 1926 onwards a trilingual supplement was also published under the title *Glasul Minorităţilor / La Voix des minorités / Die Stimme der Minderheiten* (*The Voice of Minorities*). The main contributors to this publication were Artúr Balogh, Árpád Bitay, Kelemen Gál, Elemér Gyárfás, György Kristóf, Imre Mikó, Árpád and József Willer. Elemér Jakabffy, one of the political leaders of the Hungarians in the Banat and also in Romania, was the director of both publications. In parallel with this preoccupation, central authorities in Bucharest continued to emphasise the numerical increase of the Romanian majority in cities such as Timişoara. In 1930, 15 nationalities in Timişoara were recorded and classified by the census but by 1941 these were reduced to three: Romanian, German and Hungarian. All the less numerous groups had been merged into the column referring to 'other nationalities'. The statistics of 1941 indicated for the first time the change of proportions among the local population, Romanians becoming a majority with a total population of 46,466. This accounting and establishment of a person's place in society was based on the identity theory imagined and formulated in the nineteenth century which had as its main point of reference the concept of *Völkischekultur*.[25]

We have to say that, besides being well documented and narrated, a history of the relationship between the majority and the minorities implies not only invoking or exemplifying multicultural societies – namely their life under the aegis of interculturality – but also taking into account the fact that the new identity theory, that of the ethnonation and 'nationality', accentuated differences rather than convergences. That is, the meaning of the collective mentality of the city derives from two contexts, that of the state and that of the locality, which have to be analysed simultaneously. The ethnonational and ethnocultural differentiation can be seen in the semantics attributed to the key concepts that define collectivity in the Romanian language; that is, *neam* (kinship), *popor* (people), nation, multiculturality, multi-confessionality. This aspect seems important since we are considering a city with particular characteristics resulting from its geography, its demographic movement, and its cultural references and interconnections.

THE JEWS OF INTERWAR TIMIȘOARA: THE RECOGNITION OF DIVERSITIES OR INTERCULTURAL CIVICISM?

Beyond the political discourse and decisions of interwar Romania, sociocultural realities are clearly outlined. To this end, this section will consider one of the groups living in Timișoara, namely the Jews, with the aim of revealing their status in interwar Timișoara and in Romania. Jews represent a symptomatic case for the redefinition of collective identity in the context of administrative changes taking place at state level during the transition from the Austro-Hungarian Monarchy to the Romanian state. At the end of the nineteenth century and beginning of the twentieth, Jews played a particularly important role in the profile of Timișoara: they were citizens with equal legal and political rights; they represented a bridge between communities by using three or even four languages; they had set up some of the most prestigious industrial and trade companies in the city; they had developed economic, cultural and artistic relations with other cities in Central and Western Europe.[26] Along with the Swabians,[27] they had created a bourgeois class, which became involved in the process of modernisation of the city and of the region. Consequently, the status of citizenship was fundamental for the continuity of the Jewish presence in Timişoara after the First World War, for the expansion of their activity and, to a certain extent, for the self-definition of their identity.[28]

The reorganisation of Central and Eastern Europe following the war, the creation of nation states following the Treaty of Saint-Germain and the Treaty of Trianon, had generated a crisis of conscience within the population of Timişoara and the Banat. Postwar changes provoked misunderstandings between the more cosmopolitan liberal-bourgeois Jews on the one hand and the Zionists on the other. Hildrun Glass – a researcher of the German–Jewish relationship in interwar Romania – has noticed that the main criticism of liberal groups came from the new Jewish political organisations. The same thing happened in the case of the Swabians and the Hungarians by setting up their political organisations under the emblem of ethnocultural and ethno-national identity respectively.[29] Glass's observation is credible, but internal tensions require further explanations that take into consideration the formation of the nation, the political context, economic life and social movements. Instauration of the Romanian administration in 1919 meant the need for Jews to adapt to new conditions: the administrative reorganisation of their community, taking into account the new legal framework; the political representation within Romania; redefining their identity according to the Romanian idea of nation. All this against a background in which the Jews (like the Swabians, Hungarians, Serbians, Bulgarians and Slovakians) were not considered, and did not consider themselves, foreigners in the regions belonging to the former Dual Monarchy, but rather part of the new nation's citizens.

The very first signs of the unification of the Jewish community living in Timişoara appeared in 1922 under pressure from the Orthodox Jews.[30] According to them, the interests of the Jews belonging to the former Austro-Hungarian regions should be represented by the National Union of the Jews of Transylvania and the Banat. Jewish consciousness was reborn thanks to the Zionist organisations. The progress of the movement was due to the work of Alexandru Marmorek, leader of the Zionist movement in France. A university professor and director of the Pasteur Institute in Paris, Marmorek was originally from Vienna and was familiar with the problems of Hungarian Jews. He arrived in Timişoara at the end of the First World War as a doctor attached to the French troops belonging to the Entente, sent to prevent potential conflicts among Romanians, Hungarians and Serbs in the territory of the Banat.[31] The *Uj Kelet* newspaper of Cluj claimed that Professor Marmorek drew the attention of the Jews of Timişoara to the new international political context in which they would have to deal with nationalist and anti-Semitic attacks. *Uj*

Kelet of Cluj (1918–40) and *Neue Zeit-Uj Kor* of Timișoara (1920–40) advocated reconsidering the identity issue in tune with the ideology of the time, the Timișoara newspaper becoming the mouthpiece of the Union of the Jews of Transylvania and the Banat. 'The Zionist idea was adopted by a portion of the local Jewry during the meeting held in Timișoara in 1923.'[32] In parallel, Dr Wilhelm Filderman, the representative of the Union of the Native Jews of Bucharest, addressed the Timișoara Jewry through their lawyer Adolf Vértes, with the aim of inviting them to accept the unification of the Jewish communities of Romania.[33]

Though there were similarities, the way of life and the concerns of the communities living in the Banat and Transylvania were not the same as those of the Jews living in the Old Kingdom of Romania. The Jews of Timişoara were mainly Hungarian and German speakers, and after a part of the Banat was integrated into Romania they had also acquired Romanian. The majority belonged to the Neologist (Reformist) denomination, closely attached to the idea of emancipation and the preservation of local values, which is why the political ideology promoted by the Jews of Bucharest could not be immediately assimilated by the Jews of Timişoara. Consequently, Jewish intercommunity relationships in Romania were kept on a formal level for a long time. The assembly held in Timișoara in 1923 revealed that some Jews were interested in clarifying the identity issue. If from a cultural and linguistic perspective they belonged to the cosmopolitan space of Central Europe, from the ritual viewpoint the Jews of Timişoara oscillated between Orthodox and Neolog. Against this background, it was the Zionists who formulated the first alternative to the concept of citizenship. The attendance at the assembly by both Jewish communities of Timişoara (Neolog and Orthodox) was given as an example of good cooperation. Personalities of Jewish life in the Banat and Transylvania participated, among them the chief rabbis of Timişoara and Caransebeş, the president of the National Union of the Jews of Timişoara, the president of the Neolog community of Arad, and the vice president of the National Union of the Jews of Cluj. The gathering created the conditions for a debate around the question of Jewish identity. Topics concerning religion, cultural and sports activities, national propaganda and awakening of Jewish consciousness were among the speakers' highlights. The aim of the event was stated by the president of the Neolog Community of Timişoara, Dr Adolf Vértes, who said:

> I considered that the time had come to invite delegates of the Transylvanian and Banat communities and of the national associations to the great assembly of today [23 May 1923] which is dedicated to the magnificent idea to unite our resources dispersed within various political nuances, so that we can direct them to the general benefit of the Jews.[34]

Jewish politics in Timișoara unfolded under the influence of the Jewish movements in Europe. The idea of a Jewish nation was inspired by the same differentials which were promoted by German culture in the nineteenth century and which had inspired the Czechs, Slovaks, Romanians, Hungarians, Serbs and Bulgarians a few decades before. The Romanian state required each minority group to set up its own representative body. The Jews were an exception. The two parties which the Jews of Timișoara and the Banat looked to, namely the Romanian National Party (which later became the National Peasant Party) and the Hungarian Party, had, however, ignored them. During the elections of 1927 and 1928, the Jews of the Banat and Transylvania were running on the lists of the Hungarian Party and Liberal Party respectively, and succeeded in winning only two seats in the Romanian Parliament.[35] This was quite serious, as the Jewish population in the above-mentioned regions accounted about 200,000 people.

Even though the Zionist movement was gaining ground and the spread of the majority and minority nationalist movements was felt in Timișoara, too, the majority of Jews – like the majority of the city population – were favourable to social integration and promoting a civic movement that had began a few decades earlier. Consequently, they continued to practise multilingual communication and to share values, oppose ethnicisation and nationalism, and cultivate cosmopolitan and social democratic orientations through which Timișoara entered modernity. It is also true that the Romanian state and the local administrations within it could not ignore the presence and talent of Jewish entrepreneurs, so their professional and managerial skills were capitalised on. The prestige enjoyed by the Jews for their entrepreneurship and initiative averted tendencies promoted by I.I.C. Brătianu's National Liberal Party, deterring them from replacing the old category of entrepreneurs with one of Romanian ethnic origin. The high number of the so-called minorities in Timișoara and the Banat during the interwar period meant that it was possible for economic interests to take precedence over theories and measures of ethnicism. The textile industry; the glove, hat and shoe factories; and the brewery of Timișoara benefited from the substantial contribution of Jewish entrepreneurs.[36] Their businesses were highly appreciated; cooperation among businesspeople belonging to different cultures, languages and religious denominations brought economic and political stability to the city. The Jewish presence was appreciated in the creation and running of guild associations, in the reciprocity of services provided, and in their exceptional contribution to musical and artistic life.

CONCLUSIONS

As an industrial and trade centre, interwar Timișoara had a large number of workers, important social organisations, a strong trade-union movement and a liberal bourgeoisie which was able to wisely handle business in order to maintain a relaxed environment among the employees.

Most citizens were attached to social democracy, despite the fact that left-wing movements were considered by the authorities as opposed to the national culture and identity. It was not a simple matter of capital growth, though; for example, we can observe a certain dynamic in practical matters, an extension of intergroup relationships, the creation of guilds, and the existence of a vibrant artistic and sports life.

At a time when ideologies were becoming radicalised, and racism and anti-Semitism were becoming reference points on the Romanian and European political scenes, Timișoara chose instead to cultivate an attitude of opposing conflict, a civic spirit, and a multi- and intercultural status. The aspirations of the majority of its inhabitants support the observation that social history does not simply mean division of work and state systems. In other words, as Étienne Balibar would say, non-economic social reactions play a fundamental role in such places because they represent the real historical collectivity of individuals.[37]

20

THE TREATMENT OF JEWS IN THE BANAT DURING THE SECOND WORLD WAR

The Deportation Plan

Victor Neumann

THE ROMANIAN POLITICAL BACKGROUND

In August 1940 Romania agreed to arbitration by Germany and Italy over its territorial disputes with Hungary. By the resulting award, the Vienna Diktat, Romania ceded northern Transylvania to Hungary without any armed opposition. Southern Transylvania and the Banat (along with the territories of Wallachia) remained an integral part of the Romanian state. Despite the fact that this loss – followed by administrative restructuration – was due to Nazi Germany, Romania was among the allies of the Third Reich for most of the war (1940–4). The alliance with the Axis powers was sealed by the Romanian–German treaty of November 1940.

One of the main reasons why Romania was of interest to the Nazis was its oil reserves, which the entire war machine of the Reich planned to use to its advantage in its conflict with the USSR. During such a tense political time, the Jewish population from the Banat and southern Transylvania had a very uncertain status. The government led by Marshal Ion Antonescu concentrated Jewish communities from these regions in a few important centres in order to better control them – a large number of Jews were gathered in Timișoara. This was a measure motivated by their so-called 'supervision', but also, as we shall see, by the intention to eliminate them.

As far as political decisions were concerned, these were issued in Bucharest. The state also functioned on the principle of centralisation in the years that preceded the Fascist regime, and abolished the right to elect local political representatives. This was the centralist tradition formulated by the

Constitution of 1923 (which resumed the thesis of the indivisible unity of the Old Kingdom of Romania), along with the decision issued in 1925 according to which prefectures from all over the country were to be managed by an official appointed in Bucharest.

THE OFFICIALS' SUSPICIONS REGARDING JEWS IN THE BANAT AND TRANSYLVANIA

In the 1930s, the Legionary Movement (Iron Guard) made its presence felt throughout Romania. It was inclined towards Fascism, but distinguished itself from European Fascist movements by associating the nation to a sacred community, one that validated the Church but not the State. The Legionaires identified the Romanian nation with the Orthodox Church and regarded themselves as the main mediators between God and the nation.[38] At Cluj after 1935, the movement gained momentum, Jews were beaten up on the streets, in schools and universities, and their presence in Romanian schools was drastically limited. Anti-Semitism had long been a constant of Transylvanian culture, being present in all regional, cultural-linguistic communities, whether Romanian, German or Hungarian. Officials appropriated it and applied it, often at the discretion of functionaries, army, police or gendarmerie. This attitude was visible even after the war, when the Romanian Communist authorities continued to discriminate against minorities, culminating in the sale of Germans and Jews to Germany and Israel.

In 1939 the government, led by Octavian Goga, tightened up the anti-Semitic laws. A secret provision stated:

> Jewish communities will be notified that helping refugees is forbidden and subject to severe sanctions; at the same time, they will be advised to bring to the police those refugees who would contact the [Jewish] communities or whose presence they might know of by other means.[39]

In 1940, 2.5 million people were living in north Transylvania, of whom 160,000 were Jews. Due to Romanian racial laws, a portion of Jews from the Banat and southern Transylvania migrated north, where their number rose to 165,061 in 1940–4.[40]

At the beginning of the war, there was apparent calm in Timişoara. The president of the local Jewish community was the well-known lawyer Dr Samuel Ligeti. The religious services – where the Reformed/Neolog cult was usually practised[41] – had the renowned rabbi Iacob Singer as their main representative until 1939, and in the following decade the rabbi Dr Maximilian Drechsler. During the war, Jewish community schools continued to function in Timişoara, but lacked financial support and recognition from the state. They were attended by children of Jews in the Banat and southern Transylvania.

It was the period in which the old Jewish schools had been evacuated, and classes were held in improvised spaces. In spite of these measures, there were two elementary schools at Timişoara, one in the Fabric and the other in the Josefin quarter; a boys' and a girls' high school; a commercial high school and a boarding school. Things were similar in other cities of the region. According to Professor Alfred Goldenblum's testimony, on the initiative of his father David Goldenblum, primary classes, secondary classes and an individual programme for students who were preparing for higher education were established at Sighişoara. The school functioned between 1942 and 1944 and issued certificates of graduation for the respective classes, certificates that were approved later by the schools of Sighişoara and other cities. Where such improvised institutions functioned, the teachers tried to preserve the classical norms of the teaching process. The responsibility was enormous. Despite the difficulties, the results were satisfactory.

It must be remembered that by 1938, the life of Jews had worsened in all Romanian regions. Serious threats to their communities came from the legislation adopted by Carol II's royal dictatorship regime and later by the totalitarian Legionary and military Fascist regimes. In the Banat, measures against Jews were enforced by governmental orders. The Ministry of the Interior constantly demanded reports from the prefecture and the Timiş County Police regarding the movement of the population. The documents issued by the local administrations in the Banat in 1938–42 show a great mistrust for the Jews of the region. Why was this? The documents preserved at the Timiş County Branch of the National Archives suggest that the suspicions were due to the international connections of Jewish traders; their use of the Hungarian and German languages; the attachment of some of them to Hungarian culture; and their intellectual and professional training, which could facilitate the gathering and dissemination of information.

Whoever studies the counter-intelligence reports from these years will observe that Jews from the Banat and Transylvania were considered dangerous for the policies of Carol II and Marshal Ion Antonescu because they spoke Hungarian. Due to the fact that during the Second World War Transylvania became the subject of a new territorial dispute between Hungary and Romania, the Jews from this region and the neighbouring Banat were seen as potential traitors. The information bulletins of the Romanian Secret Service stated:

> Some of them [the Jews] have strong sympathy with the Hungarian people, and are even members of the Hungarian party, which shows their feelings and attachment towards the Hungarians. The others have an expectant attitude, and are waiting for events to unfold. With all the currents started in Hungary [the anti-Jewish laws of 1939] for their removal from official functions, and also from other institutions

or enterprises, their loyalty towards the Romanian state cannot be stated with certainty.[42]

Other documents name Jews 'propagandists' and 'spies', a threat to internal order. A comparison of the Romanian and the Hungarian political thought of the time – regardless of the cultural differences – shows that Bucharest and Budapest shared a similarly mistaken perception about Jews in the Banat and Transylvania. Their reaction was not on the grounds of ensuring the integrity of the state or the safety of the Romanian and Hungarian populations. Rather, it was the result of the racist and anti-Semitic state ideology professed in Hungary and Romania.

The Hungarian authorities were dissatisfied with the fact that Jews no longer declared themselves to be Hungarians, as had been the case until 1918. On 2 August 1941, the third racial law on Jews in Hungary came into force. It was drafted while László Bárdossy was prime minister and prohibited marriage between Jews and non-Jews, and also sexual intercourse between them outside marriage. According to this law, all those who had two Jewish grandparents were considered Jews. Those who were born Christians were not considered Jews, unless they had more than two Jewish grandparents. The Hungarian churches opposed the enforcement of this law. It was proposed and accepted that the minister of justice be given the right to designate Christian-born persons as non-Jews.[43]

With regard to the attitude of the Romanian authorities, the Banat and Transylvania created difficulties for totalitarian regimes wanting to use the concept of nation only in relation to the majority ethnic group. Romania had a restrictive understanding concerning the integration of any minority, and this was not recent. In the interwar decades and during the war itself this proved to be a handicap both for politicians and for the Romanian intelligentsia. Not sufficiently concerned with essential political themes and preferring ethno-differentialism as an equivalent of the concept of nation, the Romanian political elites tackled social phenomena by notions or concepts such as ethnicity, kin/tribe and race. Ignoring regional diversity and the rights of minority linguistic groups who accounted for 30 per cent of the total population in the years 1930–40, the representatives of the National Liberal Party transformed Romania into a centralist state. When they came to power, the Fascists took advantage of the concentration of power in a single political-administrative centre to spread their radical ideology and to enforce their racist and anti-Semitic legislation rapidly and with no opposition.

At the beginning of the war, the excessive zeal of the local authorities increased as the documents from the Ministry of the Interior insisted on the supervision of any movement of the Jewish population. Even the collection of money launched by Jewish associations – known by the name of the Zionist Organisation in Romania or the New Zionist Organisation – was prohibited.

The propagandistic material used for that purpose was destroyed by order of the same ministry. If the Legionary Movement led by Corneliu Zelea Codreanu and Horia Sima took chaotic action regarding the Jews of the Banat, the Fascists led by Ion Antonescu used the state institutions – namely, the Ministry of the Interior, the army and the gendarmerie – to repress them.

IDENTITY THEORY: THE HARDSHIPS IMPOSED ON JEWS BY ION ANTONESCU'S REGIME

In the autumn of 1941, all Jewish men from the Banat region were gathered at the Electrica Stadium, near Timișoara Est railway station, to be distributed and sent to forced labour detachments. Some arrived at Chizătău-Șanovița, Ghioroc and Pâncota; others at Filiași and Piatra Olt. There are testimonies that Jews from Lugoj were sent to Făgăraș and Predeal. The main purpose of this was to 'defile human dignity' rather than to fulfil any special need.[44] The descriptions contained in the documents kept in the Timișoara Jewish Community Archives show what this form of slavery was like and how certain officers of the Romanian army disposed of the health – and even the lives – of the people who had been discriminated against on racial criteria. The archives show, for example, that in the Ghioroc camp working conditions were inhuman, beating the naked skin (between 25 and 70 times), incarceration with no explanation, and mocking treatment. Also at Ghioroc, the practice of the so-called inquisition rooms was tested.[45] Jews in these detachments worked in stone quarries, in construction, transportation, repairing roads and railway tracks, digging trenches and as porters in train stations. All this represented a kind of marginalisation and exclusion.

The decisions taken by Marshal Antonescu's government aimed at removing Jews from the social, economic and professional life of the country, and using them as a currency of exchange in relations with Germany. As already mentioned, Romania had been economically and militarily subordinate to the Third Reich from the moment it joined the Rome–Berlin Axis. As a member of this axis, Antonescu knew about the plan for Jewish extermination initiated by Hitler and known as 'the final solution'. Among the East European territories included in this project was the so-called region of the Bug, where the deportation of Romanian Jews took place. The biggest threat to those in forced labour camps was deportation to Transnistria. Every Jew knew about the horrors of Transnistria and that the chances of returning from there were negligible. Jews from the Banat and southern Transylvania knew that many of their co-religionists from Dorohoi, Bessarabia and Bukovina had died during their trip or because of the maltreatment, summary executions and general living conditions in Transnistria.

The Holocaust did not mean only the gas chambers of Auschwitz, but also the reserves set up by Hitler and his allies for other methods of mass extermination. Transnistria was among them. The 102 colonies established within the region by the Romanian administration during Antonescu's regime prove the involvement of the Romanian government in the Holocaust against Jews and Gypsies. Several hundred thousand of them disappeared there in extremely humiliating conditions. In the Hall of Remembrance at the United States Holocaust Memorial Museum in Washington, D.C., Transnistria is listed among the most atrocious camps along with Auschwitz, Majdanek, Belzec, Bergen-Belsen, Dachau and Babi Yar. This is no coincidence. The identity theory promoted by the Romanian regime was inspired by that of the Nazis. It was the basis of racist ideology and many political and military decisions. In fact, the state legislation led by Marshal Antonescu promoted the doctrine of Hitler's Reich. Here is one of Antonescu's most emblematic statements on the political thought and extermination actions he initiated and conducted:

> if we do not take advantage of the current national and European situation to purify the Romanian people, we will miss the last opportunity history offers us . . . I can bring Bessarabia back and Transylvania too, but if we don't cleanse the Romanian people we will have done nothing, because it is not borders that make the strength of a people, but the homogeneity and purity of its race. And this is my first aim.[46]

The racial doctrine stated that blood origin was the first factor that determined the future of any individual or group. That was how the Romanian dictator saw things,[47] and his speeches or interventions in the Council of Ministers show that this was the ideology that inspired his policy. His priority was not regaining north-western Transylvania or Bessarabia for the benefit of Romania, but rather 'the purification of the people'. For Antonescu, the people symbolised the tribe, and that was the equivalent of the nation

Even if the elimination method practised by the Romanian dictator was not comparable to that of the Nazis, Antonescu's practices generated mass murder based on racist principles. The name of Transnistria defines both the intentions of the Romanian Fascist regime and the actual deaths instituted by it. The statement quoted above – and there are many others expressing the same ideas, formulated by other members of Antonescu's cabinet – shows that the ethnonationalism and racism promoted in Romania between 1940 and 1944 were considered laws in interhuman and intercommunity relations.

The survivors' testimonies attest that 100 Zionist Jews from Timișoara were deported to Transnistria and never came back. One of the survivors, Doctor Paul Grünberger, saw at the Chizătău railway station (where he did forced labour) the freight train with two wagons that transported them. The railway wagons had open doors, so some of the deportees were spotted by Grünberger's colleagues. These deportees had requested transit visas through the USSR to leave for America.[48] They were exterminated in the reservation beyond the Dneister River. A few hundred more Jews, from other cities of the Banat and Transylvania, met the same tragic fate.[49] Those deportations perhaps explain why in 1941–42 the Jewish population in Timişoara decreased by almost 2,300 (from 13,610 to 11,340).[50]

Racism and anti-Semitism – which contributed to the formulation of the Fascist concept of nation – represented the most aggressive injustices committed in Romania in the years before and during the Second World War. They formed the ideological basis by which Jews from the Banat and Transylvania were deprived of their rights: they could not own radios in their own homes; they were not allowed to practise the medical profession, except to treat Jewish patients; lawyers were banned from going to court; all were forced to hand over clothes on the grounds that they were needed by the army or society. To illustrate this final case, we refer to a report of the Regional Police Inspectorate of Timişoara which mentions that in October 1941, based on Decree-Law no. 2909, published in *Official Gazette*, no. 25 on 21 October 1941, adult Jews from the Banat contributed clothing in the interest of society.

Property belonging to the Jewish community was also confiscated. The same happened to private property: shops, factories, houses, lands, forests, farms. There was continuity between the dispossession system organised by the Legionaries and that put into practice by Marshal Antonescu. In the Banat, the process of confiscation started in December 1940 and was systematically resumed in 1941 and 1942. According to the information mentioned in the reports of the Regional Police Inspectorate of Timişoara in December 1940,

> following the verbal orders of the chiefs of the Legionary county organisations without any legal basis [the decrees existed, but had been enacted from 1941], industrial and commercial enterprises were taken from the majority of the Jews which, after the [Legionary] rebellion of 21–23 January 1941, returned them.

In fact, after this rebellion which scared the Romanian Jews, a surprise occurred in the Banat and southern Transylvania. In Timişoara, for example – as stated in the document quoted above –

> the majority of the Jewish population started to sell their businesses or to associate with various Christians, thus many Jewish enterprises came into the hands of minorities, especially the Swabians [German], who wanted to take away businesses from the Jews at any cost.[51]

There are documents confirming that ethnocultural segregation had led to a decline in relations between Jewish and German communities in the Banat. In Timişoara and Sibiu, Jews were faced not only with Antonescu's decrees on the dispossession of goods, but also with members of the local German community taking unilateral action to take hold of their possessions. However, it would not be right to generalise.

According to the testimony of one of the survivors, Professor Oskar Schwartz, the Jewish population was pursued by the Romanian (Fascist) Legionaries who were active in the Banat and southern Transylvania, among them students of Timișoara Polytechnic. Discrimination against the Jewish population in the years 1941–44 was omnipresent. A report of the Romanian Secret Service entitled *International Jewish Occult Organisations: Their Action in Romania through the Cultural League, Masonic Lodges and Sport Clubs* attempted to 'justify' this anti-Semitism by saying that the Jewish Cultural League operating in different Transylvanian cities

> alongside its strictly religious role, is in close contact with Hungarian spying and irredentist organisations and it is easy to understand its attitude towards the administration of Wallachia [Romania], because the Jewish community from Ardeal [Transylvania] is completely Magyarised and imbued with the aspirations of the Hungarian nation.[52]

These kinds of prejudices were promoted by intellectuals and transformed into the ideology that would justify discrimination against Jews by the political and administrative institutions of the state.

However, even when propaganda took hold of part of the collective consciousness and a civic reaction against governmental measures was absent, Romanians did not always share the same attitude as Antonescu's regime. There were many Romanian and German citizens who not only refused to adhere to the racist ideas, but also spoke in defence of the Jews. Dr Paul Grünberger attests that during the deportations to forced labour detachments, the local population helped them with food. He said that Romanian and German villages in the Banat were rich at that time and both communities dealt admirably with the Jews. The anti-Semitic policy did not have the support of the whole Romanian population. Not only were the peasants from the Banat opposed to this way of looking at things, but so were many intellectuals. A letter addressed to Marshal Antonescu, signed by a group of Romanian intellectuals from Timișoara, stated:

> Whatever our perception towards the Jews, we are Christians and human beings . . . and we tremble at the idea that the citizens of a state could be, without any fault, stripped of all their possessions and banished from the country in which they were born, and where the bones of their parents, grandparents and great-grandparents have lain for centuries.[53]

Many of the citizens of Timișoara showed solidarity with the Jews, inviting them to listen to the radio, which had been forbidden by officials of the regime. 'Although we were at war and the risks were high, there were many good-willed people who welcomed us in their homes', said Ernest Neumann, Timișoara's chief rabbi.

The discontent at Marshal Antonescu's policy was also visible in other Romanian regions. In Oltenia and Muntenia, the southern regions of the country, the railway workers and civil servants, the population of the localities from which Romanian soldiers had been recruited for the front, expressed a critical attitude towards the regime on many occasions. This was especially the case with the railway workers and peasant families who saw their children sent to death for reasons foreign to Romania and who opposed the entrance of Romania into the anti-Soviet war. Such documentary evidence attests that the Fascism and militarism instituted by the Antonescu regime did not have the broad support of the population at all times during the war and in all regions of the country.[54]

THE PLAN FOR THE DEPORTATION AND EXTERMINATION OF JEWS FROM THE BANAT AND SOUTHERN TRANSYLVANIA

When they found out about the plans for the deportation of the Jewish communities from Timişoara, Arad and Turda to the Lublin camp, the rabbis and the president of Timişoara's Jewish community walked from one synagogue to another to boost morale in the believers. 'I was afraid of my own shadow', declared one of the survivors, but the moment called for such an attitude. The cooperation of community leaders encouraged the Jews in Timişoara but there was good reason for panic. The provisions issued at Bucharest indicated an agreement between the German Reich and Antonescu's regime on the deportation of Jews from the Banat and southern Transylvania to Poland. Wheels were in motion in three places: Timişoara, Arad and Turda, all border cities.

Representatives of the local offices of the Jewish Centre had become aware of the Romanian government's intentions. They had been instructed to draw up tables of the Jewish population according to sex, age and occupation.[55] After many discussions and agreements with the German authorities, Ion and Mihai Antonescu signed an accord on Jewish deportation from the three cities. 'Between July and October 1942, various plans were drafted concerning the ongoing deportations to Transnistria and the deportation of Jews to extermination camps. These measures were made public by the superior officer Gustav Richter (Hauptsturmführer SS), the councillor of the German Embassy in Bucharest for Jewish issues.'[56] The rumours heard by Jews in Timişoara in the summer of 1942 are confirmed by the documents and testimonies of other survivors and contributors to the cancellation of the plan.

On 10 July 1942, Colonel R. Davidescu demanded that the Ministry of the Interior draft a report on Jews in the Banat and southern Transylvania. The justification for this was that there was a need to find space to accommodate the Romanian refugees from northern Transylvania, which had been occupied by Hungary following the Vienna Diktat. Colonel Davidescu demanded the authorities prepare the land for the deportation of Jews to the Bug, excluding intellectuals and industrialists needed to manage certain factories. In his testimony, Dr Paul Grünberger confirms the measures taken by the Romanian administration. For example, he says that the Jews in Sibiu were evicted from their homes to make room for forty Romanian teachers who were refugeees from Cluj University. Even his own father went through such an experience.

In August 1942, the Romanian government sent Radu Lecca, a senior official and the so-called 'commissary' who dealt with 'Jewish issues', to Berlin to seal the Jewish deportations from the Banat and southern Transylvania to the Nazi extermination camps. From the verbal note of the German Legation in Bucharest sent to Romanian officials, it seems that, after discussions with Radu Lecca, the Germans were expecting 'a brief answer, representing the attitude of the Romanian government on all the important issues, in order to forward it to the government of the Reich'.[57]

On 18 September 1942, Radu Lecca issued the following resolution: 'The eviction of Jews from Ardeal [Transylvania] is, for the moment, only taken into consideration. It will only begin when the time is right. Until then, all the details are being prepared by the Ministry of the Interior based on the directives given by Mr Marshal Antonescu.'[58] It was in this context that the Jews made countless efforts to save themselves from deportation. Leaders of the communities from Timișoara and Sibiu went to Bucharest to find solutions to cancel the plan. After many meetings with civil servants and talks between Antonescu and some influential people, the plan was cancelled. What had happened?

In 1942 Marshal Ion Antonescu was not certain of Hitler's victory and hesitated as pressure was put on him. The ambiguity of his attitude, generated by the shift in front-line forces, was a good omen for Jews in the Banat and Transylvania. The decision was made following some joint efforts by the metropolitan bishop of Transylvania, Nicolae Bălan; the politician Iuliu Maniu; and the owner of the Arad textile factory, Franz von Neuman. They were joined by the leaders of the Jewish communities in Bucharest and Timișoara: Alexandru Șafran, chief rabbi of Romania; the lawyer Dr Wilhelm Filderman, president of the Federation of Jewish Communities in Romania; Avram Leiba Zissu, leader of the Romanian Zionist movement; Samuel Ligeti, president of Timișoara's communities; and Iosif Grünberger, a trader from Sibiu.

Raul Hilberg affirms that it was Franz von Neuman ('the baron' from Arad) who offered the Romanian army 400 million lei through a high-ranking military official to cancel the plan.[59] The story cannot be proven with documentary evidence, although the manoeuvres made by the industrialist from Arad were acknowledged by some of the survivors. Neuman had the sympathy of the locals as initiator and supporter of some of the most popular sports and had a strong influence upon the Romanian officials in Bucharest, because the textile factory he owned and managed provided war equipment needed by the troops.[60]

In the *Report on the Situation and State of Mind Regarding the Deportation of Jews from Romania* signed on 5 October 1942 by von Killinger, representative of the German Legation in Bucharest, addressed to the Ministry of Foreign Affairs of the Third Reich, the situation of the Jews from the Banat and southern Transylvania is described:

> the baptized Jew, Baron Neuman, the main shareholder of the 'Aradian Textile' factory in Arad, has been and continues to be very active. He managed to win the sympathy of the National Peasant leader, Iuliu Maniu, one of his good friends. Iuliu Maniu declared that he, as a Transylvanian Romanian, strongly opposes treating Transylvanian Jews differently from Wallachian Jews and promises to get involved by any means necessary to stop the deportation of Jews from Romania. From Jew Neuman's secretary, Jew Beiliș, it was discovered that Neuman directed the metropolitan bishop of the Transylvanian Orthodox Church, [Nicolae] Bălan, to travel to Bucharest to intervene with prominent politicians and members of the Romanian government in order to cancel the planned deportation of Jews from Romania. It is not known for certain how much Neuman paid for the success of his interventions, but some well-informed Jews declared that he paid between 100 and 400 million lei for a postponement.[61]

The decisions to halt deportations were not exclusively due to important Jewish personalities. Dr Paul Grünberger, a student of the Jewish High School of Timișoara during the war years, was very close to events and his information allows us to understand the political context. He talks about the network of interpersonal relations that made possible the survival of Jews in Timișoara, the Banat and southern Transylvania. His testimony regarding the contribution of his father, Iosif Grünberger, to the halting of the Jewish deportation, is very important. Iosif was a trader, a refugee from Sibiu who had arrived in Timișoara with all his family, and was among the Jews who read *Donauzeitung*, the daily newspaper of the German Command for the Balkans, which appeared in Belgrade. *Donauzeitung* arrived every afternoon in Timișoara. On 8 August 1942 the newspaper published an article entitled 'Jewish Resettlement in Romania', declaring that joint Romanian–German action was planned for the deportation of Jews from the Banat and southern Transylvania to Lublin camp. It also mentioned that trains with many freight wagons had been prepared at the railway stations of the Banat and Transylvania. Iosif Grünberger was very concerned about the news.

THE INTERVENTION OF ROMANIAN AND JEWISH SPIRITUAL AND POLITICAL LEADERS: CANCELLING THE DEPORTATION PLAN

A rapid mobilisation followed, the notification of anyone, including prominent personalities, who might be able to prevent the deportation plan from going ahead. It was the summer of 1942. The news published in the German newspaper in Belgrade proved to be accurate. Iosif Grünberger contacted Carol Reitter, the last president of the Zionist movement in the Banat and Transylvania, an organisation that was then illegal. Reitter was the owner of a tracing paper factory from Cărăvan. Grünberger also approached the Auscher brothers. Together, they discussed the possibilities for action in the current circumstances, and decided to go to Bucharest and Sibiu. Victor Auscher, a textile manufacturer from Timişoara, had a travel permit in his pocket. He went to Bucharest to talk with Dr Wilhelm Filderman and A.L. Zissu, while Iosif Grünberger went to Sibiu, his city of origin, to meet the metropolitan bishop Nicolae Bălan. No Jew from Timişoara was a stranger to the actions to prevent the deportations.

The relationship with Bălan – the metropolitan bishop of Transylvania, who had a great influence upon Ion Antonescu – would be crucial. It was even more important that the high Orthodox prelate should accept intervening with the marshal. Through the intercession of Ludwig Ferenc, the president of the Sephardi Jewish community of Sibiu and, incidentally, the bishop's tailor, Iosif Grünberger reached Nicolae Bălan who welcomed him and accepted his appeal to go to Bucharest to meet the head of state.[62] After his meeting with Antonescu, Metropolitan Bishop Nicolae Bălan confirmed the existence of an agreement between the Romanian government and Hitler's Reich regarding the elimination of Jews from the Banat and southern Transylvania. At the request of the high prelate, the marshal promised to cancel the plan.

Iosif Grünberger also asked Iuliu Maniu to intervene to save the Jews. The most important Romanian politician in Transylvania and one of the great democratic personalities of interwar Romania, Maniu managed to discuss the theme of Jewish deportation with Marshal Antonescu. In order to persuade him to change his decision, Maniu posed the following question: if the Germans were to lose the war and Transylvania's status were to be decided by international peace talks, how would Romania justify eliminating its Jewish population when Hungary had not? (At this time the issue of deportation was not being addressed in Hungary.)

Both interventions – those of the metropolitan bishop Nicolae Bălan and of Iuliu Maniu – were decisive in saving the Jews.[63] In the report of the German Legation in Bucharest, mentioned earlier, drafted by von Killinger, the rescuing role of the Romanian personalities was noted: 'there had been mediations to raise awareness in Romanian governmental circles and prominent politicians; Jews from the Banat and Transylvania expressed their reaction against deportation, [and] former leading politicians, democrat and liberal (Iuliu Maniu and Constantin Dinu Brătianu) intervened in their favour'.[64]

Let us not imagine that the dictator had disinterestedly accepted the cancellation of the plan. He was in a tight political spot. He could not reconcile both promises, the Jewish extermination and his pledge to Hitler, on the one hand, and the Romanian desire to recover Transylvania occupied by Hungary, on the other. Accepting the cessation of the plan was taken against the backdrop of the war that was starting to turn unfavourably against Nazi Germany. It must be understood that Jews from the Banat and southern Transylvania were considered by Antonescu as potential leverage. Despite the threat of deportation and extermination, the great majority of them survived.

The tragedy of the Jews in Bukovina, Bessarabia and Transnistria was not repeated in the other Romanian regions, which requires explanation. Beyond the suffering caused by all kinds of injustice, the survival of Jews in the Banat and southern Transylvania was real. That is why the ambiguities of Romanian domestic and foreign policy in that period have to be understood. Often tragic in content – Jews were deprived of rights, imprisoned or killed based on their racial origin – the decisions of Antonescu's regime do not exclude a lucid examination of the conditions of the the Romanian state during the war. Romania's position between Nazi Germany and USSR, two powers profoundly hostile towards each other, and also the German-Romanian military disaster in Stalingrad, encouraged the political forces in Bucharest to concentrate their attention on measures that could save and reunite the state. Sometimes, ambiguous political decisions emerged from this. After Stalingrad, Romania changed the orientation and policy concerning the Jewish population.

As the evidence presented above shows, the survival of Jews from the Banat and southern Transylvania was the result of Ion Antonescu's fears concerning the potential decisions of the peace treaties that would be signed after the end of the war, decisions that would change the territorial configuration of the Romanian state. It is also true that without the intervention of Romanian and Jewish leaders, it is unlikely that the Jews from the Banat and southern Transylvania would have been saved.[65]

21
THE RECONSTRUCTION OF CIVIL SOCIETY UNDER THE NATIONAL COMMUNIST DICTATORSHIP, 1956–89

Victor Neumann

PLURALISM AND ASPIRATION TO FREEDOM

Despite the demographic changes that followed the two world wars (especially the second) and the suspicion towards people who came from linguistic and religious minorities, citizens in the Banat of Timișoara retained the set of civic values they had held from the time of the Austro-Hungarian Monarchy. As a regional centre with a strong tradition, appreciated by all the people of the Banat, Timișoara had little in common with other Romanian cities. During the National Communist regime, it stood out for the multi- and intercultural civicism of its citizens.[1] We are not speaking of a social environment in which the majority tolerated the minorities, but of a peaceful cohabitation in which urban identity was placed above affiliation to a particular linguistic or religious community.

The desire of the largest segment of the population in Timișoara was to live freely, to trade, to travel with no restrictions inside or outside the country, and to have access to information. Concern with a stable material situation was part of the make-up of Timișoara. Preoccupation with earning money, with the household and the acquisition of material goods were not neglected even in the final years of Nicolae Ceaușescu's regime. During the food crisis caused by the policy of austerity of the late 1970s, there were still social groups in Timișoara with an acceptable standard of living. The so-called flea market, which the Communist authorities tried to close down on several occasions, and where goods from neighbouring Yugoslavia, Hungary and Austria were sold, had a role to play in preserving cultural and civilisational influences from Europe. There was a real need for information and knowledge. It was widespread practice to manufacture TV antennae in order to have access to the television channels of neighbouring countries. Television programmes from Belgrade, Novi Sad and Budapest were frequently watched by the citizens of Timişoara. Eugen Florescu, a high-ranking member of the regime and close to Nicolae and Elena Ceauşescu, the dictatorial couple, was sent from Bucharest to Timişoara to promote Romanian ethnonationalism blended with rudimentary totalitarian Communist ideas. One of the measures he intended to take was the removal of TV antennae from the roofs of houses on the grounds that information from foreign audiovisual media contravened Romanian ideology.

The intelligentsia of the Banat continued to promote the spirit of old Timişoara and the old cosmopolitan Banat, adopting a European way of thinking and cultural behaviour. They were not idolised by the masses nor did they try to impose models on them. Their air of normality was surprising compared with that of many intellectuals from other Romanian urban centres. They displayed the characteristics of an intelligentsia formed in the spirit of Central Europe[2] which is why their values were rejected and misunderstood in Bucharest. This attitude continued to manifest itself during the great anti-Ceauşescu and anti-Communist demonstrations of 1989. Fear of a different way of thinking to that of the National Communist regime was obvious, since the Banat was the westernmost region of the country, and differences in this border area were perceived as a threat to the cohesion of the Romanian state. The constant dissatisfaction of the Romanian authorities with Timişoara was also linked to the fact that a significant portion of its population spoke languages other than Romanian, thus having direct communication with the world of Europe.[3]

At the opposite pole, Communism in Romania was anti-liberal and excessively preoccupied with the ethnocultural or ethnonational identity of each inhabitant, and with ethnonationalist policies or the organic social model. The Communist Party adopted a conservative ideology which, like that of Stalin, transformed itself from time to time into xenophobia and anti-Semitism, paving the way for human trafficking, for selling Jews and Romanian Germans. These were tendencies which all Romanian authoritarian and totalitarian regimes of the twentieth century had in common. Even under these austere conditions, Timişoara continued to display the urban habits which made a more decent way of life possible. This is explained, for example, by the normality of interhuman relations and the existence of professional associations. Like Lemberg or Cernăuţi, Timişoara partially remained, until the events of 1989, a multi- and intercultural city par excellence.

How was this civic culture preserved, and how was it able to contribute to the political transformation of 1989? The cultural and civic actions that took place in Timișoara during the years of National Communism represented an avant-garde in political ideas. They carried the signs of nonconformism, of challenge to the regime. Among others, the Sigma Group of artists, the German-language writers' Aktionsgruppe Banat, Professor Eduard Pamfil's Bionic Circle, the multilingual literary circles of the Writers' Union, ecumenical meetings, cinema clubs, and the band Phoenix stand out. Each expressed popular discontent and the spirit of intellectual inquiry, rejecting wooden language and totalitarian ideology.

THE SIGMA GROUP: A REAL EUROPEAN SYNCHRONISATION

In December 1990, the artist Roman Cotoșman recalled how Group 111 (later the Sigma Group) came into being. After lengthy discussions between Ștefan Bertalan, Roman Cotoșman and Constantin Flondor in 1969, an idea emerged of establishing an experimental group of plastic artists from Timișoara with the objectives of using the principles of constructivism and implementing the prospective method. The projects were to be 'communication systems', 'designed for an environment of integration of the arts'. Collaboration with engineers, architects and scientists led the group towards an interdisciplinarity that was remarkable for the years 1960–70 within a state in which the citizens were not free.

A kidney problem necessitating an overseas operation made it possible for Roman Cotoșman to travel to the French capital.

> Parisian kinetic art was in full swing and I was impressed by Schöffer's light towers. I was hastily trying to grasp the language of structuralism and of the new novel. At the theatre, I attended some plays by Ionesco and Beckett. I had a list of books written by Livius Ciocârlie, which I managed to buy and bring back by good fortune, by escaping the customs search when I returned. Coming back home, I decided to radically change my method and means of work. I rediscovered the old official environment of conformity, blended with the fear of decadent contamination from the West. Two or three years passed before a cultural liberalisation could take place. I often met Livius Ciocârlie – our friendship had deep roots from high school days. In our discussions and work projects, we were looking for new languages in our respective fields. We were living together the adventure of creation; the disappearance of traditional art seemed irreversible.[4]

The artist returned from Paris with new experiences, new readings and impressions from the famous museums and art galleries where he had discovered the works of the pioneers of constructivism, kinetic art and lyrical abstraction. 'He walked every day, from dawn till dusk, from one gallery to another, eating once every three days, and he bought books, clothes, discs and a transistor radio. He went to see *The Bald Primadonna*, Ionescu being for us a mysterious author; we didn't dare to imagine him.'[5] He had to confront the inertia of a political system which opposed change and controlled creativity and the lives of creative people. However, he would find that, against the background of the small degree of liberalisation at the end of the 1960s, Timişoara was a place where there were enough enlightened minds with aspirations in another ideological direction. In fact, the city encouraged cultural experiments. The portrait of Cotoşman sketched by Livius Ciocârlie evokes the intellectual environment:

> He loved listening to Bach and to jazz. He stared at you in amazement when you confused Louis Armstrong's trumpet with light music. He was very preoccupied with how his clothes looked and had his own tailor where his friends went too; every suit or overcoat was for him a creative problem. He adopted the latest fashion and tried to overcome it, as it was his natural reflex to fight beyond the first line.[6]

Although the political environment was not at all favourable to experimental art, during the 1960s and 1970s Timişoara was still strongly influenced by the cosmopolitan dimension. Some of its first-ranked artists played an important part in training the new generation. One of these was the painter Professor Julius Podlipny: Dietrich Sayler, Paul Neagu, Roman Cotoşman and Ştefan Călţia all took advantage of his drawing lessons. For some – including Cotoşman – the master became too demanding and their cooperation did not yield the expected results. Podlipny was an 'interesting expressionist' who 'could only stand drawing; for him painters were just scruffy, incapable of drawing a line'.[7] He was, nevertheless, among those who stimulated the creation of plastic artists in Timişoara, imposing a systematic work method and mixed technique. The bearer of a cultural legacy and education that characterised Central Europe, he had left-wing political views – in some periods, shifting to the extreme left. His passion for art and pedagogy had an important impact on cultural ideas in Timişoara. 'He spoke Romanian poorly and, having a strong personality, any phrase he uttered became memorable. He wore a goatee; he was crippled, nervous, intransigent and sarcastic.'[8] Podlipny was, however, a personality with a strong teaching vocation, and several of the most admired Romanian artists of the second half of the twentieth century and the beginning of the twenty-first owe him a great deal.

Founded in 1966, Group III must be understood within the framework of the personalities who lived in Timişoara. It carried great expectations among not only plastic artists but also intellectuals in the city. In a short time, it proved that interdisciplinary dialogue was fundamental for adjusting to the changes that occur in our world. After Roman Cotoşman's departure for the United States in 1969, Group III became the Sigma Group. For Romanian contemporary art, it offered a different understanding and definition of man through the grammar of forms, industrial aesthetics, marketing, industrial geometry, complementary colours, design, descriptive geometry and bionic study. The five members of the Sigma Group – to whom a mathematician was added – proposed 'an art pedagogy programme, principles of correlation between form, function and environment, and form-generating principles'.[9]

Permanent points of references for the two groups were nature, the relationships between nature and numbers and between geometry and culture, and anthropology. Iosif Király – a former student of the Timişoara College of Plastic Arts, where the members of the Sigma Group were professors – recalls how, in the intellectual environment that dominated there in the late 1960s, you could consider yourself a man of the twentieth century with no interest in what had happened before 1900: 'In fact, we had no time for the past: the present was so rich, we lived the moment with such intensity that there was no room for anything else. Art, culture, was produced under my very eyes.'[10] The students read Sartre, Kafka, Joyce, Ionesco, Hesse, and also some avant-garde literature in the social sciences written by Marshal McLuhan, Alvin Töfler and Nicholas Schöffer. They listened to the music of Shostakovich, Schönberg, Bartók and Stravinsky.

The climate was stimulating, students being treated as partners with their teachers, giving them the feeling that they were walking alongside them to unknown destinations. Stimulated by art movies, books and magazines brought from Western Europe, by classes in art history and the study of visual languages, the students discovered in their immediate surroundings the activity of the Sigma Group. Iosif Király said that its influence was so strong that students started to form their own artistic groups, trying to embrace the whole world with its complex issues. The student exhibition of the College of Plastic Arts in Kalinderu Gallery in Bucharest in 1976 demonstrated the existence of a prestigious group and workshop in Timişoara. There was nothing else like it in Romania at that time. An art critic compared the exhibition to 'a living, open ensemble, surprisingly in full swing. Above it floats the dense atmosphere of a respect for tradition, along with sober and bold experiment, free from prejudice but also from snobbish affectation.'[11] The critic observed – not without indignation – the lack of publicity around the exhibition, although its content was worthy of provoking real emulation. Timişoara College of Plastic Arts was unique within the Romanian artistic environment, which begs the question: which of the art faculties would be ready to accommodate its graduates?

The Sigma Group – established around Ştefan Bertalan and Constantin Flondor, but including other artists such as Doru Tulcan, Molnár Zoltán and Dietrich Sayler – became a reference point not only for painting, where it decisively contributed to the renewal of artistic language, but also for ideological debate. The desirability of change was obvious to all of them. They had become the promoters of an alternative way of thought and communication, evading the ideological control of the National Communist regime.[12] The promotion of multi- and interdisciplinarity, an artistic pedagogy propagating openness, the overcoming of known forms and the introduction of experimental studies stimulated the cultural life of post-war Timișoara. The concerns of the group spoke of a dynamic universe, an intention to engage the receiving public in permanent dialogue. The radicalisation of individual experiment can be observed in each of the artists who were members of the Sigma Group or gravitated around it. For example, Ștefan Bertalan's scientific experimental model was a first for Romania's plastic arts.[13] The existence of an *avant la lettre* constructivism, one that would impress the specialists and the public at the Nuremberg Biennale in 1969, is indicative not only of participation in an international artistic forum, but also of a real European synchronisation of the studies made by the Timișoarans. The approach by which art had entered into an authentic dialogue with science stirred positive comments from some of the most acclaimed critics of Romania and Europe. Sigma had proved not only authenticity but also the coherence of a team. Such an environment was bound to provoke confrontation, and this was not long in coming. This 'artistic movement of Timișoara remains, even during its moments of maximum constructivism or pedagogy of the aesthetics of useful forms, under the sign of nature and universal harmony',[14] 'an effervescent galaxy', with 'its stars, Flondor and Cotoșman, Tulcan and Bertalan'.[15] The Information Tower, a 'multifunctional construction-signal' – viewed as the most important accomplishment of the Sigma Group – is conclusive proof of the attempt to blend the aesthetic and the social. The artists' maturity is reflected in their efforts to crystallise cultural and political-ideological discourse, and also in the research and resolution of the urban social network.

EDUARD PAMFIL: THE PROGRESSIVE RECONSTRUCTION OF CIVIL SOCIETY

Professor Eduard Pamfil, founder of the Romanian school of psychiatry, author of reference books, and trainer of many generations of doctors, was the great idealist of Timișoara. During the years 1960–90, he was a Western cultural landmark for the city, an inquisitive and original mind who was the intellectual opposite of the Romanian philosopher Constantin Noica. Pamfil floated above the miseries of the regime and offered models of intellectual and civic survival. He was the initiator and leader of the original Bionic Circle, which included plastic artists, musicians, philologists, historians, mathematicians and philosophers. The existence of the circle was due to a true ritual of ideas, prolific dialogue and nonconformist theory.

The meeting between painter Ştefan Bertalan – the founder and inspiration of the Sigma Group – and Eduard Pamfil was beneficial to Timişoara's creative environment. Anghel considered it to have been an ideal way of communication, where emotions and reason overlapped:

> Bertalan is [Pamfil said, defining himself too] a knight of nonconformism. Everthing, every gesture, every speech that might end in a comfortable and placid manner is avoided, if not unbearable to him. All that he does is marked by this desire to build towards something, sustained by the continuous tension of self-discontent.[16]

The civicism instilled in him by the education within his family and also during his university studies in Paris in the immediate post-war years, made Professor Pamfil one of the best loved of intellectuals. Thanks to his conferences, an entire generation of young people discovered the values of universal culture.

Eduard Pamfil was influenced by the political messages promoted by the Czech, Polish and Hungarian dissidents. This was the case of his cultural circle and of several other circles in Timişoara, but not the case of the whole Romanian intelligentsia.

The refined discourse and the thorough social analysis presented in Professor Pamfil's numerous conferences demonstrated a responsible understanding of the problems that faced the population of the city, the region and Romania as a whole. He communicated freely, pleading for the formation of personal conscience. He was a supporter of the pro-European view, opposing the traditionalist direction imposed by the regime through the media and education. The music and poetry he professed for their own sakes created the background for philosophical reflection. He had not been influenced by the essentialism of the twentieth century but could live well with pluralism, preoccupied by the multiple meanings of social relations. He deconstructed the theories that promoted the uniqueness of truth, trying to overlap public and private life. Eduard Pamfil had a liberal culture, criticising the socialist nation and the ethnonationalism of the Romanian Communists. He was inspired by French writings, being the best informed of Timişoara's intellectuals in cultural and political philosophy.

His vocabulary – influenced by his rich experience as a psychiatrist – inspired hope, imagining and anticipating the political changes that occurred in Eastern Europe in 1989. As a researcher of humanist Renaissance ideals and an enlightened thinker, Eduard Pamfil felt a responsibility towards the human aspiration to freedom. He was charming and credible. Due to his preference for speaking rather than writing, an important part of his reflections remain unpublished, but his notes are gathered in many manuscripts under the suggestive name of *Idear* (*Reflections*). His concern with debunking myths was accompanied by the establishment of his own language. A combination of the speculative and the pragmatic was present in the professor's meditations. Pamfil demonstrated the importance of convergent communication, 'the role of communication free from domination', for the purpose of open confrontation. His questions decoded contemporary issues with arguments from the social sciences. His poetry book *Arioso dolente* and *Idear* show that he understood better than any of his East European colleagues Richard Rorty's idea that 'the moral prophets of humanity were always poets, even if they expressed themselves in blank verse or parables'. This last reflection perfectly defines the humanist of Timișoara. He was a man of letters for whom the relationship between medicine, poetry and philosophy found its place in his research and understanding of the universe and the individual.

Pamfil was involved in the life of the city more than any other intellectual, and his presence at literary circles, plastic art exhibitions and conferences brought together the different cultural groups and stimulated the process of re-forming individual culture. He was the professor who animated the most profound debates. He was a constant presence in the programmes of the University House, Students' Culture House and Writers' Union literary circles. He could recite poems, play classical guitar, hold a conference or moderate debates around exciting themes of the philosophy of culture, the philosophy of history, and anthropology. Lastly, as a psychiatrist, he offered help to all those who had been kept under surveillance and humiliated by the National Communist regime. The Psychiatric Clinic in Timișoara and the Psychiatric Hospital in Gătaia provided a refuge for all the discontents, for the so-called unadaptable, for those who had the courage to oppose the aberrant measures of Ceaușescu's regime.

Eduard Pamfil symbolised a moral example that could not be called into question even by his opponents, which is why the circles he frequented continued to have a decent way of reflecting on the world. Through him, a generation of scholars who had studied in the West managed to survive in Timișoara and the Banat, and continued to promote humanist ideas as well as the nonconformist views of the time. His reflections had a strong impact upon a circle of intellectuals who, in their turn, contributed to the preservation of a civic spirit and the increase in an anti-totalitarian attitude.

AKTIONSGRUPPE BANAT: AN ARTICULATE OPPOSITION TO THE TOTALITARIAN SYSTEM

Independent of the circles mentioned above, the Universitas Literary Club of the Students' Culture House, also known as Aktionsgruppe Banat (the Banat

Action Group), was founded in 1972 and operated in Timişoara. Connected to the social and political issues of the time, the group soon provided the main intellectual opposition to National Communist ideology in Romania. Composed of young German-speaking writers – for example, Gerhardt Ortinau, William Totok, Richard Wagner, Ernest Wichner, Anton Sterbling, Rolf Bossert, Anton Bohn, Werner Kremm and Johann Lippet – the group had a short but rich period of activity. The texts written by its members were printed in many German and Romanian publications in Timişoara, Braşov, Sibiu, Cluj and Bucharest. Appreciated or criticised, they caught the attention of the Securitate, the secret police. Monitored from 1973, as can be seen from documentary evidence, Aktionsgruppe Banat was accused of plotting against the Communist regime. The young German writers had published or read in public places poems and essays criticising the Romanian totalitarian system, denouncing its form and substance. They were familiar with contemporary universal literature, and also with political debates in Germany and Austria. The pacificism of the beat generation had a strong impact upon them. They were well trained, carefully analysing Romanian legislation and Nicolae Ceauşescu's speeches in order to understand the scenario of a Communist country that officially opposed Marxist ideas. Among the poems read by William Totok at the Universitas Literary Club, there were many with evocative names such as 'Entsheidungsfragen bei einem Macht-Prozess' ('Decisive Questions at a Trial of Power'), 'Mit Chile im Herzen' ('With Chile in My Heart'), and 'Allerhand aus einem Modejournal, das ziemlich teuer und kulturausgerichtet ist' ('More Issues from a Fashion Journal That Is Quite Expensive and Has Cultural Tendencies'). Their author was one of the most harassed members of Aktionsgruppe Banat and was finally deprived of liberty.[17]

The debates of this literary circle became a clear protest against totalitarianism. They criticised populism, the propaganda that distorted reality in Romania, the passivity of the population towards a regime that abused its people.[18] Their intellectual honesty and maturity of political thought were striking and rarely encountered in intellectual environments in Romania. Conformity and opportunism had been rejected. As the literary historian Petru Motzan observed, the polemic was obvious in the poets' activist and participatory lyrics. The authoritative presence of Richard Wagner and Rolf Bossert, the reflections and interrogations of William Totok, and the family biography and questioning of the past of Johann Lippet, show how the group drew attention to a sociopolitical reality that it viewed as perfectible.[19] Aktionsgruppe Banat clearly distanced itself from the use of culture as a tool of propaganda by the Romanian authorities.

Contrary to the fact that the theme of minorities was not part of the direction of the group, the Communist Party invented and spread the idea that part of the German community in Romania had started a conflict with the state. In this manner, it justified disagreement with the protests of the German writers in Timișoara. In reality, it was an opportunity to encourage and expedite the emigration of this minority to Germany. Some of the members of Aktionsgruppe Banat were influenced by the ideology of Karl Marx, while the Romanian Communist Party promoted National Communism. Those were the years when Nicolae Ceaușescu's regime recovered some of the features of the ideology of the far Right during the interwar period. They became part of the current of protochronism. The articles published in the media in the German Federal Republic spoke of the attitude of German dissidents in Timișoara, concluding, not surprisingly, that even Marxist intellectuals were prohibited in Romania. In an article of 1976, Dieter Schlesak described the paradoxical situation of these writers, and also that of a state where political debates were prohibited, even when they were related to Karl Marx's philosophical or political thought.[20]

Even though it ceased activity only a few years after its establishment, the accomplishment of the group was that it knew how to defend not only its own dignity, but also that of a city which the regime wanted to punish for its traditional connections with people and communities from other countries and for its cosmopolitan ideas. Aktionsgruppe Banat was part of local and regional life between 1972 and 1975, but its initiatives failed to mobilise the population for a substantial protest. Instead, German-language writers formulated an articulate method of opposing the system, which was adopted as a point of reference by some of their colleagues. A few years later, Petru Ilieșu – a distinguished Romanian poet – was influenced by the activity of his German colleagues in Timișoara.

Ilieșu benefited a lot from his relationship with German writers: together they talked about the beat generation, read Western literature, and debated internal and foreign policy. It is no less true that his mood – like that of his generation – had been fed by contact with the global music movement. During his student years, he worked at the Students' Culture House, and was very receptive to Western rock music. As a consequence, in 1982 he conceived a form of protest against the regime. His manifestos, which included the slogans 'Down with the Criminal Ceaușescu' and 'Down with the Communist Party', were spread by Alexandru Gavriliu, another poet from Timișoara. Arrested shortly after he had brought his opposition out into the open, Ilieșu was interrogated and later released after the intervention of the former editor-in-chief of the German-language newspaper, Nikolaus Berwanger.[21] It is clear that the population of the city and the region had discovered that a response to the regime other than submission was possible.

The same Students' Culture House hosted other teams of young people who displayed their artistic or literary talent; for example, Pavel Dan Book Club and *Forum Stundențesc (Students' Forum)* magazine, edited in Romanian, Hungarian and German. At the end of the 1970s, there were students who understood the importance of writing a poem, an essay or a feature, the formulation of a profession of faith. The writers who attended Pavel Dan Book Club represented a generation for whom French and English literature had become the main cultural point of reference. Many read books with strong ideological content by writers banned by the Romanian Communist regime: George Orwell, Milan Kundera, Aleksandr Solzhenitsyn and others. Alexandra Indrieș, Șerban Foarță, Livius Ciocârlie, Andreas Lillin and Franyó Zoltán became models for the younger generation. These writers were inspired to talk publicly about works of world literature and philosophy. Under their guidance, there were debates on famous works by Raymond Aron, Michel Foucault and Jacques Derrida. Thus, it was possible to pursue an authentic intellectual life, and turn one's back on the ideology of the Communist Party.

PHOENIX: SPOKESMAN FOR THE PROTEST MOVEMENTS

Among the cultural activities that had a great impact on young people, was the rock band Phoenix. The group ensured great social cohesion in Timișoara, and had a positive echo throughout Romania. Phoenix was an emblem for the generations of young people who had formed within the cultural and artistic environments of the city. Including among its musicians Romanians, Germans, Hungarians, Serbians and Jews, Phoenix distinguished itself by its acute perception of social and political realities. Its texts were manifestos of the young generation of 1960–70, true protests against indoctrination and mediocrity. The band had its own style, always cultivating cross-currents between local and European cultures, and was itself inspired by the music and photography of the hippie movement.

> The ideas, the bohemian mentality and the colourful aspect of the representative of the new peaceful rebellion of flower power fascinated us. We were sure that it was the right direction for every young person to follow if he wanted to free himself from false morality. The prohibition on listening to radio stations, diffusing music and art magazines or even speciality journals from the West which were considered decadent, the more obvious wider and unchallenged censorship of cultural and social life, all tried to deflect the energy flow of profound change. But those touched by the 'microbe' of freedom found a way to overcome barriers, to inform themselves. Every issue of *Bravo*, *Musical Express* or *Rolling Stone* was read and devoured by those young people trying to identify themselves with their idols.[22]

The 1960s coincided with endless searches for personal and community-urban identity. The songs that were played expressed the thoughts and feelings of a post-war generation who wanted to express itself freely, disliking stereotypes. Phoenix proved that in Timișoara there was a movement of young people who said what they thought and ignored formality. The band's music and lyrics included political messages, subtly formulated but received by the public. The Lyra Hall, where Phoenix was based and where many of its shows took place, was ostentatiously decorated with the strangest things – chains, bicycle wheels, motorcycle cylinders, painting frames. This was the place where, thanks to the goodwill of some administrators – Phoenix could freely express itself, practising the songs that brought it fame and holding concerts three times a week during a period when the authorities had banned it.

As a result of Phoenix's rich artistic activity, Western European and American rock music became a point of reference in Romania. What Phoenix was singing derived from the expectations of their young public, their musical style being an alternative to ideological indoctrination. The emotional potential was enormous, and the world behind the Iron Curtain was being heard. The band's visionary spirit

> made them see, while the masses and even the political analysts allowed themselves to be deceived by the appearance of spiritual and material freedom, that it was all a hoax. The acute perception of reality distinguished and individualised them. The aggressive lyrics on mediocrity, indoctrination and generally against political power were taken up by the younger generation. 'Vremuri' ('Times'), 'Canarul' ('The Canary') and 'Totuși ca voi' ('Actually They Are Like You'), spoke more about the lost generation than a tome of sociological analysis.[23]

Some very talented musicians – Nicolae Covaci, Florin Bordeianu, Josef Kappl, Günter Reininger, Bela Kamocsa and Mircea Baniciu – were part of the band. Phoenix became the representative of a 'lost' generation. The surveillance of the band's concerts has been attributed to the officials responsible for propaganda in Timișoara and Timiș County. Nonconformist behaviour, clothing, lack of inhibition in interpersonal relations, the songs' messages – all generated a mood contrary to the Communist political regime. The lyrics were created by some of the brightest writers trained in the cultural and university environment in Timișoara: Vicor Cârcu, Șerban Foarță and Andrei Ujică. Between writers, musicians and public there was a communication reflecting the smouldering revolt against the authorities, the marginalisation of young people, those who banned the right to freedom of thought and action. Phoenix was an unmistakable sociocultural and ideological landmark, an opposition movement inside a totalitarian system that proclaimed itself to be eternal.

Nicolae Covaci – the leader of the band – recalls that in those years very few young people believed the Communist slogans. 'Only slippery people, whom we instinctively despised, wasted their breath trying to convince the world of things they themselves did not believe in.' The visionary content of Phoenix's songs shows why and how the group kept awake the consciousness of people facing a system with false values. Continuous improvement, periodical renewal of repertoire and use of modern musical instruments contributed to greater audiences and better concerts. In this respect, the role of musician Günter Reininger was exemplary.

Unfortunately, the multi- and intercultural originality of the Banat was little explored by the band's musicians. The emphasis on Romanian folklore – Nicolae Covaci and some music critics considered it important to the band's destiny – was not Phoenix's most inspired moment. It was an ideological choice, and one which matched – intentionally or not – protochronism and National Communist ideology. It was a trap laid by Nicolae Ceaușescu's regime, and not the only one – but one of the ablest and with long-term consequences in contemporary Romanian history.

Regardless of this shortcoming, it must be said that Phoenix created Romanian music in an authentic sense: 'Cantafabule' remains a point of reference for cultural history in Timișoara during the second half of the twentieth century. Regarding the civic sense, the band's musicians were able – although for a limited period – to express opposition to the Communist regime. Their language of protest offered hope to several generations of people from Timișoara and the Banat. When Phoenix finally left Timișoara and Romania, the citizens of the city lost not only a music that defined them, but also one of the most accessible forms of anti-totalitarian protest. Phoenix's emigration generated or accentuated the exodus of many groups from Timișoara.

AN ECHO OF THE HUNGARIAN REVOLUTION

Cultural circles influenced the civic life of the city's inhabitants. Culture offered a form of protection against the abuses of Communist authorities. However, there were cases when Timișoara's urban community had an explicitly political direction, directly opposing the Romanian totalitarian regime and the Soviet domination of the states of Central and South-East Europe. The criticism of the ideology of the extreme Left was all the more justified since hunger, low wages, ideological lies, a state-controlled economy, and an absence of management were threatening the lives of the citizens of Timișoara and the Banat who had always had a higher standard of living than the inhabitants of other regions of Romania. In 1956 the citizens of Timișoara, Lugoj, Arad, Reșița – workers, officials and students – all protested against the Soviet invasion of Hungary. Solidarity with the Hungarian revolutionaries was so strong that at one point – during the last week of October and the first of November – it seemed that the authorities had lost control over the protesters and that revolution would start in Romania, too.

The manifestos contained messages like 'We are against the USSR!', 'We don't want to learn Russian!', 'Down with Gheorgiu Dej and his clique!', 'Fight for a better life and for freedom!', 'Students, fight against the intervention of the Kremlin troops in Hungary!', 'Good job, Hungary!', 'Freedom reached Hungary and will soon reach us!'[24] The example of the actions initiated by the students of the Faculty of Medicine and Pharmacy in 1948, along with the civic conscience of the students from the Polytechnic Institute of Timișoara, who had the courage in October and November 1956 to protest against the totalitarian regime like the revolutionaries in Budapest, showed that there was a strong civic spirit in Timișoara.

News of the Hungarian revolution of 1956 simply electrified the university environments, the citizens of Timișoara spreading detailed information about what was happening in Budapest. All this panicked the regional and central Communist executives. The organisers of the student movements in Timișoara – Teodor Stanca, Aurel Baghiu, Friedrich Barth, Ladislau Nagy, Aurelian Păuna, Nicolae Balaci, Gheorghe Pop and Caius Muțiu – demonstrated a good understanding of the political issues that characterised the Central East European countries and especially Romania. They were the messengers of great social discontent.[25] By instigating demonstrations similar to those in Hungary, formulating documents with a social democrat message, informing themselves about the links between the Hungarian civic and Polish anti-totalitarian actions, the students from Timișoara had proved they had a mature political understanding. Soviet domination and USSR army intervention in Hungary were often debated by students and were criticised and denounced. The most important debate during which a political programme was promoted took place in the great hall of the Polytechnic. From the messages of the anti-Communist demonstrations, it is clear that there was great discontent with the subordination of the Central East European states in relation to the Soviet Union. It was the first time that this had been perceived in its true dimensions by the majority of people within the region. The students of Timișoara debated the shortcomings of the Communist regime in Budapest and the false information disseminated by the Romanian central media regarding the revolution in Hungary. They were critical of Romania's great political mistakes, adopting a social democratic ideology.

The information coming from Radio Kossuth in Budapest became the main credible source regarding revolutionary action in the Hungarian capital. Timișoara had Hungarian-speakers among its population, many of them risking discussions about the tragic events in Hungary. The students' civic and political culture was reflected in their 'memory books', including criticism of the Communist totalitarian system and demands for the cessation of the cult of personality; rational development of economic sectors and establishment of trade agreements with every interested country, including capitalist ones;

withdrawal of Soviet troops from Romanian territory; running the state for the benefit of its citizens and its own economic development; decent living conditions for pupils and students.

The authorities of Gheorghe Gheorghiu Dej's regime immediately sensed the danger posed by the demonstrations that took place in Timișoara during October and November 1956 and acted accordingly. During a trial, the Timișoara Military Tribunal concluded that the students had affected national security when they started the protests. It sentenced the leaders of the anti-totalitarian movement to between four and eight years of 'correctional imprisonment'.[26] In arbitrary rulings, several student groups that had participated in the protests were convicted. The prohibition on forming associations could not block the emergence of different artist and writers' circles, clubs and music bands – cultural organisations that, under various pretexts, promoted a civic spirit. Surveillance of the population was more drastic than it had been prior to the 1956 revolutionary movements, but even under these oppressive conditions, the preservation of connections with the Western world remained a priority for many citizens of the multi- and intercultural city of Timișoara.

Despite the civic effort and the cultural and artistic life that had set Timișoara apart on the Romanian and East European map of the time, after 1956 the intellectuals failed to elaborate an alternative political project to prepare for administrative change in December 1989. Did they lack pragmatism or the courage to accomplish their critical thinking? Both. The lack of concern with the formation of authentic political thought mattered. No matter how much evidence of civic culture Timișoara provided during the Communist and National Communist period, what led to the tragedy of the movements of 1989 and the ineptitude of the political-administrative and legislative changes after Communism was the absence of a democratic opposition similar to that of Charter 77 in Czechoslovakia, Solidarnosc in Poland, or dissident intellectuals in Hungary. It also has to be said that the intelligentsia were absent from any kind of debates, especially political ones. There was something else, too: Timișoara's status as Romania's second city, with no local autonomy, led to an ignorance of administrative policies.

The 1956 protest in Timișoara had been the most important to take place in Romania during Gheorghe Gheorgiu-Dej's dictatorship, showing that the population of the city and region had remarkable courage, a culture of solidarity and a freedom of expression that was opposed to the Communist totalitarian system. In spite of its shortcomings and discontent after 1989, Timișoara had been the first Romanian city to understand the necessity of changing Nicolae Ceaușescu and the Communist regime. It was because post-war Timișoara had preserved a fragment of its old civic culture that the impressive anti-Communist demonstrations in December 1989 were possible. A history of Communist Romania and Europe can never ignore their significance.

22

THE ANTI-TOTALITARIAN REVOLT OF 1989

The Role of Timișoara

Victor Neumann

THE BEGINNINGS OF POLITICAL CHANGE IN ROMANIA

The spark that lit the great demonstration of December 1989 in Timișoara is related to the multicultural and multi-confessional profile of the city. A political idea had been shaped by the destruction of Transylvanian villages, an idea that quickly became known in the international media. The same idea would play a major role in triggering the anti-Communist demonstrations in Timișoara.

Pastor László Tőkés, a chaplain of the Reformed Church in the city, protested against the destruction of Transylvanian villages – he himself was of Hungarian extraction and had previously been pastor in the Transylvanian town of Dej. This destruction formed part of the policy of 'systematisation' promoted by the National Communist government in Romania and involved restructuring towns and villages within the country, marking some for destruction and enforcing relocation of their populations. There were many German and Hungarian nationals living in these Transylvanian villages and the governments of West Germany and Hungary were concerned for their well-being. Tőkés's opposition was taken up by the members of the Reformed Church, by the international political media, by the Hungarian and German press,[1] and also by the local population.[2] The pastor's dissidence had started in 1981–82 in the clandestine publication *Ellentpontok* (*Counterpoints*) and continued in speeches held during religious services at the different parishes to which he was forced to move. At the end of the 1980s, Tőkés was chaplain of the Reformed Church of Timișoara, where he was supported by the circles of believers and the Hungarian intelligentsia in the city and the wider region.[3] Under house arrest between 1 and 15 December 1989, he was due to be evicted by the repressive apparatus of the National Communist regime.

On 15 December, the Reformed Church of Timișoara was the tensest location in the city, and in all of Romania. The next day over 1,000 citizens gathered round Tőkés's house, forming a human chain to prevent the authorities from entering. This was the trigger for the great revolt against Ceaușescu's regime. The protest of the Reformed faith group was taken up by an important segment of the city's population who understood that the suffering of the minority group was no different from that of the majority. In Piata Maria, in the immediate proximity of the Reformed Church, people chanted 'Down with Ceauşescu!' and 'Freedom!' The number of protesters reached 2,000.

The descriptions of the revolts in the city show that, at the moment when Pastor Tőkés's eviction was due to take place, the citizens of Timișoara showed unconditional solidarity with him. Initially represented by a Hungarian-speaking group, the demonstration of solidarity outside the pastor's house had quickly engaged several thousands of citizens. As someone who had campaigned for the rights of the Hungarian minority in Romania, Tőkés was impressed by the support of so many citizens for his cause. The Securitate's plans to create a Romanian–Hungarian conflict were frustrated by the demonstrators who bore the marks of a *societas civilis*, animated by the idea of liberation from the oppressive Communist regime and not by the endorsement of an obsolete historical misunderstanding.

On 17 December 1989, the forces of order opened fire on the civilians, killing 112 people and injuring 373. The anti-Ceausescu and anti-Communist demonstrations had escalated to an unprecedented extent, running beyond the control of the central authorities in Bucharest. This was confirmed by reports in the foreign press. Radio Budapest announced that the army had dispersed the demonstration in support of Tőkés, but that 'it had instead been transformed into a revolt against Ceaușescu'.[4] The well-known German newspaper *Die Welt* informed its readers on 18 December that about 4,000 demonstrators had gathered in Timișoara in front of the Reformed Calvinist church to stop Tőkés's eviction, that violent clashes between the people and the army had taken place, and that the demonstrations, which initially had a 'Hungarian ethnic character', 'later turned into rallies against Ceaușescu', involving the whole population of the city.[5] On the same day, the USA condemned the brutal repression, intending to consult NATO and the European Community with a view to adopting joint action against the authorities' violence towards Timișoara's peaceful population.[6]

In Brussels, the foreign affairs ministers of the European Community strongly condemned the supression of Timișoara's anti-totalitarian demonstrations. The European and American press extensively covered the revolts, signalling László Tőkés's relentless attitude in defence of the rights of the Hungarian population of Romania, and the ill treatment to which he was subjected by the repressive institutions of the National Communist regime. The Western media highlighted Romanian–Hungarian cooperation when the demonstrations started to intensify, underlining the fact that the spark of the revolt had been lit by Tőkés. Western diplomats, especially the British and the Americans, were very concerned about the situation of the minorities. This explains their interest in Tőkés's fate and their visit to Timişoara.[7] They knew very well that Nicolae Ceauşescu's regime was based on nationalist policy and that this was his ultimate justification for retaining power. In fact, the uprising in Timişoara did not have an ethnic character. On 19 December, the *Frankfurter Allgemeine Zeitung* drew attention to the fact that Nicolae Ceauşescu's dictatorship had upset all Romanians, not only the representatives of minorities.[8]

László Tőkés's virtues at that moment were the following: (1) he gathered the faithful around the idea of freedom of conscience; (2) he openly revealed the distress of the Hungarian minority; (3) in letters to the political media and the international press, he formulated the claims of his parishioners in credible terms; (4) he drew attention towards Timişoara as a city whose population was determined to overthrow the dictatorial regime and renounce Communist ideology.

The secret service's policy of maintaining tense relations with Romania's neighbours, especially Hungary, had blocked the idea of forming an opposition political body. The news agencies announced that during those days the Romanian–Hungarian border was closed, as were the borders with Yugoslavia and USSR. This shows that the revolt in Timişoara was spontaneous and could not be controlled by the authorities. The invocation of a foreign presence, especially nationals from Hungary coming across the border to Timişoara to stir up its population, was part of the diversion strategy of the secret service. The citizens of Timişoara did not react to these instigations, showing understanding of László Tőkés's protest, as well as the necessity to transform it into an argument for anti-totalitarian revolt. The vigil on 15 December in front of the pastor's house was transformed, between 17 and 20 December, into an impressive demonstration against Ceauşescu and Communism.

The attempt to compromise the peaceful cohabitation of the Romanian majority with the German, Hungarian, Serbian and Jewish minorities in Timişoara had been perfidious. Fragmentarily preserved, the civil society of this old urban city, built on the Central European model, did not react to the nationalist instigations of the regime.

THE INTELLECTUALS AND THE MASSES DURING THE 1989 REVOLT

Unlike cities such as Prague, Budapest and Warsaw, Timişoara had not developed a political project capable of overthrowing the Communist dictatorship. Like other Romanian cities, Timişoara was absent from the great debate of ideas and the anti-totalitarian attitudes manifested in some other Communist countries. There were no dissident literary circles, no samizdat media, no personalities capable of crystallising civil society around them, of informing and directing it politically. Even if the involvement of some intellectuals was more courageous than in other Romanian cities, the cultural and university institutions in Timişoara and the Banat did not generate political criticism or a programme for change. The universities were monitored by the repressive Party apparatus, and the teaching staff were often selected according to their loyalty to the Communist Party. Professors in the humanities – those who could have contributed to a change of attitude among the students – lived far removed from Romania's social realities and European cultural and political practices. With some notable exceptions, they represented another link in the Party's ideological propaganda. Professors of philosophy, history and sociology were employed in the departments of scientific socialism that functioned within Timişoara Polytechnic Institute. Founded after the Second World War, the University of Timişoara did not have, at that time, faculties of sociology, philosophy, psychology or political science. A modest faculty of history-geography had been suppressed in the 1980s. Though there were personalities in the fields of technical professions, medicine, philology and the arts with inclinations and results that could be admired, the idea of political change was alien to the political thought of the vast majority. Relatively insensible to the suffering of their peers, the professors received some privileges from the state: decent salaries, free houses or spacious apartments, grants, trips to foreign countries, quality medical assistance and good pensions. The new intellectual class of post-war Timişoara had borrowed something from the behavioural model of co-nationals living in poorer regions of the country. Cooperation between intellectuals and workers, which occurred during the Hungarian Revolution of 1956 or during the union battles in Poland in the 1980s, did not function in Romania. Things were similar throughout the whole country in terms of the evolution of cultural elites. One contemporary Romanian writer explained the motivation behind this ignorance on the part of the intellectuals:

> Many of the difficulties of the transition in Romania are the result – in the absence of a richer Western brother – of the inability of our intelligentsia to anticipate and prepare for change during the dictatorship. A certain excess of accommodation, a form of vague aged wisdom, and the self-satisfying rhetoric of 'resistance through culture' made us face

> the changes of 1989 with bare hands. We lived under a ridiculous decisional pressure and now we suffer the consequences.[9]

It is a convincing point of view. It is good to understand, though, that, no matter how many Western brothers Romania might have had, the answer to its problems had to be based on internal debates and intellectual directions. Ivan Evseev, one of the well-known professors from the University of Timișoara, admits that he was shocked by the change that occurred in December 1989. It was very hard for him to believe and retrace events. He witnessed the terrible battle of the crowd with the tanks and water cannons, in open confrontation with the forces of repression in one of Timișoara's central squares. His recollection is emblematic of the social category to which he belongs:

> Starting from the evening of 16 December until 22 December, for the first and maybe last time in my life, I lived the experience of another time and reality, different from the profane, common space, capable of rational modelling.[10]

The professor tried to understand the rupture that took place in his own perception of the world by the 'deep gap in time before and after the events'. However, he did not notice the absence of intellectual participation during the events. In 1989, the role of the cultural elites was minor.[11] The uprisings were due to Timișoaran society – particularly the workers (which recorded the largest number of victims) – a society which had inherited or assimilated the old cultural model. Reduced to a level which could be understood and kept alive by the actions of the avant-garde groups (which deserve a special mention for their courage), this model inspired the crowd in December 1989.

Even if psychological pressure was strong and made visible in the surveillance of all social groups, a lack of of lucidity, allied to convenience and cowardice, had taken over a large proportion of the writers, artists, journalists, priests or professors from all backgrounds – in other words, the intelligentsia that could have planned the anti-Communist revolts and Romania's peaceful transition from totalitarianism to democracy. The idea of sacrifice did not characterise the thought and actions of local and national elites. The veiled opposition to the regime of the 1960s–80s in Timișoara, such as the actions of the group coordinated by Eduard Pamfil, those represented by the Marxist German-speaking writers of Aktionsgruppe Banat, the band Phoenix, the *Forum Studențesc* magazine or the solitary gestures of poet Petru Ilieșu, could not transform the city into a pole of anti-Communism dissidence.[12] The representatives of the intelligentsia were unable to propose a political alternative. The student manifestations of 1956 against Gheorghe Gheorghiu Dej's Communist regime – an echo of the Hungarian Revolution – were not replicated in the years that followed.

The creeping paralysis of the educational institutions that had taken hold over many decades was significant. No matter how much evidence there had been of civic culture in Timişoara during the Communist period, it remains clear that at the time of the 1989 revolt, democratic opposition was not organised. There was nothing similar to the Czechoslovakian Charter 77, the Polish Solidarnosc, or Hungarian dissident intellectual circles. That is why, instead of political action prepared long before the event, what took place in December 1989 was a spontaneous revolt of Timişoara's citizens against the totalitarian regime. It did not have the benefit of well-known leaders, prepared to coordinate political change. Without either a programme or a well-defined ideal, the great mass of citizens in Timişoara confronted Nicolae Ceauşescu's totalitarian regime. Their great protest of December 1989 transformed the city into the main symbol of change in Romania. In several cities of the region, including Lugoj and Arad, citizens showed solidarity with Timişoara's protest movement.

It is important to remember that Timişoara was the first city in Romania in which civil society had become aware of the necessity for change. During the demonstrations, some transition leaders emerged. For a few days, they created and animated the events: they led the crowds of protesters, drafted strategies, opposed the use of weapons, and gave political speeches from the balcony of the Opera. They also tried to negotiate with the opposing side: for example, the meeting at the headquarters of the Communist Party County Council between the protesters' representatives led by Ioan Savu and the head of the government, Constantin Dăscălescu. There is a memorable remark relating to this meeting from one of the main actors, Savu, which is symptomatic of the events unfolding in Timişoara and later in Bucharest and other Romanian urban centres:

> Only there, in front of them [Dăscălescu and his men], I realised we were not ready to talk with them. We had organised ourselves in a committee, or whatever you want to call it . . . purely by chance – those who happened to be in front went into the hall – and then we woke up to the fact that we had no ideas, we did not know what we could do, what we had to demand as representatives of the crowd outside.[13]

In reality, there was no distribution of roles, and an essential link in constructing events was missing: that of the intelligentsia. The confusion that followed and Romania's lengthy transition towards democracy are explained by this unpardonable absence. In that watershed moment, there was only the force of the crowd, accompanied by the idea of human solidarity, the spirit of sacrifice and the belief in liberation from Communist dictatorship. It was the masses which proclaimed Timişoara as Romania's first free city. Through their spontaneous revolt and their victory, they confirm one of the most important arguments of the historian Fernand Braudel according to which the masses are sometimes able to write history. The great anti-Communist revolt of December 1989 in Timişoara was an event of the masses. As at the beginning of the twentieth century, Timișoara in 1989 did not encourage a visible difference between the citizen and the worker, which probably explains why the social segment of the workers, which the Communist regime regarded as faithful and in whose name the dictatorship had been founded, became the most discontented and the largest presence during the anti-Communist street demonstrations in 1989.

THE BANAT OF TIMIȘOARA DURING THE TRANSITION YEARS

Despite their major contribution to changing the political regime, the merits of Timișoara and the region were not acknowledged by the new government. Those who opened fire upon Timișoara's population in December 1989, killing numerous people, remained largely unknown and unpunished. Presented briefly and publicly debated once a year during the commemoration of the events of December, the revolt of Timișoara is mostly imprinted on the memory of the people who accomplished it. Remembrance of recent history is marked by partisans and centres around two revolts, in Timișoara and Bucharest. Even the asynchronous evolution of the revolts created different perspectives on them and their outcomes. The speculative or provocative manner in which the events were covered by the media or in some of the books on the revolts of 1989 (over 600 titles in 27 years), has not helped to overcome the crisis of conscience visible across the whole population.

The corruption of the central political and administrative system is acutely experienced by a majority of the inhabitants of Timișoara. There is nervousness due to centralism and the difficulties faced by the local administration. The frustrations of the population, and also of mayors and other regional leaders, have come up against the contrary interests of politicians sent from Bucharest. State institutions that survived the old regime have opposed real reform. Even the view on social issues shows that the two cultural models – those of the capital and the main regional cities – do not support a convergent perspective. The polarisation of Romanian society upon material criteria, mostly visible in Bucharest, makes interpersonal and group communication more and more difficult.

Books that offer more objective and clear information on the events of December 1989 in Timișoara include documents,[14] usually testimonies, of oral history. However, they are not able to reconstruct a full picture of events. For this reason, the way in which events unfolded in Timișoara and Bucharest, the late entry onto the stage of Bucharest (21 December) compared with Timișoara (where the revolt broke out six days earlier), and the way in which Ceaușescu was deposed, have created divergences in the minds of Romanians.

The main actors in Timişoara do not look like the main actors in Bucharest. The aspirations of the people of Timişoara included revolutionary ideas that were intended to lead to the replacement of the Communist administration. This did not and could not happen throughout Romania, as the population had not been prepared. Most of those who revolted in Timişoara refused to see this, while the political class of the new Romanian state did not give the expected explanations. This partially explains the lack of social cohesion, the suspicions, the invectives, the excessive zeal in claiming revolutionary merits, and the personal attacks through the media in the absence of legal proof.

A certain degree of radicalism and countless differences of opinions have also been felt in local and regional contexts, leading to contradictory political orientations. More than two and a half decades after the 1989 revolts, political leaders still cannot agree upon essential issues of economic strategy, social and environmental policies, rebuilding the infrastructure, and the restoration of architectural and historical heritage. The new local political class has not been able to impose itself in the eyes of the electorate or at national level. Instead, it often accepted politicians from Bucharest to represent its interests. These politicians had sporadic contacts with the city and the region, were (and are) unfamiliar with local social, cultural and economic realities, and ignored the problems of Timişoara and the Banat.

Like other Romanian cities or regions, Timişoara and the Banat are facing difficult moments in adapting to a market economy and to pluralist-democratic politics. It would have been natural, two and a half decades after the events of 1989, for the city to have gained a larger share of the country's economic, administrative and cultural life; to have earned a position equal to that of the capital; and to have imposed itself more firmly in an international context. Why did this not happen? First of all, because administrative centralism has been perpetuated; because the role Timişoara and the Banat could have played in western Romania in the development of international relations has been neglected, knowingly or out of ignorance. The refusal to take political decisions on structural reform, and the lack of attention towards the most enterprising middle class in Romania, have contributed to the dissatisfaction of the local population with the national leaders. What the government of Bucharest did not understand was that modernisation of a state always starts from its most advanced marginal region, which is from the west in Romania's case. Openness to Europe could have been ensured from Timişoara and its neighbouring cities in the Banat. The functioning of the Euro-regions implied the implementation of the model of the cross-border economy, i.e. the provision of legislation necessary for the faster and more efficient development of trade and service companies. All this has been ignored. The revival of the policy promoted a century ago by the political parties of the Old Kingdom, or that of the interwar period according to which control was exercised by officials from Bucharest, has proved counterproductive. The continued resistance of the people of Timişoara and the Banat to central government is motivated by the fact that reform of the political class and central administrative structures, of regional decentralisation and pro-European direction has been delayed. Expressed in many forms, discontent has been directed at the former Communists and their institutions. One of the fundamental documents of civil society was entitled *The Proclamation of Timişoara*. Publicly presented in March 1990, the *Proclamation* was the first act of legitimisation of the post-Communist Romanian opposition.[15]

Timişoara today is searching for a new social and cultural identity. Many of the old families who conferred a unique identity on Timişoara have gone. They were engineers, construction workers, mechanics, craftsmen, along with a portion of the intellectual elite. Most of the German-speaking population from all social classes has left. The emigration of the German community, along with the Romanian population that spoke German, together with the dissolution of the Jewish community and the movement of an important segment of the Hungarian-speaking cultural and artistic elite to Budapest, has generated a sudden change in cultural and behavioural patterns. Up to 1989, the inhabitants represented par excellence the urban category of those who had been assimilated by the city, an educated, tolerant preserver of the multicultural traditions of Timişoara and the Banat. The reasons for mass emigration were not only economic but also political. In spite of some notable renewals, the laws for private initiatives and for the regaining of private property were issued rather late. The void left after the mass migration of the old inhabitants has been suddenly occupied by a population coming from the regions of Moldavia, Oltenia and Maramureş. What is certain is that the creative potential of the multi- and intercultural society of Timişoara and the Banat was ignored. Sociological studies show that after 1989 Timişoara didn't have the necessary resources to assimilate the newcomers, as it did in the interwar period or in the post-war decades. The set of values professed by the average population, which gave personality and social cohesion to the city and region, dissolved under the pressure of very fast demographic changes. The attraction of Timişoara in recent decades is owed partly to the fact that it was here that the first step in the overthrow of the dictatorship took place, and partly because inhabitants of Romania have always felt that life is better here than in the rest of the country. It is also true that there has been political pressure to change the city's social structure.

The population of contemporary Timişoara is different from the population that initiated the revolts of December 1989. The settlement of new inhabitants coming from different regions of the country and, thus, a new demographic structure, did not create major cultural conflicts, although local administrations face certain types of behaviour that betray a lack of sensitivity to the civic pride of the city and can sometimes border on aggression. The newcomers are often ignorant of the history, architecture and common good of the city; they live on the periphery and show no curiosity about either the historical and architectural references of the region or the cultural diversity inherited from its former inhabitants. The discontinuities are identifiable by the disregard of cohabitation rules, by aggressive language and, more rarely, chauvinist slogans. Economic and financial competition is tough and often unreliable. What still ensures a certain social balance is the fact that the new elites coming from the Banat (or from Transylvanian localities close to the Banat) have some influence on the life of the city. Hence, the illusion of some that no major changes have occurred, that the basic elements of the city still survive, and that centralism alone is responsible for social disagreements, institutional inefficacity, organisational disorder, and the absence of projects regarding the restoration and repositioning of the city on the European map.

Regardless of the changes, the natural resources, the geographical position, and some markers of multi- and interculturalism and multi-confessionalism of the Banat of Timișoara still survive and are essential. Numerous private initiatives; German, French, Austrian, Hungarian and Spanish investments; and the preference of some significant Italian groups to be a part of the industrial and commercial life of the city and the region show that the dialogue regarding administrative decentralisation and European integration is still fundamental. For Timișoara to become a possible model for Romania and for other regions of East-Central Europe, its policies must avoid any form of radical discourse or behaviour. The genesis of an alternative way of thinking in the Banat of today depends on new cultural products, debates on ideas, and knowledge-based cooperation. Timișoara's opportunity to play an administrative and cultural role complementary to the attributions of Bucharest, Szeged or Novi Sad is linked to the formulation of a political ideal that is able to include the different segments of the society and the professional elites. Otherwise, Timișoara and the Banat will no longer be able to gain from their fruitful inheritance, the multiple cultural codes of previous centuries, as they did during the civic and political revolts of 1989.[16]

CONCLUSIONS

The European Community today needs not only cultural conventions,[17] but also a willingness to understand its regional histories. It needs knowledge of its Euro-regional heritage. This is to do with identifying similar values for Europeans, rather than social or economic differences. Such an understanding of the facts can ensure 'a common destiny strategy'. A historical model like that of the Banat of Timișoara offers the advantage of including the Continent's multi- and intercultural realities. Relearning the history of a Euro-region such as this goes deeper than a simple knowledge of the facts: it involves replacing a partisan way of thinking with an open, liberal one; acquiring a way of life based on traditions built on diversity and tolerance. Knowing the history of the everyday relationships between individuals and between different linguistic communities, and also the major role transnational communication plays today, can be a reference on the map of future European projects.

In the context of modernising society, the evaluation of sociocultural and political intersections that took place during the eighteenth, nineteenth and twentieth centuries will contribute to the modernising of the population's reflexes. The past of the Banat of Timișoara can inspire more flexible educational models, with ramifications in the family environment, schools and universities. The contemporary population of the region is only partially heir to the historic and architectural heritage, which is why the recovery of the past and the understanding of the present from a multi- and intercultural perspective becomes a *sine qua non* for future projects.

The history of the Banat of Timișoara offers examples useful for a balanced intellectual formation. The Habsburg experiments and the Central European local and regional demographic harmony were possible due to Vienna's mercantile policies during the eighteenth and nineteenth centuries. The Banat was the region in which these policies were clearly adopted by the whole population. The understanding of this Euro-regional history in a Continental context proves that it is possible to overcome the crises of conscience and identity in a former Communist state.

The Banat of Timișoara is a space that deserves to be known whose modern features have been formed under the influence of the Enlightenment and Austrian reforms of the eighteenth century, which need to be reinvented and reclaimed for the benefit of contemporary Europe. The fact that Timișoara has been named the 2021 European Capital of Culture demonstrates that the city has enormous potential. Its inhabitants wish to prepare for this and to reinvent themselves based on the inherited models and the convergent local, regional and European cultures.

PART VII
(CONCLUSION)

23
CONCLUSION

Victor Neumann

THE LANGUAGE DEFINING cultural and sociopolitical identity requires re-evaluation, given that the status of individuals, citizens and even communities is renewed according to their material interests, languages and culture. As with the changes that occurred in the 1900s, the changes happening today must be seen in terms of regional, national and global particularities. *The Banat of Timişoara: A European Melting Pot* shows the characteristics of a border region, past and present. This theme is evident as soon as we uncover the similarities – rather than the differences – between people and communities. In conceptualising the old and new dialogues between Occident and Orient, and evaluating the rich information regarding facts, events, social and cultural realities, we have considered what the German philosopher Hans-Georg Gadamer, famous for his work on hermeneutics, called the 'fusion of horizons'.

There are different forms and stages of modernisation throughout the world, which is why it is important to examine the languages and ideas established by the administrative and political hierarchies. It is necessary not only to highlight communitarian spirit, as the adherents of social segregation sometimes do, excessively promoting their own history and belief to the detriment of others, but also to observe the amalgamation of cultural codes. Mixed families are numerous on all the meridians of the globe, representing one of the unmistakable indications of interculturality. In the Banat of Timişoara, the practice of two or more religions within the same family or inside a community, the bi- and trilinguism defining cultural identity, cultural concerns, socio-economic and political directions, all indicate the existence of an open society. Over the last centuries, the plastic arts have often been limited by the narrow horizon of the bourgeoisie, while postmodern art values heritage, proving that the intellectual horizon and the reflexes of the individual and the collective are ambivalent.

The histories, cultures and politics of Central and Eastern Europe, as with those belonging to any other region, can be read and understood by taking into consideration relationships that transcend religious, linguistic and national uniqueness. There are states in modern Europe whose complex identity is linked to the process of continuous immigration, such as Great Britain, the Netherlands, France and Austria, and – more recently – Germany, Italy and Spain. The debut of these demographic movements in the modern era took place in the regions controlled by the Habsburg Empire. By colonising different populations, the Banat of Timișoara can be considered one of the first modern European experiments in migration within the continent. The phenomenon shows not only the cohabitation of diverse groups, but also the linguistic loans, the intersection of religious ideas and beliefs, the genesis of a multi-coded set of cultural and civilisational values. By understanding them, we will uncover the fluctuating identities of people, communities and nations. We will stop thinking in the manner of our Romantic predecessors, with their obsessive repetition of what separated them while ignoring what united them. We will understand and be able to explain not just the individual but also the collective identity, in terms of plurality and not singularity, heterogeneity not specificity. Even the relationship between the local and the universal prompts us to be mindful of the constraining ideologies promoted in the name of a majority or minority.

Speaking of the countless fruitful encounters between people, Marc Bloch observed that history equates to their multiple experiences.[1] He thought that life and science could only gain from fraternal meetings. The rewriting of history is not based on one interpretation alone, a so-called 'valid story', and that is because there are many perspectives upon the past. What we are talking about are histories that are intertwined, rather than a single history or linear story. Researching the heterogeneity of Central European cultures, Moritz Csáky recommended taking into consideration dates, facts, events or ideas that are contradictory or come about by chance. In defining collective identities, the historian must examine the complexity of social, political and cultural life. As far as the conceptualisation of the past is concerned, this includes elements that transcend the political or national sense, contradicting the communitarian aspirations or those which are considered 'purely national'.[2]

From such a perspective, *The Banat of Timișoara: A European Melting Pot* describes the meandering and fascinating past of the multi- and intercultural space situated at the intersection of the former Ottoman and Habsburg empires, of the Muslim and Christian world, of Orthodox Byzantium and the Roman Catholic Church. Although it has periodically been an object of dispute, the Banat of Timișoara has remained, for most of its history, a territory in which peaceful cohabitation was the dominant feature. How can this be explained? Firstly, its administrative organisation belonged to the Viennese imperial court and was made possible after the conquest of the region from the Ottoman Empire and in the absence of its own institutional structures. Secondly, the Viennese administration proceeded to completely reorganise the cities, the villages and the economy. It focused on building new cities, the future royal-imperial free city of Timișoara, designing and rearranging the villages and communes of the Banat with the help of Austrian cartographers, engineers and militia. Thirdly, it colonised numerous families of craftsmen, farmers and traders from all corners of Europe and reorganised the religious institutions so that each church and priest could promote religious ideas and beliefs in an ecumenical spirit. In fact, it promoted a policy quite different from the century of the Counter-Reformation, in cultivating tolerance among people and communities. Fourthly, the new region acquired in 1718 following the Treaty of Passarowitz was the site of a series of experiments conducted by the representatives of the Habsburg Empire. The local nobility had left the region during the Ottoman occupation, so that in 1552 the lands were in the possession of the Sultan, and in 1718 passed to the Habsburg Emperor. That explains the lack of opposition towards the new government and encouraged Habsburg experimentation throughout the eighteenth century, which left its mark in the following centuries on society and culture, scientific and technical achievements, and the development of industry, agriculture and trade.

The information, analysis and interpretations included for the first time in this book assist the reader eager to acquire an understanding free of constraints. The chapters that consider the origins and multiple identity of the inhabitants of the Banat, the administrative and political regimes under whose authority the region developed, the multilingual press and education, the reforms and revolutions in Timișoara and its neighbouring region, draw attention to the way in which the space has been modernised over time. Several of the chapters highlight the uniqueness of this European region during the premodern and modern era, a uniqueness consisting in the association and cooperation of its inhabitants, in multilingualism, in the assumption of a common set of values, and in the refusal of intolerant ideologies and dogmas.

To promote a good understanding of the history of this European melting pot, we have looked at the local art and architecture in a regional and European context, at the rural and urban habitat, at the genesis of the idea of a cultural nation and the manner in which the multi- and intercultural population survived despite the ethnonationalist and nationalist policies of the nineteenth and twentieth centuries. We have paid special attention to the First World War and the division of the region between Romania, Serbia and Hungary, to show how the Banat of Timișoara was repositioned along the borders of these three nations. Using comparative perspectives we can see when, how and why the local communities harmonised together, and when, how and why national interests collided.

The final chapters of *The Banat of Timişoara* concentrate upon the part of the region which, following the Treaty of Trianon, became part of Romania. It is the largest part of the region, a space where its inhabitants made an effort to preserve the cultural identity of their heritage. The phenomenon of Jewish survival in the Banat of Timişoara during the Second World War is unique in Europe and is highlighted here using information hitherto unknown to international historiography, by narrating eyewitness accounts and documentary evidence that prove the opposition of most people in Timişoara to the Romanian extremist ideologies of the years 1938–44.

In a chapter concerning the post-war years, we present examples of the intellectual, artistic and student environments which demonstrate the force of the civic spirit in Timişoara and the opposition of the population of the Banat in general towards National Communist despotism. A special chapter is devoted to the revolutionary transformation of Romania in 1989, especially since it was in Timişoara that the first large demonstrations against the totalitarian system took place. Timişoara was the only Romanian city to resist the repression of the Communist regime for a whole week. The demonstrations in December 1989 in Timişoara were important because they paved the way for the changes that followed in other Romanian cities and regions. Its multi- and intercultural inheritance, its cosmopolitan and ecumenical understanding of human relations gave Timişoara a special place at that delicate moment in history.

The Banat of Timişoara: A European Melting Pot is based on a project conceived during the 1980s and 1990s, while the research and editing took place between 2005 and 2015. The concept of the book was mine; I also wrote several chapters, as well as coordinated, structured and edited others. It presents a European perspective on local history, promoting an understanding of a fragment of Central and South-Eastern European and Romanian history. The cross-cultural and cross-border components made the region a place where experimentation was possible, a place in which people were motivated not only by competition, but also by creativity.

This is an interdisciplinary work written by historians, philologists, sociologists, architects and art historians, and historians of religion. It is the first time that a work about this region has included contributions from a number of researchers from the three countries into which it is divided today: Romania, Serbia and Hungary. The history presented here concentrates on the sociopolitical and cultural physiognomy of the region, reflecting its particular features. Without neglecting those values that explain the region's multi- and interculturality, the studies transcend any type of communitarianism.

Why is such a historical retrospective useful? Because Euroregions like the Banat of Timişoara have played, and can still play, a special role in discovering and better understanding the European dimension of Central and South-Eastern Europe, building bridges between cultures and nations. The Banat of Timişoara can promote a culture of dialogue, of integration, a European *sensus communis*. Winning the title of 2021 European Capital of Culture, following a competition with 13 other Romanian cities, is in itself a credible argument for the impressive potential of Timişoara and the surrounding region.

This book is based on information from archives and libraries in Romania, Serbia, Hungary, Austria and Germany, highlighting the past of a region whose features and identity derive from its geographical position, from the intersection of cultures and habits, and from the diversity of its civilisational strata. What we set out to achieve – a description and evaluation of the region and its city through the spectrum of some relevant themes – envisaged a history in which time and space would be researched complementarily, and where the past and the future would reveal the behavioural constants of a world, its similarities rather than its differences.

The Banat of Timişoara: A European Melting Pot often takes into account multiple social experiences, individuals and personalities capable of participating in the life of the community through association with their peers. This is not about mapping the community linguistic and religious cultures in the Banat of Timişoara, but about events and facts, administrative, economic and legislative cultures, and individual consciences. By recalling and evaluating intellectual and political ideas we have aimed to describe, understand and theorise the world of yesterday and today. We have sought to present the extraordinary history of the Banat, one that, hopefully, will motivate the transformations that Timişoara – the most important city of the region – will bring into force during the year when it holds the title of European Capital of Culture and beyond.

Timişoara, 4–5 July 2018

NOTES

Foreword

1 M. Foucher, *Fronts et frontières: Un tour du monde géopolitique* (Paris, 1988); J. Labasse, *L'Europe des régions* (Paris, 1991); E. Niemi, 'Regions and Regionalisation', in *Proceedings of the 19th International Congress of Historical Sciences, Oslo, 6–13 August 2000* (Oslo, 2000).

2 Răzvan Theodorescu, 'The Two Europes', in *Revue: Association internationale d'études du Sud-Est Européen, nos. 40–44, 2010–2014* (2nd edn., Bucharest, 2015), pp. 72–77; J. Szücs, *Les Trois Europes* (Paris, 1985).

Preface

1 Victor Neumann, *The Interculturality of the Banat Region* (3rd edn., Iași, 2015).

Chapter 1

1 *Vergangene Zukunft: Zur Semantik Geschichtlicher Zeiten* (3rd edn, Frankfurt am Main, 1995).

Chapter 2

1 For bibliography, see Karl Gutkas, *Prinz Eugene und das barocke Österreich* (Vienna, 1986); Wolfgang Oppenheimer, *Prinz Eugene von Savoy: Feldherr, Staatsmann und Mäzen 1663–1736* (Munich, 1979); Max Braubach, *Prinz Eugene von Savoy: Eine Biographie*, 5 vols (Vienna, 1963–65); Franz Herre, *Prinz Eugen: Europas heimlicher Herrscher* (Stuttgart, 1997); Hanne Egghardt, *Prinz Eugen: Der Philosoph in Kriegsrüstung* (Vienna, 2007); ead., *Auf den Spuren Prinz Eugens: Barocke Pracht in und um Vienna* (Vienna, 2008); Agnes Husslein-Arco and Marie Luise von Plessen (eds.), *Prinz Eugen: Feldherr und Philosoph* (Vienna, 2010); eid. (eds.), *Prince Eugene: General Philosopher and Art Lover* (Vienna, 2010); Stephan Peter, *Das Obere Belvedere in Vienna: Ikonographie und Arhitektonisches Konzept: Das Schloss des Prinzen Eugene als Ausdruck seines Selbsverständnisses* (Vienna, 2010).

2 For bibliography, see August Treboniu Laurian, *Temisiana sau scurtă istorie a Banatului temișan (Temesiana or a Short History of the Banat of Temesvar)* (Bucharest, 1848); Johann Heinrich Schwicker, *Geschichte des Temeser Banats* (Becicherecul Mare, 1861); Jenő Szentkláray, *Mercy kormányzata a Temesi Bánságban (Mercy's Government in the Banat)* (Budapest, 1909); id., 'Temesvár története' ('History of Temesvar'), in Samu Borovszky (ed.), *Magyarország vármegyéi és városai (Hungary's Cities and Counties)* (Budapest, n.d.); Armin Barát, *Die königliche Freistadt Temeswar: Eine monographische Skizze* (Temeswar, 1902); Leo Hoffmann, *Kurze*

Geschichte der Banater Deutschen: Von 1717 bis 1848 (Temeswar, 1925); A. Cucu, *Cetatea și harta cetății Timișoara* (*The City and the Map of Timișoara*) (Lugoj, 1931); Iosif Kinezy, *Istoricul cetății Timișoara* (*The History of the City of Timișoara*) (Timișoara, 1921); Anton Peter Petri, *Die Festung Temeschwar im 18. Jahrhundert* (Munich, 1966); Vasile V. Muntean, *Contribuții la istoria Banatului* (*Contributions to the History of the Banat*) (Timișoara, 1990); Ioan and Rodica Munteanu, *Timișoara: Monografie* (*Timișoara: Monograph*) (Timișoara, 2002).

3 A history of the historiography of Timișoara and the Banat region would be helpful, by evaluating writings, the ideological trends, the documentation and the originality of judgement in each period.

4 Francesco Griselini, *Versuch einer politischen und natürlichen Geschichte des Temeswarer Banats in Briefen und Standespersonen und Gelehrte*, vols. i–ii, trans. into German by Ignaz von Born (Vienna, 1780). See the original Italian version, *Lettere odeporiche: Ove suoi viaggi e le di lui osservazioni spettanti all storia naturale ai costumi di vari popoli e sopra piu altri interesanti oggetti si descrivono* (Milan, 1780). See also the Romanian version *Încercare de istorie politică și naturală a Banatului Timișoarei*, trans. from the German and with notes by Costin Feneșan (Timișoara, 2006). For a comparative study, see Tamara Farcaş, 'Banatul dintr-o perspectivă venețiană: *Călătoriile, corespondența și descrierile lui Francesco Griselini*' ('The Banat from a Venetian Perspective: Francesco Griselini's Travels, Writings and Descriptions'), PhD thesis (West University of Timișoara, 2011), p. 81. The Italian sources for the biography and work of Griselini are essential and they were partially and for the first time highlighted by Farcaș. For other information and the contextualisation of intellectual and political life, see my Chapter 4 in this volume.

5 Marc Bloch, *Apologie pour l' histoire ou Métier d' historien* (1949), trans. as *The Historian's Craft* (1953), p. 119.

6 The name of the Banat comes from the word *ban* which was used by the first time in c.1146 to name the representatives of the Hungarian Kingdom in Croatia and in the newly conquered Dalmatia. The *ban* was the chief administrator of this region, which then referred to the South Slavic territory. We must maintain, though, that there is no connection between medieval and modern Banat. The Banat situated between the Tisa, Mureș and Danube rivers and the Carpathian Mountains was designed as an independent region during the Turkish-Austrian peace negotiations of Karlowitz and became an administrative-territorial region following the Treaty of Passarowitz in 1718. Cf. Holm Sundhausen and Konrad Clewing (eds.), *Lexikon zur Geschichte Südosteuropas* (Vienna, 2016), 126. See also Marjanucz, Chapter 5 in this volume.

7 Banat is the region between the Tisa, Mureș and Danube rivers and the Carpathian Mountains. See also the article 'Banat' in Sundhausen and Clewing (eds.), *Lexikon zur Geschichte Südosteuropas*, pp. 127–28.

8 Cf. my Chapter 1 in this volume.

9 Griselini, *Încercare* , p .37.

10 I thank Professor Marin Marian-Bălaşa for discussions upon modernity in Western and Eastern Europe.

11 The Venetian historian's explorations, dating from the Enlightenment era, describe the people and facts of this area as a result of his direct contact with the region, and offer information necessary for the examination of events in that period. Griselini's research depicts the geography and history of the place, and engages with the demographic realities, the lifestyle of the old and new inhabitants of the area, the cultural and economic differences between Western and Eastern Europe, and the transformation made possible through the reforms of the House of Habsburg between 1719 and 1779. See Victor Neumann, *The Temptation of Homo Europaeus* (Boulder, Colorado, 1993), 125–48, 149-210; 211–39. For details, see my Chapter 4 in this volume.

12 Ilber Ortayli, 'Prince Eugene and the Ottomans: Cultural Exchange in War and Victory Encampments from 1683 to 1717', in Husslein-Arco and von Plessen (eds.), *Prince Eugene*, pp. 49–114, at pp. 52–53.

13 I would like to thank Marin Marian-Bălaşa for the discussions on this topic.

14 Ortayli, 'Prince Eugene and the Ottomans', p. 52.

15 His narrative is confined to the ideals of the age, to the invocation of Roman origins, and the continuity and unity of Romanians in a national state. Although he replicates much information from his predecessors' books or his German congeners (he was a good German-speaker) and even if his retelling of the past is dominated by a romantic tone, Treboniu Laurian notices the major changes produced by Eugene of Savoy's conquest of Timişoara and the Banat and their integration into the European sphere of influence: 'Since then a new order of things has been introduced, which was in a few times troubled until the times of Joseph II by glorious memory, but the country did not fall again under other foreign rule. But what Temisiana and Transylvania had gained by this complete passage to the Austrian sceptre, Wallachia and Moldavia had lost by the establishment of Phanariots, whose reign dates from that period.' See Treboniu Laurean, *Temisiana sau scurtă istorie a Banatului temişan*, 2.

16 Griselini, *Încercare*, pp. 122, 138–46.

17 Ibid., p. 123.

18 Victor Neumann, *Interculturalitatea Banatului* (*The Interculturality of the Banat*) (Iaşi, 2015). See also the German edn., *Die Interkulturalität des Banats* (Berlin, 2015).

19 Jenő Szentkláray, *Mercy kormányzata a Temesi Bánságban* (*Mercy's Government in the Banat*) (Budapest, 1909). This 400-page work reveals the population at the time of Eugene of Savoy's conquest, the colonisations, the appointment of the governor, the military situation, the role of the Jesuits in city life. Regardless of the subjective notes, his studies are solid, the narration reveals facts, events, outstanding people and key institutions. Szentkláray lays the figures of Prince Eugene of Savoy and Count Claude Florimond de Mercy side by side, comparing and highlighting some similitaries in the thought and political actions of the two leaders. From what this historian writes, it is clear that the two were the founders of the new Timişoara and the Banat.

20 See Nicolae Ilieşiu, *Timişoara – monografie istorică* (*Timişoara – Historical Monograph*) (Timişoara, 2003). The chapter dedicated to Eugene of Savoy's age replicates Griselini's and Szenkláray's descriptions, emphasising the names of the governors, the relationship with Vienna, and the systematisation of the new city.

21 Louis XIV's message to Duke Richelieu Sartori from Madame de Maintenon. Cited in Husslein-Arco and von Plessen (eds.), *Prince Eugene*, 23.

22 See *Memoirs of Prince Eugene, of Savoy. Written by himself. Translated from the French by William Mudford and containing all those omissions which have been detected in the recent Parisian editions (1648–1715)* (London, 1811), p. 50. See the note that accompanies the edition: 'Written not by Prince Eugene, but by Prince Charles Joseph de Ligne'.

23 Leopold Auer, 'Prince Eugene and the Ideal of "Honnête Homme": Behavioral Norms of the Elites under the Ancien Régime', in Husslein-Arco and von Plessen (eds.), *Prince Eugene*, 41–48, at p. 41.

24 See Marie Louise von Plessen, 'Prince Eugene – General Philosopher and Art Lover: The Noble Knight as Hero of the Arts', in Husslein-Arco and von Plessen (eds), *Prince Eugen*, pp. 17-21, at p. 21.

25 H. Wölfflin, *Principles of Art History: The Problem of the Development of Style in Later Art*, translated from 7th German edn. (1929) into English by M.D. Hottinger (New York 1932 and reprints).

26 Today's Novi Sad. Koloman Juhász asserts that Petrovaradin's victory meant the liberation of the entire diocese of Cenad from Ottoman domination. See Koloman Juhász, 'Jesuiten im Banat (1718–1773) ... Ein Beitrag zur Kulturgeschichte des Temeswarer Banats', *Mitteilungen des Osterreichische Staatsarchiv*, vol. 11 (1958), pp. 154–220, at p. 157.

27 Griselini, *Încercare*, p. 108. See a similar description in Johann N. Preyer, *Monographie der Königlichen Freistadt Temeswar / Monografia oraşului liber regesc Timişoara* (*Monograph on the Royal Free City of Timişoara*) (Temeswar, 1853). 'With this intention [of conquering Timişoara] 16 cavalry regiments led by Count Pálfy and 10 infantry battalions lead by the Duke of Würtemberg marched to attack this place, for the time being, until he [Prince Eugene] could personally arrive with the large army. Pálfy besieged Timişoara as best he could, but, because the garrison had 18 thousand people, he did not have enough troops to take the land.'

28 Griselini, *Încercare*, p. 118.

29 Preyer, *Mongraphie*, p. 182.

30 Ilieșiu, *Timișoara*, p. 67.

31 Griselini, *Încercare*, p. 110.

32 Ibid., p. 108.

33 Ibid., pp. 109–10.

34 Ibid., p. 111.

35 Ibid., pp. 108–9.

36 Ibid., p. 110.

37 Ibid., p. 112.

38 Ibid., See an almost identical description in Treboniu Laurian, *Temisiana sau scurtă istorie a Banatului Temișan*, pp. 135–42.

39 Juhász, 'Jesuiten im Banat (1718–1773)' p. 156.

40 Ibid. See also the main bibliographical sources regarding the moment of conquest by the imperial armies led by Eugene of Savoy. Juhász's work comprises a valuable description based on novel information gathered from the archives of Timișoara, Budapest and Vienna which present local religious life along with a series of cultural and political events from Timișoara and the Banat. The author reclaims two manuscripts found in the archive of the Roman Catholic Diocese of Timișoara, the only shortcoming resulting from the limited theme, namely the absence of comparisons with other religious and linguistic communities.

41 Griselini, *Încercare*, p. 112.

42 Požarevac, a settlement south of Belgrade.

43 Juhász, 'Jesuiten im Banat (1718–1773)', 159.

44 Griselini, *Încercare*, p. 120.

45 *Történelmi adattár (Historical Archive)* (Temesvár, 1871), pp. 379–80; see also *Izvoare și mărturii privind istoria evreilor din România (Sources and Testimonies Regarding the Jews from Romania)*, ed. Mihai Spielmann (Bucharest, 1988), document no. 39, p. 28 n. 2. See also Victor Neumann, *Istoria evreilor din Banat: O mărturie a multi- și interculturalității Europei Central-Orientale* (Bucharest, 1999), p. 11 (see the English version, *The End of a History: The Jews of Banat from the Beginning to Nowadays* (Bucharest, 2006).

46 Griselini, *Încercare*.

47 Juhász, 'Jesuiten im Banat (1718–1773)', 159.

48 Griselini, *Încercare*, pp. 118–19.

49 Ibid., p. 120.

50 Ibid., p. 113.

51 Juhász, 'Jesuiten im Banat (1718–1773)', pp. 158–59.

52 I thank the historian Miodrag Milin for the discussions we had during the making of this study.

53 Neumann, *The Temptation of Homo Europaeus*, pp. 125–48.

54 Griselini, *Încercare*, p. 117. Chroniclers before Griselini speak about the swampy terrains of Timișoara and the Banat. This is also true of documentary sources from the second half of the eighteenth century, for example, 'the geographical and economical description of Timișoara district, with special observations upon the town and the suburbs of Timișoara', by Lieutenant Philipp Elmpt – future major general and chief of staff – who had conducted and finalised the mapping of the Banat in 1768 and who presented the map to Emperor Franz Joseph II during his trip there. See Ileana Bozac and Teodor Pavel, *Călătoria împăratului Iosif al II-lea în Transilvania la 1773 / Die Reise Kaiser Josephs II. durch Siebenbürgens im Jahre 1773 (Emperor Joseph II's Trip to Transylvania in 1773)*, vol. i (2nd edn., Cluj-Napoca, 2007), document no. 39, pp. 419–22. See biographical note on Philipp Elmpt, ibid., p. 423.

55 See new documentary contributions to this topic in Marlen Negrescu and Dan Pura, *Navigația pe Bega: Secvențe istorice (Navigation on the Bega: Historical Sequences)* (Timișoara, 2006).

56 Griselini, *Încercare*, p. 120.

57 Ibid.

58 Ibid., p.124.

59 See Marjanucz, Chapter 5 in this volume.

60 Jenő Szentkláray, *Mercy kormányzata a Temesi bánságban (Mercy's Government in the Banat of Temes)* (Budapest, 1909), pp. 17–31.

61 See Marjanucz, Chapter 5 in this volume.

62 Griselini, *Încercare*, p. 121.

63 The archaeological excavations in Timișoara, during the renovation of its historic centre (2014–15) confirmed

Francesco Griselini's descriptions. Archaeologist Florin Drașovean, who coordinated the excavation of St George's Square, discovered the vestiges of a mosque and a Muslim cemetery – the same great mosque Griselini wrote about which was transformed into a Christian church after Eugene of Savoy's conquest of Timișoara. Koloman Juhász, the local and regional historian of the Catholic Church, certifies, based on the documentary evidence found in the Roman Catholic Diocesan Archive, that this transformation took place in 1718. I thank Mr Florin Drașovean for the presentation of the materials discovered on the digging site – masonry, objects and graves – and also for discussions regarding this chapter in the history of Timișoara. The recent discoveries confirm the assessments published in my books on the Banat, in which I highlighted the multicultural and the multi-civilisational realities of the city, region, Central and South-Eastern Europe. See my *Interculturalitatea Banatului (The Interculturality of Banat)* (3rd edn., Iași, 2015); id. (ed.), *Identitate și Cultură: Studii privind istoria Banatului (Identity and Culture: Studies regarding the History of the Banat)* (Bucharest, 2009). To contextualise the multi- and inter-cultural phenomena of Timișoara and Banat see id., *The Temptation of Homo Europaeus*.

64 Griselini, *Încercare*. See also Juhász, 'Jesuiten im Banat (1718–1773)'.

65 See Mihai Opriș, *Timișoara: Monografie urbanistică (Timișoara: Urban Monograph)* (Timișoara, 2007). The author observed the countless errors made by those who based their 'little histories' or 'monographs' on information from earlier writings or data gathered from ambiguous sources and translations made by unauthorised people, rather than by researching primary sources. Secondly, many local historians did not base their history of Timișoara on a critical examination of the roots or on *interdisciplinary* bases, thus making it impossible to grasp the complexity of the city, its sociocultural, religious, institutional evolutions and legacies. Even when some of their writings aspired to acknowledge diversity, they have little credit because of the lack of authenticity, the carelessness regarding the intellectual, civic and spiritual dimensions, the lack of understanding of a paradigm other than that of fictive ethnicity or simply because they 'flew above reality'. Unlike this league of storytellers who were tempted to transfer legends from one period to another, Opriș undertook thorough research. The value of what he uncovered is unique for the amplitude of documentation, the amount and precision of information, the relevance of some major aspects of Timișoara's history, the identification of the patterns and the cultural roots that influenced the city during its modernisation. In his urban history, Opriș offers a very good example of scientific research to local historiography.

66 See Szekely, Chapter 7 in this volume.

67 Ibid.

68 According to Mihai Opriș, *Timișoara: Mică monografie urbanistică (Timișoara: Small Urban Monograph)* (Bucharest, 1987), p. 42. Id., *Timișoara: Monografie urbanistică* presents the designs and histories of the most representative houses and palaces in the city and discusses Timișoara's reconstruction in the eighteenth century. There are many other reference texts. There have been numerous Romanian studies in the last two decades, and some of them – for example those of Valeriu Leu, Nicolae Bocșan and Costin Feneșan – deserve special attention. See Nicolae Bocșan, *Contribuții la istoria iluminismului românesc (Contribution to the History of the Romanian Enlightenment)* (Timișoara, 1986); Valeriu Leu, *Memorie, Memorabil, Istorie în Banat (Memory, Memorabilia, History in the Banat)* (Timișoara, 2006); Costin Feneșan, *Administrație și fiscalitate în Banatul Timișoarei (Administration and Fiscality in the Banat of Timișoara, 1717–1778)* (Timișoara, 1997).

69 See Szekely, Chapter 7 in this volume.

70 Neumann, *End of a History*, pp. 37–38.

71 Neumann, *End of a History*, p. 37.

72 See Szekely, Chapter 7 in this volume. Beside the arrangement of space in the inner city, there was concern with the expansion of the future royal free city with the creation of a few suburbs: Fabric, Josefin and Mehala. Unlike other regions, the Banat fully accepted the Central European Baroque, its medieval traits having being interrupted by the Ottoman domination between 1552 and 1716. The size and the style of the houses and palaces, and their aesthetics, suggest the

importance Vienna gave to the new regional centre.

73 Victor Neumann, 'Cultura din Banat la începutul evului modern: Primul ziar local: Temeswarer Nachrichten' ('Culture in Banat at the Beginning of the Modern Age: The First Local Newspaper: *Temeswarer Nachrichten*'), in id. (ed), *Identitate și Cultură*, pp. 25–37.

74 Id., 'Principii luministe și diferențialism etnocultural: Opera cărturarului Ștefan Stratimirović, mitropolit al ortodocșilor din Imperiul habsburgic' ('Enlightenment Principles and Ethno-cultural Differentialism: The Work of the Scholar Ștefan Stratimirović, Bishop of the Orthodox Church in the Habsburg Empire'), in id. (ed.), *Identitate și Cultură*, pp. 38–47.

75 Thanks to Eugene's interest in and passion for art, during the first half of the eighteenth century, an impressive number of baroque works were collected, which formed the core of the museums opened in Vienna in the nineteenth century. For the evolution of the Belevedere art collection and comparison with other collections, see Michael Krapf, 'Die Austellung der "Sammlung Barock": Eine Neupositionierung im Oberen Belvedere', in Agnes Husslein-Arco (ed.), *Barock: Meisterwerke im Belvedere: Katalog* (Vienna, 2008), p. 18.

76 Ernst Trost, *Prinz Eugen: Mit zahlreichen Abbildungen* (Vienna, 2013), p. 336.

77 *Reveries*, quoted in Derek Beales, *Enlightenment and Reform in Eighteenth Century Europe* (New York, 2011), pp. 169–70.

78 Bozac and Pavel, *Călătoria împăratului Iosif al II-lea*, p. 50.

79 They were both loved, one by his soldiers, the other by the simple folk.

80 See my Chapter 4 in this volume.

81 Bozac and Pavel, *Călătoria împăratului Iosif al II-lea*.

Chapter 3

1 A version of this chapter appeared in Laura Stanciu and Cosmin Popa-Gorjanu (eds.), *Transylvania in the Eighteenth Century: Aspects of Regional Identity*.

2 Theodor W. Adorno and Max Horkheimer, *Dialectic of Enlightenment: Philosophic Fragments*, trans. and ed. Edmund Jephcott (Stanford, CA, 2002), pp. 7, 18.

3 Ibid., p. 57.

4 Reinhart Koselleck, *Kritik und Krise: Ein Beitrag zur Pathogenese der bürgerlichen Welt* (Frankfurt am Main, 1973), p. 31; my translation.

5 Hans Erich Bödeker, *Aufklärung über Aufklärung? Reinhart Kosellecks Interpretation derAufklärung*, in Carsten Dutt and Reinhard Laube (eds.), *Zwischen Sprache und Geschichte: Zum Werk Reinhart Kosellecks* (Göttingen, 2013), pp. 128–74.

6 Victor Neumann, *The Temptation of Homo Europaeus* (New York, 1993), pp. 149–211.

7 Reinhart Koselleck, *Begriffgeschichten: Studien zur Semantik und Pragmatik der politischen und sozialen Sprache* (Frankfurt am Main, 2006), p. 344; see esp. 'Aufklärung und die Grenzen ihrer Toleranz', pp. 340–62. See also Victor Neumann, Introduction to Reinhart Koselleck, *The Concept of History*, trans. Victor Neumann and Patrick Lavrits (Iaşi, 2005).

8 Dominique Bourel, 'Moses Mendelssohn et l'Aufklärung', *Dix-Huitième Siècle: Qu'est ce que les Lumières?*, vol. 10 (1978), p. 13.

9 Dominique Bourel, *Moses Mendelssohn: La Naissance du judaïsme moderne* (Paris, 2004), p. 460. This is the result of rich and systematic research, using both German and Jewish historical sources, along with an extensive bibliography. The author analyses the work of Moses Mendelssohn, contributing to a better understanding of his and the interpretation of the *Auflkärung*. See also the detailed analysis in Simon Schwarzfuchs's review 'Dominique Bourel, *Moses Mendelssohn: La Naissance du judaïsme moderne*', *Revue de l'histoire des religions*, vol. 4 (2006), pp. 498–501.

10 See Bourel, *Moses Mendelssohn*, p. 458.

11 When referring to the Prussian *Aufklärung*, he identifies similarities with, but also differences to, the French *Lumières*. The well-known aspirations of the Enlightenment were in opposition to the ideologies and the vague politics of ethnonationalism promoted by the *Sturm und Drang* (Storm and Stress) movement, thus multiple confusions arise from a conceptual point of view.

12 Cf. Moses Mendelssohn, *Gesammelte Schriften*, vol. iii (Leipzig, 1843), p. 400.

13 See Mendelssohn's short description of the word *Aufklärung*, in Otto Brunner, Werner Conze and Reinhart Koselleck (eds.), *Geschichtliche Grundbergriffe: Historisches Lexikon zur politisch-sozialen Sprache in Deutschland* (Stuttgart, 2004), vol. i, pp. 272–74.

14 See also the conclusions of the thorough analysis of Mendelssohn's work in Bourel, *Moses Mendelssohn*, pp. 450–62.

15 See the contributions in Victor Neumann and Armin Heinen (eds.), *Istoria României prin concepte (The History of Romania through Concepts)* (1st edn., Iaşi, 2010).

16 In Romanian historiography, the most important work is D. Prodan, *Supplex Libellus Valachorum: Din istoria formării naţiunii române (Supplex Libellus Valachorum: The Formation of the Romanian Nation)* (3rd edn., Bucharest, 1984), which offers a variety of information on the history of Transylvanian notions related to culture and politics, mentioning both the local, central resources and the Western/Central European ones. His thematics were vast, focused on the evolution of concepts such as 'nation' among the Romanians from Transylvania; the social and political life of the inhabitants under Habsburg rule; the role of the Greek Catholic Church; the impact of the French Revolution on East and Central Europe. The starting point of the book was the primary sources from *Monumenta Comitialia Regni Transilvanie*, the magazine *Archiv des Vereins für siebenbürgische Landeskunde*, the collection of *Documente istorice translivane (Historical Transylvanian Documents)*, ed. Ioan Lupaş, as well as a vast bibliography in French, German, Romanian and Hungarian. Prodan presented the social and administrative structures as well as medieval and premodern Transylvanian politics, the evolution of the intellectual segment of the population and other political aspects of the eighteenth century.

17 The Catholic Habsburgs restored the domination of the Catholic religion in Transylvania in their own interests. See Olga Lukács and András Magyari, 'Biserică şi stat la maghiari' ('The Church and State of Hungarians'), in Ioan Aurel Pop, Thomas Nagler and András Magyari (eds.), *Istoria Transilvaniei: De la 1711 la 1918 (The History of Transylvania, 1711–1918)*, vol. iii (Cluj-Napoca, 2008), pp. 105–6.

18 Ibid., p. 105.

19 Ibid., p. 106.

20 Prodan, *Supplex Libellus Valachorum*, p. 191.

21 More examples of the preoccupations and environmental habits of the intellectual nobility are studied and analysed in Victor Neumann, 'Cultural Channels in East-Central Europe: Books and Libraries in Transylvania, Banat, Hungary and Serbia', in id., *The Temptation of Homo Europaeus*, pp. 149–211.

22 See 1778. *Praefatio ad lectorem* to *Transsilvania sive magnus Transsilvaniae Principatus olim Dacia Mediterranea doctus orbi nondum satis cognitus*. Vindobonae. Cf. Neumann, 'Cultural Channels', p. 163.

23 See Library of the Brukenthal National Museum, *The Catalogue of Transilvanicelor*, vol. ii .*Eighteenth Century*, ed. Doina Nagler. Sibiu (1982), photo no. 385, p. 113. See also photo nos. 405–6, pp. 118–19; no. 209, p. 65; no. 257, p. 78; no. 211, p. 66.

24 The paintings depicting Brukenthal and his wife are in the art collection of the Brukenthal National Museum.

25 See Adolf Armbruster, 'The Cultural Works of Samuel von Brukenthal in Sibiu', *History Magazine*, vol. 4 (1978), p. 670.

26 See Victor Neumann, *Istoria evreilor din România: Studii documentare şi teoretice (The History of Jews in Romania: Documentary and Theoretical Studies)* (Timişoara, 1996), p. 31.

27 Ibid., pp. 31, 69–93. Despite regulations introduced by some princes in Transylvania in the eighteenth century – those of Gabriel Bethlen were accompanied by protective interventions towards the Jews from Alba-Iulia by George Rákoczi and Mihai Apaffi – restrictions regarding housing and the right to practise trades continued. The imperial administration introduced tolerance fees in exchange for the right to settle in the region. In general, at that time, the restrictions regarding Jewish settlement in Transylvania were due to the conservatism of the nobility, the medieval mentality of the local population, and the fear of competition and innovation. On the other hand, Protestant intellectual circles in Transylvania showed

a constant interest in Jewish culture, which can be seen in their book collections.

28 The perspective of Prodan concerning the 'close' relationship between intellectuals and peasantry is exaggerated.

29 Cited in Prodan, *Supplex Libellus Valachorum*, p. 477.

30 Ileana Bozac and Pavel Teodor (eds), *The Journeys of Emperor Joseph the Second in Transylvania in 1773*, vol. i, (2nd edn. Cluj-Napoca, 2007); 25 March 1772. *Auersperg's Report concerning the Situation in Transylvania and the Improvements Adopted during his Rule (1 May 1771–April 1773)*, Sibiu. pp. 142–43.

31 Cf. Victor Neumann, 'Peculiarities of the Translation and Adaptation of the Concept of Nation in Eastern Central Europe: The Hungarian and Romanian Cases in the Nineteenth Century', *Contributions to the History of Concepts*, vol. 7, no. 1 (Summer 2012), pp. 71–102.

Chapter 4

1 In this chapter, the author uses 'Josephism' to refer to the *Reveries* (1765) of Joseph II (r. 1780–1848), in which he wrote of the way he envisaged changes within the Habsburg Empire, and 'Josephinism' to indicate the trends that resulted from the reforms Joseph II instituted during his reign, when administrative and economic emancipation was extended and the sociopolitical emancipation of the peoples within the Habsburg Empire took place.

2 This chapter was supported by a grant of the Romanian National Authority for Scientific Research, CNCS – UEFISCDI, project code PN-II-ID-PCE-2011-3-1042, number 457.10.2011.

3 *Reveries*, quoted in Derek Beales, *Enlightenment and Reform in Eighteenth Century Europe* (New York, 2011), pp. 169–70.

4 Cf. Cziprián Kovács Loránd, *Începuturile masoneriei la Timişoara (The Beginnings of Freemasonry in Timişoara)*, according to the website of the Alutus lodge of St George, accessed on 12 March 2012. The author duplicates in Romanian translation an important document regarding the existence of the Three White Lilies lodge of Timişoara, but does not mention the source. The credibility of the document results from the names of the initiates, their year of admittance, profession and sometimes affiliated institution.

5 Loránd, *Începuturile masoneriei la Timişoara*.

6 Vol. i (Milan, 1780).

7 Ignaz von Born was a renowned scientist, a member of the Royal Society of London, the Royal Academy of Turin, and the academies of Petersburg, Toulouse and Danzig. He was president of the Monetary and Mining Office of Prague, conservator of the Imperial Natural Science Cabinet of Vienna, councillor of the Aulic Chamber for mining.

8 Vols i–ii (Vienna, 1780).

9 According to *Giornale d'Italia* (1775), p. 194; cited in Tamara Farcaş, 'Banatul dintr-o perspectivă veneţiană: *Călătoriile, corespondenţa şi descrierile lui Francesco Griselini*' ('The Banat from a Venetian Perspective: Francesco Griselini's Journeys, Letters and Descriptions'), doctoral thesis, West University of Timişoara, 2011, p. 81. The Italian sources regarding Griselini's biography and work are essential and are emphasised in Farcaş's thesis.

10 A full Romanian translation from the German was made by Costin Feneşan and first published in Timişoara in 1984 and in a second edition in 2006. It is true that the German edition was useful for many Romanian readers and offered information for many researchers. Even the preceding fragmentary translations were useful for the development of a historiographic movement relating to the Banat. None corresponds, though, to the original Italian edition, and I think that a translation of that is overdue. Feneşan's Romanian text was formulated under the influence of the protochronist orientation that has dominated Romanian historiography from the 1970s to the time of writing (2014). A new edition would be better placed to contextualise the drafting of the book, and present the intellectual thinking of the time along with an analysis of Griselini's information. Moreover, it could investigate and appreciate the value of the work for its knowledge of the Banat, its history of the local community and the multicultural demography that has always been a feature of this space, its comments on the

economy, etc. This first history of the Banat has a first-hand connection not only to the locals' way of life but also to the imperial reformist policies. The significance of such a work must be understood according to the ideological movement of the time, and in relation to the expeditions of explorers who enriched the European culture with their research, extending and diversifying the image of Europe. See Victor Neumann, *Tentaţia lui Homo Europaeus: Geneza ideilor moderne în Europa Centrală şi de Sud-Est (Temptation of Homo Europaeus: The Genesis of Modern Ideas in Central and South-Eastern Europe)* (rev. 3rd edn, Iaşi, 2006).

11 Kenneth McKenzie, 'Francesco Griselini and His Relation to Goldoni and Molière', *Modern Philology*, vol. 14 (1 July 1916), pp. 17–27. For Goldoni's relations to Freemasonry, see Pietro del Negro, *Carlo Goldoni and Venetian Freemasonry*, www.thefreelibrary.com/Carlo+Goldoni+and+Venetian+Freemasonry.

12 McKenzie, 'Griselini'.

13 Griselini, *I liberi muratori: Commedia* (Schio, 2000), p. 47.

14 See Giuseppe Giarrizzo, *Masoneria e illuminismo nell'Europa del Settecento* (Venice, 1994).

15 *Dizionario biografico degli italiani*, Instituto della Enciclopedia italiana, vol. 59 (Rome, 2002), p. 691.

16 In another article, I set out to analyse Griselini's contribution to knowledge of the Banat, a contribution that needs to be investigated and evaluated according to Enlightenment culture and thought, in relation to the imperial policy of integrating the region with the large multicultural heterogeneity of Central Europe, but also in the sense of the new historical science that was taking shape in Europe due to Giambattista Vico's œuvre.

17 Griselini, *Lettere odeporiche*, p. iii; see Farcaş, 'Banatul dintr-o perspectivă veneţiană', pp. 81–134.

18 Griselini, *Lettere odeporiche*; see Farcaş, 'Banatul dintr-o perspectivă veneţiană', pp. 86–87.

19 Griselini, *Lettere odeporiche*, p. iv: 'volendo ch'egli rimango similmente informato delle vicende cui soggiacque rapporto al civile per ciò soggiungo l'epitome al somma ristreta di un'opera da me intrapresa e compiutta, ciò appunto della civile storia che ne lo riguarda'. Cited in Farcaş, 'Banatul dintr-o perspectivă veneţiană', p. 85.

20 Ibid. See Farcaş, 'Banatul dintr-o perspectivă veneţiană', p. 86.

21 For an analysis of Griselini's comparative linguistic research, see Eugen Coşeriu, *Limba română în faţa Occidentului. Contribuţii la istoria cunoaşterii limbii române în Europa occidentală (The Romanian Language Facing the Occident: Contributions to the History of Understanding the Romanian Language in Western Europe)* (Cluj-Napoca, 1994), esp. the chapter 'Griselini, româna şi latina vulgară' ('Griselini, Romanian and Vulgar Latin'), pp. 72–87.

22 Béla Bulla and Tibor Mendöl, *A Kárpát-medence földrajza (The Geography of the Carpatian Basin)* (Budapest, 1995), p. 170, cited by Lászlo Marjanucz, Chapter 5 in this volume.

23 Ibid.

24 Jenő Szentkláray, 'Temes vármegye története' ('The History of Timiş County'), in Samu Borovszky (ed.), *Magyarország vármegyéi és városai* (Budapest, 1897), p. 369.

25 Cf. Marjanucz, Chapter 5 in this volume.

26 Victor Neumann, 'Preliminarii la o sinteză a istoriei Banatului' ('Preliminaries to a Synthesis of the History of Banat'), in *Identitate şi Cultură: Studii privind istoria Banatului (Identity and Culture: Studies Regarding the History of Banat)*, vol. i (Bucharest, 2009), pp. 9–17. Id., 'Multiculturality and Interculturality: The Case of Timişoara', in id., *Essays on Romanian Intellectual History* (Timişoara, 2013), pp. 147–67. Id., *Istoria evreilor din Banat: O mărturie a multi- şi interculturalităţii Europei Central-Orientale (The History of the Jews from Banat: A Witness of the Central-East European Multi- and Interculturality)* (Bucharest, 1999).

27 Mihály Niámessny, *Szeged és a Délvidék (Szeged and the Southern Land)* (Szeged, 1937), p. 14; see Marjanucz, Chapter 5 in this volume.

28 *Istoria Românilor (The History of Romanians)*, vol. vi. *Românii între Europa clasică şi Europa luminilor (1711–1821) (Romanians between Classic and Enlightened Europe 1711–1821)*, edited by Paul Cernovodeanu and Nicolae Edroiu (Bucharest, 2002), p. 981.

29 Marjanucz, Chapter 5 in this volume. By contrast to nineteenth-century historians and in comparison with *Marjanucz* who is a Hungarian contemporary historian, I believe that the Banat should be looked at from a more nuanced perspective, and that its regional identity should not be associated with that of either Hungary or Transylvania. The arguments derive from the fact that the region had been ruled by the Ottoman Empire for 165 years and was later reconstructed and directly led by Habsburgs in the period in which the basis for a proper administrations, a *Landesadministration*, was laid, when the systematisation of settlements was conceived, the religious congregations were reorganised, colonisations were made and the economic modernisation started. Even if, starting in 1779, the region was managed by the Hungarian Diet of Pressburg, it had a distinct status, with social structures and hierarchies already known to the Habsburgs, with a heterogeneous culture in which the dominant languages remained Romanian and Serbian, joined by German in the eighteenth century. Finally, through its representatives, the Banat expressed a permanent aspiration to autonomy.

30 *Wienerisches Diarium*, 24 June 1778, cited in Jenő Szentkláray, *Száz év Dél-Magyarország újabb történetéből* (*A Hundred Years of the Newer History of South Hungary*), vol. i (Timişoara, 1880), 314.

31 i.e. the Baroque Palace, situated in the Dome Square (today named Union Square). From 2006, it has housed the collection of the Timișoara Museum of Art.

32 Victor Neumann, 'Reformele modernizatoare ale Iosif al II-lea şi începuturile francmasoneriei în Banatul Timişoarei' ('Joseph II's Modernising Reforms and the Beginnings of Freemasonry in the Banat of Timișoara') in *Identitate şi Cultură: Studii privind istoria Banatului* (*Identity and Culture: Studies Regarding the History of Banat*), vol. ii (Timișoara, forthcoming).

33 Cf. Marjanucz, Chapter 5 in this volume.

34 *Ephemerides sive Diarium* is a journal of the Lugoj Minorite order, partially translated and reproduced by the historian Ioan Boroș. The manuscript was later printed under the title *Repertoriul istoric despre oraşul Lugoj şi districtul sau judeţul/comitatul Caraş (vechi), începând cu 1332–1800* (*The Historical Repertoire of the City of Lugoj and the Caraș District/County, 1332–1800*). It is a work that remained in the form of manuscript, later benefiting from a partial edit by historian Valeriu Leu. See Leu, *Memorie, Memorabil, Istorie în Banat* (*Memory, the Memorable, and History in the Banat*) (Timişoara, 2006), pp. 137–50. The author reconstructs the path of the former Episcopalian secretary Ioan Boroș historical studies.

35 *Ephemerides sive Diarium*, cited in Leu, *Memorie*, p. 138.

36 Leu, *Memorie.*, p. 148.

37 Ibid., p. 142.

38 Ibid., p. 143.

39 Ibid.

40 Ibid., p. 131.

41 *Ephemerides sive Diarium*, cited in Leu, *Memorie*, p. 149.

42 Leu, *Memorie*, pp. 131–32.

Chapter 5

1 See C. Feneșan, *Administraţie şi fiscalitate în Banatul Imperial 1716–1776* (*Administration and Fiscality in the Imperial Banat 1716–1776*) (Timişoara, 1997).

2 Jenő Szentkláray, 'Temes vármegye története' ('The History of Timiș County'), in *Magyarország vármegyéi és városai* (*Counties and Towns of Hungary*): *Temes vármegye* (*Timiș County*) (Budapest, n.d.), p. 369.

3 Béla Bulla and Tibor Mendöl, *A Kárpát-medence földrajza* (*The Geography of the Carpathian Basin*) (Budapest, 1995), p. 170.

4 Pál Balogh, *A népfajok Magyarországon* (*The Population in Hungary*), ed. Royal Ministry of Cults and Education (Budapest, 1902), p. 803.

5 Victor Neumann, 'Preliminarii la o sinteză a istoriei Banatului', in id. (ed.), *Identitate şi Cultură: Studii privind istoria Banatului* ('Preliminaries to a Synthesis of the History of Banat', in *Identity and Culture: Studies on the History of the Banat*) (Bucharest, 2009), pp. 9–17. Id., 'Multi-Culturality and Interculturality: The Case of Timişoara', in id., *Essays on Romanian Intellectual History* (Timişoara, 2013), pp. 147–67. Id., *Istoria evreilor din Banat: O mărturie a multi- şi interculturalităţii Europei Central-Orientale* (*The History of the Jews from the Banat: A Testimony*

on the Multi- and Interculturality of Central-Eastern Europe) (Bucharest, 1999).

6 Mihály Niamessny, *Szeged és a Délvidék* (*Szeged and the South*) (Szeged, 1937), p. 14.

7 László Kósa, *A magyar nép történeti táji tagolódása* (*The Historical Lands of the Hungarian People*) (Budapest, 1985), p. 63.

8 For example, the German communities from the Danube regions of Europe distinguished themselves by a double migration: to America and to the Banat of Temes.

9 Annamária Jankó, 'A második katonai fölmérés' ('The Second Military Census'), *Hadtörténeti Közlemények* (*Military History Publications*), vol. 114 (Budapest, 2001), pp. 103–9.

10 Márta Fata, 'Einwanderung und Ansiedlung der Deutschen 1686–1790', in Günther Schödl (ed.), *Land an der Donau* (Berlin, 1995), p. 171.

11 Ilja Mieck (ed.), *Handbuch der europaischen Wirtscafts- und Sozialgeschichte*, vol. iv (Klett-Cotta, 1993), p. 933.

12 József Oberding, *A bánsági magyarság* (*The Hungarians of the Banat*) (Budapest, 1937), p. 40. Some of the mentioned localities can be verified in documents in the fourteenth and fifteenth centuries, such as Gătaia or Urmeniş/Armeniş (1428).

13 Veronika Novák, 'Kivándorlás Mátyusföldről Krassó megyébe' ('Emigration from Mátyusföld to Caraş County'), *Fórum*, vol. 1 (2010).

14 Sándor Bálint, 'A "szögedi nemzet" I. kötet' ('The Nation of Szöged, Part I'), in Ottó Trogmayer (ed.), *Móra Ferenc Múzeum Évkönyve* (*Yearbook of the Ferenc Móra Museum*) (Szeged, 1979), p. 135.

15 Mieck (ed.), *Handbuch der europaischen Wirtscafts- und Sozialgeschichte*, vol. iv, p. 892.

16 *Editor's Note*: The total number of colonists in Hungary in the eighteenth century was approximately 1 million, according to Mieck (ed.), *Handbuch der europaischen Wirtscafts- und Sozialgeschichte*, vol. iv, p. 893. The earliest documented mention of Jamu Mare dates from 1343; the eighteenth-century colonisation changed the demographic structure, renamed and reinvented the locality. Orţişoara dates from the beginning of the fourteenth century, going through a similar radical change in the eighteenth century. We are talking about administrative reforms, many of which aimed at the repopulation of villages or, in some cases, their modernisation with the help of the colonists brought in by imperial command. Such changes were possible in the Banat, a region where a local nobility did not then exist (this social segment had disappeared during the Ottoman occupation), and the village (and urban) administration did not oppose the imperial reforms, but assimilated them with no conditions.

17 See Ferenc Maksay, *A Magyar Kamara Archívuma* (*The Archives of the Hungarian Chamber*), ed. János Buzási (Budapest, 1992), p. 236.

18 Szentkláray, 'Temes vármegye története', p. 377.

19 Actually, the nobility of the Banat had disappeared in the sixteenth century, when the region was occupied by the Ottoman Empire. During the eighteenth century a proper nobility did not exist in Banat, the noblemen earning titles by purchasing them, starting in 1780.

20 *Wienerisches Diarium*, 24 July 1778, cited in Szentkláray, *Száz év Dél-Magyarország újabb történetéből*, p. 314.

21 Frigyes Pesty, *A Szörényi Bánság története* (*The History of the Banat of Severin*), vol. i (Budapest, 1877), p. 184.

22 S. Stojakovics, *Über die staatrechtlichen Verhältnisse der Serben*, cited in Szentkláray, *Száz év Dél-Magyarország újabb történetéből*, p. 332.

23 Ibid., p. 342.

24 Dr Gusztáv Wenczel, *Az 1848. előtti magyar magánjog* (*Private Hungarian Law before 1848*) (Budapest, 1885), pp. 255, 305.

25 During the Middle Ages, the Banat was part of the Kingdom of Hungary, while in the eighteenth century it became a component of the Habsburg Empire. During the sixteenth and seventeenth centuries the region belonged to the Ottoman Empire. Therefore, there is a historical discontinuity among these three periods in relation to policy, administration and legislation.

26 Henrik Marczali, *Magyarország története II. József korában* (*The History of Hungary in the*

Time of Joseph II) (Budapest, 1885), pp. 99, 107.

27 Szentkláray, 'Temes vármegye története', p. 367. Price for Altringen Estate was not mentioned in the document.

28 Maksay, *A Magyar Kamara Archívuma*, p. 170.

29 Szentkláray, *Száz év Dél-Magyarország újabb történetéből*, p. 331.

30 János Varga, *A jobbágyi földbirtoklás típusai 1767–1848* (*Types of Peasant Tenements 1767–1848*) (Budapest, 1967), p. 58.

31 The Hungarian State Council archives, 1992, p. 249.

32 Ernő Deák, *Ausgewählte Materialien zum Stadtwesen der Länder der ungarischen Krone (1780–1918)* (Vienna, 1979–89), vol. ii. *Theil Königliche Freistadte-Munizipialstadte*, p. 380.

33 Mihály Horváth, *Magyarország történelme* (*The History of Hungary*), vol. viii (Budapest, 1873), p. 237.

34 István Nagy and F. Kiss Erzsébet, *A Magyar Kamara és egyéb kincstári szervek* (*The Hungarian Chamber and other Treasury Institutions*) (Budapest, 1995), Protocolla Banatica 1790–1848, p. 281.

35 Bulla and Mendöl, *A Kárpát-medence földrajza*, p. 168.

36 Nagy and Erzsébet, *A Magyar Kamara*, p. 283.

37 Ibid., p. 249.

38 Ernő Deák, *Ausgewählte Materialien*, vol. ii, p. 296. Antal Szántay, *Regionalpolitik im alten Europa: Die Verwaltungsreformen Josephs II in Ungarn, in Lombardei und in den österreichischen Niederlanden 1785–1790* (*The Regional Policy in the Old Europe: Joseph II's Administrative Reforms in Hungary, Lombardy and the Austrian Low Countries*) (Budapest, 2005), p. 255.

39 'Justiz Verwaltungsbezirke um 1780 in dem Temescher Banat', in Szántay, *Regional-politik im alten Europa*, p. 97.

40 'Számok és történelem' ('Numbers and History'), in Benda Gyula, *Statisztikai adatok a magyar mezőgazdaság történetéhez 1767–1867* (*Statistical Data in the History of Hungarian Agriculture 1767–1867*), (Budapest, 1983), p. 57.

41 István Rácz, *A török világ hagyatéka Magyarországon* (*The Legacy of the Turkish World in Hungary*), (Debrecen, 1995), pp. 133–35.

42 István Petrovics, 'Módszertani problémák a középkori várostörténetünk kutatása kapcsán' ('Methodological Problems in the Research of Medieval History of Cities'), in József Vonyó (ed.), *Várostörténet-helytörténet* (*City History, Local History*) (Pécs, 2003), p. 151. The author highlights the continuity between the two eras. However, we can see that the changes introduced in the eighteenth century resulted in more discontinuities than continuities, a reason for which I invoked the visible innovations within the social, administrative and religious configurations of the Banat.

43 Sándor Bálint, 'A "szögedi nemzet" I. kötet'.

44 Deák, *Ausgewählte Materialien*, vol. ii, p. 314.

45 See Victor Neumann, 'Scurtă istorie a populaţiilor din Banat şi Trăsăturile melting pot-ului bănăţean' ('A Short History of the Populations from the Banat and Features of the Banatian Melting Pot'), in id., *Interculturalitatea Banatului* (*The Interculturality of the Banat*) (Timişoara and Iaşi, 2012), pp. 15–29, 33–42. Cf. id, 'Cultura din Banat la începutul evului modern: Primul ziar local – Temeswarer Nachrichten' ('The Culture in the Banat at the Beginning of the Modern Age: The First Local Newspaper – *Temeswarer Nachrichten*'), in id. (ed.), *Identitate şi cultură*, pp. 25–37.

46 Mieck (ed.), *Handbuch der europaischen Wirtscafts- und Sozialgeschichte*, vol. iv, p. 890.

47 Dezső Dányi (ed.), *Történeti Statisztikai Tanulmányok 2* (*Historical and Statistical Studies 2*), edition issued on the occasion of the first Hungarian census (Budapest, 1975), p. 5.

48 In the statistics of the time there is no mention of religion and nationality, because they had no relevance either from the imperial perspective or from the identity culture of the eighteenth century. The dominant features of the time were social status (nobility) or confessional status (religion). See Victor Neumann, *Conceptul de naţiune la români şi unguri: Un studiu despre identităţile politice* (*The Concept of Nation for Romanians and Hungarians: A Study on Political Identities*) (Iași, 2013).

49 Jenő Darkó, 'A karlócai érsekség egyházszervezete és görögkeleti népessége a XVIII. Században az összeírások tükrében' ('The

Organisation of the Archbishopric of Karlowitz and the Orthodox Population in the Eighteenth Century as Seen in the Censuses'), in István Zombori (ed.), *A szerbek Magyarországon* (*The Serbians of Hungary*) (Szeged, 1991), p. 116.

50 Friedrich Gottas, 'Die Deutschen in den Ländern der ungarischen Krone (1790–1867)', in Schödl (ed.), *Land an der Donau*, 266.

51 Niamessny, *Szeged és a Délvidék*, p. 6.

52 Deák, *Ausgewählte Materialien*, vol. ii, pp. 306–9.

53 Josef Vollmar Senz, *Geschichte der Donauschwaben* (*The History of the Danubian Swabians*) (Munich, 1987), p. 75.

54 Neumann, *Conceptul de națiune la români și unguri*, pp. 16–24, 54–58.

56 According to Victor Neumann, 'Trăsăturile melting pot-ului bănățean şi Timișoara interbelică: între etnicitatea fictivă" și societatea deschisă' ('The Features of the Banatian Melting Pot and Interwar Timișoara: Between "Fictional Ethnicity" and Open Society'), in id., *Interculturalitatea Banatului* (3rd edn., Iași, 2015), pp. 33–42, 45–67.

Chapter 6

1 Szabó Pál Csaba, *A magyar állam története 1711–2006* (*The History of the Hungarian State*) (Szeged, 2010).

2 The original information used for this research comes from Haus-, Hof-und Staatsarchiv, Staatsrat Protokolle, Vienna, henceforth HHStA Str Prot.

3 Eckhart Ferenc, *A Bécsi Udvari Kamrai Levéltár* (*The Viennese Court Chamber Archive*) (Budapest, n.d.), p. 60.

4 Gáll Beatrix Takaróné and Károly Tamás (eds), *A közgazdasági elméletek története* (*The History of Economic Theory*) (Budapest, Biblioteca TÉBE, nr. 94), p. 23, date unmentioned.

5 HHStA Str. Prot. 2201/1771, Vortrag der Hofkammer in Banaticis, 20 June.

6 HHStA, Str. Prot. 1300/1770, Vortrag der Hofkammer in Banaticis, 6 April.

7 Lippauer Haupt-Salz-Amt.

8 HHStA Str. Prot. 2561/1771, Vortrag der Hofkammer, 20 July, A Temesvári Tartományi Adminisztráció július 9-én kelt fölvetése alapján, Über die Verbesserung des bannatischen Salzwesens.

9 HHStA Str. Prot. 2561/1771, Vortrag der Hofkammer.

10 HHStA. Str. Prot. 2201/1771, Nota der Hofkammer, 20 June.

11 HHStA Str. Prot. 2019/1771, Vortrag der Banco-Deputation in Banaticis, 1 June.

12 HHStA Str. Prot. 86/1771, Vortrag der Hofkammer.

13 HHStA Str. Prot. 78/1770, Vortrag der Hofkammer in Banaticis und Domainenwesen.

14 HHStA Str. Prot. 19/1770, Protocollum Extract des Commerzien Rathes, fo. 543.

15 HHStA Str. Prot. 19/1770, Vortrag der Ministro-Banko-Deputation über eine Banathische Unter-Verwaltersstelle.

16 HHSta Str. Prot. 1771/2593, Vortrag der Hofkammer, Az Uradalmi Bizottmány július 10-én kelt beadványa alapján, Über Rüb-und Kohlsamen- Anbau.

17 HHStA Str. Prot. 321/1770, Vortrag der Hofkammer, 24 January.

18 Begeleitungs-Vortrag.

19 HHStA Str. Prot. 321/1770, Begleitungs Vortrag des Grafen Hatzfeld zu Protocoll der Hofkammer in Banaticis und Domänenwesen, 28 February.

20 HHStA Str. Prot. 1771/3113, Schreiben an Hofrath Raab, 6 September.

21 HHStA Str. Prot. 172/1771, Vortrag der Hofkammer.

22 HHStA Str. Prot. 1256/1771, Vortrag der Hofkammer.

23 HHStA Str. Prot. 3077/1771, Vortrag der Hofkanzley, 3 September, zu Protocolle der Sanitaet Deputation, 31. August über die Vieh-Seuche.

24 HHStA Str. Prot. 1857/1771, Protocoll der Hofkammer in Banaticis, 20 May.

25 HHStA Str. Prot. 1456/1771, Vortrag der Hofkammer, 19 April.

26 HHStA Str. Prot. 771/1973, Vortrag des Grafen Hatzfeld, 24 August zu Protocolla der Hofklammer in Banaticis, 14 August, Weltpriestern für den Bannat.

27 HHStA Str. Prot. 3594/1771, Vortrag der Hofkammer, 23 October zu Protocolla der Illyrischen Hofdeputaion, 17 October.

28 HHStA Str. Prot. 3605/1771, Vortrag der Hofkammer, 23 October, zu Protocoll der Hofdeputation in Banaticis, 16 October.

29 HHStA Str. Prot. 78/ 1771, Vortrag der Hofkammer in Banaticis und Domänen-Wesen.

30 MOL F36 7r–9v, 13. Gróf Auersperg notája 1771, 8 November.

31 HHStA Str. Prot. 3425/1770, Schreiben an Grafen Breuner.

32 Kovács Kálmán, 'A bécsi udvar erdélyi valláspolitikája az Államtanács iratai alapján' ('The Religious Policy of the Viennese Court based on the State Council Archives'), PhD dissertation (1999), p. 10.

33 HHStA Str. Prot. 1426/1770, Protocolla der Sanität-Deputation, 24 April.

34 HHStA Str. Prot. 2892/1771, Vortrag des Grafen Auersperg, 7 August.

35 HHStA Str. Prot. 1290/ 1771, Billet an Bruckenthal, 5 April.

36 HHStA Str. Prot. 37/1770, Vortrag der Illyrischen Deputatio 7 January.

37 HHStA Str. Prot. 2667/1770, Vortrag der Sanität-Deputation.

38 HHStA Str. Prot. 3684/1770, Vortrag der Illyrischen Deputation 11 October.

39 HHStA Str. Prot. 213. /1771, Vortrag des Grafen Hatzfeld 11 January.

40 HHStA Str. Prot. 2372/1771, Vortrag der Obersten Justizstelle 2 July.

41 HHStA Str. Prot. 1771/ 2749, Vortrag der Obersten Justizstelle 6 August.

42 HHStA Str. Prot. 1052/1765, Vortrag der Hofkammer 16 April.

43 HHStA Str. Prot. 578/ 1771, Vortrag der Illyrischen Deputation, 12 February, zu Protocolla des Hofkriegsrathes und der Hungarischen Kanzley.

44 Takaróné and Tamás (eds.), *A közgazdsasági elméletek története*, p. 32.

45 HHStA Str. Prot. 157/1771, Vortrag der Hofkammer Deputation in Monetariis et Montaniticis.

46 HHStA Str. Prot. 19/1771, Vortrag der Hofkammer.

47 HHStA Str. Prot. 1569/ 1772, Vortrag der Böhm-Österreichischen Kanzley.

48 HHStA Str. Prot. 4107/ 1771, Vortrag der Hofkammer in Banaticis, 27 November.

49 HHStA Str. Prot. 1771/ 2906, Vortrag der Hofkammer in Banaticis, 10 August.

50 HHStA Str. Prot. 1771/ 2766, Vortrag der Hofkammer in Banaticis, 31 July.

51 HHStA Str. Prot. 172/1771, Vortrag der Hofkammer in Banaticis, 5 January.

52 HHStA Str. Prot. 2442/ 1771, Vortrag der Hofkammer in Banaticis, 3 July.

53 HHStA Str. Prot. 1850/1771, Vortrag der Hofkammer in Banaticis, 11 May.

54 HHStA Str. Prot. 4213/1771, Vortrag der Hofkammer in Banaticis, 7 December.

55 HHStA Str. Prot. 2999/1771, Vortrag der Obersten Justizstelle, 27 August, über die Radlführer in das Banat.

56 HHStA Str. Prot. 3471/1771, Nota des Grafen Seilern, 9 October.

57 HHStA Str. Prot. 887/1771, Vortrag der Hofkammer in Banaticis, 27 February.

58 HHStA Str. Prot. 1449/1771, Vortrag des Grafen Hatzfeld, 15 April.

59 HHStA Str. Prot. 1194/1771, Vortrag der Hofkammer in Banaticis, 20 March.

60 HHStA Str. Prot. 811/1771, 932/ 1771, Vorträge des Siebenbürger- Coons, 6 March.

61 HHStA Str. Prot. 2805/1771, Vortrag der Hofkammer in Banaticis, 3 August.

62 HHStA Str. Prot. 862/1772, Vortrag der Böhm- Österreichischen Kanzley, 7 April.

63 HHStA Str. Prot. 536/ 1771, Billet an Bruckenthal.

64 HHStA Str. Prot. 1811/1771, Vortrag der Hofkammer in Banaticis 7 May.

65 HHStA Str. Prot. 2820/ 1771, Das Einrathen Stupans zu Protocolla der Hofkammer in Banaticis, 12 August.

66 HHStA Str. Prot. 3782/1771, Protocolla der Hofkammer, 9 November.

67 For further details see chapter 3 of this book entitled: 'The Enlightenment and the Policies of the Habsburg Empire', pp.41-59.

68 See Victor Neumann, *Interculturalitatea Banatului (The Interculturality of Banat)* (3rd edn, Iași, 2015).

69 Idem, 'Zwischen Osmanen und Oesterreichern.Temeswarer Banat - ein europäisches Experiment des 18. Jahrhunderts' in A. Fickers. R. Haude, S. Krebs, W. Tschacher (Hg.), Jeux sans frontières. Grenzgänge der Geschichtswissenschaft, Transcript Verlag, Bielefeld, 2017, pp. 87-97.

Chapter 7

1 Mihai Opriș, *Timişoara mică monografie urbanistică (Timişoara, Short Urban Monograph)* (Bucharest, 1987), p. 42.

2 Lewis Mumford, *The Culture of Cities* (New York, 1938), p. 88.

3 Carlo Giulio Argan, *Arte barocca* (Rome, 1989), p. 231. Cf. Hanna Derer, *Sibiu: Arhitectura în epoca barocă (Sibiu: Architecture in the Baroque Age)* (Bucharest, 2003), p. 37.

4 Opriș, *Timişoara mică monografie urbanistică*, p. 74.

5 For data on the evolution of the city of Arad, see Emil Anghel, 'Die Anordnung der Markplatze von Arad', *Historia Urbana*, vol. 1 (1993), p. 60; id., 'Distrugeri și reconstrucții la Arad' ('Destruction and Reconstruction in Arad'), *Historia Urbana*, vol. 2 (1996), p. 42. Cf. Horia Medeleanu, 'Aradul în secolul al XVIII-lea pe baza conscripțiilor străzilor din anul 1783' ('Eighteenth-Century Arad According to the Street Signs of 1783'), *Revue of Historical Monuments*, vol. 1 (1982), p. 52.

6 Hans Sedlmayr, *Pierderea măsurii (Losing the Measure)* (Bucharest, 2001), p. 42.

7 Marcela Oprescu, 'Consideraţii asupra monumentelor de for public din mediul rural' ('Considerations upon the Public Monuments in the Rural Area'), *Studii si comunicari (Studies and Presentations)*, vol. 7 (Arad Museum) (2001–2), pp. 288–97.

8 Leonardo Benevolo, *Oraşul în istoria Europei (The City in the History of Europe)* (Iaşi, 2003), p. 162.

9 Antal Palóczi, *A városok rendezése* (Urban Rules) (Budapest, 1903).

10 Nikolaus Pevsner, *An Outline of European Architecture* (London, 1966), p. 371.

11 Gheorghe Bleyer (Manuscript), 'Timişoara, The Banat Museum', cited in Pevsner, *Outline of European Architecture.*

12 Nikolaus Pevsner, *An Outline of European Architecture* (London, 2009 edn.) p. 187.

13 Bleyer (Manuscript), p. 80.

14 Karl E. Schorske, *Viena fin-de-siècle (Fin-de-Siècle Vienna)* (Iași, 1998), p. 30.

15 See the description of the synagogue, its architect, builder, opening and contextualisation in Victor Neumann, *Istoria evreilor din Banat: O mărturie a multi- și interculturalității Europei Central-Orientale (The History of Jews in the Banat: A Testimony of Central-Eastern European Multi- and Inter-culturalism)* (Bucharest, 1999), pp. 102–3.

16 Gheorghe Lanevschi, 'Rolul arhivei în elucidarea Art Nouveau-ului arădean' ('The Role of the Archive in Clarification of Arad's Art Nouveau'), *Studii si comunicari (Studies and Presentations)*, vols. 4–5 (Arad Museum) (1999), p. 247.

17 The owner of a construction business in Timișoara, Arnold Merbl accomplished numerous large-scale works. Cf. Bleyer (Manuscript), p. 17.

18 Ileana Pintilie, 'Evoluţii stilistice în creaţia arhitectului timişorean László Székely' ('Stylistic Evolution in the Creations of Architect László Székely of Timișoara'), *Studii si comunicari (Studies and Presentations)*, vols. 4–5 (Arad Museum) (1999), p. 213.

19 Lipót Baumhorn was born in 1860 at Kisber, Hungary. He studied in Vienna and worked for 12 years in Lechner Ödön's workshop in Budapest. Cf. Ileana Pintilie, 'Interferenţe regionale în arhitectura de stil 1900 reflectată în opera lui Lipót Baumhorn' ('Regional Influences on the Architecture of 1900 as Reflected in Lipót Baumhorn's Work'), *Studii si comunicari (Studies and Presentations)*, vol. 7 (Arad Museum) (2001–2).

20 Peter Puskel, *Emléklapok a régi Aradrol (Postcards from Old Arad)* (Arad, 2005), p. 107.

21 Gheorghe Lanevschi, 'Palatul Kovács Artur, un frumos edificiu secession din Arad' ('The Palace of Arthur Kovács, A Beautiful Secession Building in Arad'), *Analele Banatului (Annals of Banat)*, vol. 3 (1997), p. 61.

22 Ileana Pintilie, 'Viena, Budapesta şi Timişoara: Raportul dintre centru şi

periferie în anii întemeierii, premisă a răspândirii stilului 1900' ('Vienna, Budapest and Timişoara: The Relationship between Centre and Periphery in the Years of Foundation, Premise for Dispersion of the 1900 Style'), *Analele Banatului (Annals of Banat)*, vol. 3 (1997), p. 38.

Chapter 8

1 T.O. Gheorghiu, 'A Historical Perspective on the Process of Merging, Planning and Densification of Rural Settlements in the Banat and Crişana Regions', *Buletinul Ştiinţific al Universităţii Politehnica din Timişoara*, Seria Construcţii şi Arhitectură (*Science Bulletin of Timişoara Politehnica University*, Constructions and Architecture series), vol. 54 no. 68 (2009), pp. 5–11.

2 Francesco Griselini, *Încercare de istorie politică şi naturală a Banatului Timişoarei (An Attempt at a Political and Natural History of the Banat of Timişoara)* (Timişoara, 1984), pp. 123–42.

3 The new villages were founded on the sites of the old ones. Sânpetru mare had existed since 1333; Beşenova/Dudeşti since the fourteenth century; Peciu Nou since 1333; Deta since 1360; Pişchia since 1333. The imperial reforms of the eighteenth century changed the appearance of the villages by colonising them with a Catholic population from all over Europe. Also, their identity was recreated according to the cultural and civilisational values promoted by the Habsburgs, that being the real reason why eighteenth-century documents speak of 'new found' villages.

4 G. Hromadka, *Scurtă cronică a Banatului Montan (Short Chronicle of the Banat Mountains)* (Bonn, n.d.), pp. 21, 33–4.

5 J. Szentkláray, *Száz év Démagyarorzag ujabb történetéből (A Hundred Years of Southern Hungary's Recent History)* (Timişoara, 1878), pp. 249–54, discussed in N. Săcară, *Valori ale arhitecturii populare româneşti (Values of Romanian Folk Architecture)* (Timişoara, 1987), p. 23.

6 For Guttenbrunn, see T.O. Gheorghiu, *Locuire şi neaşezare (Habitation and Unsettlement)* (Bucharest, 2002), pp. 57–58, 211 (with some necessary corrections due to deepening study); for Sanpetrul, cf. T.O. Gheorghiu, 'Structura aşezărilor din zona Banat-Arad şi arhitectura vernaculară' ('The Structure of Settlements from the Banat-Arad Region and Vernacular Architecture)', *Transsylvania Nostra*, vol. 2 (2009), pp. 13–20.

7 M. Bel, *Compendium Hungariae geograficum* (posthumous edn., Cassoviae, 1799).

8 E. Schimscha, *Tehnik und Methoden der Theresianischen Besiedlung des Banat* (Baden, 1939), p. 93, discussed in Săcară, *Valori*, pp. 47–49.

9 Lammert and Gehl, 'Tipologia', pp. 154–55.

10 F. Milleker, *Geschichte der Gemeinde Cetad, Csatad, Lenauheim im Banat 1415–1925* (Wrschatz, 1925).

11 The villages of Săcălaz, Jimbolia and Iecea Mare were mentioned for the first time in the fourteenth century, so we can speak of their re-establishment and reorganisation by the imperial administration. I would like to thank Fr. Prof. Vasile V. Muntean for mentioning the founding dates of some of the villages from the Banat.

12 Griselini, *Încercare*, pp. 149–51.

13 Erich Lammert and Hans Gehl, 'Tipologia şi evoluţia casei şvăbeşti din Banat' ('Typology and Evolution of the Swabian House from the Banat'), *Tibiscus* – Ethnography, vol. 3 (1976–78), p. 156.

14 Ibid.; see Stela Clepea, 'Consideraţii asupra gospodăriei şi locuinţei şvabilor din Banat' ('Considerations upon the Swabian Households'), in *Banat Annals*, vol. ii. *Ethnography-Art* (Timişoara, 1984), p. 195.

15 Stela Clepea, 'Consideraţii', p. 197.

16 Cf. Săcară, *Valori*, p. 23, information taken from A. Bodor, *Délmagyarorszag telepitések története (The Historical Colonisation of Southern Hungary)* (Budapest, 1914), pp. 15–17.

17 Griselini, *Încercare*, pp. 150–51, 154–55, 327–28.

18 For data referring to the nineteenth-century Czech colonisation, see P. Rozkos, 'Contribuţie la istoria colonizării *pemilor în Banat*' ('Contribution to the History of Pems Colonisation in the Banat'), in *Banat Annals*, vol. iv. *History* (Timişoara, 1996), pp. 48–49.

19 Hromadka, *Scurtă cronică*, p. 49.

20 N.V. Cica Săcară, 'Gospodăria maghiară din Babşa de la Muzeul Banatului' ('The Hungarian Household from Babşa at the

Banat Museum',*Tibiscus – Ethnography*, vol. 3 (1976–78), pp. 167 ff.

21 A.K. Géza Roz, *Dicţionarul istoric al localităţilor din judeţul Arad (The Historical Dictionary of Arad County's Localities)* (Arad, 1997), p. 11.

22 *Atlasul culturii populare a slovacilor din România (Atlas of the Popular Culture of the Romanian Slovaks)* (Nădlac, 1998), pp. 104–17.

23 Săcară, *Valori*, p. 165.

24 T.O. Gheorghiu, 'Bánsági telepitett falvak-tipológiai megközelités' ('Colonist Villages from Banat – Typological Aspects'), in Balassa M. Iván and Cseri Miclos (eds.), *Népi epitészet erdélyben* (Szentendre, 1999), pp. 45–46.

25 *A Masodik katonai felmérés: A Magyar kiralysag és a Temesi bansag Negyfelbontasu, szines térképei- 1819–1869 (The Second Military Topographical Survey: The Colour Sections of the Maps of Hungarian Kingdom and Timiş)*, DVD, Budapest, Arcanum, 2005.

26 Timişoara State Archives, fund 104–1884.

27 A. Oişteanu, 'Antropologia locuirii tradiţionale' ('The Anthropology of Traditional Habitation'), paper, Bucharest, 1988; id., *Mythos & Logos* (Bucharest, 1997), pp. 157–58. The important results regarding the genesis and organic development of old Romanian settlements (which objectively explain centres and dispersions and also different manners of arrangement) were advertised by the Romanian rural sociological school (Dimitrie Gusti, Traian Herseni, Henri Stahl etc.), starting from the interwar period.

28 Fl. Biciuşcă, *Centrul lumii locuite (The Centre of the Habitable World)* (Bucharest, 2000), pp. 81–2.

29 For the urban models at the beginning of the Middle Ages, see T.O. Gheorghiu, *Aşezări umane: Istoria aşezărilor umane de la origini până la Renaştere (Human Settlements: The History of Human Settlements from their Origins to the Renaissance)* (Timişoara, 1997), pp. 161–74.

30 Griselini, *Încercare*, p. 154.

Chapter 9

1 This chapter was supported by a grant from the Romanian National Authority for Scientific Research, CNCS–UEFISCDI, project number PN-II-ID-PCE-2011-3-1042.

2 Jean-Baptiste Dubos, *Cugetări critice despre poezie şi pictură (Critical Thoughts upon Poetry and Painting)* (Bucharest, 1983), pp. 306–07.

3 Jan Bialostocki, *O istorie a teoriior despre artă (A History of Art Theories)* (Bucharest, 1977).

4 Ibid., p. 350.

5 John Rupert Martin, 'The Baroque from the Point of View of the Art Historian', *Journal of Aesthetics and Art Criticism*, vol. 14, no. 2 (1955), pp. 164–70.

6 Jean-Philippe Minguet, *Estetica rococoului (The Aesthetics of the Rococo)* (Bucharest, 1973), p. 52.

7 Alois Riegl, *Istoria artei ca istorie a stilurilor (Art History as Style History)* (Bucharest, 1998), p. 23.

8 Henri Focillon, *Viaţa formelor (The Life of Forms)* (Bucharest, 1995), p. 25.

9 Bialostocki, *O istorie a teoriior despre artă*, p. 327.

10 Considered decadent by the opulence of its expressions; for details, see Jacob Burckhardt, *Cicerone* (Stuttgart, 1855), p. 161.

11 Ibid., p. 348.

12 A term introduced by Hans Rose in 1921 to designate the art between 1660 and 1760, having a strong classicist base, specific to France and developed in regions of French influence.

13 Alois Riegl, *Die Entstehung der Barockkunst in Rom* (2nd edn., Vienna, 1923), p. 3.

14 Răzvan Theodorescu, 'Cuvânt înainte' ('Foreword') in Victor Neumann, *Convergenţe spiritual (Spiritual Convergences)* (Bucharest, 1986), p. 8.

15 Victor Neumann, ' "Coridoare culturale" în Europa Est-Centrală: *Cărţi şi biblioteci în mediile aulice din Transilvania, Banat, Ungaria şi Serbia*' (' "Cultural Corridors" in East-Central Europe: Books and Libraries in Aulic Environments of Transylvania, the Banat, Hungary and Serbia'), in id., *Tentaţia lui Homo Europaeus: Geneza ideilor moderne în Europa Centrală şi de Sud-Est (The Temptation of Homo Europaeus: The Birth of Modern Ideas in Central and South-Eastern Europe)* (3rd edn., Iaşi, 2006), pp. 161–229. This includes much information on the relations between the intellectuals of the aforemen-

tioned region and those of Dutch, German and Austrian cultural centres; it also shows how and why the reception of books by well-known authors published in Paris, Amsterdam, London, Leipzig, Halle, Bern and Vienna was possible; presents and comments on the life and work of some personalities, as well as the ideas that had circulated along the Continent in the seventeenth and most of the eighteenth centuries, making a brilliant career among many social groups.

16 Victor Neumann, *Interculturalitatea Banatului (Banatian Interculturality)* (2nd edn., Iaşi, 2013), pp. 15–29, 33–42. Id., 'Preliminarii la o sinteză a istoriei Banatului' ('Preliminaries towards a Synthesis of Banatian History'), in id. (ed.), *Identitate şi cultură: Studii privind istoria Banatului (Identity and Culture: Studies upon the History of the Banat)* (Bucharest, 2009), pp. 9–18.

17 Dorina Sabina Pârvulescu, *Pictura bisericilor ortodoxe din Banat (The Painting of Orthodox Churches in the Banat)* (Timişoara, 1997), p. 5.

18 Nicolae Ilieşiu, *Timişoara: Monografie istorică (Timişoara: Historical Monograph)*, vol. i (Timişoara, 1943), p. 86.

19 Ibid. The cornerstone of the city was placed on 25 April 1723 bearing the inscription: '*Imperator Carolo VI. Duce Eugenio Sabaudiae. Principe per cladem Petro – Varadini MDCCXVI a Turcis recuperata Provincia, sub praesidio Claudii Comitis a Mercy anno a partu Virginis MDCCXXIII die XXV mensis Aprilis Temesvarini moenia fondabatur.*'

20 This was the version chosen by the province's governor, Count Claude Florimond de Mercy, who submitted to the War Council a construction regulation book for the city of Timişoara in 1728, which developed during the remainder of the eighteenth century. For details, see Mihai Opriş, *Timişoara: Mică monografie urbanistică (Timişoara: Small Urban Monograph)* (Bucharest, 1987), p. 48.

21 Ibid., p. 53; for details about the city gates, see Johann Nepomuk Preyer, *Monografia oraşului liber crăiesc Timişoara (Monograph on the Royal Free Town of Timişoara)* (Timişoara, 1995), p. 188.

22 Nicolae Sabău, *Metamorfoze ale barocului transilvan: Sculptura (Metamorphoses of the Transylvanian Baroque: Sculpture)*, vol. i (Cluj-Napoca, 2002), p. 100.

23 Adriana Buzilă and Rodica Vârtaciu, *Barocul în Banat: Catalog de expoziţie (Baroque in the Banat: Exhibition Catalogue)* (Timişoara, 1995), p. 6; the church served as cathedral for the bishop of Cenad, see Ilieşiu, *Timişoara*, p. 85.

24 Preyer, *Monografia*, p. 194; Buzilă and Vârtaciu, *Barocul în Banat*, pp. 6–7.

25 Preyer, *Monografia*, p. 192.

26 Both buildings had been destroyed by the fire of 6–7 July 1849, and were rebuilt in 1851; Franz Binder, *Alt-Temeswar* (The Old Timişoara/Temeswar), Verlag der Deutschen Buchhandlung, Timişoara/Temeswar, 1934, p.110.

27 Buzilă and Vârtaciu, *Barocul în Banat*, p. 7.

28 Giulio Carlo Argan, *De la Bramante la Canova (From Bramante to Canova)* (Bucharest, 1974), pp. 174–75.

29 For the construction stages and details of the church, see *Die Domkirche in Temeswar* (Munich, 1972), pp. 90 and *passim*; A. Buzilă, 'Catedrala romano-catolică din Timişoara' ('The Roman Catholic Cathedral of Timişoara'), *Tibiscus* (History), vol. 5 (1978), pp. 237–50.

30 The largest study dedicated to the evolution of Banatian baroque architecture is Adriana Buzilă, 'Biserici baroce din Banat' ('Baroque Churches in the Banat'), doctoral dissertation (Cluj-Napoca, 1998).

31 Hans Diplich, *Die Domkirche in Temeswar* (Munich, 1972), p. 52. There are different opinions on the authorship of the construction project, see V.V. Muntean et al., *Monuments*, p. 136 n. 8.

32 Formal and stylistic analogies can be observed in the churches designed by Emanuel Fischer von Erlach in Greuze (1736), where the church of the Pauline order was built, or at Sasvár, where, together with Jean Joseph Charmant, he built Maria Theresa's palace. For details of his artistic evolution, see Pál Voit, *Der Barock in Ungarn* (Budapest, 1971), p. 48.

33 Vezi, *Plana proiectaque aedificii Viennae confecta sunt per aulicum caesare reg. celeberrimus architectum Emanuelem Fischer von Erlach*. There are different opinions regarding the plan. Robert Born, Die Domkirche in Timişoara. Eine Kunstgeschichtliche Intrepretation. *In Beitraege zur Kunstgeschichte*

Ostmitteleuropas, Verlag Herder Institut, Marburg, 2001, pp. 233, 234, 242.

34 Voit, *Der Barock in Ungarn*.

35 A. Buzilă, 'Tehnicieni constructori în Banatul secolului al XVIII-lea' ('Construction Technicians in the Eighteenth-Century Banat'), *Analele Banatului*, vol. 3 (1998), pp. 75-84.

36 Id., 'Arhitectura-oglindă a diferitelor mentalităţi bănăţene din sec. al XVIII-lea' ('Architectural Mirror of Different Banatian Mentalities in the Eighteenth Century'), in *Ars Transsilvaniae* (Bucharest, 1991), pp. 75–84.

37 See Franz Wagner, 'Die Salzburger Residenz als Gegenstand Kunstgeschichtlicher, Forschung', *Barockberichte*, vols. 5–6 (1992), p. 201.

38 Rosario Assunto, *Universul ca spectacol* (*The Universe as Performance*) (Bucharest, 1983), p. 159.

39 Silviu Anuichi, *Relaţiile bisericeşti româno-sârbe în secolul al XVII-lea şi al XVIII-lea* (*Romanian–Serbian Church Relations in the Seventeenth and Eighteenth Centuries*) (Bucharest, 1980).

40 Dorina Sabina Pârvulescu, 'Coordonate ale creaţiei artistice ortodoxe din Banat în pragul epocii modern' ('Coordinates of Orthodox Artistic Creations in the Banat at the Dawn of the Modern Age'), *AB* (Art), vol. 4, (2002), p. 138.

41 For the typology of Serbian churches from Hungary, see Dujmov Milan and Szalai-Nagy Marta, *Magyarországi Ortodox Templomok* (*Orthodox Churches in Hungary*) (Budapest, 2010), pp. 108–9.

42 Martha Nagy, 'National Self-Preservation in Eighteenth-Century Serbian Church Architecture in Hungary', *Centropa: A Journal of Central European Architecture and Related Arts*, vol. 8, no. 2 (May 2008), p. 136.

43 Vernon Hyde Minor, *Baroque and Rococo: Art and Culture* (London, 1999), p. 77.

44 Buzilă, 'Tehnicieni constructori în Banatul', p. 40.

45 Ibid.

46 Document preserved in Timiş State Archives, *Memorandum Protocol Satchinez*, I, fo. 36.

47 I.D. Suciu, Monografia Mitropoliei Banatului (Monography of the Banat Archbishop), Editura Mitropoliei Banatului, Timişoara, 1977, p. 131.

48 For details, see Teodor Octavian Gheorghiu and Radu Radoslav, 'Modele baroce coloniste bănăţene ale secolului XVIII-lea: Comparaţie cu vechile implanturi coloniste din Transilvania' ('Colonist Baroque Banatian Models of the Eighteenth Century: Comparison with the Old Colonist Implants of Transylvania)', in *Studies and Dissertations* (Arad, 1994), p. 65.

49 Eberhard Hempel, *Baroque Art and Architecture in Central Europe* (London, 1965), p. 104.

50 In 1721 the Bosnian Franciscans had established a congregation of the saint, upon the similar model in Slovakia and Bohemia; for details, see Mihaela Vlăsceanu, *Sculptura barocă în Banat* (*Baroque Sculpture in the Banat*) (Timişoara, 2005).

51 For details regarding iconography of saints, presented in Banatian baroque sculpture, see M. Vlăsceanu, 'The Iconography of Saints as Represented in Baroque Monumental Sculpture in the Banat', *Transylvanian Review*, vol. 21, suppl. no. 1 (2012), pp. 227–33.

52 Nicolae Sabău, *Sculptura barocă în România* (*Baroque Sculpture in Romania*) (Bucharest, 1992), p. 147.

53 I would like to thank Mr András Koltai, director of the Budapest Piarist Archives.

54 For details of the funeral inscription, see Vlăsceanu, *Sculptura*, pp. 38–39.

55 Anton Peter Petri, *Biographisches Lexikon des Banater Deutchtums* (Marquatstein, 1992), p. 1591.

56 Ibid., p. 100.

57 For details, see *Baroque Art in Central Europe: Crossroads* (Budapest, 1993), p. 420, where a short biography of the artist and his work is presented: 'Active in the Viennese sphere of influence during Maria Theresa's reign, J.J. Resler, educated in the Vienese academicist environnment, between 1735 and 1772 created more works, such as the statues on the altar and decoration of the Jesuit church in Gyór (1743–45); the main altar of the Trinitarian church in Poszony (Bratislava) between 1745 and 1750; in 1754 the statues of the main altar in the cathedral of Timişoara the altar of the Holy

Cross and the main altar of Trinitarian church in Vienna (1761); it is mentioned that, after the seventh decade of the eighteenth century, he adopted the rococo style, mainly for decorations, etc.'

58 Ilse Schulz, 'Leben und Werk Johann Joseph Reslers (1702–1772)', *Ein Beitrag zur Geschichte der Barokplastik in Österreich, Jahrbuch für Landesbunde von Niederösterreich* (1988/89), p. 30.

59 Voit, *Der Barock in Ungarn*, p. 113.

60 Rodica Vârtaciu, *Lucrări de sculptorul J. J. Reslers, 1700–1772 (Works by the Sculptor J. J. Reslers, 1700–1772)*, AB, NS, vol. 2 (1997), pp. 133–43.

61 Günter Brucher, *Die Kunst der Barock in Österreich* (Salzburg, 1994), p. 162, illustrating the Holy Cross altar composition from Gurk cathedral, which served as a model for the sculpture in the cathedral in Timișoara.

62 Diplich, *Die Domkirche*, pp. 260–61; in the monograph, the contract between Georg Wittman and the catheradral's authority is mentioned for the sum of 1,200 de guldens.

63 The monastery archive has preserved 16 plans of altars, of which six are for the main altar; see M. Roos, *Maria – Radna: Ein Wallfahrtsort im Sudosten Europas*, vol. i (Regensburg, 1998), p. 305, n, 50.

64 Ibid.,p. 100.

65 Ibid.

66 The documents referring to the side altars (documents 5, 6, 9 and 26 in the monastery archive) mention the beginning of the works in 1723; the votive paintings depicting Anthony of Padua were executed by Ferdinand Schiessl, who also did the fresco painting on the ceiling.

67 Information from Dr Johann Kronbichler, director of the Diocesan Museum in Salzburg; see Roos, *Maria – Radna*, p. 107.

68 N. Stoicescu, *Bibliografia localităţilor şi monumentelor medievale din Banat (Bibliography of the Banatian Medieval Settlements and Monuments)* (Timişoara, 1973), p. 22, mentions only one wooden church built in the eighteenth century.

69 Ibid., p. 113.

70 Ibid., p. 48.

71 Ibid., p. 60.

72 National Archives, Caransebeş branch, document collection St EG, no. 19–1860, Ortgeschichte von Szaska, Saszka Kohldorf und Mariaschnee, p. 1.

73 For Johann Georg Dorfmeister's artistic biography, see *Thieme-Becker*: M. Poch-Kalous, *Viennaer Plastick im 19. Jahrhundert, Geschicte der bildenden Kunst in Vienna*, in *Plastik in Vienna* (Vienna, 1970), p. 171.

74 This is attested by Sasca parish death registry, now preserved in the Archives of the Romsn Catholic Bishopric of Timișoara, *Protocollum Defunctorum Parochiae Saska*, vol. i, p. 94.

75 Buzilă and Vârtaciu, *Barocul în Banat*, p. 20.

76 Pârvulescu, *Iconostasul tradiţional în Banat (Traditional Iconostasis in the Banat)* (Timişoara, 2001), p. 5.

77 Id., *Pictura bisericilor ortodoxe din Banat între secolul al XVIII-lea şi deceniul trei al secolului al XIX-lea (Painting in Banatian Orthodox Churches between the Eighteenth Century and the Third Decade of the Nineteenth Century)* (Timişoara, 2003).

78 Fr. Griselini, *Incercare de istorie politica si naturala a Banatului Timisoarei, Editura Facla*, 1984, pp. 181–82.

79 Pârvulescu, *Iconostasul tradiţional în Banat*, p. 4.

80 Ibid., p. 5.

81 Ibid.: 'The traditional iconostasis was horizontally structured, the new iconostasis is vertically oriented, divided into three registers clearly defined by profiled cornices, decorated with simple or moulded columns, with marble or gilded pilasters and Ionic or Corinthian chapters, all contributing to a monumental aspect.'

82 Pavel Florenski, *Iconostasul (Iconostasis)* (Bucharest, 1994), p. 156.

83 Ibid., p. 10.

84 The oldest attestation of a Banatian wooden church is the *capella in honoreun Beatae Mariae Virginis*, mentioned in Ferdinand Knauz, *Monumenta Ecclesiae Strigoniensis*, vol. 1 (Strigonii, 1874), pp. 582–83, built near the village of Şemlac.

85 Ioachim Miloia, 'Din activitatea artistică a ierodiaconului Vasile' ('The Artistic Life of Deacon Vasile'), AB (October–December 1930), p. 90.

86 Nicolae Tincu Velea, *Istoria bisericească politico–națională a românilor de peste totu* (*The Political-National Church History of Romanians Everywhere*) (Sibiu, 1865), p. 202.

87 Vasile Drăguț, *Dicționar enciclopedic de artă medievală românească* (*Encyclopedic Dictionary of Romanian Medieval Art*) (Bucharest, 2000), p. 86; for the painting ensemble, see Pârvulescu, *Iconostasul tradițional*, p. 59.

88 For the iconostasis painting, see D. Medaković, *Srpska umetnost u XVIII veka* (*Serbian Art in the XVIIIth Century*) (Belgrade, 1980), p. 41; M. Jovanović, *Slikarstvo Temisvarske Eparhije* (Novi Sad, 1996), pp. 523–30; Pârvulescu, *Iconostasul tradițional*, pp. 33–34.

89 Assunto, *Universul ca spectacol*, p. 54.

90 Germain Bazin, *Clasic, baroc, rococo* (*Classic, Baroque, Rococo*) (Bucharest, 1983), p. 16.

91 Like unions from Vienna or Prague, such religious congregations were organised at Timișoara, for example those of St John Nepomuk or the Holy Virgin. For details, see Preyer, *Monografia*, p. 191.

92 Viorica Guy Marica, 'Argintari transilvăneni în Europa barocului' ('Transylvanian Silversmiths in Baroque Europe'), SCIA (Arad Museum of Art) (1994), p. 7.

93 Lorenz Dittmann, *Stil, simbol, structură* (*Style, Symbol, Structure*) (Bucharest, 1988), p. 22.

Chapter 10

1 M. Jovanoviš, *Ikonografija slikarstva u banatskim crkvama XVIII i XIX veka*, Radovi simpozijuma o srpsko/jugoslovensko-rumunskim odnosima (Vršac, 1971), pp. 165–71.

2 М. Јовановић, Л. Шелмић, Н. Кусовац, *Уметничко благо Србау Румунији...*, p. 40.

3 Д. Давидов, *Споменици Будимске епархије*, Београд, 1990, pp. 312–13.

4 М. Јовановић, *Српско сликарство у доба романтизма*, Нови Сад, 1976, pp. 120–23.

5 I. Frunzetti, *Pictorii bănățeni din secolul al XIX-lea* (*Banatian Painters in the Nineteenth Century*), ESILA, 1952, pp. 35–77.

6 Tha latter originated from Wallachia, according to V.V. Muntean, *Exegeze istorice și teologice* (*Historical and Theological Exegeses*) (2005), p. 130.

7 H. Medeleanu, *Noi precizări în legătură cu Nedelcu Popovici și pictura murală de la Lipova* (*New Explanations Regarding Nedelcu Popovici and the Mural Painting from Lipova*) (Timișoara, 1980), pp. 359–64.

8 Ibid., p. 365.

9 D. Davidov, *Ikone zografa Temišvarske i Aradske eparhije* (Novi Sad, 1981), pp. 124–25.

10 R. Staniš, *Manastir Vraćevšnica* (Kraljevo 1980). See L. Šelmiš, *Srpsko zidno slikarstvo u XVIII veku*, p. 17; id., *Slikarstvo epohe Brankoveanu i srpski živopis u XVIII veku*, p. 3.

11 M. Kašanin and V. Petroviš, *Srpska umetnost u Vojvodini* (Novi Sad, 1927), p. 192.

12 V. Țigu, *Zugravul Nedelcu Popovici* (*The Painter Nedelcu Popovici*), 'Historical Monuments Bulletin', no. 2, Bucharest, 1971, pp. 67–72.

13 D. Davidov, *Ikone zografa Temišvarske i Aradske eparhije*, pp. 124–26. Historian D. Davidov had written about Nedelcu and Şerban Popovici as Szentendre painters, with an incorrect reference regarding their origin. The correction was made by the same author in his study *Ikone zografa Temišvarske i Aradske eparhije*, p. 128, n. 26.

14 L. Mirkoviš, *Crkvene starine u srpskim crkvama Banata, Rumunije i Mađarske*, Beograd, 'Spomenik' SAN, XCIX, 1, 1950, see D. Davidov, *Ikone zografa temišvarske i Aradske eparhije*, 129; M. Jovanoviš, L. Šelmiš, N. Kusovac, *Umetničko blago Srba u Rumuniji*, Beograd-Novi Sad, 1990, p. 30; M. Jovanoviš, *Slikarstvo Temišvarske eparhije – Topografski pregled slikarstva u crkvama Temišvarske eparhije*, p. 416; see S. Bugarski, *Srpsko pravoslavlje u Rumuniji*, Temišvar-Beograd-Novi Sad, 1995, 129–30; V. Popoviš, *Srpski spomenici u Rumuniji -(Ovsenica)*, Subotica, 1996, p. 219.

15 O.M. Radosavljeviš, *Manastir Središte (prilog njegovoj istoriji)*, Pravoslavni Bogoslovni fakultet u Beogradu, XXXI, Beograd, 1987, 234. See M. Grujiš, *Prilošci istoriji srpskih banatskih manastira u drugoj polovini XVIII-og veka*, Bogoslovni glasnik, Sremski Karlovci, knj. IX, sv. 2, 1906, p. 98; J. Sentklarai, *Istorijski spomenici srpskih manastira u južnoj Ugarskoj (Ukinuti manastiri – Središte)*, Novi Sad, Zastava, 1908; see B.M. Drobnjakoviš, F. Mileker, *Letopisi opština Podunavske oblasti*, Panțevo, 1929, p. 157.

16 I.C. Panait, *Pârvu Mutu – zurgavul (Pârvu Mutu – the Painter)*, in 'Church's Voice', XXIV, 1965, br. 7–8, p. 697.

17 By working on the topography of Banatian cultural monuments in 1980, I found an icon signed *Porvul zugrav*. About this, see *Popis slikarskih i vajarskih dela u privatnoj svojini i društvenom posedu na teritoriji Banata*, knjiga V, Novi Sad, 1981, and also A. Negru's study, *O icoană necunoscută a zugravului Pârvu Mutu (An Unknown Icon by Painter Pârvu Mutu)*, in 'The Light', 4–5, Panciova, 1989.

18 V. Brătulescu, *Izvoarele picturii în Banat (The Roots of Banatian Painting)*, 'Banat Metropolitan Church', 1961, pp. 5–6, 28.

19 I.B. Mureşianu, *Colecția de artă religioasă veche a Arhiepiscopiei Timişoarei şi Caransebeşului (the Religious Art Collection of Timişoara and Caransebeş Archiepiscopate)*, Timişoara, Banat Metropolitan Church Publishing House, 1973, p. 76.

20 Središte monastery inventory from 10 June 1775 lies in the collection of Vrsac City Museum. Radu Lazăr was born in Lugoj and became priest in Caransebeş. We would like to thank Pr. Prof. Vasile V. Muntean for notifying, thus contributing to the correction of some flaws.

21 I. Stratan, V. Muntean, *Monumente istorice şi bisericeşti din Lugoj (Historical and Religious Monuments from Lugoj)*, Timişoara, Banat Metropolitan Church, 1981, p. 23.

22 O. Mikiš - L. Šelmiš, *Majstori prelaznog perioda*, Novi Sad, Galerija Matice srpske, 1981, p. 38.

23 C. Pascu, *Preotul şi zugravul Radu Lazarevici (Radu Lazarevici, Priest and Painter)*, in 'Foaia diecezană', LVI, 1941, p. 5.

24 E. Costescu, *Contribuții la cunoaşterea activității unor meşteri români care au lucrat în Banatul românesc şi sârbesc în secolul al XVIII-lea (Contributions to the knowledge of some Romanian Masters' activity, who worked in Romanian and Serbian Banat in the Eighteenth Century)*, Serbian-Yugoslavian-Romanian Relations Symposium, Panciova, 1971, p. 71.

25 N. Stoicescu, *Bibliografia localităților şi monumentelor medievale din Banat (The Bibliography of Banatian Medieval Monuments)* Timişoara 1972, pp. 23, 184, 223, 335. See 'Foaia diecezană', 1897, no. 47, year XII, 5–6; C. Diaconovici, *Enciclopedia Română (Romanian Encyclopedia)*, Sibiu, 1900, vol. II, p. 149.

26 V. Brătulescu, *Izvoarele picturii în Banat (The Roots of Banatian Painting)*, 'Banat Metropolitan Church', 1961, p. 36.

27 In her monograph *Centrele de pictură românească din Banat – secolul al XIX-lea (The Banatian Centres of Romanian Painting – the Nineteenth Century)*, Rodica Vârtaciu assumes that Velceleanu had studied at Veighel in Munich. The supposition is based on documents found in the Bishopric archive, the fund of Ramna village church, no. 307/1928, that not being a valid argument, because Miloia and Frunzetti used the same document without indicating more objective data to determine for sure the schooling period in Munich. See V. Ţigu, *Studii şi cercetări de istoria artei (Studies and Research of Art History)*, Plastic Art Series, vol. 27, Bucharest, 1980, pp. 165–75. One of the arguments was that in his later activity, Velceleanu used over 800 illustrations of Veigel's *Bible* as models. On the side of the *Bible's* pages Velceleanu signed certain translations that were used as stage directions. The text is in Romanian language, written in Cyrillic characters.

28 I. Miloia, *Din activitatea artistică a ierodiaconului Vasile (From the Artistic Activity of Deacon Vasile)*, 'Banat Annals', T, III, Timişoara, 1930, pp. 89–93; V. Cărăbiş, *Pictorii zugravi din județul Gorj în secolele XVII–XVIII (Painters from Gorj County in the eighteenth and nineteenth centuries)*, 'Revue of Museums and Monuments', no. 2, Bucharest, 1975, p. 76; Cf. O. Milanoviš-Joviš, *Autori dela likovnih i primenjenih umetnosti evidentiranih u Banatu*, 'GraTa za prouțavanje spomenika kulture Vojvodine', VIII–IX, Novi Sad, 1978, p. 322.

29 A. Cozma, *Pictorul de bisericii Filip Matei, 1853–1940 (The Religious Painter Filip Matei, 1853-1940)*, Banat Metropolitan Church Archive, Timişoara, no. archive 3; Banat Metropolitan Church Archive, Caransebeş fund, III, 328/1892.

30 A. Negru, *Contribuție la biografia pictorului Filip Matei (Contribution to the Biography of Painter Filip Matei)*, 'Lumina', br. 1–2, Panciova, 1988, pp. 64–69.

31 V. Ţigu, *Studii şi cercetări de istoria artei (Studies and Research of Art History)*, Plastic Art Series, tome 27, Bucharest, 1980, pp. 165–75.

32 I. Miloia, *Începuturile artei româneşti în Banat (The Beginnings of Romaian Art in Banat)*, in 'Banat Workshops', January–March 1930, p. 6.

33 I. Stratan-V. Muntean, *Monumente istorice şi bisericeşti din Lugoj (Historical Monuments and Churches from Lugoj)*, Timişoara, Banat Metropolitan Church, 1981, p. 20.

34 I. Frunzetti, *Pictorii bănăţeni din secolul al XIX-lea (Banatian Painters of the nineteenth Century)*, Bucharest, The Publishing House for Literature and Art, 1957, p. 39.

35 I.B. Mureşianu, *Colecţia de artă veche a Arhiepiscopiei Timişoarei şi Caransebeşului (The Old Religious Art Collection of Timişoara and Caransebeş Archiepiscopate)*, Timişoara, 1973, p. 83.

36 In *Monografia eparhiei Caransebeş (Caransebeş Diocese Monography)*, N. Corneanu mentiones Ştefan the Painter Ponerchiu (Stefan Tenecki), author of the church first iconostasis, made between the years 1759 and 1766.

37 I. Cristache Panait, *Contribuţie la cunoaşterea picturii bănăţene din bisericile de lemn de la sfârşitul secolului al XVIII-lea şi începutul secolului al XIX-lea (Contributions to the Knowledge of Banatian Painting from the Wooden Churches during the Late Eighteenth and Early Nineteenth Centuries)*, SCIA, Seria Arta plastică, I, Bucureşti, 1972, pp. 124–125.

38 R. Vârtaciu (1992), *Centre de pictură românească în Banat în secolul al XIX-lea (Romanian Painting Centers in nineteenth Century Banat)*, Timişoara, Banat Museum, p. 84.

39 C. Feneşan, *Cnezi şi Obercnezi în Banatul Imperial, 1717–1778 (Princes of Imperial Banat, 1717–1778)*, Romanian Academy Publishing House, Bucharest, 1996, pp. 70–78.

40 A. Buzilă, *Biserica Adormirii Maicii Domnului din Lugoj, ctitorie a cnezilor români din Banatul secolului al XVIII-lea, (The Assumption Church of Lugoj, Founded by the Romanian Princes of Eighteenth Century Banat)* in 'Acta Musei Napocensis', XVIII, Timişoara, 1981, p. 643.

41 Ion Frunzetti and Ion B. Mureşianu wrote superficial and inaccurate. In his study *Pictorii bănăţeni din secolul al XIX-lea (Nineteenth-Century Banatian Painters)*, Frunzetti mentiones Gerdanovici as a village painter, while Mureşianu is wrong the period and the references of some works. În *Monografia Mitropoliei Banatului (Banat Metropolitan Church Monography)*, Timişoara, 1971, Ion D. Suciu used the aforementioned studies as a foundation for the description of artistic life; hence the mistakes were inserted into this monography. Gerdanovici's value and his role in the artistic life of nineteenth-century Banat were certified by Miodrag Iovanovici in *Slikarstvo Temišvarske eparhije – Prilog topografiji banatskih slikara (Potcenjeni Georgije Đerdanović)*, pp. 174–78.

42 M. Jovanoviš, *Slikarstvo Temišvarske eparhije – Prilog topografiji banatskih slikara (Pavel Đurković u Lugošu)*, pp. 166–174.

43 A.P. Hehn, *Banater malerei*, Bucureşti, Kriterion, 1984, p. 12.

44 Hans-Georg Beck, *Kirche und theologische Literatur im Byzatinitischen Reich*, München, 1959, p.472.

45 M. Jovanoviš, L. Šelmiš, N. Kusovac, *Umetničko blago Srba u Rumuniji*, p. 24.

46 I. Frunzetti, *Pictorii bănăţeni din secolul al XIX-lea (Nineteenth-Century Banatian Painters)*, Bucharest, Publishing House for Literature and Art, 1957, p. 39. In the above work the author only slightly mentioned the existence of rural painting workshops, without analysing their activity. His judgement of the painters is arbitrary and based upon Ioachim Miloia's unfinished research. See I. B. Mureşianu, *Colecţia de artă religioasă veche a Arhiepiscopiei Timişoarei şi Caransebeşului, (The Old Religious Art Collection of Timişoara and Caransebeş Archiepiscopate)*, Timişoara, 1973, p. 80.

47 N. Stoicescu, *Bibliografia monumentelor şi localităţilor medievale din Banat (The Bibliography of Monuments and Historic Medieval Settlements from Banat)*, Timişoara, 1973, p. 17.

48 A. Negru, *Popovići iz Oravice*, în 'Zbornik', XX, LUMS, Novi Sad, 1984, pp. 271–75.

49 I.B. Mureşianu, *Colecţia de artă religioasă veche a arhiepiscopiei Timişoarei şi Caransebeşului (The Old Religious Art Collection of Timişoara and Caransebeş Archiepiscopate)*, Timişoara, Banat Metropolitan Church, 1973, p. 77.

50 The presumption according to which Baroque elements had penetrated the painting of southern Banatian workshops by Nikola Nešković's art is logical. The reasons of this supposition are Gheorghe Diaconovici's first contacts with Baroque art, in the Vrsac painter's workshop. The Vrsac Episcopalian palace chapel iconostasis and the Mesic monastery icons, in which Diaconu imitates Nikola Nešković's creations stand proof. Because Diaconovicis activity was spread on a large area inside Banat (Bocșa, Lugoj, Oravița and Caransebeș), it is obvious that Baroque elements had taken roots in the activity of the artists.

51 S. Moldovan, *Județul Caraș și orașul Oravița (Caraș County and Oravița City)*, Oravița, 1933, p. 46.

52 M. Jovanoviš, *Slikarstvo Temišvarske eparhije*, p. 14.

53 A. Cosma, *Pictura românească în Banat de la origini până azi (The Romanian Painting in Banat from Origins to Present)*, Timișoara, 1940, p. 22.

54 D. Puia, *Biserici vechi de lemn din Valea Carașului (Old Wooden Churches from Caraș Valley)*, 'Banat Metropolitan Church', 1958, nr. 4–6, p. 93.

55 A. Negru, *Pictorul Nicolae Popescu (Painter Nicolae Popescu)*, in 'Libertatea', Panciova, 1998, 35–40, see I. Frunzetti, *op. cit.*, pp. 106–10.

56 In the exhibition catalogue, Ioan B. Mureşianu presents unverified information about the place Dimitrie had been trained. The Popovici family painters' chronology on the Banatian artistic scene is often inaccurate.

57 P. Drăgălină, *Din istoria Banatului de Severin (From the History of Severin's Banat)*, vol. I, Caransebeş, 1902, 15; A. Ghidiu, I. Bălan, *Caransebeș Monography*, p. 22.

58 *Ibidem*, p. 23.

59 M. Jovanoviš, *Slikarstvo Temišvarske eparhije – Prilog topografiji dela banatskih slikara – Crkve u Karansebešu*, pp. 153–158.

60 Nicolae Popescu returns temporarily in his country, in 1867, undertaking religious painting requests for Banatian villages. For Nicolae Popescu's artistic works, the Italian press of the time, but also his contemporaries, has only words of praise. In the summer of 1867, Popescu attends the exhibition *Belle Arti di Roma* with 5 of his works that were eulogistic commented in 'Familia', Oradea, 16th of June 1867, 350–351. See Virgil Feier, *Un pictor bănăţean afirmat pe plan european (A Banatian Painter Aprreciated in Europe)*, in 'Orizont', Timişoara, 29 December 1977, p. 2. This article publishes, for the first time, valuable information from the press of the time; cf. Virgil Feier, *Dincolo de arhive (Beyond Archives)*, in 'Orizont', Timişoara, 2002, p. 6.

61 A. Negru, *Nicolae Popescu, 1835–1877 (Nicolae Popescu, 1835-1877)*, Panciova, Libertatea Publishing House, 2004, pp. 39–40.

62 The chronology of the painting execution is taken from the I.B. Mureșianu's monography *Catalogul de artă veche și religioasă... (The Old Religious Art Catalogue...)*, with the reexamination of some data.

63 I.D. Suciu, *Monografia Mitropoliei Banatului (Banat Metropolitan Church Monography)*, 130; see H. Medeleanu, *Pictorul Stefan Tenețchi, Viața și opera (Painter Stefan Tenețchi, His Life and Work)*, 'Ziridava', XV–XVI, Arad, 1987, 373–378; L. Šelmiš, *Srpsko zidno slikarstvo XVIII veka*, p. 18.

64 *Saint Barbara* icon is found in Reșița Deanery collection, inv. no. 546, being the only one that bears Trifon Achimescu's signature. About Achimescu, who made the iconostasis in 1840, the local priest stated that he has a precise hand and brush. Achimescu probably used models upon reproductions from illustrated magazines that were being printed in Banat.

65 O. Milanoviš – Joviš, *Iz slikarstva i primenjene umetnosti Vojvodine*, 'Grada za prouțavanje spomenika kulture Vojvodine', I, 1957, 49–51, 80–81. In the 1796 receipt book there is data confirming that Simeon Jakšiš, painter from Biserica Albă, was paid 175 forints for painting the iconostasis. On the iconostasis, above the Imperial Doors, Gheorghe Diaconovici's work, the mentioned inscription is found, written in black letters on a blue background, in Romanian language with Cyrillic characters. The original inscription was deteriorated, and the transcription is stylised.

66 P. Vasiš, 'Bela Crkva – centar srpskog slikarstva u XIX veku', *Politika*, 26 August 1962.

67 I.B. Mureşianu, *Colecţia de artă religioasă... (The Religious Art Collection...)*, p. 54.

68 *Popis slikarskih i vajarskid dela u društvenom posedu i privatnoj svojini u Banatu*, 2.

69 Grebenaţ, a settlement in today's Serbian Banat.

70 N. Mamuziš, *Rad na umetničkom katastru*, radni nalog 222, Narodni muzej Vršac.

71 A settlement near Biserica Albă, the same as Ulmu.

72 P. Vasiš, *Umetnsot u istočnoj Srbiji*, 'Braniţevo', sv. 4–5, July–October 1963, 55; see P. Vasiš, *Slikarska porodica Jakšić iz Bele crkve*, 270; M. Jovanoviš, *Slikarstvo Temišvarske eparhije – Ljupkova*, pp. 391–393; S. Bugarski, *Srpsko pravoslavlje u Rumuniji – Ljupkova*, 119; V. Popoviš, *Srpski spomenici u Rumuniji – Ljupkova.*

73 V. Popoviš, *Velikobečkerečki slikarski ateljeji*, Zrenjanin, 1969; idem, *Veliki Bečkerek, slikarsko središte u Banatu – prva slikarska radionica*, ZLUMS,13, Novi Sad, 1977, p. 117.

74 Pavle Vasiš, *Dimitrije Bačević ikonopisac karlovački*, 'Glasnik', Službeni list Srpske pravoslavne crkve, nr. 9, Belgrad, 1969, p. 4.

75 See D. Medakoviš, *Hristove parabole na ikonostasu Nikolajevske crkve u Zemunu*, 'Zbornik Narodnog muzeja', IV, 1964.

76 A. Negru, *Constantin Daniel*, in 'Libertatea', Panciova, 1998, pp. 24–35.

77 A. Negru, *Ugovor Konstantina Danila i crkvene opštine u Pančevu*, 'Sveske za kulturnu istoriju Matice srpske', I, Novi Sad, 1988, pp. 112–15.

78 D. Medakoviš, *Srpska umetnost u XIX veku*, Srpska knjiźevna zadruga, Beograd 1981, p. 99. M. Jovanoviš-N. Kusovac, *Škola Konstantina Danila*, Exhibition catalogue, Narodni muzej Zrenjanin, 1967, p. 25.

79 V. Popoviš, *Velikobečkerečki slikarski ateljeji*, Zrenjanin, 1969, bez paginacije; Ista, *Veliki Bečkerek, slikarsko središte u Banatu – prva slikarska radionica*, ZLUMS,13, Novi Sad, 1977, p. 117.

80 M. Jovanoš, *op. cit.*

81 R. Vârtaciu, *Centre de pictură românească în Banat în secolul al XIX-lea... (Centers of Romanian Painting in nineteenth Century Banat...)*, p. 11.

82 In the museum collection of Saint Simeon Stâlpnicul monastery, Tenecki's arguably most beautiful works are preserved – *Coronation of Virgin Mary* and *John the Evangelist at Patmos* (1790), along with *Saint Johnthe Precursor* icon from Arad's old Episcopalian church (the iconostasis is transferred to Comlăuş church).

83 M. Jovanovic, *Slikarstvo temisvarske eparhije...*, p. 229.

84 H. Medeleanu, *Documente referitoare la pictorul bănăţean Stefan Teneţchi (Documents Referring to Banatian Painter Stefan Teneţchi)* , in 'Studies and Research of Art History', 30, Bucharest, 1973, pp. 72–81.

85 M. Јовановић, *Иконостас манастира Бездина*, Зборник за ликовне уметности Матице српске 6 (Нови Сад 1970), pp. 119–32.

86 D. Davidov, *Ikone zografa Temišvarske i Aradske eparhije*, ZLUMS 17, Novi Sad, 1981, p. 119.

87 Idem, *Ikone sprpskih zografa XVIII veka*, Belgrade, 1977, pp. 33–34.

88 L. Šelmiš-O. Mikiš, *Delo Arsenija Teodorovića*, Novi Sad, 1978.

89 P. Vasiš, D. Medakoviš, *Konstantin Danil*, Katalog izložbe, Zrenjanin, 1961.

90 *Klasicizam kod Srba*, knj. VII, Beograd, 1967, p. 146.

91 K. Ambroziš, V. Ristiš, *Prilog biografijama srpskih umetnika XVIII i XIX veka (Iz Arhive Akademije likovnih umetnosti u Beču)*, 'Zbornik radova Narodnog muzeja', II, Beograd, 1959, p. 418.

92 O. Milanoviš-Joviš, *Iz slikarstva i primenjene umetnosti Vojvodine*, 'GraŤa za prouţavanje spomenika kulture Vojvodine', I, Novi Sad, 1957, pp. 73–76.

93 P. Vasiš, *Konstantin Danil i njegov krug*, în M. Jovanoviš, N. Kusovac, *Škola Konstantina Danila*, Zrenjanin, 1967, pp. 17–18.

94 M. Jovanoviš, *Srpsko slikarstvo u doba romantizma*, p. 65.

95 P. Vasiš – D. Medakoviš, *Konstantin Danil*, Zrenjanin, 1967, pp. 28–39.

96 A.P. Hehn, *Banater Malerei im wandel der Zeiten*, in 'Die Wahrheit', 1964, 12/IX, Temesvar.

97 *Ibidem*, p.18

98 In *Banater Malerei* study, at page 19, there is a mistake: Ludvig von Bersuder's father had transfered from Kőln to Timişoara in the year 1835, and the painter was born in Timișoara in 1825.

99 I. Frunzetti, *Pictorii bănățeni din secolul al XIX-lea (nineteenth Century Banatian Painters)*, ed. cit., p. 116.

100 A. P. Hehn, *Präzise Kunst, Johann Wälder, ein Banater Maler*, in 'Neue Banater Zeitung', Temesvar, 1970, pp. 1–25.

101 A.P. Hehn, *Kleine Banater Galerie*, in 'Neue Banater Zeitung', numbers 27.01.1973, up to 14.02.1974.

Chapter 11

1 Thirteen issues of *Temeswarer Nachrichten* are held in the Hofkammerarchiv (Imperial Court Archive) in Vienna. See Österreichischen Staatsarchiv: Finanz und Hofkammerarchiv, Wien, 1, Banater Akten, Rote Nr. 73, Fasz. 1 (1770–78), fols. 652–84 – Alteste Zeitung des Banat. See also Dr Joseph Wüst, *Die Anfänge des Buchdruckes und des Pressewesens im Banat* (Vienna, 1954), 47 and Franz Liebhard, *Banater Mosaik: Beiträge zur kulturgeschichte* (Bucharest, 1976), 208.

2 *Temeswarer Nachrichten*, no. 1 (18 April 1771), fols. 652–3.

3 Issue 26 (23 March 1771).

4 *Temeswarer Nachrichten*, no. 3 (2 May 1771), fol. 657.

5 Wüst, *Die Anfänge*; Liebhard, *Banater Mosaik*.

6 *Anhang zu den Temeswarer Nachrichten*, no. 2 (25 April 1771), fol. 655.

7 *Temeswarer Nachrichten*, no. 1 (18 April 1771), fol. 653.

8 *Temeswarer Nachrichten*, no. 3 (2 May 1771), fol. 658; see also no. 9 (13 June 1771), fols. 673–4.

9 Liebhard, *Banater Mosaik*, p. 223.

10 The editorial staff wished to offer as much information as possible about a province of the Habsburg Empire that was little known to the European world. See *Anhang zu den Temeswarer Nachrichten*, no. 2 (25 April 1771), fol. 655.

11 See *Anhang zu den Temeswarer Nachrichten*, no. 3 (2 May 1771), fol. 658.

12 It is possible that the inscription came from the Roman centre of Tibiscum (Jupa, near Caransebeş), the five fragments of the inscription being kept today in the Museum of Banat in Timişoara. See also I. I. Russu, M. Dušanić, N. Gudea, and V. Wollmann, *Inscripţiile Daciei Romane* (The Inscriptions of Roman Dacia), vol. iii/1 (Bucharest, 1977), no. 157, pp. 182–5 and no. 131, pp. 149–51. The author of the study published in *Temeswarer Nachrichten* has the merit of having made the first translation, even though it has a few errors, and including it in the scientific network.

13 See Victor Neumann, '*Volk* (People) and *Sprache* (Language) in Herder's Thought: The Speculative Theory of Ethno nation', in id., *Neam, Popor sau Naţiune? Despre identităţile politice europene (Group, People or Nation? Concerning European Political Identities)* (Curtea Veche, 2005), pp. 47–84.

14 See *Temeswarer Nachrichten*, no. 4 (9 May 1771), fol. 660.

15 At that date, there were no ethnonational communities, only linguistic and cultural ones. For the concepts that define the collective and political identity in modern Europe, see Neumann, *Neam, Popor sau Naţiune?*

16 It is very important to mention that the rural population of the Banat accepted borrowing and mixing foreign values. The peasants of Romanian-German, Serbian-German, Romanian-Serbian and German-Hungarian villages used two or more languages, the communication and proximity of the communities laying the foundations for mixed families. In parallel, in the cities of the Banat, the social emancipation that took place in the nineteenth century led to the assimilation of a set of values and civic norms, rather than the underlining of linguistic and religious differences. The promotion of the ideology of *Kulturnation* had begun in the Forty-Eighter period, but later managed to win over, even if only partially, the intellectual environment capable of political decisions. In the end, ethnonationalist identity theory – one contrary to the interests of the empire – was often counteracted by assimilationist policies, relatively easy to implement within a society having a mixed identity as did the Banat until the Second World War.

17 *Temeswarer Nachrichten*, no. 4 (9 May 1771), fol. 660.

18 Ibid. See J.J. Ehrler, *Banatul de la origini până în prezent* (The Banat from Its Origins to the Present Day) (1774), ed. Costin Feneşan (Timişoara, 1982). The manuscript of Ehrler's book can be found in Egyetemi Könyvtár Budapest (Budapest University Library), Kézirattár (Manuscript Cabinet), G 189.

19 The historiographical significance of this article is one of the reasons why I became interested to find out who the anonymous author was. The use of a pseudonym would have given me the chance to identify him more quickly. The first questions, searches and assumptions were made in 1953, when Joseph Wüst signalled the existence of the newspaper among the documents regarding the Banat in the Austrian State Archives. In the 1980s Franz Liebhardt (*Banater Mosaik*, 212) resumed discussion on the article. Studying the paper, I understood that it would not be insignificant to identify the name of the first chronicler of the Banat. The result of the research made by the historian Costin Feneşan coincided with my attempts. He discovered the manuscript of J.J. Ehler's work *The Banat from its Origins up to the Present Day*, 1774, at the Oetvös Loránd Budapest University Library. Comparing the text from *Temeswarer Nachrichten* with the one published by Constantin Feneşan, it became clear that the author was one and the same: Johann Jakob Ehrler. (See, in parallel, *Temeswarer Nachrichten*, nos. 3–4 and *Banatul de la origini până în prezent*.)

20 Alexander Krischan, 'Franz Griselini – erster Historiograph des Banats', in *Deutsche Forschungen in Ungarn* (Budapest, 1980), 127–86. See Francesco Griselini, *Versuch einer politischen und natürlichen Geschichte des temeswarer Banats* ... (Vienna, 1780).

21 Johann Zacharia Platner, *Gründliche Einleitung in die Chirurgie oder kurze Anweisung alle Krankheiten, so denen Chirurgis vorkommen, theils mit innerlichen und äusserlichen Medikamenten, theils durch Operationen zu curiren*, 2 pt. in 1 vol. (Leipzig, 1748).

22 *Temeswarer Nachrichten*, no. 9 (13 June 1771).

23 Tivadar Orthmayer and Jenö Szentkláray, *Történelmi adattár* (Budapest, 1871). *See* Romanian National Archives, Timişoara Branch, Fund Timişoara City Hall, file no. 2/1740.

24 Victor Neumann, 'Les Juifs de Banat entre l'Autriche-Hongrie et la Roumanie au debut du XXe siècle', in Carol Iancu (ed.), *Permanences et ruptures dans l'histoire des Juifs de Roumanie (XIXe–XXe siècles)* (Montpellier, 2004), pp. 127–39. For the process of Jewish emancipation and their involvement in urban life, see Victor Neumann, *Evreii Banatului: O mărturie a multi- şi interculturalităţii Europei Este-Centrale (The Jews of the Banat: A Testimony of East-Central Europe Multi- and Interculturality)* (2nd edn., Timişoara, 2016), pp. 85–121 and 121–63.

25 Dr Alexander Krischan, *Die 'Temeswarer Zeitung' als Banater Geschichtsquelle (1852–1949)* (Munich, 1969), p. 32.

26 Ibid.

27 See Victor Neumann, *The End of a History: Jews of Banat from the Beginning to Nowadays* (Bucharest, 2006), 93–125.

28 See Alexander Krischan, 'Ära Barat: Übernahme des "Südungarischen Lloyd" (1887–1912)', in *Die 'Temeswarer Zeitung'*, pp. 41–8.

29 Victor Neumann, 'Relaţiile româno-maghiare într-un moment de răscruce / Válaszút elött a román-magyar kapcsalatok / Romanian–Hungarian Relations at a Turning Point', in Levente Salat and Smaranda Enache (eds.), *Relaţiile româno-maghiare şi modelul de reconcilere franco-german (Romanian–Hungarian Relations and the French-German Model of Reconciliation)* (Cluj, 2004), pp. 301–25.

30 Krischan, *Die 'Temeswarer Zeitung'*, p. 45. Some historians interpreted such a manifestation as simply a sign of loyalty towards the Hungarian state, without taking into consideration the plural identity of Central European cities, the cultural nature of the locality. Hence, the generalising and simplified formulations, manifested in ethnonationalist and racist ideologies between 1900 and 1914.

31 'Wir achten und lieben die deutsche Nation, doch wir gehoren ihr nicht an'. Cf. *Temeswarer Zeitung*, no. 47 (1901), p. 1.

32 Promoted by the intellectual environment of the Reich of Kaiser Wilhelm I and picked up by some of the intellectual groups

within Central and South-Eastern Europe, the *Volkgeist* ideology conflicted with the civicism of the great cities of the Austro-Hungarian Monarchy. Gradually, this would contaminate the Hungarian elites, too. In this context, their message became a restrictive one.

33 'Das Temesvarer Theaterwesen', *Temeswarer Zeitung*, no. 75 (1896), pp. 1–2.

34 Josef Geml, 'Kulturelle Verhältnisse Temesvars', *Temeswarer Zeitung*, no. 35 (1900), pp. 6–7.

35 Ibid. By 1900, the statistics had changed: 51 per cent Germans; 32 per cent Hungarians; 11 per cent Romanians. See V. Orendi-Hommenau, *Gestern und Heute* (Temeswar, 1929), p. 6. See also A. Barat, *Die königliche Freistadt Temeswar: Eine monographische Skizze*, (Temeswar, 1902), p. 139. The city had a surface of 36 km^2; in 1890 the population density was 1,206 inhabitants/km^2, in 1900, 1,473 inhabitants/km^2. The native language spoken by the civilian and military inhabitants of the city in 1900 indicated that 55.9 per cent of Timișoara's total population spoke German, 26.7 per cent Hungarian, 9.1 per cent Romanian and 3.9 per cent Serbian. Hungarian was also spoken by another 15,135 inhabitants for whom it was not their mother tongue. According to the statistics of the time, only 16,625 of Timişoara's inhabitants could not speak Hungarian. With regard to the Banat, the demographic situation was as follows: Timiş County had a total population of 400,910 inhabitants, among whom there were 120,683 Germans, 160,585 Romanians, 57,821 Serbian, 47,518 Hungarian, 2,612 Slovaks, and so on. Torontal County had a total of 594,343 inhabitants: 158,312 Germans, 191,036 Serbians, 125,04 Hungarians, 86,168 Romanians, 15,899 Slovaks. Caraş-Severin County had a total of 466.147 inhabitants: 336,147 Romanians, 55,883 Germans, 33,787 Hungarians, 14,674 Serbians, 2,908 Slovaks. The Swabians were best represented in Torontal and Timiș, where they formed the relative majority of inhabitants; they were less represented in Caraş-Severin, where Romanians represented three-quarters of the population.

36 See Neumann, *Istoria evreilor din Banat*, p. 109; see also George Barany, 'Magyar Jew or Jewish Magyar (To the Question of the Jewish Assimilation in Hungary)', *Canadian-American Slavic Studies*, vol. 8, no. 1 (1974), pp. 1–144; cf. Hildrun Glass, *Zerbrochene nachbarschaft: Das deutsch-jüdische Verhältnis in Rumänien (1918–1938)* (Munich, 1996), p. 36.

37 It was not the number that was important, especially in the cities of the old monarchy, as much as the accepted cultural code – that is the reason why any statistic could be misleading. Individuals viewed themselves as members of one or other community according to their own interests, ideologies or intellectual level.

38 Prof. F.R., 'Südungarischer Kulturverein', *Temeswarer Zeitung*, no. 49 (1897), p. 1.

39 Anton Gokler, 'Zur Geschichte der Volksschulen', *Temeswarer Zeitung*, no. 33 (1896), pp. 1–2.

40 Josef Geml, 'Kulturelle Verhältnisse Temesvars', *Temeswarer Zeitung*, no. 35 (1900), pp. 6–7.

41 'Temesvarer Volksschulwesen', *Temeswarer Zeitung*, no. 59 (1899), pp. 1–2.

42 'Eine orientalische Akademie in Temesvar', *Temeswarer Zeitung*, no. 66 (1897), p. 4.

43 Victor Neumann, 'From the Austro-Hungarian Empire to the Romanian State: On the Jewish Question in a Disputed Territory', in id, *The End of a History*, 93–125. For similar urban cultural models in Central Europe, see also Angelo Ara, 'Juden und Jüdisches Bürgertum im Triest der Jahrhundertwende', in Andrei Corbea-Hoişie and Jacques Le Rider (eds.), *Metropole und Provinzen in Altösterreich (1880–1918)* (Polirom-Böhlau, 1996), pp. 264–74.

44 Zoltán Szász, 'Maghiari, români, saşi: Transilvania 1867–1918' ('Hungarians, Romanians and Saxons: Transylvania 1867–1918'), in *Transilvania văzută în publicistica istorică maghiară (Transylvania as Seen in the Hungarian Historical Press)* (Miercurea-Ciuc, 1999,) p. 253.

45 Ethnonationalism was present within the region, especially among pauper social segments which had benefited from emancipation and modernisation too little and too late. A type of ethnonationalism was manifested in certain intellectuals of the Banat, who had recently come into contact with the urban environment. See in

this sense Victor Neumann, 'Federalism and Nationalism in Austro-Hungarian Monarchy: Aurel C. Popovici's Theory', *East European Politics and Societies*, vol. 16, no. 3 (2002), pp. 864–98. Cf. id., 'Ecoul pogromului de la Iaşi în presa din Banat' ('The Echo of the Pogrom of Iași in the Banatian Press'), in George Voicu (ed.), *Pogromul de la Iaşi 28-30 iunie 1941: Prologul Holocaustului din România (The Pogrom of Iași 28–30 June 1941: The Prologue of the Romanian Holocaust)*, (Iaşi, 2006), pp. 205–13.

46 Josef Geml, 'Kulturelle Verhältnisse Temesvars', *Temeswarer Zeitung*, no. 35 (1900), pp. 6–7.

47 'Die 25 Jährige Tätigkeit der "Südungarischen Naturwissenschaftlichen Gesellschaft 1874 bis 1899" ', *Temeswarer Zeitung*, no. 68 (1899), pp. 2–3.

48 Zoltán Szász, 'Manchester-ul ungar: Dezvoltarea Timişoarei moderne' ('The Hungarian Manchester: The Development of Modern Timișoara'), in *Transilvania văzută în publicistica istorică maghiară (Transylvania Seen by the Hungarian Historical Press)* (Miercurea-Ciuc, 1999), pp. 244–45.

49 'Das Kleingewerbe Südungarns', *Temeswarer Zeitung*, no. 20 (1899), p. 6.

50 *Temesvarer Zeitung*, vol. 61 no. 31 (9 February 1912), p. 1.

51 Szász, 'Manchester-ul ungar', p. 247.

Chapter 12

1 B. Bengin, *Obrazovanje učitelja u Vršcu (Teacher Training at Vršac)* (Vršac, 1996), passim.

2 F. Mileker, *Povesnica slobodne kraljevske varoši Vršca (The History of the Free Royal City of Vršac)* (Pančevo, 1886), pp. 27–29.

3 Bengin, *Obrazovanje učitelja*, p. 19.

4 N. Gavrilović, *Srpske škole u Habzburškoj monarhiji u periodu pozne posvećenosti (1790–1848) (Serbian Schools under Habsburg Monarchy in the late Enlightenment (1790-1848))*, (Belgrade, 1999), pp. 21–28.

5 Ibid. 26–32.

6 Ibid.

7 S. Brankov, *Osnovna škola 'Vuk Karadžić' (The 'Vuk Karadžić' Middle School)* (Vršac, 1995), p. 16.

8 Arhiv Srpske akademije nauka i umetnosti, Sremski Karlovci (ASANUK), documents 99–1806.

9 NB in this chapter, 'alumni' is used in the original sense of male pupils or students attending a particular school or seat of learning, rather than graduates of that school. Data about the establishment of alumni within the Vršac grammar school has been gathered from the reports of meetings preserved in the Serbian Orthodox church of Vršac. The assembly establishing the alumni took place on 24 June 1799. Among the speakers was Bishop Šakabenta who announced that the monarch himself had recommended the establishment of schools in the province and in the border area as a solution to acute problems. From the first years of the Bishopric of Vršac, the bishop had founded a theological seminary for priests. Šakabenta signalled the necessity of training future teachers in methodology, thus he demanded an increased number of teachers and classes at Vršac, and that education would be accessible to *all* the young people of the Banat, not only to those from the Vršac area, with the aim of training better teachers and priests. In the same report, Abbot Ljustina praised the bishop. Professor Samoilo Martini made a presentation on German, Dutch and Hungarian schools, mentioning that in these countries, young people who went to school were financially supported by the wealthy within the community. Thus, he referred to Georgije Popović's foundation and its 200-florin donation, while the Mesic monastery promised annual support. Šakabenta himself, along with the priests, had financially supported the alumni, so that the founding of the school was possible in 1799. The most important donations were made in goods. Expectations were higher for the churches of Mehadia, Caransebeş and Lugoj, since they were the wealthiesand the majority of the beneficiaries were from the Timișoara eparchy (Vršac town archive, Vršac City Hall, Biserica Albă).

10 *Geschichte des Banater Schulwesens unter Maria Theresia*, vol. 35 (Vršac, 1882), pp. 31–32.

11 Documents from the town archive, Vršački magistrat, Bela Crkva.

12 D. Mladenović, 'Pred 50-godišnjicu otvaranja Velike realke grada Vršca', *Vojvodina*, no. 2 (20 February 1937).

13 Mileker, *Povesnica slobodne*.

14 Gavrilovic, *Srpske škole*, p. 80.

15 Ibid.

16 Ibid.

17 Ibid.

18 According to the report of the Local Council meeting, Archives of Biserica Albă/ Bela Crkva.

19 According to the report of the Local Council meeting, Archives of Biserica Albă/ Bela Crkva.

20 According to the report of the Secondary School, 1858–59.

21 According to the report of the Secondary School, 1868–69.

22 *Werschetz Geburgsbote* (1870), no. 37.

23 Ibid.

24 According to the Report of the Secondary School, 1888.

25 Ibid.

26 For the contract, which was signed in 1892, see G. Gojkov, *Vršačka gimnazija između dva rata (The High School of Vršac in the Interwar Period)* (Belgrade, 1979).

27 According to the Report of the Secondary School, 1888.

28 *Werschez Geburgsbote* (1890), no. 12.

29 N. Gavrilović, *Vršačka učiteljska škola u doba Srpskog vojvodstva i tamiškog Banata (1849–1860) (The Vršac Teacher-Training College during the Serbian Voivodeship and the Banat of Temes, 1849–1860)* (Vršac, 2006), pp. 27–36.

30 Ibid.

31 Ibid.

32 Ibid.

33 Ibid.

34 Loga was the only teacher who taught, in both Romanian and Serbian, the same disciplines that were included in the curriculum of the Sombor and Arad teacher-training colleges, after the courses were moved to Caransebeș. See ibid. p. 21.

35 For more about Romanian and Serbian schooling, see Bengin, *Obrazovanje učitelja* and G. Popi, *Školovanje učitelja i vaspitača na rumunskom nastavnom jeziku u Vršcu (The Training of Teachers in the Romanian Language in Vršac)* (Vršac, 2006).

36 For more on the subject, see Gavrilović, *Vršačka učiteljska škola*, passim.

37 Ibid.

38 R. Gava, *Apostol ljubavi (The Apostle of Love)*, vol. ii. 1931–2002 (Bela Crkva, 2002).

Chapter 13

1 Miodrag Milin, '*Între unitarism şi federalizare:* Dileme sârbeşti din veacul al XIX-lea' ('Between Unitarianism and Federalisation: Serbian Dilemmas in the Nineteenth Century', in Teodor Pavel (ed.), *Opţiuni politice la popoarele central-est europene în secolul al XIX-lea (Political Options of the Central and Eastern European Countries in the Nineteenth Century)* (Cluj-Napoca, 2006), pp. 159–66.

2 David Mackenzie, *Ilija Garasanin: Balkan Bismark* (New York, 1985); Vladimir Stojancević (ed.), *Ilija Garasanin 1812.–1874.: Medjunarodni naucni skup 9. i 10. Decembar 1987 (Ilija Garašanin 1812–1874: The International Scientific Sessions, 9–10 December 1987)* (Belgrade, 1991); see the Romanian translation by M. Milin, 'Sârbii şi croaţii (Ilija Garašanin, *Nacertanije-Plan: Programul politicii naţionale şi al celei externe a Serbiei la finele anului 1844*)' ('Serbs and Croats (Ilija Garašanin, *The Nacertanije Plan: The Serbian National and Foreign Policy Programme at the End of 1844*)'), in Teodor Pavel (ed.), *Gândire politică şi imaginar social la popoarele central-est europene: Secolul al XIX-lea. Antologie de texte (Political Thought and Social Imagination in the Central-East European People: 19th Century. Anthology of Texts)* (Cluj-Napoca, 2005), pp. 345–59.

3 Rados Ljusić, *Knjiga o Nacertaniju: Nacionalnii drzavni program Knezevine Srbije, 1844 (The Book about Nacertanije: The National State Programme of Serbian Principality, 1844)* (Belgrade, 1993).

4 Josip Juraj Strossmayer and Franjo Racki, *Politicki spisi (Political Records)*, ed. Vladimir Koščak (Zagreb, 1971).

5 Vaša Cubrilović, *Istorija politicke misli u Srbiji XIX. Veka (The History of Political Thought in 19th-Century Serbia)* (Belgrade, 1982), p. 147.

6 A.J.P. Taylor, *The Habsburg Monarchy 1809–1918: A History of the Austrian Empire and Austria-Hungary* (1948; Harmondsworth, 1990), pp. 66–9.

7 Tamás Katona, 'Conflicte naţionale în 1848–1849' ('National Conflicts in

1848–1849'), in Bárdi Nándor (ed.), *Transilvania văzută în publicistica istorică maghiare* (*Transylvania as Seen in Hungarian Historical Journalism*) (Miercurea-Ciuc, 1999), pp. 183 ff. Cf. Vladimir Stojancevic (ed.), *Istorija srpskog naroda* (*The History of the Serbian People*), vol. v/2 (Belgrade, 1981), pp. 45 ff.

8 Vasilije Krestić, *Istorija srpske stampe u Ugarskoj: 1791–1914* (*The History of the Serbian Press in Hungary: 1791–1914*) (Novi Sad, 1980), pp. 61 ff.

9 Stojancevic (ed.), *Istorija srpskog naroda*, vol. v/2, p. 46.

10 Mihailo Polit-Desancić, *Kako je to bilo u nas Srba u Buni godine 1848* (*How Was the Revolution of 1848 for Us Serbians?*), ed. Dr Slavko Gavrilović (Novi Sad, 1996), pp. 63–64.

11 For the cultural importance of the metropolitan Stefan Stratimirovic, see Victor Neumann, 'Principii luministe şi diferenţialism etnocultural: Opera cărturarului Ştefan Stratimirovici – mitropolit al ortodocşilor din Imperiul Habsburgic' ('Enlightenment Principles and Ethnocultural Differentialism: The Work of Scholar Ştefan Stratimirovici – Metropolitan of the Orthodox Church in the Habsburg Empire'), in Neumann (ed.), *Identitate şi cultură: Studii privind istoria Banatului* (*Identity and Culture: Studies upon the History of the Banat*) (Bucharest, 2009), pp. 38–47.

12 Polit-Desancić, *Kako je to bilo u nas Srba u Buni godine 1848*, pp. 64–65.

13 Ibid., p. 65.

14 I.D. Suciu, *Revoluţia de la 1848–1849 în Banat* (*The Revolution of 1848–1849 in the Banat*) (Bucharest, 1968), pp. 54–55.

15 *Transylvanian Gazette*, no. 26 (29 March 1848), p. 109 ('The Romanians and Serbs of Hungary'); Suciu, *Revoluţia de la 1848–1849 în Banat*, p. 55.

16 Slavko Gavrilović, 'Ilija Garasanin i madjari revolucionarne 1848–1849 godine' ('Ilija Garaşanin and Hungarians during the Revolutionary Years 1848–1849'), in Stojancević (ed.), *Ilija Garašanin (1812–1874)*, pp. 209–24. According to Gavrilović, a constant in Garašanin's behaviour in these difficult circumstances, which he successfully confronted, can be expressed by the slogan 'Hodi mudro, ne pogini ludo!' ('Walk wisely, don't get mad!').

17 Stojancevic (ed.), *Istorija srpskog naroda*, vol. v/2, pp. 55 ff.; D. J. Popović, *Srbi u Vojvodini* (*The Serbs of Voivodina*), vol. iii (Novi Sad, 1963), pp. 216–17; D. Pavlović, *Srbija i srpski pokret u Juznoj Ugarskoj 1848.i 1849* (*Serbia and the Serbian Movement in Southern Hungary 1848–1849*) (Belgrade, 1904), pp. 11 ff.

18 Victor Neumann, '*Temeswarer Zeitung* şi propagarea civismului Kakaniei' ('*Temeswarer Zeitung* and the Propagation of Civicism in the Dual Monarchy'), in id. (ed.), *Identitate şi cultură*, pp. 77–88.

19 Johann N. Preyer, *Monografia oraşului liber crăiesc Timişoara* (*Monograph on the Royal Free City of Timişoara*), trans. Adam Mager and Eleonora Pascu (Timişoara, 1995), pp. 213 ff.; Nicolae Ilieşiu, *Timişoara: Monografie istorică* (*Timişoara: Historic Monograph*), ed. Petru Ilieşu (Timişoara, 2003), pp. 96–99.

20 Samu Borovszky, *Temes varmegye* (Budapest, 1911), pp. 275–6; Preyer, *Monografia*, pp. 213 ff.

21 Preyer, *Monografia*, p. 214.

22 Stojancevic (ed.), *Istorija srpskog naroda*, vol. v/2, pp. 57–59.

23 Polit-Desancic, *Kako je to bilo u nas Srba u Buni godine 1848*, p. 68.

24 Jovan Hadžic-Svetić was the main exponent of the 'Orthodox' current, which linked the destiny of Serbian culture and the evolution of the Serbian language to the Slavic tradition, strongly opposing the language modernisation suggested by Vuk Karadžić. He was also a founding member of the Matica srspka academic society, along with Sava Tekelija from Arad and other Serbian pioneers from Hungary. See Zivan Milisavac, *Istorija Matice srpske* (*History of the Serbian Matrix*), vol. i. 1826–1864 (Novi Sad, 1985).

25 The contradictions regarding issues of identity were just beginning; the sociopolitical vocabulary, institutions and actions demonstrated that 1848 was not about ethnonational disputes but about some leaders' aspirations to create their own hierarchy within the great imperial hierarchy. The terms 'ethnonation' and 'nation' do not cover the social-identity themes of the time; instead, 'cultural-linguistic community' or 'religious commu-

nity' seem much closer. See Victor Neumann, *Neam, popor sau naţiune: Despre identităţile politice europene (Community, People or Nation: About European Political Identities)* (2nd edn., Bucharest, 2005), pp. 87–101, 127–45, 147–80; id., *Conceptul de naţiune la români şi unguri (The Concept of Nation to Hungarians and Romanians)* (Iaşi, 2013), pp. 16–24, 25–43, 44–54.

26 Stojancevic (ed.), *Istorija srpskog naroda*, vol. v/2, pp. 60–61.

27 Ibid.; Polit-Desancic, *Kako je to bilo u nas Srba u Buni godine 1848*, p. 98.

28 S. Kaper and S. Zdravkovic, *Srpski pokret u juznoj Ugarskoj 1848 (The Serbian Movement in Southern Hungary in 1848)*, vol. i (Belgrade, 1870), p. 93; Jovan Radonic, *Slike iz istorije i knjizevnosti (Images from History and Literature)* (Belgrade, 1938), p. 333.

29 In the press article 'Epistola unui timişorean către altul îndepărtat' ('Letter of a Man from Timișoara to a Distant Other'), cited in Suciu, *Revoluţia de la 1848–1849 în Banat*, pp. 64–65.

30 Ibid.; Stojancevic (ed.), *Istorija srpskog naroda*, vol. v/2, p. 65.

31 Suciu, *Revoluţia de la 1848–1849 în Banat*, p. 66.

32 Ibid., pp. 83–85.

33 Stojancevic (ed.), *Istorija srpskog naroda*, vol. v/2, p. 65.

34 Suciu, *Revoluţia de la 1848–1849 în Banat*, pp. 69–72.

35 Stojancevic (ed.), *Istorija srpskog naroda*,vol. v/2. pp. 69–70.

36 Polit-Desancic, *Kako je to bilo u nas Srba u Buni godine 1848*, pp. 114–16; Gavrilovic, *Srem pre i u toku Srpskog pokreta*, pp. 150–70.

37 Suciu, *Revoluţia de la 1848–1849 în Banat*, p. 110; see also Nicolae Bocşan and Valeriu Leu, *Revoluţia de la 1848 din Transilvania în memorialistică (The Revolution of 1848 in Transylvania in Memoirs)* (Cluj-Napoca, 2000), p. 19 (Kossuth wrote: 'for Romanians to have a captain in Caraș, undermines the unity of the country, which is, in fact, the only excuse for the Serbian revolt').

38 The Hungarian recruitment commission started its activity in the Banat in June. Until then, there had been a reserved attitude among Romanians towards enrolling. Thus, at the Caraș commission, of the 437 conscripted, 283 were Hungarian and German and only 153 Romanians, which was disproportionate in relation to the population, whose great majority was Romanian (I. Boroş, '*Evenimentele revoluţiei de libertate din anii 1848-1849 desfăşurate în Lugoj (Events of the Freedom Revolution of 1848-1849 in Lugoj)* (Lugoj, 1927), pp. 33–34).

39 Suciu, *Revoluţia de la 1848–1849 în Banat*, pp. 98–113; Sëbo Vukovics, *Emlékiratai Magyarországon való bujdosása és számüzetésének idejéből, sajtó alá rendezte Bessenyei Ferencz (Memoirs from Exile in Hungary under the direction of Bessenyei Ferencz)* (Budapest, 1894); Atanasie Șandor, 'Studiu asupra evenimentelor de peste munți din anii 1848–1849, cu nararea celor întâmplate în părțile Aradului' ('Study on the Events Across the Mountains from 1848 to 1849, with a Narrative of Events in Parts of Arad'), in Bocșan and Leu (eds.), *Memorialistica Revoluției de la 1848*, pp. 123–37; Partenie Gruescu, 'Evenimentele anului 1848 și 1849 prin ținutul Făgetului' ('The Events of 1848 and 1849 in *Făget* County'), in Bocșan and Leu (eds.), *Memorialistica Revoluției de la 1848*, pp. 138–51; Dimitrie Petrovici Stoicescu, 'Curgerea întâmplărilor subscrisului în timpul revoluției maghiare' ('The Flow of Events during the Hungarian Revolution'), in Bocșan and Leu (eds.), *Memorialistica Revoluției*, pp. 152–58.

40 Kaper and Zdravkovic, *Srpski pokret u juznoj Ugarskoj 1848*, vol. i, pp. 98–99; S. (Felix) Milleker, *Povesnica Vrsca (The Story of the Royal Free City of Vršac)* (1886), vol. ii, pp. 14–17; V. Krestic, 'Srpski vojni logor kod Perleza u 1848. godini' ('The Serbian Military Camp from Perlas in 1848'), *Zbornik Matice srpske za drustvene nauke*, vol. 29 (1961), pp. 34–36; Stojancevic (ed.), *Istorija srpskog naroda*, vol. v/2, pp. 76–78.

41 Mircea Măran, 'Documente despre românii din Banatul de vest în timpul Revoluției de la 1848–1849' ('Documents concerning Romanians in Western Banat during the 1848–1849 Revolution'), in Valeriu Leu, Carmen Albert and Dumitru Țeicu (eds.), *Studii bănățene (Banatian Studies)* (Timișoara, 2007), pp. 293–304.

42 Radu Flora, *Relațiile sârbo-române: Noi contribuții (Serbian-Romanian Relations: New*

Contributions) (Panciova, 1968), pp. 97–101; Nikola Gavrilovic, *Srpsko-rumunsko klirikalno uciliste u Vrscu, 1822–1867* (*The Serbian-Romanian Clerical School of Vrasac, 1822–1867*) (Novi Sad, 1983), p. 177.

43 R. Popovic-Petković, 'Dokumenti o srbijanskim dobrovoljcima u Vojvodini 1848–1849' ('Documents Regarding the Serbian Volunteers from Voivodina 1848–1849'), *Istrazivanja*, no. 2 (1973), pp. 400–10; M. Tomandl, 'Srpski vojni logor i bitka kod Perleza 2. septembra 1848. godine' ('The Serbian Military Camp from Perlas and the Battle of 2 September 1848'), *Zbornik Matice srpske za drustvene nauke*, vol. 13 (1956), pp. 135–40; Krestić, 'Srpski vojni logor kod Perleza u 1848. godini', p. 39; Kaper and Zdravkovic, *Srpski pokret u juznoj Ugarskoj 1848*, vol. ii, pp. 22–29.

44 Preyer, *Monografia*, p. 215.

45 Ibid., p. 214; Rudolf Gräf, *Timişoara sub asediu: Jurnalul feldmareşalului Gerge v. Rukawina (aprilie–august 1849): Contribuţie documentară* (*Timişoara under Siege: Field Marshal Gerge v. Rukawina's Journal, April–August 1849: Documentary Contribution*) (Cluj-Napoca, 2008).

46 A. Marchescu, *Grănicerii bănăţeni şi Comunitatea de avere* (*The Banatian Border Guards*) Caransebeş, 1941, pp. 211–23.

47 This is the estimate of the mayor at that time, Johann N. Prayer. General Commander Rukavina's Journal mentions 6,000 civil inhabitants in the city and 12,000–14,000 in its suburbs, see Gräf, *Timişoara sub asediu*, p. 102.

48 H. Geibel, *Feldzug in Ungarn und Siebenburgen im Sommer des Jahres 1849* (Pesth, 1850), pp. 372–85; Preyer, *Monografia*, pp. 214–16; Suciu, *Revoluţia de la 1848–1849 în Banat*, pp. 221–31; Gräf, *Timişoara sub asediu*, pp. 99–164.

49 Kaper and Zdravkovic, *Srpski pokret u juznoj Ugarskoj 1848*, vol. ii, pp. 41–43; Stojancevic (ed.), *Istorija srpskog naroda*, vol. v/2, p. 87.

50 Suciu, *Revoluţia de la 1848–1849 în Banat*, p. 42.

51 S. Gavrilović, *Ilija Garašanin i Madjari*, pp. 216–17; J. Thim, *A magyarországi 1848–49 iki szerb fölkelés története* (*A Hungarian History of the Serbian Revolt of 1848–1849*), vol. ii (Budapest, 1930), pp. 606–9.

52 Jean Berenger, *Istoria Imperiului Habsburgilor, 1273–1918* (*History of the Habsburg Empire, 1723–1918*) (Bucharest, 2000), pp. 414–15; Jean-Paul Bled, *Franz Joseph* (Bucharest, 2002), pp. 97–103.

53 V. Bogdanov, *Ustanak Srba u Voivodini i Madjarska revolucija* (*The Revolt of Serbs in the Voivodina and the Hungarian Revolution of 1848–1849*) (Subotica, 1929), 161–63; Ljubivoje Cerović, *Srbi u Rumuniji* (Novi Sad, 1997), pp. 200–4. Professor Cerović presents the structure of the general Council of Voivodina, established by Patriarch Rajačić on 16/28 February 1849 at Timişoara at pp. 202–3.

54 Boroş, *Evenimentele*, p. 45.

55 On 14/26 April 1849, the Hungarian Diet proclaimed the independence of Hungary, Kossuth being appointed governor.

56 Jovan Radonić, 'Patrijarh Josif Rajačić i general Djuro Rukavina' ('Patriarch Josif Rajačić and General Djuro Rukavina'), *Glas Srpske akademije nauka*, no. 193 (1949), pp. 143–68.

57 Cerović, *Srbi u Rumuniji*, p. 203; J. Savković, 'Nacrt ustava za Vojvodinu Srbiju 1849 godine' ('The Draft Constitution of 1849 for Serbian Voivodina'), *Zbornik Matice srpske za drustvene nauke*, nos. 13–14 (1956), pp. 159–66; id., 'Ferdinand Mayerhofer u srpskom pokretu 1848–1849 godine' ('Ferdinand Mayerhofer during the Serbian Movement of 1848–1849'), *Zbornik*, no. 17 (1957), pp. 76–95; Kaper and Zdravkovic, *Srpski pokret u juznoj Ugarskoj 1848*, vol. ii, pp. 68–71.

58 Gräf, *Timişoara sub asediu*, *passim*.

59 B. Schiff, *Die letzte Belagerung Temesvars* (Timişoara, 1929), *passim*.

60 Gräf, *Timişoara sub asediu*, p. 150.

61 The union of Transylvania and Hungary was enacted by the Diet of Bratislava on 18 March and legalised by the Transylvanian Diet at Cluj on 30 May 1848.

62 Liviu Maior, 'Revoluţia de la 1848–1849 în Transilvania' ('The Revolution of 1848–1849 in Transylvania'), in Ioan-Aurel Pop, Thomas Nägler and Magyari Andras (eds.), *Istoria Transilvaniei*, vol. iii. *De la 1711 până la 1918* (*The History of Transylvania*, vol. iii. *1771–1918*) (Cluj-Napoca, 2008), pp. 369–70.

63 I.D. Suciu, *Monografia Mitropoliei Banatului (The Monograph of the Banat Metropolitan Church)* (Timişoara, 1977), pp. 139–66.

64 N. Bocşan, *Contribuţii la istoria iluminismului românesc (Contributions to the History of the Romanian Enlightenment)* (Timișoara, 1986), pp. 310–61.

65 Katona, 'Conflicte naționale în 1848–1849', p. 186.

66 Ibid., p. 187.

67 Pop, Nägler and Andras (eds.), *Istoria Transilvaniei*, vol. iii, pp. 360–61; for the text *Pentru unirea tuturor românilor din statele Austriei într-o singură naţiune, de sine stătătoare (For the Unification of All Romanians from the States of Austria into a Single Nation in Its Own Right)*, see Cornelia Bodea, *1848 la Români: O istorie în date şi mărturii (1848 for Romanians: A History of Data and Testimonies)*, vol. ii (Bucharest, 1982), pp. 960–65.

68 Srem County is the new name given by the Crown. However, we will continue to use the popular name of Voivodina.

Chapter 14

1 Peter F. Sugar and Ivo J. Lederer (eds.), *Nationalism in Eastern Europe* (Far Eastern and Russian Institute Publications on Russia and Eastern Europe, no. 1; Seattle, 1969).

2 Victor Neumann, 'Peculiarities of the Tranaslation and Adaptation of the Concept of Nation in East-Central Europe: The Hungarian and Romanian Cases in the Nineteenth Century', *Contributions to the History of Concepts*, vol. 7, no. 1 (Summer 2012), pp. 72–102.

3 A. Urban, 'Agitáció a magyar köztársaságert 1848–1849 ben' ('The Movements for the Proclamation of the Hungarian Republic in 1848–1849', *Századok* (Review of the Hungarian Historical Society), vol. 2 (1999), pp. 221–52. See also Alexandru Farkas Bölöni, *Utazás Eszak Amerikában (Journey to North America)* (Cluj, 1835).

4 Lajos Kossuth, 'Nyelvkérdés' ('The Question of Language'), in *Válogatott Munkái (Selected Works)*, ed. and introd. Ferencz Kossuth (Budapest, n.d.), p. 65. See id., Discourse on 14 April 1848, in *Őszes Művei (Complete Works)*, ed István Barta, vol. xv (Budapest, 1953).

5 András Gergely, 'Kossuth nemzetiségipolitikája 1847–1853' ('Kossuth's Policy on Nationalities: 1847–1853'), *Tiszatáj*, vol. 9 (2002), pp. 78–84.

6 I. Széchenyi, *Napló (Journal)*, ed. Ambrus Oltványi (Budapest, 1978).

7 François Fejtő, *Requiem pour un empire défunt: Histoire de la destruction de l'Autriche-Hongrie* (Paris, 1992).

8 See Victor Neumann, 'Intercultural Pedagogy as an Alternative to a Monoculturally Oriented Education: The Case of Romania', in Kenneth Cushner (ed.), *International Perspectives on Intercultural Education* (Kent, Ohio, 1998).

9 Victor Neumann, 'Die bürgerliche Kultur in Siebenbürgen und im Banat: Die Rolle Temeswars in den politischen Umgestaltungsprozessen von Dezember 1989', *Halbjahresschrift für südosteuropäische Geschichte, Literatur und Politik*, vol. 11, no. 1 (1999), pp. 38–51.

10 See D. Prodan, *Răscoala lui Horea (The Uprising of Horea)* (Bucharest, 1979), pp. 13–85.

11 F.O. Salzberger, *Translating the Enlightenment: Scottish Civic Discourse in Eighteenth-Century Germany* (Oxford, 1995).

12 S. Berstein and P. Milza, *Histoire de l'Europe* (Paris, 1992).

13 B. Jelavich, *History of the Balkans* (Oxford, 1997). See also István Bibó, *A kelet-europai kisállamok nyomorusága*, cited from the French edn., *Misère des petits états d'Europe de l'Est*, trans. from Hungarian by Gyõrgy Kassai (Paris, 1981).

14 *A XIX. század uralkodó eszméinek befolyása az álladalomra* (Vienna and Pest, 1851, 1854).

15 See József Eötvös, *Ueber die Gleichberechtigung der Nationalitaeten in Oesterreich (On the Equal Rights of the Nationalities in Austria)* (Pest, 1850). See also the first booklet dedicated by Eötvös to the nationalities topic: 'A zsidók emancipátioja' ('The Emancipation of the Jews'), *Budapesti Szemle*, vol 1, no. 2 (1840). In this respect see also Victor Neumann, Chapter 15 in this volume.

16 M. Winock, *Nationalisme, fascisme, antisémitisme en France* (Paris, 1990).

17 For details, see Jenő Szűcs, *Nation und Geschichte: Studien (Nation and History: Studies)* (Cologne, 1981; Istvan Zimonyi, 'The

Concept of Nation as Interpreted by Jenő Szűcs', in *Forms of Identity: Definitions and Changes* (Szeged, 1994), pp. 1–8. See also P. Hanák, *Ungarn in der Donaumonarchie* (*Hungary in the Dual Monarchy*) (Budapest, 1984); id., *A dualizmus korának történeti problémái* (*Historical Problems of the Dual Monarchy*) (Budapest, 1971).

18 G. Vermes, *István Tisza: The Liberal Vision and Conservative Statecraft of a Magyar Nationalist* (East European Monographs; New York, 1985).

19 See O. Jászi, *Revolution and Counterrevolution in Hungary* (New York, 1969).

20 Ibid.

21 Vera Ranki, *The Politics of Inclusion and Exclusion: Jews and Nationalism in Hungary* (Sydney, 1999).

22 Richard Evans, *Rethinking German History: Nineteenth Century Germany and the Origins of the Third Reich* (London, 1987).

23 See Aurel C. Popovici, *Stat şi naţiune: Statele Unite ale Austriei Mari* (*State and Nation: The United States of Greater Austria*), trans. from the German into Romanian by Petre Pandrea (Bucharest, 1939).

24 *Diaries of Josef Pekar 1916–1933* (Prague, 2000).

25 See T.G. Masaryk's 'New Europe', in Kevin Wilson and Jan van der Dussen (eds.), *The History of the Idea of Europe* (London and New York, 1995), 92–95. 'For Masaryk, modernisation was essentially a moral and political process towards individual and national self-fulfilment. In the spirit of the poet and philosopher J.G. Herder (1744–1803) he saw the nation as the "natural" unit for the organization of society, and he wanted the state to be mere servant of the individual and the nation ... the exclusive focus on the notion of national independence compelled him to postpone his supranational schemes for conflict resolution' (p. 95).

26 R. Portal, *Les Slaves: Peuples et nations* (Paris, 1965).

27 Louis Dumont, *Essay on Individualism: Modern Ideology in Anthropological Perspective.* (Chicago, 1992), p. 130.

Chapter 15

1 This chapter was first published in Victor Neumann, *Istoria evreilor din Banat: O mărturie a multi- şi interculturalităţii Europei Central-Orientale* (Bucharest, 1999); see also the English edition, *The End of a History: The Jews of Banat from the Beginning to Nowadays* (Bucharest, 2006). I wanted to illustrate the cultural-linguistic and religious-communitarian diversity of the people of the Banat with a chapter dedicated to the most remarkable alterity in the region (and in Europe in general), namely that of the Jews. I was interested in presenting Jewish emancipation and integration within the social, economic and cultural life of East-Central Europe using the Banat as a case study. I have also considered the importance of the relationship between Christianity and Judaism in the Banat, and the way in which the secular intellectualism of the nineteenth century was related to the process of emancipation and integration. This chapter contributes to a more accurate understanding of the regional identity of the modern Banat.

2 Brukenthal Library of Sibiu, nos. 11.603 and 12.684.

3 The Library of the Protestant Theological Institute of Cluj, no. 4721; the Teleki–Bolyai Library of Târgu-Mureş (Teleki fonds), no. 02039 b4.

4 Brukenthal Library of Sibiu, no. VI, 9719.

5 Central University Library of Cluj, no. 28.249.

6 Ibid., no. 30.440; Brukenthal Library of Sibiu, no. VI, 13.579.

7 Brukenthal Library of Sibiu, no. VI, 12.844.

8 Ibid., 12.467. Although I have mentioned only a few of Mendelssohn's works (all in the Princeps edition) that are preserved in the old collections of libraries in Transylvania, they demonstrate a constant interest in Mendelssohn within the intellectual media – especially Protestant but also Catholic – of Central and Eastern Europe. I would like to thank my colleague Eugen Glück for his kindness in indicating these archive materials. I would like to add that during the nineteenth century, Mendelssohn's writings permeated Christian Orthodox circles; for example, the famous book *Jerusalem oder über religiöse Macht und Judentum* preserved in the collection of Metropolitan Bishop Nifon of Ungro-Vlahia (Wallachia), today in the fonds of the Romanian Academy Library in Bucharest.

9 'Az aradi izr. hitközség a XIX *évszázadban*' ('The Jewish Community of Arad during the Nineteenth Century'), manuscript edited in 1902 for the internal use of the community. See the Arad Jewish Community Library (henceforth ACEA), File no. 67, 1907/1911, fos. 1–10.

10 Moshe Carmilly-Weinberger, *Istoria evreilor din Transilvania (1623–1944) (The History of the Jews of Transylvania, 1623–1944)* (Bucharest, 1994), p. 110. See also Ladislau Gyémánt, *Evreii din Transilvania în epoca emancipării / The Jews of Transylvania in the Age of Emancipation (1790–1867)* (Bucharest, 2000).

11 See the explanation of this dispute in Moshe Carmilly-Weinberger, *Censorship and Freedom of Expression in Jewish History* (New York, 1977).

12 Among the works by Chorin with reform as a theme, we can mention *Shirjon Kaskasim* (Prague, 1799); *Emek Hashaveh* (Prague, 1803); *Igeret Elassaf oder Sendschreiben eines Afrikanischen Rabbi an seinen Collegen in Europa mit einem Vorworte* (Prague, 1826); *Davor Beito* (Vienna, 1820); *Jeled Zektmim* (Vienna, 1839). In *Jeled Zekunim* Chorin tells the story of his life and explains the content of the religious reforms as he sees it. For confirmation of organ music inside the Neolog synagogue of Arad (where Chorin was practising), see the request of the organ player Moricz Klein addressed to the community regarding his employment; cf. ACEA, File no. 5, fo. 74 (1845).

13 According to ACEA, File no. 67, 1902/1911, fos. 1–10. The archives of the community of Arad include many requests addressed to the Royal County Council for building a synagogue; the procedure is always based on the organisational rules and with the obligation to respect the Constitution (according to ACEA, File no. 2, 1800–29, fos. 28–31, copy). In 1822 the council gave a favourable answer to the request to build a reformed synagogue (ibid., fos. 38–39); written in German and Latin, the document is dated Arad, 22 January 1822 and signed by Emericus Gombos on behalf of the leadership of the county administration. Another document reveals that in 1820–21 9,512 guldens was collected (representing the contribution of 104 people) to build the Neolog synagogue (ibid., fos. 44–51).

14 Ibid., pp. 43–45 (copy of the document written in Latin).

15 Ibid., pp. 125–28; a letter register of the Jewish community of Arad, where Jewish institutions and societies are mentioned.

16 Many of the sources in the archives of the communities of Arad and Timişoara indicate the aspect of subordination to local authorities, but especially that of connections between communities throughout the Banat and the plain of Arad. For example, the statutes of small communities in the archives of Timişoara and Arad are conceived according to the *Landesrabbinate* in the capital of the Banat. The documents also recall elements of administration that show a mutual dependence or, at least, influence: rabbis meet and sometimes exchange letters, and take religious or administrative measures by common agreement. There is proof that Jewish representatives from the counties of Arad, Timiş and Caraş-Severin were members of the enlarged county council that met annually starting in 1888. See, for example, *Jegyzökönyve hitközségeire kiterjedő (Report of the Jewish Enlarged Community Council of the Counties)* (Temesvár, 1901) (the council was led at that time by Sternthall Salamon, representing the entire region). The commemorations of some personalities reflect not only conventional meetings, but also mutual recognition. See the very important document in ACEA, File 3, fo. 250 (1859), an edifying synthesis of the speeches made at the burial of Chief Rabbi David H. Oppenheimer by the rabbis of Szeged, Arad, Lugoj and Theresiopol (Vinga). The document was cited for the first time in Dr Moritz Löwy, *Skizzen zur Geschichte der Juden in Temesvár bis zum Jahre 1865* (Szeged, 1890), pp. 82–83.

17 ACEA, File no. 2, 1800–29, fos. 125–28 (1829). The document also gives details about organisation. For school, as for the established societies, there were financial statutes independent of each other. The school was placed close to the synagogue. That is why money earmarked for synagogues was also used for schools. The capital was managed by a representative of the community named Moses Hirschl, initially benefiting from the sum of 2,400 florins. In the case of societies, statues stated who could be a member and what rights and obligations a member had; i.e. the sum every member had to pay for the fund of the society. A president,

vice-president, cashier and secretary were appointed to manage the society.

18 ACEA, File no. 3, 1830–39, fos. 125–26 (1833).

19 Şimand was a settlement situated 25 km from Arad, where a Jewish community was established during the nineteenth century and the first half of the twentieth. After the Second World War, the Jewish community was dissolved and there are no Jews there today. However, a Jewish cemetery has been preserved in Şimand in relatively good condition – testimony to the active presence of Jews elsewhere in the region.

20 Carmilly-Weinberger, *Istoria*, p. 126.

21 See, in this sense, Peter Ujváry, *Zsidó Lexikon* (Budapest, 1929), pp. 170–71. In the recent German lexicons, Chorin is considered to be a partisan of radical reforms; see *Neues Lexikon des Judentums*, ed. Prof. Dr Julius H. Schoeps (Gütersloh and Munich, 1992), p. 95.

22 See the documentary study by Moshe Carmilly-Weinberger, 'Jewish Writers Confronted by Censorship in the Habsburg Empire and Romania in the Eighteenth–Nineteenth Century', in *Judaica*, vol. ii (Cluj, 1993), pp. 30–31.

23 Carmilly-Weinberger, *Istoria*, p. 127. The author shows that many of them suffered martyrdom, together with their communities, during deportation in 1944. For their activity, see id., *The Rabbinical Seminary of Budapest 1877–1977* (New York, 1986). The rabbis of the Banat – unlike those from Transylvania – continued to practise in more languages during the years of the Dual Monarchy and in the twentieth century. Among several remarkable examples, we can mention the rabbi of Arad, Ludovic Vagvölgy (1906–41), and the rabbi of Timişoara, Dr Miksa Drechsler (1910–66).

24 István Bibó, *Misère des petits états d'Europe de l'Est*, trans. from Hungarian by György Kassai (Paris, 1986).

25 I analysed the causes of anti-Semitism in Romanian politics during the second half of the nineteenth century in Victor Neumann, 'Repere culturale ale antisemitismului din România secolului al XIX-lea' ('Cultural Landmarks of Anti-Semitism in Nineteenth-Century Romania'), *Society and Culture* (review of the Romanian Academy Institute of Social Theory), nos. 3 and 4 (1994); repr. in *Ideea care ucide: Dimensiunile ideologiei legionare* (*The Idea that Kills: The Dimensions of Legionary Ideology*) (Bucharest, 1994), pp. 35–54.

26 Cited in Friedrich Gottas, *Ungarn im Zeitalter, des Hochliberalismus: Studien zur Tisza–Ära (1875–1890)* (Vienna, 1976), p. 164. For the same issue of emancipation, see also Lajos Venetianer, *A magyar zsidoság története* (*Torture of the Hungarian Jew*) (Budapest, 1922), p. 139.

27 I also studied an article by the historian William Marin (former professor at the West University of Timişoara), entitled 'Emanciparea civică a evreilor bănăţeni şi transilvăneni în secolele XVIII–XIX' ('The Civic Emancipation of Jews from the Banat and Transylvania during the Eighteenth and Nineteenth Centuries') (also presented as a scientific paper at the annual university session of the West University of Timişoara, 27–29 May 1983). I would like to thank Professor Marin for the numerous documentary and bibliographical details he generously offered. In some articles that I consider rewarding for their documentation, and also in his book *Unirea Banatului cu România* (*The Union of the Banat and Romania*) (Timişoara, 1978), Marin highlighted unknown facts about the history of the Banatian Jews. I am grateful to him for his important encouragement during the years of the National Communist totalitarian regime and also for recommending me for a bursary from the Friedrich Ebert Foundation of Bonn, which enabled me to enhance my information about the history of Jews from the Banat.

28 Cited in Bela Bernstein, *Az 1848–49 – iki magyar szabadságharz és a zsidók* (*The Fight for Freedom of Hungarians and Jews during the Revolution of 1848/49*) (Budapest, 1898), p. 41.

29 *Pesti Hirlap*, 7 April 1848.

30 *Der ungarischer Israelit*, 15 April 1848. The news is also reproduced in *Temesvarer Wochenblatt*, 22 April 1848, p. 136, without mentioning Jewish participation and with an incorrect transcription of Eftimie Murgu's name (Emanuel instead of Eftimie). This shows that in the German journalist circles of Timişoara neither the Jewish movement nor the Romanian

cultural and political personalities were well known – or perhaps that events that did not suit the officials were ignored. However, it was a turning point, felt as such throughout the whole empire. The appearance of a great number of journals facilitated better circulation of information. For the Jews of the Banat, *Der Südungar* (Timişoara) and *Der Patriot* (Arad) became important. For the Romanian revolutionaries in Caraş County (in the south of the Banat, with Lugoj as county seat), see the introductory study by historian I. D. Suciu, in Eftimie Murgu, *Scrieri* (*Writings*) (Bucharest, 1969), pp. 12–89. Murgu was investigated in 1845, and early in the following year he was brought under escort to Buda and taken to Neugebäude prison. The reasons given by the authorities were his actions of disturbance to state order, the fight for equal rights for the Romanian population, and the propagation a stream of ideas hostile to the aristocracy in the Diet of Pest (the same diet that had rejected Jewish emancipation). The problems of 1848, and also during the whole century of nationalities, urge us to be more reticent about an excessive, exclusive approach on the basis of national identity or membership of a nationality, an approach that is still pursued by many Central and South-East European historians. Preferring to propagate national stereotypes, some of them neglect the ideas of social equality and fraternity, which are obviously as significant as national ones, as well as the fight for the right to civil representation within the leading forums. Social and economic emancipation, though carrying significant weight, is minimised by historians to the benefit of national emancipation. I am inclined to believe that the historiographies from this part of the continent could play an important role in changing mentalities if they would only abandon the national-nationalist speculation that served the authoritarian and totalitarian regimes of the twentieth century. See Victor Neumann, *Neam, Popor sau Naţiune? Despre identităţile politice europene* (*Community, People or Nation? On European Political Identities*) (2nd edn, Bucharest, 2005); id., 'Conceptul de totalitarism în limbajele social-politice româneşti' ('The Concept of Totalitarianism in Romanian Social and Political Idioms'), *Timpul* (*Time*), no. 1 (2010).

31 Bernstein, *Az 1848–49*, pp. 114–15 and 152–53. The information was also reproduced in Marin, 'Emanciparea civică'.

32 See Daniel Ehrmann, *Betrachtungen über jüdische Verhältnise* (Pest, 1841).

33 Elias Oesterreicher, *Der Jude in Ungarn* (Pest, 1842).

34 *Pesti Hírlap*, 3 May 1848.

35 Bernstein, *Az 1848/49*, pp. 259–60.

36 See István Széchenyi, *Közjóra való törekedések* (*Aspiration Towards the Public Good*), ed. Benkő Samu (Bucharest, 1981), pp. 213–31. Cf. Széchenyi, 'Discurs ţinut la şedinţa solemnă a Academiei Ungare de Ştiinţe din 27 noiembrie 1842' ('Speech Given at the Solemn Meeting of the Hungarian Academy of Sciences on 27 November 1842'), in Cornelia Bodea (ed.), *1848 la români: O istorie în date şi mărturii* (*1848 for Romanians: A History of Data and Testimonies*) (Bucharest, 1982), pp. 199–211.

37 Széchenyi, *Közjóra*; for an evaluation of his political thinking and the involvement of Central and South-Eastern European ideas and issues, see Victor Neumann, *Convergenţe spirituale: Studii privind relaţiile culturale şi politice în Europa centrală şi de sud-est între 1750 şi 1850* (*Spiritual Convergences: Studies on Cultural and Political Relations in Central and South-Eastern Europe between 1750 and 1850*) (Bucharest, 1986), pp. 84–101. Cf. id., *Tentaţia lui homo europaeus: Geneza ideilor moderne în Europa Centrală şi de Sud-Est* (*The Temptation of Homo Europeaus: The Genesis of Modern Ideas in Central and South-Eastern Europe*) (3rd edn., Iaşi, 2006).

38 See the new Hungarian edition, edited by Szigeti Gábor (Budapest, 1981).

39 Giuseppe di Eötvös, *Dissertazione sulla emancipazione degli Ebrei* (Pest, 1842), p. 3. I refer to this Italian edition because it was made available to me by the kindness of my colleague and friend Mihai Alin Gherman from the Romanian Academy Library, Cluj branch. Note that translation into Italian indicates the intention of the author to promote his ideas on Jewish emancipation outside Hungarian intellectual circles.

40 Ibid., p. 6.

41 Ibid., p. 9.

42 Ibid., pp. 19–20.

43 Ibid., pp. 47–59.

44 Ibid., pp. 70–73.

45 Neumann, *Neam, Popor sau Naţiune*, esp. pp. 47–85, 117–46, 147–77. Cf. id., 'Conceptul de totalitarism în limbajele social-politice româneşti' ('The Concept of Totalitarianism in the Romanian Sociopolitical Language'), *Timpul*, no.1 (2010), pp. 14–16.

46 Martin Philippson, *Neueste Geschichte des jüdischen Volkes*, vol. i (Leipzig, 1907), cited in Marin, 'Emanciparea civică', p. 5. See also Zsigmond Groszmann, 'Emáncipátio a magyar zsidók polgári egyenjogusitása' ('The Emancipation of Hungarian Jews as Citizens with Equal Right'), in Ujváry, *Zsidó Lexikon*, p. 224.

47 The Banat was known in that period as Delmagyarország (South Hungary).

48 ACET, File nos. 5-8, where the Statute of the Orthodox communities, status quo (Neolog) and status quo ante may be found. The Neolog community of Timişoara was the largest at the end of the nineteenth century. Things were similar in Arad and Lugoj, with a community of the same rite coordinating religious and administrative matters.

49 *Temesvarer Zeitung*, 25 January and 4 February 1868.

50 For a balanced overview of Hungary in the period 1879–1918, see Robert A. Kann, *A History of the Habsburg Empire 1526–1918* (Berkeley and Los Angeles, 1974), pp. 452–61. With regard to the trials for so-called ritual murder, see the most recent study which contains an analysis of the trial in Tiszaeszlár: Hilel J. Kieval, 'Antisémitisme ou savoir social? Sur la génèse du procès moderne pour meurtre rituel', *Annales*, no. 5 (September–October 1994), pp. 1091–1105.

51 Kieval, 'Antisémitisme ou savoir social?' pp. 1092–93.

52 This research was carried out in the Archives of Civil Status of the City Hall of Arad and Timişoara, Registry of Marriages, 1895–1940. The data shows that a percentage of the Jewish population accepted mixed marriages such as those with Roman Catholics, Protestants, Greek Catholics and Orthodox, although most continued the tradition of homogamous marriage.

Chapter 16

1 Béla Pukánszky and András Németh, *Neveléstörténet (The History of Education)* (Budapest, 1996); Károly Vörös, 'A modern értelmiség kezdetei Magyarországon' ('The Beginnings of Modern Intellectualism in Hungary'), in id., *Hétköznapok a polgári Magyarországon (Working Days in Civic Hungary)* (Budapest, 1992), pp. 24–25.

2 István Fenyő, 'Eötvös József politikaelméleti főműve, az uralkodó eszmék' ('József Eötvös's Masterpiece of Political Theory: The Dominant Ideas'), *Századok*, no. 6 (2002), pp. 1466–68.

3 Ibid., p. 1463.

4 On federalism and nationalism, see Victor Neumann, 'Federalism şi naţionalism: O perspectivă comparativă asupra teoriilor politice din Austro-Ungaria la 1900' ('Federalism and Nationalism: A Comparative Perspective on Political Theories in Austro-Hungary around 1900'), in id., *Ideologie şi fantasmagorie: Perspective comparative asupra istoriei gândirii politice în Europa Est-centrală (Ideology and Phantasmagory: Comparative Perspectives on the History and Political Thought of East-Central Europe)* (Iaşi, 2001), pp. 68–102.

5 Law XV of 1891, §§ 15, 16, 18.

6 Ibid., § 3.

7 Ibid., § 6, pp. 22–26.

8 While Caraş-Severin County had 2 towns with official local councils, 29 large communes, 31 small civil communes and 47 settlements with over 2,000 inhabitants, in Timiş county there were 202 large communes and 121 small communes, among which 70 had more than 2,000 inhabitants, while in Torontal there were 2 towns with official local councils, 169 large communes and 42 communes, 112 settlements with more than 2,000 inhabitants: *Révai Nagy Lexikona (Révai's Great Lexicon)* (Budapest, 1911–35), vol. xii, p. 266; vol. xviii, pp. 109, 366. Data appears in *Magyar Statisztikai Évkönyv (Hungarian Annual Statistics)*, NS vol. 1 (1893) p. 317; vol. 4 (1896), pp. 422–3; vol. 5 (1897), pp. 354–55; Ibid., vol. 6 (1898), pp. 312–13; vol. 10 (1902), p. 331; vol. 14 (1906), pp. 322, 327; vol. 19 (1911), p. 332; vol. 22 (1914), p. 244.

9 See references in n. 8.

10 József Bellai, *Temesvár szab. kir. város közművelődési intézményei* (*The Educational Institutions of the Royal Free City of Timişoara*) (Timişoara, 1904), pp. 22–23; Samu Borovszky (ed.), *Magyarország vármegyéi és városai* (*The Counties and Towns of Hungary*) (Budapest, 2004) (CD-ROM). On the ethnic distribution of kindergartens the statistical data found only covers the period 1895–98, see *Magyar Statisztikai*, vol. 4 (1896), pp. 422–3; vol. 5 (1897), pp. 354–55; vol. 6 (1898), pp. 312–13.

11 Law XXXVIII of 1868, §§ 1, 48. NB in this chapter, 'popular schools' are used to designate schools open to all children as opposed to private schools.

12 Ibid., §§ 43, 44, 45.

13 *Magyar Statistikai Évkönyv* (*Hungarian Annual Statistics*) (1872), pp. 482–83.

14 Data referring to Hungary and Transylvania can be found in József Eötvös, *Kultúra és nevelés* (*Culture and Education*) (Budapest, 1976), pp. 432–33.

15 Law XXXVIII of 1868, § 34; Eötvös, *Kultúra és nevelés*, p. 436.

16 The percentage of those who attended school in 1899–1900 was as follows: in Arad County 66.58 per cent, in Arad city 81.27 per cent; in Caraş-Severin County 66.32 per cent; in Timiş County 85.61 per cent, in Timişoara 106.88 per cent; in Vršac 99.52 per cent; in Torontal County 83.81 per cent; in Pančevo 96.95 per cent (*Magyar Statisztikai Évkönyv*, NS, vol. 8 (1900), p. 326). Unfortunately, data is available only up to 1903–04, because in the following years the statistical almanacs don't mention the number of people who attended compulsory education, but only those who, contrary to their duty, did not.

17 Victor Ţârcovnicu, *Contribuţii la istoria învăţământului românesc din Banat 1780–1918* (*Contributions to the History of Romanian Education in the Banat, 1780–1918*) (Bucharest, 1970), pp. 170–72.

18 *Magyar Statistikai Évkönyv* (*Hungarian National Statistics*) (1872), pp. 482–83; *Magyar Statisztikai Évkönyv*, NS, vol. 20 (1912), pp. 368–69.

19 *Magyar Statistikai Évkönyv* (1872), pp. 434–35, 438–39.

20 Ibid.

21 Ibid.

22 Lóránt Tilkovszky, *Nemzetiségi politika Magyarországon a 20. században* (*Hungarian Politics towards Minorities in the 20th Century*) (Debrecen, 1998); Zsuzsanna Boros and Dániel Szabó, *Parlamentarizmus Magyarországon 1867–1914* (*Parliamentarianism in Hungary 1867–1914*) (Budapest, 1999), p. 35.

23 Patrick Lavrits, '*Şvabii din Banat la 1900*' (Swabians of the Banat in 1900'), in Victor Neumann (ed.), *Identitate şi cultură: Studii privind istoria Banatului* (*Identity and Culture: Studies on the History of the Banat*) (Bucharest, 2009), pp. 89–93.

24 Imre Réty, 'A csanádi egyházmegye a török hódoltság után' ('The Diocese of Csanád after the Turkish Occupation), în *Az erdélyi katholicizmus múltja és jelene* (*The Past and Present of Translyvanian Catholicism*) (Dicsőszentmárton, 1925), p. 452.

25 Law XXVI of 1893, §§ 1–7.

26 Eötvös, *Kultúra és nevelés*, pp. 438–39; Law XXXVIII of 1868, §§ 27–28.

27 Law XXXVIII of 1868, §§ 52, 54.

28 Ibid., § 11.

29 Ibid., § 58.

30 Law XVIII of 1879, §§ 1–4.

31 Law XXVII of 1907, §§ 18–19; Borovszky, *Magyarország vármegyéi és városai*; Antal Kalkbrenner, *A Karánsebesi Magyar Királyi Állami Főgimnázium első évi értesítője az 1907–08. iskolai évről* (*Information on the School Year 1907–08 of the Royal Hungarian State School of Caransebeş*) (Caransebeş, 1908), p. 63.

32 Law XXXVIII of 1868, § 55. For Romanian school curricula, see *Regulament pentru organizarea învăţământului în şcolile populare* (*Rulebook for Organizing Education in Popular Schools*) (Sibiu, 1909). See Ţârcovnicu, *Contribuţii*, p. 163.

33 Ţârcovnicu, *Contribuţii*, pp. 177–80.

34 Mihai Pârvulescu, *Şcoală şi societate: Contribuţie la cunoaşterea formării elitelor româneşti din Banat în secolul al XIX-lea* (*School and Society: Contribution to the Knowledge of the Training of the Romanian Elite in the Banat during the Nineteenth Century*) (Timişoara, 2003), p. 68.

35 Here we should mention Victor Ţârcovnicu's opinion that Law XVIII of 1879 is

unclear in relation to the learning of Hungarian in the border region.

36 Pukánszky and Németh, *Neveléstörténet*.

37 Ibid.

38. Zibolen, 'Az Organisationsentwurf és a nyolcosztályosmagyar gimnázium', pp. 18–19. Law XXX of 1883, § 1.

39 Law XXX of 1883, §§ 2, 6–8.

40 Ibid., §§ 6, 20.

41 Ibid., § 10.

42 Károly Telbisz, *25 évi polgármesteri működése alatt elmondott beszédei (Telbisz's Speeches Presented during His 25 Years as Mayor)*, ed. József Bellai (Timișoara, 1910), pp. 113–14; Antal Pfeiffeer, *A Kegyes Tanítórendiek Temesvári Társházának és a Főgymnásiumnak története (The History of the Communal School House and the Major Gymnasium of Timișoara)* (Timișoara, 1896), p 84; *Erdélyi Lexikon (Transylvanian Lexicon)*, ed. Osvtáh Kálmán (Nagyvárad, 1928), p. 288.

43 Anton Pfeiffer, *Magyar Katolikus Lexikon (Hungarian Catholic Lexicon)*, ed. Viczián János (Budapest, 1993–2010); Számek: József Szinnyei, *Magyar írók élete és munkái (The Life and Work of Hungarian Writers)*, vols. i–xiv (Budapest, 1891–1914), vol. xiii, pp. 357–58; Szentkláray: *Pallas Nagy Lexikona* (Budapest, 1893–1900), vol. xv, pp. 597–98; Imre Lukinich, 'Szentkláray Jenő', *Századok* (1925), p. 439; Körösi: Károly Erdélyi, 'A spanyol Heine' ('Heine in Spanish'), *Erdélyi Múzeum* (1902), p. 206; Slavici, *Világirodalmi Lexikon (Lexicon of Universal Literature)*, ed. Király István (Budapest, 1970–96), p. 246.

44 Pfeiffer, *Magyar Katolikus Lexikon*, pp. 86–87.

45 Telbisz, *25 évi polgármesteri működése alatt elmondott beszédei*, p. 386. *Magyar Statisztikai Évkönyv*, NS, vol. 5 (1897), p. 325; ibid., vol. 17 (1909), p. 373.

46 *Magyar Statisztikai Évkönyv*, NS, vol. 17 (1909), p. 373; ibid., vol. 22 (1914), p. 268.

47 János Szekernyés, 'A hit és a tudás várnál erősebb őrhelye' ('Faith and Science: Stronger Bastions than Any Fortress'), in 'ÚMSZ Kisebbségben', June 15, 2010, pp. 6-7.

48 Pfeiffer, *Magyar Katolikus Lexikon*, p. 84; Réty, 'A csanádi egyházmegye a török hódoltság után', pp. 450–58.

49 Béla Himpfner, *Az Aradi Királyi Főgymnasium története (The History of the Royal Major Gymnasium of Arad)* (Arad, 1896), pp. 10–39.

50 Ibid., pp. 39–44.

51 Ibid., pp. 50–51.

52 Himpfner, *Az Aradi Királyi Főgymnasium története*, p. 160; *Magyar Statisztikai Évkönyv*, NS, vol. 17 (1909), p. 373; ibid., vol. 22,(1914), p. 268.

53 Himpfner, *Az Aradi Királyi Főgymnasium története*, pp. 102–05.

54 Ibid., pp. 92–100.

55 *Magyar Statistikai Évkönyv* (1872), pp. 466–67; Borovszky, *Magyarország vármegyéi és városai*.

56 *Magyar Statistikai Évkönyv* (1872), pp. 466–67; *Magyar Statisztikai Évkönyv*, NS, vol. 17 (1909), p. 373; Miklós Putnoky, *A lugosi M. Kir. Állami Főgymnasium Értesítője az 1893–94. iskolai évről (The 1893–94 School-Year Report of the Lugoj State Major Gymnasium of the Kingdom of Hungary)* (Lugoj, 1894), pp. 19–22.

57 Kalkbrenner, *A Karánsebesi Magyar Királyi Állami Főgimnázium 1907–08*, p. 22; Putnoky, *A lugosi M. Kir. Állami Főgymnasium Értesítője az 1893–94*, pp. 47, 81.

58 Putnoky, *A lugosi M. Kir. Állami Főgymnasium Értesítője az 1893–94*, pp. 81–82.

59 *Magyar Statistikai Évkönyv* (1872), pp. 466–67.

60 MVV Torontál; János Javorik: *A pancsovai m. királyi állami főgimnázium értesítője. 1914–15. isk. év (The 1914–15 School-Year Report of the Pančevo State Major* Realschule *of the Kingdom of Hungary)* (Pančevo, 1915), 2.

61 György Tordai, *A pancsovai Magyar Királyi Állami Reál-Gymnasium Értesítője az 1884–5 tanévről (The 1884–85 School-Year Report of the Pančevo State Major* Realschule *of the Kingdom of Hungary)* (Pančevo, 1885), p. 71.

62 Telbisz, *25 évi polgármesteri működése alatt elmondott beszédei*, pp. 117–18.

63 Antal Kalkbrenner, *A Karánsebesi Magyar Királyi Állami Főgimnázium 1907–08*, pp. 22–25.

64 Ibid., pp. 31, 79–81.

65 Ibid., p. 43; Kalkbrenner, *A Karánsebesi Magyar Királyi Állami Főgimnázium VII. évi*

értesítője az 1913–14. iskolai évről (*Information on the First School Year 1913–14 of the Royal Hungarian State School of Caransebeș*) (Caransebeș,1914), pp. 86–87.

66 *Magyar Statistikai Évkönyv* (1872), pp. 478–79; ibid. (1874), pp. 604–5; Victor Neumann, *Istoria evreilor din Banat* (*The History of Jews from the Banat*) (Bucharest, 1999), pp. 52–53; *Zsidó Lexikon* (*Jewish Lexicon*), ed. Péter Ujvári (Budapest, 1924), p. 58.

67 *Magyar Statistikai Évkönyv* (1872), pp. 478–79; ibid. (1874), pp. 604–5; ibid. (1876), pp. 730–31.

68 *Zsidó lexikon*, p. 58; Borovszky, *Magyarország vármegyéi és városai*; Bellai, *Temesvár szab. kir. város közművelődési intézményei*, p. 35.

69 Bellai, *Temesvár szab. kir. város közművelődési intézményei*, pp. 47–48; István Berkeszi, *A temesvári Magyar Királyi Állami Főreáliskola története* (*The History of the Timișoara State Major Realschule of the Kingdom of Hungary*) (Temesvár, 1896), pp. 75, 81.

70 Berkeszi, *A temesvári Magyar Királyi Állami Főreáliskola története*, p. 81; Bellai, *Temesvár szab. kir. város közművelődési intézményei*, pp. 47–48.

71 Berkeszi, *A temesvári Magyar Királyi Állami Főreáliskola története*, pp. 95–96.

72 Ibid., p. 144.

73 Ibid., p. 154.

74 Ibid., pp. 271–81.

75 Himpfner, *Az Aradi Királyi Főgymnasium története*, pp. 43–44.

76 Ibid., pp. 149–51.

77 József Buday, *A verseczi m. kir. áll. Főreáliskola története* (*The History of the Vršac State* Realschule *of the Kingdom of Hungary*) (Vršac, 1896), pp. 47–119.

78 Ibid., pp. 119–33.

79 *Magyar Statisztikai Évkönyv*, NS, vol. 17 (1909), p. 375. Ibid., vol. 22 (1914), p. 270.

80 During the school year 1913–14, there were the following bilingual and non-Hungarian schools in the country: Blaj (Romanian), Beiuş (Romanian–Hungarian), Năsăud (Romanian), Bistriţa (German), Braşov (Romanian), Novi Sad (Serbian), Reghin (German), Brad (Romanian), Sibiu (German), Braşov (German). *Magyar Statisztikai Évkönyv*, NS, vol. 22 (1914), pp. 268–70; Sándor Komlósi (ed.), *Neveléstörténeti olvasókönyv* (*Educational History*) (Budapest, 1978), pp. 443–44.

81 Lajos Orosz, 'Nőnevelési reformtörekvések Magyarországon: Az intézményes nőnevelés, munkaiskolák 1777–1867') ('Trends in Women's Educational Reform in Hungary: Women's Institutionalised Education, Craft Schools 1777–1867'), *Pedagógiai Szemle* (1970), pp. 534–35.

82 Ibid., pp. 534–35; Law XXXVIII of 1868, §§ 68, 77–78.

83 Rozina Mársits, *A temesvári háztartási tanfolyammal és bentlakással egybekapcsolt Magyar Királyi Állami Felsőbb Leányiskola Értesítője az 1909–10. tanévről* (*Information upon the School Year 1909–10 of the Timișoara High School for Girls of the Kingdom of Hungary*) (Temesvár, 1910), p. 3.

84 Regarding training educators and teachers, see chapter on teacher training.

85 Ildikó Müller, *Nők iskolája: Az első magyar leánygimnázium oktatói és diákjai 1896–1917*, (*Women's School: Teachers and Pupils of the First Girls'Gymnasium*) (Budapest, 2000), pp. 202–06.

86 *Magyar Statisztikai Évkönyv*, NS, vol. 20 (1912), pp. 382–400.

87 Ibid., pp. 382–84.

88 Ibid.

89 Péter Tibor Nagy, 'A középfokú nőoktatás huszadik századi történetéhez' ('The Seconday Education of Women in the Twentieth Century'), *Iskolakultúra*, no. 3 (2003), p.3.

90 Mársits, *Magyar Királyi Állami Felsőbb Leányiskola Értesítője az 1909–10. tanévről*, pp. 49–51.

91 *Az Országos Nőképző-Egylet Tanintézetének értesítője az 1888–89-iki tanévről* (*Information upon the School of the National Association for Training Women in Budapest in the School Year 1888–1889*) (Budapest, 1889), p. 54; *Az Országos Nőképző-Egylet Tanintézetének értesítője az 1889–90-iki tanévről* (*Information upon the School of the National Association of Women Training in Budapest in the School Year 1889–90*) (Budapest, 1890), p. 54; *Az Országos Nőképző-Egylet Leánygimnáziumának értesítője az 1896–97 tanévről* (*Information upon the School the National Association of Women Training in*

Budapest in the School Year 1896–97) (Budapest, 1897), p. 67.

92 Law VIII of 1872, §. 83.

93 *Pedagógiai lexicon (Pedagogical Lexicon), vol.* 4, p. 267

94 Law XVII of 1884, § 80–82.

95 *Pedagógiai lexicon (Pedagogical Lexicon), vol.* 4, p. 268.

96 *Magyar Statisztikai Évkönyv*, NS, vol. 22 (1914), p. 244; in the school year 1904–05 the number of pupils attending these apprentice schools was as follows: 770 in Arad County, 984 in Arad, 1064 in Caraş-Severin County, 1289 in Timiş, 1005 in Timişoara, 444 in Vršac, 1482 in Torontal County, 317 in Pančevo [*Magyar Statisztikai Évkönyv*, NS, vol. 13 (1905)].

97 Bellai, *Temesvár szab. kir. város közművelődési intézményei*, pp. 34–35.

98 *Pedagógiai lexicon (Pedagogical Lexicon)*, vol., 4, p. 268; Sándor Győriványi, 'A magyar szakképzés ezeréves múltjából II' ('A Thousand History of Hungarian Vocational Training II'), Új Pedagógiai szemle vol. 1 (1996), pp. 79–80; Borovszky, *Magyarország vármegyéi és városai.*

99 Győriványi, 'A magyar szakképzés ezeréves múltjából II', pp. 80–81.

100 Ibid.

101 Bellai, *Temesvár szab. kir. város közművelődési intézményei*, pp. 38–39.

102 Telbisz, *25 évi polgármesteri működése alatt elmondott beszédei*, pp. 161–67.

103 Ede Stumpfoll, *A temesvári M. Kir. Állami Fa- és Fémipari Szakiskola értesítője az 1900 1901. tanévről (Information on the School Year 1900–01 of the State Industrial School of Wood and Metal of the Kingdom of Hungary)* (Temesvár, 1901), p. 6.

104 János Szilágyi, *Munkásmozgalom és kultúra 1867–1945 (Workers' Movement and and Culture 1867–1945)* (Budapest, 1979), pp. 52–53.

105 Győriványi, 'A magyar szakképzés ezeréves múltjából II', p.79.

106 *Magyarország Vármegyéi és Városai, Torontál Vármegye. (The Counties and Cities of Hungary. Torontál County) (Budapest, 1911)* p. 264.

107 The first deaf-blind institution in the Kingdom of Hungary was established at Vác, in 1802 on the initiative of András Cházár, while the teaching of the blind started in 1827 at Pest, due to Rafael Beitl. Szabó Anna Gordosné, *Gyógypedagógia-történet*, vol. ii. *Magyar Gyógypedagógia-történet a XX. Századig (The History of Special Pedagogy*, vol. ii. *The History of Hungarian Special Pedagogy up to the Twentieth Century)* (Budapest, 1983), p. 343; Ferenc Szőllősi, 'A vakok iskolájának múzeuma' ('The School for the Blind Museum'): www.opkm.hu/konyvesneveles/2004/3/20szollosif.html, accesed on 12 August 2010.

108 Law XXXVIII of 1868, §§ 2–3.

109 Telbisz, *25 évi polgármesteri működése alatt elmondott beszédei*, pp. 27–28; Borovszky, *Magyarország vármegyéi és városai.*

110 Telbisz, *25 évi polgármesteri működése alatt elmondott beszédei*, p. 27; Bellai, *Temesvár szab. kir. város közművelődési intézményei*, p. 41.

111 Following his activity in the Banat, between 1894 and 1898 József Roboz worked at the Blind Institute in Budapest and organised, in parallel, healing classes for those who suffered from lisps and stammering. He reached the peak of his career in 1898, when he became special inspector at the National Institute of Curative Pedagogy (*Pedagógiai Lexikon (Pedagogical Lexicon)*, gen. eds. Báthory Zoltán and Falus Iván (Budapest, 1997), p. 272).

112 Borovszky, *Magyarország vármegyéi és városai.*

113 Ibid.

114 Eötvös, *Kultúra és nevelés*, pp. 440–41; Law XXXVIII of 1868, §. 81.

115 Law XXVIII of 1868, §§ 84, 87–89, 102–04.

116 Ibid., §§ 106–11, 114.

117 Ibid., § 113.

118 József Szabó, *Az Aradi Áll. Tanítóképző Intézet rövid története. 1873–1894/5. tanév végéig (The History of Arad State Institution for Training Teachers, from 1873 until the End of the School Year 1894–95)* (Arad, 1896), pp. 3–4.

119 Ibid., pp. 24–50.

120 Ibid., pp. 14–15, 61.

121 Telbisz, *25 évi polgármesteri működése alatt elmondott beszédei*, pp. 66–69, 85–86; Bellai, *Temesvár szab. kir. város közművelődési intézményei*, pp. 42–43.

122 Pârvulescu, *Şcoală şi societate*, pp. 94–95; Pârvulescu indicated Sânandrei as foundation, although, actually, it was in Szentendre, near Buda (See Endre Arató, *Kelet-Európa története a 19. század első felében (The History of Eastern Europe in the First Half of the Nineteenth Century)* (Budapest, 1971), p. 217.

123 Pârvulescu, *Şcoală şi societate*, p. 101.

124 Ibid., p. 102.

125 Law XV of 1891, § 31.

126 Manual labour for boys was not included in the curriculum.

127 Ibid., §§ 34, 41.

128 Ibid., § 39.

129 Bellai, *Temesvár szab. kir. város közművelődési intézményei*, pp. 44–45.

130 Sándor Kováts, *A csanádi papnevelde története 1806–1906 (The History of Cenad Theology 1806–1906)* (Temesvár, 1908), pp. 430–31. A Csajághy-féle szabályzatot közli: ibid., pp. 433–43.

131 Ibid., pp. 443–44.

132 Botiş, *Istoria şcoalii normale*, p. 535.

133 Ibid., pp. 523–35.

134 Ibid., p. 537.

135 Botiş, *Istoria şcoalii normale*, p. 579.

136 Ibid., pp. 581–582.

137 Mircea Păcurariu, *Istoria Bisericii Ortodoxe Române (History of the Romanian Orthodox Church)*, vol. iii (Bucharest, 1981), p. 205; Vasile Petrica, *Institutului Teologic Diecezan Ortodox Român Caransebeş, 1865–1927 (The Romanian Orthodox Diocesan Theological Institute of Caransebeş, 1865–1927)* (Caransebeş, 2005), pp. 20–27.

138 Telbisz, *25 évi polgármesteri működése alatt elmondott beszédei*, pp. 281–83.

139 Ibid., pp. 334–37.

140 Eötvös, *Kultúra és nevelés*, p. 454.

141 Law XXXVIII of 1868, §§ 116–18.

142 Ibid., §§ 121–22.

143 Ibid., §§ 128–30.

144 *Law 1876/XXVIII*, § 1–3.

Chapter 17

1 *Drapelul*, vol. 18, no. 108 (11 October 1918).

2 *Temesvari Hirlap*, vol. 16, no. 243 (29 October 1918); József Geml, *Emlékiratok polgármesteri működésem idejéből (Memoirs from My Activity as a Lawyer)* (Timişoara, 1924), 89.

3 William Marin, *Unirea din 1918 şi poziţia şvabilor bănăţeni (The Union of 1918 and the Position of Swabians from the Banat)* (Timişoara, 1978), pp. 58–59.

4 Ibid.

5 Geml, *Emlékiratok*, p. 94.

6 Ibid., pp. 92–93; *Drapelul*, vol. 18, no. 112 (20 October 1918).

7 *Nădejdea*, vol. 9, no. 683 (26 September 1927). According to Otto Roth's interview in *Temesvarer Zeitung*, vol. 76, no. 216 (25 September 1927).

8 *Nădejdea*, vol. 9, no. 683 (26 September 1927); Ion Clopoţel, *Misiunea istorică a gărzilor naţionale în luptele de dezrobire din 1918 (The Historical Mission of the National Guards during the Fights of Emancipation in 1918)* (Bucharest, 1943), pp. 15–16.

9 *Drapelul*, vol. 18, no. 112 (20 October 1918).

10 Marin, *Unirea din 1918*, p. 63.

11 Radu Păiuşan, *Mişcarea naţională din Banat şi Marea Unire (The National Movement of the Banat and the Great Union)* (Timişoara, 1993), pp. 114–15.

12 *Nădejdea*, vol. 9, no. 683 (26 September 1927); Păiuşan, *Mişcarea naţională*, pp. 113–14.

13 *Drapelul*, vol. 18, no. 112 (20 October 1918). Zsigmond Braun, Ödön Kovács, Jenő Szenes, Károlyi Baumann, Peter Roosz and Lajos Homas were elected to the command of the Hungarian National Military Council, alongside Albert Bartha.

14 Dr Nicolae Ilieşiu, *Timişoara: Monografie istorică (Timişoara: Historical Monograph)* (Timişoara, 1943), pp. 108–9; see also the 2nd revd edn., foreword by Petru Ilieşu, preface by Victor Neumann (Timişoara, 2003).

15 *Temesvári hirlap*, vol. 16, no. 248 (3 November 1918); vol. 16, no. 249 (5 November 1918); see also *Temesvarer Zeitung*, vol. 67, no. 248 (5 Nov. 1918).

16 As well as those already mentioned, Giaconović Eta, Stoiaković Svetislav, Bogdanov Vasa, Stoicić Gheorghe and Mihailović Svetislv were noted: *Temesvári hirlap*, vol. 16, no. 246 (1 November 1918).

17 Ljubivoje Cerović, 'Srbi u Temišvarskom Banatu na istorijskom raskršću 1918–1919: Godine' ('The Serbians from the Banat of Timișoara at the Crossroads of History'), in *Prisajedinjenje Vojvodine kraljevini Srbiji 1918 (Voivodina's Reunification with Serbia)* (Novi Sad, 1993), p. 116.

18 Ibid., p. 117.

19 *Drapelul*, vol. 16, no. 112 (20 October 1918).

20 *Volkswille* (30 November 1918).

21 See Chapter 11 by Victor Neumann in this volume.

22 Cited by Victor Neumann, *The End of a History: The Jews of Banat from the Beginning to Nowadays* (Bucharest, 2006), pp. 93–124.

23 Cf. Victor Neumann, *Timișoara under the Sign of Prince Eugene of Savoy: Three Hundred Years of Europeanism* (Timișoara, 2016), pp. 55–62; id., *Die Interkulturalitaet des Banats* (Berlin, 2015), pp. 31–43.

24 See Chapter 13 by Miodrag Milin in this volume.

25 See Victor Neumann, '*Neam* (Romanian for Kin) and *Popor* (Romanian for People): The Notions of Etnocentrism', in Victor Neumann and Armin Heinen (eds.), *Key Concepts of Romanian History* (Budapest, 2013), pp. 377–403.

26 Ilieşiu, *Timișoara: Monografie istorică*, pp. 110–11; Geml, *Emlékiratok*, p. 94.

27 *Temesvári hirlap*, vol. 247 (2 November 1918); Ilieşiu, *Timișoara: Monografie istorică*, p. 111.

28 William Marin, Ioan Munteanu and Gheorghe Radulovici, *Unirea Banatului cu România (The Union of Banat with Romania)* (Timişoara, 1968), p. 274.

29 Constantin Enea, 'Aspecte ale descompunerii armatei austro-ungare: Dezertări şi răscoale ale soldaţilor din Transilvania (1914–1918)' ('Aspects of the Disintegration of the Austro-Hungarian Army: Desertions and Revolts in Transylvania, 1914–1918'), in *Acta Musei Napocensis* (Cluj-Napoca, 1968), pp. 285–86.

30 *Temesvarer Zeitung*, vol. 67, no. 256 (14 November 1918).

31 On 7 December 1914, the Serbian National Assembly, assembled at Nis, stated in the adopted *Resolution*: 'The Government declares in these moments that its most important task is to ensure victory in this great war that became, from the moment it started, both the fight for freedom and the union of all our still unreleased brothers, Serbian, Croatian and Slovene'. The Serbian government repeatedly reiterated the idea that the territories inhabited by Slavs in Austria-Hungary had to be integrated to their state, under the coordination of Belgrade.

32 Cerović, 'Srbi u Temišvarskom Banatu', p. 118.

33 G. Iancu and G. Cipăianu, *La Consolidation de l'union de la Transylvanie et de la Roumanie 1918–1919: Témoignages français* (Bucharest, 1990), pp. 21–26. K. Bogdan, 'The Belgrade Armistice of 13 November 1918', *Slavonic and East European Review*, vol. 48, no. 40 (1970), pp. 67–68.

34 *Temesvári hirlap*, vol. 16, no. 259 (16 November 1918).

35 Cerović, 'Srbi u Temišvarskom Banatu', p. 22.

36 Archives historiques militaires Vincennes, Ministère de la Guerre, État-major de l'Armée, 250/1918.

37 *Temesvarer Volksblatt* (10 December 1918).

38 Archives historiques militaires Vincennes, Ministère de la Guerre, État-major de l'Armée, 120/1919.

39 On 27 February 1919, Pavle Marinović, the Serbian minister at Bucharest, mentioned during a conversation with A. Margiloman that he was very upset that Brătianu had not even tried to reach an agreement with Serbia, creating the possibility of adversity between the two states. See Anastasie Iordache, *Ion. I.C. Brătianu* (Bucharest, 1994), p. 420.

40 Michael Kausch, *Schicksalswende im Leben des Banater deutschen Volkes* (Timişoara, 1939), pp. 30–32.

41 Ioan Munteanu, *Mişcarea naţională din Banat 1881–1918 (The National Movement of the Banat 1881–1918)* (Timişoara, 1994), p. 260.

42 See Timișoara's demographic situation according to the imperial statistics from 1910 in Victor Neumann, *Die Interkulturalitaet des Banats* (Berlin, 2015), pp. 45 ff.

43 Gheorghe I. Demian, *Pentru Banatul robit: Istoricul tratativelor duse pentru obţinerea Banatului sârbesc (1914–1923) (For the Enslaved Banat: The History of the Peace Negotiations for the Serbian Banat 1914–1918)* (Timişoara, 1933), p. 14.

44 George Popoviciu, *Memorii cu privire la integritatea Banatului (Memoirs on the Integrity of the Banat)* (Caransebeş, 1929), pp. 77–79; *Temesvarer Zeitung*, vol. 68, no. 180 (12 August 1919).

45 *Temesvarer Zeitung*, vol. 68, no. 180 (12 August 1919); see also *Banatul*, vol. 1, no. 29 (17 August 1919).

46 Neumann, *Die Interkulturalitaet des Banats* (Berlin, 2015), pp. 45 ff.

47 See id., '*Neam* (Romanian for Kin) and *Popor* (Romanian for People): The Notions of Romanian Ethno-Centrism', in id. and Armin Heinen (eds.), *Key Concepts of Romanian History: Alternative Approaches to Socio-Political Languages* (Budapest and New York, 2013), pp. 377–403.

Chapter 18

1 According to the 1910 census, around 1.5 million were living in the Torontal, Timiș and Caraș-Severin counties in the Banat, including 29.7% Germans, 22.9% Serbs and 18.7% Hungarians. See Toma Milenković, 'Banatska republika i mađarski komesarijat u Banatu (31.10.1918–20.02.1919)' ('The Banatian Republic and the Hungarian Commissariat in the Banat (31.10.1918–20.02.1919)'), *Matice Srpske (Journal of History)*, vol. 32 (1985), p. 99.

2 Toša Iskruljev, *Raspeće srpskog naroda u Sremu 1914 i Mađari (The Crucifixion of the Serbian Population from 1914 and the Hungarians)* (Novi Sad, 1936), p. 200.

3 Milorad Ekmečić, *Ratni ciljevi Srbije 1914 (Serbia's War Objectives)* (Belgrade, 1990), p. 443.

4 Ekmečić, *Ratni ciljevi Srbije 1914*, p. 274.

5 Ştefan Pascu, *The Making of the Romanian Unitary National State 1918* (Bucharest, 1989), p. 137.

6 Ştefan Pascu, *Making of the Romanian National State*, p. 153.

7 M. Milin, 'Voluntari sârbi pe frontul românesc din toamna anului 1916' ('Serbian Volunteers of the Romanian Front in the Autumn of 1916'), *The Banat Annals*, NS, archaeology-history, vol. 21 (2013), pp. 439–53.

8 Andrej Mitrović, *Razgraničenje Jugoslavije sa Madjarskom I Rumunijom 1919–1920 (The Yugoslav Border Demarcations with Hungary and Romania 1919–1920)* (Novi Sad, 1975), pp. 55–59.

9 Ljubivoje Cerović, *Srbi u Rumuniji (Serbians in Romania)* (Novi Sad, 1997), p. 400.

10 Pascu, *Making of the Romanian National State*, p. 19.

11 The 'Republicans' from Zlatița were taken by the gendarmes and brought to Biserica Albă for a public correction of 25 rod strikes, with no other consequences.

12 Cerović, *Srbi u Rumuniji*, pp. 386–91.

13 Drago Njegovan, *Prisajedinjenje Srema, Bačke I Baranje Srbiji 1918 (Unification of Srem, Bačka and Banat Regions with Serbia in 1918)* (Novi Sad, 2001), pp. 90–106.

14 Milenković, *Banatska republika*, pp. 125–27.

15 For the Banatian Republic, see Miodrag Milin, *Sârbii din România în secolul XX (Serbs from Romania in the Twentieth Century)* (Cluj-Napoca, 2012), pp. 15–16; see also Drago Njegovan and Miodrag Milin, 'Voivodina în octombrie–noiembrie 1918 (Banatul, Bacica, Barania şi Sremul – unificarea cu Serbia)' ('Voivodina in October–November 1918 (The Banat, Bačka, Baranja and Srem: The Unification with Serbia)'), *Annals of Banat*, NS, vol. 22 (2014), n. 45.

16 Ilija Petrović, *Vojvodina srpska 1918 (The Serbian Voivodina in 1918)* (Novi Sad, 1996), pp. 280–83.

17 Dr Martin Filipon was also a member of the Great National Council of Voivodina, elected on 25 November 1918 and reconfirmed on 27 February 1919 (Drago Njegovan, *Sremul, Banatul, Bacica şi Barania la 1918 – Unificarea cu Serbia (Srem, Banat, Bacica and Barania at 1918 – The Unification with Serbia)* (2nd edn., Novi Sad, 2001, pp. 125–27.

18 Milenković, *Banatska republika*, pp. 133–38.

19 Mitrović, *Razgraničenje Jugoslavije*, p. 57.

20 Cedomir Popov, *Od Versaja do Danciga (From Versailles to Danzig)* (Belgrade, 1976), p. 179.

21 Mitrović, *Razgraničenje Jugoslavije*, pp. 6–7.

22 Ibid., pp. 11–13.

23 Ibid., p. 23.

24 Cvijić's study *La Péninsule balkanique: Géographie humaine* (Paris, 1918), made a strong impression upon the delegates at the Peace Conference.

25 Mitrović, *Razgraničenje Jugoslavije*, pp. 27–28.

26 Mitrović, *Razgraničenje Jugoslavije*, p. 49.

27 Ibid., p. 99.

28 Milin, *Voluntari sârbi*, pp. 439–53.

29 Mitrović, *Razgraničenje Jugoslavije*, p. 117.

30 Ibid., p. 144.

31 Romanian sources present this incident as a means to stop barge navigation downstream the Bega and implicitly the vandalisation of the resources from Timişoara by the retreating Serbian army.

32 Mitrović, *Razgraničenje Jugoslavij*, p. 280.

33 Pascu, *Making of the Romanian National State*, p. 261.

34 Ibid.

35 Mitrović, *Razgraničenje Jugoslavije*, pp. 191–94.

Chapter 19

1 Memorandum presented at the Paris Peace Conference by the Swabian delegation of the Banat, published in *Revista Institutului Social Banat–Crişana (Banat–Crisana Social Institute Review)*, vol. 12 (November–December 1943), p. 421.

2 Benedict Anderson, *Imagined Communities: Reflections on the Origins and Spread of Nationalism* (London and New York, 1991).

3 See Chapter 11 by Victor Neumann in this volume.

4 Traian Rotariu, Maria Semeniuc, and Elemér Mezei, *Recensământul din 1910: Transilvania (The Census of 1910: Transylvania)* (Bucharest, 1999), p. 548.

5 Ibid., p. 550.

6 See the ideologised criteria and notions used by Sabin Manuilă in *Recensământul general al populaţiei României din 29 decembrie 1930 (General Census of Romania's Population of 29 December 1930)*, vols. i–x, Central Institute of Statistics (Bucharest, 1938–40).

7 Ibid., vol. ii. *Neam, limbă maternă, religie.*

8 See Anderson, *Imagined Communities.*

9 For the ethnonationalist ideological option, see Ioan Lotreanu, *Monografia Banatului, vol. i. Situaţia geografică, Locuitorii, Comunele (Monograph of Banat, vol. i. Geographical Situation, Inhabitants, Villages)* (Timişoara, 1935); Cornel Grofşorean, *Banatul de altădată şi de totdeauna: Sinteza problemelor istorice şi social-politice (The Banat of the Past and Forever: Synthesis of the Historical and Sociopolitical Questions)* (Timişoara, 1946). For the application of identity policies based on 'nationality' and for the process of Romanian assimilation of higher education in Timişoara, see the tables in Victor Vîlcovici (ed.), *Şcoala Politecnică din Timişoara: Zece ani de existenţă (octombrie 1920–octombrie 1930) (The Polytechnic of Timişoara: Ten Years of Existence – October 1920–October 1930)* (Timişoara, 1930), pp. 97–99.

10 According to 'Adresa Primăriei oraşului Timişoara către Ministerul Instrucţiunii şi al Cultelor în chestiunea înfiinţării unei Politecnice în Timişoara' ('Memorandum of the Timişoara Mayor's Office to the Ministry of Religion and Public Instruction Regarding the Establishment of a Polytechnic School in Timişoara'), in Vîlcovici (ed.), *Şcoala Politecnică din Timişoara*, pp. 7–12, cited at p. 10.

11 In 1918–20, the Council of Directors temporarily managed the question of the newly integrated regions into Romania after the Paris Peace Conference.

12 According to Onisifor Ghibu, 'Motivarea bugetului Politecnicei din Timişoara ('Motivation for the Budget of the Timişoara Polytechnic'), in Vîlcovici (ed.), *Şcoala Politecnică din Timişoar*, pp. 14–15, quote at p. 15.

13 See Alexiu Cristofor, *Ripensia* (Timişoara, 1992).

14 The first classification of the newspapers and periodicals published in interwar Timişoara can be found in Nicolae Ilieşius, *Timişoara: Monografie istorică (Timişoara: Historical Monograph)* (Timişoara, 1943). This is complemented by Thomas Mochnács, 'Cultura în Timişoara interbelică' ('Culture in Interwar Timişoara'), PhD thesis (West University of Timişoara, 2012), pp. 101–64.

15 Mochnács, 'Cultura', pp. 50–100.

16 Ibid., pp. 159–60.

17 Ibid., pp. 75–76.

18 See Ion Luca Caragiale, *Az elveszett levél* (*A Lost Letter*) (Timişoara, 1926), trans. Kádár Imre with foreword by Bánffy Miklós (Budapest, [1926]); Áron Cotruş, *Holnap* (*Tomorrow*), trans. Pál Bodó ([Timişoara], 1929); Viktor Orendi-Hommenau, *Literatur und Volkskunst der Rumänen* (*Romanian Popular Literature and Art*) (Timişoara, 1928); Mihai Eminescu, *Ausgewählte Gedichte* (*Selected Poems*), trans. Viktor Orendi-Hommenau (Timişoara, 1932); Zoltán Franyó, *A kárpáti harcokról* (*About the Fights in the Carpathians*) (Budapest, 1915); German trans. Zoltán Franyó as *Bruder Feind* (*Enemy Brother*) (Vienna, 1916); ***, *Eine Herbstsymphonie rumänischer Lyrik* (*An Autumn Symphony of Romanian Lyrics*), trans. Zoltán Franyó (Arad, 1926); ***, *Rumänische Dichter: Eine Anthologie zeitgenossischer Lyrik* (*Romanian Poets: An Anthology of Contemporary Lyrics*). ed. and trans. Zoltán Franyó (Timişoara, 1932); Ernst Toller, *Fecskekönyv* (The Book of the Swallow), trans. Zoltán Franyó (Timişoara, 1935); Mihai Eminescu, *Der Abendstern* (*The Evening Star*), trans. Zoltán Franyó (Timişoara, 1943).

19 For references concerning multilingual writers in Timişoara, see Adriana Babeţi and Cécile Kovacshazy (eds.), *Le Banat: Un Eldorado aux confins* (Paris, 2007), pp. 214–17, 199–204, 205–9.

20 Adriana Pantazi, 'Etape în istoria istoriografiei artei româneşti interbelice: Studiu de caz – Arad şi Timişoara' ('Stages in the Historiography of Romanian Art during the Interwar Period: Study Case – Arad and Timişoara'), abstract of PhD thesis (Alba-Iulia, 2012), p. 5.

21 Maria Bodó, *Creaţia bănăţeană pentru pian în perioada interbelică* (*Piano Composition in the Banat during the Interwar Period*) (Timişoara, 2005), pp. 101–18. See also Damian Vulpe, 'Învăţămîntul muzical timişorean cu şcolile lui' ('Music Instruction and the Schools in Timişoara'), lecture delivered at the symposium organised on the 10th anniversary of setting up the Music Faculty in Oradea, 13 December 2005, cf. www.deceniu-muzical-universitar.blogspot.ro/.

22 Bodó, *Creaţia bănăţeană pentru pian în perioada interbelică*, pp. 119–59.

23 The same is true of many contemporary scholars: cultural interaction is neglected. See Rodica and Ioan Munteanu, *Timişoara: Monografie* (*Timişoara: Monograph*) (Timişoara, 2002).

24 See the notions in *Recensământul general al populaţiei României din 29 decembrie 1930* (*General Census of Romania's Population of 29 December 1930*), vols. i–x (Bucharest, 1938–40).

25 For the explanation of the concepts of *neam*, *nem*, *Volk*, *Völkishekultur*, *Kulturnation*, see Victor Neumann, *Neam, Popor sau Naţiune: Despre identităţile politice europene* (*Kinship, People or Nation: On European Political Identities*) (Bucharest, 2005). For a new explanation, a comparison of the idea of nation in East Central Europe, see id., 'Peculiarities of the Translation and Adaptation of the Concept of Nation in East-Central Europe: The Hungarian and Romanian Cases in the Nineteenth Century', *Contributions to the History of Concepts*, vol. 7, no. 1 (Summer 2012), pp. 72–101.

26 Their circulation is signalled in documents within the Timiş, Caraş and Arad counties of the Banat. They had a well-established status approved by either the Ministry of Religion in Budapest or the local authorities. Many of them had a rabbi, a synagogue, a school, a cemetery, two or more cantors, administrative clerks as well as financial resources necessary to develop traditional religious activities. See also Victor Neumann, *The End of a History: The Jews of Banat from the Beginning to Nowadays* (Bucharest, 2006).

27 Elemér Jakabffy and György Páll, *A Bánsági Magyarság Husz Éve Romániában* (*The 20 Years in Romania of the Hungarians of the Banat*) (Budapest, 1939), pp. 34–35.

28 At the beginning of the twentieth century, there were Jewish communities spread out over Timişoara, Vârşeţ, Gătaia, Buziaş, Lipova, Ciacova, Recaş, Biserica Albă, Deta, Arad, Şimand, Butin, Şemlac, Pecica, Chişineu-Criş, Curtici, Sântana, Pâncota, Lugoj, Caransebeş, Bocşa, Orşova, Oraviţa, Făget, Reşiţa, Balinţ, Vinga, Ineu, Cermei and Şipet, according to the Archive of the Jewish Community in Timişoara (kept at the Centre for the Study of Jewish History in Romania, in Bucharest), File no. 56/1922–26, sheet nos. 123–24. See also Neumann, *The End of a History*.

29 Hildrun Glass, *Zerbrochene Nachbarschaft: Das Deutsch-Jüdische Verhältnis in Rumänien (1918–1938)* (*Broken Neighbourhood: The German–Jewish Relationship in Romania (1918–1938)*) (Munich, 1996), p. 291. See also the assesments and critical comments on Glass's book made by Rainer Ohliger in H-Soz-Kult, 31 October 1997, www.hsozkult.de/publicationreview/id/rezbuecher-379.

30 *Temesvarer Volksblatt*, 27 March 1922.

31 See A. Marmorek, 'Professzor a kelet es Délmagyarország zsidoság külföldi képviselöje' ('Professor Marmorek, the Representative Abroad of Southern and Eastern Hungary'), *Uj Kelet*, no. 1 (1918).

32 Archive of the Jewish Community in Timişoara, File no. 56/1922–26, sheet nos. 273–89: 'Az 1923 évi május hó 27 én megtartott bánáti es aradmegye országos zsidó nagygyülés' ('The Great Assembly of the Jews of the Banat and Arad on 27 May 1923'). The intention was explicitly formulated as early as 14 May 1923 by the presidium of the Israeli community of Timişoara in a memorandum to the Timiş prefect which reads: 'The Jews of Transylvania and the Banat wish to unify in order to support their common interests. To this end, they have organised a general assembly on 27 May of this year [1923] at 5.30 p.m. in the meeting room of the Jewish community building in Timişoara, Mărăşeşti street.' Archive of the Jewish Community of Timişoara, File no. 56/1922–26, year 1923, sheet no. 339.

33 Archive of the Jewish Community of Timişoara, File no. 56/1922–26, year 1923, sheet no. 317: 'As can be seen by anyone who carefully investigates the facts, the hard sufferings which we had to go through are owing to the lack of full cohesion between the Jews in the new territories and the Old Kingdom. The Native Jewish Union which has had up till today the cumbersome mission of giving the Jews of the Old Kingdom a lawful status by registering their emancipation in the Constitution, in the meantime in conjunction with Jewish parliamentarians protecting Jewish rights in the new territories from damage, is the one that calls today on Jews in the new territories to organise themselves, being deeply assured that this is the only and the most effective means to fight anti-Semitism. To achieve this objective, we are honoured to ask you to participate in the consultation which is to take place in Bucharest on 27 and 28 May of this year at 4.00 p.m. . . . for which we have convened personalities from all provinces. This consultation will set the background for the organisation of the Union of the Jews of Romania which comprises the sum of Jewish citizens in Romania, and the call for a general congress of the Jews of Romania will be decided upon.' On the intention of the Jewish communities of Banat and Transylvania according to the new political context, see the Archive of the Jewish Communities of Timişoara, File no. 55/1920, Sheet nos. 73–75, the copy of the letter sent by the Jewish Community of Timişoara to the Ministry of Religion and Arts as a reply to the Ministry's ordinance no. 38.095/1920.

34 Archive of the Jewish Community of Timişoara, File no. 56/1922–26, year 1923, sheet nos. 273–89.

35 See *Erdelyi Magyar Évkönyv* (*Transylvanian Hungarian Yearly*) (1930), p. 114.

36 See National Archives, Timiş County Branch, Documents on the Wool Industry. According also to F. Theiss, *Album jubiliar, 275 de ani, 1718–1993: Fabrica de bere din Timişoara* (*Jubilee Album, 275 Years, 1718–1993: The Brewery of Timişoara*) (Timişoara, 1993).

37 Étienne Balibar, Foreword to Étienne Balibar and Immanuel Wallerstein, *Race, nation, classe: Les Identités ambiugues* (Paris, 1990), p. 17. 'Ce sont ces réactions qui confèrent a l'histoire sociale une allure irréductible à la simple "logique" de la réproduction élargie du capital ou même un "jeu strategique" des acteurs définis par la division du travail et le système des États.'

Chapter 20

38 See Roland Clark, *Holy Legionary Youth: Fascist Activism in Interwar Romania* (Ithaca, NY, 2015); see also Victor Neumann, 'Neam (Romanian for Kin) and Popor (Romanian for People): The Notion of Romanian Ethno-Centrism', in Victor Neumann and Armin Heinen (eds.), *Key Concepts of Romanian History. Alternative Approaches to Socio-Political Languages* (Budapest, 2013), pp. 377–403.

39 See Arnold David Finkelstein, *Fénysugár a borzalmak ejszakájában* (*Ray of Light in the Night of Terror*) (Tel-Aviv, 1958) p. 49, cited in Zoltán Tibori Szabó, *Frontiera dintre viaţă şi moarte: Refugiul şi salvarea evreilor la graniţa româno-maghiară (1940–1944)* (*The Frontier between Life and Death: Refuge and Rescue on the Romanian-Hungarian Border, 1940–1944*), trans. Florica Perian (Bucharest, 2005), p. 96.

40 Cited in *Martiriul evreilor din România 1940–1944: Documente şi mărturii* (*The Martyrdom of Romanian Jews 1940–1944: Documents and Testimonies*) (Bucharest, 1991), p. 264.

41 In the nineteenth century, Chorin Aron, an important rabbi in the Banat, introduced sensational novelties (reforms) into religious practices, such as the use of organ music, praying with an uncovered head, and reduction in the week of mourning. Chorin initiated encyclopedic education in the sense of integrating the imperial structures and an approach to *schola universalis* (cf. Victor Neumann, *The End of a History: The Jews of Banat from the Beginning to Nowadays* (Bucharest, 2006), pp. 67–68).

42 The National Archives of Romania, Timiş County Branch, Timiş-Torontal Prefecture, dossier 107, fols. 46 and 231.

43 According to Szabó, *Frontiera dintre viaţă şi moarte*, p. 54.

44 According to the discussion with Dr Ernest Neumann, chief rabbi of Timişoara, 15 March 2002.

45 The Timişoara Jewish Community Archives (ACET), file no. 102, different documents 1943–44. See also Victor Neumann, *Istoria evreilor din Banat: O mărturie a multi şi interculturalităţii Europei est-centrale* (*The History of Jews in the Banat: A Testimony of Multi- and Interculturality in East-Central Europe*) (Bucharest, 1999), 154–55 nn. 50–51.

46 According to the National Archives of Romania, Presidency of the Council of Ministers, file 484/1941; cited in Lya Benjamin, 'Definiţia rasială a calităţii de evreu în legislaţia din România 1938–1944' ('The Racial Definition of the Jewish Condition in Romanian Legislation 1938–1944'), *Cluj-Napoca History Institute Yearbook*, vol. 34 (1995), p. 133.

47 See Lya Benjamin (ed.), *Evreii din România între anii 1940–1944* (*The Jews of Romania 1940–1944*), vol. ii. *Problema evreiască în stenogramele Consiliului de Miniştri* (*The Jewish Issue in the Shorthand Report of the Council of Ministers*) (Bucharest, 1996).

48 Dr Paul Grünberger, Oral testimony regarding the situation of the Jews from the Banat and Transylvania during the Second World War (recorded on tape by Vasile Grunea from Cluj). I would like to thank Mr Vasile Grunea, a close acquaintance of Grünberger's family, who kindly lent me the tape containing this testimony. It is one of the most trustworthy witnesses. With the help of documentary research I managed to verify some of the information, each of them confirming the same reality. Thus, I had the opportunity to understand unclear aspects and enrich the descriptions comprised in my previous book dedicated to the history of the Jews. Paul Grünberger, a medical doctor by profession, was born at Sibiu, his family moving to Timişoara during the war. He moved to Israel in 1962.

49 United States Holocaust Memorial Museum Archive (USHMMA).

50 Jean Ancel, *Documents Concerning the Fate of the Romanian Jewry During the Holocaust*, vol. vii (New York, 1986), chapter entitled 'The Activity of the Mosaic Cult of the Whole Country from 1918 to 1943'. See also ACET, file 73/1943. For the description of the conditions of Jews deported by Antonescu's regime, see Jean Ancel, *Transnistria*, vols. i–iii (Bucharest, 1999).

51 According to USHMMA, RG-2000.224, Reel 9, Trials of the Romanian Zionists, Report of the Regional Police Inspectorate of Timişoara (undated, probably from 1942), p. 14. See details and references to other sources in V. Neumann, *Istoria evreilor din Banat*, pp. 142–43.

52 USHMMA, RG-25.004M, Reel 10, Romanian Information Service Records, 1936–1966, Report of the Romanian Secret Service (Raport al Serviciilor Secrete Române) entitled *The International Jewish Occult Organizations: Their Actions in Romania by Cultural Leagues, Masonic Lodges and Sport Clubs*, p. 20.

53 Letter sent to Antonescu's office signed by circle of intellectuals from Timişoara. According to ACET, file 75/1941, fol. 105.

54 USHMMA, RG-25.010M, Reel 13, General Inspectorate of the Romanian Gendarmerie, Informative Note no. 1766 from 28 February 1942, Craiova Gendarmes Inspectorate. It describes the mood of the Romanian army, the medical and transportation conditions, the corruption, the population's discontent and critique. See also Ibid., Informative Note no. 1664 from 4 February 1942, Olt Gendarmes Legion.

55 Raul Hilberg, *The Destruction of the European Jews* (Chicago, 1967), pp. 257–66.

56 According to Benjamin (ed.), *Evreii din România între anii 1940–1944*, vol. ii, p. 452.

57 Ibid. 453.

58 Ibid.

59 Hilberg, *Destruction of the European Jews*, pp. 257–66.

60 Neumann, *Istoria evreilor din Banat*, pp. 148–59.

61 Cf. Ottmar Traşcă and Dennis Deletant (eds.), *Al Treilea Reich şi Holocaustul din România: Documente din arhivele germane (The Third Reich and the Romanian Holocaust: Documents from the German Archives)* (Bucharest, 2007), document 114, pp. 532–40.

62 Ibid.

63 Ibid.

64 Ibid.

65 See Victor Neumann, 'Between Hungary and Romania: The Case of the Southern Transylvania's Jews during the Holocaust', *East European Studies*, Woodrow Wilson International Center for Scholars (September 2001). According to Meeting Report no. 236; see www.wilsoncenter.org/publication/236-between-hungary-and-romania-the-case-the-southern-transylvanias-jews-during-the.

Chapter 21

1 Victor Neumann, 'Multicultural Identities in a Europe of Regions: The Case of Banat County', *European Journal of Intercultural Studies*, 8/1 (1997), 19–35. Franz Liebhardt, *Banater Mosaik: Beiträge zur Kulturgeschchite* (Bucharest, 1976).

2 Liebhardt, *Banater Mosaik*.

3 Victor Neumann, 'Ebrei dopo diluvio: Gli orfani della Mitteleuropa', *Lettera internazionale*, 54 (1997), 62–4.

4 See Roman Cotoşman, 'Evocation', in Ileana Pintilie, Ştefan Bertalan, Constantin Flondor, and Doru Tulcan (eds.), *Creaţie şi sincronism european: Mişcarea artistică timişoreană a anilor 60-70 (European Creation and Synchronicity: The Artistic Movement of Timişoara in the 1960s and 1970s)* (Timişoara, 1990), 39–42.

5 Livius Ciocârlie, 'Evocation', in Pintilie et al. (eds.), *Creaţie şi sincronism european*, 45.

6 Ibid.

7 Ibid.

8 Ibid. 44.

9 Constantin Flondor, 'Evocation', in Pintilie et al. (eds.), *Creaţie şi sincronism european*, 34.

10 Iosif Király, 'Evocation', in Pintilie et al. (eds.), in *Creaţie şi sincronism european*, 28.

11 Andrei Pleşu, 'Un liceu de artă plastică şi câteva întrebări' ('A College of Plastic Art and Some Questions'), in Pintilie et al. (eds.), *Creaţie şi sincronism european*, 27.

12 Ileana Pintilie, 'Cardinal Points of Timișoara's Artistic Movement 1960–1996', in *Experiment în arta românească după 1960 (Experiment in Romanian Art after 1960)* (Bucharest, 1997), pp. 1–3.

13 Ileana Pintilie, 'Evocation', in Pintilie et al. (eds.), *Creaţie şi sincronism european*, p. 2.

14 Flondor, 'Evocation', p. 34.

15 Ştefan Bertalan, 'Evocation', in Pintilie et al. (eds.), *Creaţie* şi sincronism european, p. 36.

16 Ion Nicolae Anghel, *Cartea cu Pamfil (The Book with Pamfil)* (Timișoara, 1996).

17 William Totok, *Aprecieri neretuşate: Eseuri, articole şi alte interviuri 1987–1994 (Uncensored Reflections. Essays, Articles and Other Interviews 1987–1994)* (Iași, 1997). The officials of the totalitarian regime had the ability to change the data of the problem, giving a different interpretation to his writings. For example, the documents of the County Inspectorate of the Ministry of the Interior show that he was prosecuted for promoting a bourgeois ideology in his poems, cultivating distrust in the law and the leadership of Romania. According to his criminal file no. 2899 from 1975 – drafted by the County Inspectorate – he was

arrested for the crime of 'propaganda against the socialist establishment'.

18 An explanation of the particular situation of German-language writers must consider the trials of conscience of the German community in Romania in the post-war period, their deportation, and their acutely felt condition as a minority as a result of the pressure exercised by the National Communist regime. The behaviour that distinguished the young German-speaking members of Aktionsgruppe Banat from the young Romanian-language writers was mostly due to access to German culture, to international sources of information. This explains a certain radicalisation of political ideas and a refusal to enrol in the Communist Nationalist ideology of Ceauşescu's regime.

19 See Peter Motzan, *Vânt potrivit până la tare: Zece tineri poeţi germani din România (Moderate to Strong Wind: Ten Young German Writers from Romania)* (Bucharest, 1982).

20 Dieter Schlesak, 'Kulturpolitik mit Polizeieinsatz: Marxistische Rumäniendeutsche stören die revolutionäre Ruhe ihres "sozialistischen" Staates' ('Political Culture and Police Repression: The German Marxists from Romania Disturb the Revolutionary Stillness of the "Socialist" State'), *Frankfurter Rundschau*, 10 July 1976.

21 Nikolau Berwanger, German-language journalist and poet, represented all Romania's minorities in the Central Committee of the Communist Party. Despite his collaboration with the system, he did many good things, among which was protecting many people under investigation by the secret police. Petru Ilieşu stated that, among other merits, Berwanger managed the newspaper *Neue Banater Zeitung*, for many years the most liberal paper edited in Timişoara during the years of great constraints of Ceauşescu's regime. Ilieşu admitted that he himself benefited from Berwanger's intervention during his investigation. While the papers from Timişoara and the *Orizont* magazine expressed great reservations or simply refused to publish certain articles on themes considered taboo by the system – for example, those about Jews from the Banat – Berwanger assumed responsibility for publishing such a text (1984), for which he was strongly criticised by Eugen Florescu, the propaganda representative of the Central Committee of the Communist Party in Timişoara.

22 Nicolae Covaci, *Phoenix însă eu ... (Phoenix, But Me...)* (Bucharest, 1994).

23 C. Postolache, Foreword to Covaci, *Phoenix însă eu ...*

24 M. Sitariu, *Rezistenţa anticomunistă: Timişoara 1956 (Anti-Communist Resistance: Timişoara, 1956)* (Bucharest, 1998).

25 See Caius Muţiu, Teodor Stanca, and Aurel Baghiu, '*Mişcările studenţeşti anticomuniste din octombrie 1956 din Timişoara, văzute şi prezentate de iniţiatorii şi principalii organizatori*' ('The Anti-Communist Student Movements of October 1956 in Timişoara as Seen by Their Initiators and Main Organisers'), in *Analele Sighet, no. 8. Anii 1954–1960: Fluxurile şi refluxurile stalinismului (1954–1960: The Fluxes and Refluxes of Stalinism)* (Bucharest, 2000), p. 669.

26 Ibid.

Chapter 22

1 Dennis Deletant, *România sub regimul comunist (Romania under Communist Rule)* (Bucharest, 1997).

2 Miodrag Milin, *Timişoara 15–21 decembrie 1989* (Timişoara, 1990), 1135. Cf. Milin, 'Azi în Timişoara, mîine-n toată ţara (Crîmpeie din revoluţia trăită)' ('Today in Timişoara, Tommorow in the Whole Country') (Pieces of Experienced Revolution)'), in *Timişoara: 16–22 decembrie 1989* (a collection of texts about the events of December 1989 in Timişoara) (Timişoara, 1990), pp. 45–78.

3 Mandics György, 'La vest de Doja' ('West from Doja'), in *Timişoara: 16–22 decembrie 1989*, pp. 79–84. Regarding the impressive solidarity of Timişoara's citizens, see also Tökés's testimony in Titus Suciu, *Reportaj cu sufletul la gură (Out of Breath Report)* (Timişoara, 1990), pp. 10–17.

4 See Miodrag Milin (ed.), *Timişoara în Arhivele Europei Libere: 17–20 decembrie 1989 (Timişoara in the Archives of Radio Free Europe: 17–20 December 1989)* (Bucharest, 1999), pp. 55–56. Reuter's Agency telegram sent from Budapest.

5 'Human Chain Protecting Clergyman Turns into Mass Protest', in Milin (ed.), *Timişoara în Arhivele*, pp. 60–61.

6 Ibid., pp. 151–52, Introd. (News from Romania), pp. 154–55, 'White House Condemns Romanian Use of Force'.

7 Ibid., pp. 151–52.

8 Andrei Pleşu, Preface to Wolf Lepenies, *Ascesa e declino degli intellettuali in Europa (The Ascent and Decline of Intellectuals in Europe)* (Rome, 1992), p. 10.

9 Ibid.

10 Ivan Evseev, 'Revoluţia din Timişoara ca depăşire a sinelui' ('The Revolution of Timișoara as Overcoming Self'), in *Timişoara: 16–22 decembrie 1989*, pp. 26–44.

11 This is one of the possible explanations of the fact that the role of ruling and administering the post-Communist state was given to the second tier of the Communist political class. During Bucharest's confused transition that followed Timișoara's spontaneous revolt, the reformed Communists seemed to be the only ones capable of ruling the country. For the political context of the time and for the interpretation of the 1989 revolts, see Silviu Brucan, *De la capitalism la socialism şi retur: O biografi e între două revoluţii (From Capitalism to Socialism and Back: A Biography between Two Revolutions)* (Bucharest, 1998). A former editor of the main Communist newspaper, *Scînteia (The Spark)* and the former Romanian ambassador of socialist Romania in the US, Silviu Brucan was directly involved in changing Nicolae Ceauşescu's regime and a member of the reformed Communist group that took over power. After 1990, he was one of the most important political analysts of the Romanian scene, hosting a weekly show on the ProTV channel.

12 Victor Neumann, 'Die bürgerliche Kultur in Siebenbürgen und im Banat: Die Rolle Temeswars in den politischen Umgestaltungsprozessen vom Dezember 1989', *Halbjahresschrift für südosteuropäische Geschichte, Literatur und Politik*, no. 1 (1999), pp. 38–51.

13 Suciu, *Reportaj cu sufletul la gură*, p. 216. For the political context, see also Brucan, *De la capitalism la socialism*.

14 According to *Timişoara: 16–22 decembrie 1989*; Mariana Conovici, *E un început în tot sfîrşitul... (The Beginning of the End)*, Selective collection of radio programmes aired between 17 and 25 December 1989, The Romanian Radio Society, Oral History Section, Bucharest, 1998. Milin (ed.), *Timişoara în Arhivele Europei; Procesul de la Timişoara (The Timişoara Trial)* Miodrag Milin edition, vols. i–iii (Timişoara, 2004–5).

15 Victor Neumann, *Ideologie şi fantasmagorie: Perspective comparative asupra istoriei gîndirii politice în Europa est-centrală (Ideology and Phantasmagory: Comparative Perspectives upon the History of Political Thought in Central-East Europe)* (Iaşi, 2001); see the chapter entitled 'Schimbările politice din România anului 1989: Aspiraţii contradictorii pe fondul interferenţei valorilor central, sud-est şi est europene' ('The Romanian Political Changes in 1989: Contradictory Aspirations on the Background of the Central, South-East and East European Intersection of Values'), pp. 175–97.

16 See also Victor Neumann, 'Timişoara în memoria colectivă contemporană: Perspective fragmentare' ('Timișoara in the European Collective Memory: Fragmentary Perspectives'), in Bogdan Murgescu (ed.), *Revoluţia Română din Decembrie 1989: Istorie şi Memorie (The Romanian Revolution of December 1989: History and Memory)* (Iaşi, 2007), pp. 21–44.

17 See Carolina Brossat, 'Kulturpolitischer kompetenzkonfl ikt Europarat und Europäische Union', *Dokumente, Zeitschrift für den deutsch-französischen Dialog*, vol. 4 (1995), pp. 306–13.

18 See Virgil Nemoianu, 'Cazul etosului central-european' ('The Case of the Central European Ethos'), in *Europa centrală: Nevroze, Dileme, Utopii (Central Europe: Neurosis, Dilemmas, Utopias)*, anthology by Adriana Babeţi and Cornel Ungureanu (Iași, 1997), pp. 168–94; Victor Neumann, *Istoria evreilor din Banat: O mărturie a multi-şi interculturalităţii Europei Central-Orientale (The History of the Jews of the Banat: A Testimony of Central-East European Multi- and Interculturality)* (Timișoara, 1997), pp. 97–131.

Chapter 23

1 Marc Bloch, *Combats pour l'histoire* (Paris, 1965).

2 Moritz Csáky, *Ideologie der Operette und Wiener Moderne: Ein kulturhistorische Essay* (Vìenna, 1998). Victor Neumann, *Die Interkulturalitaet des Banats* (Berlin, 2015).

INDEX

First published in 2019 by
Scala Arts & Heritage Publishers Ltd
10 Lion Yard
Tremadoc Road
London SW4 7NQ, UK
www.scalapublishers.com

ISBN 978-1-78551-124-0

Editor and co-translator Rowena Anketell
Designed by Linda Lundin
Cover design by Dieter Penteliuc-Cotoşman
Printed in Turkey

10 9 8 7 6 5 4 3 2 1

PICTURE CREDITS

Plates 3, 15 and 16: from the Banat History Museum's permanent collection;

Plate 4: original in the Hofkammerarchiv, Vienna, with copy in the Roman Catholic Diocesan Museum in Timişoara;

Plate 5: on permanent loan from the Rijksmuseum, Amsterdam to the Belvedere Museum, Vienna;

Plates 1, 6, 7, 8, 9, 10 and 17: from Andrei Herczeg's private collection;

Plates 11 and 13: from the Serbian Orthodox Eparchy of Timişoara permanent collection;

Plates 12, 22, 23 and 48: from the Art Museum Timişoara, permanent collection;

Plate 14: from the Gallery of Bishops, Roman Catholic Episcopal Palace, Timişoara;

Plate 46: donation made by the artist to the Art Museum Timişoara;

Plates 49 and 50: © Constantin Duma, from the photographic archive of 16–22 December 1989, Timişoara's Association for Memorial of Revolution, with thanks to Dr Traian Orban, President of the Association.

Plate 51: © Béla Szakáts, from the artist's photographic archive;

Plate 47: from Lucian Cotoşman's private collection;

Plates 18, 19, 20, 21 and 45: © Dieter Penteliuc-Cotoşman, private photographic archive;

Plate 24: Photography by Borsos József (c.1865-1867), © FSZEK (Fővárosi Szabó Ervin Könyvtár, Budapest Gyűjtemény), from the photographic archive of Metropolitan Ervin Szabo Library, the "Budapest" Collection, Budapest-Hungary, with thanks to Mr. Tibor Sandor, Director of the FSZEK Library, image source: https://dspace.oszk.hu/handle/123456789/692678;

Plate 25: Photography by Borsos József (c.1865-1867), © FSZEK (Fővárosi Szabó Ervin Könyvtár, Budapest Gyűjtemény), from the photographic archive of Metropolitan Ervin Szabo Library, the "Budapest" Collection, Budapest-Hungary, with thanks to Mr. Tibor Sandor, Director of the FSZEK Library, image source: https://dspace.oszk.hu/handle/123456789/692532;

Plates 26, 27, 28, 29, 30, 31, 32, 33, 34, 35, 36, 37, 38, 39, 40, 41, 42, 43 and 44: from Thomas Mohnacs private collection.